ENDLESS SUMMER

ENDLESS SUMMER

140 Years of Australian Cricket in Wisden

Edited by Gideon Haigh

Hardie Grant Books

EDITOR'S NOTE

Endless Summer is not so much a work of reference as an historical archive: accordingly, the match reports, cards and features appear as they did in the edition of *Wisden Cricketers' Almanack* from which they were extracted. Only the more obvious typographical errors in scores and names have been corrected; to foist an early twenty-first-century order on the scoreboards of yesteryear would have been misleading. This means that some players appear with a variety of initials: Wally Grout, for example, undergoes gradual augmentation and enhancement from 'W. Grout' through 'A.W.T. Grout' and 'A.T.W. Grout' to the full 'Arthur Theodore Wallace Grout' in his obituary. It also means that information such as changes to second innings batting orders is not included for matches before 1980, this being the year of its introduction to *Wisden*.

Editing of text has been limited to shortening for length, with excisions indicated by ellipses ([...]). Publication dates of extracts are indicated where they might not be immediately obvious.

The editor gratefully acknowledges the assistance of the Melbourne Cricket Club Library, especially David Studham, John Owen and David Allen, in the compilation of this treasury.

Published in 2002
by Hardie Grant Books
12 Claremont Street
South Yarra, Victoria 3141, Australia
www.hardiegrant.com.au

National Library of Australia Cataloguing-in-Publication Data:

Endless summer: 140 years of Australian cricket in Wisden.

Bibliography.
Includes index.
ISBN 1 74066 009 9.

1. Wisden cricketers' almanack. 2. Cricket – Australia –
History. I. Haigh, Gideon.

796.3580994

Edited and compiled by Gideon Haigh
Cover and text design by Andrew Cunningham, Studio Pazzo
Typeset by Lauren Statham, Alice Graphics
Printed and bound in Australia by Griffin Press

*Every effort has been made to incorporate correct information and
statistics. The publishers regret any errors and omissions, and invite
readers to contribute up-to-date or additional relevant information to
Hardie Grant Books.*

10 9 8 7 6 5 4 3 2 1

CONTENTS

1 Early Days: Australia v. England 1862–93 1
2 The Golden Age: Australia v. England 1894–1914 44
3 Between the Wars: Australia v. England 1920–38 74
4 From Bradman to Chappell: Australia v. England 1946–72 116
5 Ashes and Embers: Australia v. England 1973–2002 159
6 Routing the Prophets: Australia v. South Africa 192
7 The Big Dipper: Australia v. West Indies 210
8 Neighbours: Australia v. New Zealand 247
9 Home and Away: Australia v. India 257
10 New Frontiers: Australia v. Pakistan and Sri Lanka 277
11 Boundaries and Limits: One-day Cricket 298
12 The States' Rites: Sheffield Shield 316
13 Portrait Gallery 348
14 Issue of the Day 392
15 A Disgraceful Exhibition 426
16 The Packer Case 457
17 The Greater Game 481
18 Moments of Glory 502
19 Smokers, Non-Smokers and Others 527
20 The Long Stop 539
21 Believe It or Not 557

EARLY DAYS:
AUSTRALIA v. ENGLAND
1862–93

It is often argued that 1864 should rank as the dawn of cricket, and the year has much to recommend it. On 10 June, overarm bowling became legal, thus completing bowling's 'march of intellect' from underarm innocence – in the opinion of Sir Donald Bradman, 'possibly the greatest single change in the development of the game'. Representing South Wales Cricket Club against the Gentlemen of Sussex at Brighton a month later, a clean-shaven, fifteen-year-old William Gilbert Grace notified the game of his talent with 170 and 56 not out – his batting would revolutionise the way cricket was played, and his personality the way it was organised and watched.

That we know so many years later how many runs Grace scored in that match, meanwhile, reflects 1864's third development of significance. The publication of the first edition of *Wisden Cricketers' Almanack* was more than the minting of a distinguished imprint; it manifested the emergence of a record-keeping instinct in the game, now taken for granted, but intrinsic to its senses of continuity and context. The idea of records was a precondition for modern sport – and a compelling one. 'What is a record?' asks Allen Guttman in *From Ritual to Record: The Nature of Modern Sports*. 'It is the marvellous abstraction that permits competition not only among those gathered together on the field of sport but also among them and others distant in time and space.' In records and the games from which they are derived, a two-way process is at work: a Test match is meticulously recorded because it is important, and is important because it is meticulously recorded. Since the dawn of the age of quantification, one might say that sport has harboured a variation of that conundrum about the proverbial tree in the forest: does a game take place if no-one is around to score?

First acquaintance with *Wisden* doesn't evoke proverbial trees so much as literal ones: all that paper, all those pages. Its draft and displacement today are partly an outcome of tradition: in two dimensions, *Wisden* has remained unaltered in 140 years. Cricket's spread and sophistication, meanwhile, is indexed by *Wisden's* third dimension, its fourteen-fold expansion from the 116 pages of its first edition to the 1632 of its most recent. And while the pace of change in cricket today seems so great, it's worth noting that most of *Wisden*'s growth actually occurred between 1882 and 1922. In the year of Australia's first Test victory in England, *Wisden* came in at only 224 pages; in the course of reporting eight consecutive Australian victories at English expense forty years later, the almanack grazed 1000 pages. *Wisden* may be classified as the most English of books about the most English of games – nodding to Rudyard Kipling, Rowland Ryder once described it as 'the thin yellow line'. But its fortunes have been inseparable from the rise of international cricket in general and Australian cricket in particular. Indeed, it is difficult to think of another overseas book that has documented Australian striving in any field of endeavour so exhaustively and approvingly.

A mischievous soul could go further, and argue that Australians are likelier to read *Wisden* more closely than the English. *Wisden* is published in the northern hemisphere amid the pleasurable distractions of the cricket season's commencement; when *Wisden* navigates its way south a month or two later, it arrives as a blessed relief from winter and wall-to-wall football. And such is its transporting charm, *Wisden* might actually be better appreciated at a remove from its place of publication. In England, the name *Wisden* has authority. Away from England, it has resonance. It conjures up names, people and places. I once asked Ron Archer why he'd acclimatised to English conditions so quickly on his first tour, making a century in his first innings at Worcester in May 1953. He explained that he'd devoured his grandfather's *Wisden*s so avidly as a child that it felt as if he'd played in England before. When the firm John Wisden & Co marked its centenary, the encomium it liked most was from Australia. Prime Minister Sir Robert Menzies, whose almanacks were obtained by minions at Australia House in London for forwarding to Canberra in the diplomatic satchel, stated simply: '*Wisden* and cricket are synonymous.' Responded Lord De L'Isle: 'Let this message from Australia be the tribute of the whole British Commonwealth at once to a famous cricketer, to the great enterprise, and to the game of cricket wherever it is played.' In Australia, the word 'Wisden' is regarded as synonymous with comprehensive and compendious. In greeting Peter Coleman's history of Australian censorship *Obscenity, Blasphemy, Sedition* forty years ago, Ross Campbell described it as 'a *Wisden* of banning'.

Wisden, though, doesn't need articulated tributes; readers pay their own annual homage by trusting it as the authentic record of cricket's preceding year. Collecting it has a lore all to itself. One renowned bibliophile, Yorkshireman Karl Auty, spent most of his life in Chicago; his favoured nocturnal ritual was reaching down to the set of *Wisden*s he kept beneath his bed, and choosing a volume at random that he would then pore over for hours. In extreme circumstances, too, the almanack has even palliated hardship and horror. Cricket historian Harry Altham recalled being distracted from the death round him on the Western Front by the obituaries in his 1916 *Wisden* of W.G. Grace and Victor Trumper, 'feeling no real sorrow for W.G. passing Homeric and legendary into Elysian fields, but an almost personal pain that Trumper's gallant spirit and matchless grace should have been called so early from the world it enriched'. And possibly the most famous single almanack is a manhandled 1939 *Wisden* owned by the journalist E.W. Swanton, rebound in remnants of gas cape, glued with rice paste, and thumbed by thousands of internees in a dozen different

Japanese prisoner-of-war camps along the Burma–Siam railway. Visitors to its glass case at Lord's can still discern a fading Japanese censorship stamp on the top left of the title page; it indicates that the volume is 'not subversive'.

This book concerns how *Wisden* has, distantly but diligently, followed and featured Australian cricket over the last 140 years. It also contains subtler traces of another story, how the coverage of Australian cricket has both reflected and contributed to *Wisden*'s fortunes in that time. Before studying the game through *Wisden*'s eyes, one should understand a little about the institution itself.

It is cliché to say that John Wisden could not have foreseen how his little annual would prosper and his name be perpetuated. On the contrary, his objectives were probably short-term. A professional fast bowler, Wisden had been in various sporting enterprises throughout his career, including the joint management of a cricket ground at Leamington, secretaryship of the Cricketers' Fund Friendly Society, the very first cricket tour to the United States and Canada in 1859, and latterly a tobacconist cum sporting goods depot off the Haymarket in London, subsequently relocated to Leicester Square. In fact, in starting his almanack, Wisden was doing little more than imitate the rival Islington firm Lillywhite Brothers & Co, which had promoted its business for the fifteen preceding years with an annual *Cricketers' Guide*. The rivalry between *Wisden* and the succession of annuals bearing the Lillywhite name has been largely ignored by historians, content simply to know who won. But it was a competition with some intriguing fluctuations.

John Wisden and Fred Lillywhite had been in business together between October 1855 and December 1858, but their relations had soured in the early 1860s, after Wisden succeeded Lillywhite as secretary of the Cricketers' Fund Friendly Society. There is a hint of mischief about Wisden's move to set up in competition with his erstwhile partner, and more than a hint of malice in the brief biographical note about Wisden in *Lillywhite's Guide* in 1865: 'Was a "good 'un", but now "does nothing" for his county, England, or any other eleven, in fact, devotes his time to do [sic] a "deal of good" for promoting the manly game, for which he spends a vast amount of "coin"'.

Such remarks about Wisden and others – the great George Parr he described as an 'able manager … when out of his bedroom' – actually cost *Lillywhite's Guide* the patronage of the Marylebone Cricket Club; he was felt to have 'exceeded the fair limits of criticism upon cricketers'. But the first *Wisden* – aka *The Cricketers' Almanack for the year 1864 being the Bissextile or Leap Year, and the 28th of the Reign of Her Majesty Queen Victoria* – wouldn't have caused Lillywhite much heartache. A messy book, its scores surrounded with such factual bric-a-brac as winners of the Derby, Oaks and St Leger, a potted history of China, and the rules of pastimes such as knur and spell, it seemed destined for a short life. One can only admire the inventiveness of its compilers, or sympathise with their desperation, as they bulked their book with digressions into popular history like: 'The graces of the modern tea table were quite unknown to the country folk, although that favourite beverage, brought by the Dutch to Europe, was introduced into England by Lords Arlington and Ossory in 1666.'

These divertisements were a short-term measure: the graces of teatime would prove no match for the Graces of the green. But working out how to treat cricket in the antipodes would challenge *Wisden* some years yet. The first game in Australia that *Wisden* reported, the initial Melbourne engagement of H.H. Stephenson's trail-blazing Englishmen with a Victorian Eighteen on the first three days of 1862, was in a loose-knit grouping under the heading of 'Extraordinary Matches', which also included Shillinglee's feat of dismissing the 2nd Royal Surrey Militia for 0, and an encounter between Sixteen of Sheffield and Sixteen of the Country Round Sheffield in which all the contestants were sixty or over. Lillywhite, meanwhile, showed his experience: by slightly delaying the *Guide*'s publication, he managed to accommodate the scores of matches being played in Australia by the team that George Parr was leading there while the tour was in progress.

The first *Wisden*s were cobbled together – so far as is known, and much is not, many of *Wisden*'s records having been incinerated during the Blitz in 1940 – by the journalist W.H. Knight, in collaboration with his printer W.H. Crockford. Initially, they concerned themselves purely with scores, adjuring commentary, perhaps wary of antagonising Marylebone as had their rival: 'We, of course, make no comments upon the matches, leaving the cricketer to form his own opinion with regard to the merits of the men, since a great many of our readers are at least equal, if not superior, to ourselves in arriving at a right judgement of the play.' As their publication was far from spacious, they were also apt to condense those scores that did not absolutely demand complete recapitulation; thus, disappointingly, were the deeds of Charles Lawrence's 1868 Aboriginal visitors pared back to a puny page. Australian cricket and cricketers infiltrated those early almanacks stealthily. One of Lawrence's team, Johnny Cuzens, was the first antipodean inclusion in *Wisden*'s 'Births and Deaths' section; his death on 22 March 1871 was recorded in the 1872 edition. The second inclusion was also a death, that of Victoria's Richard Wardill on 17 August 1873, which made the 1874 edition – only to vanish rather mysteriously from the next edition, perhaps when it was learned that he had drowned himself in the Yarra after being exposed as an embezzler.

While *Wisden* was improved annually throughout the 1870s, there remained little sense of order or continuity about the almanack. Knight reported the matches played by Australia's first representative touring team in 1878 in voluminous detail, but scattered them throughout the almanack under the subsections on each county. George West, the cricket correspondent of *The Times* who succeeded to *Wisden*'s editorship on Knight's death in August 1879, drew the matches played by the team of 1880 together in their own chapter, but was much lighter on the detail, pleading limitations of space. Most bizarrely, *Wisden* ignored altogether what is today regarded as the very first Test at the Melbourne Cricket Ground in March 1877, disposing of the entire tour in a few perfunctory lines.

Why this occurred can only be speculated upon. It wasn't easy for *Wisden* to keep tabs on the early English visits to Australia. Because the undersea telegraphic cable linking Australia with Great Britain after 1872 was prohibitively expensive for all but short items, *Wisden*'s compilers would for many years depend on seaborne copies of colonial newspapers such as *The Australasian*, *The Leader* and *The Sportsman*. But circumstantial evidence suggests that *Wisden*'s lapse had a commercial cause. The captain of that English team in Australia was James Lillywhite Jnr, a scion of the famous family, and the tour coincided with another phase of chilly relations between the *Wisden* and *Lillywhite* camps. *Wisden* had issued the frankly dubious claim to have 'in circulation outstripped all its rivals, old and firmly established as some of them are'. *John Lillywhite's Cricketers' Companion*, which had absorbed the old *Cricketers' Guide* on Fred Lillywhite's death in 1866, scornfully counterclaimed 'an infinitely larger sale than any other annual work on the game', and damned statements otherwise as 'not founded on fact'. The contrast between the 1878 editions of the two annuals was then most marked: while James Lillywhite Jnr reported extensively on the tour and the inaugural Test in *Lillywhite*, *Wisden* studiously looked the other way.

Whatever the case, *Wisden*'s failure to even acknowledge the MCG match must have seemed embarrassing as Australia's famous 45-run victory was sedimented into the bedrock of cricket history. In 1930, editor C. Stewart Caine even made what looks like an attempt to justify the almanack's Homeric nod, observing airily that the forthcoming season marked Test cricket's Golden Jubilee – 'for although the representative games played in Australia by James Lillywhite's team in 1876–77 and by Lord Harris's team in 1878–79 are in these days counted as Test matches, none of those encounters should strictly be so regarded'. Lillywhite's team was dismissed as 'a financial speculation', Harris's as 'merely an amateur combination'; the Oval match of 1880 – which was in *Wisden* – should thus be accorded the status of the first 'real test'. But no move was made to adjust the almanack's records section, perhaps because Caine's statistician Sydney Southerton was actually the son of James Southerton, who had been one of Lillywhite's players. And a scorecard of the inaugural Test was finally published in the 1978 edition, where it was bracketed with the scorecard of the Centenary Test. In the meantime, *Wisden* had completed a neat double-blink by largely overlooking the first one-day international in January 1971, also at the MCG, granting it only a potted score and scorning to run a match report.

Mistakes? By *Wisden*? They do happen. One might as well acknowledge *Wisden*'s fallibility at the outset – some claims made for the almanack, as Rowland Bowen remarked, 'differ only in degree from those which the fanatical devotees of some religions make for their own revealed books'. But having said that, *Wisden*'s ignoring of the inaugural Test looks less like a mistake than a deliberate oversight; it's a pregnant silence, exemplifying the organic and arbitrary nature of cricket's growth, how its forms have been more or less arrived at rather than invented or decreed. It's a reminder, too, that Bismarck's famous advice about sausages and laws, how one should never watch their making lest one's respect for them diminish, sometimes applies equally well to cricket records.

※ ※ ※

When John Wisden died a bachelor in April 1884, he paradoxically left an orphan. With no one to inherit his sporting goods business, the future of the almanack was especially clouded. The last *Wisden* in the eponymous founder's lifetime was still markedly inferior to the competition. When the Hon Ivo Bligh's Englishmen reclaimed the still-warm Ashes in 1882–83, what had become *James Lillywhite's Cricketers' Companion* alloted the tour 23 pages, prefaced with a feature by Bligh himself. *Wisden*'s coverage ran without a covering article, and began on a page facing a calendar for the year 1844 – a rather congruous misprint.

Step forward Henry Luff, the late John Wisden's manager, who acquired the firm and perforce the almanack from the executors of the estate. Only twenty-eight, Luff was a shrewd businessman: he would broaden the company's activities from straight-forward retailing to manufacturing and branding as well. And he was also a believer in the almanack. When Billy Murdoch's Australians won their first Test match in England at the Oval in August 1882, for instance, it was Luff who arrived the next morning at Covent Garden's Tavistock Hotel to painstakingly transcribe the ball-by-ball record of the game from the visitors' own scoresheets – 'And,' he stated proudly, 'they were printed ... exactly as they were set out in the scoring book.' The almanack resumed uncertainly under the new regime. George West succumbed to a 'long-continued indisposition' – the cause of which has never been explained, though his was a sociable nature – and the 1886 edition appeared a whole year late. But this seems to have convinced Luff that *Wisden* should be run by full-time specialists – today, it would be called 'outsourcing'. The Cricket Reporting Agency was a small news agency by the standards of giants such as Reuters, Havas and Wolff. With its editorial oversight, however, *Wisden* ceased to be principally a promotional vehicle for its founder's athletic equipment and emporium, and became a force in its own right.

The Cricket Reporting Agency was chiefly the doing of brothers: Charles, Sydney and Edgar Pardon. That they were young – at the agency's founding in 1880, Charles was thirty, Sydney twenty-five, and Edgar twenty – is often overlooked. In fact, their vitality was probably fundamental to their success. At a time when Australian visits to England were still regarded with some severity, as intrusions marring the more con-genial contours of county cricket, the Pardons relished them. Edgar's first act on leav-ing school, for example, had been to follow Dave Gregory's 1878 Australians round the country, while Charles Pardon had turned his writings on the 1882 Australian tour for *Bell's Life* into a book, then collaborated on another book describing the 1884 Australian tour with Sydney, Edgar and C. Stewart Caine. Indeed, Geoffrey Moorhouse believes that there are grounds for regarding Charles Pardon as 'the first great cricket reporter'.

Though Charles Pardon's editorship spanned merely the four editions from 1887 to 1890, he accomplished much. The births and deaths pages were overhauled and expanded by that cricketing Herodotus, F.S. Ashley-Cooper, who also introduced a statistical section, 'Some Cricket Records'. *Wisden* for the first time commissioned portrait photographs and prose appreciations of the season's leading cricketers, the forerunner to its annual Five Cricketers of the Year. 'Six Great Bowlers of the Year' in the 1889 edition – including three Australians in Charlie Turner, John Ferris and Sammy Woods – proved so popular that *Wisden* for the first time sold out, necessitat-ing a reprint. Even Charles Pardon's untimely death in April 1890 left *Wisden* a legacy: the short death notice for him in *Wisden* 1891 foreshadowed the more than 10,000 obituaries to appear in succeeding editions.

The coverage that *Wisden* lavished on Anglo-Australian cricket, though, was per-haps its greatest advance, and point of product differentiation. In this, Charles Pardon and his brother Sydney who succeeded him, were far-sighted. English counties would not establish a Board of Control for Test Matches until 1899, and the Marylebone

Cricket Club not take responsibility for tours of Australia until 1903, but *Wisden* both sensed the growing importance of Ashes cricket and contributed to it. In the almanacks from 1887 to 1900, *Wisden* devoted 486 pages to reports and scores from Australian tours of England and English tours of Australia; its coverage dwarfed that of *Lillywhite*, which allocated the same games 281 pages. John Wisden & Co also dealt closely with Australian teams in England. Henry Luff was generous in tending their equipment needs, and they were generous with their names; even when the company was acting as agent for a triangular bat, Australian captain Percy McDonnell was prepared to offer an endorsement. Australian managers and scorers never failed to pay their respects at the Cricket Reporting Agency in Fleet Street. Sydney Pardon was so impressed by the 1893 Australians' teenage scorer that the agency took him on at the end of the tour: Sydney Southerton, a former ship's steward who had obtained his commission with John Blackham's side after meeting them aboard the *Liguria* en route to England, spent the rest of his life at *Wisden*, being known as 'Figure Fiend' for his astoundingly retentive memory.

Wisden's interest in cricket in Australia also grew. It began printing scores from Australian intercolonial matches in 1887–88, while *Lillywhite* persisted in the eccentric tokenism of printing averages for the East Melbourne Cricket Club in Melbourne's pennant competition. Not that *Wisden* was in any sense a globalist; on the contrary, it cheerfully acknowledged its parochialism. In toasting English success against the 1886 Australians, Charles Pardon commented: 'As, without the least ill-will towards the Australians, we in England are chiefly concerned with the prosperity and popularity of the game within our own border, it would be mere affectation to pretend to be anything but contented with the general net result of the last Australian tour.' Sydney Pardon, said C. Stewart Caine, 'mourned over any England failure', having been raised 'in an atmosphere that presumed the superiority of the Englishman in every walk of sport'. But this allegiance, always tactfully expressed and never mutating into partisanship, probably resonated with the times better than overt impartiality, tapping into the evolving sense of rivalry between England and Australia. For an Australian to have his portrait in *Wisden* – as in the 1890s did John Blackham, George Giffen, Syd Gregory, Hugh Trumble and the Trott brothers Albert and Harry – was to make it in front of the audience that mattered, as much a source of colonial satisfaction as the Royal Academy hanging Arthur Streeton's *Golden Summer: Eaglemont*, or London critics' acclaim for Tasma's *A Knight of the White Feather* and Melba's *Lucia di Lammermoor*.

By the turn of the century, meanwhile, *Wisden*'s own rivalry had been resolved. Its 1900 edition was its largest yet, its robust 650 pages encompassing the previous year's successful tour by Joe Darling's Australians, and elevating Darling, Clem Hill and Monty Noble to the Five Cricketers of the Year pantheon. *Lillywhite* followed two months later, a slighter 350 pages; it was destined to be that publication's last edition.

※ ※ ※

This book begins by ranging across the almanack's first thirty years of coverage of Anglo-Australian cricket. We're reminded that the first Australians to arrive at Lord's in May 1878 did so 'in such a quiet and unpretentious way' as to pass unrecognised. The mistake was not repeated as they left that evening having routed MCC and

Ground, W.G. Grace and all, by nine wickets. We're reminded, too, that Dave Gregory's men sent £100 of their tour takings to a fund for the bereaved in the loss of the *Princess Alice* (a Thames pleasure steamer that sank at the cost of 700 lives); the Australian team's donation of its prize money to the Sydney bushfire appeal in January 2002 was, like so much in cricket, far from a unique gesture.

Welcome to a world in which English fielders at the Sydney Cricket Ground are distracted by the blue of Australian skies then confronted by 'a field of snow', in which an English captain maims himself in a shipboard tug-o-war and a Middlesex supporter dies while spectating, where boundaries at Lord's bounce 'through the fan-light of the billiard-room door' and where a match at the Oval is stopped to allow photographs to be taken. Welcome to *Wisden*.

—GH

THE AUSTRALIANS AT LORD'S

The Australians v. M.C.C. and G. – Played at Lord's, May 27, 1878. – The showery morning of the 27th of last May, the day on which the Australians were to commence their first match at Lord's, and in London, was most discouraging to admirers of out door attractions, and when the Colonials were driven on to the ground at 11.30 there were not 500 visitors present, those who were there failing to recognise the team, and, consequently, to welcome them with that hearty good old English cheer that of a surety would have rang out clear and loud had they known who those dozen, or so, men were who at that time were being driven up to the pavilion in so quiet and unpre-tentious a way. Ten minutes after their arrival another sharp rain-fall wetted the ground; that downpour over, the sun shone out in good old fashioned early summer form, and continuing to shine the remainder of the day, visitors flocked on to the ground so continuously that by 4 o'clock there was an excellent attendance grouped round the players, in the Pavilion, and in the Grand Stand; and when the tell-tale, at the money taker's box, had been finally consulted it told of 4,742 visitors having paid and passed on to the ground, the whole of the money then taken (£119 7s.) being sub-sequently handed over to the Australians, the M.C.C. also paying all expenses attend-ing the match.

This, one of the most remarkable matches ever played at Lord's, was commenced at 3 minutes past 12, and concluded at 20 minutes past 6 the same day. Only 128 overs and 2 balls were bowled, and but 101 runs, from the bat, scored in the match. One Australian bowler (Allan) got the crack bat of England caught out from the second ball delivered in the match. Another Australian bowler (Spofforth) clean bowled the said crack for 0 in the second innings. Another Australian bowler (Boyle) finished his bowling with 8 overs and one ball for 3 runs and 5 wickets – 4 *bowled*. The aforesaid Australian bowler (Spofforth) made a distinct mark in the bowling of the match by delivering 6 overs (less one ball) for 14 runs and 6 wickets – 3 *bowled*. Alfred Shaw characteristically led off his bowling with 17 overs for one run and 2 wickets (*both bowled*). Another English bowler (Morley) obtained the first three Australian wickets ever captured at Lord's. And the decisive victory of the Australians was earnestly applauded by the members of M.C.C., and tumultuously so by the thousands of other Englishmen present, whose bones will have mouldered to dust long, long before the cricketers of the future – Colonial and English – cease to gossip about the marvellous short time match played by the Australians at Lord's on the 27th of May, 1878.

The wickets had been carefully and well prepared by Pearce, but they were wholly spoiled by soaking rain showers being followed (after the match commenced) by warm, drying sunshine, which made the top very bad to bat on. M.C.C. won choice, and started the batting (!) with W.G. Grace and Hornby, to the bowling of Allan and Boyle, two excellent head bowlers of medium pace. Allan began; the first ball he delivered Grace hit to leg for 4, the second got Grace easily caught out at short square-leg, and thereupon out rang lusty cheers, and shouts of 'Bravo, Allan', 'Well done Australia'. In Boyle's first over he bowled Booth for 0, another ringing cheer emphatically proclaiming the delight of the on-lookers at this early and great success of the Colonials. Ridley then faced Hornby, and the only stand for M.C.C. in the match was made. Ridley could not make more than singles, but Hornby gave one from Boyle such a hearty old English thump to square-leg that the ball bounded through the fan-light of the billiard-room door at the bottom of the ground; thereupon a cheer for Old England was shouted out as lustily as any given previously for the new country men. And so they went on until 25 runs had been made from 18 overs, when Allan was shunted for Spofforth, whose fast straight bowling made such havoc with the M.C.C. sticks that *in 6 overs he actually took 6 wickets (3 in one over) for 4 runs!* This wonderfully successful little bit of bowling created such extraordinary excitement among those who witnessed it that, for the full information of those who did not witness it, the compiler feels justified in giving it in detail, as follows:

...2   .w..   w...   1...   www.   .1w

As wicket after wicket went down from Spofforth's *then* perfectly unplayable bowling the cheering was of the heartiest British form, and as the Eleven returned to the Pavilion they were loudly applauded, Spofforth and Boyle being thoroughly mobbed. The fielding of the team was smart and effective, all working together admirably, their backing up being the very perfection of out cricket, and quite a pleasure to look at. Murdoch kept wicket in front rank form; his smart stumping Shaw and Mr Vernon from the fast bowling worthily elicited roars of applause. The M.C.C. innings, commenced at 3 minutes past 12, concluded at 8 past one for 33 runs, the wickets having fallen thus:

1	2	3	4	5	6, 7, 8, 9	10
4	5	27	29	30	31	33

At 25 minutes past one Charles Bannerman and Midwinter commenced the first Australian innings ever played at Lord's. [...] The English bowlers who started work in this Australian innings were Alfred Shaw and Morley, each of whom led off with a maiden over, and in Morley's second over (before a run was scored) an especially well-judged catch by young George Hearne settled Bannerman, to the evident disappointment of the many who were desirous to see how that batsman framed that had earned the great batting praise of being '*equal to Tom Humphrey in his best days*'. Horan then went to wickets, and notwithstanding Alfred Shaw continued bowling maiden over after maiden over, as he alone can bowl them, eleven runs had been scored from Morley, who, however, then had two wickets in one over, Horan being splendidly caught out – very low down at point – by W.G. Grace, and (from the following ball) A. Bannerman easily had at short square-leg by Booth. Garrett then went to wickets, and certainly no Australian batsman played better cricket in this match. He and Midwinter stayed up to luncheon call – 2 p.m. – when there had been 26 overs for 17 runs and 3 wickets – all to Morley's bowling, *Alfred Shaw then having bowled 13 overs for one run, made from the 47th ball he delivered*. After luncheon Garrett was had at mid-off, Midwinter cleverly taken at wicket for a patiently and well-played 10, and Gregory bowled, the last two wickets having fallen to the bowling of Alfred Shaw, who had *then* bowled

17 OVERS, FOR ONE RUN, AND 2 WICKETS!

Boyle and Spofforth both fell with the score at 23, making 8 wickets down, the excitement just then being great as to whether the Australians would after all beat the Englishmen's 33; but on Allan and Murdoch getting together the runs were made somehow, a loud cheer greeting the Australians when they had made 33, and a still louder cheer congratulating them on having gone a head, when they had made 34. Then Shaw bowled Murdoch for a useful 9. Bailey was last man in; he stayed for three singles whilst Allan had, in curious form, made his score 6, when he was caught and bowled by Shaw, and the innings was ended at 20 minutes to 4 for 41 runs, the Colonial wickets having given way as follows:

1	2 and 3	4	5 and 6	7 and 8	9	10
0	11	19	20	23	34	41

Morley had worked hard and bowled well for the old club; and Alfred Shaw had accomplished another and splendid bowling feat for M.C.C. by sending in 34 overs (less 2 balls) for 10 runs and 5 wickets, 3 bowled, one caught and bowled, and one caught at wicket. *The 10 runs scored from the 134 balls bowled by Shaw were eight singles and a 2, but from that hit for 2 A.J. Webbe ought to have caught out Boyle.*

At 3 minutes to 4 the second innings of M.C.C. was commenced; at 10 minutes to 5 that innings was over for 19 runs! The bowlers were Spofforth and Boyle. Spofforth commenced in a form that roused the thousands looking on to a frenzy of excitement; from the first ball he delivered W. Grace ought to have been had at wicket, the second ball thoroughly beat and clean bowled the crack, and the third ball as surely bowled A.J. Webbe; these two great and scientific bats going down before a run was scored, brought out loud and continued applause, but when (with only one run scored) Boyle in his first over bowled, with successive balls, Booth and Ridley, the cheering was tumultuous, and such as is but rarely heard at Lord's. Then a ball bowled by Spofforth painfully hurt and prostrated Hornby, compelling him to retire, the batting being continued by Wyld and Flowers, who, by plucky play, increased the score to 16, when Boyle bowled Flowers for 11, a plucky innings that included a good square-leg hit for

4 from Spofforth. With only 11 overs and 2 balls bowled, half the wickets down, and M.C.C. only 6 runs on, young Hearne went to the aid of Wyld, but neither of them could stem this amazing run of Australian success, as with the score at 17 only Spofforth bowled both of them, the Notts man for 5, and the young lad from Kent for 0. Then a storm of cheers (*in which all the Australian eleven joined*) greeted Hornby's return to the wickets with Mr Grace to run out his hits, but he was then in evident pain, and ere another run was made Spofforth bowled Vernon, and Boyle bowled Hornby, *16 overs (less one ball) having then been bowled for the 17 runs scored, and the 9 wickets down*, a really marvellous bit of cricket, considering the several skilled front rank batsmen that were out. Alfred Shaw then elicited a cheer by making a 2 from Spofforth, but in Boyle's next over Horan cleverly caught out Morley, and down went the curtain on this wonderfully small innings of M.C.C.'s, *wherein 9 of the 10 wickets had been bowled*, and Boyle had bowled 33 balls for 3 runs and 5 wickets (*4 bowled*), as follows:

l.ww   ....   .1.1   ....   .w..   ....   ..w.   w

The Australians then had but 12 runs to score to win. Midwinter and Charles Bannerman went in for these runs; Bannerman made a single from Morley, but in Shaw's second over a ball that broke in at least a foot from the off, clean bowled him, and a wicket was down for one run. Horan then went to wickets; he made a capital cut for 4 from Morley, a single, and a 2 (the winning hit), and at 20 minutes to 6 this memorable match of 4½ hours of actual cricket, was won by the Australians by 9 wickets. Thereupon a stream of at least one thousand men rushed frantically up to the pavilion, in front of which they clustered, and lustily shouted 'Well done Australia', 'Bravo Spofforth', 'Boyle, Boyle', &c., &c.; the members of the M.C.C. keenly joining in the applause of that 'maddened crowd', who shouted themselves hoarse before they left to scatter far and wide that evening the news, how in one day the Australians had so easily defeated one of the strongest M.C.C. elevens that had ever played for the famous old club. Score:

M.C.C. AND G.

W.G. Grace, c Midwinter, b Allan 4	– b Spofforth	0
A.N. Hornby, b Spofforth 19	– (*hurt*) b Boyle	1
C. Booth, b Boyle 0	– b Boyle	0
A.W. Ridley, c A. Bannerman, b Boyle 7	– b Boyle	0
A.J. Webbe, b Spofforth 1	– b Spofforth	0
F. Wyld, b Boyle 0	– b Spofforth	5
W. Flowers, c and b Spofforth 0	– b Boyle	11
G.G. Hearne, jun. (*son of George*), b Spofforth .0	– b Spofforth	0
Alfred Shaw, st Murdoch, b Spofforth 0	– not out	2
G.F. Vernon, st Murdoch, b Spofforth 0	– b Spofforth	0
F. Morley, not out 1	– c Horan, b Boyle	0
L b 1 1		
33		19

THE AUSTRALIANS

Charles Bannerman, c Hearne, b Morley 0	– b Alfred Shaw 1
W. Midwinter, c Wyld, b Alfred Shaw 10	– not out 4
T. Horan, c W. Grace, b Morley 4	– not out 7
A. Bannerman, c Booth, b Morley 0	
T.W. Garrett, c Ridley, b Morley 6	
F.E. Spofforth, b Alfred Shaw 1	
D.W. Gregory, b Alfred Shaw 0	
H.F. Boyle, c Wyld, b Morley 2	
W.L. Murdoch, b Alfred Shaw 9	
F.E. Allan, c and b Alfred Shaw 6	
G.H. Bailey, not out 3	

41   12

Umpires: A. Rylott and M. Sherwin.

AUSTRALIAN BOWLING

	Overs	Mdns	Runs	Wkts	Overs	Mdns	Runs	Wkts
Boyle	14	7	14	3	8.1	6	3	5
Allan	9	4	14	1				
Spofforth	5.3	3	4	6	9	2	16	5

M.C.C. BOWLING

	Overs	Mdns	Runs	Wkts	Overs	Mdns	Runs	Wkts
A. Shaw	33.2	25	10	5	8	6	4	1
Morley	33	19	31	5	8	4	8	–

M.C.C. BANQUET TO THE AUSTRALIANS

After the match, Lord Fitzhardinge, *the President of M.C.C.*, presided at a dinner given to the Australians by the Club, at the hotel on the ground. Particulars did not transpire.

THE AUSTRALIANS' SECOND MATCH ON THE OVAL

The Australians v. Eleven English Professionals. – Played on The Oval, September 2, 3, 1878. – The match originally set down to be played on those days on The Oval was 'The Australians v. The Players of England', of course meaning the very best eleven professionals of England available, and for that match the Committee of the Surrey C.C.C. had, with praiseworthy courtesy, placed the free use of their ground at the service of The Australians, with whom rested all arrangements, liabilities, and profits of the match. Unfortunately, owing to some very much debated, but never clearly explained, misunderstanding as to remuneration, many of the very best professionals of England did not play. It is impossible to give space in this little book to a full, and, consequently, fair expression of the published Why's and Wherefore's of this misunderstanding, and so the compiler passes it by with the expression of a regret that it ever occurred, and with a further regret that it was not amicably arranged.

The weather was as fine and warm as English weather could be expected to be in September, and the two days' attendances were so very large that the cricket critic of *The Sportsman* computed them at about 10,000 on the Monday, and about 12,000 on the Tuesday, and, inasmuch as the admission charge was 1s. each day, the result must have been highly remunerative to the Australians, and amply warranted them in generously increasing their originally agreed payment of £10 to each English player to £20, and of, furthermore, giving Barratt a bonus of £5, in compliment to the great success of his bowling in obtaining *all the 10 wickets* in Australia's first innings.

The Australians, at 12.35, commenced the batting on soft wickets, with the brothers Bannerman, to the bowling of Barratt and Watson. When the score was at 12, A. Bannerman was easily caught out at mid-on; at 14, Horan was had at slip; and, at 16, Murdoch was stumped. Then Spofforth faced Charles Bannerman, and so much of a stand was made that the score was increased to 50, when there occurred an awful smash up of Australian wickets, Spofforth being stumped for 14, and (*in one over*) Bailey had at mid-off, Gregory caught out at cover-point, and Blackham stumped, *all four wickets going down at 50*, Barratt then having bowled 17 overs for 24 runs and the 7 wickets down. Charles Bannerman stayed until the last man came in; then he was had at point for 51 (*out of 77*), an innings that won great praise for its clever timing and good hitting on such slow playing wickets. Charles Bannerman's hits included four 3's and three 4's. In that innings

BARRATT'S BOWLING CAPTURED ALL 10 WICKETS –
3 stumped, 7 caught out.

The Englishmen's innings was commenced at 3.20 by Rigley and Barlow, to the bowling of Spofforth and Garrett. The bowling had to be changed frequently before a wicket fell, and the score was hit to 23 when Rigley was well caught and bowled – hand high up, catch hot – by Allan for 18. Barlow and James Phillips made the score 44, when Barlow was stumped for 16. James Phillips and young Hearne then increased the runs to 59, when Spofforth had 4 wickets clean off the reel, as, before another run was made, he bowled Hearne, got Charlwood caught out at mid-on, bowled Wheeler first ball, and caused Watson to play the ball on, *all four English wickets falling to Spofforth's bowling with the score at 59*. H. Phillips, Lillywhite, and Barratt merely walked to the wickets and walked back again, and, when the ninth man was out, there had actually been six 0's in succession scored. William McIntyre (the last man in) then hit a bit, and, as he and James Phillips increased the score from 63 to upside the Australians' total, and then to pass that total by 5 runs, the cheering was hearty indeed, and quite as hearty for the Australians when a catch at wicket finished off the innings for 82 (*only 71 from the bat*). Time was then up, that day's cricket having consisted of 131 overs and 2 balls bowled, 148 runs from the bat and 11 extras scored, so many as thirteen 0's being attached to the 20 wickets then down.

On the Tuesday the Australians began their second innings at 12.25; they went to wickets in the same order as on the preceding day; but the Bannermans this time made 44 runs before a wicket was lost; then Charles played on for 15, and in that same over McIntyre bowled Horan. Murdoch was quickly out, and A. Bannerman c and b for 25 – the largest innings made that day; and although Gregory and Garrett increased the score by 19 runs for the last wicket, they were all out by 3.35 for 89, leaving the Englishmen 85 runs to score to win.

At 5 minutes to 4 Rigley and Barlow began the second innings of the Englishmen, to the bowling of Spofforth and Allan. Steadily was the score worked up to 13 when Spofforth bowled Barlow, and at 22 Allan bowled Rigley. James Phillips and Hearne then brought out British cheers by increasing the British score to 39, when a middle stump ball from Spofforth settled Hearne for a 12, that included a square-leg crack for 5 from the fast bowler. James Phillips and Charlwood stayed and made the score 56, when Charlwood was also bowled by Spofforth for 12; and at 60 James Phillips was c and b by Boyle for 14 – the highest score hit in that innings. At 67 Spofforth bowled Watson, the Englishmen then having four wickets to fall, and 18 runs to score to win, against frequently changed good bowling, backed up by some of the finest fielding all round by a team ever seen in this glorious old cricketing country of ours. John Wheeler and Harry Phillips then made the score 71, when a fair chance for English success was excitingly discounted by Phillips being run out, and Wheeler bowled. Two more runs only had been made when Garrett bowled Lillywhite, and there were then only McIntyre and Barratt left to make the dozen runs wanted to win. Old Mc made 3 of those runs, but then Spofforth sent in a sparkler that hit the middle stump of Barratt's wicket, and so the Australians won this closely contested match by 8 runs, whereupon the thousands on the ground rushed to the front of the Pavilion and there stood cheering the Australians so lustily, loud, and long, that the principal members of the team had to appear and bow their acknowledgments, and Conway addressed the B.P. in a brief speech. Score:

THE AUSTRALIANS

Charles Bannerman, c Barlow, b Barratt 51	– b W. McIntyre	.15
A. Bannerman, c W. McIntyre, b Barratt 4	– c and b Barlow	.25
T. Horan, c Watson, b Barratt 0	– b W. McIntyre	.4
W. Murdoch, st H. Phillips, b Barratt 0	– c G. Hearne, jun., b W. McIntyre	.0
F.E. Spofforth, st H. Phillips, b Barratt 14	– b W. McIntyre	.0
G.H. Bailey, c Lillywhite, b Barratt 0	– b Barlow	.12
D. Gregory, c J. Phillips, b Barratt 0	– not out	.9
J.M. Blackham, st H. Phillips, b Barratt 0	– b Barlow	.0
H.F. Boyle, c J. Phillips, b Barratt 8	– c and b W. McIntyre	.4
T. Garrett, c Watson, b Barratt 0	– c G. Hearne, jun., b Barratt	.10
F. Allan, not out 0	– b W. McIntyre	.4
	B 3, 1 b 3	.6
	77	**89**

ENGLISH PROFESSIONALS

W. Rigley, c and b Allan 18	– b Allan	.10
R.G. Barlow, st Murdoch, b Allan 16	– b Spofforth	.8
James Phillips, not out 19	– c and b Boyle	.14
G.G. Hearne, jun. (*son of George*), b Spofforth .8	– b Garrett	.12
H. Charlwood, c Boyle, b Spofforth 0	– b Spofforth	.12
John Wheeler, b Spofforth 0	– b Spofforth	.4
A. Watson, b Spofforth 0	– b Spofforth	.7
Henry Phillips, c Boyle, b Spofforth 0	– run out	.2
James Lillywhite, c Allan, b Boyle 0	– b Garrett	.2
E. Barratt, b Spofforth 0	– b Spofforth	.0
William McIntyre, c Murdoch, b Spofforth ..10	– not out	.3
B 4, l-b 7 11	B 2	.2
82		**76**

Umpires: W. Caffyn and Potter.

ENGLISH BOWLING

	Overs	Mdns	Runs	Wkts	Overs	Mdns	Runs	Wkts
Barratt	29	11	43	10	11.1	2	15	1
Watson	14	4	23	–				
Lillywhite	8	4	9	–				
G. Hearne, jun.	6	4	2	–	9	4	15	–
W. McIntyre					29	21	24	6
Barlow					28	18	29	3

AUSTRALIAN BOWLING

	Overs	Mdns	Runs	Wkts	Overs	Mdns	Runs	Wkts
Spofforth	34.2	18	37	7	27	11	38	5
Allan	20	13	18	2	15	8	16	1
Garrett	12	8	8	–	13	8	13	2
Boyle	8	5	8	1	8	4	7	1

On the 3rd of September, 1878, about two hours after the termination of the above match, a fearful calamity occurred on the River Thames, that overwhelmed England with sorrow. Two steamers came into collision; one ('The Princess Alice', a pleasure boat) was cut in twain and over 700 lives – then in the fullness of joy and pleasure – were sacrificed with awful suddenness, and very many families sadly and seriously bereaved.

By one who was deeply impressed by the magnitude of this calamity, and the painful and wide-spread distress that must be suffered thereby, a proposition was publicly made (with the two-fold object of Cricketers doing something to mitigate this distress, and to heal up a disruption of friendship that never should have been severed) that The Australians and the very best Eleven Players of England should play a match on The Oval, the proceeds to be equally divided between 'The Thames Calamity Fund', The Australians, and The Players. This proposition appeared to be favoured by general approval, but it was not adopted; why was never clearly understood, because, although it was stated The Australians could not find vacant days for the match, such a match – *i.e.*, The Australians v. The Players of England – *was actually played at Prince's* on the 11th and 12th of September, six days subsequent to the above proposition being made; but although that match was not played on behalf of The Fund, it is fair to repeat here that The Australians subscribed £100 in aid of that sorely needed help to the bereaved.

ENGLAND V. AUSTRALIA

Played at Kennington Oval, September 6, 7, 8, 1880. – The compiler much regrets that the limited space allotted to the Australians' matches in this book precludes the possibility of giving a lengthened account of this famous contest. He must therefore rest content to put on record the following facts anent the match: – That in the history of the game no contest has created such world-wide interest; that the attendances on the first and second days were the largest ever seen at a cricket match; that 20,814 persons passed through the turnstiles on the Monday, 19,863 on the Tuesday, and 3,751 on the Wednesday; that fine weather favoured the match from start to finish; that the wickets were faultless; that Mr Murdoch's magnificent innings of 153 *not out* was made without a chance, and contained one 5, eighteen 4's, three 3's, thirteen 2's and 41 singles; that Mr W.G. Grace's equally grand innings was made with only one hard chance, and comprised twleve 4's, ten 3's, fourteen 2's, and 46 singles; that superb batting was also shown by Mr Lucas, Lord Harris, Mr McDonnell, and Mr Steel; that the fielding and wicket-keeping on both sides was splendid; that a marvellous change in the aspect of the game was effected on the last day; that universal regret was felt at the unavoidable absence of Mr Spofforth; and that England won the match by 5 wickets. Score:

ENGLAND

Dr W.G. Grace, b Palmer	152 – *not out*	9
Dr E.M. Grace, c Alexander, b Bannerman	36 – b Boyle	0
A.P. Lucas, b Bannerman	55 – c Blackham, b Palmer	2
W. Barnes, b Alexander	28 – c Moule, b Boyle	5
Lord Harris, c Bonnor, b Alexander	52	
F. Penn, b Bannerman	23 – not out	27
A.G. Steel, c Boyle, b Moule	42	
Hon. A. Lyttelton, not out	11 – b Palmer	13
G.F. Grace, c Bannerman, b Moule	0 – b Palmer	0
A. Shaw, b Moule	0	
F. Morley, run out	2	
B 8, 1 b 11	19 N b 1	1
	420	**57**

AUSTRALIA

W.L. Murdoch, c Barnes, b Steel	0 – *not out*	153
A.C. Bannerman, b Morley	32 – c Lucas, b Shaw	8
T.U. Groube, b Steel	11 – c Shaw, b Morley	0
P.S. McDonnell, c Barnes, b Morley	27 – lbw, b W.G. Grace	43
J. Slight, c G.F. Grace, b Morley	11 – c Harris, b W.G. Grace	0
J.M. Blackham, c and b Morley	0 – c E.M. Grace, b Morley	19
G.J. Bonnor, c G.F. Grace, b Shaw	2 – b Steel	16
H.F. Boyle, not out	36 – run out	3
G.E. Palmer, b Morley	6 – c and b Steel	4
G. Alexander, c W.G. Grace, b Steel	6 – c Shaw, b Morley	33
W.H. Moule, c Morley, b W.G. Grace	6 – b Barnes	34
B 9, 1 b 3	12 B 7, 1 b 7	14
	149	**327**

Umpires: H.H. Stephenson and R. Thoms.

THE AUSTRALIANS' BOWLING

	Overs	Mdns	Runs	Wkts	Overs	Mdns	Runs	No b.	Wkts
Boyle	41	15	71	–	17	7	21	–	2
Palmer	70	27	116	1	16.3	5	35	1	3
Alexander	32	10	69	2					
Bannerman	50	12	111	3					
McDonnell	2	–	11	–					
Moule	12.3	4	23	3					

ENGLAND BOWLING

Morley	32	9	56	5	61	30	90	–	3
Mr Steel	39	9	58	3	31	6	73	–	2
Shaw	13	5	21	1	33	18	42	–	1
Mr W.G. Grace	1.1	–	2	1	28	10	66	–	2
Barnes					8.3	3	17	–	1
Mr Lucas					12	7	23	–	–
Mr Penn					3	1	2	–	–

FROM NOTES BY THE EDITOR

BIG HITTING

[…] While these tremendous drives remain chronicled because earning six runs, one may doubt if the length of carry and height of any of them equalled that by G.J. Bonnor in the first England and Australia match at the Oval in 1880. Always associated with the superb catch which G.F. Grace made, this hit was described to me quite recently by Mr S.F. Charlton, an Old Cranleighan, who saw all the match. He wrote that Shaw, the bowler from the Vauxhall end, signalled with a gesture of his hand for G.F. Grace to look out, and the next ball with this guile in it brought about the catch near the sight screen—most certainly an amazing piece of cricket. The youngest of the three Graces playing for England just waited while the batsmen twice ran up and down the pitch before the ball fell into his safe hands. Hitherto my efforts to discover in what position G.F. Grace was fielding always failed. […] (*1946*)

THE AUSTRALIANS IN ENGLAND, 1882

The third team of cricketers from Australia sailed from Melbourne for England in the Peninsular and Oriental Company's steamer *Assam* on March 16th, 1882, and after a very pleasant though not particularly speedy voyage, the vessel anchored at Plymouth at 10.30 on the morning of Wednesday, May 3rd. The manager of the team, Mr C.W. Beal, of the South Wales Cricket Association, accompanied by Messrs Murdoch, Bonnor and Garrett, left the ship and proceeded by train to London. On arriving at Paddington they at once drove to the quarters secured for them at the Tavistock Hotel, Covent Garden, by Mr Henry Perkins, Secretary of the Marylebone Cricket Club, who had been acting as their agent. The other members of the team came round to London in the steamer, and joined their companions about twelve hours after. Mr M'Donnell had had to be carried on board the vessel at Melbourne, suffering from a severe sunstroke, but he, as well as every member of the team, appeared in excellent health and spirits on landing on the shores of the Old Country. Bonnor, it may be mentioned, shortly after landing, threw a cricket ball 119 yards 5 inches, and thereby won a bet made by one of the passengers that he would not, without practice, throw 115 yards. […]

ENGLAND V. AUSTRALIA

Played at Kennington Oval, Monday, Tuesday, August 28, 29, 1882. [...] *Monday*. Murdoch beat Hornby in the toss and deputed Bannerman and Massie to commence the innings. Massie was clean bowled by a yorker on the leg-stump at 6. At 21 Murdoch played a ball from Peate on to his wicket, and, after adding a single, Bonnor was clean bowled middle stump. Horan came in, and then, at 26, Bannerman was splendidly caught by Grace at point, left hand, low down, having been in an hour and 5 minutes for 9 runs. Horan was bowled, leg-stump, at 30. Blackham joined Giffen, and, with the total unchanged, was bowled with the second ball he received. Garrett was the new batsman, and a double change of bowling was found necessary before the new comer was well caught at long-off just after luncheon. At 50 a splendid ball from Barlow just took the top of Boyle's wicket. Jones came in and rain fell for a few minutes. At 59 Blackham skied a ball and was caught, and Spofforth, the last man, joined Jones. The 'Demon' hit a 4, and then Jones was caught at third man, the innings closing for 63. At 3.30 Grace and Barlow started the first innings of England. Spofforth bowled Grace at 13, and Barlow was caught at forward point for 18. With Lucas and Ulyett together, the score was raised to 50 after half-an-hour's play, but at 56 the latter ran out to drive Spofforth and was easily stumped. At 59 Lucas was snapped at the wicket, and one run later Studd was bowled with a bailer without scoring, and half the wickets were down for 60. Read joined Lyttelton, and just when the score reached the total of the Australian innings the latter was caught at the wicket. Barnes came in and scored a single and a 4 and was then bowled by a breaking ball. Steel became Read's partner and 26 runs were added before Steel pulled a ball into his wicket. Eight wickets were down for 96 when Hornby came in. Read made a cut for 3 and Hornby scored a single, bringing up the 100. With only one run added, however, Hornby's leg stump fell, and the innings closed about five minutes before the call of time.

Tuesday. Massie and Bannerman commenced the Australians' second innings at 12.10, the Colonists being 38 to the bad. 30 went up after about 28 minutes' play, two bowling changes having been tried. At 12.45 the balance of 38 runs was knocked off. Barnes relieved Studd at 47, and from his first ball Lucas badly missed Massie at long-off, the batsman then having made 38. 50 was hoisted after 40 minutes' play. It was not until the score reached 66 that loud applause greeted the dismissal of the great hitter, bowled leg stump by Steel. Massie had made 55 out of 66 in 55 minutes, and his hits consisted of nine 4's, two 3's, three 2's, and seven singles. Bonnor took the vacant wicket, but at 70 his middle stump was knocked clean out of the ground, and Murdoch came in, but immediately lost Bannerman, caught at extra mid-off, with the total unchanged. Bannerman had played with great patience for an hour and ten minutes for his 13. Horan joined Murdoch, and the bowling was changed, with the result that the incomer was easily caught. Giffen, who took this place, was out in the same way, and the fourth and fifth wickets were down at 79. Blackham came in, and when the score had been hit up to 99 rain fell, and luncheon was taken.

Resuming at 2.45, after another shower, Blackham was well caught at the wicket without any addition to the score. Jones filled the vacancy and a single by Murdoch sent up the 100. At 114 Jones was run out in a way which gave great dissatisfaction to Murdoch and other Australians. 'Murdoch played a ball to leg, for which Lyttelton ran. The ball was returned, and Jones having completed the first run, and thinking wrongly, but very naturally, that the ball was dead, went out of his ground.' Grace put his wicket down, and the umpire gave him out. Several of the team spoke angrily of Grace's action, but the compiler was informed that after the excitement had cooled down a prominent member of Australian Eleven admitted that he should have done the same thing had he been in Grace's place. There was a good deal of truth in what a gentleman in the pavilion remarked, amidst some laughter, that 'Jones ought to thank the champion for teaching him something.' Spofforth partnered Murdoch, but was bowled middle stump at 117. Garrett came in, and very shortly after, a very smart piece of fielding on the part of Hornby, Studd and Lyttelton caused Murdoch to be run out at 122 for a very careful and good innings of 29. Boyle was last man in, but failed to score, and the tenth wicket fell at the same total at 3.25.

England, wanting 85 runs to win, commenced their second innings at 3.45 with Grace and Hornby. Spofforth bowled Hornby's off stump at 15, made in about as many minutes. Barlow joined Grace, but was bowled first ball at the same total. Ulyett came in, and some brilliant hitting by both batsmen brought the score to 51, when a very fine catch at the wicket dismissed Ulyett. 34 runs were then wanted, with seven wickets to fall. Lucas joined Grace, but when the latter had scored a 2 he was easily taken at mid-off. Lyttelton became Lucas' partner, and the former did all the hitting. Then the game was slow for a time, and 12 successive maiden overs were bowled, both batsmen playing carefully and coolly. Lyttelton scored a single, and then four maiden overs were followed by the dismissal of that batsman – bowled, the score being 66. Only 19 runs were then wanted to win, and there were five wickets to fall. Steel came in, and when Lucas had scored a 4, Steel was easily c and b. Read joined Lucas, but amid intense excitement he was clean bowled without a run being added. Barnes took Read's place and scored a 2, and 3 byes made the total 75, or 10 to win. After being in a long time for 5 Lucas played the next ball into his wicket, and directly Studd joined Barnes the latter was easily caught off his glove without the total being altered. Peate, the last man, came in, but after hitting Boyle to square-leg for 2 he was bowled, and Australia had defeated England by 7 runs.

BOWLING IN THE SECOND INNINGS OF ENGLAND
(Copied from the Australian Score Book)

Spofforth	....	11..	...1	.24.	w.1w	2...	3.4.	....
	...2	...1	1241	211.	...w	.31.	....	....
	...4	....	....	....	....	....	....	....
	....	...w	w2w.	.w..	Spofforth bowled a no ball.			

So Spofforth's last 11 overs (*10 maidens*) were bowled for *2 runs and 4 wickets!*

Garrett	11..	....	11..	1...	.3..	....	.1.1	
Boyle	...1	.4.1	...1	....	w.2.	....	.2..	1...
	....	....	....	....	....	....	...1	...
	....	..4.	....	.ww2				

Score:

AUSTRALIA

A.C. Bannerman, c Grace, b Peate	9	– c Studd, b Barnes 13
H.H. Massie, Esq., b Ulyett	1	– b Steel 55
W.L. Murdoch, Esq., b Peate	13	– run out 29
G.J. Bonnor, Esq., b Barlow	1	– b Ulyett 2
T. Horan, Esq., b Barlow	3	– c Grace, b Peate 2
G. Giffen, Esq., b Peate	2	– c Grace, b Peate 0
J. M'C. Blackham, Esq., c Grace, b Barlow	17	– c Lyttelton, b Peate 7
T.W. Garrett, Esq., c Read, b Peate	10	– not out 2
H.F. Boyle, Esq., b Barlow	2	– b Steel 0
S.P. Jones, Esq., c Barnes, b Barlow	0	– run out 6
F.R. Spofforth, Esq., not out	4	– b Peate 0
B 1	1	B 6 6
	63	**122**

ENGLAND

R.G. Barlow, c Bannerman, b Spofforth	11	– b Spofforth 0
Dr W.G. Grace, b Spofforth	4	– c Bannerman, b Boyle 32
G. Ulyett, st Blackham, b Spofforth	26	– c Blackham, b Spofforth 11
A.P. Lucas, Esq., c Blackham, b Boyle	9	– b Spofforth 5
Hon. A. Lyttelton, c Blackham, b Spofforth	2	– b Spofforth 12
C.T. Studd, Esq., b Spofforth	0	– not out 0
M. Read, not out	19	– b Spofforth 0
W. Barnes, b Boyle	5	– c Murdoch, b Boyle 2
A.G. Steel, Esq., b Garrett	14	– c and b Spofforth 0
A.N. Hornby, Esq., b Spofforth	2	– b Spofforth 9
E. Peate, c Boyle, b Spofforth	0	– b Boyle 2
B 6, l b 2, n b 1	9	B 3, n b 1 4
	101	**77**

Umpires: R. Thoms and L. Greenwood.

ENGLAND BOWLING

	Overs	Mdns	Runs	No b.	Wkts	Overs	Mdns	Runs	No b.	Wkts
Peate	38	24	31	–	4	21	9	40	–	4
Ulyett	9	5	11	–	1	6	2	10	–	1
Barlow	31	22	19	–	5	13	5	27	–	–
Mr Steel	2	1	1	–	–	7	–	15	–	2
Barnes						11	5	15	–	1
Mr Studd						4	1	9	–	–

AUSTRALIAN BOWLING

	Overs	Mdns	Runs	No b.	Wkts	Overs	Mdns	Runs	No b.	Wkts
Mr Spofforth	36.3	18	46	1	7	28	15	44	1	7
Mr Garrett	16	7	22	–	1	7	2	10	–	–
Mr Boyle	19	7	24	–	2	20	11	19	–	3

The wickets fell thus:

	1 for	2 for	3 for	4 for	5 for	6 for	7 for	8 for	9 for	10 for
Australia, 1st inns	6	21	22	26	30	30	48	50	59	63
England, 1st ″	13	18	56	59	60	63	70	96	101	101
Australia, 2nd ″	66	70	70	79	79	99	114	117	122	122
England, 2nd ″	15	15	51	53	66	70	70	75	75	77

THE HON. IVO BLIGH'S
TWELVE IN AUSTRALIA 1882–83

While taking part in the game called 'Tug of War' on board the *Peshawur* – the steamship which carried the English Cricketers to the Antipodes – the Hon. Ivo Bligh severely injured his right hand, and this mishap prevented his playing in either of the first six matches. This accident was not, unfortunately, the least serious one to befall a member of the team. On Monday, October 16th 1882, the *Peshawur* came into violent collision with the barque *Glenroy*, a short distance from Colombo. One of the crew, a Lascar, had one of his legs fractured in two places, but it was believed that scratches and bruises represented the full extent of the damage suffered by any one else on board. It was subsequently ascertained, however, that Morley had sustained a severe injury to one of his ribs, and though, with admirable pluck, he bowled in several matches, the unfortunate accident compelled him to leave the field during the progress of the second game, and prevented his taking any part in the 3rd, 7th, 8th, 9th, 10th, 14th, 15th, and 17th contests. [...]

THE HON. IVO BLIGH'S TEAM V.
MR MURDOCH'S ELEVEN

Played at Sydney, Friday, Saturday, Monday, Tuesday, January 26, 27, 29, 30, 1883.

The first match having resulted in a win for the Australian Eleven by nine wickets, and the second in a victory for the Englishmen by an innings and 27 runs, the third contest was invested with extraordinary interest, and on the opening day the attendance was the largest ever witnessed on the Moore Park ground, it being computed that from 20,000 to 23,000 spectators were present.

The Hon. Ivo Bligh again beat Murdoch in the toss, and again decided his team should have first innings, Barlow and C.T. Studd, by excellent cricket, carried the total to 41, when the latter was finely caught at the wicket. Leslie came in, but with three runs added, was clean bowled by a fast 'yorker,' making room for Steel. From the last ball bowled before luncheon Barlow was well caught, the total then standing at 67. Upon resuming Steel was bowled without adding to his score, and four wickets were down for 68 runs. At 76 Barnes was caught at the wicket, and then Read and Tylecote offered so prolonged a resistance that 115 runs were put on before the latter was run out. Tylecote's 66 was the highest score he made during the tour, and is described as, 'a most brilliant display of safe all-round hitting, without giving a possible chance to anyone in the field'. Bates partnered Read, and the total was quickly hit up to 223, when an easy catch at square-leg got rid of the Reigate amateur for a 'fine, vigorous, all-round display.' Bates was caught at 224; the English captain clean bowled at 244; and a good ball from Palmer dismissed G.B. Studd and brought the innings to a conclusion for 247. On a fresh wicket the home team scored 8 runs without losing a wicket, and then stumps were drawn for the day.

Showers fell during Friday night, and on Saturday the wicket was a trifle dead and the sky cloudy and threatening more rain. These circumstances, however, apparently in no way militated against the success of the overnight not outs – Bannerman and Giffen, who ran up the capital total of 76 for the first wicket, the latter being the first to leave, directly after luncheon, for a good innings of 41. Murdoch succeeded Giffen, and after he had been badly missed by Leslie when he had scored five, and Bannerman had had a life at the hands of Morley when he had made 39, the two batsmen brought up the 100. Then rain caused a cessation of play from 3.15 to 5.15. On the sloppy wicket 33 more runs were scored in three-quarters of an hour, during which time Bannerman was again missed, this time by Barnes. At the call of time 133 runs were totalled for the loss of only one wicket, Bannerman being *not out*, 68, and Murdoch, not out, 17.

During Saturday night and Sunday, rain fell heavily with but little intermission, and when the game was continued at 11.25 on the Monday the ground was exceedingly dead and heavy. With seven runs added to the overnight score Murdoch was out leg before wicket, and M'Donnell, who succeeded him, clean bowled at the same total. Bannerman and Horan put on 36 runs, and the former was then caught off Morley when within six of a 'century'. Despite the chances he gave his 94 was a grand innings, his off-driving and cutting being frequently brilliant. Massie filled the vacancy, but was caught at point without increasing the score. Bonnor followed, but was splendidly caught before he had scored a run, and six wickets were down for 178. Blackham and Horan added 18 to the score when the latter fell to a one-hand catch at mid-off, and Garrett, who came after him was caught in the slips before the total had been increased. Palmer stayed with Blackham while 22 runs were added, and was then caught, and the innings terminated.

When the wicket used by the visitors had been rolled C.T. Studd and Leslie commenced the second innings. Leslie was clean bowled at 13, but Barlow helped C.T. Studd to take the score to 45, when the latter shared the fate of Leslie for a freely-hit 25. Steel was lbw at 55, but Barlow and Read brought the total to 87. Then Read was bowled for 21, having given a possible chance early in his innings. At 94 Barlow was sent back for a carefully-compiled 24, and at the same total Barnes was lbw. Tylecote was caught at 97 and Bates at 98, and when 115 had been reached G.B. Studd was out in a like manner. Morley kept his wicket up for a time but was eventually bowled without scoring, and the innings closed for 153, the English captain carrying his bat for 17. Murdoch's team was set the task of scoring 123 to win, and in the little time left for play before stumps were drawn for the day Morley bowled four overs and Barlow three, without a run being scored or a wicket lost.

At 11.10 on the Tuesday the game was resumed in splendid weather. Giffen was clean bowled at 11, and Bannerman, the other overnight not-out, caught at point at 12. Murdoch was caught at 18, and without any runs being added, M'Donnell fell to a splendid catch at point. Horan was run out at 30 and Massie was caught at 33. Blackham hit with great vigour. He lost the company of Bonnor – clean bowled – at 59, and of Spofforth – caught – at 72, and then played a ball on to his wicket at 80. Garrett, the last man, came in, and when two leg-byes and a wide had been scored, Barlow bowled him, and the innings terminated for 83, the Englishmen thus winning the match by 69 runs. Score:

THE HON. IVO BLIGH'S TEAM

R.G. Barlow, c Murdoch, b Spofforth .... .28 – c Palmer, b Horan .... .24
C.T. Studd, Esq., c Blackham, b Garrett .... .21 – b Spofforth .... .25
C.F.H. Leslie, Esq., b Spofforth .... .0 – b Spofforth 8
A.G. Steel, Esq., b Garrett .... .17 – lbw, b Spofforth 6
W.W. Read, Esq., c Massie, b Bannerman ... .66 – b Horan .... .21
W. Barnes, b Spofforth .... .2 – lbw, b Spofforth 3
E.F.S. Tylecote, Esq., run out .... .66 – c Bonnor, b Spofforth 0
W. Bates, c M'Donnell, b Spofforth .... .17 – c Murdoch, b Horan 4
G.B. Studd, Esq., b Palmer .... .3 – c Garrett, b Spofforth 8
Hon. Ivo Bligh (*Captain*), b Palmer ...... .13 – not out .... .17
F. Morley, not out .... .2 – b Spofforth 0
  B 8, L b 3, n b 1 .... .12   B 5, l b 2 7

                                      247   **123**

MR MURDOCH'S ELEVEN

A.C. Bannerman, c Bates, b Morley .... .94 – c Bligh, b Barlow 5
G. Giffen, st Tylecote, b Bates .... .41 – b Barlow 7
W.L. Murdoch (*Captain*), lbw, b Steel ..... .19 – c G.B. Studd, b Morley 0
P.S. M'Donnell, b Steel .... .0 – c Bligh, b Morley 0
T. Horan, c Steel, b Morley .... .19 – run out 8
H.H. Massie, c Bligh, b Steel .... .1 – c C.T. Studd, b Barlow ...... .11
G.J. Bonnor, c G.B. Studd, b Morley ...... .0 – b Barlow 8
J. M'C. Blackham, b Barlow .... .27 – b Barlow .... .26
T.W. Garrett, c Barlow, b Morley .... .0 – b Barlow 0
G.E. Palmer, c G.B. Studd, b Barnes ...... .7 – not out 2
F.R. Spofforth, not out .... .0 – c Steel, b Barlow 7
  B 6, l b 2, w 1, n b 1 .... .10   B 6, l b 2, w 1 9

                                      218   **83**

AUSTRALIAN BOWLING

	Overs	Mdns	Runs	Wde	No b.	Wkts	Overs	Mdns	Runs	Wde	Wkts
Giffen	12	3	37	–	–	–					
Palmer	58	21	38	–	1	2	9	3	19	–	–
Spofforth	51	19	73	–	–	4	41.1	23	44	–	7
Garrett	27	8	54	–	–	2	13	3	31	–	–
Bannerman	11	2	17	–	–	1					
M'Donnell	4	–	16	–	–	–					
Horan							17	10	22	–	3

ENGLISH BOWLING

Bates	45	20	55	–	–	1					
Morley	34	16	47	–	1	4	35	19	34	–	2
Mr Steel	26	14	27	–	–	3					
Barnes	13	6	22	–	–	1					
Mr C.T. Studd	14	11	5	1	–	–					
Barlow	47.1	31	52	–	–	1	34.2	20	40	1	7

SHAW'S TEAM V.
COMBINED ELEVEN OF AUSTRALIA

Played at Sydney, Friday, Saturday, Monday, Tuesday, February 20, 21, 23, 24, 1885. – The eleven which the Englishmen had to meet on this occasion included four members of Murdoch's team – Bannerman, Scott, Bonnor and Spofforth – and of the remaining seven, five had appeared on English grounds as members of representative teams visiting the Old Country from Australia. The two notable cricketers, Evans and Trumble, completed one of the strongest combinations the Australian Colonies could produce, and after playing twenty-five matches without a single reverse, Shaw's Team sustained a defeat at the hands of this powerful eleven by the narrow majority of six runs, after one of the finest contests ever witnessed at Sydney. […]

Massie, the captain of the combined eleven, beat Shrewsbury for choice of innings, and sent in Jones and Bannerman to face the bowling of Peel and Attewell. Bannerman gave a hard chance to slip at 20, and at 36 Ulyett bowled for Peel. With 4 runs added luncheon was taken, and at two o'clock a terrific storm of lightning, thunder and hail, burst over the ground. In an incredibly short time it had the appearance of a field of snow, and then, the hail quickly melting, the ground became a sheet of water. It was scarcely to be expected that play could be resumed that day, but the water was soon absorbed, and at quarter past 4, Jones and Bannerman continued their innings, the wicket, of course, being in a sloppy condition. With the total at 45 Jones was stumped, and a run later, Bannerman was caught at short-leg. At 56 Horan was caught at the wicket, and at 73 Scott was well taken at slip. Two wickets fell with the total at 83, Bonnor being caught at slip and Jarvis clean bowled first ball. Trumble was caught in the long-field at 92, and then Garrett and Spofforth played out time, the score being 97 for eight wickets.

On the Saturday morning Spofforth was stumped at 101, and then Garrett and Evans made a splendid stand for the last wicket. Attewell, Flowers, Peel, Ulyett and Bates were all tried, but to no purpose. Flowers and Attewell bowled again but at lunch time the two batsmen were still together, and the total 175. After the interval Ulyett bowled for Bates, and when 6 runs had been added succeeded in getting Evans caught at the wicket, no fewer than 80 runs having been put on for the last wicket. The new wicket having been rolled, Shrewsbury and Scotton opened the batting for the Englishmen, Spofforth and Garrett starting the bowling. The first five overs were maidens, and then 20 soon appeared. At 25 Horan bowled for Garrett, and at 31 Shrewsbury was caught and bowled by Spofforth. Other misfortunes quickly followed, as at 33 both Ulyett and Barnes were out. Ulyett was clean bowled with a 'yorker', and the first ball Barnes received bounded from the wicket-keeper's legs, and the batsman had to retire, stumped. Bates was caught at point from a bumper at 46, and Briggs fell to forward point at 56. Scotton was given out caught at the wicket at 70, and at 82 Read was caught at point. With Flowers and Attewell together a change in the bowling was found necessary, Evans going on for Horan. At 111 Flowers was caught at the wicket, and without any addition to the total, Horan, who had relieved Evans, clean bowled Attewell with a 'yorker'. Peel and Hunter gave some trouble, and 22 runs were added before Horan bowled the latter. With the conclusion of the innings stumps were drawn for the day.

Bannerman and Bonnor began the second innings of Australia at noon on the third day, Ulyett and Peel being the bowlers. The score was slowly hit to 28 and then Bannerman gave a couple of chances which were not accepted. Bonnor having made 29 out of 37 was bowled by a 'yorker', and then Horan and Bannerman took the total to 56, when lunch was taken. Upon resuming Bannerman was caught at point, having been at the wickets an hour and a half for 16 runs. Soon after Jones came in Flowers bowled for Ulyett, but the parting came from the other end, Attewell, who had relieved Peel, bowling Jones for a well-made 22. Scott hit a 4 and was then caught at slip, Trumble filling the vacancy. When 110 had been posted Horan made a grand square-leg hit off Flowers, the ball pitching into the pavilion reserve. Flowers then gave way to Bates, who immediately bowled Horan off his thigh for 36, made in his best form. Half the wickets were now down for 119. Massie and Trumble carried the score to 151, when the former was then clean bowled by a breakback. Jarvis was caught and bowled after making a couple, and then Trumble, who had played exceedingly well, was taken at long-on for 32. Bates bowled Evans for a single, and then a splendid one-hand catch at mid-off dismissed Spofforth and brought the innings to a conclusion for 165 just after five o'clock. After an adjournment of 20 minutes Shrewsbury and Scotton faced the bowling of Spofforth and Garrett, Shaw's team wanting 214 to win. Only 14 runs were scored when one of Spofforth's fastest deliveries clean bowled Scotton, and when his successor – Ulyett – had made 4 he was thrown out by Bannerman in trying a short run. Shrewsbury and Barnes then kept their wickets intact until the call of time, the score at 6 o'clock being 29 for 2 wickets.

Before a run was scored on the last day Barnes was caught at the wicket, but Shrewsbury and Bates put on 30 before the former was clean bowled by Spofforth, who dismissed Briggs in the same way a couple of runs later. Half the wickets were now down for 61, and an easy victory for the Colonials seemed assured. Bates and Flowers took the score to 92, when the Yorkshireman fell a victim to the wicket-keeper for a fine and free 31, which included two 4's and a grand hit to long-on, off Spofforth, clean over the fence for 5. Flowers and Read then made the splendid stand which completely altered the aspect of the game. The bowling was repeatedly changed, but both batsmen played with ease and confidence and scored with great freedom. Spofforth, in particular, came in for severe punishment, but when only 20 runs were wanted, he had his revenge by clean bowling Read at 194. The outgoing batsman's score of 56 was the highest he had made in eleven-a-side matches, and his best performance in Australia. The only really bad stroke he made was off the first ball he received from Spofforth, but he gave no chances, and his innings included no fewer than nine 4's. Flowers and

Read had put on 102 runs for the seventh wicket. Attewell came in, but was run out with the total unchanged, and only 5 runs were added before Peel was caught at the wicket. When Hunter, the last man, went in only 15 runs were wanted and the excitement round the ground and in the pavilion and stand was intense. By 2's and singles the total was hit up to 207, when Spofforth took the ball, and from his first delivery Flowers was caught at point from a rising ball, and Shaw's team suffered their first defeat by 7 runs. Flowers' innings of 56 was, like Read's, the highest and best he scored in the first-class matches of the tour. Score:

THE COMBINED ELEVEN OF AUSTRALIA

A.C. Bannerman, c Peel, b Flowers . . . . .13 – c Shrewsbury, b Ulyett 16
S.P. Jones, st Hunter, b Flowers . . . . .28 – b Attewell 22
T. Horan, c Hunter, b Attewell . . . . .7 – b Bates 36
H.J.H. Scott, c Ulyett, b Attewell . . . . .5 – c Barnes, b Attewell 4
G.J. Bonnor, c Barnes, b Flowers . . . . .18 – b Ulyett 29
J.W. Trumble, c Read, b Attewell . . . . .13 – c Ulyett, b Bates 32
H.H. Massie (*Capt.*), c Scotton, b Flowers . . . . .2 – b Bates 21
A.H. Jarvis, b Attewell .0 – c and b Peel 2
F.R. Spofforth, st Hunter, b Flowers . . . . .3 – c Attewell, b Bates 0
T.W. Garrett, not out .51 – not out 0
E. Evans, c Hunter, b Ulyett . . . . .33 – b Bates 1
    B 3, l b 5 8   B 1, l b 1 2
                                        181   **165**

SHAW'S TEAM

W.H. Scotton, c Jarvis, b Horan . . . . .22 – b Spofforth 2
A. Shrewsbury, c and b Spofforth . . . . .18 – b Spofforth 24
G. Ulyett, b Spofforth .2 – run out 4
W. Barnes, st Jarvis, b Spofforth . . . . .0 – c Jarvis, b Trumble 5
W. Bates, c Evans, b Horan . . . . .12 – c Jarvis, b Spofforth 31
J. Briggs, c Scott, b Horan . . . . .3 – b Spofforth 1
W. Flowers, c Jarvis, b Spofforth . . . . .24 – c Evans, b Spofforth 56
J.M. Read, c Evans, b Horan . . . . .4 – b Spofforth 56
W. Attewell, b Horan .14 – run out 0
R. Peel, not out . . . . .8 – c Jarvis, b Trumble 3
J. Hunter, b Horan . . . . .13 – not out 5
    B 8, l b 3, n b 2 .13   B 7, l b 9, w 3, n b 1 20
                                        133   **207**

THE BOWLING OF THE COMBINED ELEVEN

	Overs	Mdns	Runs	No b.	Wkts	Overs	Mdns	Runs	Wds	No b.	Wkts
Spofforth	48	23	54	2	4	48.1	22	90	–	–	6
Horan	37.1	22	40	–	6	9	4	23	–	–	–
Garrett	6	2	17	–	–	16	8	31	–	–	–
Evans	4	1	9	–	–	4	1	8	–	1	–
Trumble						26	13	26	3	–	2
Jones						3	–	9	–	–	–

THE BOWLING OF SHAW'S TEAM

Attewell	71	47	53	–	4	58	36	54	–	–	2
Ulyett	12.2	8	17	–	1	39	25	42	–	–	2
Flowers	46	24	46	–	5	20	14	19	–	–	–
Bates	6	2	6	–	–	20	10	24	–	–	5
Peel	32	13	51	–	–	20	10	24	–	–	1

SHAW'S TEAM V. AUSTRALIA

Played at Sydney, Saturday, Monday, Tuesday, March 14, 16, 17, 1885. The very close finish recorded in the previous match between Shaw's team and a picked eleven of Australia, caused an extraordinary amount of interest to be taken in this contest, and there could not have been less than 12,000 spectators on the opening day, while 6,000 was the estimated number present on each of the other two days. The Australian team was differently constituted from that which defeated the Englishmen by the narrow majority of six runs, Palmer, M'Donnell, G. Giffen and Blackham taking the places of Scott, Massie, Jarvis and Evans. These changes, as the result unquestionably proved, greatly added to the bowling strength of the team without weakening its batting powers to any appreciable extent. The successful bowling of Giffen in the first innings, and of Palmer in the second, went, perhaps, as far towards achieving an eight wickets' victory for Australia, as the magnificent hitting of Bonnor. On the first day 11 wickets fell for 280 runs; on the second day only 7 batsmen were dismissed for an aggregate of 297 runs; while on the third day, after a night's heavy rain, 14 wickets were captured for a total of only 116 runs.

Shrewsbury won choice of innings in tossing with Blackham, and at 12.20 took Ulyett with him to the wickets. Spofforth had not arrived, so the bowling was entrusted to Giffen and Palmer. When Ulyett had made 10 he pulled a ball into his wicket, and simultaneously with his dismissal Spofforth appeared on the field. Scotton filled the vacancy; and when Shrewsbury had hit Palmer for a couple of 4's that bowler gave way to Spofforth. Shrewsbury batted in fine free form, and Scotton played a strictly defensive game as usual. At luncheon the score was 50, and upon resuming Scotton was caught at the wicket for 4 at 52. Barnes came in, and he and Shrewsbury raised the total to 76, when the English captain was clean bowled for a capital innings of 40. Barnes and Bates scored with great freedom, and a short time only elapsed before the century was hoisted. Spofforth gave way to Trumble, and Palmer relieved Giffen, but as the rate of scoring only increased with these changes, Giffen tried again in place of Palmer, and at last succeeded in clean bowling Barnes with a breakback at 159, the outgoing batsman's 50 having been made in his best form. Read became Bates' partner, and runs came just as fast. Jones bowled for Trumble, and after some time, with the score at 186, made a magnificent catch from his own bowling, which sent Bates back for a splendidly-hit 60. With Read and Flowers together the 200 was soon telegraphed, and shortly after Spofforth relieved Jones. At 219 Flowers was clean bowled, and Briggs, after making a 3 from the first ball he received, was well caught at point from the second. Giffen bowled Attewell after he had scored a single, and Peel joined Read, who then gave a chance of stumping. Later on, with his score 37, he was caught from a no ball of Spofforth's, and with the total 252 was clean bowled by Giffen for a very freely-hit and excellent innings of 47. Hunter scored 13, including two 4's in succession from Spofforth, but in trying a third he was clean bowled, and brought the innings to a conclusion for 269. Only ten minutes remained for play when the Englishmen took the field, so Garrett and Palmer were deputed to open the first innings of the Combined Eleven, to the bowling of Ulyett and Peel. Ulyett sent down the first over, and the last ball – a fast 'yorker' – clean bowled Palmer. Trumble came in, and when the total reached 11 for one wicket play ceased for the day.

Only 4 runs were added next morning before Peel bowled Trumble off his legs. M'Donnell followed, and having scored 20 out of 25, was caught at extra cover-point with the total at 40. Soon after Bannerman came in Attewell bowled for Peel, and at 66 Bates relieved Ulyett, but no other wicket was obtained before luncheon, at which time the score had reached 80. Upon resuming, Ulyett went on again, bowling against the wind, while a little later on that bowler crossed over, Barnes taking his place. Bannerman now gave a difficult chance to Scotton off Ulyett, which was not accepted, and directly after both batsmen were within an ace of being bowled by the Yorkshireman. Barnes, however, clean bowled Garrett next over for a carefully made 32, and got his successor, Giffen, caught at slip for a single. Bannerman gave another rather difficult chance to Scotton, which was also missed, and then Horan, who had taken Garrett's place, was well caught at slip off Ulyett with the total 119. Bonnor came next, and Bannerman had another life at the hands of Scotton – a very easy one this time. Flowers bowled for Ulyett, and off his second ball Bannerman was caught at point for 51, seven wickets then being down for 134. At this point the prospects of a follow-on appeared very probable, but upon Jones joining Bonnor a magnificent stand was made, and the aspect of the game underwent a complete change. Bonnor started in very indifferent form, but afterwards hit with the utmost brilliancy. After a short period of slow play Bonnor hit Barnes to the pavilion for 4, and drove the next ball over the boundary for 5. From this time to the close of the day's play the English bowling was punished with the utmost severity. Flowers gave way to Peel, and soon afterwards Attewell relieved Barnes, a hit off the last named bowler by Bonnor saving the follow-on. Ulyett was tried again, but soon gave way to Flowers. At length Barnes went on again, and from his first ball Bonnor was easily caught at third man with the total at 288. Bonnor's magnificently-hit innings of 128 was the highest made against Shaw's team, and included four 5's and fourteen 4's. Bonnor and Jones put on 154 for the 8th wicket. It was not to be expected that so long an innings should be played without chances being given, and Bonnor's fine contribution was not without blem-ishes. Though narrowly escaping being bowled several times, he gave no real chances in the field until he had made 81, when Peel misjudged a bad hit. With his score 98 he might have been caught by Barnes at slip, and later on was missed by Read at long-on. At the call of time the total stood at 308 for 8 wickets, Jones, not out, 40, and Blackham, not out, 11.

Heavy rain having fallen from a little after midnight until 9 o'clock on the morning of the third day, the wicket was altogether in favour of the bowlers when the game resumed at noon. The last two Australian wickets only added one run to the overnight total, Jones being immediately run out for a fine defensive innings of 40, while Spofforth fell to a capital catch at third man after scoring a single. Shaw's Team commenced their second innings in a minority of 40 runs, Shrewsbury and Ulyett again being the first pair. They were opposed by Spofforth and Palmer, and no change of bowling was found necessary during the innings. Ulyett was caught at cover-point after making a couple, and Scotton fell to mid-off wihtout having troubled the scorers. A fine catch at long-on got rid of Shrewsbury, and Bates was given out caught at the wicket, the fourth wicket falling with the score at 20. Read was caught at short-leg, and then Barnes and Flowers kept their wickets intact until lunch time, when the total had reached 42. Upon resumption of play Flowers was caught at third man at 46, and then 20 runs were added before Briggs, in attempting a fourth run for a bye, was run out. Barnes was caught at short mid-on from a bumper, Peel caught and bowled by Spofforth, and Hunter clean bowled, the innings closing for the poor total of 77. The Combined Eleven had therefore only 38 runs to make, but these were not obtained without the loss of two good wickets, M'Donnell being caught at third man with the total 3, and Bannerman clean bowled at 16. Horan and Jones then hit off the required runs, and Shaw's team suffered their second and last defeat by 8 wickets. Score:

SHAW'S TEAM

G. Ulyett, b Giffen	.10 – c Garrett, b Palmer	.2
A. Shrewsbury, b Giffen	.40 – c Bonnor, b Spofforth	.16
W.H. Scotton, c Blackham, b Giffen	.4 – c Jones, b Spofforth	.0
W. Barnes, b Giffen	.50 – c Bannerman, b Spofforth	.20
W. Bates, c and b Jones	.64 – c Blackham, b Palmer	.1
J.M. Read, b Giffen	.47 – c Bannerman, b Spofforth	.6
W. Flowers, b Giffen	.14 – c Jones, b Palmer	.7
J. Briggs, c Palmer, b Spofforth	.3 – run out	.5
W. Attewell, b Giffen	.1 – not out	.1
J. Hunter, b Spofforth	.13 – b Palmer	.4
R. Peel, not out	.17 – c and b Spofforth	.0
B 5, n b 1	.6 B 14, n b 1	.15
	269	77

AUSTRALIA

G.E. Palmer, b Ulyett	.0	
T.W. Garrett, b Barnes	.32	
J.W. Trumble, b Peel	.5	
P.S. M'Donnell, c Attewell, b Ulyett	.20 – c Ulyett, b Peel	.3
A.C. Bannerman, c Shrewsbury, b Flowers	.51 – b Barnes	.8
G. Giffen, c Attewell, b Barnes	.1	
T. Horan, c Barnes, b Ulyett	.9 – not out	.12
G.J. Bonnor, c Bates, b Barnes	.128	
S.P. Jones, run out	.40 – not out	.15
J. M'C. Blackham, not out	.11	
F.R. Spofforth, c Read, b Barnes	.1	
B 5, l b 1, w 2, n b 3	.11 B 2	.2
	309	38

THE BOWLING OF SHAW'S TEAM

	Overs	Mdns	Runs	Wds	No b.	Wkts	Overs	Mdns	Runs	No b.	Wkts
Ulyett	54	25	91	–	2	3					
Peel	31	12	53	–	–	1	9	4	16	–	1
Attewell	18	13	22	–	–	–	3	1	4	–	–
Flowers	14	5	27	–	–	1	3.3	2	3	–	–
Barnes	35.3	17	61	–	1	4	9	3	15	–	1
Bates	17	5	44	2	–	–					

AUSTRALIAN BOWLING

	Overs	Mdns	Runs	Wds	No b.	Wkts	Overs	Mdns	Runs	No b.	Wkts
Giffen	52	14	117	–	–	7					
Palmer	16	5	35	–	–	–	19.3	7	32	–	4
Spofforth	29	10	61	–	1	2	20	8	30	1	5
Garrett	2	1	5	–	–	–					
Trumble	12	5	16	–	–	–					
Horan	5	2	12	–	–	–					
Jones	10	5	17	–	–	1					

AUSTRALIANS V. MIDDLESEX

Played at Lord's, Thursday, Friday, Saturday, June 24, 25, 26, 1886. – The play on the opening day was thoroughly good and enjoyable. Middlesex scored a very respectable first innings, Spillman and J.G. Walker being by far the most prominent of the batsmen; and then the Australians, in an hour and a quarter, put on 96 runs without losing a wicket, Jones being not out 52, and Scott not out 42, at the close of play. The ground was in splendid condition, and the company was very large. It must be mentioned here as a matter of record that Captain Hyde, a retired captain of the Peninsular and Oriental Company's service, died suddenly on the ground during the game. The deceased gentleman was a well-known frequenter of Lord's Ground, and his face and figure were doubtless familiar to hundreds of people.

On the second day the wicket was still in grand order for run-getting, and the Australians increased their score to 155 before the first wicket fell, when Jones was caught for an altogether admirable 76. Giffen came in, and after he was missed by Spillman at the wicket, runs came at a great pace, the total at lunch-time being 237 for one wicket, Scott 115 not out. During the interval Jones was presented, in the committee-room of the pavilion, with a gold watch and chain, subscribed for him at the Gentlemen's match in the previous week. The Hon. W. Wilson, of Victoria, made the presentation on behalf of the Australian friends of the team, to whom the subscription was restricted. On the resumption of the game, the County total was soon left behind, and the score was up to 272 before the second wicket fell. Scott was then lbw for 123, a splendid display of batting, lasting four hours and twenty minutes, and including sixteen 4's, six 3's, and ten 2's. After this the Australians went out one after another in the most extraordinary way, and the whole side were out for only 354, or 95 to the good, after it had seemed as if they were set for a 500 innings. The Middlesex eleven fielded up very well, and Burton deserves a special word of praise for his excellent bowling. When the County went in for the second time they scored 83 for one wicket, A.J. Webbe being not out 33, and S.W. Scott not out 30, at the call of time. They were thus only 12 runs behind, with nine wickets to fall – one of the most extraordinary changes from lunch-time to the finish which we ever remember to have seen in a first-class match in fine weather. Cricketers and the public are familiar enough with sensational incidents on treacherous wickets, but here there was nothing to account for the fluctuations which passed over the game.

On the Saturday Webbe and Scott both played capitally, and increased the total to 129 before the second wicket fell. Then, except for G.F. Vernon's 37, no stand was made against Palmer's destructive bowling, the famous Victorian taking seven wickets for 84 runs, and bowling quite as well as ever he did in the tour. He got on his leg-break with wonderful success, and some of the batsmen could hardly look at him. The Colonists had 123 to get to win, and the 100 went up with only three wickets down. Four runs later Giffen, who had played superb cricket for 52, struck a ball into his wicket, and then followed a 'rot' which is difficult to understand or excuse. One after another the Australians went out from sheer bad cricket, and 8 runs were wanted to win with only one wicket to fall. Blackham and Pope were the last two in, and the veteran played with the utmost coolness. Burton, who had been bowling with excellent judgment and great success, was perhaps unwise to tempt Blackham to hit when matters got to the very finish, but, however that may be, he pitched a slow ball up, which the Australian jumped at and drove to the boundary, this winning the game, amidst the greatest excitement, by one wicket. English cricketers have often been blamed for exhibiting a lack of nerve at the pinch of a game, but here the Australians, with a very easy task before them, got into a condition that was much like panic. Burton's bowling in this match, 14 wickets for 192 runs, was one of the features of the season at Lord's. It may be as well to mention here, for the purposes of permanent record, that Giffen's 52 was the last of four great innings in succession. He scored, in the week which ended with this match, 72, 78, 77, and 52. Score:

MIDDLESEX

Mr A.E. Stoddart, lbw, b Palmer	.3 –	b Palmer 16
Mr A.J. Webbe, c Jones, b Palmer	.13 –	c Scott, b Palmer 61
Mr S.W. Scott, c Blackham, b Garrett	.29 –	c sub., b Giffen 68
Mr J.G. Walker, b Evans	.67 –	b Palmer 0
Spillman, c and b Evans	.87 –	st Blackham, b Palmer 6
Mr T.C. O'Brien, c Evans, b Garrett	.16 –	b Palmer 0
Mr G.B. Studd, b Evans	.1 –	st Blackham, b Palmer 3
Mr G.F. Vernon, c Bruce, b Palmer	.23 –	c Giffen, b Palmer 37
West, b Evans	.2 –	c Pope, b Giffen 0
Burton, b Evans	.5 –	c Bruce, b Giffen 1
Mr J. Robertson, not out	.2 –	not out 4
B 3, l-b 7, n-b 1 11		B 14, l-b 7 21

AUSTRALIANS

S.P. Jones, c Webbe, b Burton	76	– c Webbe, b Burton	22
H.J.H. Scott, lbw, b Robertson	123	– st Spillman, b Burton	4
G. Giffen, c Studd, b Burton	77	– b Burton	52
A.H. Jarvis, c Stoddart, b Burton	6	– c Spillman, b Burton	19
W. Bruce, c Walker, b Burton	3	– c Burton, b West	1
J.W. Trumble, c and b Burton	3	– c Webbe, b Burton	4
E. Evans, lbw, b Robertson	3	– c Walker, b West	1
J. M'C. Blackham, c and b Burton	0	– not out	6
T.W. Garrett, c Scott, b Burton	29	– c Spillman, b West	7
G.E. Palmer, c Webbe, b Burton	8	– c Robertson, b Burton	5
R.J. Pope, not out	11	– not out	0
B 9, l-b 5, n-b 1	15	L-b	2
	354		**123**

AUSTRALIAN BOWLING

	Overs	Mdns	Runs	Wkts	Overs	Mdns	Runs	Wkts
Giffen	19	7	33	0	51	20	89	3
Palmer	43	19	72	3	48.1	21	84	7
Garrett	23	3	63	2	7	3	13	0
Bruce	3	1	5	0				
Trumble	20	7	35	0	4	1	5	0
Jones	3	2	4	0				
Evans	36	18	36	5	9	6	5	0

Trumble bowled a no-ball in the first innings.

MIDDLESEX BOWLING

	Overs	Mdns	Runs	Wkts	Overs	Mdns	Runs	Wkts
Burton	72.2	24	136	8	32	13	56	6
Mr Robertson	65	28	88	2	19	7	40	0
West	33	17	62	0	13	7	25	3
Mr Webbe	14	5	29	0				
Mr Stoddart	3	1	11	0				
Mr S.W. Scott	9	5	7	0				
Mr O'Brien	1	0	6	0				

Mr Robertson bowled a no-ball in the first innings.

THE ENGLISH TEAMS IN AUSTRALIA

Two English teams visited Australia in the season of 1887–88, but it is certain that such a piece of folly will never be perpetrated again. Having regard to the fact that eleven-a-side matches are only practicable at Melbourne, Sydney, and Adelaide, it was clear from the first that two combinations would not be able to pay their way, and, though we do not know the exact result of Shaw, Shrewsbury, and Lillywhite's venture, the Melbourne Club frankly admitted a heavy loss over Mr Vernon's team. It would serve no purpose now to go into the causes of the blunder, for a blunder in every way it undoubtedly was. The Melbourne Club authorities averred that it was well known their intention of bringing out an English team had only been postponed from the previous year, while the Sydney people, who supported Shaw and Shrewsbury, declared that for all they knew, when they asked Shrewsbury and his friends to get up an eleven for the centenary celebration in New South Wales, the Melbourne Club's project had been abandoned. Wherever the blame lay, the effect was to throw a complete damper on the visits of English cricketers to the Colonies. It is satisfactory to think, however, that, apart from financial considerations, both tours were completely successful, the cricket shown being in every way creditable to the English men. Mr Vernon's team only lost one match, and in that one they played a first innings of over 300 runs, while Shaw and Shrewsbury's side suffered but two defeats. For one special occasion the two elevens joined forces, and decisively beat Combined Australia – a strong, though not quite a representative, side. The record of Mr Vernon's combination was indeed a brilliant one when we take into consideration the fact that the death of his father compelled Lord Hawke to return to England, and that Bates's services were lost through a painful accident to his eye – an accident which kept the popular Yorkshireman out of all first-class cricket in the English season of 1888, and from which, it is feared, he can never wholly recover. He was injured while practising on the Melbourne Ground, a ball hit from a neighbouring net striking him with frightful force.

SHREWSBURY'S TEAM V. NEW SOUTH WALES

Played at Sydney, Friday, Saturday, November 11, 12, 1887. – Turner and Ferris, on a bad wicket, carried all before them, and on the second day the Englishmen were beaten by ten wickets, this being one of their worst performances. It is likely enough that they had not got into form, but Turner and Ferris must have bowled wonderfully well. The New South Wales men had a little luck in rain making the wicket easier while they were batting, but they fairly outplayed their opponents at all points.

SHREWSBURY'S TEAM

A. Shrewsbury, c sub., b Ferris	20 –	lbw, b Turner	3
G. Ulyett, st Burton, b Ferris	9 –	b Turner	9
L.C. Docker, b Ferris	0 –	c Bannerman, b Ferris	7
W. Newham, b Turner	2 –	b Turner	2
M. Read, st Burton, b Ferris	2 –	c Garrett, b Turner	4
G.A. Lohmann, b Turner	4 –	b Allen	20
J. Briggs, b Turner	5 –	b Turner	2
J.M. Preston, b Ferris	0 –	not out	3
A.D. Pougher, b Ferris	0 –	b Ferris	6
R. Pilling, b Turner	0 –	c Richardson, b Ferris	3
G. Brann, not out	4 –	b Turner	3
B	3	B	4

49   66

New South Wales

R.C. Allen, c Docker, b Lohmann . . . . .0 – not out 6
A.C. Bannerman, c Pilling, b Lohmann 21
H. Moses, st Pilling, b Briggs 0
A.D. Richardson, b Pougher 2
C.T.B. Turner, c and b Pougher 13
T.W. Garrett, b Briggs 7
P.S. McDonnell, c Pougher, b Lohmann . . . . .27 – not out 15
H.W. Hiddleston, b Lohmann 3
J. Davis, lbw, b Lohmann 8
J.J. Ferris, b Briggs 5
F.J. Burton, not out 4
    B 4   B 4
                        94   **25**

New South Wales Bowling

	Overs	Mdns.	Runs	Wkts	Overs	Mdns.	Runs	Wkts
Turner	19	10	22	4	37	23	23	6
Ferris	18	7	24	6	35.1	21	35	3
Allen					2	1	4	1
Garrett					1	1	0	0

English Bowling

	Overs	Mdns.	Runs	Wkts	Overs	Mdns.	Runs	Wkts
Lohmann	26	34	26	5	5.1	1	12	0
Briggs	38	22	35	3	1	0	2	0
Pougher	12	5	29	2	4	1	7	0

MR VERNON'S TEAM v. NEW SOUTH WALES

Played at Sydney, Friday, Saturday, Monday, Tuesday, Wednesday, November 25, 26, 28, 29, 30, 1887. – A remarkable match, and the only one lost by the team during their tour. Without detracting from the merit of New South Wales's nine wickets' victory, it is only fair to say that the ground had been damaged by rain before the Englishmen played their second innings. But for this they would assuredly have made a closer fight. Some splendid cricket was shown during the game, the three famous batsmen in the New South Wales eleven – McDonnell, Moses, and Jones – being all seen to the best advantage. Not the least meritorious performance, however, was that of Abel, who, meeting Turner and Ferris for the first time in his life, played a splendid innings of 88. The two great Autralian bowlers had much to do with winning the match, Turner having a capital average when the ground was dry, and Ferris carrying all before him when it was wet.

Mr Vernon's Team

A.E. Stoddart, b Turner ....55 – b Turner 16
A. Abel, c Bannerman, b Ferris ....88 – c Bannerman, b Ferris 5
W. Bates, b Garrett ....28 – c Hiddleston, b Ferris 0
W.W. Read, l b w, b Turner ....8 – st Burton, b Ferris 14
Hon. M.B. Hawke, b Turner ....48 – c Evans, b Ferris 2
R. Peel, c and b Turner ....54 – not out 34
A.E. Newton, b Turner ....30 – c Allen, b Ferris 5
G.F. Vernon, c Moses, b Ferris ....3 – c Evans, b Ferris 4
W. Attewell, not out ....13 – c Burton, b Jones 17
J.T. Rawlin, b Turner ....4 – b Turner 5
J. Beaumont, b Turner ....2 – b Ferris 1
   B, &c 7   B, &c..........................3
                   340   **106**

New South Wales

P.S. M'Donnell, c Vernon, b Attewell ......112 – c Attewell, b Peel 2
A.C. Bannerman, b Peel 8
H. Moses, b Stoddart ....77 – not out 15
R.C. Allen, run out ....34 – not out 22
S.P. Jones, b Peel 60
H.W. Hiddleston, st Newton, b Rawlin 37
C.T.B. Turner, c Read, b Attewell 32
T.W. Garrett, c Abel, b Peel 13
E. Evans, b Peel 0
F.J. Burton, not out 13
J.J. Ferris, b Attewell 12
   B, &c 10   B 1
                   408   **40**

New South Wales Bowling

	Overs	Mdns	Runs	Wkts	Overs	Mdns	Runs	Wkts
Turner	77.3	36	106	7	31	12	40	2
Ferris	70	24	135	2	33.1	15	49	7
Garrett	24	8	40	1	6	2	7	0
Allen	6	3	10	0				
Evans	10	6	24	0				
Jones	13	3	18	0	3	0	7	1

English Bowling

	Overs	Mdns	Runs	Wkts	Overs	Mdns	Runs	Wkts
Beaumont	46	22	88	0	9	8	4	0
Peel	80	44	98	4	15	6	17	1
Rawlin	30	10	53	1				
Bates	46	15	75	0	9	4	9	0
Attewell	81.1	49	64	3	13	7	9	0
Stoddart	15	8	20	1				

Beaumont bowled one no-ball, and Stoddart and Peel each bowled a wide.

THE AUSTRALIANS IN ENGLAND, 1888

[...] The team was organised by Mr Charles W. Beal, of Sydney on the old basis of private and personal adventure: the men were, we believe, banded together in a commonwealth, though we do not profess to know, nor should we put on record if we did know, the private and financial relations that existed among the members of the eleven. It was at first hoped that Moses, the well-known left-handed batsman, who is now about thirty years of age, would be a member of the team; while down to the last moment before sailing the companionship of George Giffen was confidently expected. Disappointment followed in each case, and also in the cases of some other men who were asked to make the trip; and there can be no doubt that the team that sailed from Adelaide last March, while they did not deserve a quarter of the bitter and contemptuous things said about them by newspapers of their own Colonies, were yet far from representing Combined Australia. Four ladies journeyed with the team, the manager bringing his wife and his mother, and Mrs Bannerman and Mrs Lyons accompanying their husbands. [...]

Followers of sport are proverbially superstitious, and on the same principle that many a batsman, to 'change his luck', has gone in wearing an old cap or carrying an old bat that he used when he made some former big score, so Beal took his men to the hotel from which the great team of 1882 set out and adopted the colours worn by that famous eleven, and, also we believe for the same reason, the early practice was taken on Mitcham Green. Here naturally enough the chief interest of spectators centred in Turner and Ferris. It was no secret that this trip was an experiment, a new departure in Colonial cricket. The mighty Spofforth, the greatest bowler we had ever seen, was with the team no more; there was neither Giffen nor Palmer. The Australians of 1888 were for all practical purposes a new eleven trusting to two young bowlers. The choice of a captain had fallen upon Percy McDonnell, and it is difficult to see who else could have been selected. Not improbably when the next team comes Turner himself will be chosen, but it would have been rash in the extreme to have given the anxiety and trouble of leadership to him upon whose bowling those who knew the most about the team knew that the most depended. It was at once seen that Turner and Ferris were bowlers of high capacity and considerable resource, that their action was free from tricks of any kind, and that they both were, like all Australians we have ever seen, scrupulously and irreproachably fair. [...]

M'Donnell's conduct as captain of the eleven was by no means unanimously approved by the team or by English cricketers who took interest in the matter, and it is an open secret that but for Beal's tact, the loyalty and level-headedness of Turner, and the unswerving obedience of Ferris, there was now and then a possibility of the same sort of muffled mutiny which in some former teams has been unpleasantly apparent. Now the tour is over, and there can be no harm in speaking all one's mind, we may say that we think on many occasions M'Donnell showed want of judgment. We do not mean in his batting, though after the marvellous Manchester performance his rashness was apparent to anyone; but in the general management of his bowling.

He never seemed happy unless he had Turner on at one end and Ferris at the other. Of course we all knew very early in the tour that there were no other great bowling stars, and that it was a Turner and Ferris trip or nothing. The young bowlers stood the work magnificently. Ferris, the slighter and less robust of the two, was now and then stale and below himself, but Turner worked with superb energy, skill, and determination, and commanded the admiration of even the most lukewarm follower of the game. But what would have happened if the dry weather had come at the beginning of July instead of at the beginning of August? How would the team have fared if disease had seized one of the best bowlers instead of the best batsman? No one, save the veteran Boyle, had had any experience of English grounds, and the team had not been taught to place reliance on any one else. M'Donnell's policy said as plainly as if he had spoken the words, 'Our bowlers are Turner and Ferris; we only put the other men on to give them a rest.' [...]

AUSTRALIANS V. SURREY

Played at Kennington Oval, Monday, Tuesday, May 14, 15, 1888. – There was a large crowd to see the first big match of the London season, 14,302 paying for admission on the two days, and although regret was plainly enough shown at the county's poor form, there could be no doubt as to the cordiality of the visitors' reception. It was pretty clear by this time that M'Donnell and Bannerman, as in 1884 were the regular pair to start the batting, and in this particular game they started it wonderfully well. Lohmann and Maurice Read had only landed at Plymouth the day before, and the great bowler, besides being out of form, was lame through an injured nail, and had to give up the ball when 158 runs had been scored for five wickets. The chief feature of the first day was the superbly free hitting of Turner, who surprised cricketing England by his 103, an innings which included nineteen 4's, two 3's, and four 2's. Turner and Ferris, as in the two previous games, bowled superbly, and the Australians won by an innings and 156 runs. The new press-box at the Oval was first used for this match. The Surrey Committee, acting on suggestions made by the Editor of this Annual, extended their pavilion, and, while the reporters were given a splendid view and greater accommodation than anywhere else in England, the card-sellers and telegraph clerks were housed just inside the gates.

AUSTRALIANS

P.S. M'Donnell, b Lohmann 56	J. Worrall, b Bowley 16
A.C. Bannerman, b W. Read 43	J.J. Lyons, b Bowley 5
S.P. Jones, b Bowley 16	J.J. Ferris, not out 37
G.J. Bonnor, b Lohmann 3	H.F. Boyle, c Abel, b Beaumont 22
H. Trott, b Henderson 35	B 13, l-b 4, n-b 1 18
J. M'C. Blackham, c Key, b Bowley 9	
C.T.B. Turner, c Wood, b M. Read 103	**363**

SURREY

R. Abel, b Ferris	.11	– b Ferris	.8
Mr J. Shuter, c and b Ferris	.6	– b Turner	.8
Mr K.J. Key, b Ferris	.24	– b Ferris	.20
Mr W.W. Read, lbw, b Turner	.15	– lbw, b Turner	.4
H. Brockwell, b Turner	.3	– c Trott, b Jones	.0
M. Read, c sub., b Ferris	.12	– run out	.28
R. Henderson, b Turner	.1	– b Jones	.5
G.A. Lohmann, lbw, b Turner	.0	– lbw, b Trott	.26
H. Wood, c Boyle, b Turner	.12	– c Trott, b Turner	.7
T. Bowley, c and b Turner	.5	– not out	.0
J. Beaumont, not out	.0	– b Jones	.8
		B	.6
	89		**120**

SURREY BOWLING

	Overs	Mdns	Runs	Wkts	Overs	Mdns	Runs	Wkts
Lohmann	37	17	48	2				
Bowley	39	10	77	4				
Beaumont	23.1	6	60	1				
Abel	19	8	43	0				
Henderson	15	2	36	1				
W.W. Read	13	5	27	1				
Brockwell	14	6	32	0				
M. Read	8	2	22	1				

AUSTRALIAN BOWLING

	Overs	Mdns	Runs	Wkts	Overs	Mdns	Runs	Wkts
Turner	30.1	13	44	6	32	11	57	8
Ferris	30	12	45	4	28	17	40	2
Trott					8	5	13	1
Jones					4.3	2	4	3

Umpires: Farrands and Carpenter.

ENGLAND V. AUSTRALIA

Played at Lord's, Monday, Tuesday, July 16, 17, 1888. Although of course it was seen that the Australians were by no means equal on their merits to the best team in England, there was a considerable amount of anxiety as to the result of the first of the three great test matches. In dry weather and on a hard wicket, confidence in the strength of English batting would have been almost unlimited, but the weather for weeks had been so bad, and the Australian bowling had proved so destructive, with the condition of the turf favouring it, that many quite dispassionate judges thought the game would be so fluky, that victory would depend almost entirely upon success in the toss. It need scarcely be remarked that there had been only one previous Australian victory in this country over the full strength of England, and that that was accomplished in 1882 by a team which, by general consent, was the best that ever came here from Australia. [...] The Australians left out Lyons and Boyle, and M'Donnell, having won the toss, went in with Bannerman to commence a match about which every one's nerves were in a high state of tension, and at a time when it is not too much to say that all concerned, from batsmen, bowlers, and umpires down to the merest spectators, felt the importance of the issue, and how much was at stake. We ought, however, to say that to the best of our knowledge there was little or no betting of any consequence, and certainly, with all the eagerness and keenness of feeling, there was no bitterness or acrimony on either side.

Winning the toss was known to be a much greater advantage than is usually the case, for there had been so much rain within a few hours of the start that it was impossible the ground should be in anything like condition for good cricket. It was for some hours uncertain whether there would be any play on Monday at all and the gates were not opened until after lunch time. Some thousands of people had crowded in the St. John's Wood Road, and there was a great crush to get in, but the people had obtained places, and formed a thick ring all round the ground when play began at five minutes past three. The game has been often described, and it is not our intention to follow the play in detail. It was one in which the Australians, starting with a distinctly inferior team, played with great courage and spirit, and achieved a performance for which they were fully entitled and for which they received a large amount of credit. The Australians played quite the right game, hitting out pluckily, and never attempting to show correct cricket. The Englishmen started well enough, getting rid of Bannerman and Trott for 3 runs, but then Bonnor and M'Donnell were both missed. The total was only 82 when the ninth wicket fell, and, though this score was not a bad one under the conditions, it was not good enough to look like winning. Ferris, the last man, joined Edwards, who should have been easily run out, and then this pair, by some invaluable and fearless hitting, put on 30 runs before they were separated. The Englishmen went in in a bad light, and lost Abel, Barnes and Lohmann for 18 before stumps were drawn for the day.

On Tuesday morning play began at half-past eleven, and W.G. Grace did not add to the 10 he had made overnight. Wicket after wicket fell until eight men were out for 37, and it looked quite possible that England would have to follow on. Briggs and Peel averted this disaster, but the whole side were out before half-past twelve for 53, or 63 to the bad. The English bowling and fielding during the second innings of Australia were superb, and the ground was altogether against batsmen, so that it was no wonder the Australians were out for 60. Indeed, but for Ferris's capital hitting the total would not nearly have reached that number. But it was clear England was at a great disadvantage, and that the 124 wanted to win would be more than could be made. Mr Grace began really well, and 29 runs were made before the first wicket fell. At 34, however, the champion was out, and from that time Turner and Ferris carried everything before them. The Australians played a winning game with tremendous energy and unfailing skill, and at twenty-five minutes past four in the afternoon they were successful with 61 runs to spare. The vast crowd rushed across the ground directly the game was over, and thousands upon thousands of people formed a dense mass in front of the pavilion, and cheered with a spontaneous and genuine heartiness that could scarcely have been exceeded if the Englishmen had made the runs instead of being badly beaten. So ended a game that will never be forgotten in cricket history, and one which practically ensured the fame of the Australian team.

AUSTRALIANS

A.C. Bannerman, c Grace, b Lohmann	0 – b Peel	0
P.S. M'Donnell, c O'Brien, b Peel	22 – b Lohmann	1
H. Trott, c Lohmann, b Peel	0 – b Lohmann	3
G.J. Bonnor, b Lohmann	6 – c Lohmann, b Peel	8
J. M'C. Blackham, b Briggs	22 – run out	1
S.M.J. Woods, c Gunn, b Briggs	18 – c Grace, b Peel	3
C.T.B. Turner, c Lohmann, b Peel	3 – c Grace, b Briggs	12
J.D. Edwards, not out	21 – c Sherwin, b Lohmann	0
A.H. Jarvis, c Lohmann, b Peel	3 – c Barnes, b Peel	4
J. Worrall, c Abel, b Briggs	2 – b Lohmann	4
J.J. Ferris, c Sherwin, b Steel	14 – not out	20
B	5 B 3, l-b 1	4
	116	**60**

ENGLAND

Mr W.G. Grace, c Woods, b Ferris	10 – c Bannerman, b Ferris	24
R. Abel, b Ferris	3 – c Bonnor, b Ferris	8
W. Barnes, c Jarvis, b Turner	3 – st Blackham, b Ferris	1
G.A. Lohmann, lbw, b Turner	2 – st Blackham, b Ferris	0
Mr W.W. Read, st Blackham, b Turner	4 – b Turner	3
Mr T.C. O'Brien, b Turner	0 – b Turner	4
R. Peel, run out	8 – b Turner	4
Mr A.G. Steel, st Blackham, b Turner	3 – not out	10
W. Gunn, c Blackham, b Ferris	2 – b Ferris	8
J. Briggs, b Woods	17 – b Turner	0
M. Sherwin, not out	0 – c Ferris, b Turner	0
L-b	1	
	53	**62**

ENGLISH BOWLING

	Overs	Mdns	Runs	Wkts	Overs	Mdns	Runs	Wkts
Lohmann	20	9	28	2	14	4	33	4
Peel	21	7	36	4	10.2	3	14	4
Briggs	21	8	26	3	4	1	9	1
Barnes	6	0	17	0				
Mr Steel	3.2	2	4	1	1	1	0	0

AUSTRALIAN BOWLING

Turner	25	9	27	5	24	8	36	5
Ferris	21	13	19	3	23	11	26	5
Woods	4	2	6	1				

Umpires: Farrands and Pullin.

LORD SHEFFELD'S TEAM
IN AUSTRALIA

The tour undertaken by Lord Sheffield's team in the Australian season 1891–2 was in one respect unique. Never before in the history of visits paid by English cricketers to Australia or by Australian cricketers to the mother country had the enterprise been undertaken and carried out by a single individual. In as much as two of the three Test matches against Combined Australia ended in the defeat of the English players, the tour was in one sense a disappointment to all lovers of the game in Great Britain, but this was only the fortune of war. Moreover, our defeats had one very beneficial effect, the double triumph of the Australians restoring the game to its old place in the affections of the Colonial public.

Apart from the fact of two of the big matches having been lost, the tour was a great success, Lord Sheffield's action in arranging the trip, and the manner in which he carried it out, earning unstinted praise from every organ of public opinion in Australia. It was understood that the expenses of the tour considerably exceeded the receipts, but this was largely due to the liberal scale on which everything was done. That Lord Sheffield was well satisfied with his own reception in Australia was best proved by the fact that he presented a handsome trophy to be competed for by the different Colonies. Except for the very important fact that Arthur Shrewsbury and William Gunn declined to accept the terms offered them, the team was, on the form shown during the English season of 1891, fully representative. […]

LORD SHEFFELD'S TEAM
V. COMBINED AUSTRALIA

Played at Sydney, Friday, Saturday, Monday, Tuesday, Wednesday, January 29, 30, February 1, 2, 3, 1892. – The second of the three big matches produced one of the finest performances in the history of Australian cricket, a performance, indeed, fully comparable to the seven runs victory at the Oval in 1882, or the great, but unsuccessful fight on the same ground in 1880. The Englishmen played the same team as at Melbourne, but the Australians made one change in their side, substituting Walter Giffen for Donnan. As events turned out, they would have been wise to have chosen Sydney Gregory instead of Moses, as the latter's injured leg again gave way. The Australians proved victorious by 72 runs, and it can safely be said that the records of first-class cricket furnish few instances of a finer uphill game. Up to the end of the second day everything went in favour of the Englishmen. Thanks to Lohmann's bowling and Abel's batting, they gained indeed so commanding an advantage that the match seemed as good as over. The close of an innings on each side had left them with a lead of 162, and the Australians, on going in for the second time, lost Trott's wicket for a single run. Abel's superb innings of 132 not out lasted five hours and twenty-five minutes, and comprised eleven 4's, ten 3's, sixteen 2's, and twenty-six singles. Only once before had anyone taken his bat right through the innings in an England and Australia match, the previous instance being Dr. Barrett's performance at Lord's in 1890. On Monday, February 1, the third day of the match, there came an extraordinary change in the cricket, Lyons, Bannerman, and George Giffen batting with such success that it took the Englishmen all the afternoon to obtain two wickets, the total meanwhile being increased from 1 to 263. Lyons and Bannerman were separated at 175, their partnership having lasted two hours and three-quarters. Lyons certainly gave one chance to Abel at slip when he had made 49, and we believe he offered another to the same fieldsman, but otherwise his 134 – which included sixteen 4's, five 3's, and eight 2's – was a magnificent innings. On the fourth day the weather was unsettled and rain considerably affected the wicket. Everything went wrong with the Englishmen, who made several bad mistakes in the field. The Australians' innings closed for 391, and the Englishmen, wanting 230 to win, had to go in when the ground was in a very treacherous state. Abel, Bean, and Grace were got rid of for 11 runs, and only a downfall of rain prevented further disasters. On the following morning, the wicket rolled out much better than anyone could have expected, and the Englishmen still had a chance, Australia's bowling being weakened by the absence of M'Leod, who had been called back to Melbourne by the death of his brother. George Giffen and Turner, however, bowled wonderfully well, and despite the very fine batting of Stoddart, the innings was finished off for 156, Australia winning the game by 72 runs, and so gaining the rubber in the test matches. Bannerman's innings of 91 had much to do with the victory. Invaluable as it was, however, it would in a match of less interest have thoroughly tired out the spectators. The New South Wales batsman was actually at the wickets seven hours and twenty-eight minutes. Out of 204 balls bowled at him by Attewell he only scored from five. At the finish of the game, there was a scene of almost indescribable enthusiasm.

COMBINED AUSTRALIA

A.C. Bannerman, c Abel, b Lohmann	12 – c Grace, b Briggs	91
J.J. Lyons, c Grace, b Lohmann	41 – c Grace, b Lohmann	134
H. Moses, c Grace, b Lohmann	29 – absent hurt	0
G. Giffen, c Abel, b Lohmann	6 – lbw, b Attewell	49
C.T.B. Turner, c MacGregor, b Lohmann	15 – not out	14
W. Bruce, c Bean, b Attewell	15 – c Briggs, b Sharpe	72
H. Trott, b Lohmann	2 – c Sharpe, b Lohmann	1
R. M'Leod, c Attewell, b Lohmann	13 – c Read, b Peel	18
W.F. Giffen, c and b Lohmann	1 – b Briggs	3
S.T. Callaway, run out	1 – c Grace, b Briggs	0
J. M'C. Blackham, not out	3 – lbw, b Briggs	0
Byes, &c.	7	Byes, &c.	9
	145	**394**

LORD SHEFFIELD'S TEAM

R. Abel, not out . . . . .132 – c W. Giffen, b G. Giffen 1
W.G. Grace, b Turner . . . . .26 – c Blackham b Turner 5
A.E. Stoddart, c Blackham, b M'Leod . . . . . .27 – b Turner 69
G. Bean, b G. Giffen .19 – c Lyons, b Turner 4
M. Read, c Turner, b G. Giffen . . . . .3 – c and b G. Giffen 22
R. Peel, c G. Giffen, b Turner . . . . .20 – st Blackham, b G. Giffen 6
G.A. Lohmann, b G. Giffen . . . . .10 – c Bruce, b G. Giffen 15
G. MacGregor, lbw, b M'Leod . . . . .3 – c and b G. Giffen 12
J. Briggs, lbw, b Trott . . . . .28 – c Trott, b Turner 12
W. Attewell, b Trott . . . . .0 – c and b G. Giffen 0
J.W. Sharpe, c Bannerman, b G. Giffen . . . . .26 – not out 4
    Byes, &c. 13   Byes, &c. 6

307   156

ENGLISH BOWLING

	Balls	Mdns	Runs	Wkts	Balls	Mdns	Runs	Wkts
Lohmann	260	18	58	8	306	14	84	2
Attewell	183	20	25	1	276	24	43	1
Briggs	60	2	24	0	196	8	69	4
Sharpe	60	1	31	0	210	7	91	1
Peel					210	13	49	1
Grace					93	2	34	0
Stoddart					24	1	12	0

Lohmann bowled one wide.

AUSTRALIAN BOWLING

	Balls	Mdns	Runs	Wkts	Balls	Mdns	Runs	Wkts
Turner	222	11	90	2	140	7	46	4
M'Leod	108	6	55	2				
G. Giffen	170	5	88	4	168	10	72	6
Trott	84	3	42	2	30	0	11	0
Callaway	102	10	19	0	60	6	21	0

2

THE GOLDEN AGE: AUSTRALIA v. ENGLAND 1894–1914

Most pursuits and entertainments have a Golden Age, always in the past, glories always irrecoverable. There is a surprising degree of agreement about cricket's. The 1894–95 visit by A.E. Stoddart's team to Australia is generally viewed as its first dawning; World War I, as it did for so much, tolled the knell of passing day. Novelist A.A. Thomson wrote in *Cricket: The Golden Ages*: 'Truly great players would be great in any age, but in that age there were so many … It was a great age by any instrument of measurement. It had power; it had gusto and zest; it had elegance; it had a serenely patrician look.'

This maturation in cricket is subtly reflected in *Wisden* by the designation 'England', hitherto reserved for English teams hosting, that began to attach itself to English teams in Australia. The touring party that visited Australia in 1891–92 had been assigned the title 'Lord Sheffield's XI', reflecting its patron; Stoddart's team of 1894–95 took the field in *Wisden*'s pages as 'England', where it competed with 'Australia', a name likewise standardised after variations such as 'Combined Australia' and 'Combined Eleven of Australia'.

One shouldn't underestimate the significance of this change in nomenclature. When sporting teams wrap themselves in national flags, their victories and defeats begin to ramify beyond the sporting fields. When Stoddart's team won the 1894–95 series, it was a cause for real jubilation in England: players arriving home, like returning soldiers, were greeted by parades and testimonials. On the other hand, when Joe Darling's Australians won the 1899 rubber by the only decided Test, our first series victory in England, cricket team and country in England seemed uneasily linked. In pleading the Afrikaner case during the Boer War a year later, for instance, Kaiser Wilhelm II urged England to show the same sportsmanship in diplomacy as in sport. 'Last year in the great cricket match of England v. Australia,' he wrote to the Prince of Wales, 'the former took the latter's victory quietly with chivalrous acknowledgement of her opponent.' And it is said that the Boer leader Paul Kruger, informed that eleven

Australians were coming to South Africa who'd beaten all England, commented that the Transvaal stood no chance against such invaders.

The idea of country versus country in sport lends itself to a martial way of thinking. A hallmark of *Wisden* throughout this period is Sydney Pardon's fascination with leadership. Harry Trott, 'blessed with a temper that nothing could ruffle', became something of a benchmark, being seen as 'incomparably the best captain the Australians have ever had in this country'. Successor Darling, who 'in following Harry Trott was necessarily judged by the highest standards', was also felt to have 'exceeded all anticipations', and become 'one of the very best captains that ever took a team into the field'. The *esprit de corps* of Darling's 1902 team was deeply admired: 'All seem to be fully imbued with the idea that their one duty was to enhance, if possible, the reputation of Australian cricket.' The most lavish encomia, however, were reserved for Monty Noble: 'The method of placing the field became in Noble's hands almost an exact science, the favourite hits of the various batsmen being blocked in a way that I have never seen equalled.' Like the Golden Age, though, faith in leadership would be one of the casualties of World War I.

—GH

MR STODDART'S TEAM IN AUSTRALIA

It is perfectly safe to say that since the visit of George Parr's eleven in 1863–64 no tour of English cricketers in Australia has been from every point of view more brilliantly successful than that of Mr Stoddart's team. Leaving England in October, 1894, the band of players – with three exceptions – returned home in May last, loaded with honours and delighted with their trip. They had abundant reasons for satisfaction, inasmuch as in the series of contests with All Australia they had won the rubber by three matches to two. To these test games everything else in the tour was subordinated, even the other eleven-a-side engagements being of secondary interest, and the fixtures against the odds counting for nothing. Never, probably, have five matches excited more widespread interest. They drew such crowds of people to the Australian grounds that the Melbourne Club and the trustees of the Sydney ground, under whose joint auspices the tour was undertaken, divided between them a profit of about seven thousand pounds. In England the interest was greater than had ever been felt in matches played away from our own shores, the enterprise of the *Pall Mall Gazette*, in arranging every afternoon when the big matches were in progress for long cable messages, keeping lovers of the game in this country in closer touch with cricket in Australia than they had ever been before. It so happened that after England had been victorious at Sydney and Melbourne the Australians won at Adelaide and Sydney, the rubber thus depending on the fifth and last match, which was played on the Melbourne ground. As everyone knows, this conquering game was won by Mr Stoddart's team by six wickets, a wonderful display of batting by Brown and Albert Ward in the last stage of the contest giving them the victory. The excitement in London when the result came to hand could scarcely have been greater if the match had been played at Lord's or the Oval. [...]

English Team v. Australia

Played at Sydney, Friday, Saturday, Monday, Tuesday, Wednesday, Thursday, December 14, 15, 17, 18, 19, 20, 1894. – This was probably the most sensational match ever played either in Australia or in England. Going in first, the Australians made a poor start, losing three wickets – all bowled down by Richardson – for 21 runs. Iredale and Giffen, however, put on 171 for the fourth wicket, and Giffen and Gregory 139 for the fifth. Giffen's splendidly played 161 lasted a little over four hours and a quarter. At the close of the first day the score stood at 346 for five wickets, and in the end the total reached 586, Gregory and Blackham scoring 154 together for the ninth wicket. In recognition of his wonderful innings of 201 a collection was made for Gregory, the sum subscribed on the ground amounting to a hundred and three pounds. In face of a score of 586 the Englishmen had a dismal prospect, but they set to work with the utmost resolution and kept the Australians in the field from Saturday afternoon till the following Wednesday. Still, though they ran up totals of 325 and 437 – Albert Ward taking the chief honours in each innings – they only set Australia 177 to get. At the close of the fifth day 113 had been scored for two wickets, and the match looked all over. Drenching rain in the night, however, followed by bright sunshine, completely altered the condition of the ground, and Peel – well backed up by Briggs – proved so irresistible that the Englishmen gained an astonishing victory by 10 runs.

Australia

G.H.S. Trott, b Richardson	12	– c Gay, b Peel ... 8
J.J. Lyons, b Richardson	1	– b Richardson ... 25
G. Giffen, c Ford, b Brockwell	161	– lbw, b Briggs ... 41
J. Darling, b Richardson	0	– c Brockwell, b Peel ... 53
F.A. Iredale, c Stoddart, b Ford	81	– c and b Briggs ... 5
S.E. Gregory, c Peel, b Stoddart	201	– c Gay b Peel ... 16
J. Reedman, c Ford, b Peel	17	– st Gay b Peel ... 4
C. M'Leod, b Richardson	15	– not out ... 2
C.T.B. Turner, c Gay, b Peel	1	– c Briggs, b Peel ... 2
J. M'C. Blackham, b Richardson	74	– c and b Peel ... 2
E. Jones, not out	11	– c MacLaren, b Briggs ... 1
B, &c	12	B, &c ... 7
	586	**166**

England

Mr A.C. McLaren, c Reedman, b Turner	4	– b Giffen ... 20
A. Ward, c Iredale, b Turner	75	– b Giffen ... 117
Mr A.E. Stoddart, c Jones, b Giffen	12	– c Giffen, b Turner ... 36
J.T. Brown, run out	22	– c Jones, b Giffen ... 53
R. Peel, c Gregory, b Giffen	4	– b Giffen ... 17
Mr F.G.J. Ford, st Blackham, b Giffen	30	– c and b M'Leod ... 48
W. Brockwell, c Blackham, b Jones	49	– b Jones ... 37
W. Lockwood, c Giffen, b Trott	18	– b Trott ... 29
J. Briggs, b Giffen	57	– b M'Leod ... 42
Mr L.H. Gay, c Gregory, b Reedman	33	– b Trott ... 4
T. Richardson, not out	0	– not out ... 12
B, &c	21	B, &c ... 21
	325	**437**

ENGLISH BOWLING

	Overs	Mdns	Runs	Wkts	Overs	Mdns	Runs	Wkts
Richardson	55.3	13	181	5	11	3	27	1
Peel	53	14	140	2	30	9	67	6
Briggs	28	4	96	0	11	2	25	3
Brockwell	22	7	78	1				
Lockwood	3	2	1	0	16	3	40	0
Ford	11	2	47	1				
Stoddart	3	0	31	1				

AUSTRALIAN BOWLING

	Overs	Mdns	Runs	Wkts	Overs	Mdns	Runs	Wkts
Turner	44	16	89	2	35	14	78	1
Jones	19	7	44	1	19	0	58	1
Giffen	43	17	75	4	75	25	164	4
M'Leod	14	2	25	0	30	7	67	2
Trott	15	4	59	1	12	4	22	2
Reedman	3.3	1	12	1	6	1	12	0
Lyons	2	2	0	0	2	0	12	0
Iredale					2	0	3	0

Umpires: J. Phillips and C. Bannerman.

ENGLISH TEAM V. AUSTRALIA

Played at Melbourne, Friday, Saturday, Monday, Tuesday, Wednesday, March 1, 2, 4, 5, 6, 1895. – As was only natural, with the record standing at two victories each, the fifth and last of the test matches excited enormous interest. Indeed, it may be questioned whether any previous game in the Colonies had ever aroused such intense and widespread excitement. Numbers of people journeyed thousands of miles in order to be in Melbourne on the all-important occasion. The Australians, after anxious deliberations as to the constitution of their team, decided to leave out Turner and play Lyons. For this they were severely blamed after the match; but though they were probably averse to strengthening their already powerful batting at the expense of their bowling, the fact should be borne in mind that Turner during the earlier part of the season had met with little or no success on hard wickets. As everyone knows, Mr Stoddart's team gained a brilliant and remarkable victory for England by six wickets. It was only, however, after a desperate and protracted struggle that this result was arrived at, the game lasting well into the fifth day. From first to last the match was played on a perfectly true wicket, which gave no advantage to one side over the other. The Australians, who had the good fortune to win the toss, led off in splendid style, scoring on the opening day 282 runs for four wickets. Darling and Gregory, not out with 72 and 70 respectively, were soon got rid of on the second morning, but the total reached 411. In face of this big score the Englishmen made 385, MacLaren and Peel playing very finely and putting on 162 runs for the fifth wicket. The Australians opened their second innings well, but on the fourth day, when a dust storm caused considerable discomfort both to players and spectators, Richardson bowled superbly, and the eleven were all out for 267. This left Mr Stoddart's team 297 to get to win, and it was anybody's match. At the call of time the score stood at 28 for one wicket, and to the dismay of the Englishmen, Mr Stoddart was out l-b-w from the first ball bowled next morning. The position was desperate, but at this point Albert Ward and Brown made the stand which, if they are never to do anything more, will suffice to keep their names famous in the history of English and Australian cricket. By wonderful batting – Ward's patient defence being scarcely less remarkable than Brown's brilliant hitting – they put on 210 runs together, their partnership practically ensuring the success of their side. After the fourth wicket had fallen, the end soon came, MacLaren and Peel being in at the finish. Though the crowds of spectators were, of course, greatly disappointed, they cheered the Englishmen most heartily.

AUSTRALIA

G.H.S. Trott, b Briggs	42	– b Peel ... 42
W. Bruce, c MacLaren, b Peel	22	– c and b Peel ... 11
G. Giffen, b Peel	57	– b Richardson ... 51
F.A. Iredale, b Richardson	8	– b Richardson ... 18
S.E. Gregory, c Philipson, b Richardson	70	– b Richardson ... 30
J. Darling, c Ford, b Peel	74	– b Peel ... 50
J.J. Lyons, c Philipson, b Lockwood	55	– b Briggs ... 15
H. Graham, b Richardson	6	– lbw, b Richardson ... 10
A.E. Trott, c Lockwood, b Peel	10	– b Richardson ... 0
A.H. Jarvis, not out	34	– not out ... 14
T.R. M'Kibbin, c Peel, b Briggs	23	– c Philipson, b Richardson ... 13
B 3, l-b 10	13	B 5, l-b 6, n-b 2 ... 13
	414	**267**

ENGLAND

A. Ward, b M'Kibbin	32	– b H. Trott ... 93
W. Brockwell, st Jarvis, b H. Trott	5	– c and b Giffen ... 5
Mr A.E. Stoddart, st Jarvis, b H.Trott	68	– lbw, b H. Trott ... 11
J.T. Brown, b A.E. Trott	30	– c Giffen, b M'Kibbin ... 140
Mr A.C. McLaren, h.w., b H. Trott	120	– not out ... 20
R. Peel, c Gregory, b Giffen	73	– not out ... 15
W. Lockwood, c H. Trott, b Giffen	5	
Mr F.G.J. Ford, c A.E. Trott, b Giffen	11	
J. Briggs, c H. Trott, b Giffen	0	
Mr H. Philipson, not out	10	
T. Richardson, lbw, b H. Trott	11	
B 8, l-b 8, w 4	20	B 6, l-b 5, w 2, n-b 1 ... 14
	385	**298**

ENGLISH BOWLING

	Overs	Mdns	Runs	Wkts	Overs	Mdns	Runs	Wkts
Richardson	42	7	138	3	45.2	7	104	6
Peel	48	13	114	4	46	16	89	3
Lockwood	27	7	72	1	16	7	24	0
Briggs	23.4	5	46	2	16	3	37	1
Brockwell	6	1	22	0				
Ford	2	0	9	0				

AUSTRALIAN BOWLING

	Overs	Mdns	Runs	Wkts	Overs	Mdns	Runs	Wkts
Giffen	45	13	130	4	31	4	106	1
H. Trott	24	5	71	4	20	1	63	2
A.E. Trott	30	4	84	1	19	2	56	0
M'Kibbin	19	6	73	1	14	2	47	1
Bruce	5	1	7	0	39	1	10	0
Lyons					1	0	2	0

Umpires: J. Phillips and T. Flynn.

THE AUSTRALIANS IN ENGLAND 1896

[...] We are by no means convinced that, man for man, the eleven of last season were richer in individual skill than that of 1893, but there can be no possible question that they worked much more cordially together, and, taking one match with another, played vastly better cricket. To a very large extent the improvement was, we think, due to the change in the leadership. We would yield to no one in admiration for Blackham as a cricketer, but the experience of 1893 showed clearly that he was not well fitted by temperament to captain a travelling eleven. Anxious and nervous to a degree he lacked, both on the field and off it, the calm self-control which is almost the first essential of a leader. Not for a moment would we hold him directly responsible for the comparative non-success of a side from which so much was expected, but we feel convinced that under a different captain in 1893 much better results would have been obtained. The absolute antithesis to Blackham was Trott, who, with the exception of Murdoch, proved himself to be incomparably the best captain the Australians have ever had in this country. We have his own testimony to the fact that he was by no means anxious for the post, but almost from the first match it was perfectly clear that he was in every way fitted for it. Of course the continuous success of his side made his duties far more pleasant and easy than those of some previous captains, but we feel quite sure that in a season of ill-fortune he would have earned just as great a reputation. Blessed with a temper that nothing could ruffle, he was always master both of himself and his team whatever the position of the game. More than that his judgment in changing the bowling was rarely or never at fault. [...]

ENGLAND v. AUSTRALIA

Played at Manchester, Thursday, Friday, Saturday, July 16, 17, 18, 1896. – The second of the three great test matches, which ended in a well-earned victory for the Australians by three wickets, was in many ways one of the most remarkable matches of the season, for though the Englishmen were defeated at the finish, the two best performances of the game were accomplished for them, Ranjitsinhji playing perhaps the greatest innings of his career, and Richardson bowling in a style he has seldom approached. [...] With the ground in such excellent condition for run-getting it was a fortunate circumstance for Trott to win the toss, and his team made admirable use of their opportunity. Richardson often puzzled the batsmen, and was many times unlucky in just failing to hit the wicket, but on the whole the English bowling looked anything but deadly, and the Australians started so well that they seemed, in the first three hours, to have rendered themselves practically secure against defeat. Following up his recent success, Iredale played a beautiful innings of 108, and so excellent was the assistance afforded him by Giffen, Trott and Darling that at one time the score stood at 294 with only three men out. At this point the prospects of the Englishmen were particularly gloomy, but Richardson came with a fine effort, and before the call of time, eight Australian wickets were down for 366. On the following morning, thanks to a useful stand by Kelly and M'Kibbin, the Australian total was carried to 412. With the conditions still most favourable and the wicket practically as good as ever, it seemed quite possible that the Englishmen would get very near to their opponents' total, but with a few exceptions the batting was particularly feeble and the whole side were out for 231. Trott changed his bowling with remarkable skill and judgement, and it was quite a stroke of genius to go on first himself with Jones. [...] England had to follow on against a majority of 181, and the start of their second innings was disappointing, as despite some admirable batting by Stoddart and Ranjitsinhji, four of the best wickets on the side had fallen before the drawing of stumps for 109. At the close of the second day's play therefore, the Englishmen with six wickets to go down were still 72 runs behind, and nothing seemed less likely than that they would before the end of the game, hold practically a winning position. Such however proved to be the case, the Englishmen playing a wonderful uphill game and struggling hard, though without success, to atone for the shortcomings of the two previous afternoons. Much depended upon Ranjitsinhji, and the famous young Indian fairly rose to the occasion, playing an innings that could, without exaggeration, be fairly described as marvellous. He very quickly got set again, and punished the Australian bowlers in a style that, up to that period of the season, no other English batsman had approached. He repeatedly brought off his wonderful strokes on the leg side, and for a while had the Australian bowlers quite at his mercy. Could the other English batsmen have rendered him any material assistance, there is no saying to what extent the English total might have been increased, but as it was, there was no other score on the Saturday morning higher than nineteen. Ranjitsinhji's remarkable batting, and the prospect of the Englishmen after all running their opponents close, worked the spectators up to a high pitch of excitement, and the scene of enthusiasm was something to be remembered when the Indian cricketer completed the first hundred hit against the Australians last season. MacLaren, Lilley and Hearne all tried hard to keep up their wickets for Ranjitsinhji, but Briggs after making sixteen, could not resist the temptation of jumping out to try and drive a slow ball from M'Kibbin. The innings came to an end for 305, Ranjitsinhji carrying his bat for 154. [...] He was at the wickets for three hours ten minutes, and among his hits were twenty-three 4's, five 3's and nine 2's.

The Australians were left with 125 to get to win, and with the ground showing very few signs of wear, most people looked forward to seeing the number hit off for the loss of perhaps three or four batsmen. As it turned out, the Australians had many very anxious moments, Richardson making a magnificent effort in bowling, which was quite worthy of comparison with Ranjitsinhji's batting earlier in the day. Almost before one could realise what was happening, four of the best Australian wickets had fallen for 45, and with the prospect of a keenly exciting finish, the remainder of the game was watched with breathless interest. Another failure for the Colonials might have been attended with most serious results, but Gregory and Donnan played with splendid nerve at the critical time, and the score reached 79 before the former was caught at short leg for an invaluable 33. Still the match was far from over. Donnan was out at 95 and Hill at 100, the position being that the Australians with three wickets to fall, wanted 25 runs to win. With Richardson bowling in his finest form, and nearly all the best Australian batsmen gone, the Englishmen at this point seemed to have actually the best of the game, and the excitement was intense. Everything rested upon Trumble and Kelly, and it would be difficult to speak too highly of the manner in which they got through a terribly trying ordeal. The bowling was so good that they could only score at rare intervals, and generally by singles, but they surely and slowly placed their side on the high road to victory. When only nine runs were required to win, Lilley, who up to that time had kept wicket absolutely without a mistake, failed to take a chance offered him by Kelly. Had this come off, there is no saying what might have happened, but as it was, Trumble and Kelly hit off the remaining runs, and a splendid match ended in favour of Australia by three wickets. Some idea of the excellence of the bowling may be gathered from the fact that the last 25 runs took just an hour to obtain. There was a scene of great enthusiasm at the finish, the Australians being received with a heartiness that reflected immense credit on the Manchester public. [...]

AUSTRALIA

F.A. Iredale b Briggs	.108	– b Richardson 11
J. Darling c Lilley b Richardson	.27	– c Lilley b Richardson 16
G. Giffen c and b Richardson	.80	– c Ranjitsinhji b Richardson 6
G.H.S. Trott c Brown b Lilley	.53	– c Lilley b Richardson 2
S.E. Gregory c Stoddart b Briggs	.25	– c Ranjitsinhji b Briggs 33
H. Donnan b Richardson	.12	– c Jackson b Richardson 15
C. Hill c Jackson b Richardson	.9	– c Lilley b Richardson 14
H. Trumble b Richardson	.24	– not out 17
J.J. Kelly c Lilley b Richardson	.27	– not out 8
T. M'Kibbin not out	.28	
E. Jones b Richardson	.4	
B 6, l-b 8, w 1	.15	L-b 3
	412	**125**

ENGLAND

Mr W.G. Grace st Kelly b Trott	.2 – c Trott b Jones	.11
Mr A.E. Stoddart st Kelly b Trott	.15 – b M'Kibbin	.41
K.S. Ranjitsinhji c Trott b M'Kibbin	.62 – not out	.154
R. Abel c Trumble b M'Kibbin	.26 – c M'Kibbin b Giffen	.13
Mr F.S. Jackson run out	.18 – c M'Kibbin b Giffen	.1
J.T. Brown c Kelly b Trumble	.22 – c Iredale b Jones	.19
Mr A.C. MacLaren c Trumble b M'Kibbin	.0 – c Jones b Trumble	.15
A. Lilley not out	.65 – c Trott b Giffen	.19
J. Briggs b Trumble	.0 – st Kelly b M'Kibbin	.16
J.T. Hearne c Trumble b Giffen	.18 – c Kelly b M'Kibbin	.9
T. Richardson run out	.2 – c Jones b Trumble	.1
B	.1 B 2, l-b 3, w 1	.6
	231	**305**

ENGLISH BOWLING

	Overs	Mdns	Runs	Wkts	Overs	Mdns	Runs	Wkts
Richardson	68	23	168	7	42.3	16	76	6
Briggs	40	18	99	2	18	8	24	1
Jackson	16	6	34	0				
Hearne	28	11	53	0	24	13	22	0
Grace	7	3	11	0				
Stoddart	6	2	9	0				
Lilley	5	1	23	1				

AUSTRALIAN BOWLING

Jones	5	2	11	0	17	0	78	2
Trott	10	0	46	2	7	1	17	0
Giffen	19	3	48	1	16	1	65	3
Trumble	37	14	80	2	29.1	12	78	2
M'Kibbin	19	8	45	3	21	4	61	3

Umpires: J. Phillips and A. Chester.

MR STODDART'S TEAM IN AUSTRALIA

To speak the plain truth there has not for a very long time been anything so disappointing in connection with English cricket, as the tour of Mr Stoddart's team in Australia last winter. The team left England in September, 1897, full of hope that the triumph of three years before would be repeated, but came home a thoroughly beaten side. Following the precedent of the previous tour five test matches were played against the full strength of Australia, and of these the Englishmen only won the first, severe defeats being suffered in all the other four. Twice they were beaten in a single innings, once by eight wickets, and finally at Sydney on the 2nd of March by six wickets. [...] The financial success was immense, the test matches attracting an extraordinary number of people, and the public were delighted – as they had every reason to be – with the cricket shown by their own players. Above all the others in batting stood out the two left-handers – Clement Hill and Darling – while in a group of fine bowlers Noble shone conspicuously. Almost unknown as a bowler when the season began, he developed surprising skill and several times on perfect wickets quite puzzled the Englishmen, keeping a fine length with a little work on the ball and being curiously deceptive in the flight. Of Hill and Darling it would be impossible to say too much, their play in match after match being wonderful. As in England in 1896, the Australians owed much to the unfailing skill and tact of Trott as a captain.

ENGLISH TEAM V. AUSTRALIA

Played at Melbourne, Saturday, Monday, Tuesday, Wednesday, January 29, 31, February 1, 2, 1898. – Of the five test matches this was perhaps the most eventful. The Englishmen started in wonderful form by getting six wickets down for 57 runs, but after that they were quite outplayed, the Australians gaining a brilliant victory by eight wickets. The turning point of the Australians' first innings was the partnership of Clement Hill and Trumble, 165 runs being put on for the seventh wicket. Never before had Hill given quite so fine a display as his 188. He was batting a little over five hours and all things considered his innings may be described as perhaps the best seen in the Colonies during the season. With only a total of 323 to face on a perfectly sound wicket, the Englishmen seemed to have very good prospects, but they failed miserably, their dismissal for 174 marking the lowest point reached by their batting during the whole trip. They did not do very much better when they followed on, and it is no more than the truth to say that they richly deserved to be beaten. The Australians played their winning game wonderfully well, the variety and excellence of their bowling calling forth a high compliment from Mr Stoddart when the match was over.

AUSTRALIA

C. McLeod (V.) b Hearne	1	– not out 64
J. Darling (S.A.) c Hearne b Richardson	12	– c Druce b Hayward 29
C. Hill (S.A.) c Stoddart b Hearne	188	– lbw, b Hayward 0
S.E. Gregory (N.S.W.) b Richardson	0	– not out 21
F.A. Iredale (N.S.W.) c Storer b Hearne	0	
M.A. Noble (N.S.W.) c and b Hearne	4	
G.H.S. Trott (V.) (capt.) c Storer b Hearne	7	
H. Trumble (V.) c Mason b Storer	46	
J.J. Kelly (N.S.W.) c Storer b Briggs	32	
E. Jones (S.A.) c Hayward b Hearne	20	
W. Howell (N.S.W.) not out	9	
Extras	4	Extra 1
323		**115**

ENGLISH TEAM

Mr A.C. MacLaren b Howell	.8 –	c Iredale b Trumble .... .45
E. Wainwright c Howell, b Trott	.6 –	c McLeod b Jones 2
K.S. Ranjitsinhji c Iredale b Trumble	.24 –	b Noble .... .55
T. Hayward c Gregory b Noble	.22 –	c and b Trumble .... .25
W. Storer c and b Trumble	.2 –	c Darling b McLeod .... .26
Mr N.F. Druce lbw b Jones	.24 –	c Howell b Trott .... .16
Mr J.R. Mason b Jones	.30 –	b Howell .... .26
Mr A.E. Stoddart c Darling b Jones	.17 –	b Jones .... .25
J. Briggs not out	.21 –	c Darling b Howell .... .23
J.T. Hearne c Trott b Jones	.0 –	not out 4
T. Richardson b Trott	.20 –	c Trumble b McLeod 2
		Extras .... .14
	174	**263**

ENGLISH BOWLING

	Overs	Mdns	Runs	Wkts	Overs	Mdns	Runs	Wkts
Richardson	26	2	102	2				
Hearne	35.4	13	98	6	7	3	19	0
Hayward	10	4	24	0	10	4	24	2
Briggs	17	4	38	1	6	1	31	0
Stoddart	6	1	22	0				
Storer	4	0	24	1				
Wainwright	3	1	11	0	9	2	21	0
Mason					4	1	10	0
Ranjitsinhji					3.4	1	9	0

AUSTRALIAN BOWLING

	Overs	Mdns	Runs	Wkts	Overs	Mdns	Runs	Wkts
Howell	16	7	34	1	30	12	58	2
Trott	11.1	1	33	2	12	2	39	1
Noble	7	1	21	1	16	6	31	1
Trumble	15	4	30	2	23	6	40	2
Jones	12	2	56	4	25	7	70	2
McLeod					8.2	4	11	2

Umpires: J. Phillips and C. Bannerman.

ENGLAND V. AUSTRALIA

Played at Lord's, Thursday, Friday, Saturday, June 15, 16, 17, 1899. – The second of the Test matches was the only one of the five brought to a definite conclusion, and its result was a heavy blow to English cricket, the Australians gaining a brilliant victory on the third afternoon by ten wickets. They played a winning game all the way through, fairly beating the Englishmen at every point. The match, indeed, furnished one of the most complete triumphs gained by Australian cricketers in England since Gregory's team came over and astonished us in 1878. [...]

The Englishmen really lost the match during the first hour or so on the opening day. They won the toss and when they went in to bat on a carefully-prepared wicket it was confidently expected they would stay for the whole of the afternoon. To the dismay of the crowd, however, six wickets went down for 66 runs – a deplorable start from which the team were never able to recover. Jackson and Jessop by putting on 95 runs together saved their side from complete collapse, but Jackson, who played a superb innings, might have been run out by several yards when England's score stood at 70. It was felt when the innings ended for 206 – Jones's terrific bowling being the chief cause of the breakdown – that the Australians had an immense advantage, and so it proved. For a little time there seemed some chance of an even game, Worrall, Darling and Gregory being got rid of for 59 runs, but thenceforward the Australians were always winning. The turning point of the game was the partnership of Clement Hill and Noble. The two batsmen had carried the score from 59 to 156 at the drawing of stumps, and on the following morning they took the total to 189 before Noble left. Then came another good partnership, Hill and Trumper putting Australia well in front with six wickets in hand, and increasing the score to 271. At this point Hill was brilliantly caught by Fry in the deep field. Later on Trumper found a valuable partner in Trumble, and it was not until after four o'clock that the Australian innings ended, the total reaching 421, or 215 runs ahead. In their different styles Hill and Trumper, who curiously enough made exactly the same score, played magnificent cricket. Trumper's innings was by far the more brilliant of the two, but inasmuch as Hill went in while there was still a chance of an even game, and had to play the English bowling at its best, it is only right to say that the left-handed batsman had the greater share in the ultimate success of his side. Hill, who was missed at slip by Ranjitsinhji when he had made 119, was batting just over four hours, and hit seventeen 4's, seven 3's and eighteen 2's. Trumper, who so far as could be seen gave no chance whatever, hit twenty 4's, four 3's and six 2's, and was at the wickets for three hours and a quarter.

Going in for the second time against a balance of 215, the Englishmen had a very gloomy outlook, and their position was desperate when at 23 their third wicket went down, the batsmen out being Fry, Ranjitsinhji and Townsend. Hayward and Jackson made things look a little better, but just before the time for drawing stumps Jackson was easily caught and bowled in playing forward at Trumble, the total at the close being 94. Hayward batted well, but when he had made a single he was palpably missed by the wicket-keeper, standing back to Jones. On the third morning MacLaren joined Hayward, and so long as these two batsmen stayed together there was still a chance of England making something like a fight. Indeed, things were looking comparatively cheerful when 150 went up without further loss. However, on Laver being tried Hayward, Tyldesley and Jessop were caught in quick succession, and with seven wickets down for 170 the match was as good as over. MacLaren, who so long as Hayward stayed in had been steadiness itself, hit in wonderful form from the time that Lilley joined him, but despite his efforts England were all out for 240. Never has MacLaren played a greater innings. The Australians only required 26 runs – a trifling number, which after lunch Darling and Worrall obtained without being separated.

ENGLAND

Mr C.B. Fry c Trumble b Jones	13	– b Jones	4
Mr A.C. MacLaren b Jones	4	– not out	88
K.S. Ranjitsinhji c and b Jones	8	– c Noble b Howell	0
Mr C.L. Townsend st Kelly b Howell	5	– b Jones	8
Mr F.S. Jackson b Jones	73	– c and b Trumble	37
T. Hayward b Noble	1	– c Trumble b Laver	77
J.T. Tyldesley c Darling b Jones	14	– c Gregory b Laver	4
Mr G.L. Jessop c Trumper b Trumble	51	– c Trumble b Laver	4
A.A. Lilley not out	19	– b Jones	12
W. Mead b Jones	7	– lbw, b Noble	0
W. Rhodes b Jones	2	– c and b Noble	2
B 2, l-b 6, w 1	9	B 2, l-b 2	4
	206		**240**

AUSTRALIA

J. Worrall c Hayward b Rhodes	18	– not out	11
J. Darling c Ranjitsinhji b Rhodes	9	– not out	17
C. Hill c Fry b Townsend	135		
S.E. Gregory c Lilley b Jessop	15		
M.A. Noble c Lilley b Rhodes	54		
V. Trumper not out	135		
J.J. Kelly c Lilley b Mead	9		
H. Trumble c Lilley b Jessop	24		
F. Laver b Townsend	0		
E. Jones c Mead b Townsend	17		
W.P. Howell b Jessop	0		
L-b 4, n-b 1	5		
	421		**28**

AUSTRALIAN BOWLING

	Overs	Mdns	Runs	Wkts	Overs	Mdns	Runs	Wkts
Jones	36.1	11	88	7	36	15	76	3
Howell	14	4	43	1	31	12	67	1
Noble	15	7	39	1	19.4	8	37	2
Trumble	15	9	27	1	15	6	20	1
Laver					16	4	36	3

ENGLISH BOWLING

	Overs	Mdns	Runs	Wkts	Overs	Mdns	Runs	Wkts
Jessop	37.1	10	105	3	6	0	19	0
Mead	53	24	91	1				
Rhodes	39	14	108	3	5	1	9	0
Jackson	18	6	31	0				
Townsend	15	1	50	3				
Ranjitsinhji	2	0	6	0				
Hayward	6	0	25	0				

Umpires: T. Mycroft and W.A.J. West.

THE AUSTRALIANS IN ENGLAND 1902

From a cricket point of view the Australians had a triumphant tour, and as regards material reward they got on, I believe, quite as well as could have been expected in such a deplorable summer. In going through a programme of thirty-nine fixtures with only two defeats, they beat the records of all their predecessors in this country, and no one who followed their tour or, like myself, saw only a section of the matches, will deny that they richly deserved all the success they obtained. No travelling team ever strove harder for victory or more completely subordinated all personal considerations to the prime object of winning matches. They formed a splendid all-round combination, the players new to England having been picked with the nicest judgment, but the team would not, with all their ability, have been able to show such consistently fine form week after week throughout a long tour, if the men had not taken scrupulous care of themselves when off the field. I make no apology for insisting rather strongly upon this point. Everyone who is at all behind the scenes in cricket knows perfectly well that in the case, both of English elevens in Australia and Australian elevens in England, the brightest hopes have sometimes been wrecked through want of self-control on the part of players on whom the utmost dependence was placed. In this connection it is, of course, impossible to mention names, but the famous cricketers who have captained elevens in this country and the Colonies will know perfectly well the cases I have in mind. […]

In his own sphere of action, Darling is a born leader. When he comes to England, he comes simply and solely to play cricket, and he has the rare power of being able to keep a whole team up to something approaching his own standard. He has immense concentration of purpose and under his guidance the players were just as keen at the end of three months' cricket as they had been at the beginning of their tour. […] All seemed to be fully imbued with the idea that their one duty was to enhance, if possible, the reputation of Australian cricket. […]

Just at one period of their tour the team must have felt despondent. Immediately after their collapse at Birmingham in the first Test match for a score of 36 and their defeat by Yorkshire at Leeds, when Hirst and F.S. Jackson got them out for 23, several of the players, unable to withstand the atrocious weather, fell victims to influenza and for the moment the general outlook was dark in the extreme. Rain day after day had had a deplorable effect upon the receipts at the various matches and the outbreak of illness, coming at a time when there seemed no immediate prospect of an improvement in the weather, sent the spirits of the players down to zero. Indeed it was said that one or two of the men new to England were so thoroughly downhearted that, had such a thing been possible, they would have been quite willing to pack up their bags and return home. On the day of the Test match at Lord's, Howell and Trumble, the latter of whom had only just commenced playing after a dislocated thumb had lost him a month's cricket, was down with influenza; Darling and Noble were only just getting over the same complaint and Saunders, though pressed into the service at the last moment, had hardly recovered from an inflamed eye and an attack of tonsilitis. No wonder in the circumstances that a somewhat forlorn and dispirited set of cricketers went into the field at Lord's, on the 12th of June. Suddenly, however, both in a figurative and a literal sense, the clouds lifted. The invalids quickly regained health and strength, and, after continous rain had restricted the Test match to something under two hours' play on the opening day, the weather became decently favourable. The Australians easily beat an England eleven at Eastbourne and from that time they never looked back, the remainder of the trip being in the nature of a triumphal march. [...]

Coming to the individual work of the various players, one is struck first by the preeminence of Victor Trumper as a batsman and next by the extremely fine form shown by nearly all the members of the team who were new to England. Trumper stood alone among the batsmen of the season, not only far surpassing his own colleagues, but also putting into the shade everyone who played for England. In the course of the tour he obtained, despite the wet weather, 2570 runs, thus easily beating Darling's 1941 in the glorious summer of 1899, which up to this year was a record aggregate for any Colonial batsmen touring in this country. Pages might be written about Trumper's batting without exhausting the subject. Having regard to the character of the season, with its many wet days and soft wickets, it is safe to say that no one – not even Ranjitsinhji – has been at once so brilliant and so consistent since W.G. Grace was at his best. Trumper seemed independent of varying conditions, being able to play just as dazzling a game after a night's rain as when the wickets were hard and true. All bowling came alike to him and on many occasions, notably in the Test matches at Sheffield and Manchester and the first of the two games with the M.C.C. at Lord's, he reduced our best bowlers for the time being to the level of the village green. They were simply incapable of checking his extraordinary hitting. Only a combination of wonderful eye and supreme confidence could have rendered such pulling as his at all possible. The way in which he took good length balls off the middle stump and sent them round to the boundary had to be seen to be believed. Though this exceptional faculty, however, was one of the main sources of his strength on soft wickets, he was far indeed from being dependent on unorthodox strokes. His cutting and off-driving approached perfection and he did everything with such an easy grace of style that his batting was always a delight to the eye. Risking so much, he plays what I should call a young man's game, lightning quickness of eye and hand being essential to his success, and for this reason I should not expect him after twenty years or more of first-class cricket to rival such batsmen as Shrewsbury, A.P. Lucas and W.L. Murdoch, but for the moment he is unapproachable. He was not in the smallest degree spoilt by his triumphs, bearing himself just as modestly and playing the game as sternly at the end of a long tour as at its beginning. Incidentally I may express my extreme satisfaction that the efforts to secure him for an English county failed. It would have been a paltry and unworthy thing to deprive Australia, by means of a money bribe, of her finest batsman. [...]

ENGLAND V. AUSTRALIA

Played at Manchester, Thursday, Friday, Saturday, July 24, 25, 26, 1902. – The fourth of the Test games produced one of the most memorable matches in the whole history of cricket, the Australians, after some extraordinary fluctuations of fortune, winning by three runs. At the end of the first day they looked to have the game in their hands, and at the end of the second it seemed equally certain that they would be beaten.

Superb bowling and fielding pulled them through at the finish, but they would probably be the first to admit that fortune was very kind to them, five or six hours' rain
during Friday night making the task of the Englishmen in the last innings twice as
difficult as it had promised to be. In the opinion of most people England ought,
despite the damaged pitch, to have won the match, but defeat by three runs after such
a tremendous struggle certainly carried with it no discredit. [...] In picking twelve
men for England the Selection Committee left out Fry and Jessop, restored
Ranjitsinhji to the place he had not been able to take at Sheffield, and brought in
L.C.H. Palairet and Tate. As Fry had failed in three matches it was only right to drop
him, but it was a mistake not to play Jessop as his absence, apart from all question of
run-getting, sadly weakened the fielding on the off-side. On the morning of the
match another blunder was committed, Tate being played in preference to Hirst. The
condition of the ground – very soft and slow after a lot of rain – offered some excuse
for the course adopted, but it meant playing a bowler pure and simple in preference to
a first-rate all-round man, and the result proved anything but happy.

The Australians derived great advantage from winning the toss as up to lunch
time the ball did nothing at all on the soft turf. Trumper, Duff and Hill, made splendid use of their opportunities, but it must be said that the English bowlers did very
poor work, pitching so short that it was often an easy matter to pull them. By magnificent hitting Trumper and Duff scored 135 in an hour and twenty minutes for the first
wicket and when lunch time came the total without further loss had reached 173, the
Australians seeming already on the high road to victory. After the interval Rhodes got
rid of Trumper, Noble and Gregory in quick succession, but Darling punished him
tremendously and while in with Hill made an invaluable stand for the fifth wicket.
With only five men out for 256 the Australians seemed sure to make considerably
over three hundred, but the last few batsmen could do nothing against Lockwood,
and the innings ended for 299. It should be stated that owing to the soft ground
Lockwood was not tried at all until the score had reached 129. Duff, Hill and Darling
all played fine cricket, but the chief batting honours rested with Trumper, who scored
his 104 without making a mistake of any kind. His pulling was a marvel of ease and
certainty. The wicket had been drying fast since luncheon and the Englishmen on
going in to bat could do little or nothing against Trumble and Saunders, five wickets
going down in three-quarters of an hour for 44. Jackson and Braund then played out
time, the total at the drawing of stumps being 70.

Friday was England's day, the cricket shown by the home side, apart from one lamentable blunder in the field, being magnificent. To begin with Jackson and Braund
pulled the game round into quite a respectable position, carrying the overnight score of
70 to 185 before they were separated. Altogether they put on during their partnership
141 runs. It was a splendid performance, for although the wicket had improved a great
deal and was in good condition, runs were very hard to get, the Australian bowlers
being always able to get break on the ball. Lunch time had nearly arrived, when
Braund, in stepping out to drive Noble, turned on to his wicket a ball that would have
missed the off stump. A better morning's play all-round was not seen during the whole
season. Braund made a wretched stroke with his score at 58 but otherwise his innings
was quite beyond reproach, the way in which he punished Armstrong on the leg side
being most refreshing. After luncheon Jackson did not get much support, but he

played a great game himself, seizing every opportunity of scoring and forcing the hitting in the most skilful way while the last two men were in with him. In fourth wicket down on Thursday, with the score at 30 he was the last man out, England finishing up with a total of 262 or only 37 runs behind. He was at the wickets nearly four hours and a half, playing all the time with superb judgment and skill. [...]

Excitement was at its highest point when shortly after four o'clock the Australians entered upon their second innings, everyone feeling that the result of the match might depend on the next hour's play. As it happened Lockwood's bowling was even more remarkable in quality than Jackson's batting had been, and the game went entirely in England's favour. Trumper, Hill and Duff were out for ten runs, Trumper being caught at slip by Braund at the second attempt, and the fourth wicket would have fallen at sixteen if Darling had not been missed at square leg off Braund's bowling by Tate. If the catch had been held it is quite likely, as Lockwood was bowling in such wonderful form, that the Australians would have been out for a total of fifty or sixty. As it was, Darling and Gregory stayed together for an hour, their partnership producing 54 runs. Gregory was the first to go, and Darling left at 74. Then Lockwood, who had been indulged with a rest, got rid of Hopkins and Noble, and when the time came for drawing stumps eight wickets were down for 85. The Australians were only 122 runs ahead with two wickets to fall, and it is only reasonable to assume that if the weather had kept fine during the night, England would have won the match comfortably enough. Rain poured down for five or six hours however, and on Saturday morning the position had completely changed. Owing to the state of the ground nothing could be done until shortly after twelve, and for the addition of a single run the Australian innings ended, England being left with 124 to get to win. For Lockwood, as a bowler, the match was nothing less than a triumph, his analysis for the two innings coming out at eleven wickets for 76 runs. Finer bowling than his on Friday afternoon can rarely have been seen.

As no one could tell how the wicket would play, the Englishmen entered upon their task under very anxious circumstances. At first, however, everything went well, MacLaren and Palairet scoring 36 runs in fifty minutes, and being still together at lunch time. Still, though they started so well, the difficulty they experienced in playing the bowling made one apprehensive as to what would happen after the interval. Palairet was bowled at 44, and then with MacLaren and Tyldesley together runs for a few overs came so fast that England seemed likely to win hands down. However, at 68 or only 56 to win, Tyldesley was caught in the slips. Another misfortune quickly followed, MacLaren, after playing very fine cricket for an hour and a quarter, hitting out rashly at a ball from Trumble and being caught in the long field at 72. At this point Ranjitsinhji was joined by Abel, and after the latter had been missed by Saunders at mid-on, a slight shower stopped the game for a quarter of an hour. The weather looked very threatening and it was clear, on cricket being again proceeded with, that Abel had received strict injunctions to hit. He played a game quite foreign to his ordinary methods, and for a time got on very well. Ranjitsinhji, however, was altogether at fault and did not seem to have the least confidence in himself. He was always in front of the stumps in trying to play Trumble, and at 92 he was leg-before-wicket to that bowler. With six wickets in hand and only 32 runs wanted, England still seemed sure of victory, but from this point everything changed, Trumble and Saunders, backed up by superb fielding, bowling so finely that in fifty minutes five more wickets went down for 24 runs. Abel was bowled in trying to drive; Jackson was caught at mid-off from a full pitch; Braund beautifully stumped, and Lockwood bowled, the eighth wicket falling at 109. With fifteen runs required, Rhodes joined Lilley and in three hits, one of them a big drive over the ring by Rhodes, the score was carried to 116 or only eight to win. At this point, Lilley, from a fine hit, was splendidly caught by Hill at square-leg, the fieldsman just reaching the ball when running at full speed. Heavy rain then drove the players from the field and there was a delay of three-quarters of an hour before the match could be finished. Tate got a four on the leg-side from the first ball he received from Saunders, but the fourth, which came a little with the bowler's arm and kept low, hit the wicket and the match was over, Australia winning by three runs. Trumble and Saunders bowled extraordinary well, combining a lot of break with almost perfect length, and the fielding that did so much to win the match was unsurpassable.

AUSTRALIA

V. Trumper c Lilley b Rhodes	104 –	c Braund b Lockwood 3
R.A. Duff c Lilley b Lockwood	54 –	b Lockwood 4
C. Hill c Rhodes b Lockwood	65 –	b Lockwood 0
M.A. Noble c and b Rhodes	2 –	c Lilley b Lockwood 4
S.E. Gregory c Lilley b Rhodes	3 –	lbw, b Tate 24
J. Darling c MacLaren b Rhodes	51 –	c Palairet b Rhodes 37
A.J. Hopkins c Palairet b Lockwood	0 –	c Tate b Lockwood 2
W.W. Armstrong b Lockwood	5 –	b Rhodes 3
J.J. Kelly not out	4 –	not out 2
H. Trumble c Tate b Lockwood	0 –	lbw, b Tate 4
J.V. Saunders b Lockwood	3 –	c Tyldesley b Rhodes 0
B 5, l-b 2, w 1	8	B1, l-b 1, n-b 1 3
	299	**86**

ENGLAND

Mr L.C.H. Palairet c Noble b Saunders	6 –	b Saunders 17
R. Abel c Armstrong b Saunders	6 –	b Trumble 21
J.T. Tyldesley c Hopkins b Saunders	22 –	c Armstrong b Saunders 16
Mr A.C. MacLaren b Trumble	1 –	c Duff b Trumble 35
K.S. Ranjitsinhji lbw, b Trumble	2 –	lbw, b Trumble 0
Hon. F.S. Jackson c Duff b Trumble	128 –	c Gregory b Saunders 4
L.C. Braund b Noble	65 –	st Kelly b Trumble 7
A.A. Lilley b Noble	7 –	c Hill b Trumble 3
W.H. Lockwood run out	7 –	b Trumble 4
W. Rhodes c and b Trumble	5 –	not out 4
F.W. Tate not out	5 –	b Saunders 4
B 6, l-b 2	8	B 5
	262	**120**

ENGLISH BOWLING

	Overs	Mdns	Runs	Wkts	Overs	Mdns	Runs	Wkts
Rhodes	25	3	104	4	14.4	5	26	3
Jackson	11	0	58	0				
Tate	11	1	44	0	5	3	7	2
Braund	9	0	37	0	11	3	22	0
Lockwood	20.1	5	48	6	17	5	28	5

AUSTRALIANS' BOWLING

Trumble	43	16	75	4	25	9	53	6
Saunders	34	5	104	3	19.4	4	52	4
Noble	24	8	47	2	5	3	10	0
Trumper	6	4	6	0				
Armstrong	5	2	19	0				
Hopkins	2	0	3	0				

Umpires: T. Mycroft and J. Moss.

ENGLAND V. AUSTRALIA

Played at Kennington Oval, Monday, Tuesday, Wednesday, August 11, 12, 13, 1902. – Australia having already won the rubber, the fifth and last of the Test matches had not at starting the same importance that would under other circumstances have attached to it, but it produced a never-to-be-forgotten struggle and a more exciting finish, if that were possible, than the one at Manchester. In face of great difficulties and disadvantages England won by one wicket after the odds had been fifty to one on Australia. Some truly wonderful hitting by Jessop made victory possible after all hope had seemed gone, and Hirst and Rhodes got their side home at the close. In its moral results the victory was a very important one indeed, as no one interested in English cricket could have felt other than depressed and low spirited if all the Test matches played out to a finish had ended in favour of Darling's team. In making up the English side the Selection Committee restored Jessop and Hirst to the places they ought to have filled at Manchester, and for the first time in the series of games gave a place to Hayward, Ranjitsinhji, Tate and Abel being left out. Hayward had done enough to deserve a trial, but, as it happened, he proved a great failure as a batsman and was by no means lively in the field. The Australians of course kept to the team that had been victorious at Sheffield and Old Trafford. The wicket, though a trifle slow from the effects of recent rain, was in very good condition, and the Australians, staying in for the whole of the first day, made the highly satisfactory score of 324. At one time they did not seem likely to do nearly so well as this for, though Trumper and Duff scored 47 for the first partnership, there were four wickets down for 82 and five for 126. The change in the game was brought about by Hirst, who for a time bowled in quite his form of 1901. Duff was out to a marvellous catch by the wicket-keeper standing back, Lilley jumping a yard or more on the leg side and holding a ball that would have gone for four. Noble and Armstrong by putting on 48 runs considerably improved the Australians' position, but with seven wickets down for 175 the outlook was none too promising. However, all these disasters were so well retrieved that the three remaining wickets added 149 runs, an invaluable partnership by Hopkins and Trumble putting on 81. The batting was very painstaking, but an unlucky mistake by Lilley at the wicket when Trumble had made nine had, from England's point of view, a deplorable effect on the game.

If the weather had kept fine the Englishmen would not on an Oval wicket have been afraid of facing a score of 324, but the bad luck that had handicapped them at Sheffield and Manchester still pursued them, heavy rain during the early hours of Tuesday morning making a great difference in the pitch. Under the circumstances they did not do at all badly to score 183, but apart from some bright hitting by Tyldesley there was nothing remarkable in the efforts of the early batsmen. At lunch time six wickets were down for 83, and it seemed certain that the side would follow on and be beaten. Braund and Hirst made a great effort, the latter hitting with the utmost free-dom, but when he left the total had only reached 137, England still wanting 38 runs to avoid going in again. Thanks, however, to a bad blunder by Hill, who palpably missed Lockwood at long-on when the batsman had made eleven, the follow-on was saved, the innings ending for 183 or 141 runs behind. Braund was often beaten by balls that missed the wicket, but in staying in for an hour and a half he did invaluable work for his side. Trumble bowled throughout the innings in splendid form and took eight wickets for just over eight runs apiece. Possessing such a big lead the Australians looked, when they went in for the second time, to have the match in their hands. They opened their innings with a great misfortune, Trumper throwing away his wicket in attempting a foolish run, and for the rest of the afternoon the batting was marked by such extreme care that at the drawing of stumps the score, with eight men out, had only reached 114, two hours and three-quarters being occupied in getting these runs. The wicket was still rather difficult and Lockwood bowled very finely. Hill was out to a magnificent catch low down in the slips in one hand by MacLaren, and Noble bowled off his pads by a ball that he did not attempt to play with his bat.

On Wednesday morning Lockwood quickly obtained the two outstanding wick-ets, bringing the Australian innings to a close for 121, and then England went in with 263 wanted to win the match. Tuesday's cricket, while the turf was still soft after the rain, had damaged the pitch to no small extent, and up to a certain point the batsmen were so helpless against Saunders and Trumble that the easiest of victories for Australia appeared in prospect. Three wickets fell to Saunders for ten runs and but for Gregory missing Hayward badly at short-leg there would have been four wickets down for 16. Even as it was half the side were out for 48 and the match looked all over. At this point, Jackson, who had gone in third wicket down, was joined by Jessop and a stand was made which completely altered the game. At first, however, Jessop's cricket was far from suggesting the wonderful form he afterwards showed. When he had made 22 Kelly missed stumping him and at 27 he gave a rather awkward chance to Trumper at long-off. At lunch time the two batsmen were still together, Jackson, who had played superb cricket, being 39 and Jessop 29. After the interval Jackson was far indeed from keeping up his previous form, being repeatedly in difficulties and giving a palpable chance to Armstrong at slip. Jessop, on the other hand, settled down at once, and hit as he only can. At one point he scored four 4's and a single off successive balls from Saunders. The partnership had added 109 runs in sixty-five minutes when Jackson was easily caught and bowled. Jessop went on hitting for some little time longer, but at 187 he closed his extraordinary innings by placing a ball gently into short-leg's hands. He scored, in just over an hour and a quarter, 104 runs out of 139, his hits being a 5 in the slips, seventeen 4's, two 3's, four 2's and seventeen singles. [...] Hirst played a great game and, after Lockwood's dismissal at 214, received such help from Lilley that victory gradually came in sight. The score was advanced to 248, or only 15 to win, and then from a good hard drive Lilley was finely caught at deep mid-off. Rhodes as last man had a trying crisis to face, but his nerve did not fail him. Once, however, he nearly lost his wicket, Armstrong at slip getting a catch in his hand, but being partly overbalanced, dropping the ball. Hirst went on imperturbably, scoring again and again by means of cleverly placed singles, and at last he had the extreme satisfaction of making the score a tie. Then Rhodes sent a ball from Trumble between the bowler and mid-on, and England won the match by one wicket. [...]

AUSTRALIANS

V. Trumper b Hirst	.42 – run out	.2
R.A. Duff c Lilley b Hirst	.23 – b Lockwood	.6
C. Hill b Hirst	.11 – c MacLaren b Hirst	.34
J. Darling c Lilley b Hirst	.3 – c MacLaren b Lockwood	.15
M.A. Noble c and b Jackson	.52 – b Braund	.13
S.E. Gregory b Hirst	.23 – b Braund	.9
W.W. Armstrong b Jackson	.17 – b Lockwood	.21
A. Hopkins c MacLaren b Lockwood	.40 – c Lilley b Lockwood	.3
H. Trumble not out	.61 – not out	.7
J.J. Kelly c Rhodes b Braund	.39 – lbw, b Lockwood	.0
J.V. Saunders lbw, b Braund	.0 – c Tyldesley b Rhodes	.2
B 5, l-b 3, n-b 2	.10 B 7, l-b 2	.9
	324	**121**

ENGLAND

Mr A.C. MacLaren c Armstrong b Trumble	.10 – b Saunders	.2
Mr L.C.H. Palairet b Trumble	.20 – b Saunders	.6
J.T. Tyldesley b Trumble	.33 – b Saunders	.0
T. Hayward b Trumble	.0 – c Kelly b Saunders	.7
Hon. F.S. Jackson c Armstrong b Saunders	...2 – c and b Trumble	.49
L.C. Braund c Hill b Trumble	.22 – c Kelly b Trumble	.2
Mr G.L. Jessop b Trumble	.13 – c Noble b Armstrong	.104
G.H. Hirst c and b Trumble	.43 – not out	.58
W.H. Lockwood c Noble b Saunders	.25 – lbw, b Trumble	.2
A.A. Lilley c Trumper b Trumble	.0 – c Darling b Trumble	.16
W. Rhodes not out	.0 – not out	.6
B 13, l-b 2	.15 B 5, l-b 6	.11
	183	**263**

ENGLISH BOWLING

	Overs	Mdns	Runs	Wkts	Overs	Mdns	Runs	Wkts
Lockwood	24	2	85	1	20	6	45	5
Rhodes	28	9	46	0	22	7	38	1
Hirst	29	5	77	5	5	1	7	1
Braund	16.5	5	29	2	9	1	15	2
Jackson	20	4	66	2	4	3	7	0
Jessop	6	2	11	0				

AUSTRALIANS' BOWLING

	Overs	Mdns	Runs	Wkts	Overs	Mdns	Runs	Wkts
Trumble	31	13	65	8	33.5	4	108	4
Saunders	23	7	79	2	24	3	105	4
Noble	7	3	24	0	5	0	11	0
Armstrong					4	0	28	1

Umpires: C.E. Richardson and A.A. White.

FROM M.C.C. IN AUSTRALIA

IMPRESSIONS OF THE TOUR

By B.J.T. Bosanquet

[...] Queensland gave us a good game, and produced a fast aboriginal bowler. Leonard Braund was selected to open the innings for us and didn't much fancy it. The first ball hit the bat somehow and went to fine leg for two; the second, passed batsman, wicket-keeper, *and longstop,* and hit the screen about the time Braund finished his shot. The third was slower, and the batsman, retiring gracefully, placed it gently into point's hands. His own account of the proceedings is worth giving, it is as follows:

> 'I took first ball from the aboriginal, Henry, supposed to be the fastest bowler in the world, and certainly I will say that the first three balls he gave me were indeed the fastest I have ever seen. I *got him* away for two on the leg side, but the next ball, in cutting him, I was splendidly caught at point!'

[...] West Maitland provided an interesting draw. Their fielding and bowling were a bit slack, and Foster remonstrated. Unfortunately when we took the field, I had an off-day, and at the close of the match their captain said quietly to Foster, 'Well, I don't think our bowling was much worse than Bosanquet's!' Newcastle produced another draw, and here George Hirst was insulted. Having adjourned for a drink, he was just in time to hear someone say, 'that Hirst is a —— rotten player!' Leaving his drink he retired, being with difficulty restrained from wreaking summary vengeance, and never knew a happy moment till, having persuaded Foster to send him in first, he had taken 50 of the very best in our second innings.

[...] Another important factor in our success was the personality of our captain [P.F. Warner]. The keenest of enthusiasts, and, as he would say, a 'cheerful optimist' he infected the whole team with his own spirit, and in addition never spared himself if he could do anything for the comfort, or pleasure, of the men under him. His sole thought was for us, and no one of us can ever properly appreciate, or be sufficiently grateful for, all he did for us. A wise, and most successful captain on the field, his tact and kindly influence in less strenuous moments had even more to do with his final triumph. Most of the hard work of the tour, and most of the troubles and worries incidental to such a trip, fell on his shoulders. He never shirked and never complained, and herein performed the greater portion of a captain's duty. In his own words the day on which we won the rubber constituted 'the happiest moment of his life,' and never was happiness more deserved. We could have wished him better luck with the bat, but personal success was the last consideration with him. In other fields he earned distinction, notably as an orator. In this connection we suffered, if I may use the word, from excess of hospitality. Much as we appreciated the kindly feelings which prompted the welcome extended to us on all hands, one *can* have too much of a good thing, and speeches, when one has just arrived after a fatiguing journey, sometimes about 10 p.m., can hardly be too short. The kindness and hospitality shown to us by private individuals all over the country could not have been surpassed and everybody did their best to give us the best of good times, which we certainly had, and we can never be sufficiently grateful for all that was done for us on every hand. [...]

FIRST TEST MATCH

Played at Sydney, Friday, Saturday, Monday, Tuesday, Wednesday, Thursday, December 11, 12, 14, 15, 16, 17, 1903. – The first of the five Test matches was in many ways the best of the series. Indeed a finer game has rarely been seen in Australia. It lasted into the sixth day, and attracted in all about 95,000 people. The Australians, on winning the toss, lost Trumper, Duff and Hill for a dozen runs, Trumper being out to a wonderful catch at slip. Thanks to Noble these disasters were retrieved, but when at the end of the day the score stood at 259 for six wickets, the Australians did not seem to have done anything out of the common. However, rain in the night made their total look far more formidable.

Next day the Australian innings ended for 285 and the Englishmen went in under very anxious conditions, as no one could tell how the wicket would play. Tyldesley, batting with the utmost skill, saved his side from a break-down before lunch, and by four o'clock the wicket had practically recovered. At the drawing of stumps the total had reached 243 for four wickets, Foster being not out 73, and Braund not out 67. Noble was at the wickets four hours and three-quarters for his 133, and hardly made a mistake. The third day was marked by the most brilliant and sensational cricket seen during the tour, R.E. Foster, with a magnificent innings of 287, beating all records in Test matches. Altogether he was batting for seven hours, among his hits being thirty-eight 4's. The latter part of his innings was described on all hands as something never surpassed. Foster and Braund added 192 runs together, Braund playing an admirable innings, but with eight men out the Englishmen were only 47 ahead. Then came the startling play, Relf and Rhodes helping Foster to put on respectively 115 and 130 runs for the ninth and tenth wickets. The last wicket partnership set up a new record in Test games. Foster's triumph was the more remarkable as he had never before played in an England and Australia match. He did not begin his great innings at all well, and ought to have been caught when he had made 51, but his batting on the third day was beyond criticism. Going in against a balance of 292 runs, Australia had scored 17 without loss when stumps were pulled up.

Next day they did great things, carrying their score to 367 and only losing five wickets. There was a very regrettable and indeed disgraceful demonstration on the part of a large section of the crowd when Hill was given run out, a storm of hooting and booing going on for a long time. On the fifth day the Australian innings ended for 485, Trumper taking out his bat for a faultless 185. His hits included twenty-five 4's, and during a stay of three hours and fifty minutes he gave no chance. Rhodes bowled with the utmost steadiness on the hard ground, and in writing home Mr Warner said he did not know what the side would have done without him.

England wanted 194 to win, and found the task a very heavy one. They won on the sixth day by five wickets, but they would very probably have been beaten if, after four wickets had fallen for 83, Laver at short leg had not missed Hirst before that batsman had scored a run. As it was Hayward and Hirst made a great stand, and almost won the game together. Hayward was batting just over four hours for his beautifully-played 91.

AUSTRALIA

R.A. Duff c Lilley b Arnold	3	– c Relf b Rhodes	84
V. Trumper c Foster b Arnold	1	– not out	185
C. Hill c Lilley b Hirst	5	– run out	51
M.A. Noble c Foster b Arnold	133	– st Lilley b Bosanquet	22
W.W. Armstrong b Bosanquet	48	– c Bosanquet b Rhodes	27
A.J. Hopkins b Hirst	39	– c Arnold b Rhodes	20
W.P. Howell c Relf b Arnold	5	– c Lilley b Arnold	4
S. Gregory b Bosanquet	23	– c Lilley b Arnold	43
F. Laver lbw, b Rhodes	4	– c Relf b Rhodes	6
J.J. Kelly c Braund b Rhodes	10	– b Arnold	13
J.V. Saunders not out	11	– run out	2
Byes, &c.	3	Byes, &c.	28
	285		**485**

ENGLAND

P.F. Warner c Kelly b Laver	0	– b Howell	8
T. Hayward b Howell	15	– st Kelly b Saunders	91
J.T. Tyldesley b Noble	53	– c Noble b Saunders	9
E. Arnold c Laver b Armstrong	27		
R.E. Foster c Noble b Saunders	287	– st Kelly b Armstrong	19
L.C. Braund b Howell	102	– c Noble b Howell	0
G.H. Hirst b Howell	0	– not out	60
B.J.T. Bosanquet c Howell b Noble	2	– not out	1
A.A. Lilley c Hill b Noble	4		
A.E. Relf c Armstrong b Saunders	31		
W. Rhodes not out	40		
Byes, &c.	16	Byes, &c.	6
	577		**194**

ENGLISH BOWLING

	Overs	Mdns	Runs	Wkts	Overs	Mdns	Runs	Wkts
Hirst	24	8	47	2	29	1	79	0
Arnold	32	7	76	4	28	3	93	2
Braund	26	9	39	0	12	2	56	0
Bosanquet	13	0	52	2	24	1	100	1
Rhodes	17.2	3	41	2	40.2	10	94	5
Relf	6	1	27	0	13	5	35	0

AUSTRALIAN BOWLING

	Overs	Mdns	Runs	Wkts	Overs	Mdns	Runs	Wkts
Saunders	36.2	8	126	2	10.5	3	51	2
Laver	37	12	116	1	16	4	37	0
Howell	31	7	113	3	31	18	35	2
Noble	34	8	99	3	12	2	37	0
Armstrong	23	3	47	1	18	6	28	1
Hopkins	11	1	40	0				
Trumper	7	1	12	0				
Gregory	2	0	8	0				

THIRD TEST MATCH

Played at Adelaide, Friday, Saturday, Monday, Tuesday, Wednesday, Thursday, January 10, 11, 13, 14, 15, 16, 1908. – The Englishmen lost the third Test Match by 245 runs, allowing the game to slip out of their hands after it had seemed twenty to one on them. They played the same eleven as at Melbourne, but the Australians made two changes, Hartigan the Queensland batsman and O'Connor taking the places of Hazlitt and Cotter, the last named player being kept away by a bad strain. Clem Hill, suffering from influenza, was too unwell to field, but fighting against his illness he played a wonderful innings. Winning the toss the Australians scored 285, runs coming at the rate of just under one a minute. Macartney batted finely for two hours and a quarter, and Hartigan's first appearance was a great success. The innings ended on the second morning the English bowling, despite the intense heat, having been maintained at a high standard.

The Englishmen batted very consistently and when play ceased they were only 26 behind with five wickets in hand. The Australians missed Cotter on the fast wicket. Crawford played finely the next morning, and the innings closed for 363 or 78 ahead. On Australia going in for second time Barnes soon got rid of Trumper and Macartney, and at the drawing of stumps the Australians, with four wickets down, were 55 runs to the good. Noble, who played splendidly, left with two runs added next morning, and though Ransford and O'Connor put on 44 together the seventh wicket fell at 180. The Englishmen were in a tremendously strong position, but as events turned out a couple of dropped catches destroyed their chance. Hartigan, when 32, should have been caught by Fielder at point, and Hill, when 22, was badly missed by Barnes at mid-off.

Making the most of their luck the two batsmen played superbly and at the close of the afternoon they were still together, the score having been raised to 397. In all the partnership added 243 runs, Hartigan being out on the fifth morning at 423. In his 116 he hit a dozen 4's. Hartigan's success in making a hundred in his first Test Match was much appreciated. Hill was batting for five hours and twenty minutes for his 160 – a great effort considering his illness. He hit eighteen 4's. Fielder, who had been unwell all through the match, could not play on the fifth day. The innings ended for 506 the Englishmen being left with 429 to get to win. There never seemed the least chance of this enormous task being accomplished. Hardstaff played very finely, but five wickets were down for 139 and on the following morning the match was finished off in less than an hour.

AUSTRALIA

V. Trumper b Fielder	.4	– b Barnes	.0
M.A. Noble c Hutchings b Barnes	.15	– c Gunn b Fielder	.65
C.G. Macartney lbw, b Braund	.75	– b Barnes	.9
P.A. McAlister c Hutchings b Crawford	.28	– c Hutchings b Crawford	.17
W.W. Armstrong c Humphries b Fielder	.17	– c Hutchings b Braund	.34
V. Ransford b Barnes	.44	– c Rhodes b Braund	.25
C. Hill c Humphries b Barnes	.5	– c Gunn b Crawford	.160
R. Hartigan b Fielder	.48	– c sub b Barnes	.116
H. Carter lbw, b Hutchings	.24	– not out	.31
J.A. O'Connor not out	.10	– b Crawford	.20
J.V. Saunders b Fielder	.1	– run out	.0
B 3, l-b 5, w 3, n-b 3	.14	B 20, l-b 7, w 2	.29
	285		**506**

ENGLAND

J.B. Hobbs c Carter b Saunders	.26	– not out	.23
F.L. Fane run out	.48	– b Saunders	.0
G. Gunn b O'Connor	.65	– c Trumper b O'Connor	.11
K.L. Hutchings c and b Macartney	.23	– b O'Connor	.0
L.C. Braund b Macartney	.0	– c Hartigan b O'Connor	.47
J. Hardstaff b O'Connor	.61	– c Macartney b Saunders	.72
W. Rhodes c Carter b O'Connor	.38	– c Armstrong b O'Connor	.9
S.F. Barnes c and b Armstrong	.12	– c McAlister b Saunders	.8
J.N. Crawford b Armstrong	.62	– c and b Saunders	.7
J. Humphries run out	.7	– b O'Connor	.1
A. Fielder not out	.0	– c Ransford b Saunders	.1
B 12, l-b 2, w 2, n-b 5	.21	B 3, n-b 1	.4
	363		**183**

ENGLAND BOWLING

	Overs	Mdns	Runs	Wkts	Overs	Mdns	Runs	Wkts
Barnes	27	8	60	3	42	9	83	3
Fielder	27.5	5	80	4	23	3	81	1
Rhodes	15	5	35	0	27	9	81	0
Crawford	14	0	65	1	45.5	4	113	3
Braund	9	1	26	1	23	3	85	2
Hutchings	2	1	5	1	7	0	34	0

AUSTRALIA BOWLING

Saunders	36	6	83	1	21.4	4	65	5
Macartney	18	3	49	2	4	1	17	0
O'Connor	40	8	110	3	21	6	40	5
Noble	18	4	38	0	7	1	14	0
Armstrong	18	4	55	2	10	1	43	0
Hartigan	2	0	7	0				

THE AUSTRALIANS IN ENGLAND 1909

[…] Coming to the merits of the Australians as an all-round combination, I am convinced that never before in the history of cricket has a fine side been so under-rated. Even after the rubber had been decided, critics, ordinarily possessed of sound judgment, were loth to admit that the Australians deserved their success. So grudging was the praise for the winners, and so many were the excuses urged on behalf of the beaten team, that it was not surprising to find the English press accused in the Australian papers of being one-sided. In expressing my personal belief that the Australians were estimated at far below their proper worth, I know that I am, if I may use the expression, rowing in the same boat as Mr C.B. Fry. When the England team for the fourth Test Match was being selected, Mr Fry told me that the trouble was wholly due to the fact that the Australians had been absurdly under-rated. When towards the end of May the Australians lost three matches in a fortnight, a good many people who ought to have known better, jumped to the conclusion that the tour was going to be a failure. […] Apart from the breakdown at Birmingham, the batting was maintained at a very high level, the small totals at Leeds and Manchester being fully accounted for by the state of the wickets, and never, I think, in a series of Test Matches in England has the fielding of any eleven been so consistently fine. If there were any means of calculating the number of runs saved the records of the five Test Matches in 1909 would indeed be illuminating. The method of placing the field became in Noble's hands almost an exact science, the favourite hits of the various batsmen being blocked in a way that I have never seen equalled. […]

    A better piece of bowling than Armstrong's on the third day at Lord's no one could wish to see. Again and again he made the ball do enough to beat the bat, and once or twice, unless I am mistaken, he varied his leg-breaks by turning a little the reverse way. For accuracy of length he remains unapproached among leg-break bowlers. It is the fashion in England to under-rate Cotter, the fact being overlooked that he is appreciably faster than any other bowler now before the public. This extra pace more than makes up for his occasional vagaries of direction. Macartney may not be a first rate left-handed bowler every day, but he was beyond doubt first-rate at Leeds, having the best English batsmen at his mercy in both innings. […]

SECOND TEST MATCH

Played at Lord's, Monday, Tuesday, Wednesday, June 14, 15, 16, 1909. – The second Test Match marked the turning point in the Australians' fortunes. Faced as they were with a possibility of the tour being a failure they were on the eve of the game much depressed, the extreme difficulty they had experienced in beating Somerset having greatly shaken their confidence in themselves. However, they beat England in most brilliant fashion by nine wickets and only once more – after an interval of over three months – did they suffer defeat. [...]

Rightly judging that the wicket in the absence of further rain would improve, Noble on winning the toss decided to put England in. His policy was justified by results, the wicket, never so difficult as was expected, being much faster on the second day than on the first. All things considered England gave a very creditable display of batting, staying in until just upon six o'clock for a total of 269. The highest and best innings was played by King, who not only showed the value of left-handed batting, but did much to justify his selection. He played a good strong game, hitting cleanly on the off side and placing the ball well to leg. He and Tyldesley put on 79 runs for the fourth wicket, taking the score from 44 to 123, but they had to work very hard for their runs, the partnership lasting an hour and twenty-five minutes. [...]

On the second day the match went all in favour of the Australians. The wicket rolled out very well and not until a quarter to six did the innings end, the total reaching 350 or 81 runs ahead. Then in the last twenty-five minutes England lost Hobbs's wicket for 16 runs. In gaining their big advantage the Australians owed nearly everything to Ransford who, like Harry Graham in 1893 and Victor Trumper in 1899, had the satisfaction of making a hundred in his first Test Match at Lord's. Going in third wicket down with the score at 90 he withstood the England bowling for a little over four hours and took out his bat for 143. For the most part he played wonderfully well but fortune was kind to him. When 13 he was missed by MacLaren at slip, when 56 he might have been caught at the wicket and with his score 61 he gave a chance at second slip to Jones. Had any one of these three chances been taken the whole course of the game might have been different. Ransford was strong on the leg side, but the feature of his innings was his brilliant hitting past cover-point. He was a little rash now and then in going for the off ball, but apart from this his judgment was seldom at fault. His great innings included twenty-one 4's, three 3's and nine 2's. He found valuable partners in Trumper and Noble, the fifth wicket putting on 79 runs and the sixth 71. [...]

The last day was a triumph for Australia and nothing less than humiliating for England. As the wicket had quite recovered from its drenching on Saturday most people thought that England would have little difficulty in saving the game, but in less than half an hour all hopes of this kind were destroyed. Tyldesley and George Gunn were out in one over from Armstrong at 22; with one run added Hayward was run out; and then Armstrong, who was in wonderful form, clean bowled King and Hirst with splendid balls, six wickets being down for 41. In the meantime Jones had been missed low down in the slips by Laver. Had this catch been held England would in all probability have been beaten in a single innings. As it was, Jones and MacLaren doubled the score, putting on 41 runs together in fifty minutes. MacLaren, beaten at last by a fine break back, played well, but Jones never inspired confidence. Lilley, as on the first day, hit freely, but at half-past two the innings was all over for 121. Never perhaps has Armstrong bowled quite so finely. More than once he varied his leg breaks by making the ball turn a little the other way, and his length was a marvel of accuracy. At one point he had taken five wickets for eight runs, and in the whole innings his record was six wickets for 35. [...] The match proved an enormous attraction, 50,166 people paying for admission during the three days.

ENGLAND

T. Hayward st Carter b Laver	16	– run out	6
J.B. Hobbs c Carter b Laver	19	– c and b Armstrong	9
J.T. Tyldesley lbw, b Laver	46	– st Carter b Armstrong	3
G. Gunn lbw, b Cotter	1	– b Armstrong	0
J.H. King c Macartney b Cotter	60	– b Armstrong	4
Mr A.C. MacLaren c Armstrong b Noble	7	– b Noble	24
G.H. Hirst b Cotter	31	– b Armstrong	1
Mr A.O. Jones b Cotter	8	– lbw, b Laver	26
A.E. Relf c Armstrong b Noble	17	– b Armstrong	3
A.A. Lilley c Bardsley b Noble	47	– not out	25
S. Haigh not out	1	– run out	5
B 8, l-b 3, w 3, n-b 2	16	B 2, l-b 3, n-b 10	15
	269		**121**

AUSTRALIA

P.A. McAlister lbw, b King	22	– not out	19
F. Laver b Hirst	14		
W. Bardsley b Relf	46	– c Lilley b Relf	0
W.W. Armstrong c Lilley b Relf	12		
V.S. Ransford not out	143		
V.T. Trumper c Maclaren b Relf	28		
M.A. Noble c Lilley b Relf	32		
S.E. Gregory c Lilley b Relf	14	– not out	18
A. Cotter run out	0		
C.G. Macartney b Hirst	5		
H. Carter b Hirst	7		
B 16, l-b 8, w 1, n-b 2	27	B	4
	350		**41**

AUSTRALIA BOWLING

	Overs	Mdns	Runs	Wkts	Overs	Mdns	Runs	Wkts
Laver	32	0	75	3	14	5	24	1
Macartney	8	2	10	0				
Cotter	23	1	80	4	18	3	35	0
Noble	24.2	9	42	3	5	1	12	1
Armstrong	20	6	46	0	24.5	10	35	6

ENGLAND BOWLING

	Overs	Mdns	Runs	Wkts	Overs	Mdns	Runs	Wkts
Hirst	26.5	2	83	3	8	1	28	0
King	27	5	99	1				
Relf	45	14	85	5	7.4	4	9	1
Haigh	19	5	41	0				
Jones	2	0	15	0				

Umpires: J. Moss and C.E. Dench.

3

BETWEEN THE WARS: AUSTRALIA v. ENGLAND 1920–38

Interwar Ashes cricket was an era of unparalleled scores and, at least on a per capita basis, perhaps unrepeated public interest in the game in Australia and England. Bradman's statistics still boggle our minds, but the idea that more than 350,000 of his countrymen thronged the MCG to watch him lead Australia in the New Year's Test of 1937 is nearly as remarkable.

Both eventualities played to *Wisden*'s strengths. The record section of *Wisden* doubled in size between the wars, as did circulation of the almanack's limp edition. This was in spite of a resumption to international cricket after World War I that, at least in England, was inauspicious in the extreme. *Wisden* had no compunction about describing England's visit to Australia in 1920–21 as a 'disaster', and remarked of Australia's reciprocal visit to England in 1921 that 'there has never been a season so disheartening'. The might of Warwick Armstrong's Australians at the time is exemplified not only in the reports of their Test matches, overshadowed by the marauding Jack Gregory and Ted McDonald, but in feats like Charlie Macartney's 345 in 'rather less than four hours' against Nottinghamshire and Arthur Mailey's 10–66 against Gloucestershire.

When England finally threw off the Australian yoke at the Oval in August 1926, *Wisden*'s C. Stewart Caine felt delightedly vindicated, having foreseen in that year's edition 'that the dark days are coming to an end'. He could not, of course, have forseen the rise of Bradman, a one-man English-day redarkener. Anglo-Australian cricket exchanges throughout the 1930s essentially turned on his performances, and gates fluctuated according to the likelihood of his appearances: more than 900,000 attended his first series as captain, and he rewarded them with 810 runs at an average of 90. The expectation of something big accompanied him everywhere; the mere mention of his name became almost enough. Allied soldiers were warned of the bombardment of the Monte Cassino monastery in March 1944 with the code: 'Bradman will be batting tomorrow'.

Bradman was a *Wisden* reader as well as a rewriter. In *The Art of Cricket*, he joined to summarise it as 'usually referred to as 'The Cricketer's Bible' – a hackneyed line, but from him a meaningful tribute. There's further evidence from this period, indeed, that the well-prepared cricketer always has a *Wisden* handy. When England declared late on the first day of the abbreviated Old Trafford Test of July 1921, Hanson Carter had an almanack handy to show his skipper that the closure was illegal under Law 55 (1914).

Contrast this to seventy years later when Dean Jones was adjudged run out in a Test at Bourda while walking from his wicket after being bowled by a 'no ball'. Coach Bob Simpson and manager Lawrie Sawle had then to borrow an almanack from the press box to confirm that Clyde Cumberbatch was in error under Laws 27 (5) and 38 (2). And by then, alas, it was too late. QED.

—GH

THE MCC IN AUSTRALIA 1920–21

The tour of the M.C.C.'s team in the winter of 1920–21 resulted, as everyone knows, in disaster, all the Test matches being easily won by Australia. Never before in the history of English or Australian trips since Test matches were first played had one side shown such an overwhelming superiority. As the news came to hand of defeat after defeat people thought the Englishmen must be playing very badly. Not till the Australians came here in the summer and beat us three times in succession on our own grounds did we fully realise the strength of the combination that had set up such a record. The M.C.C. were very doubtful as to the wisdom of renewing the interchange of visits so soon, feeling that English cricket had not had time to regain its pre-war standard, and it will be remembered that they declined a pressing invitation to send out a team in the winter of 1919–20. However, in face of Australia's keen desire, they could not insist on further delay. That the Australian authorities had judged the situation rightly was proved by results. In a financial sense the tour was an immense success, the Test matches attracting bigger crowds than ever. [...]

FIRST TEST MATCH

Played at Sydney, Friday, Saturday, Monday, Tuesday, Wednesday, December 17, 18, 20, 21, 22, 1920. – Though the first Test Match ended in disaster for them, the Englishmen started uncommonly well, bowling and fielding so finely that the Australians took the whole of the first afternoon to score 250 for eight wickets. The great chance for England came the next day, but it was hopelessly missed. In facing a modest total of 267 the team were in a far better position than they could have expected, and when 140 went up with only three men out the prospect was very hopeful. So dismally did the batting collapse, however, that the innings was all over for 190. Hobbs and Woolley alone showed much ability to deal with the skilful bowling, Hendren, in scoring his 28, being let-off in the slips when he had made a single. For the failure in batting there was no forgiveness. Going in for the second time with a lead of 77 the Australians before the drawing of stumps on the second day scored 46 without loss, and on Monday they carried their total to 332 for five wickets. Following up his 70 in the first innings Collins gave a splendid display, hitting ten 4's and completing his hundred in just over three hours and a half. Macartney, after a curiously slow start, was very brilliant. The most remarkable cricket of the match came on the fourth day, Armstrong playing a magnificent innings. Getting runs at the rate of 45 an hour, he scored 158 in less than three hours and a half out of the 246 put on while he was in. His hits included seventeen 4's, most of them splendid drives. For their huge total of 581 the Australians were at the wickets just upon nine hours. The Englishmen were left with the impossible task of getting 659 to win and, considering their hopeless position, they did not do badly to score 281.

AUSTRALIA

C.G. Macartney b Waddington	.19	– b Douglas	.69
H.L. Collins run out	.70	– c Waddington b Douglas	.104
W. Bardsley c Strudwick b Hearne	.22	– b Hearne	.57
C. Kelleway run out	.33	– c Russell b Woolley	.78
W.W. Armstrong st Strudwick b Woolley	.12	– b Parkin	.158
J.M. Gregory c Strudwick b Woolley	.8	– run out	.0
J.M. Taylor lbw, b Hearne	.34	– c Woolley b Parkin	.51
C.E. Pellew c Hendren b Hearne	.36	– lbw, b Woolley	.16
J. Ryder run out	.5	– run out	.6
W.A. Oldfield c Hobbs b Parkin	.7	– c Strudwick b Parkin	.16
A.A. Mailey not out	.10	– not out	.0
B 4, l-b 6, n-b 1	.11	B 17, l-b 7, n-b 2	.26
	223		**581**

ENGLAND

J.B. Hobbs b Gregory	.49	– lbw, b Armstrong	.59
A.C. Russell b Kelleway	.0	– c Oldfield b Gregory	.5
J.W. Hearne c Gregory b Mailey	.14	– b Gregory	.57
E. Hendren c Gregory b Ryder	.28	– b Kelleway	.56
F.E. Woolley c Mailey b Ryder	.52	– st Oldfield b Mailey	.16
Mr J.W.H.T. Douglas st Oldfield b Mailey	.21	– c Armstrong b Mailey	.7
W. Rhodes c Gregory b Mailey	.3	– b Mailey	.45
W. Hitch c Kelleway b Gregory	.3	– c Taylor b Gregory	.19
A. Waddington run out	.7	– b Kelleway	.3
C. Parkin not out	.4	– b Kelleway	.4
H. Strudwick lbw, b Gregory	.2	– not out	.1
B 3, l-b 4	.7	B 6, l-b 3	.9
	190		**281**

ENGLAND BOWLING

	Overs	Mdns	Runs	Wkts	Overs	Mdns	Runs	Wkts
Hitch	10	0	37	0	8	0	40	0
Hearne	34	8	77	3	42	7	124	1
Parkin	26.4	5	58	1	35.3	5	102	3
Waddington	18	3	35	1	23	4	53	0
Woolley	23	8	35	2	36	11	90	2
Douglas	3	0	14	0	26	3	79	2
Rhodes					22	2	67	0

AUSTRALIA BOWLING

Kelleway	6	2	10	1	15.5	3	45	3
Gregory	23.1	3	56	3	33	6	70	3
Mailey	23	4	95	3	24	2	105	3
Ryder	6	1	20	2	17	6	24	0
Armstrong	1	0	2	0	10	0	21	1
Macartney					3	0	7	0

FROM NOTES BY THE EDITOR

During all the years I have edited *Wisden* there has never been a season so disheartening as that of 1921. England was not merely beaten but overwhelmed. The drawn games at Manchester and The Oval did something to restore our self-respect, but at best they afforded small consolation for the crushing defeats at Nottingham, Lord's, and Leeds. We had, of course, wretched luck in having to play without Hobbs – when at last he took the field at Leeds he was suddenly attacked by serious illness – but the loss of his invaluable batting, though a tremendous handicap, did not wholly account for our failure. We had no Test match bowlers of the pre-war standard, Parkin being by far the best of the various men tried, and our fielding compared with the brilliant work of the Australians was very second-rate. At Lord's the contrast was humiliating. Never before was an England side so slow and slovenly. I cannot help thinking that if when the fixtures were arranged in December 1920, our authorities had had any idea of the Australians' strength, something in the nature of systematic preparation for the Test matches would have been decided on. The five defeats in Australia of the M.C.C.'s team showed us plainly enough what we should have to face, but the revelation came too late. Everything had been left to chance and we paid the penalty. [...] In saying all this I have no wish or intention to depreciate the Australians. Far from that, I was among those who regarded them, at any rate on hard wickets, as one of the finest all-round teams that ever went into the field. All I contend is that our cricket authorities played into their hands by treating the Test matches from the first so casually. [...] It is easy to be wise after the event but, as Mr Spofforth pointed out, it would perhaps have been better from the first not to lean so much on the players who went to Australia. The fact of having been on the losing side five times was not calculated to inspire confidence. [...]

In one respect things turned out exactly as I ventured to predict a year ago. The Australians, even more than in previous tours, made everything subordinated to the Test matches, Armstrong seeing to it that Gregory and McDonald should be fresh and able to keep up their full pace on the big occasions. [...] I notice that on reaching home Armstrong paid a well-deserved compliment to his two fast bowlers for the splendid way in which they stuck to their work till the rubber was won. Of course, it is a comparatively easy task to lead a team when all the men can get runs and nearly everyone is a star fieldsman, but Armstrong struck me as being in every way a first-rate captain. Leading off with a run of success, only checked by the drawn game at

Attleborough, he was never faced by the troubles and difficulties that Noble sur-
mounted so triumphantly in 1909, but he always seemed to do the right thing at the
right time. In particular he managed his bowling changes with the nicest skill. In
retiring from the game he will leave behind him a record that is never likely to be
approached. Under him Australia won eight Test matches in succession – five at
home and three in this country. [...] (*1922*)

Second Test Match

Played at Lord's, Saturday, Monday, Tuesday, June 11, 13, 14, 1921. – In the second of
the Test Matches the Englishmen were not disgraced as at Nottingham, putting up
indeed a more creditable fight in face of tremendous odds, but they again suffered a
heavy defeat, the Australians winning easily on the third afternoon by eight wickets.
The match proved an enormous attraction, but on the Saturday the arrangements for
dealing with the crowd proved inadequate, many ticket-holders being greatly
delayed and inconvenienced in getting through the gates. The M.C.C. came in for
some sharp criticism, and were compelled to put forward an explanation. Things
went quite smoothly after the first day, but a good deal of soreness was felt. In choosing the England eleven the selection committee made drastic changes from the side
that did so badly at Trent Bridge. They were disappointed with regard to C.B. Fry,
who begged off on the ground that he did not feel satisfied with his form. Up to the
last moment the exact constitution of the team was uncertain, and on the Saturday
morning a surprise was sprung on the public by bringing in Tennyson, who had not
even been mentioned as a candidate. [...]

   As at Nottingham, England won the toss, and again practically lost the match at
the start, three wickets being down for 25 runs. Dipper was bowled in trying to turn
McDonald; Knight from a ball very wide of the off stump gave the simplest of catches
at slip, and Hendren was quite lost with one of McDonald's fastest. The result of these
disasters was that the Englishmen at the end of half-an-hour found themselves playing an uphill game. Woolley and Douglas made a great effort, and as long as they
stayed together there was hope of the position being retrieved. Both played
Armstrong with extreme caution, and when lunch-time came the score had reached
only 77. Things went well after the interval, till at 108 Douglas mistimed a palpable
long-hop that he tried to pull and was clean bowled. After Douglas left Woolley continued to play superb cricket, but he could get no one to help him. He was the last man
to go – England being all out for 187. Nothing finer in English batting was seen last
season than Woolley's 95. His innings lasted three hours and included ten 4's.

   The Australians went in with extreme confidence, and in little more than two
hours scored 191 for three wickets, thus leaving off with an overwhelming advantage.
The English bowling had neither length nor spin, and from the first the batsmen

made very light of it. Bardsley was at his best, and Macartney and Pellew hit away as they liked. The second day opened well for England, Bardsley being caught at slip with the score unaltered, and Armstrong clean bowled at 192. Here, however, our success ended, the Australians hitting freely and cleanly to carry their score to 342. Gregory had some luck, but the two chances he gave were very difficult. The England bowling was up to a point far better than it had been on the Saturday, Parkin in particular sending down some splendid overs. England had to go in against a balance of 155, and it was felt that the position was almost hopeless. Still, thanks chiefly to Woolley and Dipper, who put on 94 runs together, the arrears were cleared off soon after the tea interval with seven wickets in hand. Hopes were rising, but at 165 Woolley, in trying to hit a palpable long hop to the boundary, was out to a wonderful catch by Hendry at forward short leg. Woolley again missed his 100, but his second innings was no less admirable than his first. His only mistake was a chance in the slips when 36. With Woolley out the bowlers soon re-asserted themselves. Tennyson hit vigorously after being missed by the wicket-keeper, and at the drawing of stumps England's score stood at 243 with eight wickets down.

On the third morning Tennyson made a gallant effort, seizing every chance to score, but despite his efforts the innings was all over for 283. Scoring his 74 not out in an hour and forty minutes, Tennyson hit ten 4's, most of them powerful drives, and showed that he, at any rate, was not afraid of the fast bowlers.

The Australians only required 129 to win – a trifling task for such a side on a pitch that showed scarcely any signs of wear. Bardsley and Andrews settled the matter by sending up 101 together, but before the end came Macartney pulled a ball on to his wicket. Bardsley again played finely, but he had a narrow escape off Douglas's bowling in the second over, the ball going into Hendren's right hand wide in the slips and out again – a hard chance, but a possible one.

ENGLAND

Mr D.J. Knight c Gregory b Armstrong 7	– c Carter b Gregory	.1
A.G. Dipper b McDonald 11	– b McDonald	.40
F.E. Woolley st Carter b Mailey 95	– c Hendry b Mailey	.93
E. Hendren b McDonald 0	– c Gregory b Mailey	.10
Mr J.W.H.T. Douglas b McDonald 34	– b Gregory	.14
Mr A.J. Evans b McDonald 4	– lbw, b McDonald	.14
Hon. L.H. Tennyson st Carter b Mailey 5	– not out	.74
Mr N. Haig c Carter b Gregory 3	– b McDonald	.0
C. Parkin b Mailey 0	– c Pellew b McDonald	.11
H. Strudwick c McDonald b Mailey 8	– b Gregory	.12
T.J. Durston not out 6	– b Gregory	.2
B 1, l-b 11, w 1, n-b 1 14	B 4, l-b 3, n-b 5	.12
187		**283**

AUSTRALIA

W. Bardsley c Woolley b Douglas	.88	– not out	.63
T.J.E. Andrews c Strudwick b Durston	.9	– lbw, b Parkin	.49
C.G. Macartney c Strudwick b Durston	.31	– b Durston	.8
C.E. Pellew b Haig	.43	– not out	.5
J.M. Taylor lbw, b Douglas	.36		
W.W. Armstrong b Durston	.0		
J.M. Gregory c and b Parkin	.52		
H.L. Hendry b Haig	.5		
H. Carter b Durston	.46		
A.A. Mailey c and b Parkin	.5		
E.A. McDonald not out	.17		
B 2, l-b 5, n-b 3	.10	B 3, l-b 2, n-b 1	.6
	342		**131**

AUSTRALIAN BOWLING

	Overs	Mdns	Runs	Wkts	Overs	Mdns	Runs	Wkts
Gregory	16	1	51	1	26.2	4	76	4
McDonald	20	2	58	4	23	3	89	4
Armstrong	18	12	9	1	12	6	19	0
Mailey	14.2	1	55	4	25	4	72	2
Hendry					4	0	15	0

ENGLAND BOWLING

	Overs	Mdns	Runs	Wkts				
Durston	24.1	2	102	4	9.3	0	34	1
Douglas	9	1	53	2	6	0	23	0
Parkin	20	5	72	2	9	0	31	1
Haig	20	4	61	2	3	0	27	0
Woolley	11	2	44	0	3	0	10	0

Umpires: J. Moss and W. Phillips.

NOTTS V. AUSTRALIANS

Played at Nottingham, Saturday, Monday, June 25, 27, 1921. – In the long history of Notts cricket there has perhaps never been such a deplorable match as this. The county began well when Richmond clean bowled Bardsley, but for the rest of the game they were hopelessly outplayed, and in the end they suffered defeat by an innings and 517 runs. On the admission of the Notts batsmen themselves nothing in the condition of the ground offered the least excuse for such miserable scores as 58 and 100. Indeed, the pitch was so good that even Gregory could not make the ball get up. Despite Bardsley's failure the Australians on the first day scored 608 for seven wickets. Notts had to pay a terribly high price for one blunder, Macartney being missed in the slips when he had made nine. Never afterwards at fault, he went on to play the highest innings of the season, scoring his 345 in rather less than four hours. He simply did as he liked with the bowling, hitting four 6's and forty-seven 4's. One of the 6's – off John Gunn – went clean out of the ground. Pellew was also very brilliant, getting his 100 in an hour and three quarters. While he was in with Macartney 291 runs were put on. After lunch the Notts bowling was weakened by the absence of Barratt, who had injured his hand. Though batting a man short, Oates having damaged his thumb, Notts ought to have saved the game, but the batting was dreadfully feeble. When they followed on George Gunn showed good defence for an hour and a quarter, and Carr made a few fine hits, but that was all.

AUSTRALIANS

W. Bardsley b Richmond 0
T.J.E. Andrews c Oates b Barratt 29
C.G. Macartney lbw, b Hardstaff 345
J.M. Taylor c Whysall b Barratt 50
C.E. Pellew c Oates b Staples 100
J.M. Gregory c G. Gunn b Hardstaff 19
J. Ryder b Hardstaff 20

H.L. Hendry st Oates b Hardstaff 51
W.A. Oldfield b Staples 40
E.A. McDonald b Hardstaff 1
A.A. Mailey not out 0

B 8, l-b 10, w 1, n-b 1 20

675

NOTTS

G. Gunn b McDonald .4 – c Oldfield b Mailey 20
G.M. Lee c Pellew b Gregory . . . . .1 – run out 9
J. Gunn c McDonald b Gregory . . . . .0 – b Gregory 1
J. Hardstaff b Gregory . . . . .16 – b McDonald 6
Mr A.W. Carr b McDonald . . . . .15 – c Oldfield b Mailey 31
W. Payton lbw, b McDonald . . . . .2 – lbw, b Gregory 14
W. Whysall b Gregory . . . . .15 – b Gregory 9
S.J. Staples b Mailey .2 – c Andrews b Mailey 3
F. Barratt not out . . . . .2 – c Gregory b Mailey 1
L. Richmond st Oldfield b Mailey . . . . .0 – not out 1
T. Oates absent hurt . . . . .0 – absent hurt 0
    L-b 1   B 1, n-b 1 .2
                                58   100

NOTTS BOWLING

	Overs	Mdns	Runs	Wkts	Overs	Mdns	Runs	Wkts
Barratt	23	4	89	2				
Richmond	36	1	193	1				
Staples	27	3	131	2				
J. Gunn	9	1	71	0				
Lee	2	0	14	0				
Carr	1	0	24	0				
Hardstaff	28.2	3	133	5				
Whysall	1	1	0	0				

AUSTRALIAN BOWLING

Gregory	8	1	23	4	11	1	26	3
McDonald	10	0	24	3	13	6	25	1
Ryder	7	2	9	0	1	1	0	0
Mailey	1.4	1	1	2	13.5	1	36	4
Hendry					3	0	11	0

Umpires: G.P. Harison and W.A.J. West.

GLOUCESTERSHIRE V. AUSTRALIANS

Played at Cheltenham, Saturday, Monday, Tuesday, August 20, 22, 23, 1921. – The Australians were bound to beat Gloucestershire, and their victory by an innings and 136 runs was in no way surprising. Still, they might not have won quite so easily if the wicket on the second day had not helped their bowlers. Winning the toss, the Australians were batting the whole of Saturday afternoon, and scored 425 for eight wickets. Bardsley and Macartney were seen at their very best, putting on 218 runs during their partnership. Macartney, who hit twenty-three 4's, was at the wickets for two hours and five minutes and Bardsley half-an-hour longer. No other batting in the innings was of the same class, but Gregory hit well, scoring at the rate of just over a run a minute. On Monday morning the Australian innings soon ended, and then on a pitch damaged by rain Gloucestershire had a very bad time. Keigwin showed fine defence, withstanding the bowlers for two hours, but that was all. In the follow-on Keigwin again took the honours, being 48 not out at the drawing of stumps. Mailey took the six wickets that fell, and on the following morning he obtained the other four, he being the fifth bowler in the season to take all ten wickets in an innings. The Australians proved a big attraction at Cheltenham, the gate receipts beating all records.

AUSTRALIANS

H.L. Collins c Barnett b Bessant 15	J. Ryder not out 39
W. Bardsley lbw, b Bessant 127	H.L. Hendry b Mills 0
C.G. Macartney b Parker 121	H. Carter b Mills 9
C.E. Pellew c Mills b Parker 1	A.A. Mailey c Dipper b Parker 3
J.M. Gregory b Mills 78	B 12, l-b 3, n-b 16
W.W. Armstrong lbw, b Parker 22	
E.R. Mayne b Parker 7	**438**

GLOUCESTERSHIRE

Mr C.S. Barnett b Armstrong	.3	– b Mailey	.25
A.G. Dipper b Gregory	.7	– b Mailey	.4
Mr R.P. Keigwin c Carter b Hendry	.47	– c Mayne b Mailey	.65
H. Smith lbw, b Armstrong	.2	– c and b Mailey	.0
W.R. Hammond b Gregory	.0	– b Mailey	.1
Mr F.G. Robinson b Hendry	.18	– b Mailey	.4
Mr W.H. Rowlands c Mayne b Hendry	.19	– b Mailey	.23
Mr F.J. Seabrook b Mailey	.6	– c and b Mailey	.30
P. Mills not out	.18	– c Pellew b Mailey	.3
C. Parker st Carter b Mailey	.2	– not out	.8
J.G. Bessant b Mailey	.2	– b Mailey	.0
B 1, l-b 2	.3	B 5, l-b 6, n-b 1	.12
	127		**175**

GLOUCESTERSHIRE BOWLING

	Overs	Mdns	Runs	Wkts	Overs	Mdns	Runs	Wkts
Parker	50.2	9	148	5				
Bessant	19	2	106	2				
Mills	37	4	129	3				
Keigwin	3	0	16	0				
Hammond	3	0	23	0				

AUSTRALIAN BOWLING

	Overs	Mdns	Runs	Wkts	Overs	Mdns	Runs	Wkts
Gregory	19	6	37	2	12	2	38	0
Armstrong	21	5	53	2	12	1	54	0
Hendry	11	4	13	3				
Mailey	8.3	1	21	3	28.4	5	66	10
Ryder					5	3	5	0

Umpires: B. Brown and A. Millward.

AN ENGLAND XI v. AUSTRALIANS

Played at Eastbourne, Saturday, Monday, Tuesday, August 27, 29, 30, 1921. – This was the match that produced the sensation of the season. Unbeaten up to the closing days of August, it seemed certain that the Australians, surpassing the record of all the previous teams, would go through their tour without suffering defeat, but, as events turned out, the side selected by MacLaren won the game after a tremendous struggle by 28 runs. MacLaren all through the summer had maintained that he could pick a side good enough to overcome the Australians, but all hope of victory seemed gone when on winning the toss, and taking first innings on a perfect wicket, the Englishmen went down in an hour and a quarter for a score of 43. Probably the strong wind that was blowing accounted in some measure for the failure, but be that as it may, McDonald and Armstrong were irresistible. Gregory started the bowling with McDonald, but he hurt the thumb of his bowling hand after sending down two overs and had to retire. With the match to all appearance in their hands the Australians possibly regarded their task too lightly. Thanks to Bardsley and Macartney the score was up to 80 with only one man out, but the last eight wickets went down for 91 runs, Falcon bowling finely. Still, though the total only reached 174, there did not seem the least cause for apprehension, especially as the Englishmen lost a wicket for eight runs before the drawing of stumps. Bardsley played a beautiful innings, making his 70 in two hours without giving a chance. On the Monday Faulkner and Hubert Ashton brought about a marvellous change in the game. Becoming partners with the score at 60 for four wickets, they put on 154 runs together, both playing superbly. Ashton was out lbw at 214, and Faulkner left, eighth wicket down, at 307. Not since the first match of the Triangular Tournament in 1912 had Faulkner played such an innings as his 153. He hit a 6 and twenty 4's, and was at the wickets for three hours and a half without making a mistake. Ashton did not hit so hard, but his innings also was flawless. The Australians were left with only 196 to get, and at the close of play they had scored 21 for the loss of Collins' wicket. Most people took it for granted that the Australians would win readily enough, nothing in their record suggesting failure in the last innings. If what happened could in any way have been foreseen the Eastbourne ground would hardly have accommodated the crowd. Bardsley was bowled at 52, and at the same total Carter was caught at point. Then at 73 a fine ball clean bowled Macartney, this being perhaps the turning point of the game. Andrews and Pellew added 30 runs together, but at lunch time the Australians had five wickets down, and still required 87 runs to win. For some little time after resuming things went well for them, Andrews and Ryder taking the score to 113 before Ryder left. Gregory, who followed, was out leg-before-wicket to the second hall he received, and the chances veered round. Andrews was out at 153, and amidst intense excitement Armstrong was lbw. Mailey, the last man, joined McDonald with 42 runs still wanted. Thirteen runs were added, and then Gibson clean bowled Mailey and won the match. When it was all over there was a scene of wild enthusiasm, MacLaren, in particular, coming in for endless congratulations. For once last season the English fielding was magnificent, and it was said that Gibson, in taking six wickets for 64 runs, scarcely sent down a bad length ball. So fine was the fielding of both sides that no catch which went to hand was dropped.

An England XI

Mr G.N. Foster c Gregory b McDonald	5	– c and b McDonald 11
Mr G.A. Faulkner b Armstrong	3	– c Mailey b Armstrong 153
Mr G. Ashton lbw, b Armstrong	6	– lbw b Armstrong 36
Mr H. Ashton b McDonald	0	– lbw, b Armstrong 75
Mr A.P.F. Chapman b McDonald	16	– b McDonald 11
Mr C.T. Ashton c Ryder b Armstrong	1	– b McDonald 0
Mr M. Falcon b McDonald	8	– c and b McDonald 17
Mr G.E.C. Wood lbw, b Armstrong	1	– b McDonald 2
Mr A.C. Maclaren b McDonald	0	– b McDonald 5
Mr C.H. Gibson not out	1	– not out 0
Mr W. Brearley b Armstrong	1	– run out 0
N-b	1	B 10, l-b1, n-b 5 16

43

326

AUSTRALIANS

H.L. Collins b Falcon .... .19 –	c H. Ashton b Gibson .... .12
W. Bardsley lbw, b Faulkner .... .70 –	b Gibson .... .22
C.G. Macartney b Faulkner .... .24 –	b Falcon ....'.14
T.J.E. Andrews b Faulkner .... .0 –	b Faulkner .... .31
C.E. Pellew c H. Ashton b Falcon .... .1 –	c H. Ashton b Gibson .... .16
J. Ryder b Falcon .... .10 –	c G. Ashton b Gibson .... .28
W.W. Armstrong b Falcon .... .13 –	lbw, b Faulkner .... .11
H. Carter c H. Ashton b Faulkner .... .10 –	c C.T. Ashton b Falcon .... .16
J.M. Gregory not out .... .16 –	lbw, b Gibson 0
E.A. McDonald b Falcon .... .4 –	not out 9
A.A. Mailey b Falcon .... .4 –	b Gibson 0
B 1, l-b 2 3	L-b 3, n-b 5 8
174	**167**

AUSTRALIAN BOWLING

	Overs	Mdns	Runs	Wkts	Overs	Mdns	Runs	Wkts
Gregory	2	0	6	0	9	0	51	0
McDonald	10	2	21	5	31	3	98	6
Armstrong	8.1	4	15	5	24.5	6	74	3
Ryder					5	1	11	0
Mailey					22	3	76	0

AN ENGLAND XI'S BOWLING

	Overs	Mdns	Runs	Wkts	Overs	Mdns	Runs	Wkts
Falcon	18.4	2	67	6	18	2	82	2
Gibson	14	2	54	0	22.4	6	64	6
Faulkner	16	1	50	4	5	1	13	2

Umpires: H. Butt and J.P. Whiteside.

THIRD TEST MATCH

Played at Melbourne, Saturday, Monday, Tuesday, Wednesday, Thursday, Friday, Saturday, December 29, 31, 1928, January 1, 2, 3 ,4, 5, 1929. – England, having proved successful in the two previous Test games, naturally approached the third with a certain amount of confidence. In the end they won by three wickets, this victory giving them the rubber and the retention of The Ashes. There were many changes of fortune in the course of a great struggle but scarcely anything in the whole tour approached the long, drawn-out tension of the last innings before the winning hit was made. In ordinary circumstances, little might have been thought of the task of getting 332, but these runs had to be made on a rain-ruined wicket and anybody who knows the Melbourne ground will appreciate the stupendous effort required. As at the Oval in 1926, the judgment and skill of Hobbs and the stubbornness of Sutcliffe really carried England to victory, but in awarding great praise to them for wonderful batting under difficult conditions, it must not be forgotten the part that, earlier in the match,

Hammond, with his innings of 200, the bowling of Larwood, Tate, Geary and White, and the high standard of the fielding all round, played in the success.

England had the same eleven as at Sydney, but Australia made further changes, bringing in Bradman, a'Beckett, and Oxenham for Ponsford, Nothling and Ironmonger. These alterations undoubtedly made Australia a better combination, for Blackie, expensive at Sydney, met with marked success as a bowler in the first innings, while Bradman, with two fine displays of batting, showed what a mistake had been made in leaving him out of the second match. Ryder, winning the toss, Australia made such a poor start as to lose the first three wickets for 57 runs but then came a great stand by Kippax and Ryder who, at the rate of a run a minute, added no fewer than 161. Kippax had played well for an hour before lunch and directly afterwards he hit four 4's to leg off Larwood, three of them in one over. Ultimately he was caught at long leg in repeating this profitable stroke. Stylish and effective in all he did, he batted for over three hours and a half in beautiful fashion. Bradman next helped Ryder to put on 64 in less than an hour. Ryder, who drove well, was in for three hours and forty minutes. Bradman and a'Beckett added 86, but nobody else did much towards the total of nearly 400. Bowled by a yorker at 373, Bradman scored well in front of the wicket, hitting nine 4's during his stay of over three hours. Although he took only one wicket, White bowled with wonderful steadiness while Tate's work was beyond praise. On the second day 62,259 people witnessed the play, this being a record attendance for one afternoon.

England headed their opponents' total by 20 runs after losing Hobbs with 28 on the board. The batting honours went to Hammond who, going in first wicket down, was fifth to leave at 364, brilliantly caught behind the bowler. Batting for nearly six and three-quarter hours, Hammond, in a masterly display, hit only seventeen fours, but he had to face a lot of steady bowling and accurate fielding. As at Sydney, he made great use of his favourite stroke through the covers, with an occasional square drive. Sutcliffe, very restrained, helped him to add 133 and after the fall of the fourth wicket at 238 Hammond and Jardine put on 126. Jardine was in for over three hours, concentrating mainly on defence. Following Hammond's dismissal, however, the last five wickets fell in seventy minutes for 53 runs. Blackie, who came out with the fine record of six wickets for 94 runs, obtained after going on at 351, four for 34 in his last spell of bowling.

When Australia went in a second time, Richardson again failed and although Woodfull batted uncommonly well and Kippax helped to add 78, there were four wickets down for 143. England then stood in a good position, but Bradman – nearly bowled by White when seven – assisted Woodfull to put on a valuable 58, and subsequently proceeded to make his first hundred in a Test match. Woodfull, fifth out at 201, hit only seven 4's during his stay of four hours and a half. His defence all through was wonderful. There were seven men out for 252, but Oxenham helped to add 93 at the rate of a run a minute before Bradman's innings closed at 345. Bradman batted over four hours, hit eleven 4's and brought off many splendid drives. Australia had two wickets to fall on the sixth day when, owing to rain during the night, play could not be resumed until nearly one o'clock, and it was noticed that Ryder did not have the wicket rolled. England, wanting 332 to win, had to go in for five minutes before lunch. This period was safely tided over, but on resuming Hobbs, with his score 3 and the total 10, was given a life by Hendry at slip. For that blunder a heavy price had to be paid. The ball was turning and at other times getting up almost straight, but Hobbs and Sutcliffe contented themselves for the most part in playing it, realising that the longer they stayed the better was England's chance of making the runs. Only 75 were obtained between lunch and tea but altogether the two batsmen made 105 before Hobbs was leg before. He hit only one four in his 49, but the value of his innings could not be measured by the mere runs he made. Remarkable footwork, masterly defence and unerring skill in a difficult situation were the memories this innings left. England were still a long way from victory, but Sutcliffe and Jardine, with the wicket steadily becoming less awkward, added 94. Incidentally, Jardine had been sent in next on the advice of Hobbs, who, signalling for a new bat, took the opportunity of suggesting this to Chapman. Jardine, before getting out next morning, played his part with the utmost fidelity. Sutcliffe and Hammond put on 58 and Hendren, missed when 21 at long-on by Bradman, helped in a stand which produced an invaluable 61, before Sutcliffe was leg before at 318. For his 135 – in the circumstances a great innings – Sutcliffe batted nearly six hours and a half. England then had the match in their hands, but just before tea Hendren was bowled and afterwards Chapman and Tate lost their wickets before Geary made the winning hit at half-past four. Without belittling the splendid batting of England and particularly of the first pair, it can be said that the Australian bowlers failed to make the most of their opportunity. Blackie, for the most part, bowled a dead length instead of pitching the ball up, and a'Beckett sent down ball after ball wide of the off stump. The total attendance at the match reached 262,467, the receipts being £22,561 18s. The attendance was easily a record.

AUSTRALIA

W.M. Woodfull c Jardine b Tate 7	– c Duckworth b Tate 107
V.Y. Richardson c Duckworth b Larwood 3	– b Larwood 5
H.L. Hendry c Jardine b Larwood 23	– st Duckworth b White 12
A.F. Kippax c Jardine b Larwood 100	– b Tate 41
J. Ryder c Hendren b Tate 112	– b Geary 5
D.G. Bradman b Hammond 79	– c Duckworth b Geary 112
W.A. Oldfield b Geary 3	– b White 7
E.L. a'Beckett c Duckworth b White 41	– b White 6
R.K. Oxenham b Geary 15	– b White 39
C.V. Grimmett c Duckworth b Geary 5	– not out 4
D.J. Blackie not out 2	– b White 0
B 4, l-b 3 7	B 6, l-b 7 13
397	**351**

ENGLAND

J.B. Hobbs c Oldfield b a'Beckett	20	– lbw, b Blackie	49
H. Sutcliffe b Blackie	58	– lbw, b Grimmett	135
W.R. Hammond c a'Beckett b Blackie	200	– run out	32
Mr A.P.F. Chapman b Blackie	24	– c Woodfull b Ryder	5
E. Hendren c a'Beckett b Hendry	19	– b Oxenham	45
Mr D.R. Jardine c and b Blackie	62	– b Grimmett	33
H. Larwood c and b Blackie	0		
G. Geary lbw, b Grimmett	1	– not out	4
M.W. Tate c Kippax b Grimmett	21	– run out	0
G. Duckworth b Blackie	3	– not out	0
Mr J.C. White not out	8		
B 1	1	B 15, l-b 14	29
	417		**332**

ENGLAND BOWLING

	Overs	Mdns	Runs	Wkts	Overs	Mdns	Runs	Wkts
Larwood	37	3	127	3	16	3	37	1
Tate	46	17	87	2	47	15	70	2
Geary	31.5	4	83	3	30	4	94	2
Hammond	8	4	19	1	16	6	30	0
White	57	30	64	1	56.5	10	107	5
Jardine	1	0	10	0				

AUSTRALIA BOWLING

	Overs	Mdns	Runs	Wkts	Overs	Mdns	Runs	Wkts
A'Beckett	37	7	92	1	22	5	39	0
Hendry	20	8	35	1	23	5	33	0
Grimmett	55	14	114	2	42	12	96	2
Oxenham	35	11	67	0	28	10	44	1
Blackie	44	13	94	6	39	11	75	1
Ryder	4	0	14	0	5.5	1	16	1

Umpires: D. Elder and G. Hele.

THE AUSTRALIANS IN ENGLAND 1930

By S.J. Southerton

Coming to England while the experience of four consecutive defeats in Test Matches in their own land was still fresh in their memories, the seventeenth Australian team to visit this country accomplished a very fine performance. They not only achieved the great object of the tour by winning the rubber and so regaining possession of 'The Ashes' but, in the course of thirty-one engagements against first-class sides, they were beaten but once — in the opening Test Match at Nottingham.

It is true that in the general results of the tour their record was unimpressive, for of the thirty-one important games they won only eleven, lost one and drew eighteen, while the encounter with Gloucestershire towards the latter part of August ended in a tie. Outside these fixtures there were three others of which one was won, one drawn, and one abandoned without a ball being bowled. The large proportion of drawn games was due to the fact that in most of them bad weather interfered. Indeed, the weather placed the Australians at a considerable disadvantage. In a number of their early matches they had to contend against not only a lot of wet but a decidedly low temperature, feeling the cold so much that heavy underclothing under flannel shirts, and a couple of sweaters in addition, failed to keep them reasonably warm in the field. As no fewer than eleven of the fifteen who made the trip had not visited England before, the handicap under which they laboured may be imagined. Still, they triumphed in a remarkable fashion over the discomforts of a wet and cheerless English summer, and a chosen few of the newcomers adapted themselves, in a manner of which few people thought them capable, to the varying paces of the different wickets on which they had to play. [...]

This particular tour will always be remembered by reason of the amazing batting successes which attended the efforts of Bradman. It is not too much to say that he took both England and the whole cricket world by storm. Those who, like myself, had seen him play in Australia against the team captained by A.P.F. Chapman were fully prepared for something out of the common but little did we dream that his progress would be of such a triumphal nature. Nothing like his series of colossal innings in the Test Matches had ever before been witnessed. He put the coping-stone on a – so far – very brief career when in the Third Test Match at Leeds, following innings of 131 at Nottingham and 254 at Lord's, he made 334 which eclipsed the previous highest score ever obtained in Test Matches between England and Australia – 287 by the late R.E. Foster at Sydney during the M.C.C. tour of 1903–4. As if that were not sufficient, Bradman, although failing at Manchester, wound up with 232 in the final Test Match at Kennington Oval. [...]

While the Australians undoubtedly owed much of their success to Bradman's batting, it cannot be denied that an almost equally potent factor in the overthrow of England was the bowling of Grimmett. Curiously enough, Grimmett did not in the victory at the Oval bear anything like the great part that he had done in the previous encounters but long before that he had established over most of the England batsmen an ascendancy which they never really overcame. He took twenty-nine wickets in the Test Matches, but his average of nearly 32 does not convey a real idea of his effectiveness. Taking part in no engagement other than first-class, Grimmett obtained 144 wickets at an average of less than 17 runs apiece and, in so doing, headed the bowling – a position he most thoroughly deserved. He started the season so well that when five matches had been played he had taken thirty-nine wickets, including all ten for 37 runs against Yorkshire at Sheffield. By the beginning of July he had dismissed over a hundred men, and although in August – probably owing to a bruised finger – he accomplished nothing out of the ordinary, his bowling never lost its anxieties for English batsmen. [...] Practically every time he went on he at once brought about a diminution in the rate of run-getting. Generally speaking, his length was flawless; even better than when he was here four years previously. To begin with he obtained most of his wickets with leg-breaks but as the season advanced he bowled the googly more often and he got plenty of batsmen leg before with a well disguised top-spinner. [...]

SECOND TEST MATCH

Played at Lord's, Friday, Saturday, Monday, Tuesday, June 27, 28, 30, July 1, 1930. – Beating England, after a memorable struggle, by seven wickets Australia took an ample revenge for their overthrow a fortnight previously at Trent Bridge. The batting of the Australians and particularly that of Bradman will assuredly live long in the minds of those who saw it but, while giving the visitors the fullest praise for winning so handsomely after having to face a first innings total of 425, it is only proper to observe that to a large extent England played right into the hands of their opponents. Briefly, the Englishmen lost a match, which, with a little discretion on the last day, they could probably have saved. The result of this encounter had a strong bearing on the rubber for, if England had made a draw and the Leeds and Manchester games ended as they did, the final match at the Oval would have been limited to four days. It can with truth be said, however, that the England bowling in no other game not only looked but actually was so entirely lacking in sting and effect.

Records went by the board. Australia, in putting together a total of 729 before declaring with only six wickets down, broke four – the highest score by Australia in England, 551 at Kennington Oval in 1884; the highest score by England in this country, 576 at the Oval in 1899; the highest score by Australia, 600 at Melbourne in 1924; and the highest score in the whole series of Test Matches, 636 by England at Sydney in December, 1928. Bradman himself, with a score of 254, played the second highest individual innings in the whole series of Test matches between England and Australia, while Duleepsinhji, not only made a hundred on the occasion of his first appearance in a Test match against Australia but scored the highest number of runs ever obtained by an England player in these matches at Lord's. There was one other notable point, A.P.F. Chapman, after leading England to victory six times, captaining the losing side. As some set off against that he enjoyed, for the first time in his career, the distinction of making a hundred in a Test Match. In addition to Duleepsinhji, J.C. White and G.O. Allen came into the home team, Sutcliffe – owing to injury – Larwood and Richard Tyldesley standing down.

Chapman again won the toss and England, batting for five hours and fifty minutes, scored on the first day 405 runs for nine wickets. This, seeing that with the score only 13 Hobbs was out and that despite some delightful driving by Woolley and Hammond three wickets were down for 105, was a distinctly fine performance. Duleepsinhji and Hendren obtained the first real mastery over the attack, adding 104 runs in ninety minutes. The batting of these two after lunch was delightful, Duleepsinhji driving with fine power and Hendren scoring by cleverly executed strokes to the on. Chapman and Allen failing, the game took a strong turn in favour of Australia and, while the 200 had gone up with only three wickets down, six men were out for 239. Duleepsinhji, however, found a valuable partner in Tate who hit so hard as to make 54 out of 98 in seventy minutes with eight 4's – chiefly drives – as his most important strokes. Duleepsinhji seemed certain to play out time after he had lost Robins at 363 but at quarter past six, with the score at 387, he was caught at long-off. It seems ungracious to say it, but Duleepsinhji was guilty of a bad error of judgment. He had twice driven Grimmett to the boundary in glorious fashion and in the same over lashed out wildly. Batting for four hours and three-quarters he gave a magnificent display. When the occasion demanded it he exercised restraint and at other times hit beautifully all round the wicket, having twenty-one 4's among his strokes. His innings was not faultless, for at 65 he was missed at short-leg by Woodfull from a very simple chance, while at 98 he was let off by Wall at third slip. Had Duleepsinhji been patient and stayed in until the close of play there is no telling what would have been the subsequent course of events.

The next morning another 20 runs were added and then Australia, by skilful and judicious batting, remained in for the rest of the day and scoring 404 for the loss of only two batsmen left off no more than 21 runs behind – a very great performance. Tate bowled with great pluck and determination but, generally, the England attack was indifferent, Allen especially being innocuous and expensive. The Australians batted to a set plan, Woodfull and Ponsford steadily wearing down the bowling for Bradman later on to flog it. Nearly three hours were occupied over the first 162 runs, but in another two hours and three-quarters no fewer than 242 came. While in the end Bradman made most runs very great credit was due to Woodfull and Ponsford who, when England's bowling was fresh, put on 162 for the first wicket. Curiously enough the partnership terminated almost directly after a break in the play while the members of both teams were presented to the King in front of the pavilion, Ponsford, who had batted very soundly, being caught at slip. Woodfull, who was always restrained but who showed rare judgment, stayed in until twenty minutes past six, having withstood the attack for five hours and a half. His defence was remarkable and he scarcely ever lifted the ball but he enjoyed one great stroke of fortune. Just before the King arrived, Woodfull, with his score at 52 playing forward to Robins, dragged his foot over the crease. Duckworth gathered the ball and swept it back to the stumps but omitted to remove the bails. That little error cost England dear. Bradman, who went in when Ponsford was out and the bowling had been mastered, seized his opportunity in rare style and, hitting all round the wicket with power and accuracy, scored in two hours and forty minutes 155 runs and was not out at the close. The Englishmen fielded well and often brilliantly.

On the Monday, Australia kept England in the field for another four hours and a half and added 325 runs for the loss of four more batsmen before declaring their innings closed at the tea interval. The partnership between Bradman and Kippax which did not end until ten minutes to three when Bradman was caught right-hand at extra-mid-off, produced 192 runs in less than three hours. In obtaining his 254, the famous Australian gave nothing approaching a chance. He nearly played on at 111 and, at 191, in trying to turn the ball to leg he edged it deep into the slips but, apart from those trifling errors, no real fault could be found with his display. Like Woodfull, he scarcely ever lifted the ball and, while, his defence generally was perfect, he hit very hard in front of the wicket. Altogether he batted five and a half hours, his chief strokes being twenty-five 4's, three 3's, and twenty-six 2's. Kippax, who was in for three hours, left three runs later at 588, but England's troubles were not over, Richardson and McCabe adding 55, and Oldfield and Fairfax 57 in the last forty-five minutes before the closure was put into force. For their huge total Australia batted ten hours and ten minutes.

England thus found themselves requiring 304 runs to escape an innings defeat. At their second attempt they lost Hobbs at 45 and Woolley at 58 but in the last forty minutes Hammond and Duleepsinhji added 40 runs. The score was up to 129 the next morning before Hammond left but when, shortly before twelve o'clock, the fifth wicket fell at 147 England looked like losing in an innings. Indeed, but for an unaccountable misunderstanding between Richardson and Ponsford, this would probably have happened. Chapman, before he had scored, mishit a ball and the two fieldsmen mentioned stood and watched it fall to the ground between them. Eventually settling down, Chapman hit in rare style, being especially severe on Grimmett. Allen, too, batted with marked skill and aggression and 125 runs were added before he was out. It was about this time that, with a little care and thoughtfulness, England might have saved the game for at the luncheon interval, with, five men out, they had cleared off all but 42 of the arrears. So far from devoting their energies to defence they continued hitting away, adding another 113 runs in an hour and a quarter afterwards but losing their last five wickets. Chapman, eighth to leave at 354, obtained his runs in just over two hours and a half. Four 6's and twelve 4's were among his strokes. He drove and pulled with tremendous power in a very wonderful display. A foolish call by Robins cost a valuable wicket when White was run out and the innings closed just before half-past three for 375.

Australia thus had to make only 72 to win but in twenty minutes there was much excitement. Ponsford was bowled at 16, Bradman caught low down at backward-point at 17, and Kippax taken at the wicket at 22. Visions of a remarkable collapse arose but Woodfull, exercising sound generalship by taking most of Robins' bowling himself, tided over an anxious period and by five o'clock he and McCabe had obtained the remaining runs. In the course of the four days, 110,000 people watched the cricket, the takings being roughly £14,500.

ENGLAND

J.B. Hobbs c Oldfield b Fairfax	1	– b Grimmett 19
F.E. Woolley c Wall b Fairfax	41	– hit wkt, b Grimmett 28
W.R. Hammond b Grimmett	38	– c Fairfax b Grimmett 32
K.S. Duleepsinhji c Bradman b Grimmett	173	– c Oldfield b Hornibrook 48
E. Hendren c McCabe b Fairfax	48	– c Richardson b Grimmett 9
Mr A.P.F. Chapman c Oldfield b Wall	11	– c Oldfield b Fairfax 121
Mr G.O. Allen b Fairfax	3	– lbw, b Grimmett 57
M.W. Tate c McCabe b Wall	54	– c Ponsford b Grimmett 10
Mr R.W.V. Robins c Oldfield b Hornibrook	5	– not out 11
Mr J.C. White not out	23	– run out 10
G. Duckworth c Oldfield b Wall	18	– lbw, b Fairfax 0
B 2, l-b 7, n-b 1	10	B 16, l-b 13, w 1 30
	425	**375**

AUSTRALIA

W.M. Woodfull st Duckworth b Robins . . . .155 – not out 26
W.H. Ponsford c Hammond b White . . . . . . .81 – b Robins 14
D.G. Bradman c Chapman b White . . . . . . .254 – c Chapman b Tate 1
A.F. Kippax b White . . . . .83 – c Duckworth b Robins 3
S. McCabe c Woolley b Hammond . . . . .44 – not out 25
V.Y. Richardson c Hobbs b Tate 30
W.A. Oldfield not out 43
A. Fairfax not out 20
    B 6, l-b 8, w 5 19   B 1, l-b 2 .3
                                        *729   72

*Innings declared closed
C.V. Grimmett, P.M. Hornibrook and T.W. Wall did not bat.

AUSTRALIA BOWLING

	Overs	Mdns	Runs	Wkts	Overs	Mdns	Runs	Wkts
Wall	29.4	2	118	3	25	2	80	0
Fairfax	31	6	101	4	12.4	2	37	2
Grimmett	33	4	105	2	53	13	167	6
Hornibrook	26	6	62	1	22	6	49	1
McCabe	9	1	29	0	3	1	11	0
Bradman					1	0	1	0

ENGLAND BOWLING

	Overs	Mdns	Runs	Wkts	Overs	Mdns	Runs	Wkts
Allen	34	7	115	0				
Tate	64	16	148	1	13	6	21	1
White	51	7	158	3	2	0	8	0
Robins	42	1	172	1	9	1	34	2
Hammond	35	8	82	1	4.2	1	6	0
Woolley	6	0	35	0				

Umpires: F. Chester and T. Oates.

THIRD TEST MATCH

Played at Leeds, Friday, Saturday, Monday, Tuesday, July 11, 12, 14, 15, 1930. – The third Test Match, while it afforded that remarkable young batsman, Bradman, the opportunity of leaving all individual batting records in representative matches far behind, was in many respects an unsatisfactory affair. England had the worst of it from start to finish but escaped with a draw, a heavy storm on Sunday night, followed by further rain on the Monday restricting the third day play's to forty-five minutes while, on the Tuesday, further delay occurred owing to defective light.

The game will go down to history on account of the wonderful batting perform-ance accomplished by Bradman who, with an innings of 334, beat the previous highest – 287 by R.E. Foster for England at Sydney – which had stood since December, 1903. In the course of this, Bradman achieved fame in other directions. Like C.G. Macartney on the same ground four years previously, he reached three-figures before lunch-time on the first day. Not out 309 at the close he had then exceeded a total of a thousand runs in Test cricket and reached an aggregate of exactly 2,000 runs for the season. In playing two consecutive innings of over 200 in Test matches he equalled the performance of Hammond during the previous tour in Australia. He also equalled Macartney's performance of 1926 in scoring three separate hundreds in successive Test matches. Truly could it be called 'Bradman's Match'. Bigger though it was and characterised by splendid stroke play, Bradman's innings did not quite approach his 254 at Lord's in freedom from fault but as to its extraordinary merit there could be no two opinions. As usual, he rarely lifted the ball and when making two or more consecutive scoring strokes seldom sent it in the same direction. His footwork was admirable as was the manner in which he played his defensive strokes to balls just short of a length.

Australia, who had played the same eleven in the previous two games, had to make two changes. Suffering from gastritis, Ponsford stood down and Fairfax had not completely recovered from an operation he had had to undergo at Nottingham. Jackson and à Beckett, therefore, played in their first Test Match in England. […] This time, Woodfull won the toss and Australia led off so brilliantly that, when the first day's play ended, they had 458 runs on the board with only three wickets down. The pitch, like those at Nottingham and Lord's, was, on the first day at any rate, lacking in life and pace and all in favour of batsmen. Opening the innings with Woodfull, Jackson off the fifth ball of the second over was caught at forward-short-leg but England had to wait until five minutes past three before they took another wicket, Woodfull and Bradman, in the meantime, putting on 192 runs in two hours and thirty-five minutes. This was very largely the work of Bradman who, quick to settle down, completed 102 out of the first 127 in ninety-five minutes. All the same, Woodfull, by another great display of defensive cricket, rendered his side invaluable assistance. After Woodfull left, bowled in trying to hook a shortish ball, Bradman found another admirable partner in Kippax who if overshadowed by his colleague, played uncommonly well in helping to add 229 in rather less than two and three-quarter hours. The next day McCabe, who had batted twenty minutes overnight, stayed until 63 runs had been put on but nothing of any consequence was accomplished by the rest, the last seven wickets falling in a hundred minutes for 108 runs. Bradman, sixth out at 508, obtained his 334 in six hours and a quarter, his score being made up of forty-six 4's, six 3's, twenty-six 2's, and eighty singles. When he had made 141 he put up a ball towards mid wicket and at 202 he skied a ball over Tate's head at mid-on. Indeed, a man a little quicker on his feet than Tate might have made a catch of it. Actually, Bradman gave only one chance, being missed at the wicket off Geary at 273 when the total was 385. He hit very hard in front of the wicket, scored splendidly on the leg side and very often cut in dazzling fashion. Nobody could have had a better reception than that accorded to Bradman on his return to the pavilion.

Before lunch Hobbs and Sutcliffe scored 17 runs for England but the total was only 53 when Hobbs was out in a manner which provoked considerable discussion. à Beckett, fielding very close in on the on-side to Grimmett's bowling, took the ball from a gentle stroke very low down, turning a complete somersault but retaining possession. Hobbs was about to walk away but stepped back into his crease on overhearing a remark by Oldfield and an appeal from other members of the side. An appeal having been made, Hobbs was perfectly justified in waiting for the decision. Oates, the umpire at the bowler's end, was unable to give one, à Beckett in falling over obscuring his view, so he referred to Bestwick standing at square-leg. Unhappily, Bestwick hesitated before holding up his finger, and the great majority of the crowd took the view that à Beckett had not properly made the catch. [...] England at the close of play, with five wickets down for 212, found themselves 354 behind and requiring 205 to save the follow-on. On the Monday the weather following a storm in the night, which resulted in water lying in patches on the ground, was very bad. So long a delay occurred that not until half past five was play proceeded with. From the manner in which the pitch rolled out it was quite obvious that cricket would have been possible at least an hour earlier. Thirty runs were scored before an appeal against the light at a quarter past six was upheld.

On Tuesday morning Duckworth, who had gone in for ten minutes on Saturday evening, batted so well that the score was up to 289 before he was caught at the wicket, 83 runs having been added in rather more than two hours. Hammond stayed until the score was 319 after resisting the bowling for five hours and twenty minutes. He hit only fourteen 4's but gave a splendid display of skilful batting, neglecting very few opportunities of scoring off anything in the nature of a punishable ball. Chapman, hitting hard, put on 51 runs with Tate but England were all out at a quarter to three for 391, their innings lasting nearly eight hours. The last three wickets fell in half an hour for 36 runs.

England followed on 179 behind and, as over three hours remained for cricket, there was always a possibility of them losing. Hobbs and Sutcliffe opened the innings in a very poor light. After a quarter of an hour, they appealed against it and the players went in. For some extraordinary reason the crowd took this in very bad part, booing the batsmen and cheering the Australians, while on the game being resumed there was a continuance of this unseemly behaviour. With 24 scored, Hobbs was brilliantly thrown out by Bradman from deep-mid-off but Sutcliffe and Hammond stayed nearly an hour to add 50. After Duleepsinhji had been caught at point off a ball which he afterwards confessed he did not see, another appeal against the light was made at ten minutes to six and no further cricket took place. The total attendance reached 77,500, and the gate receipts £8,597.

AUSTRALIA

W.M. Woodfull b Hammond	50	
A. Jackson c Larwood b Tate	1	
D.G. Bradman c Duckworth b Tate	334	
A.F. Kippax c Chapman b Tate	77	
S. McCabe b Larwood	30	
V.Y. Richardson c Larwood b Tate	1	
E.L. à Beckett c Chapman b Geary	29	

W.A. Oldfield c Hobbs b Tate 2
C.V. Grimmett c Duckworth
    b Tyldesley 24
T.W. Wall b Tyldesley 3
P.M. Hornibrook not out 1
    B 5, l-b 8, w 1 14

ENGLAND

J.B. Hobbs c à Beckett b Grimmett	29	– run out	13
H. Sutcliffe c Hornibrook b Grimmett	32	– not out	28
W.R. Hammond c Oldfield b McCabe	113	– c Oldfield b Grimmett	35
K.S. Duleepsinhji b Hornibrook	35	– c Grimmett b Hornibrook	10
M. Leyland c Kippax b Wall	44	– not out	1
G. Geary run out	0		
G. Duckworth c Oldfield b à Beckett	33		
Mr A.P.F. Chapman b Grimmett	45		
M.W. Tate c Jackson b Grimmett	22		
H. Larwood not out	10		
R. Tyldesley c Hornibrook b Grimmett	6		
B 9, l-b 10, n-b 3	22	L-b	8
	391		**95**

ENGLAND BOWLING

	Overs	Mdns	Runs	Wkts	Overs	Mdns	Runs	Wkts
Larwood	33	3	139	1				
Tate	39	9	124	5				
Geary	35	10	95	1				
Tyldesley	33	5	104	2				
Hammond	17	3	46	1				
Leyland	11	0	44	0				

AUSTRALIA BOWLING

	Overs	Mdns	Runs	Wkts	Overs	Mdns	Runs	Wkts
Wall	40	12	70	1	10	3	20	0
à Beckett	28	8	47	1	11	4	19	0
Grimmett	56.2	16	135	5	17	3	33	1
Hornibrook	41	7	94	1	11.5	5	14	1
McCabe	10	4	23	1	2	1	1	0

Umpires: W. Bestwick and T. Oates.

FIRST TEST MATCH

Played at Nottingham, Friday, Saturday, Monday, Tuesday, June 8, 9, 11, 12, 1934. – Australia began the series of Test matches with a splendid victory by 238 runs. On the first three days, at any rate, the fortunes of the game changed sufficiently to keep interest at its highest pitch, while on the last afternoon everyone was on the tip-toe of excitement in watching England's desperate but unavailing effort to stave off defeat. Thus it came about that the decision of the contest was not determined until only ten more minutes remained for play. For a long time before this, however, the impression generally existed that England were engaged in a somewhat hopeless task. It is very easy to be wise after the event, but one could not resist the feeling that with 380 runs required to win, with rather less than five hours left for cricket, the England batsmen, having made up their minds to strive for a draw rather than go for the runs – the success of the latter policy being most unlikely – played into the hands of bowlers like O'Reilly and Grimmett by failing to realise that bolder methods rather than passive resistance might have achieved their object.

Before the match, England were in difficulties about the captaincy, Wyatt, selected for that position, having had his thumb fractured in the Test Trial just previously. In the circumstances, it was properly considered wise not to include him, and the leadership of the eleven devolved upon Walters – appearing for the first time in a Test Match against Australia. Three fast bowlers were present but only one, Farnes, was included, Bowes being left out and Nichols acting as twelfth man. As events proved, England could have done very well with either of the men omitted, but Farnes was a distinct success, taking five wickets in each innings at a cost of 179 runs. Unfortunately for England, Mitchell of Derbyshire caused no trouble to the Australian batsmen; the match revealed that Australia as a team fielded better than England; but the most disappointing features were the breakdowns in England's batting after the first or second wickets had fallen. Seeing that in the course of their earlier engagements, the Australians had had no fewer than ten centuries scored against them it looked as though they were taking a risk by going into the field without Ebeling, so that their attack rested upon O'Reilly, Grimmett and Wall with McCabe and Chipperfield to help. The course the game took justified the Selectors of the team in their action.

As a matter of fact, England up to a point fared quite satisfactorily, for, after Woodfull and Ponsford had made 77 together in ninety-five minutes, two wickets fell before lunch, and shortly before quarter to four Australia had five men out for 153. Ponsford made his runs by varied strokes and hit eight 4's; Woodfull was very stolid for nearly two hours; Bradman hit six 4's in half an hour; and Brown stayed for eighty minutes, but the fact remained that Australia, up to then, had scarcely made sufficient use of their opportunity of batting first on a nice easy wicket. As it happened, no further wicket fell during the afternoon, McCabe, who played a bold confident game, and Chipperfield carrying the score to 207 when rain and bad light ended the day's cricket at quarter to six. On Saturday McCabe was out at 234, having made 65 out of 81 in eighty minutes, but unexpected assistance was given to Chipperfield by Oldfield and Grimmett, and the innings did not end until nearly quarter to three, seven hours play yielding a total of 374. Chipperfield, in his first Test match, just missed the distinction of making a hundred. He was 99 at lunch time, and out third ball afterwards. He and Oldfield added 47, and with Grimmett as his partner 74 runs were added for the eighth wicket. Batting three hours and twenty minutes, Chipperfield obtained his runs largely by cutting, his innings, while eminently useful, being nothing like so attractive as that of McCabe. Going in at three o'clock, England fared well for a time, despite the loss of Walters at 45, for Sutcliffe was in his best form, cutting and off-driving so finely as to score 62 out of 102 in two hours and ten minutes.

Then the game turned. Hammond was out four runs later, and Leyland left at 114, and these three quick reverses caused Pataudi and Hendren to adopt such cautious methods that in forty minutes before the end only 14 runs came, and England at the close found themselves 246 behind with six wickets to fall. Matters on Monday again went badly for England who soon after twelve o'clock had six men out for 165. Then, however, came the one real stand of the innings, Geary giving Hendren such valuable assistance that in an hour and fifty minutes 101 runs were added before Hendren left. Both men played finely in their effort to pull the game round. Geary, indeed, hit with pronounced freedom, and, if possibly a little more restrained, Hendren scarcely made a bad stroke. He was in for three hours and forty minutes, doing great work during a most anxious period. England, however, were all out by three o'clock, and they found themselves 106 runs behind.

Still, Australia at their second attempt lost their first three wickets for 69 before the game turned once more with a partnership between McCabe and Brown. Brown, when 33 and with the total 102, gave a chance of stumping and that probably had a very big effect upon the subsequent course of events, for the two men played out time and altogether added 112 in a hundred minutes, McCabe hitting a six and fifteen 4's in a very fine display. Brown, although playing with a very straight bat, did not approach his colleague in brilliance, but his cricket was always high class. Seventh out at 244, he was in nearly four hours and hit only three 4's. All the other batsmen on the Tuesday morning went out for runs in order to give Woodfull the chance of declaring at the earliest possible moment. He did not do this until half-past twelve when 114 had been added to the overnight score in ninety minutes. By this time the wicket was showing signs of wear, and when England went in a second time Grimmett and O'Reilly were seen to be turning the ball. Sutcliffe and Walters put on 51, but after Sutcliffe had been caught at slip for the second time in the match the batting broke down, and by tea-time five men were out for 115. Leyland and Ames tried their hardest and stayed for seventy minutes, but wickets fell at regular intervals and with O'Reilly taking the last three very quickly the innings closed at twenty past six for 141. O'Reilly, following his four wickets in the first innings, took seven for 54 and bowled superbly. Clever variation in flight and pace combined with spin off the worn turf made him very difficult, and he deserved all the congratulations showered upon him at the close by his delighted colleagues.

AUSTRALIA

W.M. Woodfull c Verity b Farnes	26	– b Farnes	2
W.H. Ponsford c Ames b Farnes	53	– b Hammond	5
W.A. Brown lbw, b Geary	22	– c Ames b Verity	73
D.G. Bradman c Hammond b Geary	29	– c Ames b Farnes	25
S.J. McCabe c Leyland b Farnes	65	– c Hammond b Farnes	88
L.S. Darling b Verity	4	– c Hammond b Farnes	14
A.G. Chipperfield c Ames b Farnes	99	– c Hammond b Farnes	4
W.A. Oldfield c Hammond b Mitchell	20	– not out	10
C.V. Grimmett b Geary	39	– not out	3
W.J. O'Reilly b Farnes	7	– c Verity b Geary	18
T.W. Wall not out	0		
B 4, l-b 5, n-b 1	10	B 22, l-b 9	31
	374	(Eight wkts, dec.)	**273**

ENGLAND

Mr C.F. Walters lbw, b Grimmett . . . . .17 – b O'Reilly 46
H. Sutcliffe c Chipperfield b Grimmett . . . . .62 – c Chipperfield b O'Reilly 24
W.R. Hammond c McCabe b O'Reilly . . . . . .25 – st Oldfield b Grimmett 16
Nawab of Pataudi c McCabe b Wall . . . . .12 – c Ponsford b Grimmett 10
M. Leyland c and b Grimmett . . . . .6 – c Oldfield b O'Reilly 18
E. Hendren b O'Reilly . . . . .79 – c Chipperfield b O'Reilly 3
L.E.G. Ames c Wall b O'Reilly . . . . .7 – b O'Reilly 12
G. Geary st Oldfield b Grimmett . . . . .53 – c Chipperfield b Grimmett 0
H. Verity b O'Reilly . . . . .0 – not out 0
Mr K. Farnes b Grimmett . . . . .1 – c Oldfield b O'Reilly 0
T.B. Mitchell not out . . . . .1 – lbw, b O'Reilly 4
 B 5   B 4, l-b 3, n-b 1 8

                        268   **141**

ENGLAND BOWLING

	Overs	Mdns	Runs	Wkts	Overs	Mdns	Runs	Wkts
Farnes	40.2	10	102	5	25	3	77	5
Geary	43	8	101	3	23	5	46	1
Hammond	13	4	29	0	12	5	25	1
Verity	34	9	65	1	17	8	48	1
Mitchell	21	4	62	1	13	2	46	0
Leyland	1	0	5	0				

AUSTRALIA BOWLING

	Overs	Mdns	Runs	Wkts	Overs	Mdns	Runs	Wkts
Wall	33	7	82	1	13	2	27	0
McCabe	7	2	7	0	2	0	7	0
Grimmett	58.3	24	81	5	47	28	39	3
O'Reilly	37	16	75	4	41.4	24	54	7
Chipperfield	3	0	18	0	4	1	6	0

FALL OF THE WICKETS

Australia – First Innings

1	2	3	4	5	6	7	8	9	10
77	88	125	146	153	234	281	355	374	374

Australia – Second Innings

1	2	3	4	5	6	7	8
2	32	69	181	219	231	244	267

England – First Innings

1	2	3	4	5	6	7	8	9	10
45	102	106	114	145	165	266	266	266	268

England – Second Innings

1	2	3	4	5	6	7	8	9	10
51	83	91	103	110	134	135	137	137	141

Umpires: A. Dolphin and F. Chester.

FIFTH TEST MATCH

Played at Kennington Oval, Saturday, Monday, Tuesday, Wednesday, August 18, 20, 21, 22, 1934. – Each side having won once with two games left drawn, the fifth and concluding Test Match was entered upon without any restrictions as to the time involved in reaching a definite result. As it happened four days proved sufficient for Australia to win by 562 runs. Thus they regained The Ashes. Being successful in the rubber by two victories to one, they brought their number of wins in the whole series of encounters between the two countries to 52 as against 51 by England. Under conditions which, apart from the winning of the toss, favoured neither side unduly the result was a fitting tribute to the superior all-round skill of Australia. [...]

The law of averages suggested that it was Woodfull's turn to win the toss. This he did and when Clark, coming on at 20, bowled Brown at 21 with the best ball sent down all day long, it seemed as though the England attack on a hard wicket was about to come into its own. Never were hopeful anticipations more rudely dispelled. Between them Ponsford and Bradman gave another glorious display of batting, staying together until nearly half-past six and engaging in a partnership which left that of Leeds far behind and produced 451 runs in five hours and a quarter. This time Bradman was the first to leave, hitting over his head at a bouncing ball and being caught behind the wicket at 472. McCabe went in and played out time, Australia, as the result of the first day's cricket, having 475 runs on the board with only two men out. It would be hard to speak in too high terms of praise of the magnificent displays of batting given by Ponsford and Bradman. Before Bradman joined him Ponsford had shown an inclination to draw away from the bowling of Bowes but he received inspiration afterwards from the example of his partner, who from the very moment he reached the centre and took up his stance was coolness and mastery personified.

The pitch did not help bowlers at all. Those with a command of spin found it extremely difficult to make the ball turn in the slightest and only by dropping it short could the fast bowlers make the ball rise above stump high. Clark tried leg-theory with a packed leg-side field but as, for the most part, he maintained a good length, his bowling, even if he now and again dropped the ball short, scarcely came under the category of what is known 'body-line'. Incidentally Clark and the others tried all sort of theories but they had no effect on Bradman who, as the afternoon wore on, invested his batting with increasing daring. He drove, and cut with the utmost certainty and power and when the ball did bounce he just stepped back and hooked it. Included in his hits were a six and thirty two 4's and, having regard to the rate at which he, as well as Ponsford scored, a better display has rarely been seen. Ponsford was not quite so sure as Bradman and he frequently turned his back to the ball to receive blows on the thigh. All the same, he drove with great power and was clever in getting the ball away between the fieldsmen placed close in. Just after the new ball was brought into use at 200 the England bowling was at its best but generally speaking it never looked quite good enough for the task at hand and it was noticeable that scarcely a single yorker was sent down all day long while the bowlers of pace failed to keep their deliveries just that little bit short of a length to compel batsmen to play the forward defensive stroke. As during the day about 80 runs an hour were obtained it can be realised that too many long-hops and half-volleys were sent down. This great partnership meant that in consecutive representative encounters Bradman and Ponsford in two stands scored 839 runs in ten hours and three-quarters. Ponsford offered three very difficult chances and one when 115 comparatively easy; Bradman's batting, as far as was seen, was flawless.

On Monday England had further trouble before the innings which lasted nearly ten hours closed at twenty minutes to five for 701 runs – the second highest in the history of Test Matches between England and Australia. On this day 226 runs were made in four and a quarter hours for eight wickets – evidence of an improvement in the England attack. Of the fast bowlers Clark was the best from the point of sustained effort and real class but he had no luck. Allen was faster and more virile and Bowes had an inspired period when, going on at 605, he took three wickets in five overs and a ball for 19 runs. McCabe was out early at 488 and Ponsford gave another chance before once more hitting his wicket in drawing back to Allen. Fourth out at 574, he batted seven hours and thirty-five minutes for his workman-like innings of 266 and he hit a five and twenty-seven 4's. Woodfull gave a plodding display which lasted two hours and a half, Kippax was in for just over fifty minutes and none of the batting approached in class that of the opening afternoon. [...]

Tuesday was a black day for England and except for a superbly aggressive display by Maurice Leyland the batting proved deplorable. Sutcliffe and Walters were separated at 104, Sutcliffe being out to a good catch at the wicket on the leg-side when the partnership had lasted an hour and fifty minutes and then followed a series of disasters. Walters and Woolley left in one over at 108 and 111; Wyatt playing on at 136 gave Grimmett his 100th wicket in Test cricket and Hammond went at 142. Leyland and Ames put a better appearance on affairs but when they had added 85 in less than an hour, Ames retired with a strained back. After that Leyland dominated the proceedings. He drove splendidly and when at length bowled at 321 he had made 110 out of 185 in two hours and forty minutes. He hit a six and fifteen 4's, nearly all drives.

Australia, 380 ahead, scored 186 for two wickets before the end of the day, Brown leaving at 13 and Ponsford at 42. [...] Bradman and McCabe scored at a fine pace, making 144 together in ninety minutes. Light rain fell during the night but the wicket the next morning was not greatly affected. Ames was still away but Bowes returned and went on to bowl. He soon dismissed Bradman who, with McCabe, had added 150 in ninety-five minutes and then for the first time England's bowling got really on top so that, although the last partnership between Ebeling and O'Reilly produced 55 in forty minutes, Australia were all out by half-past two for 327, the last eight wickets having produced 141 in two hours and ten minutes. Clark and Bowes shared the wickets, both bowling extremely well. Woolley kept wicket and made a catch standing back.

England were thus left with no fewer than 708 to get to win – only 34 short of the number England had set Australia in the First Test Match at Brisbane during the 1928-29 tour. England made a shocking start, Walters leaving at one and Woolley at three but Sutcliffe and Hammond added 64 in sixty-five minutes. Hammond was fourth to leave after tea at 89 and following that it only became a question as to whether the match would be over or not before half-past six. Apart from an easy chance of stumping, Hammond certainly played very well but the tea interval proved his undoing. Leyland left at 109 and Wyatt at 122 and shortly before six o'clock with Allen stumped the innings was all over for 145 and as was the case four years previously Australia won the rubber on the anniversary of Woodfull's birthday. [...]

AUSTRALIA

W.A. Brown b Clark	10	– c Allen b Clark	1
W.H. Ponsford hit wkt, b Allen	266	– c Hammond b Clark	22
D.G. Bradman c Ames b Bowes	244	– b Bowes	77
S.J. McCabe b Allen	10	– c Walters b Clark	70
W.M. Woodfull b Bowes	49	– b Bowes	13
A.F. Kippax lbw, b Bowes	28	– c Walters b Clark	8
A.G. Chipperfield b Bowes	3	– c Woolley b Clark	16
W.A. Oldfield not out	42	– c Hammond b Bowes	0
C.V. Grimmett c Ames b Allen	7	– c Hammond b Bowes	14
H.I. Ebeling b Allen	2	– c Allen b Bowes	41
W.J. O'Reilly b Clark	7	– not out	15
B 4, l-b 14, w 2, n-b 13	33	B 37, l-b 8, w 1, n-b 4	50
	701		**327**

ENGLAND

Mr C.F. Walters c Kippax b O'Reilly	64	– b McCabe	1
H. Sutcliffe c Oldfield b Grimmett	38	– c McCabe b Grimmett	28
F.E. Woolley c McCabe b O'Reilly	4	– c Ponsford b McCabe	0
W.R. Hammond c Oldfield b Ebeling	15	– c and b O'Reilly	43
Mr R.E.S. Wyatt b Grimmett	17	– c Ponsford b Grimmett	22
M. Leyland b Grimmett	110	– c Brown b Grimmett	17
L.E.G. Ames retired hurt	33	– absent ill	0
Mr G.O. Allen b Ebeling	19	– st Oldfield b Grimmett	26
H. Verity b Ebeling	11	– c McCabe b Grimmett	1
E.W. Clark not out	2	– not out	2
W.E. Bowes absent ill	0	– c Bradman b O'Reilly	2
B 4, l-b 3, n-b 1	8	L-b 1, n-b 2	3
	321		**145**

ENGLAND BOWLING

	Overs	Mdns	Runs	Wkts	Overs	Mdns	Runs	Wkts
Bowes	38	2	164	4	11.3	3	55	5
Allen	34	5	170	4	16	2	63	0
Clark	37.2	4	110	2	20	1	98	5
Hammond	12	0	53	0	7	1	18	0
Verity	43	7	123	0	14	3	43	0
Wyatt	4	0	28	0				
Leyland	3	0	20	0				

AUSTRALIA BOWLING

Ebeling	21	4	74	3	10	5	15	0
McCabe	6	1	21	0	5	3	5	2
Grimmett	49.3	13	103	3	26.3	10	64	5
O'Reilly	37	10	93	2	22	9	58	2
Chipperfield	4	0	22	0				

FALL OF THE WICKETS

Australia – First Innings

1	2	3	4	5	6	7	8	9	10
21	472	488	574	626	631	638	676	682	701

Australia – Second Innings

1	2	3	4	5	6	7	8	9	10
13	42	192	213	224	236	236	256	272	327

England – First Innings

1	2	3	4	5	6	7	8
104	108	111	136	142	263	311	321

England – Second Innings

1	2	3	4	5	6	7	8	9
1	3	67	89	109	122	138	141	145

Umpires: F. Chester and F. Walden.

THIRD TEST MATCH

At Melbourne, January 1, 2, 4, 5, 6, 7, 1937. Australia won by 365 runs.

England were not disgraced even though the margin was a large one: outside influences had much to do with the result. [...] As things turned out Bradman won the match for Australia when he won the toss and his tactics influenced the result. On the second day he took the unusual procedure in a played-to-a-finish Test Match of declaring his first innings closed and sent England in to bat on a pitch from which the ball often reared up almost straight and at other times kept low. It is important to mention that on the first day, when Australia were batting, the wicket was lifeless and unhelpful to spin bowling and yet England got down six wickets for 130 and would probably have done still better had not rain set in and led to the bowlers being handicapped by the wet ball. Next day rain held up a resumption of the match until after lunch. The difficulties of the wicket quickly became apparent, and batsmen experienced such an unhappy time that in about three hours thirteen wickets fell.

England after losing nine wickets for 76, also declared so that for the first time in Test cricket each side closed its first innings. It is possible England would have done better had Allen's declaration been made earlier but, as one authority put it, the England captain could not be expected to possess second sight. At the close of play on the second day, one Australian – O'Reilly – had been dismissed for three runs and a Sunday without rain enabled the wicket to recover so that when Australia took up their second innings again the conditions were more favourable for batting than at any previous time in the match.

Following the dismissal of Fingleton from a weak stroke after he had promised great things, McCabe was Australia's hero on the first day. Towards the end of the afternoon, with six wickets down, McCabe suddenly found his best form and revelled in a hectic ten minutes of big hitting, in which he was joined enthusiastically by Oldfield. The England bowlers were steady all day and the field gave nothing away.

Play on the second day, Saturday, was sensational throughout. On the 'glue-pot wicket' Australia's apparently feeble total of 200 assumed formidable proportions. Leyland was the one real success for England. Hammond scored more runs, and made some daring if desperate shots with a close ring of fieldsmen almost within touch of his bat; Leyland never seemed in difficulties. Both men were out to extraordinary catches by Darling at short-leg; just as Rigg had fallen to Verity on the first day – catches that would have been missed ninety-nine times out of a hundred.

Australia batted all the third day. It was inevitable that Bradman should find his form soon, and he chose the moment of his county's greatest need to do so. Rain fell in the afternoon and between – and during – the showers the England bowlers were handicapped by a wet ball which they wiped with a towel between each delivery. Bradman took full advantage of this and, though not quite his old scintillating self, and eschewing the off drive, he thrilled the crowd and subdued the bowlers. Scoring 270 he played his highest innings against England in Australia. Not until the evening was it revealed that Bradman was suffering from a severe chill. That explained his sedateness. In Rigg he found a splendid partner; a man who had been on the fringe of the Australian XI for a long time and looked good enough a cricketer to have gained a place earlier. Rigg, reputed a poor starter, showed none of this failing, and the free use of his arms and wrists proved his class. Hereabouts came the first glimpse during the tour of the Bradman known to England. It was after a stoppage for rain and he faced Voce. He took 13 off the over (of eight balls) and 2 and 3 off the first two balls of Allen's next over. Another shower cut short the burst of hitting.

The fact, on the fourth day, Bradman and Fingleton put up a sixth wicket record of 346 – actually the highest stand for any wicket in a Test match in Australia – was due to Bradman sending in his tail-end batsmen first. Usually those two players would have been associated for the second wicket. The pitch had become as perfect as any batsman could wish, and though the England bowlers remained steady they had little chance of beating Bradman or Fingleton. [...] Bradman, still suffering from mild influenza, was quickly dismissed on the morning of the fifth day, and immediately after lunch England opened their second innings wanting 689 runs to win. Such a task had never been achieved in Test history but the wicket was still very easy and a dour fight was anticipated. However, Leyland alone of the earlier batsmen, and Robins, towards the end of the day, batted really well. Hammond made a splendid 50 and then was out to a rather careless stroke. The scoring was certainly fast and delighted the spectators, but this was not quite the type of cricket the situation demanded.

On the sixth morning Leyland and Robins rose to their greatest heights. Previously, Leyland had carried such responsibility that he had repressed many of his most spectacular shots, but this time he exploited them all, his hitting through the covers being reminiscent of his finest innings in England. With Robins out England virtually were all out, and Leyland remained undefeated with a noteworthy 111. [...]

AUSTRALIA

J.H. Fingleton c Sims b Robins	38 – c Ames b Sims	136
W.A. Brown c Ames b Voce	1 – c Barnett b Voce	20
D.G. Bradman c Robins b Verity	13 – c Allen b Verity	270
K.E. Rigg c Verity b Allen	16 – lbw (N) b Sims	47
S.J. McCabe c Worthington b Voce	63 – lbw (N) b Allen	22
L.S. Darling c Allen b Verity	20 – b Allen	0
M. Sievers st Ames b Robins	1 – not out	25
W.A. Oldfield not out	27 – lbw b Verity	7
W.J. O'Reilly c Sims b Hammond	4 – c and b Voce	0
F. Ward st Ames b Hammond	7 – c Hardstaff b Verity	18
L. O'B. Fleetwood-Smith (did not bat)	0 – c Verity b Voce	0
B 2, l-b 6, n-b 2	10 B 6, l-b 2, w 1, n-b 10	19

Nine wkts, dec. **200**   **564**

ENGLAND

T.S. Worthington c Bradman b McCabe	0 – c Sievers b Ward	16
C.J. Barnett c Darling b Sievers	11 – lbw b O'Reilly	23
W.R. Hammond c Darling b Sievers	32 – b Sievers	51
M. Leyland c Darling b O'Reilly	17 – not out	111
J. Sims c Brown b Sievers	3 – lbw (N) Fleetwood-Smith	0
L.E.G. Ames b Sievers	3 – b Fleetwood-Smith	19
Mr R.W.V. Robins c O'Reilly b Sievers	0 – b O'Reilly	61
J. Hardstaff b O'Reilly	3 – c Ward b Fleetwood-Smith	17
Mr G.O. Allen not out	0 – c Sievers b Fleetwood-Smith	11
H. Verity c Brown b O'Reilly	0 – c McCabe b O'Reilly	11
W. Voce not out	0 – c Bradman b Fleetwood-Smith	0
B 5, l-b 1, n-b 1	7 L-b 3	3

Nine wkts, dec. **76**   **323**

ENGLAND BOWLING

	Overs	Mdns	Runs	Wkts	Overs	Mdns	Runs	Wkts
Voce	18	3	49	2	29	2	120	3
Allen	12	2	35	1	23	2	84	2
Sims	9	1	35	0	23	1	109	2
Verity	14	4	24	2	37.7	9	79	3
Robins	7	0	31	2	11	2	46	0
Hammond	5.3	0	16	2	22	3	89	0
Worthington					4	0	18	0

AUSTRALIA BOWLING

	Overs	Mdns	Runs	Wkts	Overs	Mdns	Runs	Wkts
McCabe	2	1	7	1	8	0	32	0
Sievers	11.2	5	21	5	12	2	39	1
O'Reilly	12	5	28	3	21	6	65	3
Fleetwood.Smith	3	1	13	0	25.6	2	124	5
Ward					12	1	60	1

FALL OF WICKETS

Australia – First Innings

1	2	3	4	5	6	7	8	9
7	33	69	79	122	130	183	190	200

Australia – Second Innings

1	2	3	4	5	6	7	8	9	10
0	3	38	74	97	443	511	511	549	564

England – First Innings

1	2	3	4	5	6	7	8	9
0	14	56	68	71	71	76	76	76

England – Second Innings

1	2	3	4	5	6	7	8	9	10
29	65	117	155	179	195	306	322	323	323

Umpires: G. Borwick and J.D. Scott.

FOURTH TEST MATCH

Played at Adelaide, January 29, 30, February 1, 2, 3, 4, 1937. Australia won by 148 runs.

Two factors lost England the match, which might have been won despite Bradman succeeding in the toss. One was England's batting collapse on the Monday, when the immense advantage gained by getting Australia out for the small total of 288 was frittered away by a deplorable display after Barnett and Leyland had put the side in a splendid position. The other was Bradman's second innings of 212. [...] The wicket was perfect throughout the match, and for the only time in the series, no rain came to interfere with play. The batting failures, therefore, were inexplicable. Australia's win roused cricket enthusiasm in the country to a high pitch because it meant the final Test being the decider of the rubber.

The first day's play was witnessed by 39,000 people. Australia won the toss and in the five hours allotted scored 267 for the loss of seven wickets; a good day's work by England. Fingleton was run out at 26, a foolish sacrifice of his wicket that had been foreshadowed by faulty running, but Brown and Rigg stayed together until the first over after lunch when Farnes dismissed both batsmen. McCabe came to the rescue and played a grand innings, but Bradman, who, unusually restrained, took 68 minutes to score 26 runs, was clean bowled by Allen when trying one of his favourite hook shots. Gregory, making his Test debut at the age of 20, showed promise, and McCabe indulged in an exhilarating burst of scoring immediately after the tea interval, and played Verity more confidently than anyone else had done during the tour. When in trying to hook Robins he was magnificently caught by Allen at deep square leg, McCabe had batted two and a quarter hours and hit nine 4's. Chipperfield played a resolute innings and was not out at the close with 45. At twenty minutes to one on the second day Australia were out for 288 and by the close of play England had hit 174 for two wickets, Barnett being 92 and Leyland 35. England appeared to be in a very strong position and Barnett's first Test century was completed early on the morning of the third day but prior to that, in the same over from Fleetwood-Smith, Leyland had been taken in the slips. Then the game swung Australia's way. Wyatt failed, immediately after lunch Barnett left, and five England wickets were lost for 259 with Australia still 29 runs on – not as comfortable a position as had been promised.

Barnett batted nearly five and three quarter hours and hit one 6 and thirteen 4's. It was a great innings, illustrative of the progress the Gloucestershire man had made on the tour. Ames also batted well but there was a long 'tail' and England finished only 42 ahead. By close of play Australia were 21 on with nine wickets in hand, and Bradman in his most dangerous mood. The fourth day's play virtually settled the issue; a stubborn stand between Bradman and McCabe realised 109, and a big fifth wicket partnership ensued between Bradman and Gregory. This, producing 135, was not broken until the fifth day when Bradman showed signs of tiredness. Bradman's innings was not one of his most brilliant efforts but he has never looked more sure of himself. He seemed to go in to bat with the fixed determination of winning the match, and though England bowled with any amount of skill and heart he hit 212 in 437 minutes. In that score there were only fourteen 4's – an indication of the dourness of the fight. Incidentally, it was Bradman's seventh double century in Tests against England. On his dismissal the four remaining wickets went down for 11 runs and Hammond returned the very creditable analysis of five for 57.

At the close of the fifth day there was still a ray of hope for England because Hammond and Leyland were together with 148 of the 392 runs required already scored and seven wickets in hand. The wicket, considering the amount of play on it, was in wonderful order. Fleetwood-Smith, however, was in an inspired mood and utilised the pitch to his needs as no bowler on the English side could have done. Neither of the overnight batsmen survived long and it was left to Wyatt to carry on while others failed. Wyatt, on reaching an excellent fifty, gave up defensive tactics and fell to a catch at the wicket. That was the end of a match in which Bradman's batting and the skilful spin bowling of Fleetwood-Smith confounded England's prospects.

AUSTRALIA

J.H. Fingleton run out	10 – lbw b Hammond	12
W.A. Brown c Allen b Farnes	42 – c Ames b Voce	32
K. Rigg c Ames b Farnes	20 – c Hammond b Farnes	7
D.G. Bradman b Allen	26 – c and b Hammond	212
S.J. McCabe c Allen b Robins	88 – c Wyatt b Robins	55
R. Gregory lbw b Hammond	23 – run out	50
A.G. Chipperfield not out	57 – c Ames b Hammond	31
W.A. Oldfield run out	5 – c Ames b Hammond	1
W.J. O'Reilly c Leyland b Allen	7 – c Hammond b Farnes	1
E.L. McCormick c Ames b Hammond	4 – b Hammond	1
L.O'B. Fleetwood-Smith b Farnes	1 – not out	4
L-b 2, n-b 3	5 B 10, l-b 15, w 1, n-b 1	27
	288	433

ENGLAND

H. Verity c Bradman b O'Reilly	19	– b Fleetwood-Smith	17
C.J. Barnett lbw b Fleetwood-Smith	129	– c Chipperfield b Fleetwood- Smith	21
W.R. Hammond c McCormick b O'Reilly	...20	– b Fleetwood-Smith	39
M. Leyland c Chipperfield		– c Chipperfield	
b Fleetwood-Smith	45	– b Fleetwood-Smith	32
Mr R.E.S. Wyatt c Fingleton b O'Reilly	3	– c Oldfield b McCabe	50
L.E.G. Ames b McCormick	52	– lbw b Fleetwood-Smith	0
J. Hardstaff c and b McCormick	20	– b O'Reilly	43
Mr G.O. Allen lbw b Fleetwood-Smith	11	– c Gregory b McCormick	9
Mr R.W.V. Robins c Oldfield b O'Reilly	10	– b McCormick	4
W. Voce c Rigg b Fleetwood-Smith	8	– b Fleetwood-Smith	1
Mr K. Farnes not out	0	– not out	7
B 6, l-b 2, w1, n-b 4	13	B 12, l-b 2, n-b 6	20
	330		**243**

ENGLAND BOWLING

	Overs	Mdns	Runs	Wkts	Overs	Mdns	Runs	Wkts
Voce	12	0	49	0	20	2	86	1
Allen	16	0	60	2	14	1	61	0
Farnes	20.6	1	71	3	24	2	89	2
Hammond	6	0	30	2	15.2	1	57	5
Verity	16	4	47	0	37	17	54	0
Robins	7	1	26	1	6	0	38	1
Barnett					5	1	15	0
Leyland					2	0	6	0

AUSTRALIA BOWLING

McCormick	21	2	81	2	13	1	43	2
McCabe	9	1	18	0	5	0	15	1
Fleetwood.Smith	41.4	10	129	4	30	1	110	6
O'Reilly	30	12	51	4	26	8	55	1
Chipperfield	9	1	24	0				
Gregory	3	0	14	0				

FALL OF WICKETS

Australia – First Innings

1	2	3	4	5	6	7	8	9	10
26	72	73	136	206	226	249	271	283	288

Australia – Second Innings

1	2	3	4	5	6	7	8	9	10
21	88	197	237	372	422	426	427	429	433

England – First Innings

1	2	3	4	5	6	7	8	9	10
53	108	190	195	259	299	304	318	322	330

England – Second Innings

1	2	3	4	5	6	7	8	9	10
45	50	120	149	190	190	225	231	235	243

Umpires: G. Borwick and J.D. Scott.

FIRST TEST MATCH

At Trent Bridge, June 10, 11, 13, 14, 1938. Drawn. England, in a match memorable for the setting-up of many new records including seven individual hundreds, put together the highest innings total ever hit against Australia. Not until half past three on the second day did Australia have an opportunity of batting and with 151 scored half their wickets had fallen. McCabe then played an innings the equal of which has probably never been seen in the history of Test cricket; for the best part of four hours he maintained a merciless punishment of the bowling. Although his phenomenal effort did not save his side from the indignity of having to follow on, it broke the control of the play which England had held from the outset and by concentrating upon defence in their second innings Australia saved the game.

In a magnificent contest of skill, the excellence of the wicket always counted heavily in favour of batsmen. First innings conferred upon England a very important advantage. Australia put their faith in spin bowlers, but hardly ever did a ball turn and the bowlers who had so confused county sides came in for harsh treatment. On the opening day Barnett shared with Hutton in a first-wicket partnership of 219 which surpassed the previous best against Australia in England by the Hon. F.S. Jackson and Tom Hayward, who made 185 for England's first wicket at the Oval in 1899. The full value of Barnett's dashing attack on Australia's bowling was probably not appreciated at the time. Besides easing the task of the batsmen who followed, it provided a heartening influence on the play of Hutton, who, together with Compton, had the distinction of hitting a century on a first appearance against Australia. For the first time in a Test match, four individual hundreds were registered in one innings for, following the success of Barnett, Hutton and Compton, Paynter made the highest score against Australia in England and also shared with Compton in a record fifth wicket partnership of 206. The previous best figure for this wicket was 192 by R.E. Foster and Braund (L.C.) at Sydney in 1903.

As the result of two hours' batting by Barnett and Hutton before lunch on Friday 169 runs were scored. The Gloucestershire man drove and cut in magnificent style and was particularly severe on Fleetwood-Smith. In view of the kind of innings he played, it was not surprising that he made false strokes; he was almost caught in the gulley when three, when 51 he hit a ball back hard towards Fleetwood-Smith and next over offered a difficult chance to Bradman, running from deep mid-off. The satisfaction of making a hundred before lunch-time was denied to Barnett, but off the first ball bowled after the interval he completed three-figures and altogether he made 126, batting nearly three hours and hitting eighteen 4's. Some of his drives off the back foot were splendidly executed. Hutton batted about half an hour longer and if, compared with Barnett, he looked slow, he was very sure of himself. An incident that occurred soon after the match began, when the ball rolled against the middle and leg stumps without displacing a bail, did not disturb him. He summed up the length of every delivery to a nicety, and three fieldsmen close to the bat did not have the least chance to snap up. Hutton placed his strokes particularly well and his hitting to the on-side and to leg and his late-cutting was admirably done. He hit fourteen 4's.

The next ball after the completion of his hundred ended Hutton's innings and then Australia made better progress; Edrich played on and Hammond, after a few forcing shots, was bowled neck and crop, but England finished the day with a score of 422 for four wickets, the last hour and a half producing 141 runs from Paynter and Compton. Some fine running between wickets featured this stand. Compton's stylish and confident play created a big impression and Paynter by quick footwork mastered the spin bowling.

When on Saturday, Compton was fifth out, England had 487 runs on the board. In a stand with Paynter lasting two hours, twenty minutes Compton hit finely on the leg side, also excelling with the drive and square cut, and in scoring 102, including fifteen 4's, he batted without a mistake. Owing to the ball lodging in the wicket-keeper's pads, Paynter escaped being stumped when 88 and the one other opportunity Australia had of getting him out occurred with his score 163, Fleetwood-Smith at fine leg making a creditable but unavailing effort to hold a hard hit. Some good cover driving by Ames featured a sixth wicket stand of 90 and with Wright batting steadily after the eighth wicket fell, Paynter completed 200. When Hammond declared England's innings and Paynter left the crease about quarter-past three on Saturday, 30,000 spectators rose to their feet, cheering the Lancashire left-hander all the way to the pavilion. Just as the effort of Barnett was the foundation of England's batting triumph after an innings lasting ten minutes less than nine hours, so Paynter during five hours, twenty minutes' batting most efficiently consolidated the work of the early batsmen. Often jumping in to drive he forced runs well, hit Ward for a 6 and also included a 5 and twenty-six 4's among his figures. During the innings four of Australia's bowlers each had a hundred runs hit off him.

No such inspiring start as had been given to England by the first wicket pair was enjoyed by Australia. Going on at 29, Wright, with his fourth ball in a Test match, dismissed Fingleton who played a long hop on to his wicket. By subdued and not altogether certain batting, Brown and Bradman raised the score to 111 and then Bradman, deceived in the flight of a ball, played it against his pads from which it glanced into the wicket-keeper's hands, Two appeals against the light were unsuccessful and before time Australia also lost Brown, who batted extremely well for two hours and a half. Ward went in as 'stop-gap' and played through the last two overs despite the intimidating effect of an arc of nine fieldsmen within nine yards of his bat and Farnes bowling at top speed.

As a result of this most successful day for England, Monday's play began with Australia's score 138 for three, McCabe being 19 not out, made in 35 minutes. A record of these facts is a necessary preliminary to a description of the amazing batting which followed from McCabe and gave such an epic turn to the game. Six wickets were down for 194 and then McCabe, assisted in turn by three left-hand batsmen – Barnett, O'Reilly and McCormick – altered the whole aspect of affairs. In a little less than four hours, McCabe scored 232 out of 300 – his highest score in a Test match. His driving was tremendously hard, he hooked short balls with certainty and power, one off Farnes yielding a six, and he showed real genius in beating Hammond's efforts to keep him away from the bowling. While McCabe was running riot, the England captain delayed calling for the new ball and took other measures in the hope of keeping down runs, but the Australian, having completed his first hundred in two hours, twenty minutes, proceeded to score 4's much more readily. Wright was hit for 44 runs off three successive overs. Although he travelled so fast, McCabe did not offer a real chance, but once Edrich made a plucky effort to hold a ball hooked with terrific power. In the last ten overs bowled to him, McCabe took the strike in eight and hit 16 of his thirty-four 4's and in a last wicket stand of 77 with Fleetwood-Smith he scored 72 in 28 minutes. His glorious innings ended in a fitting way for in attempting a big hit off Verity he skied the ball to cover.

The probability that he would be in a position to enforce a follow-on influenced Hammond to conserve Verity's energies and the Yorkshireman bowled no more than 45 balls during the innings. England's fielding remained sure and enthusiastic all the time and although McCabe's rate of scoring might suggest the attack was demoralised that was not the case. When Australia followed on 247 behind, batting of a much different character was seen. Brown and Fingleton adopted stone-walling tactics which called forth mild barracking from some of the spectators and Fingleton followed the extraordinary procedure of stepping away from his wicket, taking off his gloves and laying down his bat. A good left-hand slip catch by Hammond disposed of Fingleton after an opening partnership of 89 in two and a quarter hours and Tuesday's play was notable for a dour resistance by Brown and Bradman who, making a hundred apiece, batted with grim patience and admirable skill. In view of the position Australia were of course justified in playing this type of game and by adding 170 in three hours, ten minutes they robbed England of practically all chance of winning. Brown stayed nearly five hours and a half, and hit thirteen 4's – a splendid performance for his side. He played Verity admirably. Troubled by a leg strain, Bradman was never seen as an attacking batsman, but he amazed everyone by the power of his concentration while batting the whole day. His second innings, begun twenty minutes before Monday's play closed, lasted six hours and there were only five 4's in his not out 144 which, being his thirteenth hundred in England–Australia matches, allowed him to take the record from Jack Hobbs, who hit twelve hundreds in the series. Verity bowled with precision and Wright sometimes made a ball turn, but the pitch was too good for England to force a win. Shortly after the tea interval Australia stood only 114 ahead with half their wickets gone and they saved the match, although the Englishmen stuck gamely to their task. Annoyed by the wearisome cricket, spectators late in the day indulged in ironical cheering, whereupon Bradman showed disapproval of this slight demonstration by standing clear of his wickets until the noise subsided. The total attendance was 89,681 and the receipts £15,293 2s. 9d.

ENGLAND

L. Hutton lbw b Fleetwood-Smith	....	100
C.J. Barnett b McCormick	....	126
W.J. Edrich b O'Reilly	....	5
Mr W.R. Hammond (Capt.) b O'Reilly	......	26
E. Paynter not out	....	216
D. Compton c Badcock b Fleetwood-Smith	.	102
L.E.G. Ames b Fleetwood-Smith	.....	46
H. Verity b Fleetwood-Smith	....	3
R.A. Sinfield lbw b O'Reilly	....	6
D.V.P. Wright not out	....	1
B 1, l-b 22, n-b 4	....	27
	Eight wkts, dec.	**658**

Mr K. Farnes did not bat.

AUSTRALIA

J.H. Fingleton b Wright 9	– c Hammond b Edrich 40
W.A. Brown c Ames b Farnes 48	– c Paynter b Verity 133
D.G. Bradman (Capt.) c Ames b Sinfield 51	– not out 144
S.J. McCabe c Compton b Verity 232	– c Hammond b Verity 39
F. Ward b Farnes 2	– not out 7
A.L. Hassett c Hammond b Wright 1	– c Compton b Verity 2
C.L. Badcock b Wright 9	– b Wright 5
B.A. Barnett c Wright b Farnes 22	– lbw b Sinfield 31
W.J. O'Reilly c Paynter b Farnes 9	
E.L. McCormick b Wright 2	
L. O'B. Fleetwood-Smith not out 5	
B 10, l-b 10, w1 21	B 5, l-b 16, n-b 5 26
411	Six wkts, dec. **427**

AUSTRALIA BOWLING

	Overs	Mdns	Runs	Wkts	Overs	Mdns	Runs	Wkts
McCormick	32	4	108	1				
O'Reilly	56	11	164	3				
McCabe	21	5	64	0				
Fleetwood.Smith	49	9	153	4				
Ward	30	2	142	0				

ENGLAND BOWLING

	Overs	Mdns	Runs	Wkts	Overs	Mdns	Runs	Wkts
Farnes	37	11	106	4	24	2	78	0
Hammond	19	6	44	0	12	6	15	0
Sinfield	28	8	51	1	35	8	72	1
Wright	39	6	153	4	37	8	85	1
Verity	7.3	0	36	1	62	27	102	3
Edrich					13	2	39	1
Barnett					1	0	10	0

FALL OF THE WICKETS

England – First Innings

1	2	3	4	5	6	7	8
219	240	244	281	487	577	597	626

Australia – First Innings

1	2	3	4	5	6	7	8	9	10
34	111	134	144	151	194	263	319	334	411

Australia – Second Innings

1	2	3	4	5	6
89	259	331	337	369	417

Umpires: F. Chester and E. Robinson.

FOURTH TEST MATCH

At Leeds, July 22, 23, 25, 1938. Australia won by five wickets. Their success enabled them to retain the 'Ashes'. [...] At no time was the wicket easy for batting and Australia won largely because they possessed better spin bowling. For O'Reilly, the match provided a big triumph, for he took five wickets in each innings for altogether 122 runs. Exactly why the pitch, even during the early stages of the game, played so queerly was hard to understand. A likely explanation was that it was kept on the damp side through moisture being drawn to the surface in the humid weather pre-vailing. At any rate bowlers were able to turn the ball and as the match progressed spin acted more quickly; by Monday the wicket had worn and O'Reilly took full advantage of this state of affairs. [...]

To see England's batsmen struggling for runs after Hammond, for the third suc-cessive match, won the toss was at once unexpected and perplexing. In the course of five hours, and despite a splendid effort by Hammond, the innings was over. The Australian bowling had far more accuracy about it than in the two previous Tests and from his first over O'Reilly puzzled the batsmen. Barnett, after offering two chances, was entirely responsible for Hardstaff being run out and although he batted through the two hours up to lunch, during which only 62 runs were scored, he looked strangely uncertain. Not until after the interval did Hammond attempt to change the character of the cricket and then, having hit a no-ball from McCormick for 6, he lost Barnett to a fine one-hand catch at the wicket. Barnett stayed nearly two hours and a half and his stand with Hammond realised 54. With Paynter batting steadily, as many runs came from the next wicket. How much Hammond dominated the cricket can be gathered from the fact that he scored 76 out of 108 and hit ten 4's. Another clever piece of wicket-keeping by B.A. Barnett began a minor collapse for after Paynter, losing his balance, was stumped, Compton, next over, was bowled and, with one added, Price left to a slip catch. [...]

When Wright, with the first ball he bowled in Australia's innings, got rid of Brown, B.A. Barnett was sent in to play out time with Fingleton and the outcome of this move far exceeded expectations. Barnett, indeed, played a most valuable innings and England bowled for nearly an hour and a half next morning before gaining further reward. The second wicket partnership yielded 59 and Fingleton batted in dogged style for over two hours; Barnett, who made his highest score in Test cricket, was in ten minutes longer. The attack of Farnes and Bowes after lunch was accurate and full of danger; McCabe and Badcock in turn were clean bowled and Australia's first five wickets fell for 145. The light at this time was none too good but Bradman, as in each of the two previous Tests, did not let the occasion pass without placing to his name another three-figure score – his twelfth of the tour. Although a beautiful length leg-break led to Hassett being caught at slip after helping to add 50, Waite stayed long enough to see Australia take an innings lead. Shielding his successive partners, Bradman astutely nursed the bowling and he made every possible run against high-class fielding. His stroke-play and his defence were alike admirable. [...]

Bad light once interrupted this innings and when England went in 19 runs behind an appeal was upheld. Barnett and Edrich survived an awkward fifty minutes prior to close of play and they put 60 runs on the board before being separated next morning. This in fact was the most productive stand of the whole match. For the collapse which afterwards set in no one could have been prepared. O'Reilly, on a worn pitch, and ably supported by Fleetwood-Smith, finished off the innings before lunch-time, England's full ten wickets actually going down for the addition of 74 runs to the overnight score. Successive balls accounted for Hardstaff and Hammond, the latter being finely caught close in at short square-leg, and Compton had the ill-luck to be caught off his wrist. Paynter, after going in third wicket down, made a gallant effort and, not out, batted over an hour, but the sixth, seventh and eighth wickets all fell at 116, Fleetwood-Smith dismissing Verity and Wright with consecutive balls, a feat which O'Reilly performed at the expense of Farnes and Bowes. Except when he changed ends, O'Reilly bowled fifteen overs without a rest and he took five wickets for nine runs apiece. With six men on the leg side close to the bat, and with no-one in the long field, he demoralised the majority of the batsmen. England's 123 represented their lowest total against Australia for 17 years.

Left to get 105, Australia had to struggle hard for success. Farnes kept up a splendid attack but misfielding gave Australia valuable runs. Intense excitement came into the cricket when Wright, after going on at 48, quickly sent back Bradman and McCabe. With the first four batsmen in the order all out, Australia had to contend with atrocious light but the batsmen refrained from appealing and, as Hassett began to drive and pull in an easy, confident style, England's chance of turning the tables gradually slipped away. A storm threatened and Hassett, no doubt anxious to settle the match before the rain came, tried to drive a leg-break and skied the ball to point. His brave innings, however, in company with Badcock had carried the total to within 14 of victory and there were five wickets to fall. Rain interrupted the play with nine runs needed but Australia got home without further loss, making the required runs in an hour and fifty minutes. [...]

ENGLAND

W.J. Edrich b O'Reilly .12	– st Barnett b Fleetwood-Smith 28	
C.J. Barnett c Barnett b McCormick 30	– c Barnett b McCormick 29	
J. Hardstaff run out 4	– b O'Reilly 11	
Mr W.R. Hammond (Capt.) b O'Reilly 76	– c Brown b O'Reilly 0	
E. Paynter st Barnett b Fleetwood-Smith 28	– not out 21	
D. Compton b O'Reilly 14	– c Barnett b O'Reilly 15	
W.F. Price c McCabe b O'Reilly 0	– lbw b Fleetwood-Smith 6	
H. Verity not out 25	– b Fleetwood-Smith 0	
D.V.P. Wright c Fingleton		
b Fleetwood-Smith .22	– c Waite b Fleetwood-Smith 0	
Mr K. Farnes c Fingleton b Fleetwood-Smith .2	– b O'Reilly 7	
W.E. Bowes b O'Reilly 3	– lbw b O'Reilly 0	
L-b 4, n-b 3 7	L-b 4, w 1, n-b 1 6	

223   123

AUSTRALIA

J.H. Fingleton b Verity	30	– lbw b Verity	9
W.A. Brown b Wright	22	– lbw b Farnes	9
B.A. Barnett c Price b Farnes	57	– not out	15
D.G. Bradman (Capt.) b Bowes	103	– c Verity b Wright	16
S.J. McCabe b Farnes	1	– c Barnett b Wright	15
C.L. Badcock b Bowes	4	– not out	5
A.L. Hassett c Hammond b Wright	13	– c Edrich b Wright	33
M.G. Waite c Price b Farnes	3		
W.J. O'Reilly c Hammond b Farnes	2		
E.L. McCormick b Bowes	0		
L.O'B. Fleetwood-Smith not out	2		
B 2, l-b 3	5	B 4, n-b 1	5
	242		**Five wkts 107**

AUSTRALIA BOWLING

	Overs	Mdns	Runs	Wkts	Overs	Mdns	Runs	Wkts
McCormick	20	6	46	1	11	4	18	1
Waite	18	7	31	0	2	0	9	0
O'Reilly	34.1	17	66	5	21.5	8	56	5
Fleetwood.Smith	25	7	73	3	16	4	34	4
McCabe	1	1	0	0				

ENGLAND BOWLING

	Overs	Mdns	Runs	Wkts	Overs	Mdns	Runs	Wkts
Farnes	26	3	77	4	11.3	4	17	1
Bowes	35.4	6	79	3	11	0	35	0
Wright	15	4	38	2	5	0	26	3
Verity	19	6	30	1	5	2	24	1
Edrich	3	0	13	0				

FALL OF THE WICKETS

England – First Innings

1	2	3	4	5	6	7	8	9	10
29	34	88	142	171	171	172	213	215	223

Australia – First Innings

1	2	3	4	5	6	7	8	9	10
28	87	128	136	145	195	232	240	240	242

England – Second Innings

1	2	3	4	5	6	7	8	9	10
60	73	73	73	96	116	116	116	123	123

Australia – Second Innings

1	2	3	4	5
17	32	50	61	91

Umpire: E.J. Smith and F. Chester.

4

FROM BRADMAN
TO CHAPPELL:
AUSTRALIA v. ENGLAND
1946–72

Any cricket history nowadays that emphasises the Ashes courts the displeasure of the game's globalists. Yet history is precisely the forum in which it should be recognised and understood. Cricket's growth as an international game is exceptionally recent. Australia did not lose a series to a team other than England until 1965; not, in other words, until *Wisden* was more than a hundred years old.

Their primacy may not have been an unmitigated good for the Ashes. Certainly there were periods throughout the 1950s and 1960s where the gravity and ceremony surrounding Anglo-Australian cricket seemed to stifle enterprise and imagination. Even the best rubber of the period, 1961, contained two inconclusive and forgettable encounters. And it is hard today to conceive of games as pointless as 1964's Old Trafford Test – Bob Simpson 311 on one side, Ken Barrington 256 on the other, and eighteen wickets in five days. They seem more remote from us than Tests at the turn of the twentieth century.

Not that the quarter-century from cricket's resumption after World War II was as grim as it has sometimes been painted. As this section reveals, cricket also touched some lofty heights, and no period enfolding the careers of Ray Lindwall, Keith Miller, Arthur Morris, Neil Harvey, Norm O'Neill, *inter alia*, could not have its vivid phases. Bradman's last efflorescence dominated the immediate post-war period, culminating in the helter-skelter Headingley Test of July 1948. *Wisden* missed nothing on his final tour, including his decision to donate the surplus on his testimonial to 'the provision of concrete pitches similar to those on which he learned his cricket'. The almanack is also at its starchiest in discussing the mercurial Miller: 'His habit of wheeling round, flying into an abnormally fast start and tossing back his head before releasing the ball gave an impression that petulance more than cricket tactics dictated his methods at such times.'

Some matches in this period are unrepeatable. The Brisbane Tests of December 1946 and December 1950, misshapen by rain in the era of uncovered pitches, seem to belong to another sport. But the shape of cricket's future can be discerned in the increasing influence of fast bowling: the triumphs of Frank Tyson and Brian Statham in 1954–55, of Alan Davidson and Ian Meckiff in 1958–59, then John Snow and Dennis Lillee on opposite sides in the early 1970s proved more indicative of trends than the feats of Jim Laker and Richie Benaud. It would take Shane Warne to restore slow bowling's cachet, and in a later era, by which time it was acknowledged that the Ashes was not the only game in town.

—*GH*

FIRST TEST MATCH

At Brisbane, November 29, 30, December 2, 3, 4, 5, 1946. Australia won by an innings and 332 runs. [...] England began the match well enough after Bradman won the toss. From the third ball of Bedser's second over Morris was caught at first slip. Bradman entered, and immediately was in trouble against Bedser, edging the fifth ball of the same over to the slips and popping up the seventh to square leg. Barnes, hooking brilliantly, did his best to shield Bradman from the bowling until at 46 he was splendidly caught at square leg off a short ball. Bedser, like a goalkeeper, knocked the ball up and caught it at the second attempt. At this point Bradman had made only seven in forty minutes very shakily. There followed the Ikin incident. After lunch, taken with the total 77 for two wickets, Bradman and Hassett gradually wore down the bowling in the relentless heat. Bedser bowled nobly for long spells, but could not return after tea owing to stomach trouble – a legacy of his war service in Italy. Hassett always remained subdued, but Bradman found his true form, and the first day ended with Australia 292 for two – Bradman 162, Hassett 81.

Bedser reappeared next day, when Edrich broke the long stand by clean bowling Bradman with his fourth ball. Bradman hit nineteen 4's. Then Miller joined Hassett in another long stand, during which the England fielding deteriorated. The total reached 428 before Hassett, who hit ten 4's, was caught at mid-on after batting six and a half hours, about the same time as Bradman. Altogether Hassett was dropped three times. Even at this early stage of the match the England bowlers had been no-balled twenty times, but even worse was the failure of Gibb to catch McCool who, when only one, offered a chance off Bedser. That proved a most expensive mistake. Meanwhile Miller, if subdued, drove brilliantly while at the wicket for two hours forty minutes. His best strokes yielded one 6 and six 4's. After tea, McCool and Johnson hammered the bowling freely, taking the total to 595 for five wickets by Saturday evening, when McCool was 92 and Johnson 47.

Rain and bad light limited cricket on Monday to ninety-nine minutes. Bradman did not have the pitch mown and Australia lost their five remaining wickets for 50 runs. Playing back, McCool was leg-before when wanting only five for a century on his Test début. In an enterprising innings of two hours thirty-five minutes McCool hit fourteen 4's and his stand with Johnson produced 131. Always venturesome, Lindwall hit two 6's and three 4's. England now faced Lindwall and Miller; both occasionally pitched short. During lunch the sky became overcast and thunder was heard when, with the second ball after the interval, Lindwall bowled Hutton playing back.

Bad light and showers caused many stoppages, and the day ended with England 21 for one wicket. Late that evening a violent thunderstorm broke, and next day, when cricket was resumed after a delay of only ten minutes, England on a nightmare pitch took their score to 117 for five wickets before another thunderstorm flooded the ground. During this shortened day's play of three hours England fought valiantly. Lindwall, Miller and even Toshack made the ball lift alarmingly. Washbrook soon left, but Compton batted bravely; Edrich was struck repeatedly, and when Hammond came in nearly every ball from Lindwall rose head high. When taken at first slip immediately after lunch, Edrich had withstood the bowling for one and three-quarter hours. He scored only 16, but his was one of the most skilful batting displays I have ever seen. With Ikin going cheaply, half the side were out for 56. The bowling became even more difficult with the Australians pitching a better length, but Hammond, at his best, and Yardley raised the score to 117 without further loss when, following several appeals against the light, the players left the field. Then came the second storm, with hailstones as big as golf balls.

Contrary to expectations, the ground made a remarkable recovery next day in the brilliant sunshine, but the pitch proved more treacherous than ever, and, though England never gave up the unequal struggle, fifteen wickets fell in three and a half hours. So Australia won at ten minutes to five. An attack of chicken-pox robbed Australia of Lindwall, but Miller and Toshack were enough for England. The big shock was the fall of Hutton to the first ball of the second innings. He left to one of three catches by Barnes at short leg. The only real stand in the follow-on was between Ikin and Gibb, who put on 47. Miller achieved a fine all-round performance in his first Test by making 79 and taking nine wickets for 77. Toshack, the tall left-arm medium bowler, who was given plenty of advice by Bradman, responded so well that his figures were nine wickets for 99 runs. [...]

AUSTRALIA

S.G. Barnes c Bedser b Wright 31	D. Tallon lbw b Edrich 14
A. Morris c Hammond b Bedser 2	R. Lindwall c Voce b Wright 31
D.G. Bradman b Edrich 187	G. Tribe c Gibb b Edrich 1
A.L. Hassett c Yardley b Bedser 128	E. Toshack not out 1
K.R. Miller lbw b Wright 79	B 5, l-b 11, w 2, n-b 11 29
C. McCool lbw b Wright 95	
I.W. Johnson lbw b Wright 47	**645**

ENGLAND

L. Hutton b Miller 7	– c Barnes b Miller	0
C. Washbrook c Barnes b Miller 6	– c Barnes b Miller	13
W.J. Edrich c McCool b Miller 16	– lbw b Toshack	7
D. Compton lbw b Miller 17	– c Barnes b Toshack	15
W.R. Hammond lbw b Toshack 32	– b Toshack	23
J.T. Ikin c Tallon b Miller 0	– b Tribe	32
N.W.D. Yardley c Tallon b Toshack 29	– c Hassett b Toshack	0
P.A. Gibb b Miller 13	– lbw b Toshack	11
W. Voce not out 1	– c Hassett b Tribe	18
A.V. Bedser lbw b Miller 0	– c and b Toshack	18
D.V.P. Wright c Tallon b Toshack 4	– not out	10
B 8, l-b 3, w 2, n-b 3 16	B 15, l-b 7, w 1, n-b 2 25
141	**172**

ENGLAND BOWLING

	O	M	R	W	O	M	R	W
Voce	28	9	92	0				
Bedser	41	4	159	2				
Wright	43.6	4	167	5				
Edrich	25	2	107	3				
Yardley	13	1	47	0				
Ikin	2	0	24	0				
Compton	6	0	20	0				

AUSTRALIA BOWLING

Lindwall	12	4	23	0				
Miller	22	4	60	7	11	3	17	2
Toshack	16.5	11	17	3	20.7	2	82	6
McCool	1	0	5	0				
Tribe	9	1	19	0	12	2	48	2
Barnes	1	0	1	0				

FALL OF WICKETS

Australia

1	2	3	4	5	6	7	8	9	10
9	46	322	428	465	596	599	629	643	645

England – First Innings

1	2	3	4	5	6	7	8	9	10
10	25	49	56	56	121	134	136	136	141

England – Second Innings

1	2	3	4	5	6	7	8	9	10
0	13	33	62	65	65	112	114	143	172

Umpires: J.D. Scott and G. Borwick.

AUSTRALIANS IN ENGLAND, 1948

When announcing retirement from first-class cricket, D.G. Bradman claimed that the 1948 side bore comparison with any of its predecessors, he accurately reflected the majority of opinion on the 19th Australian team visiting England. In retaining 'The Ashes' held by Australia since 1934, these Australians enjoyed almost uninterrupted success, while becoming the first side to go unbeaten through an English tour: certainly they achieved all that could be expected of a combination entitled to the description *great*. Yet they gave cause for reservation of such sweeping judgment as the Tests were by no means so one-sided as results suggested, and Yorkshire and Hampshire played themselves into positions arousing visions of the first Australian defeat by a county since Hampshire beat the 1912 team. Still, for the most part, victory followed victory so inevitably for the Australians that at times opponents took on an air of defeat almost before the match had been in progress more than an hour or two. Once or twice that impression extended even to the Tests.

A summary of their achievements proved the might of probably the most united Australian party sent to England. Not only did they win exactly half their 34 matches with an innings to spare, two by ten wickets, one by nine wickets, two by eight wickets and one by 409 runs, but eleven batsmen between them hit 50 centuries, and in first-class games seven of their seventeen players completed 1,000 runs, with Loxton only 27 short when he broke his nose while batting at Scarborough. Comparisons of totals reveal even more. The Australians made 350 or more in 24 innings whereas, apart from the Tests, the highest total against them was Nottinghamshire's 299 for 8. Twice the Australians failed to reach 200, but they dismissed opponents for less than that figure no fewer than 37 times, and in seven innings for under 100. [...]

From whichever angle the Tests were and are studied, the speed bowling of Lindwall, ably backed by Miller and Johnston, constituted the biggest single weapon on either side. Undoubtedly, Lindwall bore a major part in England's defeats. Not only did he combine controlled pace and accuracy, which allowed batsmen few moments of respite, but he helped bowlers at the other end to their triumphs because, worried by Lindwall, batsmen often took undue risks in their efforts to score from his colleagues. Lindwall introduced an additional source of concern to batsmen by the employment of the extra fast bumper. Unlike Australia, where the bumper, pitched much shorter, usually goes through at uniform height, there were variations of lift on the English pitches when Lindwall bounced the ball and batsmen found no easy choice in deciding whether to attempt to hook, to play a dead bat or to duck. The speed of the ball from the turf left little time for the batsman to change his mind or his stroke for, most important, Lindwall bowled this ball with remarkable precision of length and direction. Proof that batting against Lindwall in England was not enviable was given by the accidents at various times to Compton, Washbrook, Keeton, Robertson, Todd and Watkins. Yet although Miller did no comparable physical damage, his bumpers created more annoyance to those spectators and cricket-lovers who disliked this type of bowling. His habit of wheeling round, flying into an abnormally fast start and tossing back his head before releasing the ball gave an impression that petulance more than cricket tactics dictated his methods at such times. To many people it seemed a pity that such a fine player and one of the game's personalities should have caused the only sign of displeasure, minor as it was, by crowds during the tour; but he could not expect otherwise when he bowled five bumpers in eight balls, as against Hutton at Nottingham. [...] Both Lindwall and Miller were helped in bowling by the lack of practice afforded the majority of English batsmen against such speed since before the war; but this could not be advanced as a reason for the consistent success of Johnston, who shared with Lindwall the distinction of equalling the fast-bowling record which E.A. MacDonald established by taking 27 wickets in the 1921 Test series. Bradman worked nobody harder than Johnston, who responded by dismissing 102 batsmen in first-class matches, and generally proving such a vital cog in the wheel that probably he would have been missed more than any other bowler had he been injured. [...]

For Bradman the tour provided the most fitting climax possible to an illustrious career. Apart from leading Australia to continued Test dominance, he made more hundreds than any batsman in the country and for the second time – he hit 13 in 1938 – he emulated Trumper's performance of 1902 with eleven first-class centuries on a tour in England. In addition to this supreme batting ability, Bradman demonstrated his knowledge of the game in captaincy and generalship. Most pleasing to him must have been the warmth of the reception accorded him by crowds everywhere, particularly in his last two Tests, at Leeds and The Oval. The British public paid striking tribute to his popularity, and they made such big response to a newspaper fund for a Bradman testimonial that, after receiving a silver trophy, he asked that the surplus money should go towards the provision of concrete pitches similar to those on which he learned his cricket.

Behind Bradman was a batting combination of almost unlimited strength so that, no matter the side chosen, runs could be expected from all except the last one or two men. Not only did the Australians score 15,120 runs for the loss of 304 wickets in first-class games, an average of just under 50 per wicket, but they maintained a remarkably fast scoring rate which was reduced only in awkward periods during Tests. The dashing Miller and exuberant Harvey typified the Australian attitude when at Leeds they set about the English attack at a most difficult time and made 121 runs in ninety minutes, a stand which caused England to lose a firm grip on the game. Several times the Australians scored over 500 in a day against the counties, and they made the highest total in a day's play of six hours when they flogged the Essex bowling for 721 at Westcliff. Their 774 against Gloucestershire was the highest score of the summer and the second biggest by Australians in England. For the most part the Australians exuded confidence which the flow of easy victories at the start must have inspired and in batting no one showed this inestimable quality more than Morris, the most consistent batsman on either side in the Tests. He surpassed his first triumphant Test season in Australia by heading the batting figures with 696 runs, average 87.00, his innings including centuries in the Second, Fourth and Fifth Tests, and he gave no better display than that at Leeds, where he and Bradman made 301 for the second wicket in Australia's second innings. [...] Through the nature of his duties as opening batsman, Barnes imposed upon himself limitations in stroke-play, relying mainly on powerful fore-armed square-cuts and hooks for his runs, but when the situation warranted he revealed all the aggression which made him such an attractive batsman in former seasons. For instance, at Scarborough Barnes scored 50 in twenty-five minutes after reaching his century, and 6's followed 4's in a whirlwind display of hitting. In addition to his batting Barnes exercised a big influence on opposing batsmen through his fielding at forward short-leg, or point, as at Leeds. [...]

ESSEX V. AUSTRALIANS

At Southend, May 15, 17, 1948. Australians won by an innings and 451 runs. In light-hearted vein, they made history by putting together the highest total scored in a day of six hours in first-class cricket. Bradman led the run-getting revel on the Saturday. Complete master of the Essex bowlers on a fast pitch, he scored 187 in two hours five minutes, and by a wide variety of orthodox and unorthodox strokes hit thirty-two 4's and a 5. Brown's 153 occupied three hours and contained seventeen 4's. Loxton (fourteen 4's and a 6) and Saggers (nine 4's) also scored centuries. The biggest partnerships were 219 in ninety minutes between Brown and Bradman for the second wicket, 166 in sixty-five minutes by Loxton and Saggers for the sixth, and 145 in ninety-five minutes between Barnes and Brown for the first. Bailey dismissed Brown and Miller with successive balls, but generally the bowlers failed to stem the scoring. Because of injury Bailey did not bat in either innings. Essex, dismissed twice on Monday, first failed against the pace of Miller and the cleverly varied left-arm deliveries of Toshack; then in the follow-on – apart from Pearce and P. Smith, who made a stand of 133 – they broke down in face of Johnson's off-spinners. The attendance and receipts – 32,000 and £3,482 – were ground records.

AUSTRALIANS

S.G. Barnes hit wkt b R. Smith 79
W.A. Brown c Horsfall b Bailey 153
D.G. Bradman b P. Smith 187
K.R. Miller b Bailey 0
R.A. Hamence c P. Smith b R. Smith 46
S.J. Loxton c Rist b Vigar 120
R.A. Saggers not out 104

I.W. Johnson st Rist b P. Smith 9
D. Ring c Vigar b P. Smith 1
W.A. Johnston b Vigar 9
E.R.H. Toshack c Vigar b P. Smith 4
B 7, n-b 2 .9

721

ESSEX

T.C. Dodds c Ring b Miller . . . . .0 – b Toshack 16
S.J. Cray b Miller . . . . .5 – b Johnson 15
A.V. Avery b Johnston . . . . .10 – c Brown b Johnson 3
F.H. Vigar c Saggers b Miller . . . . .0 – c Johnson b Toshack 0
R. Horsfall b Toshack . . . . .11 – b Johnson 8
T.N. Pearce c Miller b Toshack . . . . .8 – c and b Johnson 71
R. Smith c Barnes b Toshack . . . . .25 – c Ring b Johnson 0
T.P.B. Smith b Toshack . . . . .3 – lbw b Barnes .54
F. Rist c Barnes b Toshack . . . . .8 – b Johnson 1
E. Price not out . . . . .4 – not out 4
T.E. Bailey absent hurt . . . . .0 – absent hurt 0
B 2, l-b 6, n-b 1 9   B 6, l-b 3, n-b 6 15

83   **187**

ESSEX BOWLING

	O	M	R	W		O	M	R	W
Bailey	21	1	128	2					
R. Smith	37	2	169	2					
P. Smith	38	0	193	4					
Price	20	0	156	0					
Vigar	13	1	66	2					

AUSTRALIAN BOWLING

	O	M	R	W		O	M	R	W
Miller	8	3	14	3		2	1	4	0
Johnston	7	1	10	1		10	4	26	0
Toshack	10.5	0	31	5		17	2	50	2
Ring	11	4	19	0		7	3	16	0
Loxton						12	3	28	0
Johnson						21	6	37	6
Barnes						9.4	5	11	1

Umpires: W.H. Ashdown and D. Hendren.

FOURTH TEST MATCH

At Leeds, July 22, 23, 24, 26, 27, 1948. Australia won by seven wickets. By the astonishing feat of scoring 404 for three wickets on the fifth day of the match when the pitch took spin, Australia won the rubber. Until that fatal last stage England were on top, but a succession of blunders prevented them gaining full reward for good work on the first four days. [...] When Yardley won the toss for the third time in four matches, England gained first use of a perfect pitch. Without Barnes, Bradman did not place a fieldsman close in at forward short leg and the batsmen welcomed their freedom. After their disappointing starts together in the earlier games, Hutton and Washbrook gave England a great send-off with an opening stand of 168, their best partnership in any Test Match. Hutton completely justified his recall to the side and Washbrook successfully eliminated the dangerous high hook stroke which often caused his downfall in earlier Tests. He completed an almost faultless hundred out of 189 and fell in the last over of the day after batting five hours twenty minutes. His second stand with Edrich produced 100.

Bedser, sent in to play the last four balls overnight, proved such an efficient stopgap that the third successive century partnership resulted. For the second day running the Australians met with no success before lunch, and the third wicket realised 155 before Bedser, who made his highest score in any Test, gave a return catch. Edrich left three runs later after batting five hours ten minutes. This quick fall of wickets revitalised the Australians and the England batting broke down badly. From a total of 423 for two, England were all out 496.

Hassett and Morris opened the Australian innings, but did not shape confidently. Morris left at 13, and next morning Pollard, in his first over, sent back Hassett and Bradman in three balls, making Australia 68 for three. Then nineteen-year-old Neil Harvey joined Miller, and, delivering a terrific onslaught on the England attack, they rescued Australia from their precarious position. In just over an hour and a half they put on 121 by glorious stroke-play. Loxton carried on the big hitting and, with Harvey, added 105 in ninety-five minutes. Harvey hit seventeen 4's while making 112 – his second successive Test century. Loxton's terrific driving brought five 6's and nine 4's. Yet despite this punishment England held the upper hand, for with eight wickets down Australia were 141 behind. Then occurred a similar experience to that at Lord's, where Australia's tail-end batsmen could not be dislodged. Johnston and an injured Toshack, who batted with the aid of a runner, in turn helped Lindwall with such success that the last two wickets added 103 and England's lead was restricted to 38.

Hutton and Washbrook opened with a century stand for the second time in the match and created a new world record for Test cricket in accomplishing the feat twice. Both left at 129, but England consolidated their position by rapid scoring. Edrich and Compton put on 103 at more than one a minute and, although a slight collapse followed, Evans, with help from Bedser and Laker, punished the bowling. At the close of the fourth day England led by 400 with two wickets left.

To most people Yardley's decision to continue batting for five minutes next day came as a surprise and the reason for it aroused plenty of comment. The main idea was to break up the pitch by the use of the heavy roller. Three runs were added in two overs, and then Yardley declared, leaving Australia to score 404 in 345 minutes. The pitch took spin and the ball lifted and turned sharply. Unfortunately, Laker was erratic in length. Compton, bowling his left-hand off-breaks and googlies, baffled the batsmen several times, but without luck. Evans should have stumped Morris when 32, and Compton only gained reward when he held a return catch from Hassett at 57, but he ought to have dismissed Bradman, Crapp dropping a catch at first slip. In half an hour before lunch Morris and Bradman put on 64, and after the interval, against a succession of full tosses and long hops, runs continued to flow. When 59 Bradman had another escape off Compton, and Yardley, in despair, called for the new ball even though the pitch favoured spin. Evans should have stumped Bradman when 108, and Laker at square leg dropped Morris when 126. Not until 301 had been put on did England break the stand, and by that time the match was as good as won. Morris batted four hours fifty minutes for 182. Miller did not last long, but Harvey made the winning stroke within fifteen minutes of time. No fewer than 66 fours were hit in the innings, 33 by Morris and 29 by Bradman.

The attendance figures of 158,000 created a record for any match in England. Receipts amounted to £34,000.

ENGLAND

L. Hutton b Lindwall	.81	– c Bradman b Johnson .... .57
C. Washbrook c Lindwall b Johnston	.143	– c Harvey b Johnston .... .65
W.J. Edrich c Morris b Johnson	.111	– lbw b Lindwall .... .54
A.V. Bedser c and b Johnson	.79	– c Hassett b Miller .... .17
D.C.S. Compton c Saggers b Lindwall	.23	– c Miller b Johnston .... .66
J.F. Crapp b Toshack	.5	– b Lindwall .... .18
N.W.D. Yardley b Miller	.25	– c Harvey b Johnston 7
K. Cranston b Loxton	.10	– c Saggers b Johnston 0
T.G. Evans c Hassett b Loxton	.3	– not out .... .47
J.C. Laker c Saggers b Loxton	.4	– not out .... .15
R. Pollard not out	.0	
B 2, l-b 8, w 1, n-b 1	.12	B 4, l-b 12, n-b 3 .... .19
	496	Eight wkts, dec. **365**

AUSTRALIA

A.R. Morris c Cranston b Bedser	.6	– c Pollard b Yardley .... .182
A.L. Hassett c Crapp b Pollard	.13	– c and b Compton .... .17
D.G. Bradman b Pollard	.33	– not out .... .173
K.R. Miller c Edrich b Yardley	.58	– lbw b Cranston .... .12
R.N. Harvey b Laker	.112	– not out 4
S.J. Loxton b Yardley	.93	
I.W. Johnson c Cranston b Laker	.10	
R.R. Lindwall c Crapp b Bedser	.77	
R.A. Saggers st Evans b Laker	.5	
W.A. Johnston c Edrich b Bedser	.13	
E.R.H. Toshack not out	.12	
B 9, l-b 14, n-b 3	.26	B 6, l-b 9, n-b 1 .... .16
	458	Three wkts **404**

AUSTRALIA BOWLING

	O	M	R	W	O	M	R	W
Lindwall	38	10	79	2	26	6	84	2
Miller	17.1	2	43	1	21	5	53	1
Johnston	38	13	86	1	29	5	95	4
Toshack	35	6	112	1				
Loxton	26	4	55	3	19	2	29	0
Johnson	33	9	89	2	21	2	85	1
Morris	5	0	20	0				

ENGLAND BOWLING

	O	M	R	W	O	M	R	W
Bedser	31.2	4	92	3	21	2	56	0
Pollard	38	6	100	2	22	6	55	0
Cranston	14	1	51	0	7.1	0	28	1
Edrich	3	0	19	0				
Laker	30	8	113	3	32	11	93	0
Yardley	17	6	38	2	13	1	44	1
Compton	3	0	15	0	15	3	82	1
Hutton					4	1	30	0

FALL OF WICKETS

England – First Innings:

1	2	3	4	5	6	7	8	9
168	268	423	426	447	473	486	490	496

England – Second Innings:

1	2	3	4	5	6	7	8
129	129	232	260	277	278	293	330

Australia – First Innings:

1	2	3	4	5	6	7	8	9
13	65	68	189	294	329	344	355	403

Australia – Second Innings:

1	2	3
57	358	396

Umpires: F. Chester and H.G. Baldwin.

FIFTH TEST MATCH

At Kennington Oval, August 14, 16, 17, 18, 1948. Australia won by an innings and 149 runs, so completing their triumph in the rubber with four victories and one draw. [...] Extraordinary cricket marked the opening day. So saturated was the ground by copious rain during the week that the groundsmen could not get the pitch into a reasonable state for a punctual start. The captains agreed that play should begin at 12 o'clock, and Yardley, having won the toss, chose to bat – an inevitable decision with the conditions uncertain and the possibility of more rain. As it happened, apart from local showers early on Sunday morning, the weather proved fine until England fared badly for the second time. All things considered, the Australians found everything favourable for them, as was the case at Lord's. […] Hutton, the one exception to complete failure, batted in his customary stylish, masterful manner throughout the innings, being last out from a leg glance which Tallon held with the left hand close to the ground as he fell – a great finish to Australia's splendid performance.

Lindwall, with his varied pace and occasional very fast ball, excelled. Always bowling at the stumps, he made the ball rise at different heights. Four times he clean bowled a hesitant opponent. Except that Watkins received a blow on the shoulder that destroyed his supposed value as a bowler, the batsmen escaped injury during a most pitiful display. After lunch Lindwall bowled 8.1 overs, four maidens, and took five wickets at a cost of 8 runs!

Everything became different when Australia batted. Barnes and Morris, with controlled assurance and perfect stroke play, made 117, and shortly before six o'clock Bradman walked to the wicket amidst continued applause from the standing crowd. Yardley shook hands with Bradman and called on the England team for three cheers, in which the crowd joined. Evidently deeply touched by the enthusiastic reception, Bradman survived one ball, but, playing forward to the next, was clean bowled by a sharply turning break-back – possibly a googly. As if to avenge the fall of these two wickets in an over, Morris twice hooked Hollies to the boundary and the score rose to 153, while on Monday it reached 226 before Hassett left – 109 for the third wicket. That those runs occupied two hours and a quarter testified to good bowling and fielding by a side in a forlorn position, and the next best partnership was the sixth, which added 39.

Morris missed the special distinction of making 200 through his own ill-judged call for a sharp run, Simpson, fielding substitute for Watkins, with a good return from third man causing his dismissal for 196. Scoring these runs out of 359 in six hours forty minutes, Morris hit sixteen 4's. His strokes past cover-point were typical of the highest class left-handed batsman. His drives and hooks beat the speediest fieldsmen, and he showed marked skill in turning the ball to leg. He was eighth out, and Tallon got most of the 30 runs added before Bedser at last earned reward for steady bowling by taking the tenth wicket.

Facing arrears of 337, England lost Dewes with 20 scored, but Hutton and Edrich raised the total to 54 before bad light stopped play. The conditions remained anything but good on Tuesday, when the early fall of Edrich to a fine ball from Lindwall preceded the only stand of consequence, Compton and Hutton putting on 61 in an hour and fifty minutes before Lindwall, with his left hand at second slip, held a hard cut from Compton. Hutton maintained his sound form until a bumper from Miller struck Crapp on the head, soon after which the Yorkshireman gave Tallon a catch. Batting four hours and a quarter for 64 out of 153, Hutton was always restrained but admirable in defence.

After he left three wickets fell in deepening gloom for 25 runs. Evans, from the way he shaped without attempting a stroke, obviously could not see the ball which bowled him. Lindwall, with the pavilion behind him, sending down something like a yorker at express speed. The umpires immediately responded to the appeal against the light, and rain at four o'clock delayed the finish until Wednesday morning, when the remaining three wickets realised only ten runs in a sad spectacle for England. […]

ENGLAND

L. Hutton c Tallon b Lindwall	.30 –	c Tallon b Miller	.64
J.G. Dewes b Miller	.1 –	b Lindwall	.10
W.J. Edrich c Hassett b Johnston	.3 –	b Lindwall	.28
D.C.S. Compton c Morris b Lindwall	.4 –	c Lindwall b Johnston	.39
J.F. Crapp c Tallon b Miller	.0 –	b Miller	.9
N.W.D. Yardley b Lindwall	.7 –	c Miller b Johnston	.9
A. Watkins lbw b Johnston	.0 –	c Hassett b Ring	.2
T.G. Evans b Lindwall	.1 –	b Lindwall	.8
A.V. Bedser b Lindwall	.0 –	b Johnston	.0
J.A. Young b Lindwall	.0 –	not out	.3
W.E. Hollies not out	.0 –	c Morris b Johnston	.0
B 6	.6	B 9, l-b 4, n-b 3	.16

52   **188**

AUSTRALIA

S.G. Barnes c Evans b Hollies	.61	R.R. Lindwall c Edrich b Young	.9
A.R. Morris run out	.196	D. Tallon c Crapp b Hollies	.31
D.G. Bradman b Hollies	.0	D. Ring c Crapp b Bedser	.9
A.R. Hassett lbw b Young	.37	W.A. Johnston not out	.0
K.R. Miller st Evans b Hollies	.5	B 4, l-b 2, n-b 3	.9
R.N. Harvey c Young b Hollies	.17		
S.J. Loxton c Evans b Edrich	.15	**389**	

AUSTRALIA BOWLING

	O	M	R	W	O	M	R	W
Lindwall	16.1	5	20	6	25	3	50	3
Miller	8	5	5	2	15	6	22	2
Johnston	16	4	20	2	27.3	12	40	4
Loxton	2	1	1	0	10	2	16	0
Ring					28	13	44	1

ENGLAND BOWLING

	O	M	R	W
Bedser	31.2	9	61	1
Watkins	4	1	19	0
Young	51	16	118	2
Hollies	56	14	131	5
Compton	2	0	6	0
Edrich	9	0	38	1
Yardley	5	1	7	0

FALL OF WICKETS

England – First Innings:

1	2	3	4	5	6	7	8	9
2	10	17	23	35	42	45	45	47

England – Second Innings:

1	2	3	4	5	6	7	8	9
20	64	125	153	164	167	178	181	188

Australia – First Innings:

1	2	3	4	5	6	7	8	9
117	117	226	243	265	304	332	359	389

Umpires: D. Davies and H.G. Baldwin.

FIRST TEST MATCH

At Brisbane, December 1, 2, 4, 5, 1950. Australia won by 70 runs. How much the events of the Brisbane Test influenced the remainder of the series could be only a matter of conjecture, but certainly England were entitled to feel that their misfortune here added to their subsequent tasks. Most Australians agreed with the general view that the intervention of a typical Brisbane storm brought in its train defeat for the side which batted better, bowled better and fielded better than the winners. The realisation that on the play they were superior made defeat particularly galling for a team conceded so little chance before the cricket began.

Virtually the game was won and lost at the toss of the coin. When Brown called incorrectly to Hassett, he allowed Australia first use of a good pitch more suited to batting, even though its slow pace did not encourage forcing strokes. Yet the first day belonged to England. They surprised everybody by dismissing Australia for such a meagre total in the conditions.

Compensation for losing the toss came swiftly. From the fourth ball of the day Hutton, at backward short-leg, smartly held Moroney. That was just the tonic needed. For the rest of the innings England's fielding touched the highest class and Evans, behind the wicket, was inspired. No better catches were seen in the Tests than those by which he dismissed Harvey and Loxton. When Loxton cut Brown, the ball struck Evans hard on the glove and rebounded forward. His reaction instantaneous, Evans dived headlong and grasped the catch with his left hand inches from the turf as his body struck the ground with force. [...] Well as England bowled and fielded, Australia's batting was not convincing. Apart from Harvey, few of the batsmen gave the impression of being at ease. Harvey put his usual vigour into a thrilling sequence of his most spectacular left-handed strokes before being caught at the wicket on the leg side when glancing Bedser off the middle of the bat. His 74, made out of 118, contained ten sparkling 4's. Lindwall was solid and watchful, but impatience cost the wickets of at least three early batsmen.

To the end of the Australian innings the cricket was exciting enough. It became more so. A successful appeal against the light by England's new opening pair, Washbrook and Simpson – Brown decided to put Hutton at five to give strength to the middle – was the final act on that dramatic Friday.

Inside a few hours the storm broke, and cricket could not be resumed until half an hour before lunch on Monday. For thirty minutes Washbrook and Simpson provided skill and courage so far unsurpassed in the match. In that time they scored 28 runs together on a pitch just as treacherous as it played through the remainder of the day, in which twenty wickets went down for 102.

True to tradition, the pitch was the game's villain. Medium-paced bowling of good length presented a wellnigh insoluble problem. Sometimes the ball reared head high, at other times it kept horribly low. Both captains placed nearly all their fieldsmen in a circle a few yards from the bat, and twelve of the wickets resulted from catches close to the wicket.

When the back of England's innings had been broken, Brown declared. His one hope was to force Australia in again as soon as possible. Moroney, who experienced the disaster of a 'pair' on his Test debut, Morris and Loxton were out before a run was scored, and wickets continued to go down so quickly that Hassett retaliated by a declaration which gave England an hour and ten minutes to bat before the close. They required 193 to win. If only two or three men had been lost then their prospects might have been bright. It was not to be.

A lightning yorker by Lindwall wrecked Simpson's wicket with the first ball of the innings. There followed half an hour of sound defence by Washbrook and Dewes. Each left within a few minutes of the other, but England's most crushing blow that evening occurred in the last ten minutes when three wickets were lost. Anxiety caused at least two of these dismissals, McIntyre, for example, being run out trying a fourth run when preservation of wickets was of paramount importance. Wicket-keeper Tallon ran ten to fifteen yards before catching a bad throw-in and, with his gloved hand, hurling down the wicket.

So England entered the last day wanting 163 to win with only four wickets left. [...] Evans helped Hutton add sixteen before he and Compton pushed successive balls from Johnston into the hands of forward short-leg. Australia were within sight of victory, but it was not theirs until Hutton had given yet another exhibition of his wonderful batsmanship on tricky turf. Aided first by Brown and then by Wright, Hutton thrashed the fast bowlers majestically and played the turning or lifting ball with the ease of a master craftsman. When assisted by Wright in a last-wicket stand of 45, Hutton even looked capable of carrying England through, but Wright succumbed to temptation to hook the last ball before lunch. Hutton's was an innings to remember.

AUSTRALIA

J. Moroney c Hutton b Bailey	.0 –	lbw b Bailey 0
A.R. Morris lbw b Bedser	.25 –	c Bailey b Bedser 0
R.N. Harvey c Evans b Bedser	.74 –	c Simpson b Bedser 12
K.R. Miller c McIntyre b Wright	.15 –	c Simpson b Bailey 8
A.L. Hassett b Bedser	.8 –	lbw b Bailey 3
S.J. Loxton c Evans b Brown	.24 –	c Bailey b Bedser 0
R.R. Lindwall c Bedser b Bailey	.41 –	not out 0
D. Tallon c Simpson b Brown	.5	
I.W. Johnson c Simpson b Bailey	.23 –	lbw b Bailey 8
W.A. Johnston c Hutton b Bedser	.1	
J. Iverson not out	.1	
B 5, l-b 3, n-b 3 11		N-b 1 1

1/0 2/69 3/116 4/118 5/129   **228**   1/0 2/0 3/0 4/12   (7 wkts, dec.) **32**
6/156 7/172 8/219 9/226   5/19 6/31 7/32

ENGLAND

R.T. Simpson b Johnston	.12 –	b Lindwall 0
C. Washbrook c Hassett b Johnston	.19 –	c Loxton b Lindwall 6
T.G. Evans c Iverson b Johnston	.16 –	c Loxton b Johnston 5
D.C.S. Compton c Lindwall b Johnston	.3 –	c Loxton b Johnston 0
J.G. Dewes c Loxton b Miller	.1 –	b Miller 9
L. Hutton not out	.8 –	not out 62
A.J. McIntyre b Johnston	.1 –	run out 7
F.R. Brown c Tallon b Miller	.4 –	c Loxton b Iverson 17
T.E. Bailey not out	.1 –	c Johnston b Iverson 7
A.V. Bedser (did not bat)	–	c Harvey b Iverson 0
D.V.P. Wright (did not bat)	–	c Lindwall b Iverson 2
B 2, n-b 1 3		B 6, n-b 1 7

1/28 2/49 3/52 4/52   (7 wkts, dec.) **68**   1/0 2/16 3/22 4/23 5/23   **122**
5/56 6/57 7/67   6/30 7/46 8/46 9/77

ENGLAND BOWLING

	O	M	R	W	O	M	R	W
Bailey	12	4	28	3	7	2	22	4
Bedser	16.5	4	45	4	6.5	2	9	3
Wright	16	0	81	1				
Brown	11	0	63	2				

AUSTRALIA BOWLING

	O	M	R	W	O	M	R	W
Lindwall	1	0	1	0	7	3	21	2
Johnston	11.2	1	35	5	11	2	30	2
Miller	10	1	29	2	7	3	21	1
Iverson					13	3	43	4

Umpires: H. Elphinston and A. Barlow.

THIRD TEST MATCH

At Melbourne, December 31, 1954, January 1, 3, 4, 5, 1955. England won by 128 runs at nineteen minutes past one on the fifth day with a day to spare. As in the previous Test, the combined speed of Tyson and Statham proved too much for Australia and again the two young amateur batsmen, Cowdrey (102) and May (91), carried the England batting on a sporting pitch which was said to have been doctored on the Sunday. Certainly large cracks were evident on Saturday yet on Monday these had closed and for a time the surface behaved more kindly to batsmen. The Victorian Cricket Association and the Melbourne Cricket Club held an inquiry into a report published in *The Age* alleging watering and issued the following statement:

'After a searching inquiry it is emphatically denied that the pitch or any part of the cricket ground has been watered since the commencement of the Third Test match on Friday, December 31.'

With Compton fit England had their strongest side (Bedser again being omitted) and Australia welcomed back Ian Johnson, their captain, and Miller, but Langley, the wicket-keeper, stood down through injury which gave Maddocks his opportunity to make his debut in Test cricket.

This time Hutton, winning the toss, decided to bat, but apart from Cowdrey, Evans and Bailey England made a sorry show. [...] Miller bowled magnificently throughout the ninety minutes before lunch when his figures were 9 overs, 8 maidens, 5 runs, 3 wickets. There were only two scoring strokes against him, a cover drive for 3 by Compton and one for 2 by Cowdrey. As Miller's knee was still suspect Johnson later preferred to conserve his energy for batting. Hutton, troubled by a heavy cold, decided only at the last minute to play.

So England faced the second day knowing that yet again the bowlers must rescue them from a crisis, and thanks to Tyson and Statham ably assisted by Bailey and Appleyard the first eight Australian wickets fell for 151. Hutton used his bowlers in short spells, for the heat was stifling. As Compton could not field, having bruised his thumb when he fell to a bouncer, Wilson acted as substitute, excelling in the leg trap.

Maddocks, who had kept wicket neatly and efficiently, rallied Australia. Arriving when six men had gone for 115 he saw the total to 188 for eight at the close, having made 36 in two and a quarter hours. Maddocks batted another half-hour making top score, 47. He and Johnson added 54 and with Johnson lasting altogether two hours Australia gained a lead of 40, their last four wickets adding 116 against England's 22.

It was essential that the early England batsmen did not let down their side a second time and the arrears were cleared before a turning ball across the wicket took Edrich's off stump. So at eight minutes to three May joined Hutton and proceeded to play masterly cricket in which the straight drive predominated. There was always the possibility that he might be trapped by a 'creeper', but May watched the ball intently. At 96 he saw Hutton fall to one which moved fast and low from outside the off stump. The captain had served his side well by remaining nearly two and a half hours and giving a fine example of watchfulness and concentration. [...] On the fourth day May soon left having batted three hours twenty minutes and hit eight 4's. Bailey defended for two and three-quarter hours but Evans and Wardle hit gaily, Wardle taking 16 in one over from

Johnston and 14 from the next by Johnson. Actually Wardle hit 38 out of 46 in forty minutes, but this time the rest of the tail failed so that Australia were left to make 240 to win.

A superb right-hand catch by Cowdrey at forward short-leg when he disposed of Morris brought England their first success at 23, but in order to keep Miller fresh, Benaud came next and both he and Favell exercised great care until Appleyard yorked Favell. Nearly half an hour remained that day and Benaud (19) and Harvey (9) raised the total to 79 for two.

This meant that Australia still required 165, a task that seemed far from impossible. The pitch was worn and the experts predicted that England must look to Appleyard, pointing out that the conditions were made for his off spin, and probably they were right, but Tyson and Statham saw England home without Hutton having to look elsewhere for any bowling. [...] A wonderful leg-side catch by Evans when Harvey glanced the seventh ball of the day heralded the collapse. The loss of Harvey was a terrible blow to Australia and with Benaud hooking too soon and Edrich catching Miller at slip from a ball which lifted, Tyson claimed three wickets in 21 balls in the first half-hour. [...] Evans took his third catch, this time from Johnston high with the left hand, Australia being all out in three hours and five minutes. [...]

ENGLAND

L. Hutton c Hole b Miller 12	– lbw b Archer 42
W.J. Edrich c Lindwall b Miller 4	– b Johnston 13
P.B.H. May c Benaud b Lindwall 0	– b Johnston 91
M.C. Cowdrey b Johnson 102	– b Benaud 7
D.C.S. Compton c Harvey b Miller 4	– c Maddocks b Archer 23
T.E. Bailey c Maddocks b Johnston 30	– not out 24
T.G. Evans lbw b Archer 20	– c Maddocks b Miller 22
J.H. Wardle b Archer 0	– b Johnson 38
F.H. Tyson b Archer 6	– c Harvey b Johnston 6
J.B. Statham b Archer 3	– c Favell b Johnston 0
R. Appleyard not out 1	– b Johnston 6
B 9 9	B 2, l-b 4, w 1 7

1/14 2/21 3/29 4/41 5/115   **191**   1/40 2/96 3/128 4/173 5/185   **279**
6/169 7/181 8/181 9/190   6/211 7/257 8/273 9/273

AUSTRALIA

L. Favell lbw b Statham 25	– b Appleyard 30
A.R. Morris lbw b Tyson 3	– c Cowdrey b Tyson 4
K.R. Miller c Evans b Statham 7	– c Edrich b Tyson 6
R.N. Harvey b Appleyard 31	– c Evans b Tyson 11
G.B. Hole b Tyson 11	– c Evans b Statham 5
R. Benaud c sub b Appleyard 15	– b Tyson 22
R.G. Archer b Wardle 23	– b Statham 15
L. Maddocks c Evans b Statham 47	– b Tyson 0
R.R. Lindwall b Statham 13	– lbw b Tyson 0
I.W. Johnson not out 33	– not out 4
W.A. Johnston b Statham 11	– c Evans b Tyson 0
B 7, l-b 3, n-b 2 12	B 1, l-b 13 14

1/15 2/38 3/43 4/65 5/92 6/115   **231**   1/23 2/57 3/77 4/86 5/87   **111**
7/134 8/151 9/205   6/97 7/98 8/98 9/110

AUSTRALIA BOWLING

	O	M	R	W	O	M	R	W
Lindwall	13	0	59	1	18	3	52	0
Miller	11	8	14	3	18	6	35	1
Archer	13.6	4	33	4	24	7	50	2
Benaud	7	0	30	0	8	2	25	1
Johnston	12	6	26	1	24.5	2	85	5
Johnson	11	3	20	1	8	2	25	1

ENGLAND BOWLING

	O	M	R	W	O	M	R	W
Tyson	21	2	68	2	12.3	1	27	7
Statham	16.3	0	60	5	11	1	38	2
Bailey	9	1	33	0	3	0	14	0
Appleyard	11	3	38	2	4	1	17	1
Wardle	6	0	20	1	1	0	1	0

Umpires: M.J. McInnes and C. Hoy.

SECOND TEST MATCH

At Lord's, June 21, 22, 23, 25, 26, 1956. Australia won by 185 runs and gained their first Test victory in England since 1948 at The Oval. They went in to the match still without a win against a county side, but proved conclusively that their early form could not be taken as a true guide. The team played splendidly together, took a firm grip on the game and never relaxed. There were several splendid individual performances, notably by Miller, Benaud and Langley, but it was really a triumph of teamwork. England, well served in bowling and fielding, twice failed with the bat. [...]

After nearly three weeks of intermittent rain the weather improved shortly before the match and the pitch rolled out firm and easy-paced, but throughout the game fast and fast-medium bowlers were able to make the ball move appreciably off the ground and this resulted in many snicks. In addition batsmen frequently attempted strokes but missed the ball altogether.

McDonald and Burke did Australia a great service when, after Johnson won the toss, they opened with a stand of 137. This was the best start for Australia against England for 26 years. In 1930 Woodfull and Ponsford began with 162 at The Oval. Although they had one or two anxious moments later, Australia never really looked back after this promising send-off. Burke, who batted so well in the second innings at Nottingham, again showed his soundness. The score reached 70 at lunch time but might have ended soon afterwards, May missing a sharp chance in the gully off Statham with McDonald 43. Burke, when 45, cut a ball only a little above May, crouching at second slip, another possible chance, and not until the stand had lasted three hours fifty minutes did England gain their first success. Then Bailey, in the course of four balls, sent back McDonald and Harvey and eased England's anxieties.

Trueman, at second slip, hampered somewhat by Cowdrey at first slip, held an excellent catch low with his left hand to dismiss McDonald. Soon after tea, Burke, who batted four hours ten minutes, was drawn forward by Laker and stumped. That ended England's success on the first day. Bad light held up play for fifty-two minutes until ten past six and in the last twenty minutes May, who had an unhappy time, missed another sharp chance at second slip offered by Burge, when 16, off Trueman.

Australia finished with 180 for three, the outcome of six hours' play, but next day lost their last seven wickets for 105. England fought back splendidly, only one stand checking them, that between Mackay and Archer, who put on 53 for the sixth wicket. Mackay, the left-hander, relied on dead-bat tactics and rarely attempted a scoring stroke. He stayed two hours forty minutes for 38.

As in the first Test, Australia were soon plagued by injury. After sending down only 29 balls at the start of his Test career, Crawford pulled a muscle at the back of his thigh and could not bowl again in the match. That made Australia's eventual victory even more creditable, but once more it threw a heavy strain on Miller and Archer, who again responded magnificently.

Richardson and Cowdrey failed to repeat their first Test success. Richardson, repeatedly sparring at off-side balls, eventually touched one to the wicket-keeper and Graveney was soon bowled. England looked to be recovering from these two early disasters with Cowdrey and May batting well, but the first of three really brilliant catches in the match ended the stand. Cowdrey hit a ball with tremendous power, but Benaud, in the gulley, flung up his hands and held on to it with everyone looking towards the boundary. The force of the ball knocked Benaud backwards.

At the close of the second day England were 211 behind, only 179 having been scored throughout the six hours. Saturday provided a most exciting day's cricket as first one side and then the other gained the upper hand. May, missed at first slip off Miller when 45, batted two and a half hours for 63 and Bailey gave a typically defiant display, but the others failed and England out for 171 were 114 behind. Miller, bowling for long spells and moving the ball either way at varying pace, took half the wickets for 72.

Australia's long lead looked like being decisive, but great-hearted bowling by Trueman and fine fielding put England back in the game. First Cowdrey in the gulley held a fine low right-handed catch almost as good as that by Benaud, to break the opening stand. Harvey took ten off the first three balls he received and was out to the fourth, brilliantly taken at short fine leg by Bailey, who dived full length and held a genuine leg-glide with his right arm outstretched just off the ground.

These two great efforts inspired the Englishmen, particularly Trueman, who put every ounce of energy into his work and bowled really fast. He had Burke caught at first slip, yorked Burge and after Bailey had dismissed Archer, returned for a final spell and sent back Miller, Evans holding another fine catch at the wicket. Australia finished the third day with six men out for 115, only 229 ahead. Trueman took four of the wickets for 38.

At that point the game looked evenly balanced, but from Monday morning Australia took control. Benaud set about the bowling so wholeheartedly that England's chances soon waned. Mackay made a passive partner for Benaud. Between them they put on 117 for the seventh wicket of which Benaud made 97, including one 6 and fourteen 4's. Trying a big hit to complete his century shortly after Trueman took the new ball, Benaud skied a catch behind the stumps. He batted two hours twenty-three minutes and was one of the few batsmen in the match willing to attack. His previous best score against England was only 34. Mackay, even more stubborn than in the first innings, spent four hours twenty-five minutes over 31, one of the slowest Test innings on record. He averaged seven runs an hour.

England were set the formidable task of scoring 372 to win with eight hours forty minutes to bat. They soon ran into trouble, Richardson again being caught at the wicket. Cowdrey and Graveney showed no inclination to force matters, but their caution did not help and Graveney was second out at 59. The final day began with England 72 for two and again they were forced to struggle. Their lack of enterprise enabled the Australians to throw all their efforts into winning the match without worrying about the possibilities of England getting the runs. Watson was bowled when hitting across a full toss and Cowdrey, after batting just over three hours for 27, was lbw at 91.

Johnson set a close, attacking field, particularly to Cowdrey, and Burge stood astonishingly close at forward short leg, barely two yards from the bat. At one point May, after a word with Cowdrey, spoke to Johnson, but apart from moving round a little squarer, Burge remained almost in touching distance from Cowdrey. While May and Bailey were together there seemed a faint chance that England might save the game, but the end was in sight when Bailey fell just before lunch. May, missed at the wicket when 35, continued his stubborn resistance, but apart from a quickly hit 20 by Evans, no one else did much.

May had just passed his third fifty in successive innings against Australia when he edged a catch to the wicket-keeper. He batted a little over two hours. The remaining three wickets went down for six runs and at seven minutes to three o'clock the match was over. Miller took five more wickets and made his match analysis ten for 152, a great performance for a 36-year-old fast-medium bowler.

No fewer than 21 wickets fell to catches behind the stumps. Evans did well at the wicket for England, holding six catches and making one stumping, but Langley achieved an even better performance for Australia. He established a new Test record for a wicket-keeper by helping to dismiss nine men in the match. [...]

AUSTRALIA

C.C. McDonald c Trueman b Bailey	78	– c Cowdrey b Bailey	26
J.W. Burke st Evans b Laker	65	– c Graveney b Trueman	16
R.N. Harvey c Evans b Bailey	0	– c Bailey b Trueman	10
P. Burge b Statham	21	– b Trueman	14
K.R. Miller b Trueman	28	– c Evans b Trueman	30
K. Mackay c Bailey b Laker	38	– c Evans b Statham	31
R.G. Archer b Wardle	28	– c Evans b Bailey	1
R. Benaud b Statham	5	– c Evans b Trueman	97
I.W. Johnson c Evans b Trueman	6	– lbw b Bailey	17
G.R. Langley c Bailey b Laker	14	– not out	7
P. Crawford not out	0	– lbw b Bailey	0
L-b	2	B 2, l-b 2, n-b 4	8

1/137 2/137 3/151 4/185 5/196   **285**   1/36 2/47 3/69 4/70 5/79   **257**
6/249 7/255 8/265 9/285   6/112 7/229 8/243 9/257

ENGLAND

P.E. Richardson c Langley b Miller 9	– c Langley b Archer .... .21
M.C. Cowdrey c Benaud b Mackay .... .23	– lbw b Benaud .... .27
T.W. Graveney b Miller 5	– c Langley b Miller .... .18
P.B.H. May b Benaud .... .63	– c Langley b Miller .... .53
W. Watson c Benaud b Miller 6	– b Miller .... .18
T.E. Bailey b Miller .... .32	– c Harvey b Archer .... .18
T.G. Evans st Langley b Benaud 0	– c Langley b Miller .... .20
J.C. Laker b Archer .... .12	– c Langley b Archer 4
J.H. Wardle c Langley b Archer 0	– b Miller 0
F.S. Trueman c Langley b Miller 7	– b Archer 2
J.B. Statham not out 0	– not out 0
L-b 14 14	L-b 5 5

1/22 2/32 3/60 4/87 5/128   **171**   1/35 2/59 3/87 4/91 5/142   **186**
6/128 7/161 8/161 9/170   6/175 7/180 8/184 9/184

ENGLAND BOWLING

	O	M	R	W	O	M	R	W
Statham	35	9	70	2	26	5	59	1
Trueman	28	6	54	2	28	2	90	5
Bailey	34	12	72	2	24.5	8	64	4
Laker	29.1	10	47	3	7	3	17	0
Wardle	20	7	40	1	7	2	19	0

AUSTRALIA BOWLING

	O	M	R	W	O	M	R	W
Miller	34.1	9	72	5	36	12	80	5
Crawford	5	2	4	0				
Archer	23	9	47	2	31.2	8	71	4
Mackay	11	3	15	1				
Benaud	9	2	19	2	28	14	27	1
Johnson					4	2	3	0

Umpires: E. Davies and F.S. Lee.

FOURTH TEST MATCH

At Manchester, July 26, 27, 28, 30, 31, 1956. England won by an innings and 170 runs, with just over an hour to spare and so retained the 'Ashes'. This memorable game will always be known as 'Laker's Match' because of the remarkable performance by the Surrey off-break bowler in taking nine wickets for 37 runs in the first innings and ten wickets for 53 in the second. Laker broke all the more important bowling records in the history of cricket. [...] The excitement came towards the last day, first when England were trying hard to make up for the time lost by rain to gain the victory which would settle the destination of the 'Ashes', and later as Laker drew nearer and nearer his ten wickets in the innings. The controversy arose over the preparation of the pitch and for days cricketers, officials, critics and the general cricketing public could talk of little else. [...]

May won the toss for the third time in the series and he gave England a big advantage. The pitch was completely useless to fast and fast-medium bowlers and Richardson and Cowdrey, as at Nottingham, gave delightful displays. They took command from the first over and in three hours ten minutes scored 174 for the opening stand. This was England's best start against Australia since 1938 when L. Hutton and C.J. Barnett began with 219 at Trent Bridge. Both batsmen went all out for their strokes and their perfect understanding in running enabled them to offset the value of Australia's defensive field.

Cowdrey, strong in driving, was first to leave, but Richardson did not survive much longer, batting three hours forty minutes for 104, his first Test century. Most of eleven 4's, the same number as Cowdrey, came from well-timed leg-side strokes, but he also brought off some good cover drives, notably two in an over from Lindwall which were models of execution.

Sheppard and May continued the mastery of the Australian attack, but towards tea time, puffs of dust became noticeable when the ball landed and it seemed that the pitch was breaking up unusually early. Johnson and Benaud, the Australian spin bowlers, were unable to exploit the conditions and England finished the first day with a total of 307 for three. Towards the close May was caught off a quickly spun and lifting leg-break after helping Sheppard add 93. A curiosity was that the first five England batsmen were all amateurs, something that had last happened against Australia in 1899 when C.B. Fry, A.C. MacLaren, K.S. Ranjitsinhji, C.L. Townsend and F.S. Jackson were the men concerned.

Mutterings about the pitch could be heard that evening, but they rose to full fury next day. [...] Australia began their reply just after half-past two and before play ended on the second day they had lost eleven wickets. McDonald and Burke began steadily with a stand of 48, but they had to fight hard against the spin of Laker and Lock, who were brought on early. Laker did not start his devastating work until switched to the Stretford end, from where he took each of his nineteen wickets. McDonald and Harvey fell at the same total and after tea, taken at 62 for two, the last eight wickets went in thirty-five minutes for 22 runs. Lock took his only wicket with the first ball after the interval and Laker did the rest, his after tea spell being seven wickets for eight runs in 22 balls. While admitting that Laker spun his off-breaks appreciably, the Australian batsmen gave a sorry display and appeared to give up too easily.

Following on 375 behind, Australia were unfortunate to lose McDonald, who retired with a knee injury after scoring 11. Harvey replaced him and was out first ball, hitting a full toss into the hands of short mid-on. Harvey failed to score in either innings. Australia finished the day with one wicket down for 51 and the controversial storm broke that night.

Accusations were made that the pitch had been prepared specially for England's spin bowlers and these were denied by the Lancashire authorities. The Australians were said to be extremely bitter over the condition of the pitch, but their captain, Johnson, declined to comment on the subject. The arguments continued over the week-end and not until Laker's wonderful bowling on the last day overshadowed everything did they abate.

The weather changed completely on Saturday, when rain allowed only three-quarters of an hour's cricket between ten minutes past two and five minutes to three.

In that brief period Australia added six runs and lost the wicket of Burke. Sunday was an atrocious day and Monday was almost as bad. In two spells of forty-five minutes and fifteen minutes Australia took their score to 84 without further loss. Conditions were terrible for cricket, a fierce wind making batting and bowling extremely difficult. Lignum bails were used and were most successful, not once being blown off.

England looked like being robbed of victory by the weather but it improved considerable on the last day and play began only ten minutes late. The soaking the pitch received left it slow and easy-paced and by fighting, determined cricket, McDonald and Craig remained together until lunch time when the score was 112 for two with four hours left.

Shortly before the interval the sun appeared and almost immediately the ball began to spin quickly. Afterwards Laker began another devastating spell, sending back Craig, Mackay, Miller and Archer in nine overs for three runs. Craig, who helped McDonald add 59, gave a fine, courageous display for four hours twenty minutes; the other three failed to score, Mackay, like his fellow left-hander, Harvey, for the second time in the match. Benaud stayed with McDonald for an hour and a quarter to tea when, with an hour and fifty-five minutes left, England needed to capture four wickets.

Occasionally Laker changed ends, but only when he returned to the Stretford end did he continue his success. After tea the ball spun quicker than at any time in the match and Australia's last hope vanished when McDonald fell to the second ball. His 89, made in five hours thirty-seven minutes, showed that the bowling could be played by determined concentration and he deserved the highest praise for his great effort.

The tension mounted as Laker captured his eighth and ninth wickets. There was never a question of giving Laker his tenth wicket for England's only thought was victory. Lock repeatedly beat the bat, but it was not his match and at twenty-seven minutes past five a great cheer went up as Laker successfully appealed to the umpire, Lee, for lbw against Maddocks. The match was over and Laker had taken all ten wickets.

He earned his triumph by remarkable control of length and spin and it is doubtful whether he bowled more than six bad length balls throughout the match. As Johnson said afterwards: 'When the controversy and side issues of the match are forgotten, Laker's wonderful bowling will remain.'

That night the rain returned and the following day not a ball could be bowled in any of the first-class matches, so it can be seen how close was England's time margin, and how the greatest bowling feat of all time nearly did not happen.

ENGLAND

P.E. Richardson c Maddocks b Benaud	104	
M.C. Cowdrey c Maddocks b Lindwall	80	
Rev. D.S. Sheppard b Archer	113	
P.B.H. May c Archer b Benaud	43	
T.E. Bailey b Johnson	20	
C. Washbrook lbw b Johnson	6	
A.S.M. Oakman c Archer b Johnson	10	

T.G. Evans st Maddocks b Johnson 47
J.C. Laker run out 3
G.A.R. Lock not out 25
J.B. Statham c Maddocks b Lindwall 0

B 2, l-b 5, w 1 8

1/174 2/195 3/288 4/321 5/327   **459**
6/339 7/401 8/417 9/458

AUSTRALIA

C.C. McDonald c Lock b Laker	.32 – c Oakman b Laker	.89
J.W. Burke c Cowdrey b Lock	.22 – c Lock b Laker	.33
R.N. Harvey b Laker	.0 – c Cowdrey b Laker	.0
I.D. Craig lbw b Laker	.8 – lbw b Laker	.38
K.R. Miller c Oakman b Laker	.6 – b Laker	.0
K. Mackay c Oakman b Laker	.0 – c Oakman b Laker	.0
R.G. Archer st Evans b Laker	.6 – c Oakman b Laker	.0
R. Benaud c Statham b Laker	.0 – b Laker	.18
R.R. Lindwall not out	.6 – c Lock b Laker	.8
L. Maddocks b Laker	.4 – lbw b Laker	.2
I.W. Johnson b Laker	.0 – not out	.1
	B 12, l-b 4	.16

1/48 2/48 3/62 4/62 5/62   **84**   1/28 2/55 3/114 4/124 5/130   **205**
6/73 7/73 8/78 9/84   6/130 7/181 8/198 9/203

AUSTRALIA BOWLING

	O	M	R	W	O	M	R	W
Lindwall	21.3	6	63	2				
Miller	21	6	41	0				
Archer	22	6	73	1				
Johnson	47	10	151	4				
Benaud	47	17	123	2				

ENGLAND BOWLING

	O	M	R	W	O	M	R	W
Statham	6	3	6	0	16	9	15	0
Bailey	4	3	4	0	20	8	31	0
Laker	16.4	4	37	9	51.2	23	53	10
Lock	14	3	37	1	55	30	69	0
Oakman					8	3	21	0

Umpires: F.S. Lee and E. Davies.

SECOND TEST MATCH

At Melbourne, December 31, 1958 January 1, 2, 4, 5, 1959. Australia won by eight wickets. England were set back on their heels from the start when Davidson took threee wickets in a sensational over and although Statham also bowled finely the tourists never really recovered. The match produced a hostile bowling effort by the left-arm Meckiff whose jerky action brought much criticism. [...] May, winning the toss on a fairly well-grassed pitch, again decided to bat first. The start was amazing for in the third over of the day Davidson sent back Richardson, Watson and Graveney with the first, fifth and sixth deliveries. Richardson snicked a catch to the wicket-keeper. Watson fell to a full-toss and Graveney mistimed the pace of the ball off the pitch. Davidson took these wickets in his first fourteen balls for four runs, all conceded in his first over.

Bailey and May fought back gallantly. Though instructed to keep up an end and give the strike to freer stroke-makers, Bailey realised that the situation demanded aggressiveness and he brought off many forceful drives and cuts. Cowdrey then helped May hold the fort against the best bowling Benaud could bring against them. Off-driving stylishly, May mastered pace and spin bowlers and the fifth pair were still together at the close with the total 173 for four. May had been fortunate to receive a life when 20 for Benaud, diving to take a return catch, missed the ball when his knee knocked against his hand.

The second day produced exciting fluctuations of fortune. In the first eight overs May and Cowdrey hit 33, then the new ball, taken at 206, brought about a second collapse. May fell to a ball which moved in quickly, Evans was caught at backward short-leg, and Cowdrey snicked a catch to the wicket-keeper. May hit eleven 4's in his meritorious display which lasted five and a quarter hours; his stand with Cowdrey occupied just over three hours. [...]

Australia, going in at ten minutes past three, lost Burke to a deadly ball which came back and left him offering no stroke, but McDonald and Harvey defied England till the close while taking the score to 96. Harvey, who ran into his best form, had hit ten 4's in his 60 not out.

On the third day, when the attendance reached 71,295, England fought back in determined fashion. [...] Harvey, forced to struggle for his century, scored twenty singles and only two more 4's while adding the necessary runs, but on passing the hundred he drove and cut more freely. McDonald fell at slip just after lunch, then O'Neill stayed with Harvey till tea. At five o'clock the score stood at 255 for two, but in five dramatic overs O'Neill, Harvey, Simpson and Benaud were out for seven more runs. O'Neill flashed and paid the penalty, Harvey was yorked and Simpson and Benaud were leg-before, wholehearted fast bowling by Statham and Loader thus earning justified reward. Harvey hit sixteen 4's in his highest innings against England and stayed six hours and ten minutes. His partnership with McDonald added 126 in three hours forty minutes and that with O'Neill, who was contained by Lock using six on-side fielders, 118 in two hours and twenty minutes. Australia finished the day 282 for six.

On the Saturday fast bowlers were supreme and fifteen wickets went down for 122 runs, all to the quick men with the exception of Evans who was run out. The day began with Australia losing their last four wickets for 26 runs before lunch. [...]

England had a golden chance after lunch to wipe off their arrears of 49 and gain a grip on the game for the pitch was still unhelpful to spin, but another breakdown ensued. Richardson, flashing at a ball outside the off-stump, was magnificently caught by Harvey diving at slip, and with Watson, Graveney, Bailey – caught off a lifting ball – and Cowdrey leaving in a quick succession half the side were out for 44. May resisted without ever finding it possible to take the offensive but there was no recovery and at 87 Meckiff finished the innings by sending Loader's off-stump cartwheeling yards. [...] The winning hit – a straight drive for four by Burke off Lock – gave Australia victory just before one o'clock. Attendance 230,948; receipts £A46,791 13s. 6d.

ENGLAND

P.E. Richardson c Grout b Davidson	.3 – c Harvey b Meckiff	.2
T.E. Bailey c Benaud b Meckiff	.48 – c Burke b Meckiff	.14
W. Watson b Davidson	.0 – b Davidson	.7
T.W. Graveney lbw b Davidson	.0 – c Davidson b Meckiff	.3
P.B.H. May b Meckiff	.113 – c Davidson b Meckiff	.17
M.C. Cowdrey c Grout b Davidson	.44 – c Grout b Meckiff	.12
T.G. Evans c Davidson b Meckiff	.4 – run out	.11
G.A.R. Lock st Grout b Benaud	.5 – c and b Davidson	.6
J.C. Laker not out	.22 – c Harvey b Davidson	.3
J.B. Statham b Davidson	.13 – not out	.8
P.J. Loader b Davidson	.1 – b Meckiff	.0
B 1, l-b 2, w 3	.6 B 1, l-b 1, n-b 2	.4

1/7 2/7 3/7 4/92 5/210 6/218   **259** 1/3 2/14 3/21 4/27 5/44   **87**
7/218 8/233 9/253   6/57 7/71 8/75 9/80

Bowling: FIRST INNINGS – Davidson 25.5-7-64-6; Meckiff 24-4-69-3; Mackay 9-2-16-0; Benaud 29-7-61-1; Kline 11-2-43-0. SECOND INNINGS – Davidson 15-2-41-3; Meckiff 15.2-3-38-6; Benaud 1-0-4-0.

AUSTRALIA

C.C. McDonald c Graveney b Statham	.47 – lbw b Statham	.5
J.W. Burke b Statham	.3 – not out	.18
R.N. Harvey b Loader	.167 – not out	.7
N. O'Neill c Evans b Statham	.37	
K. Mackay c Evans b Statham	.18	
R. Simpson lbw b Loader	.0	
R. Benaud lbw b Statham	.0	
A.K. Davidson b Statham	.24	
W. Grout c May b Loader	.8 – st Evans b Laker	.12
I. Meckiff b Statham	.0	
L. Kline not out	.1	
L-b 3	.3	

1/11 2/137 3/255 4/257 5/261   **308** 1/6 2/26   **42**
6/262 7/295 8/300 9/300

Bowling: FIRST INNINGS – Statham 28-6-57-7; Loader 27.2-4-97-3; Bailey 16-0-50-0; Laker 12-1-47-0; Lock 17-2-54-0. SECOND INNINGS – Statham 5-1-11-1; Loader 5-1-13-0; Laker 4-1-7-1; Lock 3.1-1-11-0.

Umpires: M.J. McInnes and R. Wright.

FROM NOTES BY THE EDITOR

THE TRUE SPIRIT OF CRICKET

The summer of 1961 brought much satisfaction even if England failed to regain the Ashes from Australia and small attendances at County matches caused alarm. The presence of Richie Benaud and his Australian team contributed to a rekindling of all that is best in cricket. The pattern was set at the end of the previous year at Brisbane where Australia and West Indies played the first tie in the history of Test cricket.

As soon as Benaud arrived in this country, he said his aim was to do away with dull cricket by keeping the game moving and bowling as many overs as possible. He promised there would be no dawdling in the field; the players would move briskly to their positions and in this way keenness and efficiency would be attained. On all controversial issues he and his players intended to leave matters entirely in the hands of the umpires. Benaud proved as good as his word.

THE GAME'S THE THING

Good fellowship and friendliness pervaded the tour and for once the importance of winning a game or a series was not allowed to impinge upon the true spirit of cricket. I have been watching Test cricket for forty years and I cannot recall a more pleasant atmosphere. I am sure that all cricket-lovers will say: Long may it continue.

As for the standard of play in the Tests, both England and Australia have been represented in the past by much stronger sides; yet day after day the struggle was intense, first one side and then the other gaining the upper hand. Surely, there can have been few more dramatic days than the last at Old Trafford, where twice England appeared to have obtained a stranglehold only for Australia to fight back in great style, first with the bat and then with the ball. (*1962*)

SECOND TEST MATCH

At Lord's, June 22, 23, 24, 26, 1961. Australia won by five wickets. They were well on top until a startling collapse occurred when they went in to get 69 for victory. Even so, there seemed little chance of England snatching the match from the fire and the game was over a day and a half early.

Almost throughout, batsmen were worried by the fast bowlers on a lively pitch and there were several cases of knocks and bruises, although fortunately none serious. There were talks from the first day of a ridge at the Nursery end and immediately the match ended M.C.C. called in a team of experts to survey the pitch. They discovered several depressions and M.C.C. stated that they would make an attempt to put things right before the start of 1962. Most of the time the ball flew at the Nursery end but even at the other end the fast bowlers were able to get plenty of lift and anyone who stayed at the crease a long time needed plenty of good fortune, besides determination and courage. [...]

The Australians were without Benaud, because of his damaged shoulder, and Harvey led the side for the first time. [...] Cowdrey retained the captaincy, despite the return of May and yet again he won the toss. That made twelve in succession for England, nine by Cowdrey and three by May. As at Edgbaston, the toss did not help England, for they were soon in difficulties. Davidson made the ball rear around the batsmen's ribs when pitching just short of a length and even off a length at times. Dropped catches looked like being costly. Pullar, when five, offered a simple chance to Burge in the gulley off Davidson, but he added only six. Lawry, at short leg, missed a sharp catch from Dexter off Misson and the same bowler had Subba Row dropped on the leg side by Grout. England appeared to have made the most of these escapes but in the last five minutes before lunch both men were out at the same total, 87.

The Duke of Edinburgh watched the morning's cricket and the players were presented to The Queen before the resumption. Five more wickets fell before tea for only 80 runs, Davidson, McKenzie and Misson all being dangerous. [...] Davidson well earned his five wickets and McKenzie, the only newcomer to Test cricket in the match, supported him well. In the last hour of the first day Australia lost McDonald and Simpson cheaply but Lawry and Harvey prevented further disaster. When bowling McDonald, Statham took his 200th Test wicket, a feat previously accomplished for England only by Alec Bedser.

The second day belonged to Lawry, the tall 24-year-old left-handed batsman from Victoria. He gave a magnificent display of tenacity in his second Test Match and he stayed six hours, ten minutes for 130. During the course of it he became the first Australian to complete 1,000 runs on the tour. The pitch was still awkward, although not quite so bad as on the first day. Harvey helped Lawry add 75 before being caught at first slip after receiving two successive blows in the body.

Dexter captured the valuable wicket of O'Neill without any undue help from the pitch and with four wickets down for 88 Australia were struggling. Then Burge joined Lawry and they added 95. Lawry, extremely strong on the leg-side and solid in defence, completed his maiden Test century in four and three-quarter hours. He was still there when Australia went ahead with four wickets to fall, but was out at 238. He hit eighteen 4's and did not give a chance, although he was occasionally beaten outside the off-stump by Statham.

The last two wickets added 102 and practically ended England's chances of victory. Mackay played another of his stubborn innings and McKenzie and Misson showed remarkably good style and skill for numbers ten and eleven. McKenzie, celebrating his twentieth birthday on the Saturday, helped in a stand of 53 and Misson stayed with Mackay while 49 came for the last wicket.

England, 134 behind, made a lively start, Pullar scoring 24 out of 31 in twenty-five minutes before lunch. Then England's troubles began. Subba was quickly out, Dexter was bowled off his body, Pullar gave a catch at the wicket and Cowdrey presented an easy catch to cover. They were then 84 for four. May and Barrington improved matters with a stand of 47 before Grout held a brilliant one-handed catch when May received another rising ball.

The arrears were cleared with five wickets left, but Illingworth did not last long. Practically everything depended on Barrington, who settled down to a determined effort. Murray provided good support and at the close of the third day England were 44 on with four wickets left. These soon went. Barrington added only seven more, having batted three hours twenty minutes and hit eleven 4's in 66. McKenzie ended the innings by taking three wickets in twelve balls and he finished with five for 37 off 29 overs. Grout held five catches in the innings and eight in a Test for the second time in his career. During the second innings he claimed his 100th Test victim.

Australia needed only 69 for victory, but suddenly ran into trouble against Statham and Trueman, who made the most of the still lively pitch. McDonald and Lawry both went at 15 and two more wickets, those of Harvey and O'Neill, fell at 19.

With their leading batsmen gone Australia unexpectedly found themselves on the run. Had Lock held a difficult chance offered by Burge from the last ball before lunch Australia would have been 35 for five.

Burge ended England's faint hopes with a confident display and although Simpson left with eleven still needed the result was never again in doubt. Burge finished the match with two successive fours off Statham, the game ending at ten minutes to three on the fourth day. Burge made 37 of the last 52 runs in an hour. [...]

ENGLAND

G. Pullar b Davidson	11	c Grout b Misson	42
R. Subba Row lbw b Mackay	48	c Grout b Davidson	8
E.R. Dexter c McKenzie b Misson	27	b McKenzie	17
*M.C. Cowdrey c Grout b McKenzie	16	c Mackay b Misson	7
P.B.H. May c Grout b Davidson	17	c Grout b McKenzie	22
K.F. Barrington c Mackay b Davidson	4	lbw b Davidson	66
R. Illingworth b Misson	13	c Harvey b Simpson	0
†J.T. Murray lbw b Mackay	18	c Grout b McKenzie	25
G.A.R. Lock c Grout b Davidson	5	b McKenzie	1
F.S. Trueman b Davidson	25	c Grout b McKenzie	0
J.B. Statham not out	11	not out	2
L-b 9, w 2	11	B 1, l-b 10, w 1	12

1/26 2/87 3/87 4/111 5/115   **206**   1/33 2/63 3/67 4/80 5/127   **202**
6/127 7/156 8/164 9/167   6/144 7/191 8/199 9/199

Bowling: FIRST INNINGS – Davidson 24.3-6-42-5; McKenzie 26-7-81-1; Misson 16-4-48-2; Mackay 12-3-24-2. SECOND INNINGS – Davidson 24-8-50-2; McKenzie 29-13-37-5; Misson 17-2-66-2; Mackay 8-6-5-0; Simpson 19-10-32-1.

AUSTRALIA

W.M. Lawry c Murray b Dexter	130	c Murray b Statham	1
C.C. McDonald b Statham	4	c Illingworth b Trueman	14
R.B. Simpson c Illingworth b Trueman	0	c Illingworth b Statham	15
*R.N. Harvey c Barrington b Trueman	27	c Murray b Trueman	4
N.C. O'Neill b Dexter	1	b Statham	0
P.J. Burge c Murray b Statham	46	not out	37
A.K. Davidson lbw b Trueman	6	not out	0
K.D. Mackay c Barrington b Illingworth	54		
†A.W.T. Grout lbw b Dexter	0		
G.D. McKenzie b Trueman	34		
F.M. Misson not out	25		
B 1, l-b 12	13		

1/5 2/6 3/81 4/88 5/183   **340**   1/15 2/15 3/19 4/19 5/58   **(5 wkts) 71**
6/194 7/238 8/238 9/291

Bowling: FIRST INNINGS – Statham 44-10-89-2; Trueman 34-3-118-4; Dexter 24-7-56-3; Lock 26-13-48-0; Illingworth 11.3-5-16-1. SECOND INNINGS – Statham 10.5-3-31-3; Trueman 10-0-40-2.

Umpires: C.S. Elliott and W.E. Phillipson.

FOURTH TEST MATCH

At Old Trafford, July 27, 28, 29, 31, August 1, 1961. Australia won by 54 runs and made certain of retaining The Ashes. They deserved great credit for fighting back three times when in difficulties, but England, on top for a large part of the match, disappointed, particularly on the last day. Dropped catches proved costly to England and had an important bearing on the result. The game was intensely keen throughout and was the best of the series. [...]

Benaud won the toss for Australia, who batted on a green pitch which helped the faster bowlers appreciably on the first day. Simpson fell in Statham's first over and, switching ends, the Lancashire fast bowler also dismissed Harvey at 51. O'Neill, never happy, was struck frequently on the thigh and body when facing Flavell and the game had to be held up occasionally while he recovered. Once he vomited when at the bowler's end, but he continued. O'Neill was out when he fell into his wicket in trying a hook. The ball hit him on the wrist and broke a blood vessel in his left forearm, but it was not serious and he continued for the rest of the match. Flavell took his first Test wicket when he bowled Burge shortly after lunch and Australia, despite the sound batting of Lawry, were 106 for four. A little later rain ended play for the day, three and a half hours being lost. Next morning the remaining six wickets fell in an hour and a half for 66, Statham and Dexter each claiming three. Lawry's splendid 74 took three hours. Statham thoroughly deserved his five wickets for 53, frequently beating the batsmen with his swing and movement off the ground.

England lost Subba Row and Dexter cheaply, but gained the upper hand with a third-wicket stand of 111 between Pullar and May. By the close of the second day England, with seven wickets left, were only three runs behind, but they ran into trouble first thing on Saturday, losing May and Close at the same total with 25 added. May missed a century by five runs, being caught at first slip when Grout dived and scooped the ball up for Simpson. May batted just over three and three-quarter hours and hit fourteen 4's. Barrington and Murray carefully put England back on top by adding 60 and another good stand came for the seventh wicket, Barrington and Allen adding 86. Then Simpson quickly ended the innings, but England led by 177.

Lawry and Simpson knocked off 63 of the arrears before the end of play, but England should have ended the stand at 38, Subba Row, at second slip, missing Lawry (25) off Trueman. This proved an expensive mistake for Lawry went on to his second century of the series. The opening stand reached 113. Another fielding lapse occurred when Harvey was dropped in the slips by Close when two and he was missed again in the slips, this time by Barrington off Flavell when 26.

Australia cleared their deficit for the loss of two wickets, but a fine catch by Trueman at backward short leg ended Lawry's stay of four and a half hours. Firm drives and, as usual powerful hooks and leg-side deflections, brought Lawry most of his thirteen 4's. Although O'Neill again received a painful blow on the thigh, he fought hard, but England steadily captured wickets. On the last morning Australia lost three men while adding three runs and the total went from 331 for six to 334 for nine. Allen took all three without cost in 15 balls.

At that point Australia were only 157 on and England looked to have the game comfortably won, but there developed a splendid last-wicket stand between Davidson and

McKenzie. Davidson took 20 in an over off Allen and removed his menace on a pitch taking a fair amount of spin. The other bowlers could make no impression and 98 were added before the innings closed. It was Australia's highest last-wicket Test stand in England. This not only made England's task harder in terms of runs, but it took valuable time away from them. They were set to get 256 in three hours, fifty minutes.

Pullar and Subba Row began with a brisk partnership of 40. Then came a glorious display of controlled hitting by Dexter which put England right up with the clock. Driving with tremendous power and cutting and hooking splendidly, Dexter took only eighty-four minutes to score 76, which included one 6 and fourteen 4's. The second-wicket stand with Subba Row produced 110 in that time.

Suddenly the position changed completely. Benaud, bowling round the wicket and pitching into the rough of Trueman's footholds, brought such a collapse that in twenty minutes to tea England virtually lost the game. After getting Dexter caught at the wicket, Benaud bowled May round his legs, had Close, following one drive for 6, caught at backward square leg and bowled the solid Subba Row.

England resumed after tea needing 93 in eighty-five minutes with only Barrington of their leading batsmen left. When Murray and Barrington fell for the addition of eight all thoughts of an England victory had gone and it became only a question of whether Australia could finish the match in time. They did so with twenty minutes to spare and thus Australia gained their first Test win at Old Trafford since 1902. Benaud claimed six for 70, his best performance against England. Owing to his shoulder trouble he attempted little spin, being content to let the ball do its work on dropping into the rough. [...]

AUSTRALIA

W.M. Lawry lbw b Statham	74	– c Trueman b Allen	102
R.B. Simpson c Murray b Statham	4	– c Murray b Flavell	51
R.N. Harvey c Subba Row b Statham	19	– c Murray b Dexter	35
N.C. O'Neill hit wkt b Trueman	11	– c Murray b Statham	67
P.J. Burge b Flavell	15	– c Murray b Dexter	23
B.C. Booth c Close b Statham	46	– lbw b Dexter	9
K.D. Mackay c Murray b Statham	11	– c Close b Allen	18
A.K. Davidson c Barrington b Dexter	0	– not out	77
*R. Benaud b Dexter	2	– lbw b Allen	1
†A.W.T. Grout c Murray b Dexter	2	– c Statham b Allen	0
G.D. McKenzie not out	1	– b Flavell	32
B 4, l-b 1	5	B 6, l-b 9, w 2	17

1/8 2/51 3/89 4/106 5/150   **190**   1/113 2/175 3/210 4/274 5/290   **432**
6/174 7/185 8/185 9/189   6/296 7/332 8/334 9/334

Bowling: FIRST INNINGS – Trueman 14-1-55-1; Statham 21-3-53-5; Flavell 22-8-61-1; Dexter 6.4-2-16-3. SECOND INNINGS – Statham 44-9-106-1; Trueman 32-6-92-0; Flavell 29.4-4-65-2; Allen 38-25-58-4; Dexter 20-4-61-3; Close 8-1-33-0.

ENGLAND

G. Pullar b Davidson	.63	– c O'Neill b Davidson	.26
R. Subba Row c Simpson b Davidson	.2	– b Benaud	.49
E.R. Dexter c Davidson b McKenzie	.16	– c Grout b Benaud	.76
*P.B.H. May c Simpson b Davidson	.95	– b Benaud	.0
D.B. Close lbw b McKenzie	.33	– c O'Neill b Benaud	.8
K.F. Barrington c O'Neill b Simpson	.78	– lbw b Mackay	.5
†J.T. Murray c Grout b Mackay	.24	– c Simpson b Benaud	.4
D.A. Allen c Booth b Simpson	.42	– c Simpson b Benaud	.10
F.S. Trueman c Harvey b Simpson	.3	– c Benaud b Simpson	.8
J.B. Statham c Mackay b Simpson	.4	– b Davidson	.8
J.A. Flavell not out	.0	– not out	.0
B 2, l-b 4, w 1	.7	B 5, w 2	.7

1/3 2/43 3/154 4/212 5/212 **367** 1/40 2/150 3/150 4/158 5/163 **201**
6/272 7/358 8/362 9/367   6/171 7/171 8/189 9/193

Bowling: FIRST INNINGS – Davidson 39-11-70-3; McKenzie 38-11-106-2; Mackay 40-9-81-1; Benaud 35-15-80-0; Simpson 11.4-4-23-4. SECOND INNINGS – Davidson 14.4-1-50-2; McKenzie 4-1-20-0; Benaud 32-11-70-6; Simpson 8-4-21-1; Mackay 13-7-33-1.

Umpires: John Langridge and W.E. Phillipson.

FROM NOTES BY THE EDITOR

AUSTRALIA'S DEBT TO SIMPSON

[…] That Australia won the rubber and, by virtue of their victory at Headingley, retained The Ashes was due mainly to the ability and leadership of their captain, Bobby Simpson. England looked to be the more likely winners at Trent Bridge and Lord's, but when the weather kept fine at Headingley, Simpson had already imbued his men with a fine team spirit and Burge played the innings of his life, being splendidly supported by Hawke and Grout. Simpson took over the Australian captaincy when his country's resources had been weakened by the departure of Benaud, Davidson, Harvey and Mackay. Then, coming to England, he lost the toss four times to Dexter, but won it when it mattered most, in the vital fourth Test at Old Trafford.

With Australia then one up in the series with two to play, Simpson knew that he had only to avoid defeat in one match to keep those Ashes. So he defied the England bowling for hour after hour while compiling his memorable 311; but by batting into the third day he played into the hands of those critics who see little that is good in cricket. Some blamed the pitch; it was too placid; it lasted too long, and so on. The fact of the matter was that there was a deficiency of bowling in both teams. No one complained about the pitches when Lindwall and Miller were about, or Larwood and Voce, or Tate. Nor when Hammond and Bradman were batting. (*1965*)

THIRD TEST MATCH

At Leeds, July 2, 3, 4, 6, 1964. Australia won by seven wickets with more than a day to spare. At last the weather was fine throughout and Australia, despite a period of tremendous anxiety, finished easy winners of a contest which will always be known as 'Burge's Match'. Fierce controversy raged for several days because many people considered that England lost their chance just after five o'clock on Friday when Titmus was bowling superbly and seven Australian wickets were down for 187. Dexter took the second new ball and relied on Trueman and Flavell to demolish the tail. At that stage, Burge was 38, but Trueman fed him with a generous supply of medium pace long hops and not only did Burge finish with 160, but the last three wickets put on 211 runs thanks to the help he received from Hawke and Grout. So Australia gained a valuable lead of 121 and they never looked back.

[…] Dexter set England a splendid example by his daring stroke play, but Simpson handled his attack astutely and the fielding reached the highest Australian standards. Eight catches – some quite brilliant – were held and none were missed. The bowling honours went to Hawke and McKenzie who attained steady pace and accuracy and were never found wanting in stamina. Australia achieved their most deadly work in the seventy minutes after lunch when they disposed of Dexter, Barrington and Taylor. Hawke's round-the-wicket attack perplexed several batsmen, an exception being Parks who never looked in difficulty and drove especially well, but after tea Hawke ran through the tail with the new ball, taking four wickets for 30 in 13.3 overs. Australia were left to bat for ten minutes, but no sooner had Simpson and Lawry reached the crease than the umpires upheld their appeal for bad light.

Next day, Trueman and Flavell were unable to make any impression and with Simpson and Lawry giving Australia their best start so far with a stand of 50 it seemed almost certain that the England total of 268 would be passed without much difficulty. Timid batsmanship by Redpath led Australia into trouble and although the pitch did not encourage spin at this stage Titmus and Gifford managed to gain control. Titmus proved such a model of accuracy that he bowled from 1.20 p.m. until 5.50 p.m., his figures being 29–17–27–3 and while he operated Australia's fortunes swayed from a total of 95 for one to 187 for seven.

Lawry served Australia splendidly for three hours. He hit ten 4's before Redpath called him for a sharp single and Boycott returned the ball in a flash from third man to the bowler's end. It was on Lawry's departure that Burge began his valuable display. At this stage Titmus's figures were 10–8–3–0. Australia had mustered only four runs in half an hour and Redpath had been batting for two hours, ten minutes when he hit his second boundary only for Gifford to knock back his middle stump in the same over.

Even Burge needed twenty minutes to open his score. Burge broke free with a powerful straight drive at the end of an hour's spell by Gifford during which he conceded only 16 runs in eleven overs. Booth, Cowper (in his first Test), Veivers and McKenzie all failed and so at 187 when Burge had made only 38, Trueman took the new ball in the 89th over. Australia were on their knees, but in the next seven overs from Trueman and Flavell, Burge and Hawke helped themselves to 42 runs and they proceeded to add 105 for the eighth wicket in ninety-nine minutes of which Hawke made 37. So at the end of the second day, Australia's total reached 283 for eight with Burge 100 not out. He reached three figures out of 159 in just over three hours, having excelled with the cut, hook and drive.

Grout is no stranger to helping Australia through a crisis and accompanying Burge to the crease on Saturday morning he promptly showed Trueman that he could punish the long hop as effectively as his partner. Three of these he despatched to the boundary when Trueman's first two overs of the day cost 14. The Burge-Grout partnership produced 89 and England needed a third new ball before a very fine catch by A. Rees (Glamorgan) at mid-wicket ended Burge's great innings. Burge, whose display was reminiscent of S.J. McCabe's 232 at Trent Bridge in 1938, batted five and a quarter hours and hit twenty-four 4's. The whole innings lasted eight hours, ten minutes.

Little went right for England in their second innings. Boycott for the third time in his three Test knocks was caught by Simpson at first slip (a very fine catch) off Corling. Parfitt came next and off the very first ball had a knuckle broken whereupon Edrich and Barrington battled bravely until tea when England were 88 for one. A careless stroke to the very first ball after the interval resulted in Edrich being taken on the leg side but Barrington carried on with commendable enterprise. Dexter, strangely subdued, contributed only 17 in seventy-five minutes and on his departure Barrington, too, decided to concentrate solely on defence. After an appeal against the light was turned down, Barrington, with six minutes to go, was leg-before and so England finished with a total of 157 for four – 36 runs ahead.

England had plenty of time during the week-end to dwell on where they went wrong and plan a recovery. It was reckoned they needed to set Australia about 200 in the fourth innings, but they added no more than 72 more runs on Monday so that Australia had to make only 109 for victory. They owed much to McKenzie who had never bowled better in this country. [...] Lawry soon went, but time was on Australia's side and they had no need to hurry. Apart from a break of two overs which allowed him to switch ends, Titmus bowled through the innings of two and a half hours and at tea when Australia wanted only 18 his figures read: 24–18–12–2. Redpath, almost passive at one period, batted well for his side and he settled the issue with his tenth four, having completed his first Test fifty in England.

ENGLAND

G. Boycott c Simpson b Corling	.38 – c Simpson b Corling	.4
J.H. Edrich c Veivers b McKenzie	.3 – c Grout b McKenzie	.32
*E.R. Dexter c Grout b McKenzie	.66 – c Redpath b Veivers	.17
K.F. Barrington b McKenzie	.29 – lbw b Veivers	.85
P.H. Parfitt b Hawke	.32 – c Redpath b Hawke	.6
K. Taylor c Grout b Hawke	.9 – b Veivers	.15
†J.M. Parks c Redpath b Hawke	.68 – c Booth b McKenzie	.23
F.J. Titmus c Burge b McKenzie	.3 – c Cowper b Corling	.14
F.S. Trueman c Cowper b Hawke	.4 – not out	.12
N. Gifford not out	.1 – b McKenzie	.1
J.A. Flavell c Redpath b Hawke	.5 – c Simpson b Corling	.5
L-b 9, n-b 1	.10 B 6, l-b 6, w 1, n-b 2	.15

1/17 2/74 3/129 4/138 5/163   **268**   1/13 2/88 3/145 4/157 5/169   **229**
6/215 7/232 8/260 9/263   6/184 7/192 8/199 9/212

Bowling: FIRST INNINGS – McKenzie 26-7-74-4; Hawke 31.3-11-75-5; Corling 24-7-50-1; Veivers 17-3-35-0; Simpson 5-0-24-0. SECOND INNINGS – McKenzie 28-8-53-3; Corling 17.5-6-52-3; Hawke 13-1-28-1; Veivers 30-12-70-3; Simpson 1-0-11-0.

AUSTRALIA

W.M. Lawry run out	.78	– c Gifford b Trueman	.1
*R.B. Simpson b Gifford	.24	– c Barrington b Titmus	.30
I.R. Redpath b Gifford	.20	– not out	.58
P.J. Burge c sub b Trueman	.160	– b Titmus	.8
B.C. Booth st Parks b Titmus	.4	– not out	.12
R.M. Cowper b Trueman	.2		
T.R. Veivers c Parks b Titmus	.8		
G.D. McKenzie b Titmus	.0		
N.J.N. Hawke c Parfitt b Trueman	.37		
†A.T.W. Grout lbw b Titmus	.37		
G.E. Corling not out	.2		
B 1, l-b 8, w 2, n-b 6	.17	B 1, l-b 1	.2

1/50 2/124 3/129 4/154 5/157   **389**   1/3 2/45 3/64   **(3 wkts) 111**
6/178 7/178 8/283 9/372

Bowling: FIRST INNINGS – Trueman 24.3-2-98-3; Flavell 29-5-97-0; Gifford 34-15-62-2; Dexter 19-5-40-0; Titmus 50-24-69-4; Taylor 2-0-6-0. SECOND INNINGS – Trueman 7-0-28-1; Titmus 27-19-25-2; Gifford 20-5-47-0; Dexter 3-0-9-0.

Umpires: C.S. Elliott and W.F. Price.

FOURTH TEST MATCH

At Old Trafford, July 23, 24, 25, 27, 28, 1964. Drawn. For all the remarkable personal achievements in the match, a bad taste was left in the mouth of the cricket enthusiasts who saw Australia retain the Ashes. Simpson's strategy, with his team one up and two to play, was to make certain that Australia did not lose. Dexter, with England kept in the field until the third morning was well advanced, had no hope of winning and so a boring situation resulted in which twenty-eight and a quarter hours of play were needed to produce a decision on the first innings! […] Simpson's first Test century in 30 matches was the highest ever made at Old Trafford. Lasting twelve and three-quarter hours, it was also the longest innings ever played against England. […] What would have happened had Dexter won the toss can only be conjectured, for McKenzie, following a severe stomach upset a few days earlier, was not at his fittest. On the easy-paced turf Australia, setting themselves to build a formidable total to stop England winning, scored 253 for two wickets on the first day.

There was no encouragement to bowlers from the opening delivery sent down by Rumsey to his rival left-hander Lawry, and although Cartwright, by control of length at medium-pace with some movement off the pitch occasionally worried the batsmen – he had Simpson when 33 missed at the wicket on the leg side – the attack posed no real danger. Lawry adept in hooking, took a 6 apiece off Price, Cartwright and Rumsey before hitting his first four with his score at 64, but the stroke-play generally was far from forceful. Methodically, the batsmen wore down the toiling bowlers in sunshine. Titmus had a long bowl, but Dexter who set largely defensive fields did not employ Mortimore until twenty past three with the score 173 and Lawry, with a cover-drive off the Gloucestershire bowler, reached his third hundred against

England out of 179 in five minutes under four hours. His sound, but unenterprising innings, ended three quarters of an hour later when, for the third time in Tests in the current series, and for the fifth time in the season, he was run out when Mortimore, the bowler, made a brilliant stop. The partnership produced 201, and Lawry included five 4's besides the three 6's, in his 106. […]

On the second day, Simpson and his colleagues maintained their dominance yet seldom became free-scoring. Simpson again batted in subdued, if almost faultless, fashion and was barracked before displaying some of his characteristic cuts and drives. O'Neill had given promise of brightening proceedings before a ball which swung across knocked back his leg-stump at 318. […] In company with Booth, Simpson, who had reached 160 at rather less than 20 an hour since he began, at last decided to open his shoulders. He took 11 in an over off Price with the new ball, but soon reverted to his sedate mood. When 203, Simpson could have been run out backing-up if Titmus, about to bowl, had not been chivalrously inclined, and the Middlesex bowler inappropriately suffered when the Australian captain, bestirring himself again, hit 14 off him in one over.

At the end of another hot day, Simpson had been in twelve hours for 265 out of a score of 570 for four, and Booth, who had scored with firm strokes, was 82 in an unfinished partnership of 188. Cartwright, England's best bowler, had sent down 77 overs for 118 runs and two wickets.

Simpson continued Australia's and his own innings next morning and in the light of subsequent events his policy, however unpalatable it was to cricket lovers, proved correct. Had he declared the previous evening and managed to snatch a couple of wickets a way to victory might have been open to him, but that again is mere surmise. In the event, Simpson made sure that Australia would not lose by extending his team's innings for another hour and raising the total 656 for eight before declaring. In that time, the batting, for the first time in the match, was consistently entertaining, bringing 86 runs for four wickets. Simpson had a chance of passing the world record Test score of 365 not out by G.S. Sobers, but this did not affect his attitude. He made no attempt to play safe for the purpose and after straight-driving Mortimore for 6 and hitting four more 4's he fell at the wicket paying the penalty for a slashed stroke played off Price with rather reckless abandon.

The crowd, having overlooked the dull spells of his batting, generously gave him an ovation for his score of 311 out of 646 for six. He defied England for three minutes under twelve and three-quarter hours, and in addition to his 6 he hit twenty-three 4's. His stand with Booth, fifth to leave, well caught off a stiff return at 601, added 219 in just over three and a half hours. Booth, who missed a hundred by two, hit one 6 and ten 4's. The innings lasted thirteen hours. Price took three for 183. He, like his teammates, had his edge blunted by the unresponsive pitch. Barrington, with his leg-breaks, was never tried, a tactical shortcoming by Dexter.

When England began batting at twenty to one on Saturday, there seemed little hope of them making 457 to avoid following-on, and what optimism did exist soon received a check when Edrich edged the now fully-recovered fast-medium McKenzie to second slip with the score 15. Then came a renewal of hope with Boycott and Dexter driving and cutting excellently. Simpson unavailingly challenged Dexter with spin and flight and the second wicket brought 111 before Boycott, having stayed three hours, played too soon at a slower ball from McKenzie and was bowled. A shaky start sent Barrington into his shell and Dexter, too, became so restrained that slow handclapping broke out. At one stage Barrington's disinclination to make a forcing stroke encouraged Simpson to employ four short-legs, for Veivers. With the score carried to 162 for two, Dexter 71 and Barrington 20, bad light stopped play fifty minutes early – a disappointing end to the day for a crowd of 30,000.

Wanting 295 more to make Australia bat again, England had far their best day on Monday when Dexter carried his score to 174 and Barrington reached 153 not out. Dexter, who hit his eighth Test hundred, was missed twice by McKenzie at backward short leg when 74 and 97, and narrowly escaped being given out at 108 when Burge said he did not really know whether he had made a catch low down at cover, but the later part of Dexter's innings provided much pleasure for the onlookers. From lunch, taken at 247 for two, the batsmen were masters. In turn they forced the game with drives, square-cuts, late-cuts and full-blooded leg-side strokes which punished quick and slow bowlers alike. Poor fielding swelled the scoring and Barrington was fortunate, when 99, that McKenzie, at short-slip failed to hold a cut.

Barrington had played 44 Test innings in England without making more than 87. In one spell of ten overs, Simpson conceded 38 runs and the partnership passed 200 in ten minutes over four hours. Dexter, with a majestic cover-drive off Veivers, exceeded K.S. Ranjitsinhji's 154 not out for England at Old Trafford in 1896, and at tea, with 111 runs having come since lunch, England wanted 99 more to save the follow-on. Afterwards, England's rising hopes received an unexpected setback in the dismissal of Dexter, third out, at 372. Hawke and Veivers, doing sufficient to keep the batsmen watchful, made runs scarce enough to set impatient onlookers slow handclapping, and whether or not Dexter had his concentration disturbed he eventually played across, in somewhat casual style, at a ball pitched well up to him and was bowled.

He, too, was given an ovation for his fine innings, including twenty-two 4s, for which he had kept the Australians at bay for eight hours. The stand of 246 in five hours and twenty-five minutes fell 16 short of the record England third-wicket partnership against Australia of 262 by W.R. Hammond and D.R. Jardine at Adelaide, in 1928–29. [...] Dexter's example counted for nothing. Barrington pushed and deflected when he could have driven powerfully and the opportunity to encourage his partners and thoroughly discourage his rivals was lost. Parks hit only three 4's in his 60 which occupied three hours and twenty minutes, Titmus made nine runs in almost an hour and when Barrington was lbw, seventh to go, at 594 he had been at the crease for eleven hours and twenty-five minutes. He hit twenty-six 4's in his 256.

With McKenzie enlivened and Veivers still pitching a length, the issue was soon settled after Barrington's departure on the stroke of tea, and England, though having kept Australia in the field over two hours longer than the tourists had kept them, finished 45 behind. McKenzie's late successes, achieved by change of pace and deceptive movement, gave him a fine analysis in such a huge total, but the endurance of Veivers, who sent down 46.1 overs unchanged on the last day, was just as remarkable. The Australians had to bat a second time for the closing five minutes, and it was a suitable ending, seeing what indecisive cricket had gone before, that Simpson and Lawry were bowled to by Barrington and Titmus using an old ball. [...]

AUSTRALIA

W.M. Lawry run out .106	– not out 0
*R.B. Simpson c Parks b Price 311	– not out 4
I.R. Redpath lbw b Cartwright 19	
N.C. O'Neill b Price 47	
P.J. Burge c Price b Carwright 34	
B.C. Booth c and b Price 98	
T.R. Veivers c Edrich b Rumsey 22	
†A.T.W. Grout c Dexter b Rumsey 0	
G.D. McKenzie not out 0	
B 1, l-b 9, n-b 9 19	

1/201 2/233 3/318 4/382   (8 wkts, dec.) **656**   (no wkt.) **4**
5/601 6/646 7/652 8/656

N.J.N. Hawke and G.E. Corling did not bat.

Bowling: FIRST INNINGS – Rumsey 35.5-4-99-2; Price 45-4-183-3; Cartwright 77-32-118-2; Titmus 44-14-100-0; Dexter 4-0-12-0; Mortimore 49-13-122-0; Boycott 1-0-3-0. SECOND INNINGS – Barrington 1-0-4-0; Titmus 1-1-0-0.

ENGLAND

G. Boycott b McKenzie 58	T.W. Cartwright b McKenzie 4
J.H. Edrich c Redpath b McKenzie 6	J.S.E. Price b Veivers 1
*E.R. Dexter b Veivers 174	F.E. Rumsey not out 3
K.F. Barrington lbw b McKenzie 256	
P.H. Parfitt c Grout b McKenzie 12	
†J.M. Parks c Hawke b Veivers 60	B 5, l-b 11 16
F.J. Titmus c Simpson b McKenzie 9	
J.B. Mortimore c Burge b McKenzie 12	1/15 2/126 3/372 4/417 5/560 **611**
	6/589 7/594 8/602 9/607

Bowling: McKenzie 60-15-153-7; Corling 46-11-96-0; Hawke 63-28-95-0; Simpson 19-4-59-0; Veivers 95.1-36-155-3; O'Neill 10-0-37-0.

Umpires: J.S. Buller and W.F. Price.

SEVENTH TEST MATCH

At Sydney, February 12, 13, 14, 16, 17, 1971. England won by 62 runs. A very different pitch from that on which bowlers toiled in Adelaide made sure that the final match would reach a definite result. It did so early on the fifth day, the extra day allowed on this occasion not being necessary. On the first day twelve wickets fell. Ian Chappell, Australia's new captain, sent England in first and the batsmen fell to spin, despite another fine, resolute innings by Illingworth. There was time for Lever and Snow to shoot out Eastwood and Stackpole for 13.

Australia slumped to 66 for four, but England let their strong position slip, largely because Walters was missed three times. He and the stubborn Redpath, who batted over three and a quarter hours, put on 81, and Greg Chappell's three-hour innings carried Australia to a lead of 80. During the closing stages of the innings Jenner ducked into a ball from Snow and was hit on the face. Snow was warned by Umpire

Rowan against the use of persistent bumpers, which led to a protest by Illingworth. The crowd demonstrated against Snow and Illingworth led his side off the field, but returned after being warned by the umpires that the match would otherwise be awarded to Australia.

Edrich and Luckhurst more than countered Australia's lead with an opening stand of 94, and a series of useful scores finally set Australia to make 223 with the pitch helpful to spinners and not unfriendly to pace bowlers. Snow bowled Eastwood with his sixth ball, but in the fifth over, going for a high hit to long leg off Lever, he broke his right hand on the boundary fencing and was put out of action. Nevertheless, the other bowlers, with Illingworth himself playing a notable part, had half the side out for 96. Only Stackpole, hitting two 6's and six 4's, prospered, and he seemed fortunate not to be given out caught by Knott off Lever when he was 13.

On the final day Greg Chappell was Australia's last hope, and he was winkled out by Illingworth, who pulled out his best to compensate for Underwood being disappointing in conditions expected to make him the match winner. For England to win without Boycott, their top batsman, and then without Snow at the climax of the game was a great achievement. Australia had recast their side, dropping Lawry and, as stated, giving the captaincy to Ian Chappell. Lawry's batting was sorely missed. The 35-year-old Eastwood, who was not even in the Victoria side at the start of the season, was no adequate replacement.

ENGLAND

J.H. Edrich c G.S. Chappell b Dell	30	– c I.M. Chappell b O'Keeffe 57
B.W. Luckhurst c Redpath b Walters	0	– c Lillee b O'Keeffe 59
K.W.R. Fletcher c Stackpole b O'Keeffe	33	– c Stackpole b Eastwood 20
J.H. Hampshire c Marsh b Lillee	10	– c I.M. Chappell b O'Keeffe 24
B.L. d'Oliveira b Dell	1	– c I.M. Chappell b Lillee 47
*R. Illingworth b Jenner	42	– lbw b Lillee 29
†A.P.E. Knott c Stackpole b O'Keeffe	27	– b Dell 15
J.A. Snow b Jenner	7	– c Stackpole b Dell 20
P. Lever c Jenner b O'Keeffe	4	– c Redpath b Jenner 17
D.L. Underwood not out	8	– c Marsh b Dell 0
R.G.D. Willis b Jenner	11	– not out 2
B 4, l-b 4, w 1, n-b 2	11	B 3, l-b 3, n-b 6 12

1/5 2/60 3/68 4/69 5/98 6/145   **184**   1/94 2/130 3/158 4/165 5/234   **302**
7/156 8/165 9/165   6/251 7/276 8/298 9/299

Bowling: FIRST INNINGS – Lillee 13-5-32-1; Dell 16-8-32-2; Walters 4-0-10-1; G.S. Chappell 3-0-9-0; Jenner 16-3-42-3; O'Keeffe 24-8-48-3. SECOND INNINGS – Lillee 14-0-43-2; Dell 26.7-3-65-3; Walters 5-0-18-0; O'Keeffe 26-8-96-3; Jenner 21-5-39-1; Eastwood 5-0-21-1; Stackpole 3-1-8-0.

AUSTRALIA

K.H. Eastwood c Knott b Lever	.5	– b Snow	.0
K.R. Stackpole b Snow	.6	– b Illingworth	.67
†R.W. Marsh c Willis b Lever	.4	– b Underwood	.16
*I.M. Chappell b Willis	.25	– c Knott b Lever	.6
I.R. Redpath c and b Underwood	.59	– c Hampshire b Illingworth	.14
K.D. Walters st Knott b Underwood	.42	– c d'Oliveira b Willis	.1
G.S. Chappell b Willis	.65	– st Knott b Illingworth	.30
K.J. O'Keeffe c Knott b Illingworth	.3	– c sub b d'Oliveira	.12
D.K. Lillee c Knott b Willis	.6	– c Hampshire b d'Oliveira	.0
T.J. Jenner b Lever	.30	– c Fletcher b Underwood	.4
A.R. Dell not out	.3	– not out	.3
L-b 5, w 1, n-b 10	.16	B 2, n-b 5	.7

1/11 2/13 3/32 4/66 5/147 6/162   **264**   1/0 2/22 3/71 4/82 5/96   **160**
7/178 8/235 9/239   6/131 7/142 8/154 9/154

Bowling: FIRST INNINGS – Snow 18-2-68-1; Lever 14.6-3-43-3; d'Oliveira 12-2-24-0; Willis 12-1-58-3; Underwood 16-3-39-2; Illingworth 11-3-16-1. SECOND INNINGS – Snow 2-1-7-1; Lever 12-2-23-1; d'Oliveira 5-1-15-2; Willis 9-1-32-1; Underwood 13.6-5-28-2; Illingworth 20-7-39-3; Fletcher 1-0-9-0.

Umpires: T.F. Brooks and L.P. Rowan.

FIFTH TEST MATCH

At The Oval, August 10, 11, 12, 14, 15, 16, 1972. Australia won by five wickets with half a day to spare. This was a splendid match with fortune swaying first to one side and then to the other. The result remained in the balance until the last half hour when England, having lost Illingworth their captain the previous afternoon, were finally mastered. Among the several notable personal performances that of Lillee, Australia's demon fast bowler, was the keynote to his side's success. From the moment Illingworth won the toss for the fourth time in the series and gave England first innings on an excellent pitch which lasted well throughout the six days, Lillee, by his sheer pace coupled with the occasional shock-telling bouncer, was the man England feared most. […]

England were always fighting an uphill battle for yet again their specialist batsmen let them down and soon after tea on the first day eight wickets had fallen for 181, by which time Lillee had well-nigh exhausted himself as Knott came to the rescue with a daring display. […] Two hours cricket before lunch produced only 27 overs while England made 50 for the loss of Edrich and Wood. Then Parfitt and Hampshire settled down to a confident stand until just after the ball had been changed for the 'umpteenth' time in this series, when Hampshire cut a high bouncer of good length to

Inverarity at short third man. Then came a landslide, only relieved on the appearance of Knott, who ably assisted by Arnold saw the total to 267 for nine at the close. Besides Lillee's pace, which brought him three wickets in four balls for the second time in the rubber, England had also been troubled by Mallett, whom let the wiseacres of Headingley note, turned the ball quite a lot early on this first day to take three for 80.

Knott continued to thrash away next morning, but when Lillee flung a bouncer at Underwood, possibly England's ace bowler in a six-day match, and struck his arm, Knott called it a day, having hit seventeen boundaries in a grand knock that brought him 92 in two and a quarter hours.

Arnold and Snow soon disposed of Australia's opening pair, Watson and Stackpole, for 34 and then began the highest stand of the rubber between the Chappells, who in just over four hours put on 201 – each reached three figures, the first time two brothers had hit a hundred in the same innings of a Test match. Ian Chappell played the captain's part, paying strict attention to defence – he had a rare duel with the two slow bowlers, Underwood and Illingworth, and there were few false strokes in a memorable day's cricket watched by a full house of 28,000. In fact, the gates were closed on this Friday and the next two days. Eventually, Greg Chappell hit too soon at a shorter ball from Illingworth and was well caught at mid-on, having struck seventeen 4's. Ian Chappell, not out 107, had seen his side within 10 runs of England's 284 and Australia still had seven wickets intact to start the third day, Edwards having stayed the last forty-four minutes of Friday for 16.

On Saturday, the game veered England's way, for Australia were seeking a total of 500, but Snow and Underwood, ably backed by Arnold and Greig, bowled splendidly. […] Underwood showed his class with some immaculate bowling on a firm true surface with four men besides Knott close to the bat. Underwood undid Edwards – three hours, forty minutes at the crease with nine 4's in his 79 – Sheahan, Marsh and Inverarity, taking his four wickets on this day in 13 overs for 29 runs – a masterly effort. So, at the week-end Australia were 394 for eight.

With the game equally poised at the half-way stage, bearing in mind that Australia faced fourth innings, England continued their strong challenge to win the rubber. They soon captured the two outstanding Australian wickets for the addition of five runs and the lead was restricted to 115. A stupendous effort by the England batsmen was required and considering that all the first nine proceeded to acquire double figures, this was forthcoming but really only Wood, and later Knott again, answered the call as their supporters hoped. […] Wood stayed four hours, thirty-five minutes and he hit fifteen 4's. After such a grand effort, he was unfortunate to miss by 10 runs a hundred on his Test debut. It was good to see again someone present a straight bat to Lillee and Massie and someone who was not afraid to get behind the line of the ball, ready to hook the bouncer. At the end of the fourth day England stood only 112 runs in front with half their wickets standing.

Australia had delivered 82 overs and so Ian Chappell resumed next day with his slow bowlers Mallett and Inverarity. Illingworth, accompanied by Greig, helped himself to 12 before Lillee and Massie went into action after three overs. Lillee soon removed both men, but Snow kept up his end sensibly while Knott plundered freely for a memorable hour as he helped himself to nine 4's, being last out, and not giving Underwood a chance to face Lillee. [...]

By tea, Australia were 56 for one, chasing 242. Then Illingworth shared the attack with Underwood and a rare tussle ensued, despite some aggression by Stackpole against Underwood who once more bowled superbly, as indeed did the captain round the wicket until he slipped on delivering and sprained his right ankle an hour before the close. The leadership fell on Edrich who relied on Greig to replace the injured captain. At the drawing of stumps Australia were 116 for one, with Stackpole 70, Ian Chappell 29. The loss of Illingworth, coupled with an injury to d'Oliveira who could not bowl, proved the death knell for England well as Underwood and his colleagues maintained the challenge. Snow, too, took no part in the attack, having received a severe blow on his left arm when facing Lillee with the bat. Nevertheless, within half an hour of resuming on the last morning England accounted for Stackpole, Ian Chappell and Edwards for five runs. Stackpole (nine 4's) had batted three hours and twenty minutes.

Australia still wanted 71 and between them Sheahan and Marsh in their differing styles saw them home. Sheahan, so often disappointing, was the man of the moment with his straight bat and upright stance. He batted two hours and twenty minutes. Marsh began carefully until the new ball was taken at 210 when he sensed victory at hand and unleashed many exciting leg hits which sent Australia hurrying to square the rubber and for the first time in their history without a single player from New South Wales in their eleven.

ENGLAND

B. Wood c Marsh b Watson	.26 – lbw b Massie	.90
J.H. Edrich lbw b Lillee	.8 – b Lillee	.18
P.H. Parfitt b Lillee	.51 – b Lillee	.18
J.H. Hampshire c Inverarity b Mallett	.42 – c I.M. Chappell b Watson	.20
B.L. d'Oliveira c G.S. Chappell b Mallett	.4 – c I.M. Chappell b Massie	.43
A.W. Greig c Stackpole b Mallett	.16 – c Marsh b Lillee	.29
*R. Illingworth c G.S. Chappell b Lillee	.0 – lbw b Lillee	.31
†A.P.E. Knott c Marsh b Lillee	.92 – b Lillee	.63
J.A. Snow c Marsh b Lillee	.3 – c Stackpole b Mallett	.14
G.G. Arnold b Inverarity	.22 – lbw b Mallett	.4
D.L. Underwood not out	.3 – not out	.0
L-b 8, w 1, n-b 8	.17 B 11, l-b 8, n-b 7	.26

1/25 2/50 3/133 4/142 5/145   **284**   1/56 2/81 3/114 4/194 5/205   **356**
6/145 7/159 8/181 9/262   6/270 7/271 8/333 9/356

Bowling: FIRST INNINGS – Lillee 24.2-7-58-5; Massie 27-5-69-0; Watson 12-4-23-1; Mallett 23-4-80-3; G.S. Chappell 2-0-18-0; Inverarity 4-0-19-1. SECOND INNINGS – Lillee 32.2-8-123-5; Massie 32-10-77-2; Watson 19-8-32-1; Mallett 23-7-66-2; Inverarity 15-4-32-0.

AUSTRALIA

G.D. Watson c Knott b Arnold	13	– lbw b Arnold	6
K.R. Stackpole b Snow	18	– c Knott b Greig	79
*I.M. Chappell c Snow b Arnold	118	– c sub b Underwood	37
G.S. Chappell c Greig b Illingworth	113	– lbw b Underwood	16
R. Edwards b Underwood	79	– lbw b Greig	1
A.P. Sheahan c Hampshire b Underwood	5	– not out	44
†R.W. Marsh b Underwood	0	– not out	43
R.J. Inverarity c Greig b Underwood	28		
A.A. Mallett run out	5		
R.A.L. Massie b Arnold	4		
D.K. Lillee not out	0		

G.D. Watson c Knott b Arnold ....13 – lbw b Arnold 6
K.R. Stackpole b Snow ....18 – c Knott b Greig 79
*I.M. Chappell c Snow b Arnold ....118 – c sub b Underwood 37
G.S. Chappell c Greig b Illingworth ....113 – lbw b Underwood 16
R. Edwards b Underwood ....79 – lbw b Greig 1
A.P. Sheahan c Hampshire b Underwood ....5 – not out 44
†R.W. Marsh b Underwood ....0 – not out 43
R.J. Inverarity c Greig b Underwood 28
A.A. Mallett run out 5
R.A.L. Massie b Arnold 4
D.K. Lillee not out 0
   L-b 8, w 1, n-b 7 16   L-b 6, n-b 10 16

1/24 2/34 3/235 4/296 5/310   **399** 1/16 2/132 3/136   (5 wkts) **242**
6/310 7/383 8/387 9/399   4/137 5/171

Bowling: FIRST INNINGS – Arnold 35-11-87-3; Snow 34.5-5-111-1; Greig 18-9-25-0; d'Oliveira 9-4-17-0; Underwood 38-16-90-4; Illingworth 17-4-53-1. SECOND INNINGS – Arnold 15-5-26-1; Snow 6-1-21-0; Greig 25.3-10-49-2; Underwood 35-11-94-2; Illingworth 8.5-2-26-0; Parfitt 2-0-10-0.

Umpires: A.E. Fagg and A.E.G. Rhodes.

5

ASHES AND EMBERS: AUSTRALIA v. ENGLAND 1973–2002

Anglo-Australian cricket in the late twentieth century has in some respects mirrored Anglo-Australian relations. As England has gradually ceased to be our cultural benchmark, so is the desire to beat England no longer the paramount objective of our cricket. But the Ashes occupy a more solid place in Australian thinking than some jeremiahs will allow.

This section chonicles some of the better moments from the last quarter-century or so of Ashes cricket, beginning with the summer of 1974–75. The Ashes were unpredictable then. As John Thicknesse put it in his *Wisden* 1976 tour report, the unexpected emergence of Dennis Lillee and Jeff Thomson as a pace bowling partnership gave England an 'unpleasant surprise'. The unpredictability persisted, though, in that England won the next full series at home; in fact, England lost only one Ashes series on its own shores, and then somewhat unluckily, between 1965 and 1988.

In *Wisden* 1989, Matthew Engel of the *Guardian* extolled the virtues of competition between England and Australia, which he depicted as a brand leader among cricket 'products'. The words now have a melancholy ring. When they saw the light of day, England's hold on the Ashes had four months to run. Since then, cricket's oldest trophy has been held fast and firmly by Australia. During Engel's subsequent period as editor of *Wisden*, custody of the Ashes was seemingly a matter for periodic ratification rather than outright dispute; England won only a single 'live' Test.

The almanack has rather agonised over this. In *Wisden* 1994, Ian Chappell was asked to explain 'Why we Beat the Poms'. In *Wisden* 1995 the editor even called for the physical Ashes urn to change domicile. Curiously, though, Anglo-Australian contests have continued to produce their share of memorable cricket – as much, if not more, than the 1960s, when the teams were possibly stronger and certainly far more closely matched. The modern dynamic, of catchweight contest rather than heavyweight title bout, holds its own appeals. Games such as the Adelaide Test of January 1995, the Edgbaston Test of May 1997, the Melbourne Test of December 1998 and the Headingley Test of August 2001 – not included here because it's in the current *Wisden*

– have been the more memorable for overthrowing what appears the natural order. Nor have the exchanges been marred by such malign modern phenomena as throwing, sledging or match-fixing. A Bombay police inspector quoted in Mihir Bose's 'The Corruption of Cricket' in *Wisden* 1999 lamented: 'Every side with the exception of Australia and England can be bought.' True or not, and the remark even at the time seemed a little extreme, it nonetheless affirms the Ashes' abiding appeal.

—GH

M.C.C. IN AUSTRALIA AND NEW ZEALAND, 1974–75

By John Thicknesse

An unpleasant surprise was in store for M.C.C. on their eighth post-war tour of Australia. Having been selected on the assumption that as a consequence of Dennis Lillee's back injury in West Indies early in 1973, Australia were unlikely to call upon a genuinely fast bowler, Denness's side in fact found themselves confronting two – Lillee and a youngster from Sydney, Jeff Thomson, who up to that time had made a bigger name for himself by what he had said in a magazine about hurting batsmen than by anything he had done on the cricket field. […] Thomson, six feet tall, 24 years old, and equipped with the extremely powerful V-shaped back that characterises many fast bowlers, Thomson took 33 wickets in four and a half Tests and looked sure to break Arthur Mailey's longstanding record, 36 in 1920-21, when he hurt himself playing tennis on the rest day of the Adelaide Test and was unable to bowl again in the series. […] Lillee, within himself at Brisbane, bowled with a hostility that bordered on savagery throughout the series, steadily gaining pace as he gained confidence in his back. And his pace was comparable to Thomson's, so that England had no respite.

By one of those accumulating coincidences that have no connection with logic and therefore no explanation, four Tests passed before Lillee took other than two wickets in an innings. He got a better reward at Adelaide, with four in each innings, and finished the series with 25, eight behind Thomson. In its way, Lillee's was an even more remarkable achievement because less than two years earlier it was open to doubt whether he would ever bowl fast again. Ambition and iron determination carried him back to the peaks of fitness and success he had achieved as a 23-year-old in England in 1972. He spent weeks in a plaster-cast to take the strain off his back after Australia's tour of West Indies and in 1973-74, patiently following medical advice, hardly bowled at all in the hope that if he did everything he was told he might yet battle back to open Australia's bowling in the series against England.

Watching the two in action, it was easy to believe they were the fastest pair ever to have coincided in a cricket team. They would have been too good for better batting sides than Denness's even without the superb standard of catching set by Greg Chappell and Mallett in the slips and gully, or without the help they got from the pitches. Of the first four Tests – Brisbane, Perth, Melbourne, Sydney – only the Perth pitch could be described as true. Overall, they were unevenly grassed and fast, giving variable bounce, especially at Brisbane.

The catching reached its zenith at Perth, where the Chappell brothers, Mallett and Redpath shared 13 in the slips and gully, compared to one by Marsh, the wicket-keeper. At least a quarter of those catches would have stood out as the 'catch of the match' in most Tests. Twenty-three of the fast bowlers' 58 wickets fell in that segment, while from all Australia's bowlers, the total rose to 38, with another 18 to Marsh.

On top of those advantages, the umpires, Brooks and Bailhache, gave Thomson and Lillee considerable freedom in respect of short-pitched bowling. Thomson's tremendous strength – or perhaps some feature of his perfectly fair but 'hurling' action – enabled him to get the ball up from a fuller length that any fast bowler I had seen. But even from him, there were often two unmistakable bouncers an over, while Lillee sometimes bowled three or even four. [...] When Thomson and Lillee were bowling, the atmosphere was more like that of a soccer ground than of a cricket match, especially at Sydney, where England's batsmen must have experienced the same sort of emotion as they waited for the next ball as early Christians felt as they waited in the Colosseum for the lions. Passions were occasionally roused by the fact that during the season Lillee had published *Back to the Mark*, a book in which he openly admitted that when he bowled a bouncer he aimed to hit the batsman and make him think twice about the wisdom of going on batting. No fast bowler had been as explicit as that in print (although it stands to reason that a bouncer has to be straight to be effective) and there was no doubt that the comment played its part in provoking the exultant chants of 'Lill...lee, Lill...lee' from the jam-packed Hill that accompanied him along the 30-yard walk to his mark, and up the first half of his run-up...to be followed by an expectant hush as he neared the bowling crease. [...]

SECOND TEST MATCH

At Perth, December 13, 14, 15, 17, 1974. Australia won by nine wickets. The match was virtually decided on the first day when England, put in, collapsed in two and three-quarter hours from 99 for one to 208 all out. Australia, batting for one over on the first evening, built a lead of 273 by mid-afternoon on the third day, bowled England out for 293, and won fifty-three minutes from stumps on the fourth day to go two up in the series.

England were handicapped by the absence of Amiss and Edrich, but poor batting against Thomson and Lillee was again at the root of their defeat. Thomson added seven wickets to his nine at Brisbane, generating great speed on a pitch that gained pace after the first day, and Lillee again had four – a bag that would have been bigger if the luck had run for him. England's troubles were accentuated by Australia's brilliant catching in the slips and gully, 13 being taken out of 14 offered. Greg Chappell established a Test record with seven catches in the match, all but two of them at second slip.

On the second day England were briefly in contention when Australia were 192 for four, but a spectacular 103 by Walters, who made exactly a hundred between tea and stumps, reversed the situation. Ross Edwards also played an important part in consolidating Australia's position, batting five hours twenty minutes and helping Walters to add 170 in two hours, twenty minutes for the fifth wicket. [...]

Thomson needed only five balls to inflict his first injury, hitting Luckhurst on the top hand off a good length. Luckhurst was able to bat on, but the hand swelled overnight, preventing him from fielding, and in the second innings he batted number seven. Both he and Lloyd were lucky to survive Lillee's new-ball spell, but Thomson was wildly erratic and the opening stand lasted eighty minutes before Luckhurst slashed Walker hard into the gulley where Mallett held the first of Australia's fine catches.

Cowdrey stepped out for his 188th Test innings (and first for 3½ years) to as warm an ovation as he is accustomed to at Canterbury and having narrowly survived his first three balls gave a demonstration of defensive technique against fast bowling that was subsequently equalled only by Knott, in the first innings, and Titmus, who was playing his first test since February 1968. Only these three consistently observed the principle of moving their bodies into line against Thomson and Lillee, thus minimising the danger of being caught in the slips. [...]

On the second day a crowd of 23,000 saw Australia add 351 off 76 overs, Walters highlighting the performance with a vicious exhibition of pulling against Greig, Arnold and Old. In the hour after tea he made 67, including the majority of his eleven 4's; but despite Edwards's co-operation he lost the strike for lengthy periods against the second new ball and faced the last ball of the day at 97, needing a six to complete a hundred in a session for the second time in his test career. (The first was against West Indies at Port-of-Spain in 1973). Willis delivered a fast long-hop and Walters exultantly hooked it into the crowd at square-leg.

Edwards (79) began the third day with five successive twos off Arnold, and went on to score the first Test hundred by a Western Australian at Perth. But Walters was caught at slip off Willis's second ball of the day and the threatened massacre did not materialise. Old polished off the tail and Australia's last six wickets fell for 129.

So just before the Test's halfway point Lloyd and Cowdrey opened England's second innings. Thomson ended a staunch partnership of 52 when a good-length ball cut back to hit Lloyd in the abdomen, causing him to retire hurt, but in 36 overs before stumps England lost only Cowdrey and began the fourth day at 102 for one, needing 171 to make Australia bat again.

Their slim hopes of making a close match vanished in Thomson's first three overs, when Greig and Denness were caught in the slips playing a long way from their bodies, and Fletcher touched his first ball, a lifting outswinger, to Marsh. Lloyd and Luckhurst held on well despite their injuries, but it was left to Titmus, playing his 50th Test, to underline the technical deficiencies of his more exalted team-mates with a nearly flawless 61 in three hours twenty minutes. When he was last out, brilliantly caught on the run by Greg Chappell at wide long-off, Australia needed only 21 to win and knocked them off inside four overs for the loss of Wally Edwards.

ENGLAND

D. Lloyd c G.S. Chappell b Thomson	49	– c G.S. Chappell b Walker	35
B.W. Luckhurst c Mallett b Walker	27	– c Mallett b Lillee	23
M.C. Cowdrey b Thomson	22	– lbw b Thomson	41
A.W. Greig c Mallett b Walker	23	– c G.S. Chappell b Thomson	32
K.W.R. Fletcher c Redpath b Lillee	4	– c Marsh b Thomson	0
*M.H. Denness c G.S. Chappell b Lillee	2	– c Redpath b Thomson	20
†A.P.E. Knott c Redpath b Walters	51	– c G.S. Chappell b Lillee	18
F.J. Titmus c Redpath b Walters	10	– c G.S. Chappell b Mallett	61
C.M. Old c G.S. Chappell b I.M. Chappell	7	– c Thomson b Mallett	43
G.G. Arnold run out	1	– c Mallett b Thomson	4
R.G.D. Willis not out	4	– not out	0
W 3, n-b 5	8	L-b 4, w 1, n-b 11	16

1/44 2/99 3/119 4/128 5/132   **208**   1/62 2/106 3/124 4/124 5/154 6/156   **293**
6/132 7/194 8/201 9/202   7/219 8/285 9/293

Bowling: FIRST INNINGS – Lillee 16-4-48-2; Thomson 15-6-45-2; Walker 20-5-49-2; Mallett 10-3-35-0; Walters 2.3-0-13-2; I.M. Chappell 2-0-10-1. SECOND INNINGS – Lillee 22-5-59-2; Thomson 25-4-93-5; Walker 24-7-76-1; Walters 9-0-17-0; Mallett 11.1-4-32-2.

AUSTRALIA

I.R. Redpath st Knott b Titmus	41	– not out	12
W.J. Edwards c Lloyd b Greig	30	– lbw b Arnold	0
*I.M. Chappell c Knott b Arnold	25	– not out	11
G.S. Chappell c Greig b Willis	62		
R. Edwards b Arnold	115		
K.D. Walters c Fletcher b Willis	103		
†R.W. Marsh c Lloyd b Titmus	41		
M.H.N. Walker c Knott b Old	19		
D.K. Lillee b Old	11		
A.A. Mallett c Knott b Old	0		
J.R. Thomson not out	11		
B 7, l-b 14, n-b 2	23		

1/64 2/101 3/113 4/192 5/362   **481**   1/4   (1 wkt.) **23**
6/416 7/449 8/462 9/462

Bowling: FIRST INNINGS – Willis 22-0-91-2; Arnold 27-1-129-2; Old 22.6-3-85-3; Greig 9-0-69-1; Titmus 28-3-84-2. SECOND INNINGS – Willis 2-0-8-0; Arnold 1.7-0-15-1.

Umpires: R.C. Bailhache and T.F. Brooks.

THE CENTENARY TEST MATCH

By Reg Hayter

At Melbourne, March 12, 13, 14, 16, 17, 1977.

An occasion of warmest reunion and nostalgia, the cricket continuously compelling, a result straining credulity. Hans Ebeling, former Australian Test bowler and the inspiration of it all, should have been christened Hans Andersen Ebeling.

From Ebeling, a vice-president of the Melbourne Cricket Club, originated the suggestion to signalise 100 years of Test Cricket by a match between England and Australia on the same ground – in 1877 the Richmond Police Paddock – on which David Gregory's team beat James Lillywhite's all-round professional England side.

The Victorian Cricket Association and the Melbourne Cricket Club co-operated to bring this about and, with sponsorship from Qantas, T.A.A., Benson & Hedges and the Melbourne Hilton Hotel, a masterpiece of organisation resulted in an event which none fortunate enough to be present could forget. Unlucky were those who missed it.

Arrangements were made for the England team visiting India to extend their tour to play an official Test in the same month as the 1877 Test, and invitations to attend as guests were sent to the 244 living cricketers who had played for Australia or England in the series. All but 26 of these were able to accept for an event unique in history.

The oldest Australian Test player present was the 87-year-old Jack Ryder. Even though suffering from near blindness, the 84-year-old Percy Fender made the enervating air journey from Britain as the oldest English representative. He was accompanied by his grandson, Jeremy, who became his cricketing eyes. Poor health alone prevented E.J. ('Tiger') Smith and Herbert Sutcliffe to travel and, for the same reason, Frank Woolley could not leave Canada.

Of those who went to Melbourne many told unusual stories. Colin McCool was marooned in his Queensland home by floods and had to be hauled up from his front lawn by helicopter for the airport. Jack Rutherford's train broke down and he finished the journey to the airport by taxi. Denis Compton – who else? – left his passport in a Cardiff hotel and, but for the early start to the pre-flight champagne party at London Airport which enabled a good friend to test the speed limits on the M4, would have missed the plane. Some ex-England players – Harold Larwood, Peter Loader, Tony Lock, Barry Knight, Frank Tyson – already lived in Australia and the Australian Neil Hawke flew home from England. The gradual gathering of all at the Hilton Hotel, 200 yards across the Jolimont Park from the Melbourne Oval, brought meetings and greetings of unabated happiness. Not a hitch, not one.

Fittingly, this was also Melbourne's Mardi Gras, a week called 'Moomba', the aboriginal word for 'let's get together and have fun'. After a champagne (much was drunk between London and Melbourne and back) breakfast and an opening ceremony on which ex-Test captains accompanied the teams on to the field, the crowd were also given the opportunity of a special welcome to all the former Test players.

Greig called correctly to Greg Chappell's spin of the specially-minted gold coin and chose for England to field first. Probably he felt apprehension about his batsmen facing Lillee while moisture remained in the pitch. The resolute fast-medium bowl-ing of Willis, Old and Lever, helped by Underwood's customary left-handed accuracy and breathtakingly supported in the field, appeared to justify Greig's decision in Australia's dismissal for 138 in front of a crowd of over 61,000. Australia, handi-capped by the early departure of McCosker, who fractured his jaw when a ball from Willis flew off his hand into his face, were always on the defensive. England's batting buckled even more swiftly against Lillee, at the zenith of his form and speed, and Walker – Australia's fielding being no whit inferior to that of England.

That was the last of the bowling mastery. On the second, third and fourth days Australia increased their first innings lead of 43 so much that their declaration left England 463 to win at 40 an hour. Marsh, who had already beaten Grout's record of 187 Test victims, added to his triumph by his first Test century against England, and Walters joyfully rode his fortune in the manner that has charmed so many cricket admirers of the cavalier approach to batsmanship. Yet the spotlight centred on the 21-year-old David Hookes who won his place on the forthcoming tour to England with an innings straight from the fount of youth. This six feet, two inches powerful left-handed batsman, who had scored five centuries in 1976–77 Sheffield Shield cricket, strode to the crease with a confidence even more apparent when he struck Greig for five 4's in an over – off, pull, cover, mid-wicket, cover.

Then it was England's turn. And, in the presence of the Queen and the Duke of Edinburgh – during an interval they drove round the ground and were hugely acclaimed – royally did they apply themselves. Well as Amiss, Greig, Knott and Brearley batted, however, the innings to remember was played by Randall, a jaunty, restless, bubbling character, whose 174 took England to the doorstep of victory. The Australian spectators enjoyed his approach as much as Indian crowds had done on the tour just finished.

Once, when Lillee tested him with a bouncer, he tennis-batted it to the mid-wicket fence with a speed and power that made many a rheumy eye turn to the master of the stroke, the watching Sir Donald Bradman. Words cannot recapture the joy of that moment. Another time, when Lillee bowled short, Randall ducked, rose, drew him-self to his full five feet eight, doffed his cap and bowed politely. Then, felled by another bouncer, he gaily performed a reverse roll. This helped to maintain a friendly atmosphere in what, at all times, was a serious and fully competitive match.

The Australians responded. When Randall was 161, umpire Brooks gave him out, caught at the wicket. Immediately Marsh intimated that he had not completed the catch before dropping the ball. After consultation, the umpire called Randall back. Would that this spirit was always so! At the end of the game Randall was awarded the first prize of 1,600 dollars as the Man of the Match. To be chosen ahead of the superb Lillee, whose colleagues chaired him from the field when he finished the match with an analy-sis of eleven for 165, was a feat indeed. Some time after it was over someone discovered that the result of the 226th Test between the two countries – victory by 45 runs – was identical, to the same side and to the very run, with that of the 1877 Test on the same ground. Hans Andersen Ebeling had even scripted the final curtain.

AUSTRALIA

I.C. Davis lbw b Lever	.5 –	c Knott b Greig	.68
R.B. McCosker b Willis	.4 –	c Greig b Old	.25
G.J. Cosier c Fletcher b Lever	.10 –	c Knott b Lever	.4
*G.S. Chappell b Underwood	.40 –	b Old	.2
D.W. Hookes c Greig b Old	.17 –	c Fletcher b Underwood	.56
K.D. Walters c Greig b Willis	.4 –	c Knott b Greig	.66
†R.W. Marsh c Knott b Old	.28 –	not out	.110
G.J. Gilmour c Greig b Old	.4 –	b Lever	.16
K.J. O'Keeffe c Brearley b Underwood	.0 –	c Willis b Old	.14
D.K. Lillee not out	.10 –	c Amiss b Old	.25
M.H.N. Walker b Underwood	.2 –	not out	.8
B 4, l-b 2, n-b 8	.14	L-b 10, n-b 15	.25

1/11 2/13 3/23 4/45 5/51 **138**   1/33 2/40 3/53 4/132   (9 wkts, dec.) **419**
6/102 7/114 8/117 9/136   5/187 6/244 7/277 8/353
                        9/407

Bowling: FIRST INNINGS – Lever 12-1-36-2; Willis 8-0-33-2; Old 12-4-39-3; Underwood 11.6-2-16-3. SECOND INNINGS – Lever 21-1-95-2; Willis 22-0-91-0; Old 27.6-2-104-4; Greig 14-3-66-2; Underwood 12-2-38-1.

ENGLAND

R.A. Woolmer c Chappell b Lillee	.9 –	lbw b Walker	.12
J.M. Brearley c Hookes b Lillee	.12 –	lbw b Lillee	.43
D.L. Underwood c Chappell b Walker	.7 –	b Lillee	.7
D.W. Randall c Marsh b Lillee	.4 –	c Cosier b O'Keeffe	.174
D.L. Amiss c O'Keeffe b Walker	.4 –	b Chappell	.64
K.W.R. Fletcher c Marsh b Walker	.4 –	c Marsh b Lillee	.1
*A.W. Greig b Walker	.18 –	c Cosier b O'Keeffe	.41
†A.P.E. Knott lbw b Lillee	.15 –	lbw b Lillee	.42
C.M. Old c Marsh b Lillee	.3 –	c Chappell b Lillee	.2
J.K. Lever c Marsh b Lillee	.11 –	lbw b O'Keeffe	.4
R.G.D. Willis not out	.1 –	not out	.5
B 2, l-b 2, w 1, n-b 2	.7	B 8, l-b 4, w 3, n-b 7	.22

1/19 2/30 3/34 4/40 **95**   1/28 2/113 3/279 4/290   **417**
5/40 6/61 7/65 8/78 9/86   5/346 6/369 7/380 8/385 9/410

Bowling: FIRST INNINGS – Lillee 13.3-2-26-6; Walker 15-3-54-4; O'Keeffe 1-0-4-0; Gilmour 5-3-4-0. SECOND INNINGS – Lillee 34.4-7-139-5; Walker 22-4-83-1; Gilmour 4-0-29-0; Chappell 16-7-29-1; O'Keeffe 33-6-108-3; Walters 3-2-7-0.

Umpires: M.G. O'Connell and T.F. Brooks.

THIRD CORNHILL TEST

At Leeds, July 16, 17, 18, 20, 21, 1981. England won by 18 runs. A match which had initially produced all the wet and tedious traits of recent Leeds Tests finally ended in a way to stretch the bounds of logic and belief. England's victory, achieved under the gaze of a spellbound nation, was the first this century by a team following on, and only the second such result in the history of Test cricket. The transformation occurred in less than 24 hours, after England had appeared likely to suffer their second four-day defeat of the series. Wherever one looked, there were personal dramas: Brearley, returning as captain like England's saviour; Botham, who was named Man of the Match, brilliant once more in his first game back in the ranks; Willis, whose career has so often heard the distant drums, producing the most staggering bowling of his life when his place again seemed threatened. [...]

Australia, having chosen to bat, ended the first day in fine health at 203 for three, the extra hour having reduced lost time to only fifty minutes. Dyson batted diligently for his century, playing chiefly off the back foot, and survived one chance, to Botham in the gully, when 57. Chappell, who supported Dyson staunchly in a stand of 94 for the second wicket, was twice reprieved – by Gower and Botham again – so England, not for the first time this summer, suffered for their ineptitude in the field. [...] It will come as a surprise when, in future years, people look back on a Test of such apparently outrageous drama, to know that the second day was pedestrian in the extreme. Botham, to some degree, salvaged English pride by taking five more wickets, all of them in an after-tea spell costing 35 runs, and finishing with six for 95. Naturally, the assumption was drawn that he is a more effective player without leadership duties. Despite his efforts, Australia extended their score to 401 for nine, thanks to half-centuries from Hughes and Yallop. [...]

At this stage, the odds seemed in favour of a draw. An England win was on offer generously, though by no means as extravagantly as 24 hours later when Ladbrokes, from their tent on the ground, posted it at 500 to 1. The reason for their estimate was a truncated day on which England were dismissed for 174 and, following on 227 behind, lost Gooch without addition. Australia's seamers had shown what could be done by bowling straighter and to a fuller length than their counterparts. Other than Botham, who opted for all-out aggression and profited by a swift 50, England at no stage commanded and were occasionally undone by deliveries performing contortions at speed. Botham fell victim to just such a ball from Lillee and the catch by Marsh was his 264th in Tests, beating Knott's record.

The third day ended with unhappy scenes similar to those seen at Lord's, when spectators hurled cushions and abuse at the umpires. On this occasion, Messrs Meyer and Evans had walked to the middle, wearing blazers, at five to six, after a lengthy stoppage for poor light. They consulted their meters and summoned the covers, abandoning play just before the hour. With cruel irony, the light improved instantly, the sun was soon breaking through and the large crowd was incited to wrathful demands for explanations as to why they were not watching the prescribed extra hour. Once more, it seems, confusion in interpretation of the playing regulations was the cause of the ill feeling: they stated only that conditions must be fit for play at the scheduled time of finish and not, as the umpires thought, that play must actually be in motion. Whether it was, in fact, fit at six o'clock is open to doubt, but the TCCB soon adjusted the ruling so that play in future Tests in the series could restart at any stage of the extra hour.

This heated diversion seemed likely to achieve nothing more than a stay of sentence for England, a view which appeared amply confirmed by late afternoon on the

Monday. England were then 135 for seven, still 92 behind, and the distant objective of avoiding an innings defeat surely their only available prize. Lillee and Alderman had continued where Saturday's disturbances had forced them to leave off, and for all Boycott's skilful resistance, the cause seemed lost. Boycott, who batted three and a half hours, was sixth out to an lbw decision he seemed not to relish, and when Taylor followed quickly, the England players' decision to check out of their hotel seemed a sound move. Three hours later, the registration desks around Leeds were coping with a flood of re-bookings, Botham having destroyed the game's apparently set course with an astonishing, unbeaten 145, ably and forcefully aided by Dilley. Together, they added 117 in 80 minutes for the eighth wicket, only 7 short of an England record against Australia. Both struck the ball so cleanly and vigorously that Hughes's men were temporarily in disarray; when Dilley departed after scoring 56 precious runs, Old arrived to add 67 more with Botham, who still had Willis as a partner at the close, with England 124 ahead.

Botham advanced his unforgettable innings to 149 not out before losing Willis the next morning, but Australia, needing 130, still remained clear favourites. Then, at 56 for one, Willis, having changed ends to bowl with the wind, dismissed Chappell with a rearing delivery and the staggering turnabout was under way. Willis bowled as if inspired. It is not uncommon to see him perform for England as if his very life depended on it, but this was something unique. In all, he took eight wickets for 43, the best of his career, as Australia's last nine wickets tumbled for 55 runs despite a stand of 35 in four overs between Bright and Lillee. Old bowled straight and aggressively and England rose to the need to produce an outstanding show in the field. Yet this was Willis's hour, watched or listened to by a vast invisible audience. At the end, the crowd gathered to wave their Union Jacks and chant patriotically, eight days in advance of the Royal Wedding. (*Alan Lee*)

AUSTRALIA

J. Dyson b Dilley	.102	– (2) c Taylor b Willis 34
G.M. Wood lbw b Botham	.34	– (1) c Taylor b Botham 10
T.M. Chappell c Taylor b Willey	.27	– c Taylor b Willis 8
*K.J. Hughes c and b Botham	.89	– c Botham b Willis 0
R.J. Bright b Dilley	.7	– (8) b Willis 19
G.N. Yallop c Taylor b Botham	.58	– (5) c Gatting b Willis 0
A.R. Border lbw b Botham	.8	– (6) b Old 0
†R.W. Marsh b Botham	.28	– (7) c Dilley b Willis 4
G.F. Lawson c Taylor b Botham	.13	– c Taylor b Willis 1
D.K. Lillee not out	.3	– c Gatting b Willis 17
T.M. Alderman not out	.0	– not out 0
B 4, l-b 13, w 3, n-b 12	.32	L-b 3, w 1, n-b 13 18

1/55 2/149 3/196 4/220 ?5/322   (9 wkts dec.) **401**   1/13 2/56 3/58 4/58 5/65   **111**
6/354 7/357 8/396 9/401   6/68 7/74 8/75 9/110

Bowling: FIRST INNINGS – Willis 30-8-72-0; Old 43-14-91-0; Dilley 27-4-78-2, Botham 39.2-11-95-6; Willey 13-2-31-1; Boycott 3-2-2-0. SECOND INNINGS – Botham 7-3-14-1; Dilley 2-0-11-0; Willis 15.1-3-43-8; Old 9-1-21-1; Willey 3-1-4-0.

ENGLAND

G.A. Gooch lbw b Alderman	.2	– c Alderman b Lillee	.0
G. Boycott b Lawson	.12	– lbw b Alderman	.46
*J.M. Brearley c Marsh b Alderman	.10	– c Alderman b Lillee	.14
D.I. Gower c Marsh b Lawson	.24	– c Border b Alderman	.9
M.W. Gatting lbw b Lillee	.15	– lbw b Alderman	.1
P. Willey b Lawson	.8	– c Dyson b Lillee	.33
I.T. Botham c Marsh b Lillee	.50	– not out	.149
†R.W. Taylor c Marsh b Lillee	.5	– c Bright b Alderman	.1
G.R. Dilley c and b Lillee	.13	– b Alderman	.56
C.M. Old c Border b Alderman	.0	– b Lawson	.29
R.G.D. Willis not out	.1	– c Border b Alderman	.2
B 6, l-b 11, w 6, n-b 11	.34	B 5, l-b 3, n-b 5	.16

1/12 2/40 3/42 4/84 5/87 **174**   1/0 2/18 3/37 4/41 5/105 **356**
6/112 7/148 8/166 9/167   6/133 7/135 8/252 9/319

Bowling: FIRST INNINGS – Lillee 18.5-7-49-4; Alderman 19-4-59-3; Lawson 13-3-32-3. SECOND INNINGS – Lillee 25-6-94-3; Alderman 35.3-6-135-6; Lawson 23-4-96-1; Bright 4-0-15-0.

Umpires: B.J. Meyer and D.G.L. Evans.

FOURTH TEST MATCH

At Melbourne, December 26, 27, 28, 29, 30, 1982. England won by 3 runs. A magnificent Test match, to be ranked among the best ever played, produced a finish of such protracted excitement that it had the whole of Australia by the ears. Needing 292 to win, Australia were 218 for nine when Border and Thomson embarked on a last-wicket partnership of epic proportions. At close of play on the fourth day they had taken the score to 255 for nine, leaving another 37 runs to be found on the last morning for Australia, there and then, to regain the Ashes.

Although, on this last day, the match could have been over within moments, 18,000 spectators, admitted free of charge, went to the Melbourne Cricket Ground in the hope of seeing Border and Thomson achieve their improbable goal. All things considered, among them a new ball taken at 259 for nine, Thomson was rarely in trouble; Border never was. By the time Botham began the eighteenth over of the morning Australia were within 4 runs of victory. His first ball was short of a length and wide of the off stump. Thomson, sparring at it, edged a none-too-difficult catch to Tavaré, the second of Botham's two slips. Tavaré managed only to parry it, the ball bouncing away behind him but within reach of Miller, fielding at first slip, deeper than Tavaré. With a couple of quick strides Miller reached the catch and completed it, the ball still some eighteen inches off the ground.

No-one who played in the game or watched it, or who saw it on television, or who listened to it on the radio, many of them from halfway across the world, could have been left unmoved. In terms of runs, the only closer Test match ever played was the Brisbane tie between Australia and West Indies in 1960–61. In 1902, at Old Trafford, the margin between England and Australia was also 3 runs, on that occasion in Australia's favour.

England made two changes from the side that had lost the third Test in Adelaide, one optional, the other not. Randall, having been hit in the face by a short ball from Holding during England's one-day match in Launceston, was unfit, his place being taken by Cook. Cowans was preferred to Hemmings. Australia were unchanged. For the fourth time in the series the captain winning the toss chose to field. With the match being played on a pitch that had been laid only nine months before, Chappell took a calculated gamble when he committed Australia to batting last. In the event the pitch lasted surprisingly well and was, as Chappell expected, damp enough on the first day for England to be in early trouble. When Gower was third out, immediately after lunch, they were 56 for three. The innings was saved by a brilliant fourth-wicket partnership of 161 in only 32 overs by Tavaré and Lamb.

With Cook and Fowler going in first, Tavaré was able to bat at number three, which he much prefers to opening. After his usual slow start Tavaré began to attack the bowling, especially Yardley's, with unaccustomed vigour. By the time he was very well caught in the gully, England had fairly galloped to 217. But Lamb soon followed Tavaré, a fine innings ending a little unworthily when he got himself out to Yardley, and by close of play England, having fallen right away, were all out for 284. Cook, when first out, had given Chappell, at slip, his 111th Test catch, a new Australian record.

Each of the first three days saw one full innings completed. On the second Australia were bowled out in their first innings for 287, on the third England, in their second innings, for 294. By taking the wickets of Dyson and Chappell with successive balls in Australia's first innings, Cowans made his first impact on a match from which he was to emerge as a hero. Chappell hooked the first ball he received to deep square leg, where Lamb had just been carefully stationed. In the end Australia owed their narrow first-innings lead to Hughes's application, Hookes's good fortune laced with strokes of fine timing, and Marsh's belligerence. By now the umpiring of Rex Whitehead was becoming an irritant. On the second day, when they were in the field, and on the third, when they were batting, England were in danger of allowing it to undermine their resolve. After the match it was forgotten, all else being dwarfed by the climax, but it was undoubtedly erratic.

At 45 for three in their second innings England faced their next crisis. This time, however, after Botham had made 46 in 46 balls, their last five wickets made a vital contribution. Pringle and Taylor added 61 together, every run of some concern to Australia, faced by the prospect of batting last. Fowler, too, until hit on the foot by Thomson and forced to have a runner (the injury was to put him out of the next Test match) had played much his best innings of the tour. When Lawson found the edge of Pringle's bat Marsh claimed his 27th victim of the series, a new record for Test cricket.

Although the occasional ball was keeping very low, Australia's final target of 292, on an uncommonly fast Melbourne outfield (a prolonged and serious drought had restricted the watering of the ground), was eminently attainable. The equality of the four totals – 284, 287, 294 and 288 – tells of the unyielding nature of the match, with first one side, then the other, holding the advantage. When, as in Australia's first innings, Chappell fell cheaply to Cowans, splendidly caught low down in the covers by Gould (fielding as substitute for Fowler) off a hard slash from a short ball, England were in front, Wessels having already been bowled off his pads by Cowans. When, at 71, Dyson was beautifully caught at slip, by Tavaré off Botham, it remained that way. Hughes and Hookes then added 100, which gave Australia the initiative. Hughes's departure to a tumbling catch by Taylor off Miller, followed quickly by Hookes's, restored it to England. With Cowans, inspired by his successes over Chappell and generously encouraged by the crowd, claiming Australia's fifth (Hookes), sixth (Marsh), seventh (Yardley) and ninth (Hogg) wickets for 19 runs in seven overs, England had all but won when Thomson, his hair dyed platinum blond, joined Border.

As Thomson took root and Border switched to the attack, Willis adopted tactics which, though they brought final victory, were much criticised at the time. When Border had the strike Willis placed all his fielders in a far-flung ring, which meant that if England were to win they would almost certainly have to get Thomson out. Even for the last two overs of the fourth day, after a brief stoppage for rain, Border was allowed to bat unharassed by close fielders. It was the same next morning, even when England took the new ball.

Thus flattered, Border, whose previous fifteen Test innings had brought him only 245 runs, was now at his fighting best. Thomson, growing in confidence, occasionally pierced England's off-side field, his feet spreadeagled. As Australia slowly closed the gap, every run was cheered to the echo. England, in their fielding, showed understandable signs of panic. Cowans, though he continued to bowl well, failed to find quite his best rhythm; Willis, though admirably accurate, lacked his old pace. In the end, all hope for England almost gone, Botham, their great all-rounder, produced the ball that not only won the match but revived the tour. Botham's dismissal of Thomson made him only the second Englishman, Wilfred Rhodes being the other, to have scored 1,000 runs and taken 100 wickets against Australia. [...]

ENGLAND

G. Cook c Chappell b Thomson	10	– c Yardley b Thomson	26
G. Fowler c Chappell b Hogg	4	– b Hogg	65
C.J. Tavaré c Yardley b Thomson	89	– b Hogg	0
D.I. Gower c Marsh b Hogg	18	– c Marsh b Lawson	3
A.J. Lamb c Dyson b Yardley	83	– c Marsh b Hogg	26
I.T. Botham c Wessels b Yardley	27	– c Chappell b Thomson	46
G. Miller c Border b Yardley	10	– lbw b Lawson	14
D.R. Pringle c Wessels b Hogg	9	– c Marsh b Lawson	42
†R.W. Taylor c Marsh b Yardley	1	– lbw b Thomson	37
*R.G.D. Willis not out	6	– not out	8
N.G. Cowans c Lawson b Hogg	3	– b Lawson	10
B 3, l-b 6, w 3, n-b 12	24	B 2, l-b 9, n-b 6	17

1/11 2/25 3/56 4/217 5/227   **284**   1/40 2/41 3/45 4/128 5/129   **294**
6/259 7/262 8/268 9/278 9/282   6/160 7/201 8/262

Bowling: FIRST INNINGS – Lawson 17-6-48-0; Hogg 23.3-6-69-4; Yardley 27-9-89-4; Thomson 13-2-49-2; Chappell 1-0-5-0. SECOND INNINGS – Lawson 21.4-6-66-4; Hogg 22-5-64-3; Yardley 15-2-67-0; Thomson 21-3-74-3; Chappell 1-0-6-0.

AUSTRALIA

K.C. Wessels b Willis 47	– b Cowans 14
J. Dyson lbw b Cowans 21	– c Tavaré b Botham 31
*G.S. Chappell c Lamb b Cowans 0	– c sub b Cowans 2
K.J. Hughes b Willis 66	– c Taylor b Miller 48
A.R. Border b Botham 2	– (6) not out 62
D.W. Hookes c Taylor b Pringle 53	– (5) c Willis b Cowans 68
†R.W. Marsh b Willis 53	– lbw b Cowans 13
B. Yardley b Miller 9	– b Cowans 0
G.F. Lawson c Fowler b Miller 0	– c Cowans b Pringle 7
R.M. Hogg not out 8	– lbw b Cowans 4
J.R. Thomson b Miller 1	– c Miller b Botham 21
L-b 8, n-b 19 27	B 5, l-b 9, w 1, n-b 3 18

1/55 2/55 3/83 4/89 5/180   **287**   1/37 2/39 3/71 4/171 5/173   **288**
6/261 7/276 8/276 9/278   6/190 7/190 8/202 9/218

Bowling: FIRST INNINGS – Willis 15-2-38-3; Botham 18-3-69-1; Cowans 16-0-69-1; Pringle 15-2-40-1; Miller 15-5-44-3. SECOND INNINGS – Willis 17-0-57-0; Botham 25.1-4-80-2; Cowans 26-6-77-6; Pringle 12-4-26-1; Miller 16-6-30-1.

Umpires: A.R. Crafter and R.V. Whitehead.

SECOND CORNHILL TEST

At Lord's, June 27, 28, 29, July 1, 2, 1985. Australia won by four wickets. This was Border's match. The Australian captain scored 43 per cent of his side's runs, 237 out of 552, and led them superbly to maintain Australia's unbeaten run at cricket's headquarters since Verity bowled them to defeat in 1934. [...] A fine match was played in a good atmosphere with none of the noises-off that had marred the enjoyment of many people at the Test matches against West Indies the previous year. It was remarkable that play was able to start to time on the first day, for on the afternoon before, an MCC assistant secretary had worn wellington boots to inspect the sodden outfield. However, Mick Hunt, the groundsman, and some of his staff worked through the night to remove surface water and, although the pitch was soft and the square still wet, the umpires allowed the game to begin at the appointed time. Border won the toss and asked England to bat. The pitch being too slow at that stage for his leg-spinner, the 38-year-old Holland, Border was gambling on his three pace bowlers to bowl England out, and he was not disappointed. England brought in Edmonds and Foster for Cowans and Willey, and omitted Sidebottom from their original twelve players.

McDermott bowled magnificently for his six wickets. He had both England's openers, Gooch and Robinson, leg before, though Gooch's decision appeared a harsh one, the point of impact looking to be outside the line of the off stump as he played his shot. Gower dominated the England first innings with batting which persuaded the selectors to confirm him in the captaincy for the remaining four Tests. Lawson, still not bowling as fast or aggressively as he is able to, took the crucial wicket of Botham, having him caught on the cover boundary, driving at a slower delivery.

Play on the second day was interrupted five times and finally curtailed by bad light, to the annoyance of a capacity crowd. Loud disapproval was expressed when play was halted for the last time with England's spinners, Edmonds and Emburey, in action. Border, then 92 out of Australia's 183 for four, might have gone at 87 when his pull off Edmonds struck Gatting's wrist at short leg. As the fielder strove to control the ball, he seemed, prematurely, to try to throw it up in celebration of what would have been a remarkable catch. The ball escaped Gatting's despairing lunge, and in response to a somewhat half-hearted appeal umpire Bird ruled that it had not been retained in such a way as to satisfy Law 32.

Border's fifth-wicket stand of 216 with Ritchie ended soon after lunch on the third day when Botham, kept out of the attack in the morning to protect a slightly strained ankle, upset Ritchie's equanimity with a couple of bouncers and followed them with a straight delivery which had him leg before. Botham bowled as fast as for some time and his five wickets prevented the Australians from running away with the match. It was the 25th time he had claimed five wickets in an innings in a Test, a record for any country.

Trailing by 135, England needed a sound start to their second innings; but Gooch was caught behind, trying to leg glance McDermott, and Robinson's bat caught in his pad as he defended against Holland. Gower then took the controversial decision to send in not one, but two night-watchmen, Emburey and Allott. The promotion of two tailenders meant that a major batsman was likely to be left stranded later in the innings, and so it proved. On the Monday morning Lawson reduced England to 98 for six when he removed Emburey, Allott and Lamb, Gower having gone for a one-day-style 22. But Botham, suffering from a bruised toe sustained when he was hit by a golf ball at Wentworth the day before, added 131 with Gatting. They were on the way to turning likely defeat into possible victory when Holland went round the wicket at the Nursery End, aiming for the rough created by McDermott outside the right-hander's leg stump. McDermott had been officially warned by umpire Bird for running down the pitch. Botham's reply was to keep padding the ball away until, going for a big hit, he was caught just backward of point. Downton went next ball, caught at slip. Holland's five wickets on his first appearance in a Test in England were a splendid reward for accurate, intelligent bowling.

Australia faced 21 overs before the close, by when they were 46 for three, needing 127. Hilditch was caught hooking, Wood in the gully off a lifter, both off Botham, and Ritchie was bowled by the accurate Allott. Wood's wicket was Botham's 326th in Tests, making him England's most prolific wicket-taker. On the last morning Border's nerve held after Australia had declined to 65 to five, Wessels, the striker, being run out by a quick return from Gower at short leg and Boon bowled. Border was made Man of the Match and the game of cricket enhanced by a pleasurable Test.

ENGLAND

G.A. Gooch lbw McDermott	.30	– c Phillips b McDermott	.17
R.T. Robinson lbw b McDermott	.6	– b Holland	.12
*D.I. Gower c Border b McDermott	.86	– (5) c Phillips b McDermott	.22
M.W. Gatting lbw b Lawson	.14	– (6) not out	.75
A.J. Lamb c Phillips b Lawson	.47	– (7) c Holland b Lawson	.9
I.T. Botham c Ritchie b Lawson	.5	– (8) c Border b Holland	.85
†P.R. Downton c Wessels b McDermott	.21	– (9) c Boon b Holland	.0
J.E. Emburey lbw b O'Donnell	.33	– (3) b Lawson	.20
P.H. Edmonds c Border b McDermott	.21	– (10) c Boon b Holland	.1
N.A. Foster c Wessels b McDermott	.3	– (11) c Border b Holland	.0
P.J.W. Allott not out	.1	– (4) b Lawson	.0
B 1, l-b 4, w 1, n-b 17	.23	B 1, l-b 12, w 4, n-b 3	.20

1/26 2/51 3/99 4/179 5/184 **290** 1/32 2/34 3/38 4/57 5/77 **261**
6/211 7/241 8/273 9/283 6/98 7/229 8/229 9/261

Bowling: FIRST INNINGS – Lawson 25-2-91-3; McDermott 29.2-5-70-6; O'Donnell 22-3-82-1; Holland 23-6-42-0. SECOND INNINGS – McDermott 20-2-84-2; Lawson 23-0-86-3; Holland 32-12-68-5; O'Donnell 5-0-10-0.

AUSTRALIA

G.M. Wood c Emburey b Allott	.8	– (2) c Lamb b Botham	.6
A.M.J. Hilditch b Foster	.14	– (1) c Lamb b Botham	.0
K.C. Wessels lbw b Botham	.11	– run out	.28
*A.R. Border c Gooch b Botham	.196	– (5) not out	.41
D.C. Boon c Downton b Botham	.4	– (6) b Edmonds	.1
G.M. Ritchie lbw b Botham	.94	– (4) b Allott	.2
†W.B. Phillips c Edmonds b Botham	.21	– c Edmonds b Emburey	.29
S.P. O'Donnell c Lamb b Edmonds	.48	– not out	.9
G.F. Lawson not out	.5		
C.J. McDermott run out	.9		
R.G. Holland b Edmonds	.0		
L-b 10, w 1, n-b 4	.15	L-b 11	.11

1/11 2/24 3/80 4/101 5/317 **425** 1/0 2/9 3/22 4/63 **(6 wkts) 127**
6/347 7/398 8/414 9/425 5/65 6/116

Bowling: FIRST INNINGS – Foster 23-1-83-1; Allott 30-4-70-1; Botham 24-2-109-5; Edmonds 25-4-85-2; Gooch 3-1-11-0; Emburey 19-3-57-0. SECOND INNINGS – Botham 15-0-49-2; Allott 7-4-8-1; Edmonds 16-5-35-1; Emburey 8-4-24-1.

Umpires: H.D. Bird and D.G.L. Evans.

ENGLAND V. AUSTRALIA – THE BRAND LEADER?

By Matthew Engel

The first Australian team to visit England after the war was welcomed in the 1948 *Wisden* by the writer, Vivian Jenkins, who described the Test matches between the two nations as 'an ever-recurring wonder that stirs the blood of each succeeding generation as they see it come to light anew.' Jenkins's generation had just suffered a conflict infinitely more important than any game, and there was indeed a sense of wonder about the renewal of cricket. The Editor's Notes in that volume, referring to the 1947 season, were headed 'A Wonderful Season' and the sub-headings included the phrases 'Bowlers of Many Types', 'Batsmen Excel', 'Close Finishes' and 'Great Crowds'. Despite the present editor's best intentions, the 1989 edition is inevitably a little less upbeat.

This is, in part, the penalty for more than 40 years of peace. Sport has fallen into a routine. Every four years – immediately after leap year, the American presidential election and the quadrennial shellacking of English cricket by West Indies – the Australians arrive. Is that such a big deal any more?

Modern cricket, professional and problematical, cannot recapture the delight people felt in the late 1940s simply in being alive and, incidentally, involved in the game again. We have come to take the good things in life for granted. Players and journalists secretly rejoice when a tour is cancelled because it gives them a break from Test matches. Meanwhile, cricket has become a competing brand name in the leisure industry; it has to be sponsored, marketed and packaged for television.

England v. Australia is a product. And if it remains the brand leader, it is hard to pretend that is anything to do with superior quality. It is highly improbable that the Test series this summer will be won by the world's best cricket team. If *Which?* magazine was conducting a survey, it would probably rate India against New Zealand a better buy. And yet. Ad-men understand better than anybody the importance of mystique, and in cricket we are absolute suckers for it. Somehow this spring is a little different from last spring, the one before and the one before that. The first grass cuttings smell just a mite sweeter; the tang of anticipation is that tiny bit keener. The Ashes are at stake. In spite of everything, England v. Australia is an ever-recurring wonder, even in 1989.

But if it is to stay that way, we perhaps ought to understand the phenomenon a little better. It is probably 28 years since the two teams met as the best cricket teams on earth. Even so, there have been a stack of series and individual games since then that have stirred the blood in a way no other contest could have.

Part of this is because, somehow, England and Australia understand each other's cricket. Thinking about this, I wondered whether this might be something to do with the unfashionable concept of kith 'n' kin. But it is not. That rapport is never there with the New Zealanders. Lovely people, of course – but on a tour of New Zealand it soon becomes clear that everyone there would be far more interested if you were playing rugby or, worse, a best-of-50 one-day series. With England and Australia, there is a shared instinct. For more than a century, cricket's founder-nations have managed to rub along together. The relationship has often been terse, even gruff, because both countries prefer it that way. But when problems have arisen – bodyline, the chuckers and drag artists of the fifties, even the Packer intervention – they have been settled in the end with a mutual regard and sympathy.

It happens that in the 1980s there has been a great deal of personal friendship between the dressing-rooms. This is partly a reaction to the sledging 1970s, and partly due to the personal qualities of the leading players of the era, Allan Border in particular. We have grown used to the sight of Australia's captain playing for Essex, though it would have been inconceivable for his predecessors. On the whole, I am inclined to think that it is a precedent which ought not be encouraged. This is nothing to do with the desperate theory that England's prospects of winning Test matches are being ruined by the small number of overseas players now allowed to appear in county cricket. It is everything to do with the freshness that Australians still bring to every fourth English summer.

Dean Jones, who was established as one of the world's leading players until he lost form in 1988, is still only a rumour to most English cricket-watchers. Ditto Bruce Reid. One feels that the appeal of the West Indians, for instance, would have been infinitely greater through the 1980s if the sight of Richards and Marshall had been rationed, instead of being on offer seven days a week, summer after summer, to those who bothered to turn up at Taunton and Southampton.

Australian touring teams really do arrive still, unlike Indians and West Indians who sort of coalesce over the course of a few days from exotic winter quarters in places like Oldham. Even with the Aussies, it is not quite the same as in the old days, when the liner would dock at Tilbury, and Woodfull or Bradman would stand on a windswept quayside in a full-length macintosh and make a brief but graceful speech (having had a month on board for preparation, with only formal dinners and deck quoits as distractions) about making friends, playing bright cricket and winning the series. Nowadays, the players arrive at Heathrow, shortly after finishing their latest set of utterly forgettable one-day internationals against somebody or other. They will be driven to a hotel in central London and troop into a function room, probably with chandeliers. The team will be green-blazered, bleary-eyed, unshaven; if precedent is followed exactly, one or two may be suffering from very severe hangovers indeed. The captain will then make a brief but graceful speech about making friends, playing bright cricket and winning the series.

It is not necessary for anyone to believe this, even the captain. After all, in the past 25 years, Australia have won only one series in Britain – on the hastily arranged tour of 1975. However, he is probably being utterly insincere only if he says he intends to win all the county matches as well. The Australian tour, alone of them all, still retains a sense of occasion outside the Test matches; it remains an event when the team arrives in Northampton or Southampton. It would be an event in Hove or Canterbury, too, but this year Kent and Sussex are likely to get a fixture only by being knocked out of the NatWest Bank Trophy before the semi-finals, which is not something they are going to contrive on purpose. Among spectators, the enthusiasm remains; but it represents the triumph of hope and folk-memory over recent experience. The 1977, 1981 and 1985 Australians played 42 first-class matches between them outside the Tests and drew 31 of them. The last two visiting teams were unbeaten in first-class matches outside the Tests, just as the 1953 team was. It would be nice to see this as a tribute to their strength. Unfortunately, it has more to do with a truncated fixture list, appalling weather and pathetic attitudes on the part of both touring teams and counties.

I hereby propose a minor amendment to either the Laws of the Game or the tour conditions, to apply to (a) any touring captain who says he would have declared but thought that so-and-so needed the batting practice, and (b) any county captain who, on the first morning of the tourists' game, suddenly discovers that all his adult fast bowlers and front-line batsmen happen to have hay fever or groin stains; viz., that they should be taken at once to the traditional beneficiary's barbecue and served up roasted whole with the jacket potatoes.

However, these are the 1980s. If something is to be done, it will probably require a form of sponsorship. An attempt was made a decade ago, with an improbable £100,000 jackpot offered to the touring team if they won every county match. The 1980 West Indians actually got almost halfway – five wins out of eleven – towards scooping the pool before being confounded by that very wet summer. It seems to me that something similar may have to be devised again, this time with an equally juicy bone for the counties to gnaw.

Occasionally, a classic match still happens. For the opening game of first-class cricket on the 1985 tour, the Australians went to Taunton and there were 507 runs on the first day, a marvellous duel between Botham and the visiting attack, and then a burst of fast bowling from Jeff Thomson which implied that he and his team were ready to storm through the summer. It was an illusion, in various ways; but the tour as a whole was unforgettable none the less. One way or another, it always is. Pray heaven it always will be. (*1989*)

FIFTH CORNHILL TEST

At Nottingham, August 10, 11, 12, 14, 1989. Australia won by an innings and 180 runs. Toss: Australia. The bad luck which seems to accompany a side guilty of bad play (or should it be the other way round?) struck again for England when Small withdrew on the eve of the match, thus preserving their 100 per cent record of being unable to choose from the originally selected squad in every Test in 1989. Although Thomas was called up in Small's place, in the event he was named as twelfth man, which left England with the inexperienced new-ball pairing of Fraser, playing in his third Test, and Malcolm, winning his first cap. Atherton was the only other débutant, the selectors having responded to calls for a major transfusion of new blood with little more than a smear. No player contracted to go to South Africa had been considered for selection, and Gooch had been omitted to rediscover his form with his county.

On a flat, grassless pitch expected to assist the spinners as the match wore on, England named both Cook and Hemmings in their final eleven, and Cook it was who took the first Australian wicket. As it arrived at twelve minutes past twelve on the second day, this was not a matter for great rejoicing. Border, having won an important toss, had then spent the best part of four sessions joining in the applause as Marsh and Taylor went past numerous records in their opening partnership of 329.

The milestones (gravestones?) began just after lunch on the first day with the comparatively modest figure of 89 – Australia's previous highest opening partnership at Trent Bridge – and ended at 323, the highest by two openers in Ashes history, a record that had stood to Hobbs and Rhodes since 1911–12. In between the following were passed: 135 – Australia's best opening partnership of the series; 170 – the highest Australian partnership at Trent Bridge; 201 – the highest Australian opening partnership in England; 244 – the highest Australian opening partnership against England; and 319 – the highest partnership in a Test at Trent Bridge. Moreover, by stumps on Thursday, Marsh and Taylor had become the first pair to bat through a full day's play in a Test match in England, and only the ninth in Test cricket anywhere. They were the third opening pair to bat through the first day of a Test match, the others being V. Mankad and P. Roy, for India v. New Zealand in 1955–56, and W.M. Lawry and R.B. Simpson, for Australia v. West Indies in 1964–65. As for individual landmarks, Marsh made his first century in 22 Tests since the 1986–87 Ashes encounter in Brisbane, while Taylor continued his remarkable summer with a career-best 219 in nine hours ten minutes (461 balls, 23 fours) to take his aggregate for the series to 720 runs at an average of 90. Only three Australian totals in Ashes history remained above that, all of them compiled by D.G. Bradman.

Despite the fact that Australia eventually put together a total of 602 for six declared, their highest at Trent Bridge, England for once had not totally let themselves down. Malcolm bowled with genuine hostility when fresh, the batsmen's apprehension augmented by the fact that Malcolm's uncertainty as to where the ball was going led to several accidental beamers. Fraser's contrasting accuracy allowed him to bowl for a quarter of the innings at a cost of no more than 2 runs per over, and Cook rediscovered the flight and control that had deserted him in the previous Test. Nor did the fielding, as it had on previous occasions, disintegrate.

With the notable exception of Smith, however, there was not much consolation from the batting. The first wicket went down after four deliveries (740 fewer than England had required to remove the first Australian), and when Atherton made a second-ball 0 on his début, Smith arrived for the start of the second over with the scoreboard reading 1 for two. His strokeplay, particularly around the off stump, was little short of ferocious. Hughes took a beating, and a pull off Hohns resulted in Boon, at short leg, literally having the helmet torn from his head. It was a miracle that he was helped off in need of nothing more than a couple of aspirin and a lie-down.

Smith's magnificent 150-ball century, bracketed alongside Waugh's unbeaten 177 at Headingley as among the great innings in England v. Australia Tests, none the less stood alone amidst another familiarly depressing tale. Such was England's gruesome technique that Australia had little more to do than bowl at the stumps, certain in the knowledge that sooner or later either a crooked bat would miss the ball or a front pad – planted not far enough down the pitch to confuse the umpire – would get in its way. England had suffered more bad luck when Botham dislocated a finger on his right hand, failing to take a sharp chance in the slips. Coming in at No. 9 he could bat more or less only one-handed, and having already been informed that the injury would prevent him from playing at The Oval, he did not bat in the second innings.

Following on 347 in arrears on Monday morning, England were bowled out for 167 soon after tea. Atherton, batting almost three hours (127 balls) for his 47, was the one batsman to make a half-decent fist of it. Only once before, to Bradman's 1948 side, had England lost four home Tests in an Ashes series, and the final ignominy for them in the statistical avalanche was the fact that an innings and 180 runs represented their heaviest defeat in England by Australia. (*Martin Johnson*)

Man of the Match: M.A. Taylor.

Close of play: First day, Australia 301-0 (G.R. Marsh 125*, M.A. Taylor 141*); Second day, Australia 560-5 (A.R. Border 46*, I.A. Healy 5*); Third day, England 246-9 (N.G.B. Cook 1*, D.E. Malcolm 1*).

AUSTRALIA

G.R. Marsh c Botham b Cook 138
M.A. Taylor st Russell b Cook 219
D.C. Boon st Russell b Cook 73
*A.R. Border not out 65
D.M. Jones c Gower b Fraser 22
S.R. Waugh c Gower b Malcolm 0

†I.A. Healy b Fraser 5
T.V. Hohns not out 19
   B 6, l-b 23, w 3, n-b 29 61

1/329 (1)   (6 wkts, dec.) **602**
2/430 (2) 3/502 (3) 4/543 (5)
5/553 (6) 6/560 (7)

M.G. Hughes, G.F. Lawson and T.M. Alderman did not bat.

Bowling: Fraser 52.3-18-108-2; Malcolm 44-2-166-1; Botham 30-4-103-0; Hemmings 33-9-81-0; Cook 40-10-91-3; Atherton 7-0-24-0.

ENGLAND

T.S. Curtis lbw b Alderman ....1 – (2) lbw b Alderman 6
M.D. Moxon c Waugh b Alderman ....0 – (5) b Alderman 18
M.A. Atherton lbw b Alderman ....0 – c and b Hohns 47
R.A. Smith c Healy b Alderman ....101 – b Hughes 26
*D.I. Gower c Healy b Lawson ....11 – (1) b Lawson 5
†R.C. Russell c Healy b Lawson ....20 – b Lawson 1
E.E. Hemmings b Alderman ....38 – lbw b Hughes 35
A.R.C. Fraser b Hohns ....29 – b Hohns 1
I.T. Botham c Waugh b Hohns ....12 – absent injured
N.G.B. Cook not out ....2 – (9) not out 7
D.E. Malcolm c Healy b Hughes ....9 – (10) b Hughes 5
   L-b 18, n-b 13 31   B 3, l-b 6, w 1, n-b 6 16

1/1 (2) 2/1 (3) 3/14 (1) 4/37 (5)   **255**   1/5 (1) 2/13 (2) 3/67 (4)   **167**
5/119 (6) 6/172 (4) 7/214 (7)   4/106 (5) 5/114 (6) 6/120 (3)
8/243 (8) 9/244 (9) 10/255 (11)   7/134 (8) 8/160 (7) 9/167 (10)

Bowling: FIRST INNINGS – Alderman 19-2-69-5; Lawson 21-5-57-2; Hohns 18-8-48-2; Hughes 7.5-0-40-1; Waugh 11-4-23-0. SECOND INNINGS – Alderman 16-6-32-2; Lawson 15-3-51-2; Hughes 12.3-1-46-3; Hohns 12-3-29-2.

Umpires: N.T. Plews and D.R. Shepherd.

FIRST CORNHILL TEST

At Manchester, June 3, 4, 5, 6, 7, 1993. Australia won by 179 runs. Toss: England. Test debuts: A.R. Caddick, P.M. Such; B.P. Julian, M.J. Slater.

An enthralling match of splendid individual achievements was won by Australia with 9.4 overs to spare. A rarity among modern Tests in England, it was shaped by slow bowling and finally decided by leg-spin. Warne, the 23-year-old Victorian, returned match figures of eight for 137, the best in England by an Australian leg-spinner since W.J. O'Reilly took ten for 122 at Leeds in 1938. One particular delivery from Warne set the tone for the series. His first ball in an Ashes contest pitched outside leg stump and hit the top of Gatting's off stump. Gatting looked understandably bewildered as he dragged himself off the field. Thereafter only Gooch played Warne with conviction: never, perhaps, has one delivery cast so long a shadow over a game, or a series.

Warne also produced a stunning catch at backward square leg to dismiss Caddick in the tense final stages as England tried to salvage a draw. [...]

The opening pair, both from the New South Wales town of Wagga Wagga, began with a stand of 128 but then Australia lost three wickets for 11 in the final hour, including Steve Waugh, who was bowled off stump trying to drive – a classic off-spinner's dismissal. On the second day, Such moved on to take six for 67 and his cool and control compared favourably with the palpable lack of confidence shown by Tufnell.

With Australia out for 289 and Gooch and Atherton resuming their sequence of reassuring opening partnerships England briefly looked like a team ready to compete for the Ashes. Then Atherton was out, Warne came on for the 28th over, bowled what became known as The Ball from Hell and the series really began. Gatting's departure was followed by that of Smith, caught at slip, and Gooch, who hit a full-toss to mid-on. By the close England had eight down and Keith Fletcher, the England manager, was saying he had never seen a Test pitch in England turn so much.

The third day began with another flurry of wickets. Such came on to bowl the ninth over of the Australian innings and with his fifth ball had Taylor lbw, sweeping. But Boon then batted with his customary pragmatism while Mark Waugh unleashed a series of glittering strokes. The cricket was more attritional after Waugh was out but Australia were just as sure-footed: Steve Waugh and Healy batted England out of the match with an unbroken stand of 180 in 164 minutes. Healy became the first Australian to make his maiden first-class century in a Test since H. Graham, exactly a hundred years earlier, at Lord's. [...] The declaration came at 3 p.m. and England were left to score 512 in a day and a half. Gooch and Atherton again batted securely, with the captain notably authoritative. Then Gatting played with freedom until he was bowled off his pads from the last ball of the day by the indefatigable Hughes, a due reward for his willingness to vary his line and length. Gooch was understandably more circumspect on the final morning and – although Smith was tormented and then bowled by Warne – he reached his 18th Test hundred and England had the chance of a draw. Yet half an hour after lunch Gooch became the fifth cricketer, and the first Englishman, to be dismissed 'handled the ball' in a Test as he instinctively flicked out with a glove at a ball dropping on to his stumps. Umpire Bird had no hesitation in giving Gooch out, with the moral victory, if not the wicket, going to Hughes for extracting extra bounce on an increasingly lifeless pitch.

Although the first ten English batsmen all batted for at least half an hour in the second innings, none could match the technical skill and authority of Gooch. For a time Caddick and Such threatened an unlikely stalemate but brilliant catches by Warne and Border completed their downfall. The Australians embarked on some typically committed celebrations. (*Patrick Murphy*)

Man of the Match: S.K. Warne. *Attendance*: 55,788; *receipts* £812,100.

Close of play: First day, Australia 242-5 (A.R. Border 9*, I.A. Healy 6*); Second day, England 202-8 (A.R. Caddick 6*, P.M. Such 9*); Third day, Australia 231-3 (D.C. Boon 85*, A.R. Border 29*); Fourth day, England 133-2 (G.A. Gooch 82*).

AUSTRALIA

M.A. Taylor c and b Such	.124 –	(2) lbw b Such	.9
M.J. Slater c Stewart b DeFreitas	.58 –	(1) c Caddick b Such	.27
D.C. Boon c Lewis b Such	.21 –	c Gatting b DeFreitas	.93
M.E. Waugh c and b Tufnell	.6 –	b Tufnell	.64
*A.R. Border st Stewart b Such	.17 –	c and b Caddick	.31
S.R. Waugh b Such	.3 –	not out	.78
†I.A. Healy c Such b Tufnell	.12 –	not out	.102
B.P. Julian c Gatting b Such	.0		
M.G. Hughes c DeFreitas b Such	.2		
S.K. Warne not out	.15		
C.J. McDermott run out	.8		
B 8, l-b 8, n-b 7	.23	B 6, l-b 14, w 8	.28

1/128 (2) 2/183 (3) 3/221 (4) 4/225 (1)   **289**   1/23 (2) 2/46 (1)   (5 wkts, dec.) **432**
5/232 (6) 6/260 (5) 7/264 (8)   3/155 (4) 4/234 (5)
8/266 (9) 9/267 (7) 10/289 (11)   5/252 (3)

Bowling: FIRST INNINGS – Caddick 15-4-38-0; DeFreitas 23-8-46-1; Lewis 13-2-44-0; Such 33.3-9-67-6; Tufnell 28-5-78-2. SECOND INNINGS – Caddick 20-3-79-1; DeFreitas 24-1-80-1; Such 31-6-78-2; Tufnell 37-4-112-1; Hick 9-1-20-0; Lewis 9-0-43-0.

ENGLAND

*G.A. Gooch c Julian b Warne	.65 –	handled the ball	.133
M.A. Atherton c Healy b Hughes	.19 –	c Taylor b Warne	.25
M.W. Gatting b Warne	.4 –	b Hughes	.23
R.A. Smith c Taylor b Warne	.4 –	b Warne	.18
G.A. Hick c Border b Hughes	.34 –	c Healy b Hughes	.22
†A.J. Stewart b Julian	.27 –	c Healy b Warne	.11
C.C. Lewis c Boon b Hughes	.9 –	c Taylor b Warne	.43
P.A.J. DeFreitas lbw b Julian	.5 –	lbw b Julian	.7
A.R. Caddick c Healy b Warne	.7 –	c Warne b Hughes	.25
P.M. Such not out	.14 –	c Border b Hughes	.9
P.C.R. Tufnell c Healy b Hughes	.1 –	not out	.0
B 6, l-b 10, n-b 5	.21	L-b 11, w 1, n-b 4	.16

1/71 (2) 2/80 (3) 3/84 (4)   **210**   1/73 (2) 2/133 (3) 3/171 (4)   **332**
4/123 (1) 5/148 (5) 6/168 (7)   4/223 (1) 5/230 (5) 6/238 (6)
7/178 (8) 8/183 (6) 9/203 (9)   7/260 (8) 8/299 (7) 9/331 (9)
10/210 (11)   10/332 (10)

Bowling: FIRST INNINGS – McDermott 18-2-50-0; Hughes 20.5-5-59-4; Julian 11-2-30-2; Warne 24-10-51-4; Border 1-0-4-0. SECOND INNINGS – McDermott 30-9-76-0; Hughes 27.2-4-92-4; Warne 49-26-86-4; Julian 14-1-67-1.

Umpires: H.D. Bird and K.E. Palmer. Referee: Mansur Ali Khan (India).

WHY WE BEAT THE POMS

By Ian Chappell

Why do Australia beat England? In general, because Australia play an aggressive brand of cricket and, when the talent is there, they get in position to seek victory more often. Notwithstanding that, Australia couldn't have lost the last three Ashes series even if they had bet heavily on the opposition. England played badly, often. In particular, the bowling was abysmal. .

During the summer of 1993 I constantly heard the lament, 'What is wrong with English cricket?' In part, the answer is the inability of people directing the English game to recognise the good that there is. For instance, one of the more common moans was 'Where are all the England fast bowlers?' Answer: Devon Malcolm was playing for Derbyshire for the first five Tests. Or 'What has happened to the old-fashioned English seamer?' Answer: Steve Watkin was playing for Glamorgan for the first five Tests. Or 'Why were England 4-0 down after five Tests?' Answer: From the time of the second one-day international when, as captain, Graham Gooch froze like a rabbit caught in the headlights, it was obvious he wasn't the man to lead England to an Ashes victory.

England's ability to over-theorise and complicate the game of cricket is legendary. Ever since I became involved in Ashes battles, I've felt that Australia could rely on some assistance from the England selectors. In 1993 they ran truer to form than many of the players they picked. Their magnanimity gave Australia a four-game start before the penny dropped. They then promoted Mike Atherton to the captaincy and, in no time, England picked a reasonably well-balanced side with an attack that bore some semblance of hostility.

Atherton had one piece of good fortune which every captain needs to be successful. Angus Fraser chose the appropriate moment to return to full form and fitness. But even before that Atherton had displayed considerable cricket wisdom. He said at Edgbaston after only three days in the job: 'Our most important task is to identify the talent to win games. Then we must be prepared to stick with them.' He was as good as his word in helping to select the touring party for the Caribbean and in addition he cleverly used his new-found power to make important adjustments to the balance of the side.

Until the advent of Atherton, England's selections had often lacked rhyme or reason. A classic case was the predicament of 21-year-old Mark Lathwell in the one-day international series. At Lord's, Australia had an unbeatable 2-0 lead, so the selectors took the opportunity to play their talented 21-year-old, Damien Martyn. As he made mincemeat of the bowling on his way to a glorious half-century, an MCC member said to me, 'How come you Australians always produce good young batsmen?' With Lathwell needlessly sitting in the pavilion watching his third match in a row, the answer wasn't difficult. 'We play them,' I replied.

Maybe Atherton doesn't need assistants like Keith Fletcher. The England cricket manager seems typical of a mentality that pervades county cricket – if it's difficult, take the easy way out. Fletcher's illogical call during the Ashes series for groundsmen to help England by producing seaming pitches went as it should have done: unheeded. However, Fletcher's behaviour should have caught the attention of officials and received a reprimand.

Not only was the suggestion unfair, his reasoning was astray. This was proved at The Oval where a well-balanced side, capably led and playing good, aggressive cricket, beat Australia on one of the best cricket wickets I've seen in England. There was pace and bounce in Harry Brind's pitch (as usual) and it produced the best match of the series. If the counties followed the examples of Brind and Old Trafford's Peter Marron and, where possible, produced similar pitches, then England's good cricketers would benefit substantially at international level. Unfortunately, the county mentality is often similar to Fletcher's: pitches are prepared either to assist the home side or to blunt a strength in the opposition.

Fletcher incorrectly suggested that England is the only country where helping the home side with pitch preparation is not accepted practice. I haven't played on or seen any green-top fliers in the Caribbean, and my brother Greg has often said: 'If you have to bat against four West Indies pace bowlers then the best place to do it is on their own turf.' And in more than thirty years of playing and watching cricket in Australia, I can honestly say that I've never seen a Test pitch that varies greatly from its behaviour during the Sheffield Shield season. In fact, one of the strengths of the Shield competition is that the players perform on pitches which are very close to Test standard. Under this system it's easy to identify the players who stand a chance at Test level, the ones who are capable of playing only first-class cricket and those who will soon return to club cricket.

When Australia hit rock bottom through the 1984-87 period, the standard of Sheffield Shield cricket was low. The problem was addressed because talented and gutsy young players were encouraged. Now it is a vibrant competition and an excellent breeding ground. England are on the right track with four-day first-class games, but it will take time for the benefits to accrue. I think they should go a step further and reduce the number of teams to make it more competitive, as there are players in the county structure who are not up to first-class standard. Any system that protects incompetence needs changing. If this means having a first and second division then that could be the way to accommodate part-time players who want to combine business and cricket.

These changes could be part of a package to convince the counties that they must put England's needs at the top of their list, rather than on a level with deciding which colour to paint the pavilion roof.

Any move to improve the structure should be aimed at increasing pride in playing for the national team. Encouragingly, since Atherton has become involved in the selection process, I detect a move back to the feeling that the England team is for English players. If this is the case it's good news: England was in danger of becoming a haven for career cricketers who were unsure of making it in their own country.

Lack of pride manifests itself in a number of ways and in England's case the most serious has been to capitulate in a Test when trouble loomed. Their players used to be the best in the world at extricating themselves from trouble. This generation needs to rediscover that urge. The inability to save Tests must also have something to do with technique and mental strength. In an age where we have more coaches than ever throughout the cricket world, I query how much good they are doing. I believe in good coaching, but I think players are better to have none (i.e. work it out for themselves) than to have bad coaching.

In Australia, I believe the Cricket Academy could be run more effectively by not removing the young players from their home environment. However, many of the players leaving the Academy are mentally tough and primed for first-class cricket. This is exactly what you would expect with Rod Marsh as head coach and there is no doubt it is having a positive effect on the depth of Australian first-class cricket.

Also, apart from a brief period when Australia, like other teams, were bluffed by West Indies into thinking that pace was the almighty weapon, there has been a broad-brush approach to bowling the opposition out. This includes having leg-spinners once again. In the period when they were forgotten in Australia, Bill 'Tiger' O'Reilly was furious. But just as he did in his playing days, O'Reilly saved his most lethal delivery for the old enemy. 'I can never forgive English cricket,' he said, 'for attempting to kill off leg-spin bowling.' O'Reilly thought English captains had no idea how to handle leg-spinners.

This brings me in a roundabout way to uncovered pitches. This is often suggested as a recipe for helping English cricket. I say codswallop. Uncovered pitches at first-class level would encourage the expectancy of easy pickings for the bowlers. Leg-spinners are the antithesis of easy pickings. Another suggestion is that there is too much one-day cricket. This is codswallop too. If young players are taught *properly* as they progress in the game, the smarter ones learn to adapt their thinking to all sorts of different pitches, bowlers and playing conditions.

Prior to the 1993–94 season, the Australian Cricket Board gave the selectors power to rest a jaded or slightly injured player from one-day internationals, while still receiving full pay. This is recognition that Test cricket is the true measuring stick for a player's skill, but also acknowledges the contribution made by one-day cricket to the game's finances and spreading popularity. It could also be a solution to the vexing problem of the right balance in a touring team's itinerary.

The ACB's edict is an interesting development in the gradual evolution of the professional game, in places other than England. Like so many things, the English invented one-day cricket and other countries have improved on their system, leaving them languishing. There are some signs of modern thinking in the marketing of English cricket but it has taken an inordinate amount of time to occur. In the end, though, the marketing men need a strong England side. So does the whole of cricket. (*1994*)

from NOTES BY THE EDITOR

THE ASHES REALLY SHOULD GO TO AUSTRALIA

[…] As every schoolboy used and ought to know, the urn and its contents rest permanently in the museum at Lord's. This is, of course, legally as it should be: they were given to MCC in 1927. But the Ashes is no longer a contest between a mother-country and its colonial offshoot, far from it; it is a battle between two independent nations. Works of art are transported round the world. It would be in keeping with MCC's historic mission if it were to agree that the trophy should be displayed in the country that holds them.

Such a move would generate enormous public interest in both nations and give a huge emotional charge to the moment the Ashes changed hands. This would not just be an act of generosity. It would be terrific for English cricket's long-term well-being: children could then be taken to Lord's, forced to stare at the empty plinth and swear that they would help bring about the urn's return. There is no single reason why England lose so often at cricket, but it is easy to underestimate the power of symbolism and patriotism and passion.

It cannot be irrelevant to England's long-term failures that so many of their recent Test players were either born overseas and/or spent their formative years as citizens of other countries. In the heat of Test cricket, there is a difference between a cohesive team with a common goal, and a coalition of individuals whose major ambitions are for themselves. Successive England captains have all been aware of this. It is not a question of race. And of course there have been many fine and committed performances from players with all kinds of disparate backgrounds. But several of these players only came to England to play as professionals. There is a vast difference between wanting to play Test cricket and wanting to play for England. The overall effect has been to create a climate in which, as *The Independent* put it, 'some of our lot play for their country because they get paid for it.' (*1995*)

THIRD CORNHILL TEST

At Manchester, July 3, 4, 5, 6, 7, 1997. Australia won by 268 runs. Toss: Australia. Test debut: D.W. Headley.

The slumbering giant, aroused by the unaccustomed situation of trailing in a Test series, awoke, flexed its not inconsiderable muscle and demolished the opposition with brutal efficiency. Australia's emphatic triumph put them back on track after a stuttering start and weeks of depressing grey skies and rain. Suddenly, the weather resembled something vaguely like summer, but England's first defeat in eight Tests dampened the optimism springing from their resounding victories in the one-day series and the First Test. The contest had high achievement and occasional drama, but, from the moment Steve Waugh put his stamp on it, the whip hand was held by Australia. Waugh became the first batsman to score twin Ashes hundreds for 50 years; backed up by Warne, who convincingly returned to his best form, he well and truly wrested the initiative from England.

Australia had reinforced McGrath's intimidating pace with Gillespie, who replaced Kasprowicz after proving his recovery from a hamstring strain. England gave Dean Headley a historic debut: he was the third generation of his family to play Test cricket, following his grandfather George and his father Ron, who both represented West Indies. Malcolm was dropped, and Tufnell and the Gloucestershire left-armer Mike Smith were also omitted from a squad of 14.

Headley was straight into the action, striking Taylor on the helmet as he ducked into a bouncer in his opening over. England had hardly concealed their joy when Taylor chose to bat on a moist, green pitch with bare patches at either end. It seemed a foolish gamble; it proved a brave and calculated decision – one made easier for a captain with Warne's genius at his disposal. But Taylor was the first sufferer. Headley pressed home the advantage in his third over, squaring him up with a fiery delivery which was edged to first slip. Taylor's headache worsened as Australia declined to 42 for three. That was when Steve Waugh entered the fray, but he got little support from the middle order. The total was a miserable 160 for seven when Reiffel joined him, just before tea.

Their luck changed, shortly after a break for bad light, when Reiffel was dropped on 13 by Stewart, off Headley. This could be construed as the turning point of the entire season. Reiffel contributed 31 to a tremendously important stand of 70 before he finally fell next morning, to Gough's trademark in-swinging yorker. By then, Waugh had completed a century of enormous skill and character. With his lucky red handkerchief poking from his trouser pocket like a matador's cap, he faced the charging attack for four hours, and later called it his finest Test innings. When he was ninth out, edging Gough's delivery on to his middle stump, he had seen Australia to 235, an admirable total in testing conditions. Headley ensured it went no higher with his fourth wicket, thanks to Stewart, whose sixth catch equalled England's record for an innings against Australia; later, he added two more to break the record for a match. His opposite number, Healy, soon retaliated. A brilliant leg-side stumping off a full toss from Bevan removed Butcher and provided Healy's 100th dismissal in 25 England–Australia Tests. Only Rod Marsh (148 in 42 games) and Alan Knott (105 in 34) had previously reached this landmark.

Healy's 99th victim had been Atherton, who, for the third time in three Tests, went cheaply in the first innings to McGrath. This time, he gloved a seemingly erratic leg-side delivery. But Butcher, possibly sensing his last chance to justify his place, and his brother-in-law Stewart steered England serenely to 74. Then Warne made his first telling impact and sent shivers of apprehension through the home camp. Recalling his 'ball from hell' to dismiss Mike Gatting here four years earlier, he bowled a sharply spinning leg-break; Stewart, nonplussed, jabbed desperately and jerked his head back to see Taylor fling himself sideways at slip and snaffle a superb low catch. Now Warne was ready to put Australia in charge, and he had just the pitch to encourage him. The green demon of the previous day had been transformed into a brown strip, already scarred by footmarks. Flighting the ball cleverly and getting some vicious spin, he dismissed Thorpe, Hussain and Crawley for one run in a magical spell of 26 balls, as the baffled Englishmen slumped to 111 for six with barely a whimper. He and McGrath mopped up the final two wickets in 22 balls of the third morning, and England were all out for 162. Warne finished with six for 48 from 30 overs, his first haul of five or more since he took seven for 23 against Pakistan at Brisbane in November 1995.

Australia led by 73, but Headley and Croft removed their top three for 39 by the 14th over. Controversy enveloped the second wicket: Hussain, at slip, lunged forward as Blewett drove at Croft, and the ball bounced out of his right hand before he clasped it with his left. Umpire Venkataraghavan was unsure whether the edge had carried and consulted George Sharp before giving Blewett out. But the Waughs combined to guide Australia into safer waters. Mark played a sublime two-hour 55, with seven fours and a six, while the flint-eyed Steve, often wincing in pain as he snatched a badly bruised right hand away from his bat, held firm for more than six hours. In that time, he became the third Australian to score a century in each innings against England in 288 Tests, and the first right-hander, joining Warren Bardsley, at The Oval in 1909, and Arthur Morris, at Adelaide in 1946–47. Though Bevan failed again, the lower order did themselves proud. Taylor finally declared 20 minutes after Sunday lunch.

He left England a theoretical target of 469 in a minimum of 141 overs – 63 more than any Test team had made to win. The pressure was overwhelming and England buckled. Butcher and Atherton opened aggressively, Atherton hooking Gillespie for six; the angry bowler struck back by trapping him lbw as he snapped up three for five in 19 balls. Warne and McGrath completed the rout. On bowling Stewart, Warne became the third Australian bowler, after Dennis Lillee and Craig McDermott, to take 250 Test wickets, in his 55th match; his legend was further enhanced when Healy put on a helmet, complete with grille, to keep to him. Only Crawley resisted, but he emulated Atherton at Lord's by treading on his wicket when in sight of a century. England were all out for 200 at 12.30 on the final day. Australia's champagne celebrations were in stark contrast to the glum atmosphere in the home camp; the series was level at 1–1, but the momentum now was all one-way. *(Ken Casellas)*

Man of the Match: S.R. Waugh. *Attendance*: 87,829; *receipts* £1,621,959.

Close of play: First day, Australia 224-7 (S.R. Waugh 102*, P.R. Reiffel 26*); Second day, England 161-8 (M.A. Ealham 23*, A.R. Caddick 15*); Third day, Australia 262-6 (S.R. Waugh 82*, S.K. Warne 33*); Fourth day, England 130-5 (J.P. Crawley 53*, M.A. Ealham 5*).

AUSTRALIA

*M.A. Taylor c Thorpe b Headley	2	– (2) c Butcher b Headley	1
M.T.G. Elliott c Stewart b Headley	40	– (1) c Butcher b Headley	11
G.S. Blewett b Gough	8	– c Hussain b Croft	19
M.E. Waugh c Stewart b Ealham	12	– b Ealham	55
S.R. Waugh b Gough	108	– c Stewart b Headley	116
M.G. Bevan c Stewart b Headley	7	– c Atherton b Headley	0
†I.A. Healy c Stewart b Caddick	9	– c Butcher b Croft	47
S.K. Warne c Stewart b Ealham	3	– c Stewart b Caddick	53
P.R. Reiffel b Gough	31	– not out	45
J.N. Gillespie c Stewart b Headley	0	– not out	28
G.D. McGrath not out	0		
B 8, l-b 4, n-b 3	15	B 1, l-b 13, n-b 6	20

1/9 (1) 2/22 (3) 3/42 (4) 4/85 (2) 5/113 (6)　　**235**　1/5 (2) 2/33 (3) 3/39 (1)　(8 wkts, dec.) **395**
6/150 (7) 7/160 (8) 8/230 (9) 9/235 (5)　　　　　　4/131 (4) 5/132 (6) 6/210 (7)
10/235 (10)　　　　　　　　　　　　　　　　　　　7/298 (8) 8/333 (5)

Bowling: FIRST INNINGS – Gough 21-7-52-3; Headley 27.3-4-72-4; Caddick 14-2-52-1; Ealham 11-2-34-2; Croft 4-0-13-0. SECOND INNINGS – Gough 20-3-62-0; Headley 29-4-104-4; Croft 39-12-105-2; Ealham 13-3-41-1; Caddick 21-0-69-1.

ENGLAND

M.A. Butcher st Healy b Bevan	.51	– c McGrath b Gillespie	.28
*M.A. Atherton c Healy b McGrath	.5	– lbw b Gillespie	.21
†A.J. Stewart c Taylor b Warne	.30	– b Warne	.1
N. Hussain c Healy b Warne	.13	– lbw b Gillespie	.1
G.P. Thorpe c Taylor b Warne	.3	– c Healy b Warne	.7
J.P. Crawley c Healy b Warne	.4	– hit wkt b McGrath	.83
M.A. Ealham not out	.24	– c Healy b McGrath	.9
R.D.B. Croft c S.R. Waugh b McGrath	.7	– c Reiffel b McGrath	.7
D. Gough lbw b Warne	.1	– b McGrath	.6
A.R. Caddick c M.E. Waugh b Warne	.15	– c Gillespie b Warne	.17
D.W. Headley b McGrath	.0	– not out	.0
B 4, l-b 3, n-b 2	.9	B 14, l-b 4, w 1, n-b 1	.20

1/8 (2) 2/74 (3) 3/94 (1) 4/101 (5)   **162**   1/44 (2) 2/45 (3) 3/50 (4) 4/55 (2)   **200**
5/110 (4) 6/111 (6) 7/122 (8) 8/123   5/84 (5) 6/158 (7) 7/170 (8) 8/177 (6)
(9) 9/161 (10) 10/162 (11)   9/188 (9) 10/200 (10)

Bowling: FIRST INNINGS – McGrath 23.4-9-40-3; Reiffel 9-3-14-0; Warne 30-14-48-6; Gillespie 14-3-39-0; Bevan 8-3-14-1. SECOND INNINGS – McGrath 21-4-46-4; Gillespie 12-4-31-3; Reiffel 2-0-8-0; Warne 30.4-8-63-3; Bevan 8-2-34-0.

Umpires: S. Venkataraghavan (India) and G. Sharp.
Referee: R.S. Madugalle (Sri Lanka).

CHRONICLE OF 1997

[...] Australia's Anti-Discrimination Board reported that Britons complained of racial abuse more than any other ethnic group in the country, and said the level of complaints rose during England cricket tours. Chris Puplick, the board chairman, said expatriates were often upset by TV commentators saying that Poms would play better cricket if they washed more. He added that most complaints were unjustified, and indicated hypersensitivity rather than racial hatred. *(Daily Telegraph,* January 3, 1997) [...]

FOURTH TEST MATCH

At Melbourne Cricket Ground, Melbourne, December 26 (no play), 27, 28, 29, 1998. England won by 12 runs. Toss: Australia. Test debuts: M.J. Nicholson; W.K. Hegg.

This was the very best that Test cricket has to offer, a veritable jumbo pack of drama and incident. All three days were played at an allegro tempo – 40 wickets and more than 1,000 runs in more than 300 overs – and the finale in lengthening shadow at 7.33 p.m. on December 29 was unforgettable. It was the closest Ashes contest since the corresponding match at the MCG 16 years earlier, and again involved England coming back from a 2–0 deficit. Although the urn itself wasn't at issue, you'd scarcely have known it. [...]

The toss was transacted on Boxing Day before an expectant 60,000, but no sooner had Taylor elected to insert than a downpour commenced. Rain fell in such quantity that you expected to see an ark bobbing in the distance. Play was finally abandoned at 4.15 p.m. and – rain insurance premiums having been considered prohibitive – the cost to the Australian Cricket Board ran into seven figures. Fortunately, the playing conditions allowed for lost time to be recovered by prolonging match times 30 minutes at each end to allow 105 overs per day.

McGrath struck twice in his first two overs when play finally commenced under mackerel skies and in a bone-chilling wind on Sunday, but Stewart was so determined that you could almost hear his teeth grind. Finding stoical partners in Hussain and Ramprakash, he ended eight years and 23 Tests of Ashes under-achievement with a 160-ball innings of absolute conviction. A surprisingly fast outfield ensured full value for his edges as well as his resonant pulls and drives, and the crowd of 25,099 welcomed his landmark with a rousing ovation, a gesture springing from both appreciation and a desire to keep warm.

Passing 200 for the loss of three wickets, England were in a position of unaccustomed affluence. [...] But again the visitors frittered away their advantage with dilatory batting against Steve Waugh and MacGill either side of tea. Hick threatened temporarily to fill the breach by hoisting the game's only six at least 120 metres into the Barmy Army precinct, but promptly widened it by flailing to mid-on; the fifth of seven casualties in the span of 70 runs. Mullally's sixth nought of the tour met with hysterics.

Gough saw off Australia's openers that evening with the speediest spell of the match, one delivery being clocked at 150 kmh. And after Mark Waugh had succumbed rather unluckily to Fraser next morning, the Yorkshireman continued making inroads. Australia were five for 151 at the first break, and the competitive equilibrium was such that the lunchtime stripper in the nearby Royal Hotel obligingly hastened to finish by 1.35 p.m., allowing sufficient time for drinkers to wend their way back to the MCG and not miss a ball.

Healy threatened to reprise his Brisbane heroics, then mishooked, and Sunday's leading bowlers had to become Monday's leading batsmen for Australia to secure a lead. Steve Waugh's 17th Test century and seventh against England was one of his most authoritative, spiced with 13 hard-hit boundaries and including an uncharacteristic overhead hook to achieve the milestone. At 40, he overhauled Sir Donald Bradman to become Australia's fifth-highest run scorer, and it testifies to his stature that there was about the innings an almost Bradmanesque inevitability. MacGill, meanwhile, brazened out one Gough over where his exploratory edge was passed six times to help his senior partner add 88 in 98 minutes of pure exasperation for England. [...]

When Stewart succumbed again to MacGill after a spunky two-hour fifty, his team was only eight runs to the good with six wickets to call on. Hussain grafted capably and Hick played with uncustomary sureness of touch, but Australia were firm favourites when the latter was yorked: England had then only 151 to protect on a surface showing few signs of deterioration.

The prospect of a tantalising finish was first raised by Mullally. England's most transitory tailender swung bravely at McGrath – who interspersed his deliveries with a stream of invective, for which he later received a £2,500 fine suspended for four months from referee John Reid. Mullally helped Fraser add 23 for England's last wicket in 21 minutes. When Australia started positively on their pursuit after an early tea, Mullally then curbed their progress with an importunate spell from the members' end that kept his team in touch.

Television news bulletins at 6 p.m. foresaw a comfortable Australian triumph and, despite a gymnastic Ramprakash catch at square leg to arrest a screaming Langer pull, the hosts advanced steadily to three for 130. Centrebet odds on an English upset stretched to 50 to 1. The Barmy Army was maintaining a noisy vigil, but more from high spirits than high hopes. Then, quite without warning, Dean Headley shredded the script, upending four wickets in a dozen deliveries for four runs. It was Test fast bowling of the highest quality. English fans greeted him at deep fine leg with lusty salaams.

Australia, only 35 runs shy of victory, were still not out of it by any means. Steve Waugh, in his 110th Test, and Nicholson, in his first, aligned so nervelessly in adding 21 runs that Stewart consulted the umpires at 7.20 p.m. about terminating a session then almost four hours in duration. Waugh dissented and spellbound spectators cheered the game's continuation. Shadows were now encroaching on the centre square, however, and Nicholson touched Headley to Hegg. When Steve Waugh then nudged a single, MacGill and McGrath perished in three Gough deliveries amid scenes of English ecstasy on both sides of the boundary.

Headley claimed the individual award, although many others had contributed to the contest's splendour: Stewart, responsible for almost a third of England's runs; Steve Waugh, who batted for more than seven hours without hint of error; Gough, with 43.4 overs of manful toil; Hick, with two useful innings and four smart catches; MacGill, taker of 7/143 in unsympathetic conditions; even Mullally, whose unexpected runs had delighted all bar McGrath. Umpires Bucknor and Harper also had excellent matches. The Englishmen's only pang as they celebrated, meanwhile, was that they had not exhibited such resolve in the two preceding Tests. (*Gideon Haigh*)

Man of the Match: D.W. Headley. *Attendance*: 159,031.
Close of play: First day, no play; Second day, Australia (1) 2-59 (Langer 26, M.E. Waugh 12); Third day, England (2) 2-65 (Stewart 43, Headley 0).

ENGLAND

M.A. Atherton c Healy b McGrath	0 – b Fleming	0
*A.J. Stewart b MacGill	107 – c Slater b MacGill	52
M.A. Butcher c Langer b McGrath	0 – c Slater b MacGill	14
N. Hussain c Healy b Nicholson	19 – (5) c Slater b Nicholson	50
M.R. Ramprakash c McGrath b S.R. Waugh	63 – (6) b Nicholson	14
G.A. Hick c Fleming b MacGill	39 – (7) b Fleming	60
†W.K. Hegg c Healy b S.R. Waugh	3 – (8) c MacGill b Nicholson	9
D.W. Headley c Taylor b McGrath	14 – (4) b McGrath	1
D. Gough b MacGill	11 – c Slater b MacGill	4
A.R.C. Fraser not out	0 – not out	7
A.D. Mullally b MacGill	0 – c and b McGrath	16
L-b 7, w 1, n-b 6	14 B 2, l-b 4, n-b	17

(76 overs, 309 mins)   **270**   (80.2 overs, 333 mins)   **244**

Fall: 0 4 81 200 202 206 244 266 270 270   Fall: 5 61 66 78 127 178 202 221 221 244

Bowling: FIRST INNINGS – McGrath 22-5-64-3; Fleming 19-3-71-0; Nicholson 10-0-59-1; MacGill 19-2-61-4; S.R. Waugh 6-2-8-2. SECOND INNINGS – McGrath 20.2-5-56-2; Fleming 17-4-45-2; Nicholson 15-4-56-3; MacGill 27-3-81-3; M.E. Waugh 1-1-0-0.

AUSTRALIA

*M.A. Taylor c Hick b Gough	.7 –	(2) c Headley b Mullally 19
M.J. Slater lbw b Gough	.1 –	(1) lbw b Headley 18
J.L. Langer c Hussain b Gough	.44 –	c Ramprakash b Mullally 30
M.E. Waugh lbw b Fraser	.36 –	c Hick b Headley 43
S.R. Waugh not out	.122 –	not out 30
D.S. Lehmann c Hegg b Gough	.13 –	c Hegg b Headley 4
†I.A. Healy c Headley b Fraser	.36 –	c Hick b Headley 0
D.W. Fleming c Hick b Mullally	.12 –	lbw b Headley 0
M.J. Nicholson b Gough	.5 –	c Hegg b Headley 9
S.C.G. MacGill c Hegg b Mullally	.43 –	b Gough 0
G.D. McGrath b Mullally	.0 –	lbw b Gough 0
B 4, l-b 6, n-b 11 21		B 4, l-b 1, n-b 4 9

(98.3 overs, 452 mins)   **340** (46.4 overs, 241 mins)   **162**

Fall: 13 26 98 127 151 209 235 252 340 340   Fall: 31 41 103 130 140 140 140 161 162 162

Bowling: FIRST INNINGS – Gough 28-7-96-5; Headley 25-3-86-0; Mullally 21.3-5-64-3; Ramprakash 2-0-6-0; Fraser 22-0-78-2. SECOND INNINGS – Gough 15.4-2-54-2; Headley 17-5-60-6; Mullally 10-4-20-2; Fraser 4-0-23-0.

Umpires: S.A. Bucknor (West Indies) and D.J. Harper.
TV Umpire: G.T.D. Morrow.
Referee: J.R. Reid (New Zealand).

6

ROUTING THE PROPHETS: AUSTRALIA v. SOUTH AFRICA

Cricket contestants for a hundred years, Australia and South Africa have only met on seventy-one occasions in Test cricket. For this, there are good reasons. Australia's visit to South Africa in 1914–15 was abandoned after the outbreak of World War I, a proposed South African trip to Australia never eventuated because of World War II, and there were the two barren decades when South Africa met nobody at international level save a succession of rather motley rebel teams who preferred their superannuation payouts in Krugerrands.

These long hiatuses have lent cricket meetings between the two countries an unpredictable quality. And South Africa, in particular, has shown an aptitude for surprising Australia, notably with young teams in 1952–53 and 1963–64, then the exceedingly powerful combinations of 1966–67 and 1969–70.

This summer marks the fiftieth anniversary of the first of those series, one now little recalled, but quite remarkable. One–nil down against an Australian team that had won twenty-six and lost only two of thirty-two post-war Tests, Jackie Cheetham's team of tyros, emphasising fitness and fielding, came back to draw two–all. As *Wisden* 1954 gushed: 'Rarely in the history of international cricket has a team so thoroughly routed the prophets as did the young and markedly inexperienced side, led by J.E. Cheetham, which made South Africa's third visit to the Antipodes so momentous.' And if Australian cricket has suffered another humbling as absolute as 1969–70, it doesn't spring readily to mind; had it been repeated here in 1971–72, rather than being replaced by a more politically expedient Rest of the World tour, a few outstanding Australian careers might have been nipped in the bud.

Perhaps the outstanding series between these countries, however, remains their meeting in 1910–11, almost a last burnishing of the Golden Age. Australia's margin of victory, 4–1, is distorted by the Tests' timeless nature. The teams were actually well-matched, and in their attacking instincts similar. On the rubber's first day, Australia looted six for 494 in five hours – still our biggest total in a day's play. In the Second and Third Tests, played inside a fortnight, Australia won after trailing by 158 on the first

192

innings, then lost after a first innings of 465. First Aubrey Faulkner then Victor Trumper experienced the unusual distinction of compiling double centuries in losing causes. It's a series to rank with the far more famous one that occured fifty years later, at least on the field, and amply repays a visit to *Wisden* 1912.

—GH

SECOND TEST MATCH

Played at Melbourne, Saturday, Monday, Tuesday, Wednesday, December 31, 1910, January 2, 3, 4, 1911. – This was the sensational match of the tour, the South Africans suffering defeat by 89 runs when everyone thought they had the game in their hands. Pegler was given a place in their team to the exclusion of Vogler. The Australians led off with a score of 348, their batting being very good but, considering the perfection of the wicket, not exceptionable. Clem Hill was bowled by a ball that he did not attempt to play. Nourse brought off a wonderful catch on the boundary, and was presented with the ball as a memento of his feat. When the South Africans went in, Faulkner played the innings of his life. Batting for five hours and a quarter, he scored 204 runs out of 368 put on while he was in, and hit twenty-six 4's. He might have been caught when 64 and again at 126, but these were his only mistakes. Zulch, Nourse, and Snooke helped him to put on 107, 110, and 90 runs respectively for the second, third, and sixth wickets. In the second innings of Australia Trumper played superbly, scoring 159 out of 237 in less than three hours, but no one else gained any real mastery over Schwarz and Llewellyn. South Africa only required 170 to win, but the occasion proved too much for them. They were soon in a losing position, half the wickets being down for 46, and the innings ended for 80, Australia winning the match by 89 runs. Whitty's bowling was described as beyond praise. No excuse could be offered for the failure but it was thought that Faulkner flattered the bowlers by his extreme caution. Zulch left a sick bed in order to take his innings.

AUSTRALIA

V.T. Trumper b Pegler	34	– b Faulkner ... 159
W. Bardsley c Snooke b Sincalir	85	– st Sherwell b Schwarz ... 14
C. Hill b Llewellyn	39	– b Schwarz ... 0
D.R.A. Gehrs b Llewellyn	4	– st Sherwell b Schwarz ... 22
C.G. Macartney run out	7	– c Snooke b Llewellyn ... 5
V.S. Ransford run out	58	– c Sinclair b Schwarz ... 23
W.W. Armstrong c Sherwell b Faulkner	75	– b Llewellyn ... 29
C. Kelleway c Faulkner b Stricker	18	– b Pegler ... 48
H. Carter not out	15	– c Sherwell b Llewellyn ... 0
A. Cotter c Stricker b Schwarz	3	– c sub (Commaille) b Llewellyn ... 15
W.J. Whitty c Nourse b Faulkner	6	– not out ... 5
L-b 3, n-b 1	4	L-b 6, n-b 1 ... 7
	348	**327**

SOUTH AFRICA

P.W. Sherwell c Carter b Cotter	24	– b Whitty	16
J.W. Zulch b Cotter	42	– not out	6
G.A. Faulkner c Armstrong b Whitty	204	– c Kelleway b Whitty	8
A.D. Nourse b Kelleway	33	– lbw, b Cotter	2
L. Stricker b Armstrong	26	– lbw, b Cotter	0
C.B. Llewellyn b Armstrong	5	– b Cotter	17
S.J. Snooke b Whitty	77	– c Armstrong b Whitty	9
J.H. Sinclair not out	58	– lbw, b Whitty	3
R.O. Schwarz b Whitty	0	– c Kelleway b Cotter	7
O.C. Pearse b Armstrong	6	– c Kelleway b Whitty	0
S.J. Pegler lbw, b Armstrong	8	– lbw, b Whitty	0
B 2, l-b 10, w 2, n-b 9	23	B 6, l-b 3, n-b 3	12
	506		**80**

SOUTH AFRICA BOWLING

	Overs	Mdns	Runs	Wkts	Overs	Mdns	Runs	Wkts
Nourse	8	3	24	0	5	1	18	0
Snooke	5	1	19	0	8	1	24	0
Pegler	10	0	43	1	6.3	1	24	1
Schwarz	13	0	66	1	22	2	76	4
Llewellyn	10	0	69	2	16	0	81	4
Sinclair	13	1	53	1	8	0	32	0
Stricker	10	0	36	1	2	1	10	0
Faulkner	10-4	0	34	2	12	1	55	1

AUSTRALIA BOWLING

	Overs	Mdns	Runs	Wkts	Overs	Mdns	Runs	Wkts
Cotter	43	5	158	2	15	3	47	4
Whitty	29	6	81	3	16	7	17	6
Kelleway	17	3	67	1				
Armstrong	48	9	134	4	1	0	4	0
Macartney	16	5	43	0				

THIRD TEST MATCH

Played at Adelaide, Saturday, Monday, Tuesday, Wednesday, Thursday, Friday, January 7, 9, 10, 11, 12, 13, 1911. After a tremendous struggle, the match lasting into the sixth day, the South Africans beat Australia by 38 runs. Their victory was the reward of most patient and determined batting. They led off well by scoring 482, but the innings lasted nearly eight hours and a quarter. Zulch had more than a fair share of luck in his 105, but Snooke only gave a single chance and that a difficult one. In Australia's first innings Trumper gave a display that even he has never surpassed. In third wicket down he scored 214 out of 354 in four hours, hitting twenty-six 4's, and taking out his bat. The South Africans were enthusiastic in his praise, Sherwell, who was keeping wicket, and thus had the best means of judging, saying that he gave no chance of any kind and made no false strokes. When the South Africans went in the second time, Faulkner played a fine innings of quite a different type, batting nearly four hours for his 115. The Australians, left with 378 to get, tried very hard, but the wicket was beginning to show signs of wear, and the task proved a bit too much for them.

SOUTH AFRICA

P.W. Sherwell lbw, b Armstrong	.11	– lbw, b Whitty	.1
J.W. Zulch c Macartney b Whitty	.105	– c Carter b Whitty	.14
G.A. Faulkner c Hill b Armstrong	.56	– c Armstrong b Whitty	.115
A.D. Nourse b Cotter	.10	– c Armstrong b Kelleway	.39
M. Hathorn b Whitty	.9	– b Whitty	.2
C.B. Llewellyn run out	.43	– b Whitty	.80
S.J. Snooke c Kelleway b Cotter	.103	– run out	.25
J.H. Sinclair c Armstrong b Kelleway	.20	– c Hill b Whitty	.29
L. Stricker c Kelleway b Armstrong	.48	– b Macartney	.6
R.O. Schwarz b Armstrong	.15	– not out	.11
S.J. Pegler not out	.24	– c Cotter b Kelleway	.26
B 6, l-b 10, w 4, n-b 18	.38	B 4, l-b 2, w 1, n-b 5	.12
	482		**360**

AUSTRALIA

C.G. Macartney b Llewellyn	.2	– lbw, b Schwarz	.0
C. Kelleway c Sherwell b Llewellyn	.47	– c Sherwell b Sinclair	.65
V.S. Ransford b Llewellyn	.50	– c Llewellyn b Schwarz	.0
W. Bardsley lbw, b Nourse	.54	– c and b Faulkner	.58
V.T. Trumper not out	.214	– b Llewellyn	.28
D.R.A. Gehrs c Schwarz b Faulkner	.20	– c Sherwell b Schwarz	.22
C Hill c Snooke b Schwarz	.16	– c Schwarz b Sinclair	.55
W.W. Armstrong b Sinclair	.30	– b Schwarz	.48
H. Carter lbw b Schwarz	.17	– c Llewellyn b Faulkner	.11
A. Cotter c Snooke b Llewellyn	.8	– not out	.36
W.J. Whitty c Sherwell b Sinclair	.1	– c Schwarz b Pegler	.11
B 4, l-b 2	.6	L-b	.5
	465		**339**

AUSTRALIA BOWLING

	Overs	Mdns	Runs	Wkts	Overs	Mdns	Runs	Wkts
Cotter	38	4	100	2	23	3	64	0
Whitty	34	7	114	2	39.2	5	104	6
Armstrong	42.4	9	103	4	33	9	90	0
Kelleway	24	6	72	1	23	4	64	2
Macartney	27	9	51	0	12	3	26	1
Gehrs	1	0	4	0				

SOUTH AFRICA BOWLING

Llewellyn	31	4	107	4	12	0	48	1
Schwarz	19	2	68	2	15	3	48	4
Sinclair	25.5	3	86	2	21	2	72	2
Pegler	20	2	92	0	10.4	0	58	1
Faulkner	11	0	59	1	15	3	56	2
Nourse	12	2	43	1	5	0	31	0
Stricker	1	0	4	0				
Snooke					5	0	21	0

THIRD TEST MATCH

At Durban, January 20, 21, 23, 24, 1950. Australia won by five wickets.

After at one time looking almost certain to be defeated, Australia staged a dramatic recovery and gained a glorious victory with only twenty-five minutes to spare. This success gave them the rubber, the first two Tests having been won by convincing margins. The luck of the toss forsook Hassett and South Africa on a good pitch scored easily. E. Rowan showed determination typical of his character in completing his hundred during the first day, and Nourse made runs with characteristic assurance. South Africa reached a respectable total, and no one could have anticipated the remarkable cricket which followed. Yet when the second day was over South Africa had established a lead of 236, Australia having been dismissed for 75 – their lowest total in a Test match against South Africa. The player largely responsible for this astonishing collapse was Tayfield, a newcomer to Test cricket this season. This Natal off-break bowler worried all the batsmen and took seven for 23 in 8.4 overs. Nourse was left with the week-end in which to decide whether to enforce the follow-on. Probably influenced by the threat of rain, he decided to bat a second time, and though the turf now aided spin the failure of the South African batsmen was difficult to understand. The side were all out for 99, and Australia began the final day needing 256 to win with seven wickets in hand.

The odds still favoured South Africa, but Harvey refused to be deterred by the immensity of the task. Helped by Loxton and McCool, he adopted a dogged style quite out of keeping with his normal game and stayed five hours thirty minutes without making a mistake. This innings of extraordinary patience and skill, which enabled Australia to record their remarkable victory, left a lasting impression upon all who witnessed it. The history of Test cricket provides few comparable feats.

SOUTH AFRICA

E.A.B. Rowan c Johnston b Miller	.143	– c Saggers b Lindwall	.4
O. Wynne b Johnston	.18	– b Johnson	.29
J. Nel c and b Johnson	.14	– lbw b Johnston	.20
A.D. Nourse c Saggers b Johnston	.66	– c McCool b Johnson	.27
W.W. Wade b Lindwall	.24	– b Johnston	.0
N.B.F. Mann b Johnston	.9	– lbw b Johnson	.0
J. Cheetham c Hassett b Johnston	.4	– c Hassett b Johnson	.1
J. Watkins b Lindwall	.5	– st Saggers b Johnson	.2
H. Tayfield run out	.15	– b Johnston	.3
V.I. Smith b Lindwall	.1	– b Johnston	.4
C. McCarthy not out	.0	– not out	.2
B 3, l-b 7, n-b 2	.12	B 5, l-b 1, n-b 1	.7
	311		**99**

AUSTRALIA

A.R. Morris c Smith b Tayfield	.25	– hit wkt b Tayfield	.44
J.R. Moroney b Tayfield	.10	– lbw b Tayfield	.10
I.W. Johnson lbw b Tayfield	.2		
K.R. Miller b Tayfield	.2	– lbw b Mann	.10
A.L. Hassett lbw b Tayfield	.2	– lbw b Mann	.11
R.A. Saggers c Cheetham b Mann	.2		
C.L. McCool lbw b Mann	.1	– not out	.39
R.R. Lindwall b Mann	.7		
R.N. Harvey c and b Tayfield	.2	– not out	.151
S.J. Loxton c Cheetham b Tayfield	.16	– b Mann	.54
W.A. Johnston not out	.2		
B 3, l-b 1	.4	B 7, l-b 9, n-b 1	.17
	75	Five wkts	**336**

AUSTRALIA BOWLING

	O	M	R	W	O	M	R	W
Lindwall	19	3	47	3	4	1	7	1
Miller	24	5	73	1	7	0	12	0
McCool	13	3	35	0				
Johnston	31.2	5	75	4	18.2	6	39	4
Loxton	6	1	31	0				
Johnson	16	5	38	1	17	2	34	5

SOUTH AFRICA BOWLING

	O	M	R	W	O	M	R	W
McCarthy	6	2	8	0	12	3	32	0
Watkins	4	1	9	0	6	2	10	0
Mann	10	1	31	3	50.6	13	101	3
Tayfield	8.4	1	23	7	49	5	144	2
Smith					5	0	32	0

FALL OF WICKETS

South Africa – First Innings:

1	2	3	4	5	6	7	8	9
32	75	242	264	283	289	293	304	308

South Africa – Second Innings:

1	2	3	4	5	6	7	8	9
9	51	85	85	88	90	93	93	93

Australia – First Innings:

1	2	3	4	5	6	7	8	9
31	35	37	39	42	45	46	53	63

Australia – Second Innings:

1	2	3	4	5
14	33	59	95	230

SOUTH AFRICANS IN AUSTRALIA AND NEW ZEALAND, 1952–53

Rarely in the history of international cricket has a team so thoroughly routed the prophets as did the young and markedly inexperienced side, led by J.E. Cheetham, which made South Africa's third visit to the Antipodes so momentous. The atmosphere in which the South Africans sailed could scarcely have been more gloomy. Many acknowledged as sound and dispassionate judges had suggested that the tour should be cancelled rather than allow South Africa's cricket, admittedly at a low ebb, to suffer a sequence of seemingly inevitable crushing defeats which could cause long-standing damage. The Australian Board of Control, remembering the financial failure of the previous year's tour by West Indies, expressed apprehension of the public reaction to a side which, by general agreement, stood in danger of being overwhelmed.

This fear was met immediately by the South African Board of Control with the reply that they were prepared to lose as much as £10,000 on an educational tour which they hoped would put their cricket on the right road for the future. How wise they were! Yet the same officials must have been just as surprised as, and even more delighted than, anyone that, without so many of the men who had formed the backbone of their country's cricket in preceding years, Cheetham's team finished with a better Test record than any in Australia since D.R. Jardine's in 1932–33 – and with a profit of £3,000. [...]

Two reasons contributed above all towards South Africa's success. One was a standard of fielding which truly deserved the description of brilliant. The other was a fighting determination and team spirit which won the admiration of all. From the start South Africa's new captain and his trusted friend the team manager, K.G. Viljoen, left no doubt that they would give every fraction of their energies and thought to the task confronting them. By example and speech they were equally clear that they expected nothing less from anyone else. They were not disappointed.

On arrival in Australia Cheetham told friends that he might not be leading a strong batting or bowling side, but he was resolved they should excel in the field. At times in the opening fortnight at Perth the South Africans devoted three to four hours a day at fielding alone, and to the end of the tour they practised fielding as assiduously as batting and bowling. Before many matches had been played spectators went just as much to see the fielding of these superbly fit young men as to watch them bat and bowl. [...]

SECOND TEST MATCH

At Melbourne, December 24, 26, 27, 29, 30, 1952. South Africa won by 82 runs. Their first victory over Australia for forty-two years came as reward for superior allround cricket. Endean and Tayfield played specially notable roles, but the whole side deserved praise for two fielding performances which drew favourable comparison with some of the best teams of the past. Little indication of the events which were to lead to Australia's third defeat in thirty-three post-war Tests – all in the last eight matches – was contained in the early play. South Africa ran into immediate trouble against Miller and Lindwall, and the total only became respectable through solid rescue work by Murray, top scorer, Mansell and Tayfield.

Throughout the series South Africa gave no finer display of out-cricket than on the second day. Although their attack was depleted by the absence of Murray (fibrositis) and Watkins (strained back) they held Australia to a purely nominal lead. The stand of 84 by McDonald and Morris was Australia's first-wicket best in twenty-two Test innings but, apart from the hard-driving Miller, the middle batsmen failed against the off-breaks of Tayfield and the leg-spin of Mansell. By steady length and bowling to his field, Tayfield gave nothing away in an unchanged spell of nearly four hours, at one stage of which he took the wickets of Ring, Miller and Johnston for one run. The spectacular catch which dismissed Morris set South Africa's standard for the innings. A drive hit Cheetham's upflung hands close to the wicket but bounced away from him. Tayfield spun round, raced after the ball, and caught it in a full-length dive. Cheetham and McGlew made other excellent catches, and Endean, with his back to the iron fence, held a drive by Miller above his head.

The last three days went all in favour of South Africa. When Lindwall and Miller used the new ball the bowling presented some menace, but Endean, Waite, who shared a second-wicket stand of 111, Funston and McLean faced them calmly. Most of the other bowling was made to look innocuous. Endean, though unattractive in style and relying chiefly on strokes behind the wicket, withstood the attack for seven and a half hours without giving a chance. His 162 not out was the second highest innings for South Africa against Australia, the best being G.A. Faulkner's 201 on the same ground in 1910–11. On account of sore feet Miller was used sparingly, but even so he caused most batting problems and when he dismissed Waite he completed his Test double of 1,000 runs and 100 wickets. Poor light did not help Australia when they started the last innings, but more high-class bowling by Tayfield was the chief reason for their failure to score the 373 required to win. In one period of nine maiden overs he sent back Miller,

Langley and Hole, and he richly merited his match record of thirteen wickets for 165. Once again Harvey stood out as Australia's best batsman and the lofted stroke which brought his innings to a close resulted from his only error of timing. [...]

SOUTH AFRICA

D.J. McGlew b Lindwall	.46	– st Langley b Ring ... .13
J.H.B. Waite c Lindwall b Miller	.0	– c Hole b Miller ... .62
W.R. Endean c Benaud b Lindwall	.2	– not out ... .162
K.J. Funston c Ring b Miller	.9	– run out ... .26
R.A. McLean c Lindwall b Ring	.27	– lbw b Miller ... .42
J.E. Cheetham c Johnston b Miller	.15	– lbw b Johnston 6
J.C. Watkins c Langley b Benaud	.19	– b Johnston 3
P.N.F. Mansell b Lindwall	.24	– b Miller ... .18
A.R.A. Murray c Johnston b Benaud	.51	– st Langley b Ring ... .23
H.J. Tayfield c Langley b Miller	.23	– lbw b Lindwall ... .22
M.G. Melle not out	.4	– b Lindwall 0
B 4, l-b 3 7		B 1, l-b 5, w 4, n-b 1 ... .11

1//2 2/9 3/27 4/63 5/93 6/112   **227**   1/23 2/134 3/196 4/261 5/284   **388**
7/126 8/156 9/207   6/290 7/319 8/353 9/388

AUSTRALIA

C.C. McDonald c Fuller b Mansell	.82	– c Mansell b Murray ... .23
A.R. Morris c and b Tayfield	.43	– c Watkins b Melle 1
R.N. Harvey c Cheetham b Tayfield	.11	– c Watkins b Tayfield ... .60
A.L. Hassett c Melle b Mansell	.18	– lbw b Tayfield ... .21
K.R. Miller c Endean b Tayfield	.52	– b Tayfield ... .31
G.B. Hole c Waite b Mansell	.13	– b Tayfield ... .25
R. Benaud b Tayfield	.5	– c Melle b Tayfield ... .45
R.R. Lindwall run out	.1	– b Melle ... .19
D. Ring c McGlew b Tayfield	.14	– c Melle b Tayfield ... .53
G.R. Langley not out	.2	– b Tayfield 4
W.A. Johnston lbw b Tayfield	.0	– not out 0
N-b 2 2		B 1, l-b 6, n-b 1 8

1/84 2/98 3/155 4/158 5/188   **243**   1/3 2/34 3/76 4/131   **290**
6/211 7/219 8/239 9/243   5/139 6/148 7/181 8/216 9/277

AUSTRALIA BOWLING

	O	M	R	W	O	M	R	W
Lindwall	14	2	29	3	31.5	4	87	2
Miller	21	3	62	4	22	5	51	3
Johnston	12	2	37	0	31	9	77	2
Ring	18	1	72	1	31	5	115	2
Benaud	6.6	1	20	2	6	0	23	0
Hole					7	0	24	0

SOUTH AFRICA BOWLING

Melle	14	0	73	0	11	2	39	2
Watkins	6	1	15	0	10	2	34	0
Murray	3	1	11	0	23	7	59	1
Tayfield	29.4	9	84	6	37.1	13	81	7
Mansell	19	3	58	3	14	2	69	0

Umpires: H. Elphinston and M. McInnes.

FOURTH TEST MATCH

At Johannesburg, February 7, 8, 10, 11, 12, 1958. Australia won by ten wickets and made certain of the rubber. [...] Craig won the toss for the third successive time in Tests and the Australians did not take long to establish a strong position. They began slowly and after two and a half hours had scored no more than 52 for the loss of McDonald and Harvey. Craig made a wise move in promoting Benaud to number four and he and Burke thoroughly mastered the attack. South Africa were handicapped after lunch when Adcock retired with influenza and Heine reduced his pace because of ankle trouble. Benaud, after playing himself in, attacked the bowling and completed an excellent century before he skied a hook. Heine followed this success by causing Craig to play on and by the close Australia, 217 for four, had lost some of their advantage. Burke, who played a sound defensive role in helping Benaud add 158, batted all day for 79 not out. Adcock was able to bowl next morning and at one time Australia were 234 for seven. Mackay and Davidson led the recovery with a stand of 81 and Meckiff also gave Mackay useful support.

South Africa lost McGlew in scoring 19 overnight and on the third day only Funston did well for them. Because of hand injuries to van Ryneveld and Waite, the batting order had to be changed, but even so the failures came as a surprise under such ideal batting conditions. That Tayfield, the 'night watchman', stayed three hours emphasised this fact. [...] Following on 198 behind, South Africa scored seven without loss before the close and on the fourth day made a determined effort to save the game. They lost only two wickets, but added no more than 119 runs in five hours. McGlew refused to depart from rigid defence and his first 50 took five hours thirteen minutes, the slowest on record. Two fine slip catches by Simpson accounted for Endean and Goddard and South Africa began the last day 72 behind with eight wickets in hand. The match was over immediately after lunch, the remaining wickets falling for 72. McGlew batted six hours for 70 and Funston again made a gallant effort, but the other batsmen disappointed.

AUSTRALIA

J.W. Burke c Waite b Heine	81	– not out	0
C.C. McDonald lbw b Tayfield	26	– not out	1
R.N. Harvey c Waite b Goddard	5		
R. Benaud c Endean b Heine	100		
I.D. Craig b Heine	3		
W. Grout lbw b Adcock	7		
K. Mackay not out	83		
R. Simpson c Waite b Adcock	6		
A.K. Davidson c Burger b Heine	62		
I. Meckiff c Endean b Heine	26		
L. Kline c Waite b Heine	1		
L-b 1	1		

1/43 2/52 3/210 4/213 5/222 6/222   **401**   (No wkt) **1**
7/234 8/315 9/393

SOUTH AFRICA

D.J. McGlew c Grout b Meckiff	1	– c Simpson b Benaud	70
W.R. Endean lbw b Davidson	22	– c Simpson b Benaud	38
H.J. Tayfield lbw b Benaud	27	– st Grout b Kline	0
T.L. Goddard c and b Meckiff	9	– c Simpson b Benaud	0
K.J. Funston c Craig b Kline	70	– not out	64
R.A. McLean c Grout b Davidson	9	– c Grout b Davidson	0
C. Burger st Grout b Kline	21	– c McDonald b Kline	1
J.H.B. Waite lbw b Benaud	12	– c Grout b Benaud	10
P. Heine c and b Benaud	24	– c Meckiff b Benaud	1
N.A.T. Adcock b Benaud	0	– run out	3
C.B. van Ryneveld not out	0	– lbw b Kline	0
B 3, w 2, n-b 3	8	L-b 8, w 2, n-b 1	11

1/17 2/27 3/46 4/104 5/115 6/166   **203**   1/78 2/78 3/147 4/147 5/161 6/180   **198**
7/166 8/186 9/194   7/180 8/182 9/183

SOUTH AFRICA BOWLING

	O	M	R	W	O	M	R	W
Heine	37.5	7	96	6				
Adcock	17	3	37	2				
Goddard	43	10	136	1				
Tayfield	49	18	107	1				
van Ryneveld	3	0	24	0				
McLean					0.4	0	1	0

AUSTRALIA BOWLING

	O	M	R	W	O	M	R	W
Meckiff	21	3	38	2	13	2	24	0
Davidson	19	2	39	2	20	4	44	1
Mackay	11	5	11	0				
Benaud	20.2	0	70	4	41	8	84	5
Kline	9	1	37	2	16	6	27	3
Burke					15	10	8	0

FOURTH TEST MATCH

At Adelaide, January 24, 25, 27, 28, 29, 1964. South Africa won by ten wickets, so bringing the series level at one-all with one to play. They gained this well-deserved victory with cricket much more lively in character and of a higher standard than that of the Australians. Peter Pollock, squeezing every ounce from the pitch, set the pattern with the valuable wickets of Lawry and O'Neill in his fifth over and had Burge not escaped three times, Australia would have been unable to show what appeared to be a reasonable total. In fact, their 345 soon looked inadequate as South Africa started on the path to their highest total against Australia. Barlow and Graeme Pollock were never in any trouble as with pleasant aggressiveness they went merrily on their way to South Africa's largest stand in Test cricket, 341 in four hours forty-three minutes for the third wicket.

Barlow followed in the footsteps of such illustrious cricketers as Aubrey Faulkner and Dudley Nourse in hitting a double century against Australia, 108 of his runs coming in 4's, and this was his third three-figure innings of the series. The 19-year-old Pollock threw his bat at the ball even more joyously than his partner, three 6's and eighteen 4's being included in his 175, which took him past 1,000 runs for the tour. Barlow's total rose to 1,439, 519 of them in Tests. Back came the bowlers to capitalise on South Africa's lead of 250 and fittingly it was Barlow, with his first bowl of the game, who took three wickets for six runs as Australia lost four wickets in the last half hour of the fourth day. So South Africa needed only part of the final morning to complete their win.

AUSTRALIA

*R.B. Simpson b Goddard	78	– c Lindsay b Halse	34
W.M. Lawry c Partridge b P. Pollock	14	– c Goddard b P. Pollock	38
N.C. O'Neill c Goddard b P. Pollock	0	– c Partridge b Halse	66
P.J. Burge c Halse b P. Pollock	91	– run out	20
B.C. Booth c Lindsay b Goddard	58	– lbw b P. Pollock	24
B. Shepherd lbw b Goddard	70	– c Lindsay b Barlow	78
R. Benaud b Partridge	7	– b Barlow	34
G.D. McKenzie c Lindsay b Goddard	12	– c and b Barlow	4
†A.T.W. Grout c Partridge b Goddard	0	– c Pithey b Halse	23
N. Hawke not out	0	– c Carlstein b Seymour	0
R.A. Gaunt run out	1	– not out	2
B 1, l-b 8, n-b 5	14	L-b 4, w 1, n-b 3	8

1/35 2/37 3/141 4/225 5/279 6/290   **345**   1/72 2/81 3/125 4/178 5/210 6/301   **331**
7/333 8/333 9/344   7/301 8/301 9/310

Bowling: FIRST INNINGS – P. Pollock 21-1-96-3; Partridge 22-4-76-1; Halse 13-1-54-0; Seymour 12-2-38-0; Goddard 24.6-4-60-5; Bland 1-0-7-0. SECOND INNINGS – P. Pollock 14-1-73-2; Partridge 17-3-76-0; Goddard 21-3-64-0; Halse 13.3-1-50-3; Seymour 19-1-54-1; Barlow 5-2-6-3.

SOUTH AFRICA

*T.L. Goddard b Hawke	.34	– not out ...... .34
E.J. Barlow lbw b Hawke	.201	– not out ...... .47
A.J. Pithey c Grout b Hawke	.0	
R.G. Pollock b Hawke	.175	
K.C. Bland c Grout b Gaunt	.33	
P.R. Carlstein c Benaud b Gaunt	.37	
†D. Lindsay b Simpson	.41	
P.M. Pollock c Benaud b Hawke	.21	
M.A. Seymour c Simpson b Hawke	.3	
J.T. Partridge b McKenzie	.6	
C. Halse not out	.19	
B 7, l-b 8, w 3, n-b 7	.25	w 1 1

1/70 2/70 3/411 4/437 5/500   **595**   (no wkt.) **82**
6/501 7/559 8/568 9/575

Bowling: FIRST INNINGS – McKenzie 30.1-2-156-1; Gaunt 24-1-115-2; Hawke 39-5-139-6; Benaud 20-1-101-0; Simpson 10-1-59-1. SECOND INNINGS – Gaunt 2-0-22-0; McKenzie 4-0-22-0; Hawke 6-0-20-0; Benaud 3-1-17-0.

Umpires: C. Egar and L. Rowan.

SECOND TEST MATCH

At Kingsmead, Durban, February 5, 6, 7, 9, 10, 1970. South Africa won by an innings and 129 runs. [...] The match produced a host of new records, pride of place going to Graeme Pollock for his mammoth 274 which gave him the individual record for a South African in Test matches. This was Pollock's first century on the Kingsmead ground; he reached 100 in two hours, fifty minutes and 200 in five hours, seven minutes and altogether batted three minutes under seven hours, before he played a tame return to Stackpole. He hit one 5 and forty-three 4's. His concentration never wavered and he attacked continuously and with merciless efficiency.

The total exceeded by two runs the previous highest total made by South Africa in the 170 Tests played against Australia, England and New Zealand. England's 654 for five wickets in the Timeless Test on the same ground in 1938–39 is the only score for or against these countries to surpass the latest total. Another highlight of the match was Richards' maiden Test hundred in only his second Test. In an exhibition of technical perfection the 24-year-old Natal and Hampshire batsman scored 140 of the 229 runs on the board. He reached his hundred off 116 deliveries and his only false stroke in a three-hour innings was his last one. He had Pollock as a partner for the last hour and the spectators were treated to a superb display as the pair added 103 runs for the third wicket. Between them they scored 414 runs of South Africa's gigantic total. Pollock, with Lance as his partner, also established a new South African sixth-wicket Test record of 200.

The Australians, thoroughly demoralised and with victory out of the question, failed to match the 164 they scored in the first innings at Newlands. Lawry and Stackpole put on 44 in even time and survived some hair-raising moments. The dynamic Barlow was then given the ball and in ten deliveries, with Goddard at the other end, the total slumped to 48 for four wickets. Sheahan batted beautifully, but it was a lone battle as Pollock and Procter accounted for the tail and the touring team followed-on 465 runs behind.

In the second innings Walters, Redpath and Stackpole all reached the seventies and at times the visitors' prospects seemed quite encouraging. Both Lawry and Chappell had succumbed to the fatal touch and Sheahan's batting, during a short stay, bore no resemblance to his first innings effort. In the latter stages Bacher again called on Barlow, whose figures at that point read nought for 50; the all-rounder staged a repeat performance and captured three wickets in quick succession for only four runs. This put paid to Redpath's hopes of assistance and any thoughts of an Australian recovery. Redpath was the hero of the innings but was unable to find a reliable partner and the match ended with South Africa two up and a full day to spare.

SOUTH AFRICA

B.A. Richards b Freeman 140	†D. Gamsy lbw b Connolly 7
T.L. Goddard c Lawry b Gleeson 17	P.M. Pollock not out 36
*A. Bacher b Connolly 9	A.J. Traicos not out 5
R.G. Pollock c and b Stackpole 274	
E.J. Barlow lbw b Freeman 1	
B.L. Irvine b Gleeson 13	B 1, l-b 3, n-b 23 27
H.R. Lance st Taber b Gleeson 61	
M.J. Procter c Connolly b Stackpole 32	1/88 2/126 3/229 (9 wkts, dec.) **622**

4/231 5/281 6/481 7/558 8/575 9/580

Bowling: McKenzie 25.5-3-92-0; Connolly 33-7-104-2; Freeman 28-4-120-2; Gleeson 51-9-160-3; Walters 9-0-44-0; Stackpole 21-2-75-2.

AUSTRALIA

*W.M. Lawry lbw b Barlow ....15 – c Gamsy b Goddard 14
K.R. Stackpole c Gamsy b Goddard ....27 – lbw b Traicos 71
I.M. Chappell c Gamsy b Barlow ....0 – c Gamsy b P.M. Pollock 14
K.D. Walters c Traicos b Barlow ....4 – c R.G. Pollock b Traicos 74
I.R. Redpath c Richards b Procter ....4 – not out 74
A.P. Sheahan c Traicos b Goddard ....62 – c Barlow b Procter 4
E.W. Freeman c Traicos b P.M. Pollock .....5 – b Barlow 18
†H.B. Taber c and b P.M. Pollock ....6 – c Lance b Barlow 0
G.D. McKenzie c Traicos b Procter ....1 – lbw b Barlow 4
J.W. Gleeson not out ....4 – c Gamsy b Procter 24
A.N. Connolly c Bacher b Traicos ....14 – lbw b Procter 0
L-b 5, n-b 10 15   B 9, l-b 8, n-b 22 39

1/44 2/44 3/44 4/48 5/56   **157**   1/65 2/88 3/151 4/208 5/222   **336**
6/79 7/100 8/114 9/139   6/264 7/264 8/268 9/336

Bowling: FIRST INNINGS – Procter 11-2-39-2; P.M. Pollock 10-3-31-2; Goddard 7-4-10-2; Barlow 10-3-24-3; Traicos 8.2-3-27-1; Lance 2-0-11-0. SECOND INNINGS – Procter 18.5-5-62-3; P.M. Pollock 21.3-4-45-1; Goddard 17-7-30-1; Barlow 31-10-63-3; Traicos 30-8-70-2; Lance 7-4-11-0; Richards 3-1-8-0; R.G. Pollock 3-1-8-0.

Umpires: J.G. Draper and C.M.P. Coetzee.

SECOND TEST MATCH

AT Sydney, January 2, 3, 4, 5, 6, 1994. South Africa won by five runs. Toss: South Africa. [...] South Africa's unlikely hero was de Villiers, in only his second Test: he took ten wickets, and his second-innings six for 43 included the first four as Australia slumped to 56 for four before the end of the fourth day. By then they might well have been celebrating victory but for some late-order South African resistance organised by Rhodes, who came in at 107 for four and saw 132 added.

The last part of South Africa's stunning success was presided over by Cronje after Wessels broke a finger attempting a slip catch. The young deputy marshalled his troops well on the tense final morning, and his turn, throw and direct hit to run out Warne from wide mid-off was a devastating blow for Australia. The Australians, who brought in McGrath for Reiffel, had seemed to be in control from the first day, when only a second-wicket stand of 90 between Kirsten and Cronje stood in the way of another dazzling display of leg-spin variations from Warne. Two years to the day after his undistinguished Test debut, when he took one for 150 against India in Sydney, Warne swept away the middle order, finishing with seven for 56. The flipper accounted for Cullinan, Rhodes and Kirsten; Richardson and Matthews fell to classic leg-breaks which found the edge and curled to slip; Symcox was fooled by the massive behind-the-legs turner – and Wessels fell for the sucker punch, driving a full toss back to the bowler.

Slater made light of an untrustworthy pitch to score 92 and led Australia to 292, a lead of 123. Border, who passed Greg Chappell's record of 1,150 runs in Sydney Tests – and needed stitches after top-edging Symcox into his face – lasted four hours for 49, and Martyn contributed 59. There were four wickets apiece for Donald and de Villiers, while the burly off-spinner Symcox bowled 46 overs – 33 in one spell – without looking unduly threatening.

Wessels, despite his broken finger and a still-painful knee, came in at No. 4 to steady the tourists, but soon became the first of another five victims for Warne – the first time he had taken ten wickets in any match. South Africa lost five wickets before clearing the first-innings deficit, but Rhodes organised the tail to good effect, sharing stands of 72 with Richardson and 36 for the last wicket with Donald. His unbeaten 76 in 195 minutes included six fours and a hooked six off McDermott.

Needing only 117 to win, Australia looked to have shrugged off the early loss of Slater, reaching 51 before de Villiers rocked them with three wickets in five balls. South Africa felt victory depended on the quick removal of Border. They got their wish in the first over of the final day, when he played no shot at one from Donald which cut back and clipped his off bail. Waugh – leg-before to Donald's Waqar-like yorker – and Healy soon followed, as did Warne, needlessly run out. In came McDermott, a veteran of a similarly pulsating situation at Adelaide the previous season. He spanked four quick fours on his way to 29, the top score of the innings, but his partner Martyn's nerve failed after 106 minutes and six singles. He holed out to cover, and McGrath (whose first-innings nine represented the sum total of his first-class runs on his home ground) soon followed, sparking off emotional scenes in the South African dressing-room. UCBSA managing director Ali Bacher – who led his country to the 4–0 thrashing of Australia when the two last met in 1969–70 – called it 'our finest achievement ever'. [...]

Man of the Match: P.S. de Villiers. *Attendance*: 107,587.

Close of play: First day, Australia 20-1 (M.J. Slater 5*, D.C. Boon 7*); Second day, Australia 200-5 (D.R. Martyn 15*, I.A. Healy 6*); Third day, South Africa 94-2 (W.J. Cronje 37*, K.C. Wessels 7*); Fourth day, Australia 63-4 (M.E. Waugh 4*, A.R. Border 7*).

SOUTH AFRICA

A.C. Hudson lbw b McGrath	.0 –	c Healy b McDermott 1
G. Kirsten st Healy b Warne	.67 –	b McDermott 41
W.J. Cronje c Waugh b McDermott	.41 –	b McDermott 38
D.J. Cullinan b Warne	.9 –	(5) lbw b Warne 2
J.N. Rhodes lbw b Warne	.4 –	(6) not out 76
*K.C. Wessels c and b Warne	.3 –	(4) b Warne 18
†D.J. Richardson c Taylor b Warne	.4 –	lbw b McGrath 24
P.L. Symcox b Warne	.7 –	c Healy b McDermott 4
C.R. Matthews c Taylor b Warne	.0 –	c Waugh b Warne 4
P.S. de Villiers c Waugh b McDermott	.18 –	lbw b Warne 2
A.A. Donald not out	.0 –	c Healy b Warne 10
B 1, l-b 4, n-b 11	.16	B 13, l-b 1, n-b 5 19

1/1 (1) 2/91 (3) 3/110 (4) 4/133 (5)   **169**   1/2 (1) 2/75 (2) 3/101 (3) 4/107 (4)   **239**
5/134 (2) 6/141 (7) 7/141 (6)   5/110 (5) 6/182 (7) 7/188 (8)
8/142 (9) 9/152 (8) 10/169 (10)   8/197 (9) 9/203 (10) 10/239 (11)

Bowling: FIRST INNINGS – McDermott 18.1-2-42-2; McGrath 19-5-32-1; Warne 27-8-56-7; May 10-1-34-0. SECOND INNINGS – McDermott 28-9-62-4; McGrath 14-3-30-1; May 22-4-53-0; Warne 42-17-72-5; Border 3-1-8-0.

AUSTRALIA

M.J. Slater b Donald	.92 –	(2) b de Villiers 1
M.A. Taylor c Richardson b Donald	.7 –	(1) c Richardson b de Villiers 27
D.C. Boon b de Villiers	.19 –	c Kirsten b de Villiers 24
M.E. Waugh lbw b Symcox	.7 –	(5) lbw b Donald 11
*A.R. Border c Richardson b de Villiers	.49 –	(6) b Donald 7
D.R. Martyn c Richardson b de Villiers	.59 –	(7) c Hudson b Donald 6
†I.A. Healy c Richardson b Donald	.19 –	(8) b de Villiers 1
S.K. Warne c Rhodes b Symcox	.11 –	(9) run out 1
C.J. McDermott c Cronje b de Villiers	.6 –	(10) not out 29
T.B.A. May not out	.8 –	(4) lbw b de Villiers 0
G.D. McGrath b Donald	.9 –	c and b de Villiers 1
B 1, l-b 2, n-b 3	.6	L-b 3 3

1/10 (2) 2/58 (3) 3/75 (4) 4/179 (5)   **292**   1/4 (2) 2/51 (3) 3/51 (4) 4/56 (1)   **111**
5/179 (1) 6/229 (7) 7/250 (8)   5/63 (6) 6/72 (5) 7/73 (8)
8/266 (9) 9/281 (6) 10/ 292 (11)   8/75 (9) 9/110 (7) 10/111 (11)

Bowling: FIRST INNINGS – Donald 31.2-8-83-4; de Villiers 36-12-80-4; Matthews 28-11-44-0; Symcox 46-11-82-2. SECOND INNINGS – Donald 17-5-34-3; de Villiers 23.3-8-43-6; Matthews 6-5-9-0; Symcox 10-3-22-0.

Umpires: S.G. Randell and W.P. Sheahan. Referee: J.L. Hendriks (West Indies).

SECOND TEST MATCH

At Port Elizabeth, March 14, 15, 16, 17, 1997. Australia won by two wickets. Toss: Australia. Mark Waugh's magnificent fourth-innings 116 clinched a wildly fluctuating Test and, with it, the series – South Africa's first home defeat in six series since resuming Test cricket in 1992. Australia began and finished strongly, but for much of the match South Africa seemed bound to square the series. […]

Australia were unchanged, but South Africa dropped Hudson, Rhodes and Klusener and brought in Bacher, Gibbs and McMillan, now fit again. This meant three inexperienced batsmen in the top six, and they were swept aside by Gillespie's first five-wicket haul for his country. Bowling an impeccable line and length at high speed, he helped to reduce South Africa to 95 for seven. Then the Australians were convinced Richardson was caught behind before scoring, but he remained to add 85 for the eighth wicket with McMillan. A total of 209 was a good one on that pitch. Again, the lack of a third pace bowler hampered Australia, although Warne bowled beautifully in conditions entirely against wrist-spin.

The Australians lost Hayden on the first evening and their reply next day was a peculiar one. They somehow got through the morning with only three wickets down, despite inordinate movement off the greentop. They were helped when Pollock was forced out after tearing a hamstring. The turning point came when Bacher ran out Elliott for 23, the top score of the innings. That started a collapse of seven wickets for 44, and Australia trailed by 101. Donald bowled with fearsome hostility and frequently beat the bat, but Blewett was his only victim in the Test – a statistic almost as extraordinary as the fact that Healy took only one catch. The tourists complained because hessian mats were not used under the tarpaulin covers to reduce overnight sweating, as they were in the First Test. Raman Subba Row exonerated the ground authorities, though he recommended to ICC that covering be uniform in each country.

South Africa's openers extended their advantage to 184 as batting conditions improved, which put them almost out of sight. But on the third day, a red mist cost them all ten wickets for 85. Bacher was responsible for another run-out, but this time the victim was his partner, Kallis, and five more dismissals from rash strokes gave Australia a hope of victory. Only Cronje displayed the necessary obduracy, batting for 21 overs until he failed to read a googly from Bevan.

Australia needed 270. Though two and a half days remained, another 40 or 50 might have defeated them. The chance was there and Mark Waugh took it. He later described it as his best innings in any cricket: it lasted nearly five and a half hours and included a six and 17 fours. Stern defence was twinned with innate elegance after he arrived in a crisis – 30 for two. Taylor failed again, and Hayden was comically run out when he and Elliott lunged for the same crease as Cronje burst between them to knock down the other wicket.

Waugh reached his fifty by the close, when Australia were an encouraging 145 for three, with his brother Steve digging in at the other end. But Kallis had Steve caught in the covers and, when Adams bowled Blewett, at 192 for five, South Africa were back in the match. The crowd, though disappointingly small, was close to delirium. Bevan came in to help Waugh to the brink of victory but, with 12 still wanted, Kallis dismissed Waugh and Cronje had Bevan caught at slip. Warne soon followed. Two wickets were left, five needed. But not for Healy the Hirst–Rhodes tactic of getting them in singles – he swung Cronje high over long leg for six.

Man of the Match: M.E. Waugh. *Attendance*: 44,782.

Close of play: First day, Australia 10-1 (M.A. Taylor 7*, M.T.G. Elliott 1*); Second day, South Africa 83-0 (G. Kirsten 41*, A.M. Bacher 38*); Third day, Australia 145-3 (M.E. Waugh 54*, S.R. Waugh 11*).

SOUTH AFRICA

G. Kirsten c Hayden b Gillespie	.0 –	b Gillespie ...43
A.M. Bacher c Elliott b McGrath	.11 –	c McGrath b Gillespie ...49
J.H. Kallis c Blewett b Gillespie	.0 –	run out ...2
D.J. Cullinan c Warne b Gillespie	.34 –	lbw b Gillespie ...2
*W. J. Cronje b McGrath	.0 –	c Healy b Bevan ...27
H.H. Gibbs b Gillespie	.31 –	c M.E. Waugh b McGrath ...7
B.M. McMillan c S.R. Waugh b Warne	.55 –	lbw b Bevan ...2
S.M. Pollock lbw b Gillespie	.0 –	lbw b Warne ...17
†D.J. Richardson c McGrath b Warne	.47 –	not out ...3
A.A. Donald c and b Warne	.9 –	c Warne b Bevan ...7
P.R. Adams not out	.5 –	c Taylor b Warne ...1
B 8, l-b 8, w 1 ...17		B 1, l-b 5, n-b 2 ...8

1/13 (1) 2/17 (3) 3/21 (2) 4/22 (5) **209** 1/87 (1) 2/98 (3) 3/99 (2) 4/100 (4) **168**
5/70 (4) 6/95 (6) 7/95 (8)   5/122 (6) 6/137 (7) 7/152 (5)
8/180 (9) 9/204 (7) 10/209 (10)   8/156 (8) 9/167 (10) 10/168 (11)

Bowling: FIRST INNINGS – McGrath 22-7-66-2; Gillespie 23-10-54-5; Warne 23.4-5-62-3; Blewett 4-2-3-0; Bevan 2-0-8-0. SECOND INNINGS – McGrath 13-3-43-1; Gillespie 18-4-49-3; S.R. Waugh 4.3-0-16-0; Blewett 7.3-3-16-0; Warne 17.4-7-20-2; Bevan 13-3-18-3.

AUSTRALIA

M.L. Hayden c Cullinan b Pollock	.0 –	(2) run out ...14
*M.A. Taylor c Richardson b Pollock	.8 –	(1) lbw b McMillan ...13
M.T.G. Elliott run out	.23 –	c and b Adams ...44
M.E. Waugh lbw b Cronje	.20 –	b Kallis ...116
S.R. Waugh c Richardson b McMillan	.8 –	c Cronje b Kallis ...18
G.S. Blewett b Donald	.13 –	b Adams ...7
M.G. Bevan c Richardson b McMillan	.0 –	c Cullinan b Cronje ...24
†I.A. Healy c Bacher b Cronje	.5 –	not out ...10
S.K. Warne lbw b Adams	.18 –	lbw b Kallis ...3
J.N. Gillespie not out	.1 –	not out ...0
G.D. McGrath c Richardson b Kallis	.0	
B 1, l-b 7, w 2, n-b 2 ...12		B 11, l-b 8, w 3 ...22

1/1/ (1) 2/13 2 3/48 (4) 4/64 (3) **108** 1/23 1) 2/30 (2) 3/113 (3) (8 wkts) **271**
5/66 (5) 6/70 (7) 7/85 (8)   4/167 (5) 5/192 (6) 6/258 (4)
8/86 (6) 9/106 (9) 10/108 (11)   7/258 (7) 8265 (9)

Bowling: FIRST INNINGS – Donald 23-13-18-1; Pollock 6-3-6-2; Adams 4-0-5-1; McMillan 14-2-32-2; Cronje 14-7-21-2; Kallis 9.4-2-18-1. SECOND INNINGS – Donald 26-6-75-0; McMillan 21-5-46-1; Cronje 9.3-1-36-1; Kallis 16-7-29-3; Adams 21-4-66-2.

Umpires: S. Venkataraghavan (India) and R.E. Koertzen.
Referee: R. Subba Row (England).

7

THE BIG DIPPER:
AUSTRALIA v. WEST INDIES

When cricket writer Ray Robinson referred to matches between Australia and West Indies as 'Big Dipper Cricket' in 1975 to evoke their extraordinary fluctuations, he was writing before the biggest change of all in their conduct. In 1975–76, Australia annihilated a visiting team from the Caribbean by five Tests to one. Who could then have foreseen that Australia would not win another series against West Indies for almost two decades?

Robinson was already on solid ground in volunteering his description. Who could forget the glories of 1960–61, including what *Wisden* 1962 referred to unequivocally as 'The Greatest Test Match': the tie at Brisbane. West Indies had been the third international team to defeat Australia in a Test (at Sydney in February 1931) and the second to beat Australia in a series (in 1964–65), on the receiving end of our biggest total (eight for 758 at Kingston in May 1955) and least generous declaration (a Bill Lawry special, setting the visitors 735 to win in ten hours at Sydney in February 1969).

Yet what amounts to the greatest shift in the international cricket order over the last century and a quarter is that between 1975 and 1995: the rise of West Indian cricket tilted cricket permanently from its Anglo-Australian axis. The cause was not far to seek. West Indian players benefited more than those of any other international team from Packer-inspired professionalism, not to mention the proliferation of one-day cricket – a form of the game suited to their explosive batting, fast bowling and fielding. The effect was dramatic. Australia has not lost so consistently to any other international team: at one stage fifteen of twenty-seven Tests.

It could not and did not last forever. But even since Mark Taylor's team recovered the Frank Worrell Trophy in April 1995, West Indies have proven capable of administering shocks. The most recent Kingston and Bridgetown Tests were both classics, adorned by the batting of a reborn Brian Lara. 'Seldom in the august annals of Test cricket,' commented Peter Roebuck in *Wisden Australia* 1999, 'has any batsman had a month to set beside the amazing performance of Brian Lara in March 1999.' It is in the nature of Big Dippers that they leave the biggest surprises for when they are least expected.

—GH

SECOND TEST MATCH

At Sydney, November 30, December 1, 3, 4, 5, 1951. Australia won by seven wickets. The West Indies, victims of the Australians' 'bumper' tactics, lost a great chance of nullifying their defeat at Brisbane. After scoring 362 they had Australia's opening pair out for 27 when Walcott made a fatal error behind the wicket, dropping Hassett. From then the initiative escaped their grasp. Hassett and Miller added 235 for the fourth stand and established a record Australian partnership for any wicket against the West Indies.

Hassett gambled on the state of the pitch. Rain seeped under the covers during the night and conditions looked unfavourable for run-making. When Rae went at 33 none would decry Hassett's decision to field, but the later batsmen changed the outlook. Worrell showed little concern for either the reputed hostile attack or the nature of the turf, and Walcott, strong off the back foot, looked equally confident. Then came Christiani. With a glorious display of wristy strokes he looked set for a century, but a lapse in concentration brought his downfall off the last ball of the day. He attempted a cover drive and played into his wicket. When play recommenced Goddard and Gomez hit 73 of the last 76 runs. Lindwall, when bowling Ramadhin, took his 100th Test wicket. Australia replied with 131 for three before stumps were drawn on Saturday, and during the rest day Goddard could reflect with a good deal of satisfaction on his side's position. However, he was to regret deeply that dropped catch off Hassett, against whom one cannot afford to make mistakes, and who on Monday reached 100 in just under five hours. Miller, who forced Ramadhin to place three fieldsmen on the leg boundary, was an hour quicker completing his century, having enjoyed a generous amount of luck. He hit fifteen boundaries before, like Christiani, playing on. After this the West Indies attack wilted noticeably. Lindwall and Ring, dropped when 18, added 79 in the last hour, and next day Johnston and Langley scored another 32 runs in helping Australia to lead by 155.

Nearly two days remained and the West Indies still had the opportunity of averting defeat, but several of their leading batsmen were removed by the bumpers which Lindwall and Miller relentlessly sent down. Two injured players, Stollmeyer and Weekes, refused to be intimidated. Stollmeyer, who pulled a muscle fielding and used a runner, ducked too slowly in Lindwall's second over and was struck on the top of his head, but he carried on. Not so his partner, Rae, who, after obvious discomfort when two deliveries rose chest high, fell to a simple catch to silly mid-off. Worrell flashed unsuccessfully at a ball high over the stumps. Weekes, suffering from leg trouble, played each ball on merit. One bumper was promptly hit to the boundary and he made some glorious strokes through the covers before becoming the third man to deflect a ball with fatal results. [...]

WEST INDIES

A.F. Rae c Johnson b Johnston	.17	– c Ring b Miller 9
J.B. Stollmeyer c Johnson b Lindwall	.36	– b Johnson 35
F.M. Worrell b Johnson	.64	– c Langley b Lindwall 20
E.D. Weekes b Lindwall	.5	– b Johnson 56
C.L. Walcott c Langley b Ring	.60	– st Langley b Johnson 10
R.J. Christiani b Hole	.76	– c Hassett b Miller 30
G.E. Gomez lbw b Johnston	.54	– c Miller b Lindwall 41
J.D. Goddard c Johnson b Johnston	.33	– not out 57
P.E. Jones lbw b Lindwall	.1	– c Miller b Johnston 7
S. Ramadhin b Lindwall	.0	– b Johnston 3
A.L. Valentine not out	.0	– b Miller 1
B 12. l-b 3, n-b 1	.16	B 9, b 12 21

1/33 2/85 3/99 4/139 5/228 6/286   **362**   1/19 2/52 3/102 4/130 5/141 6/210   **290**
7/359 8/360 9/360   7/230 8/246 9/268

AUSTRALIA

K. Archer c Weekes b Gomez	.11	– lbw b Worrell 47
A.R. Morris c Walcott b Jones	.11	– st Walcott b Ramadhin 30
A.L. Hassett c Christiani b Jones	.132	– not out 46
R.N. Harvey c Gomez b Goddard	.39	– lbw b Worrell 1
K.R. Miller b Valentine	.129	– not out 6
G. Hole b Valentine	.1	
R. Lindwall run out	.48	
I.W. Johnson c Walcott b Jones	.5	
D. Ring c Ramadhin b Valentine	.65	
G. Langley not out	.15	
W.A. Johnston b Valentine	.28	
B 16, l-b 14, n-b 3	.33	B 6, l-b 1 7

1/19 2/27 3/106 4/341 5/345 6/348   **517**   1/49 2/123 3/125   (3 wkts) **137**
7/372 8/457 9/485

AUSTRALIA BOWLING

	O	M	R	W	O	M	R	W
Lindwall	26	2	66	4	17	3	59	2
Johnston	25.4	2	80	3	24	5	61	2
Johnson	14	3	48	1	23	2	78	3
Miller	21	3	72	0	13.2	2	50	3
Ring	17	1	71	1	7	0	21	0
Hole	4	1	9	1				

WEST INDIES BOWLING

	O	M	R	W	O	M	R	W
Jones	27	5	68	3	5	1	16	0
Gomez	18	2	47	1	5	1	9	0
Worrell	11	0	60	0	2	0	7	2
Valentine	31.5	3	111	4	10	0	45	0
Ramadhin	41	7	143	0	12.3	1	53	1
Goddard	24	6	55	1				

FIFTH TEST MATCH

At Kingston, June 11, 13, 14, 15, 16, 17, 1955. Australia won by an innings and 82 runs a game in which more records were established. First and foremost was the performance of Walcott in hitting for the second time during the series two separate centuries in a match, a feat never before accomplished. Furthermore he became the first player to reach three figures on five occasions in a Test rubber. The Australian total, besides being the biggest ever recorded in a Test match by a team from the Commonwealth, yielded two other records – the scoring of five centuries in an innings and the highest third wicket stand in history for Australia.

By the end of the opening day West Indies appeared likely to make a better fight, for with six wickets down they had 327 runs on the board. They began badly on a pitch full of runs, losing two wickets, including that of the new opening batsman, Furlonge, for 13. Then Walcott led a recovery in which Weekes and Worrell rendered able support. Let off when 21 by Johnston, who twisted a knee in attempting the catch and did not bowl in the match, Walcott offered only one more chance, at 105, during a stay of nearly five hours. While always strong in defence, he drove, cut and pulled with great power. Weekes, who injured a thigh muscle early in his innings, hit so fiercely all round that in scoring 56 of the 82 added for the third wicket, he registered no fewer than ten boundaries. Worrell, with a discriminating display, helped Walcott to put on 110 before falling to a splendid left-handed catch on the leg side behind the wicket by Langley, who gave a capital exhibition and in the two innings allowed only eight byes. Next day Miller bowled so effectively that the remaining four wickets went down for 30 runs. Three of them fell to Miller at a cost of 15 runs, and he finished with six for 107.

Australia in turn made a poor start, losing two men for seven runs, but from that point they were the masters. McDonald and Harvey, proceeding unhurriedly, put on 295 in a little over five hours. Harvey, staying till his side stood 16 ahead, batted for seven hours five minutes and hit one 6 and twenty-four 4's. Very slow at first, Miller shared with Archer in a stand which realised 220, and there followed a dazzling display of forcing batsmanship by Benaud. So mercilessly did Benaud flog a tiring attack that, with two 6's and fifteen 4's among his figures, he reached 100 in seventy-eight minutes. Upon his dismissal Johnson declared with Australia 401 ahead.

Three West Indies wickets went down for 65, but again Walcott checked the success of bowlers. He found a steady partner in Sobers, who stayed three hours while 179 runs were added, but when they were parted such a breakdown occurred that the innings and the match were all over for another 75 runs early on the sixth day.

WEST INDIES

J.K. Holt c Langley b Miller	4	– c Langley b Benaud	21
H. Furlonge c Benaud b Lindwall	4	– c sub b Miller	28
C.L. Walcott c Langley b Miller	155	– c Langley b Lindwall	110
E.D. Weekes b Benaud	56	– not out	36
F.M. Worrell c Langley b Lindwall	61	– b Johnson	12
O.G. Smith c Langley b Miller	29	– c and b Benaud	16
G. Sobers not out	35	– c Favell b Lindwall	64
D. Atkinson run out	8	– c Langley b Archer	4
C. Depeiza c Langley b Miller	0	– b Miller	7
F. King b Miller	0	– c Archer b Johnson	6
T. Dewdney b Miller	2	– lbw b Benaud	0
L-b 2, w 1	3	B 8, l-b 6, w 1	15

1/4 2/13 3/95 4/205 5/268 6/327   **357**   1/47 2/60 3/65 4/244 5/244 6/268   **319**
7/341 8/347 9/347   7/273 8/283 9/289

AUSTRALIA

C.C. McDonald b Worrell	127	R. Benaud c Worrell b Smith	121
L. Favell c Weekes b King	0	I.W. Johnson not out	27
A.R. Morris lbw b Dewdney	7		
R.N. Harvey c Atkinson b Smith	204	B 8, l-b 7, w 9, n-b 1	25
K.R. Miller c Worrell b Atkinson	109		
R.G. Archer c Depeiza b Sobers	128	1/0 2/7 3/302 (8 wkts, dec.) **758**	
R.R. Lindwall c Depeiza b King	10	4/373 5/593 6/597 7/621 8/758	

G.R. Langley and W.A. Johnston did not bat.

AUSTRALIA BOWLING

	O	M	R	W	O	M	R	W
Lindwall	12	2	64	2	20	5	56	2
Miller	25.2	2	107	6	19	3	58	2
Archer	11	1	39	0	26	6	68	1
Benaud	24	5	75	1	30	10	76	3
Johnson	22	7	69	0	23	10	46	2

WEST INDIES BOWLING

Dewdney	24	4	115	1
King	31	1	126	2
Atkinson	55	21	132	1
Smith	52.4	17	145	2
Worrell	45	10	116	1
Sobers	38	12	99	1

Umpires: P. Burke and T. Ewart.

WEST INDIES IN AUSTRALIA, 1960–61

Never has it been more apparent that the game is greater than the result than in Melbourne on February 17, 1961. Commerce in this Australian city stood almost still as the smiling cricketers from the West Indies, the vanquished not the victors, were given a send-off the like of which is normally reserved for Royalty and national heroes. Open cars paraded the happy players from the Caribbean among hundreds of thousands of Australians who had been sentimentalised through the media of cricket as it should be played. Worrell, the handsome West Indies captain, Hall, a bowler big in heart as well as stature, Kanhai, a fleet-footed batsman in the best tradition, and the suave Ramadhin, who had come a long way since he was introduced to cricket at the Canadian Mission School in Trinidad, were among those whom it was said, were moved to tears by the enthusiasm of the farewell.

Four months earlier these same players had arrived almost unsung but vowing, through their captain, that they were going to re-instil some lost adventure into cricket, which for several years had in the main been a dull, lifeless pastime to watch internationally. The forthright Australian captain, Benaud, supported him. Cynics, and the not so cynical, who had witnessed so much drab play over the last decade or so, thought they had heard it all before. Too much was at stake nationally, they argued, for any lightness of heart to prevail.

Worrell and Benaud and their associates happily proved them wrong. The opening match between the countries produced grand cricket and the first tie in a Test; Australia won the second, West Indies the third and the fourth was drawn. So the series built up to a magnificent climax at the vast Melbourne stadium. The struggle intensified and support grew and grew. A world record crowd of 90,800 saw play on the Saturday of this vital match, watched in all by 274,404 people who paid £A48,749, the highest receipts for any Australian match.

Over 40,000 were present on a drama-charged final day. A fair percentage of that crowd became allies of the opposition when a debatable decision at the vital moment went against West Indies and, as Australia finally squeezed victory and the rubber by a mere margin of two wickets, the batsmen had the crowd surging towards them as they went through for the winning single – a bye. Such was the intensity of the occasion. Summer's glorious pastime had returned as a spectacle of some consequence and faith in the game was restored among the all-important younger fraternity on whom its popularity, and indeed its very existence, depends. That Worrell and Benaud were the leaders cannot be stressed too much. Upon their insistence on attractive, sensible cricket was laid the foundations of a true demonstration of this great game.

Yet without support their aims would have been meaningless. This came in full measure on both sides, with Kanhai, Sobers, Hunte, Alexander, Hall and Gibbs most successful for the West Indies and O'Neill, Simpson, Grout and Davidson in particular backing up the efforts of Benaud. [...] The fact that the West Indies took home £30,000 was indicative of the support received, and the institution of the Frank Worrell Cup commemorating the Brisbane tie – to be played for regularly between West Indies and Australia – ensured that there would remain something tangible to remind all of the most enjoyable cricket contest for many years.

THE GREATEST TEST MATCH

AUSTRALIA AND WEST INDIES TIE AT BRISBANE

By E.M. Wellings

I was there. I saw it all. That is something that countless thousands would give much to be able to say. For it was The Greatest Test Match, The Greatest Cricket Match and surely The Greatest Game ever played with a ball. Australia v. West Indies at Brisbane from December 9 to December 14 1960 was already a great match before it bounded explosively to its amazing climax to produce the only tie in the history of Test cricket.

Some time has elapsed since the remarkable events of Hall's last over, in which the final three Australian wickets fell, five runs were made to bring the scores level and one catch dropped. But the picture of those events is more vivid now than it was at the time. Then all was confusion, for so much happened and thrill followed thrill so rapidly that everything became an exciting jumble. Even Meckiff, the last man out, was confused and thought West Indies had won by a run.

THE FINAL OVER

Six runs were wanted by Australia when Hall began what had to be the final over. The first ball hit Grout high on the leg, dropped at his feet, and he and Benaud scampered a single. Now the odds were heavily on Australia for Benaud was 52 and batting in match-winning vein. But immediately the odds were levelled. The next ball was a bouncer and Benaud aimed to hook it, as Davidson a few minutes earlier had superbly hooked a similar ball. He merely nicked it, and every West Indian leapt for joy as Alexander took the catch. So Meckiff arrived to play his first ball quietly back to Hall, and Australia needed a run off each ball.

A bye was run, and Grout skied the fifth ball just out on the leg side. Fielders converged from all directions, but Hall was the tallest and most determined, and he alone put his hands to it as the batsmen were running a single. It bounced out, and the fielders drooped in despair. The next delivery almost completed their despair, for Meckiff courageously clouted it loftily away to leg. He and Grout ran one, then another, and staked all on a third to win the match as Hunte was preparing to throw from the square-leg boundary. It was a glorious low throw, fast and true, and though Grout hurled himself at the line and skidded home on severely grazed forearms he could not counter the speed of the ball.

Umpire Hoy flung his right arm high to announce the decision immediately to everyone anxiously looking towards him, and again the West Indies leapt and flung their arms in triumph. A minute or so later umpire and fielders repeated their actions, only more so. At the fall of the last wicket the joy of the West Indies was so expressed in leaps and bounds and running about that the scene might have served for a ballet of ultramodern abandon. The man who sent them into transports of delight and tied the match was little Solomon when Kline smoothly played the seventh ball of that fateful last over towards square-leg. Meckiff at the other end was well launched on a run, but he never made it. With little more than one stump's width to aim at, Solomon threw the wicket down, as he had done some dozen minutes earlier from farther away to run out Davidson and give his side the chance to save themselves.

THREE RUN OUT

That was not the least remarkable feature of this very remarkable match. Three of the last four batsmen were run out by a fielding side whose throwing often had their wicket-keeper racing yards from the target area to retrieve the ball. At the crisis the throws straightened themselves, or perhaps they were made by the right men, for Hunte and Solomon were not often among the wild throwers.

That final over lasted nine minutes and ended four minutes after the appointed time. Not so long ago it would have been cut short at the dismissal of Grout. But for a comparatively recent law amendment, which provided for the last over being played out whatever the time, we lucky spectators would not have palpitated to the last tremendous thrill of that last tremendous over. Nor perhaps would spectators, bounding with excitement no less than the fielders, have raced across the ground to cheer and call for the heroes of the day, and repeat their cheers again and again in front of the players' pavilion.

UNFORGETTABLE SIGHT

That, like the freely expressed delight of the West Indies fielders, was an unforgettable sight. They were not so numerous as that gathered rapturously in front of The Oval pavilion in 1953, when Hutton's team at last recovered the Ashes from Australia, but the Queenslanders made up for their relative lack of numbers by their enthusiasm. We all recognised that this was more than a tied match. It was tied by teams playing in Homeric manner.

At the climax neither side made the slightest attempt to play for safety. Both were set on winning or perishing in the attempt. With three wickets standing, including that of Benaud, Australia could surely have coasted home to safety, and since they had gallantly pulled themselves up from a position of imminent defeat only two hours earlier, we could hardly have blamed them if they had.

On the other side Hall, who had earlier wasted many deliveries barely within the batsman's reach, bowled straight more consistently than at any previous time in the match. Australia and West Indies played out the game in a spirit which should serve as an example to all others.

There have been other Test matches not far removed from being tied. Perhaps the most momentous was that at The Oval in 1902, when Australia were cantering home until Jessop hit a hurricane century and Hirst and Rhodes, the last pair, scored the final runs with typical Yorkshire unconcern in singles to give England the win by one wicket. Now in 1960 the Brisbane Test eclipsed that and all other close and thrilling finishes.

RIGHT EXAMPLE

From first to last the spirit of enterprise was in striking contrast to the play in most other recent Tests. Almost coinciding with it a bitter defensive contest was waged by India and Pakistan without ever any prospects of a definite result.

Only two years earlier Brisbane had been the scene of the dullest ever England–Australia Test. England based their sketchy plans entirely on defensive batting and restrictive practices, and there was hardly a hint at batting enterprise until, on the last afternoon, O'Neill hit out for an Australian win. More recently West Indies and England opposed each other with nothing but negative intentions.

Test cricket had come to a sorry pass. Unpalatable though it is to admit, England developed the tight, restrictive tactics. Having then superior forces, they proved victorious for a time. It is not, therefore, surprising that others followed their lead and, in particular, sought to play England at their own game. Hence the tedium of many recent matches. Now Australia and West Indies have given a new lead, which England can neglect to follow only at the risk of grave loss of prestige.

SOBERS' CENTURY

England's recently defensive opponents in the West Indies were very different players against Australia at Brisbane. From the outset their batsmen were attacking, and they hoisted the first 50 off only 58 balls. That their batting attack was somewhat undisciplined cost wickets, but, in the course of a magnificent stand of 174, Sobers and Worrell proved how fruitful discreet aggression can be.

They were superb, and the hundred by Sobers in just over two hours, from no more than 29 overs, was the fastest Test century for many years. Sobers had the glory in his team's innings of 453, which brought runs at the rare average rate of 4.5 per eight-ball over. But Worrell was the man of great cricketing character who imposed discipline on his side's play throughout the match. In this respect, Solomon's well-judged batting gave him valuable assistance.

Before the end Hall hit furiously and played amusingly. A partnership between him and Trueman would be enormous fun. Then Australia played an innings of 505 which, by comparison with that of their opponents, did not entirely commend itself to the home critics. Without that comparison, however, it would have been very well received by spectators disillusioned by other Tests. Yet O'Neill's 181, his highest Test score at the time, was not up to the standard of his innings on the same ground in 1958. In the meantime he had apparently fallen into the stultifying groove of current Test cricket.

GREAT PACE

A second West Indies innings of 284, maintained largely by Worrell and Solomon after some of the earlier batsmen had shown suicidal tendencies, left Australia 310 minutes in which to make 233. And so to the final remarkable chapter.

It began with Hall, a bowler of great pace and enormous, though sometimes misplaced enthusiasm, bowling now with greater discipline and taking West Indies to the brink of success. Half Australia were out for 57, and Hall had four for 37. Then a sixth wicket fell at 92, and those watchers who lived in Sydney were planning to catch the 5.45 plane. They had to wait until the following morning.

Most batting sides, I think, would have tried to play for a draw in these circumstances. Australia did not. They had their captain at the wicket, and he and Davidson set off for victory. Davidson had already had a great match. He had taken 11 wickets and scored 44. Moreover, while the general standard of Australia's fielding was below their best standards, his own work in the field had been flawless. Now he added 80 more vigorous runs to his fine record and, after playing himself through a sticky period at the start, earned every single of them. Such was his all-round success that in normal circumstances the Test would rightly go down to history as Davidson's Match. As it is, this is to be known as The Greatest Test Match, but it was big enough to carry also a sub-title recognising Davidson's performance.

UP WITH THE CLOCK

He and Benaud batted with outstanding judgment. They played the bowling strictly on its merits and brought off some sterling strokes, among which Davidson's hook off a head-high bumper from Hall stands out as a vivid memory. And they ran like whippets. Time after time they had the West Indies hurling fiercely at their stumps and missing. It would not have mattered if the stumps had been hit, for their judgment was splendid and their understanding perfect. It was astonishing that, after all the hard work Davidson had done, he was running as keenly and as rapidly at the end as at the start. He was tremendously fit.

After tea Australia had to score just above one run a minute, which was not easy when the average tally of overs per two-hour session was around 27. But they kept well up with the clock, and with 12 minutes to go only seven were needed. The story seemed cut and dried. Australia were going to win, and Worrell would perhaps regret not having used the left-arm off-breaks and googlies of Sobers earlier. When Sobers did arrive to use spin after a spell at medium pace, Davidson and Benaud were in full blast and he could not part them.

DEADLY AIM

It was Solomon who did that when 12 minutes remained. Davidson went for an extra run. Perhaps this was the one and only time during the partnership when a direct hit by a fielder could have been effective. Solomon achieved the direct hit from some 25 yards and square with the wicket on the leg side. There followed the two other run-out wickets, and when the dust of excitement had settled there was some talk that Australia had only themselves to blame for faulty running. That is ungenerous to both sides and takes no account of the daring running of Benaud and Davidson, without which they could not have levelled the scores. The attempted runs by Grout and Meckiff in the last over were fully justified.

Post-mortems on such a match are out of place. I am happily content to have been one of the company of 4,100 who saw the thrilling and inspiring end of this greatest match. It serves as a challenge to all cricketers and calls to them to tackle their matches in the same spirit of sporting enterprise. This was essentially a sporting game, as the crowd recognised when they called for the 22 victors in the cause of cricket to show themselves on the patio of their pavilion.

WEST INDIES

C.C. Hunte c Benaud b Davidson . . . . .24 – c Simpson b Mackay 39
C. Smith c Grout b Davidson . . . . .7 – c O'Neill b Davidson 6
R. Kanhai c Grout b Davidson . . . . .15 – c Grout b Davidson 54
G. Sobers c Kline b Meckiff . . . . .132 – b Davidson 14
*F.M. Worrell c Grout b Davidson . . . . .65 – c Grout b Davidson 65
J. Solomon hit wkt b Simpson . . . . .65 – lbw b Simpson 47
P. Lashley c Grout b Kline . . . . .19 – b Davidson 0
†F.C.M. Alexander c Davidson b Kline . . . . .60 – b Benaud 5
S. Ramadhin c Harvey b Davidson . . . . .12 – c Harvey b Simpson 6
W. Hall st Grout b Kline . . . . .50 – b Davidson 18
A.L. Valentine not out . . . . .0 – not out 7
    Extras 4   Extras .23

1/23 2/42 3/65 4/239 5/243   **453**   1/13 2/88 3/114 4/127 5/210   **284**
6/283 7/347 8/366 9/452   6/210 7/241 8/250 9/253

Bowling: FIRST INNINGS – Davidson 30-2-135-5; Meckiff 18-0-129-1 Mackay 3-0-15-0; Benaud 24-3-93-0; Simpson 8-0-25-1; Kline 17.6-6-52-3. SECOND INNINGS – Davidson 24.6-4-87-6; Meckiff 4-1-19-0; Benaud 31-6-69-1; Mackay 21-7-52-1; Kline 4-0-14-0; Simpson 7-2-18-2; O'Neill 1-0-2-0.

AUSTRALIA

C.C. McDonald c Hunte b Sobers . . . . .57 – b Worrell 16
R.B. Simpson b Ramadhin . . . . .92 – c sub b Hall 0
R.N. Harvey b Valentine . . . . .15 – c Sobers b Hall 5
N.C. O'Neill c Valentine b Hall . . . . .181 – c Alexander b Hall 26
L. Favell run out . . . . .45 – c Solomon b Hall 7
K.D. Mackay b Sobers . . . . .35 – b Ramadhin .28
A.K. Davidson c Alexander b Hall . . . . .44 – run out 80
* R. Benaud lbw b Hall . . . . .10 – c Alexander b Hall 52
†A.W.T. Grout lbw b Hall . . . . .4 – run out 2
I. Meckiff run out . . . . .4 – run out 2
L.F. Kline not out . . . . .3 – not out 0
    Extras 15   Extras .14

1/84 2/138 3/194 4/278 5/381   **505**   1/1 2/7 3/49 4/49 5/57 6/92   **232**
6/469 7/484 8/489 9/496   7/226 8/228 9/232

Bowling: FIRST INNINGS – Hall 29.3-1-140-4; Worrell 30-0-93-0; Sobers 32-0-115-2; Valentine 24-6-82-1; Ramadhin 15-1-60-1. SECOND INNINGS – Hall 17.7-3-63-5; Worrell 16-3-41-1; Sobers 8-0-30-0; Valentine 10-4-27-0; Ramadhin 17-3-57-1.

FOURTH TEST MATCH

At Adelaide, January 27, 28, 30, 31, February 1, 1961. Drawn. In a finish almost as exciting as the First Test, a defiant last-wicket partnership prevented West Indies taking the lead in the series. When Kline joined Mackay, an hour and fifty minutes remained with the West Indies total beyond reach. Two minutes later, Sobers, four yards from the bat, appealed confidently for a catch from Mackay off Worrell but it was turned down by Egar, the umpire, and the pair not only played out time but added 66 runs.

The match was full of incident. Gibbs, the West Indies off-spinner, did the hat-trick in Australia's first innings – the first against Australia this century – and Kanhai scored a hundred in each innings.

West Indies won the toss and after losing Hunte at 12 scored freely on an easy-paced pitch. The best batting came from Kanhai and Worrell who added 107 in just over an hour. Kanhai's first hundred came in a little over two hours and included two 6's and eleven 4's. Benaud kept the score in check with his accurate spin and captured five wickets for 96.

Australia also suffered a quick reverse when Favell was dismissed, but McDonald played doggedly for 71 and Simpson, after a shaky start, scored 85. Mackay never appeared comfortable and eventually was leg-before to Gibbs. Grout and Misson were the other victims in the hat-trick when Australia slumped from 281 for five to 281 for eight. Benaud appeared unperturbed and, receiving unexpected help from Hoare, took the score to 366. The Australian bowling offered few terrors when the West Indies batted a second time and Kanhai scored his second hundred of the match. With Hunte, he put on 163 – a record second-wicket partnership for West Indies against Australia.

Worrell declared and set Australia to score 460 in just over six and a half hours. Australia lost three wickets for 31 and anxiously faced the last day. Their hopes were raised by a determined stand by O'Neill and Burge, who justified his return to Test cricket. This lasted almost until lunch. Yet all seemed lost until the splendid fighting resistance of Mackay and Kline. For the last over Worrell recalled Hall to bowl to Mackay, but the Queenslander survived.

WEST INDIES

C.C. Hunte lbw b Hoare	6	– run out	79
C. Smith c and b Benaud	28	– c Hoare b Mackay	46
R. Kanhai c Simpson b Benaud	117	– lbw b Benaud	115
G. Sobers b Benaud	1	– run out	20
*F.M. Worrell c Misson b Hoare	71	– c Burge b Mackay	53
S. Nurse c and b Misson	49	– c Simpson b Benaud	5
J. Solomon c and b Benaud	22	– not out	16
†F.C.M. Alexander not out	63	– not out	87
L. Gibbs b Misson	18		
W. Hall c Hoare b Benaud	5		
A.L. Valentine lbw b Misson	0		
Extras	13	Extras	11

1/12 2/83 3/91 4/198 5/271 6/288   **393**   1/66 2/229 3/263   (6 wkts, dec.) **432**
7/316 8/375 9/392   4/270 5/275 6/388

Bowling: FIRST INNINGS – Hoare 16-0-68-2; Misson 17.5-2-79-3; Mackay 2-0-11-0; Benaud 27-5-96-5; Kline 21-3-109-0; Simpson 5-0-17-0. SECOND INNINGS – Hoare 13-0-88-0; Misson 28-3-106-0; Mackay 12-0-72-2; Benaud 27-3-107-2; Kline 12-2-48-0.

AUSTRALIA

C.C. McDonald c Hunte b Gibbs	71	– run out 2
L. Favell c Alexander b Worrell	1	– c Alexander b Hall 4
N.C. O'Neill c Alexander b Sobers	11	– c and b Sobers 65
R.B. Simpson c Alexander b Hall	85	– c Alexander b Hall 3
P.J. Burge b Sobers	45	– c Alexander b Valentine 49
*R. Benaud c Solomon b Gibbs	77	– c and b Sobers 17
K.D. Mackay lbw b Gibbs	29	– not out 62
†A.W.T. Grout c Sobers b Gibbs	0	– lbw b Worrell 42
F.M. Misson b Gibbs	0	– c Solomon b Worrell 1
D. Hoare b Sobers	35	– b Worrell 0
L.F. Kline not out	0	– not out 15
Extras 12		Extras 13

1/9 2/45 3/119 4/213 5/221 6/281   **366**   1/6 2/7 3/31 4/113 5/129   (9 wkts) **273**
7/281 8/281 9/366   6/144 7/203 8/207 9/207

Bowling: FIRST INNINGS – Hall 22-3-85-1; Worrell 7-0-34-1; Sobers 24-3-64-3; Gibbs 35.6-4-97-5; Valentine 21-4-74-0. SECOND INNINGS – Hall 13-4-61-2; Worrell 17-9-27-3; Sobers 39-11-87-2; Gibbs 28-13-44-0; Valentine 20-7-40-1; Solomon 3-2-1-0.

Umpires: C. Hoy and C.J. Egar.

FIFTH TEST MATCH

At Melbourne, February 10, 12, 13, 14, 15, 1961. Australia won by two wickets. When late on the afternoon of February 15, 1961, Valentine spun a ball past batsman and wicket-keeper it was swallowed up by the crowd as they swarmed on to the Melbourne stadium while Mackay and Martin were going through for the winning run. Thus ended an enthralling series which appropriately culminated in excitement and drama.

The drama occurred when Australia, needing 258 to win, were 254 for seven. Grout late-cut Valentine and the off-bail fell to the ground. Alexander, the wicket-keeper, did not turn round to follow the ball's flight but instead stood pointing at the broken wicket. The batsmen went through for two runs, after which the umpire at the bowler's end, Egar, went over to speak to Hoy at square leg. They decreed that Grout was not out. What caused the bail to fall off can only be conjecture but those two runs remained fact and the value of two runs at such a vital stage cannot be calculated. The umpires' ruling brought forth some hostility from the crowd of 41,186, who, however, soon had other events to occupy their minds. Grout was eighth out without addition and at the same total the West Indies missed a chance of dismissing Martin. Hall at mid-on failed to react quickly enough to a fairly easy catch. This lapse gave Martin a single and brought the scores level. Then came that final extra.

The beginning matched the end. Though rain fell over the city two days earlier it was generally considered that the side winning the toss would bat first. But Australia had a captain brave in Benaud. With the atmosphere heavy and Hall on the other side, he sent a murmur of surprise round the ground by telling the West Indies to take first innings. In the event, Davidson, the one bowler who, it was hoped, would do most to prove Benaud right, accomplished practically nothing. Instead the spinners worried all except Kanhai and Sobers and there was no cause for complaint from Australia when at the end of the first day West Indies were 252 for eight.

A world record crowd of 90,800 saw McDonald, at his very best, and Simpson serve Australia well on Saturday with an opening partnership of 146, the best send-off for either side in the series, but at 236 for six the lead stood 57 runs away when stumps were drawn. Thus far the cricket had been interesting but not so engrossing as much of the play in the earlier matches. The game really began to tick again on Monday. Then the batsmen, including Harvey, who injured a leg muscle catching Kanhai, were wound on the web of Sobers and Gibbs and Australia were thankful for the aggressiveness of broad shouldered Burge in helping them to finish their innings 64 ahead. Sobers went on to bowl at 124 for no wicket, half an hour before the tea interval on Saturday, and did not come off until the score stood at 335 for nine. He bowled slow at first, opened with the new ball on Monday and bowled all morning and for an hour afterwards. In all, his marathon effort lasted 41 overs and final figures of five for 120 in 44 overs spoke eloquently of an unflagging performance.

The first-innings deficit did not worry West Indies. Indeed, it seemed to spur them to greater effort. Smith hooked the second ball from Misson over fine leg for six and he and Hunte had 50 on the board in as many minutes, so that runs soon began to count again. Kanhai sent the fieldsmen scurrying with some delightful stroke play and by the end of the third day the match had regained its even keel. West Indies were 62 runs on with eight wickets left. Some of the balance tilted Australia's way as they fought with all their natural tenacity but once more they found an 'enemy' of comparable toughness in Alexander, who maintained his record of having exceeded 50 in each of the Tests. For two and a half hours he defied the bowlers. Then he was caught off Davidson, who when he had Hall taken behind the stumps brought his aggregate wickets to 33 in four Tests of the series. This catch, and three more taken during the day despite a damaged wrist, enabled Grout to match the record of helping in 23 dismissals in a rubber.

So came the final phase with Australia needing 258 for victory. Simpson began as enthusiastically as Smith, taking 24 runs off the first ten balls sent down to him, including 18 from the opening over. He was just as convincing when the spinners wrought havoc later and to him more than any other went the main accord on this final day of a memorable series. Both sides agreed before the start that an extra day should be added so as to minimise the chances of a stalemate but enterprising cricket from all made it unnecessary.

WEST INDIES

C. Smith c O'Neill b Misson	11	– lbw b Davidson ... 37
C.C. Hunte c Simpson b Davidson	31	– c Grout b Davidson ... 52
R. Kanhai c Harvey b Benaud	38	– c Misson b Benaud ... 31
G. Sobers c Grout b Simpson	64	– c Grout b Simpson ... 21
*F.M. Worrell c Grout b Martin	10	– c Grout b Davidson ... 7
P. Lashley c Misson b Benaud	41	– lbw b Martin ... 18
†F.C.M. Alexander c McDonald b Misson	11	– c Mackay b Davidson ... 73
J. Solomon run out	45	– run out ... 36
L. Gibbs c Burge b Misson	11	– c O'Neill b Simpson ... 8
W. Hall b Misson	21	– c Grout b Davidson ... 21
A.L. Valentine not out	0	– not out ... 3
Extras	9	Extras ... 14

1/18 2/75 3/81 4/107 5/200 6/204 **292** 1/54 2/103 3/135 4/173 5/201 6/238 **321**
7/221 8/235 9/290 7/262 8/295 9/304

Bowling: FIRST INNINGS – Davidson 27-4-89-1; Misson 14-3-58-4; Mackay 1-0-1-0; Benaud 21.7-5-55-2; Martin 8-0-29-1; Simpson 18-3-51-1. SECOND INNINGS – Davidson 24.7-4-84-5; Misson 10-1-58-0; Mackay 10-2-21-0; Benaud 23-4-53-1; Martin 10-1-36-1; Simpson 18-4-55-2.

AUSTRALIA

R.B. Simpson c Gibbs b Sobers	75	– b Gibbs ... 92
C.C. McDonald lbw b Sobers	91	– c Smith b Gibbs ... 11
N.C. O'Neill b Gibbs	10	– c Alexander b Worrell ... 48
P.J. Burge c Sobers b Gibbs	68	– b Valentine ... 53
K.D. Mackay c Alexander b Hall	19	– not out ... 3
R.N. Harvey c Alexander b Sobers	5	– c Smith b Worrell ... 12
A.K. Davidson c Alexander b Sobers	24	– c Sobers b Worrell ... 12
*R. Benaud b Gibbs	3	– b Valentine ... 6
J. Martin c Kanhai b Sobers	15	– not out ... 1
F.M. Misson not out	12	
†A.W.T. Grout c Hunte b Gibbs	14	– c Smith b Valentine ... 5
Extras	20	Extras ... 15

1/146 2/181 3/181 4/244 5/260 **356** 1/50 2/75 3/154 4/176 **(8 wkts) 258**
6/309 7/309 8/319 9/335 5/200 6/236 7/248 8/256

Bowling: FIRST INNINGS – Hall 15-1-56-1; Worrell 11-2-44-0; Sobers 44-7-120-5; Gibbs 38.4-18-74-4; Valentine 13-3-42-0. SECOND INNINGS – Hall 5-0-40-0; Worrell 31-16-43-3; Sobers 13-2-32-0; Gibbs 41-19-68-2; Valentine 21.7-4-60-3.

Umpires: C. Hoy and C.J. Egar.

FIFTH TEST MATCH

At Sydney, February 14, 15, 16, 18, 19, 20, 1969. Australia won by 382 runs. As the series had not been decided, the final Test was played over six days and it contained all the lessons of the last three matches. Australia again outclassed the West Indies, who revealed their familiar failings in all departments and particularly in the fielding. Griffith came into the West Indies side for Holford and for the last time in a Test match partnered Hall. Sobers put Australia in and almost achieved the crucial break-through himself. After Stackpole had played Hall into his stumps Sobers dismissed Chappell and Redpath in the same over and Australia were 51 for three. The West Indies chance of pressing home this advantage went when Lawry (44) drove at Sobers and was badly dropped by Nurse at second slip.

Lawry and Walters then retrieved the situation for Australia. [...] In all they added 336 in six and three-quarter hours, the second highest stand for Australia against the West Indies for any wicket. Lawry batted eight hours, twenty minutes hitting twelve 4's in his 151 while Walters' 242, his highest in Test cricket, took eight hours with twenty-four 4's. [...] With their chance of victory irrevocably gone the West Indies once again carelessly threw away their wickets, although they were given a fine start by Carew and Fredericks, who put on 100 in an hour and three-quarters. Then only Lloyd and Kanhai showed any fight and the West Indies finished 340 behind. But Lawry, mindful of their recovery at Adelaide, did not enforce the follow-on. Walters made another hundred, the first batsman to make a double century and a century in the same Test, and Redpath batted attractively for his first hundred in Test cricket. Eventually Lawry's declaration left the West Indies to score 735 in ten hours and although Sobers and Nurse both made defiant centuries, Australia won after only forty-three minutes play on the sixth morning.

AUSTRALIA

*W.M. Lawry b Griffith	151	– c Fredericks b Griffith	17
K.R. Stackpole b Hall	20	– c Carew b Hall	6
I.M. Chappell lbw b Sobers	1	– c Hendriks b Hall	10
I.R. Redpath c Nurse b Sobers	0	– c Sobers b Gibbs	132
K.D. Walters b Gibbs	242	– c Fredericks b Gibbs	103
A.P. Sheahan c Fredericks b Griffith	27	– c Hendriks b Sobers	34
E.W. Freeman c Hendriks b Griffith	56	– c Carew b Sobers	15
G.D. McKenzie b Gibbs	19	– c Carew b Sobers	40
†H.B. Taber lbw b Hall	48	– not out	15
J.W. Gleeson c Hendriks b Hall	45	– not out	5
A.N. Connolly not out	1		
L-b 2, w 1, n-b 6	9	B 4, l-b 6, w 1, n-b 6	17

1/43 2/51 3/51 4/387 5/435   **619**   1/21 2/36 3/40 4/249   (8 wkts, dec.) **394**
6/453 7/483 8/543 9/614   5/301 6/329 7/329 8/388

Bowling: FIRST INNINGS – Hall 35.7-3-157-3; Griffith 37-1-175-3; Sobers 28-4-94-2; Gibbs 40-8-133-2; Carew 10-2-44-0; Lloyd 2-1-7-0. SECOND INNINGS – Hall 12-0-47-2; Griffith 14-0-41-1; Gibbs 33-2-133-2; Sobers 26-3-117-3; Carew 5-0-26-0; Lloyd 2-0-13-0.

WEST INDIES

R.C. Fredericks c Taber b Connolly	39 – c Taber b McKenzie	0
M.C. Carew c Taber b Freeman	64 – b Connolly	3
R.B. Kanhai c Taber b Connolly	44 – b Connolly b McKenzie	18
*G.S. Sobers c Taber b Connolly	13 – c Redpath b Gleeson	113
B.F. Butcher c Sheahan b McKenzie	10 – c Gleeson b Stackpole	31
C.H. Lloyd b McKenzie	53 – c Freeman b Stackpole	11
S.M. Nurse c Stackpole b Connolly	9 – b Gleeson	137
†J.L. Hendriks c Taber b McKenzie	1 – c Stackpole b McKenzie	16
C.C. Griffith c Freeman b Gleeson	27 – b Gleeson	15
W.W. Hall b Gleeson	1 – c Sheahan b Chappell	0
L.R. Gibbs not out	4 – not out	0
B 2, l-b 4, n-b 8	14	B 1, l-b 5, n-b 2	8

1/100 2/154 3/159 4/179 5/179	**279**	1/0 2/10 3/30 4/76 5/102	**352**
6/190 7/193 8/257 9/259		6/220 7/284 8/351 9/352	

Bowling: FIRST INNINGS – McKenzie 22.6-2-90-3; Connolly 17-2-61-4; Freeman 12-2-48-1; Gleeson 19-8-53-2; Chappell 6-1-13-0. SECOND INNINGS – McKenzie 16-1-93-3; Connolly 18-4-72-1; Stackpole 7-0-57-2; Gleeson 15.2-1-84-3; Freeman 2-0-16-0; Chappell 6-0-22-1.

Umpires C.J. Egar and L. Rowan.

THIRD TEST MATCH

At Port of Spain, March 23, 24, 25, 27, 28, 1973. Australia won by 46 runs. In one of the most exciting of contemporary Test matches Australia won on the last afternoon just when it had looked as if Kallicharran was going to lead the West Indies to an astonishing victory after they had been left to score 334 to win on a turning wicket. West Indies suffered the big handicap of losing Rowe when he pulled the ligaments in his ankle in the field on the first day and was unable to bat in either innings.

Fredericks gave the West Indies a good start in the final innings and after a wild and irresponsible stroke by Kanhai and some predictable agonies by Lloyd against spin, Kallicharran and Foster came together. By lunch on the last day they had taken the score to 268 for four and only 66 more were needed. With Ian Chappell keeping his slips up and attacking to the last, Kallicharran played a slightly casual back shot to Walker's first ball of the afternoon and was caught behind. Soon afterwards Foster pushed O'Keeffe gently into forward short leg's hands and that was that. [...]

The shape of the game was established on the first morning after Ian Chappell had won the toss for the third consecutive time. Within thirty-five minutes of the start Gibbs was bowling to three short legs. Australia had begun badly, losing Stackpole to the third ball of the innings, but Ian Chappell and Redpath put on 107 for the second wicket before Chappell was out in the last over before lunch. This brought in Walters, who produced the best innings of the series. Reputedly it is a difficult wicket to play strokes on and yet in the two hours between lunch and tea Walters scored exactly 100, hitting sixteen 4's. By any standards it was a magnificent innings. His driving was quite glorious and he cut and pulled with power and certainty. In all he batted for two hours, twenty-eight minutes, hitting one 6 and sixteen 4's.

West Indies made a bad start, but Kallicharran scored an attractive fifty and Kanhai produced a more careworn half century. The Australian leg-spinners, Jenner and O'Keeffe, did not bowl particularly well and the side badly missed an off spinner. There was another important innings by Murray, who took West Indies to within 52 of Australia's score.

By the time Australia went in again the ball was turning a long way, but increasingly slowly. Redpath and Walters made useful runs and there was a glorious innings of 97 by Ian Chappell, who held the innings together at a time when it seemed that the West Indies spinners would win the match. His 97 took him three hours, fifty minutes, but it was not an entirely defensive innings, for he never wasted any chance of scoring runs. He was seventh out at 231 and then some strange bowling by Gibbs allowed the last three wickets to add 50, which was slightly more than the margin between the two sides at the end.

Against the main batsmen Gibbs had been pushing the ball through with his short legs up for the catch. Now he put his fielders back on the boundary and tried to buy the remaining wickets. Walker with his huge shoulders took advantage of this and swung his bat for 23 priceless runs and he and Hammond added 33 for the last wicket. If Gibbs had gone on pushing the ball through he might have given away the odd edged single, but he would surely have restricted the batsmen to very few runs. As it was the runs he gave away made the difference between victory and defeat.

AUSTRALIA

K.R. Stackpole c Foster b Boyce	0	c Fredericks b Boyce	18
I.R. Redpath run out	66	c Kanhai b Willett	44
G.S. Chappell c Kallicharran b Gibbs	56	c and b Gibbs	1
K.D. Walters c Fredericks b Inshan	112	c Gibbs b Willett	32
R. Edwards lbw b Boyce	12	b Gibbs	14
*I.M.Chappell c and b Inshan	8	c Fredericks b Willett	97
†R.W. Marsh b Inshan	14	b Inshan	8
K.J. O'Keeffe run out	37	c Kallicharran b Gibbs	7
T.J. Jenner lbw b Gibbs	2	b Gibbs	6
M.H.N. Walker b Gibbs	0	not out	23
J.R. Hammond not out	2	c Kanhai b Gibbs	19
B 10, l-b 7, n-b 6	23	B 5, l-b 7	12

1/1 2/108 3/181 4/240 5/257   **332**   1/31 2/96 3/99 4/156 5/185   **281**
6/2362 7/312 8/321 9/321   6/208 7/231 8/231 9/248

Bowling: FIRST INNINGS – Boyce 18-4-54-2; Lloyd 7-3-13-0; Gibbs 38-11-79-3; Willett 19-3-62-0; Inshan 41.1-11-89-3; Foster 6-2-12-0. SECOND INNINGS – Boyce 10-1-41-1; Lloyd 3-1-11-0; Gibbs 45-14-102-5; Willett 28-15-33-3; Inshan 21-2-82-1.

WEST INDIES

R.C. Fredericks c I.M. Chappell b Jenner	.16	– c Redpath b Stackpole	.76
M.L.C. Foster lbw b Jenner	.25	– c G.S. Chappell b O'Keeffe	.34
A.I. Kallicharran c G.S. Chappell b Jenner	.53	– c Marsh b Walker	.91
C.H. Lloyd c and b G.S. Chappell	.20	– c Stackpole b O'Keeffe	.15
*R.B. Kanhai c Redpath b O'Keeffe	.56	– b G.S. Chappell	.14
†D.L. Murray lbw b Hammond	.40	– c Redpath b Walker	.7
K.D. Boyce c Marsh b O'Keeffe	.12	– c I.M. Chappell b O'Keeffe	.11
Inshan Ali c Marsh b Walker	.15	– b Walker	.2
E.T. Willett not out	.4	– b O'Keeffe	.0
L.R. Gibbs c O'Keeffe b Jenner	.6	– not out	.0
L.G. Rowe absent hurt	.0	– absent hurt	.0
B 17, l-b 11, w 1, n-b 4	.33	B 19, l-b 13, n-b 7	.39

1/33 2/44 3/100 4/149 5/206   **280**   1/39 2/141 3/177 4/219 5/268   **289**
6/230 7/265 8/267 9/280   6/274 7/281 8/288 9/289

Bowling: FIRST INNINGS – Walker 30-8-55-1; Hammond 7-3-7-1; Jenner 38.3-7-98-4; O'Keeffe 28-10-62-2; G.S. Chappell 14-8-16-1; Stackpole 2-0-8-0; I.M. Chappell 2-1-1-0. SECOND INNINGS – Walker 25-6-43-3; Hammond 6-3-12-0; Jenner 15-2-46-0; O'Keeffe 24.1-5-57-4; G.S. Chappell 32-10-65-1; Stackpole 11-4-27-1.

Umpires: D. Sang Hue and R. Gosein.

FIRST TEST MATCH

At Brisbane, November 28, 29, 30, December 2, 1975. Australia won by eight wickets. For the second year running a Test Match at the Gabba began with a controversy over the pitch. The former Lord Mayor of Brisbane, Alderman Clem Jones, was still in charge and after the Queensland match which was played on a badly underprepared wicket, he came in for a great deal of criticism, especially as the Test pitch seemed to be in a similar condition. In the four days before the match two fierce electrical storms broke over Brisbane and each time the covers were inadequate and the pitch was flooded. After a lot of hard work, which included blowing hot air on to the pitch with a machine which was normally used for incubating eggs, it made a remarkable recovery. [...] This was Greg Chappell's first Test Match as captain of Australia and he could hardly have had a better start, for not only did Australia win the match, but also he made a hundred in each innings. [...]

When Lloyd won the toss he gave the West Indies an important advantage which their batsmen threw away in an astonishing first morning's cricket. They all went for their strokes as if playing a forty-over match, and after two hours play and eighteen overs they came into lunch at 125 for six. Gilmour was the most hostile of the bowlers and neither Thomson nor Lillee were as impressive in this match as they had been in the corresponding one against England twelve months earlier. The West Indies were taken past 200 through bold innings by Murray and Holding.

McCosker had stomach trouble and so Redpath opened for Australia with Turner and they made a good start although both had some luck against Roberts and Holding, who were both very fast. Turner was dropped by Rowe at second slip off Roberts when he was 12. Redpath was spectacularly thrown out by Holding at the start of the second day and when he had made one Ian Chappell was dropped by Richards at forward short leg off Roberts. He then began to bat extremely well and with Turner going on to make a solid 81, Australia were assured of a good lead. Later in the day Greg Chappell was seen at his best. He drove beautifully, especially on the on side and reached a hundred in three hours, twenty-five minutes. He and Marsh added 122. The innings was then quickly finished off by Gibbs who bowled splendidly, taking five for 102 in 38 overs.

The West Indies began their second innings badly, losing Greenidge for his second nought of the match, and Fredericks and Holding, the nightwatchman, were soon out on the third morning. Both Rowe and Kallicharran survived chances off Lillee. They then began to bat splendidly although it was surprising that Gilmour was given only eleven overs in the innings, for he badly worried Rowe outside the off stump. He and Kallicharran added 198, a fourth wicket record for the West Indies against Australia. While Rowe's cover driving was the feature of his innings, Kallicharran played many exciting cuts and hooks. While they were together it looked as if the West Indies might set Australia more than 300 in the final innings.

Then, in twenty minutes, carelessness cost them three wickets. After batting four and a half hours Rowe played a wild pull at Jenner and was caught at slip and four balls later Lloyd drove when not to the pitch and was caught at extra cover. Soon afterwards Richards, who seemed badly affected by nerves, ran himself out by half the length of the pitch and when Kallicharran was bowled sweeping at Mallett the score had gone from 248 for three to 275 for seven. Another brave innings by Murray took the West Indies' lead to 218.

Australia soon lost McCosker and then Gibbs began a wonderful spell of bowling on a pitch which was turning a long way if only slowly. Australia were 60 for two when he bowled Turner, but then the Chappell brothers began to bat magnificently, though when Ian was twelve, he drove a full toss from Inshan Ali back to the bowler, who dropped a none-too-difficult catch. While Greg batted superbly in his upright elegant way and went on to reach his second hundred of the match, Ian played probably the most important innings for it was he who coped with Gibbs when he first came on and was bowling brilliantly. Although the match ended in four days it could hardly have been a more eventful and fascinating game of cricket.

WEST INDIES

R.C. Fredericks c Marsh b Gilmour	.46 – c Marsh b Gilmour	.7
C.G. Greenidge lbw b Lillee	.0 – c McCosker b Gilmour	.0
L.G. Rowe run out	.28 – c I.M. Chappell b Jenner	.107
A.I. Kallicharran c Turner b Lillee	.4 – b Mallett	.101
I.V.A. Richards c Gilmour b Lillee	.0 – run out	.12
*C.H. Lloyd c Marsh b Gilmour	.7 – c Redpath b Jenner	.0
†D.L. Murray c Mallett b Gilmour	.66 – c and b Mallett	.55
M.A. Holding c G.S. Chappell b Gilmour	.34 – c Turner b Lillee	.19
Inshan Ali c Redpath b Thomson	.12 – b Lillee	.24
A.M.E. Roberts c I.M. Chappell b Mallett	.3 – lbw b Lillee	.3
L.R. Gibbs not out	.11 – not out	.4
L-b 1, n-b 2	.3 B 4, l-b 15, w 5, n-b 14	.38

1/3 2/63 3/70 4/70 5/81 **214** 1/6 2/12 3/50 4/248 5/248 **370**
6/99 7/171 8/199 9/199 6/269 7/275 8/346 9/348

Bowling: FIRST INNINGS – Lillee 11-0-84-3; Thomson 10-0-69-1; Gilmour 12-1-42-4; Jenner 4-1-15-0; Mallett 0.5-0-1-1. SECOND INNINGS – Lillee 16-3-72-3; Gilmour 11-4-26-2; Thomson 18-3-89-0; Mallett 21.4-6-70-2; Jenner 20-2-75-2.

AUSTRALIA

A. Turner b Roberts	.81 – b Gibbs	.26
I.R. Redpath run out	.39	
I.M. Chappell lbw b Gibbs	.41 – not out	.74
*G.S. Chappell c Greenidge b Roberts	.123 – not out	.109
R.B. McCosker c Kallicharran b Inshan	.1 – c Murray b Roberts	.2
†R.W. Marsh c Murray b Gibbs	.48	
G.J. Gilmour c Lloyd b Gibbs	.13	
T.J. Jenner not out	.6	
D.K. Lillee b Roberts	.1	
J.R. Thomson lbw b Gibbs	.4	
A.A. Mallett c Fredericks b Gibbs	.0	
L-b 5, n-b 4	.9 B 5, l-b 2, n-b 1	.8

1/99 2/142 3/178 4/195 5/317 **366** 1/7 2/60 (2 wkts) **219**
6/350 7/354 8/361 9/366

Bowling: FIRST INNINGS – Roberts 25-2-85-3; Holding 20-4-81-0; Gibbs 38-7-102-5; Inshan Ali 17-1-67-1; Lloyd 6-1-22-0. SECOND INNINGS – Roberts 14-2-47-1; Holding 10-0-46-0; Gibbs 20-8-48-1; Inshan Ali 10-0-57-0; Fredericks 2-0-12-0; Kallicharran 0.2-0-1-0.

Umpires: T.F. Brooks and R.C. Bailhache.

SECOND TEST MATCH

At Perth, December 12, 13, 14, 16, 1975. West Indies won by an innings and 87 runs. This was one of the most remarkable Test Matches which can ever have been played and was a complete reversal of the First in Brisbane. The West Indies batsmen and their fast bowlers found that the fastest pitch they came across in Australia exactly suited their methods and just as everything had failed in the First Test now everything came off. The two strongest memories of the match will always be Fredericks's 169 and Roberts's fast bowling, but Ian Chappell's 156 and Lloyd's 149 were scarcely less memorable. This match came as a sharp reminder that when everything is going right for them there is no side on earth which could stop the West Indies. […] It looked a good toss for Australia to win, but Roberts soon sent back both openers. Julien and Boyce benefited from the pace and bounce, and Australia lost half their wickets for 189.

Meanwhile, Ian Chappell, who had come in during the first over, was batting superbly. He had just a little luck early on but was soon timing the ball beautifully as he hooked, pulled and drove. He was well supported by Gilmour later on and their stand of 88 came in only sixty-five minutes. Chappell's hundred took four and a half hours and it was one of the best innings that even he can have played, for he held the Australian batting together on his own. The next morning Holding finished off the innings in his second over with the second new ball when with the first, second and seventh balls of the over he bowled Chappell, Thomson and Mallett.

The West Indies had ninety minutes batting before lunch and, remarkably, Julien came out to open with Fredericks. Fredericks began by hooking Lillee's second ball for 6 off the edge although from then on he never made any sort of mistake. Runs came at a bewildering pace as he hooked and drove and cut at Thomson and Lillee. It was thrilling batting and the Australians could only stand and watch.

Julien had a lot of luck as he flashed and missed, but when in the tenth over he fended Gilmour into the gully, 91 runs had already been scored. At lunch after only 14 overs the West Indies were an incredible 130 for one. Fredericks went on and on through the afternoon as one astonishing stroke was followed by the next. His hundred came in one hour, fifty-six minutes off 71 balls with one 6 and eighteen 4's and when soon after tea he drove at Lillee and was caught at slip he had made 169 out of 258. Soon after that Kallicharran, who was batting well, hooked at Lillee and the ball flew off the edge and broke his nose. The Australian fielding had grown careless and before the end of the day Lloyd had been dropped twice and Murray once.

The next day these two took their stand to 164 in two and a half hours. Murray's 50 had been exciting, and Lloyd produced his own special display of pyrotechnics which if not quite matching Fredericks' was very impressive. His 149 took three hours, thirty-eight minutes and he hit one 6 and twenty-two 4's. Later, Kallicharran, who continued his innings, and Boyce played some good strokes.

The West Indies had a lead of 256 and when in a wonderful spell of controlled fast bowling Roberts took four wickets before the close, the match was as good as over. Greg Chappell and Marsh continued their resistance for a while the next morning before Roberts dismissed them both and the last six wickets put on only another 65 runs. Roberts finished with seven for 54. It had been a match which had expressed vividly the full joy and exuberance of West Indies cricket and when compared to what went on before and afterwards its inconsistency as well.

AUSTRALIA

R.B. McCosker lbw b Roberts	.0	– c Rowe b Roberts	.13
A. Turner c Gibbs b Roberts	.23	– c Murray b Roberts	.0
I.M Chappell b Holding	.156	– c sub b Roberts	.20
*G.S. Chappell c Murray b Julien	.13	– c Rowe b Roberts	.43
I.R. Redpath c Murray b Julien	.33	– lbw b Roberts	.0
†R.W. Marsh c Julien b Boyce	.23	– c Murray b Roberts	.39
G.J. Gilmour c Julien b Gibbs	.45	– c Fredericks b Roberts	.3
M.H.N. Walker c Richards b Holding	.1	– c sub b Julien	.3
D.K. Lillee not out	.12	– c Lloyd b Julien	.4
J.R. Thomson b Holding	.0	– b Julien	.9
A.A. Mallett b Holding	.0	– not out	.18
B 12, l-b 5, n-b 6	.23	B 13, l-b 2, n-b 2	.17

1/0 2/37 3/70 4/149 5/189 6/277   **329**   1/0 2/25 3/45 4/45 5/124 6/128   **169**
7/285 8/329 9/329   7/132 8/142 9/146

Bowling: FIRST INNINGS – Roberts 13-1-65-2; Boyce 12-2-53-1; Holding 18.7-1-88-4; Julien 12-0-51-2; Gibbs 14-4-49-1. SECOND INNINGS – Roberts 14-3-54-7; Holding 10.6-1-53-0; Julien 10.1-1-32-3; Boyce 2-0-8-0; Gibbs 3-1-3-0; Fredericks 1-0-2-0.

WEST INDIES

R.C. Fredericks c G.S. Chappell		†D.L. Murray c Marsh b Lillee	.63
b Lillee	.169	M.A. Holding c Marsh b Thomson	.0
B.D. Julien c Mallett b Gilmour	.25	K.D. Boyce not out	.49
A.I. Kallicharran c I.M. Chappell		A.M.E. Roberts b Walker	.0
b Walker	.57	L.R. Gibbs run out	.13
I.V.A. Richards c Gilmour b Thomson	.12	B 2, l-b 16, n-b 11	.29
*C.H. Lloyd b Gilmour	.149		**585**

Bowling: Lillee 20-0-123-2; Thomson 17-0-128-3; Gilmour 14-0-103-2; Mallett 26-4-103-0; I.M. Chappell 1.4-1-0-0.

Umpires: R.R. Ledwidge and M.G. O'Connell.

FIRST TEST MATCH

At Melbourne, December 26, 27, 28, 29, 30, 1981. Australia won by 58 runs. […] In the fifth over of the match, after Australia had chosen to bat, Holding dismissed Laird and Chappell with successive balls, this being the Australian captain's fourth successive 0 for Australia since the last Test against Pakistan. Soon Australia were 26 for four, and it needed a superb innings by Hughes to effect some sort of recovery.

Holding, in particular, was extremely fast. Yet Hughes was determined not just to concentrate on passive defence. When the ninth wicket fell at 155 Hughes had reached 71, but Alderman kept his head down and his bat straight while his partner played some marvellous strokes, reaching his hundred with a thrilling square cut for 4 off Garner. Hughes batted for 262 minutes and hit eleven 4s.

West Indies were left with 35 minutes' batting on the first evening, which produced most dramatic cricket as Alderman and Lillee took four wickets for 10 runs. Alderman had Bacchus, opening in place of Greenidge whose knee injury had not mended, caught at fourth slip; Lillee, who began the match needing five wickets to beat Lance Gibbs's record of 309 Test wickets, then had Haynes splendidly caught by Border above his head at second slip. Croft, the night-watchman, was leg before, shuffling across his stumps in the same over. And with the last ball of the day Lillee bowled Richards off the inside edge as he tried to drive.

Lillee thus began the second day needing two more wickets for his record. Dujon, having batted excitingly well, was the first, being caught at deep backward square leg off a hook that would have been a big 6 on many grounds. Lillee got his record when Gomes was caught by Chappell at first slip. West Indies were eventually all out for 201, which gave them a first-innings lead of 3. But by then the pitch had dried after the rain storms which had punctuated the second day, and for the next four hours Australia seemed to be building a sizeable score as Wood, Laird and Border all played useful innings. Chappell failed again, this time being caught behind glancing at Garner. Four wickets fell in the last hour of the third day as the pitch began to behave awkwardly, and Holding quickly finished off the innings the next morning. His eleven for 107 in the match was a fine reward for some wonderful bowling and the best ever by a West Indian against Australia. David Murray, behind the stumps, took his tally of catches for the match to nine, a figure exceeded in Test cricket only by Bob Taylor's ten at Bombay in 1979–80.

West Indies final target was 220, but after Alderman had had Bacchus leg before and bowled Richards in the second over of the innings they never looked likely to win. The only time Australia had any anxiety was when Dujon played a second fine innings, this time concentrating for the most part on defence, though never wasting the chance to play a stroke that did not involve a risk.

During the match the Melbourne Cricket Club announced that the committee had decided to relay the square over the next three years, beginning as soon as the current Australian season was over. This was also the last match before the old MCG scoreboard was taken down, to be replaced by an electronic one.

Attendance: 136,464.

AUSTRALIA

B.M. Laird c Murray b Holding	4	– (2) lbw b Croft	64
G.M. Wood c Murray b Roberts	3	– (1) c Murray b Garner	46
*G.S. Chappell c Murray b Holding	0	– c Murray b Garner	6
A.R. Border c Murray b Holding	4	– b Holding	66
K.J. Hughes not out	100	– b Holding	8
D.M. Wellham c sub (Logie) b Croft	17	– lbw b Holding	2
†R.W. Marsh c Richards b Garner	21	– c Murray b Holding	2
B. Yardley b Garner	21	– b Garner	13
D.K. Lillee c Gomes b Holding	1	– c Murray b Holding	0
G.F. Lawson b Holding	2	– not out	0
T.M. Alderman c Murray b Croft	10	– b Holding	1
B 1, l-b 5, n-b 8	15	B 5, l-b 4, w 1, n-b 4	14

1/4 2/4 3/8 4/26 5/59 6/115   **198**   1/82 2/106 3/139 4/184 5/190 6/199   **222**
7/149 8/153 9/155   7/215 8/218 9/220

Bowling: FIRST INNINGS – Holding 17-3-45-5; Roberts 15-6-40-1; Garner 20-6-59-2; Croft 16.1-3-39-2. SECOND INNINGS – Holding 21.3-5-62-6; Roberts 18-4-31-0; Garner 18-5-37-3; Croft 20-2-61-1; Richards 5-0-17-0.

WEST INDIES

D.L. Haynes c Border b Lillee	1 –	c Lillee b Yardley	28
S.F.A. Bacchus c Wood b Alderman	1 –	lbw b Alderman	0
C.E.H. Croft lbw b Lillee	0 –	(11) not out	0
I.V.A. Richards b Lillee	2 –	(3) b Alderman	0
*C.H. Lloyd c Alderman b Yardley	29 –	(4) c Border b Lawson	19
H.A. Gomes c Chappell b Lillee	55 –	(5) b Yardley	24
P.J. Dujon c Hughes b Lillee	41 –	(6) c Marsh b Yardley	43
†D.A. Murray out	32 –	(7) c Marsh b Yardley	10
A.M.E. Roberts c Marsh b Lillee	18 –	(8) lbw b Lillee	10
M.A. Holding c and b Alderman	2 –	(9) lbw b Lillee	7
J. Garner c Laird b Lillee	7 –	(10) lbw b Lillee	0
B 1, l-b 3, n-b 9	13	B 1, l-b 10, n-b 9	20

1/3 2/5 3/6 4/10 5/62   **201**   1/4 2/4 3/38 4/80 5/88   **161**
6/134 7/147 8/174 9/183   6/116 7/150 8/154 9/154

Bowling: FIRST INNINGS – Lillee 26.3-3-83-7; Alderman 18-3-54-2; Lawson 9-2-28-0; Chappell 2-2-0-0; Yardley 7-2-23-1. SECOND INNINGS – Lillee 27.1-8-44-3; Alderman 9-3-23-2; Lawson 17-3-36-1; Yardley 21-7-38-4.

Umpires: A.R. Crafter and R.C. Bailhache.

SECOND TEST MATCH

At Port-of-Spain, March 16, 17, 18, 20, 21, 1984. Drawn. Two epic innings by Border stood between Australia and defeat. His undefeated 98 in the first innings lasted 5 hours 49 minutes, his undefeated century in the second another four and threequarter hours. He offered not a single chance although batting, each time, under great pressure.

Border received crucial assistance in Australia's cause from other sources. The weather accounted for the equivalent of almost a full day, and finally the tailenders, Hogg and then Alderman, batted with him for the last 160 minutes to frustrate their opponents. In addition, Garner, West Indies' most penetrative bowler, was off the field for half the last day with stomach cramps.

Richards, leading the team in place of the injured Lloyd (pulled hamstring), sent Australia in on a well-grassed pitch; and by the time rain halted play at lunch on the first day, Garner had taken four wickets and Australia were 55 for four. Garner added a fifth early next day, but Jones, in his first Test, helped Border prevent a complete rout with a century stand. Border was denied his century when he was held scoreless on 98 for twelve deliveries, ten from Garner, while the last two wickets fell.

With the early moisture out of the pitch, West Indies took a sizeable first-innings lead through two partnerships of brilliant strokeplay. Richards and Logie added 100, then Dujon, from 187 balls, scored 130 runs by exquisite batting which featured two 6s (hooks off successive balls from Hogg) and fifteen 4s. Logie, a last-minute replacement for Lloyd, was Dujon's partner while 158 were added, but he fell 3 short of his century after an unsteady period in the 90s.

Richards's declaration left his bowlers just over an hour of the fourth day and all of the fifth to win the match. Australia entered the last day 55 for three and were all but beaten when their eighth wicket fell 55 minutes before tea, still 17 in arrears. By now, however, Garner was off the field, Richards delayed taking the new ball for 10.2 overs, and Border and his last two partners clung on to deny West Indies a victory which had appeared theirs. Hogg stayed for 55 minutes, and Alderman, whose previous highest Test score was 12, had been batting for 95 minutes when Border reached his century by hitting the last ball of the match to the boundary.

AUSTRALIA

K.C. Wessels c Gomes b Garner	.4	– lbw b Garner ..4
†W.B. Phillips c Dujon b Garner	.4	– run out ..0
G.M. Ritchie b Garner	.1	– b Small ..26
*K.J. Hughes c Dujon b Garner	.24	– lbw b Marshall ..33
A.R. Border not out	.98	– (6) not out ..100
D.W. Hookes b Garner	.23	– (7) c Richardson b Gomes ..21
D.M. Jones c and b Richards	.48	– (8) b Richards ..5
G.F. Lawson c and b Daniel	.14	– (9) b Marshall ..20
T.G. Hogan c Greenidge b Daniel	.0	– (5) c Logie b Daniel ..38
R.M. Hogg c Marshall b Daniel	.11	– c Garner b Richards ..9
T.M. Alderman c Richardson b Garner	.1	– not out ..21
B 6, l-b 4, n-b 17	.27	B 6, l-b 1, w 1, n-b 14 ..22

1/4 2/7 3/16 4/50 5/85 **255** 1/1 2/35 3/41 4/114   (9 wkts) **299**
6/185 7/233 8/233 9/253   5/115 6/153 7/162 8/196 9/238

Bowling: FIRST INNINGS – Garner 28.1-9-60-6; Marshall 19-4-73-0; Daniel 15-3-40-3; Small 10-3-24-0; Gomes 10-0-33-0; Richards 10-4-15-1. SECOND INNINGS – Marshall 22-3-73-2; Garner 15-4-35-1; Small 14-2-51-1; Daniel 9-3-11-1; Richards 25-5-65-2; Gomes 27-5-53-1; Logie 0.1-0-4-0.

WEST INDIES

C.G. Greenidge c Phillips b Hogg ..24
D.L. Haynes run out ..53
R.B. Richardson c Wessels b Alderman ..23
*I.V.A. Richards c Phillips b Alderman ..76
H.A. Gomes b Lawson ..3
A.L. Logie lbw b Hogan ..97
†P.J. Dujon b Hogan ..130
M.A. Small did not bat.

M.D. Marshall lbw b Lawson ..10
J. Garner not out ..24
W.W. Daniel not out ..6
B 7, l-b 12, w 2, n-b 1 ..22

1/35 2/93 3/124 4/129   (8 wkts, dec.) **468**
5/229 6/387 7/430 8/462

Bowling: Lawson 32-3-132-2; Hogg 31-2-103-1; Alderman 35-9-91-2; Hogan 28-3-123-2. *Wides and no-balls debited to bowlers' analyses.*

Umpires: D.M. Archer and C. Cumberbatch.

FOURTH TEST MATCH

At Sydney, January 26, 27, 28, 29, 30, 1989. Australia won by seven wickets. Toss: West Indies. As had happened in 1984–85, on West Indies' last full visit to Australia, a bare and slow Sydney pitch, on which the ball turned from the start, gave Australia the chance to attack West Indies at their weakest point and inflict on them a rare defeat, their first for eleven Tests. West Indies departed from their usual formula by bringing in a spinner, Harper, in place of a fourth fast bowler, Patterson, and against every current trend the match produced 279.3 overs of spin, the most in a Test match in Australia for 57 years. To take advantage of the conditions, Australia chose Hohns, the Queensland leg-spinner. Mark Taylor, an opening batsman from New South Wales, replaced Wood. For both Hohns and Taylor it was their first cap.

When Richards won the toss and West Indies reached 144 before losing their second wicket, the match looked to be slipping away from Australia at an early stage. But Border then embarked on an all-round performance seldom surpassed by a captain in Test cricket. Having bowled only two overs in the first three Tests, he now destroyed West Indies' first innings, with some co-operation from the batsmen, by taking seven for 46 with the orthodox left-arm slows he had never thought worth taking seriously. Richards, Hooper, Harper and Marshall were all out to long-hops; Richards, given out caught at short leg, got a dubious decision. West Indies were all out just before the close of play on the first day, and on the second Boon's first century against them allowed Australia to consolidate their advantage.

As Australia built a crucial lead on the third day, chiefly through a fourth-wicket partnership of 170 between Boon and Border, it was slow going. Border's 50 took 262 balls; in terms of time (five hours ten minutes) it was the fifth slowest in Test cricket. Richards, unlike his opposite number, did not have a good match, partly for the way he gave Marshall only seven overs of the first 94 in Australia's first innings and Walsh only five of the first 123, although his own off-breaks, like those of Harper and Hooper, were bowled too negatively to be effective. When, belatedly, Marshall did get his chance, his final analysis was remarkable enough to compound Richards's misjudgement and make him think that even on this pitch he would have done better to have had a fourth fast bowler in his side.

West Indies' second innings followed much the same course as their first. Although they had wiped out Australia's lead of 177 with seven wickets in hand, they finished by leaving Australia with only 80 to win. Again carelessness had much to do with their downfall, especially in the case of Hooper and Richards, both caught at deep mid-off trying to loft Hohns for six. The one outstanding exception was Haynes, whose 143 was considered by both captains to be among the finest innings they had seen. Haynes batted almost faultlessly for five and a quarter hours, assiduously smothering the spin and making good use of the loose ball. Hohns justified his selection with three valuable wickets, and Border took his tally for the match to eleven for 96. Border had never taken more than four wickets in a first-class match before; now, only Hughes (thirteen for 217 at Perth the month before) had ever taken more than Border in a Test match for Australia against West Indies. Despite a brief hiccup at the start of their second innings, when they lost Taylor and Boon cheaply, Australia won a quarter of an hour after lunch on the last day. Fittingly enough, Border hit the winning runs.

Man of the Match: A.R. Border. *Attendance*: 83,729

Close of play: First day, West Indies 224; Second day, Australia 200-3 (D.C. Boon 110*, A.R. Border 18*); Third day, Australia 401; Fourth day, West Indies 254-9 (C.E.L. Ambrose 4*, C.A. Walsh 6*).

WEST INDIES

C.G. Greenidge c Waugh b P.L. Taylor	56	– c and b Hughes 4
D.L. Haynes c Boon b Hohns	.75	– c M.A. Taylor b Border 143
R.B. Richardson c P.L. Taylor b Border	28	– c Hughes b P.L. Taylor 22
C.L. Hooper c Marsh b Border	.0	– c Jones b Hohns 35
*I.V.A. Richards c Boon b Border	.11	– c Jones b Hohns 4
A.L. Logie b Border	.0	– c P.L. Taylor b Hohns 6
†P.J.L. Dujon c Hughes b Border	.18	– run out 9
R.A. Harper c P.L. Taylor b Border	.17	– lbw b Border 12
M.D. Marshall c Marsh b Border	.9	– c P.L. Taylor b Border 3
C.E.L. Ambrose c Jones b P.L. Taylor	.1	– c Boon b Border 5
C.A. Walsh not out	.4	– not out 7
L-b 1, w 1, n-b 3	.5	B 1, w 1, n-b 4 6

1/90 2/144 3/156 4/174 5/174   **224**   1/17 2/56 3/167 4/188 5/198   **256**
6/174 7/199 8/213 9/220   6/225 7/232 8/244 9/247

Bowling: FIRST INNINGS – Alderman 10-2-17-0; Hughes 10-3-28-0; P.L. Taylor 25.2-8-65-2; Hohns 24-8-49-1; Border 26-10-46-7; Waugh 4-0-18-0. SECOND INNINGS – Hughes 18-6-29-1; Alderman 2-0-6-0; Waugh 3-0-10-0; P.L. Taylor 29-4-91-1; Hohns 34-11-69-3; Border 18.4-3-50-4.

AUSTRALIA

G.R. Marsh c Dujon b Marshall	.2	– (2) b Richards 23
M.A. Taylor b Ambrose	.25	– (1) c Haynes b Ambrose 3
D.C. Boon c Dujon b Walsh	.149	– c Harper b Marshall 10
D.M. Jones b Richards	.29	– not out 24
*A.R. Border b Marshall	.75	– not out 16
S.R. Waugh not out	.55	
†I.A. Healy c Logie b Marshall	.11	
P.L. Taylor lbw b Marshall	.0	
T.V. Hohns b Marshall	.0	
M.G. Hughes c Dujon b Walsh	.12	
T.M. Alderman run out	.9	
B 6, l-b 14, n-b 14	.34	B 3, l-b 1, n-b 2 6

1/14 2/43 3/114 4/284 5/335   **401**   1/3 2/16 3/55   (3 wkts) **82**
6/355 7/357 8/357 9/388

Bowling: FIRST INNINGS – Marshall 31-16-29-5; Ambrose 33-5-78-1; Harper 37-9-86-0; Walsh 22.5-5-48-2; Hooper 37-10-72-0; Richards 31-1-68-1. SECOND INNINGS – Marshall 8-2-17-1; Ambrose 7-1-16-1; Hooper 10.3-2-24-0; Walsh 3-0-9-0; Richards 7-2-12-1.

Umpires: L.J. King and T.A. Prue.

FOURTH TEST MATCH

At Adelaide, January 23, 24, 25, 26, 1993. West Indies won by one run. Toss: West Indies. Test debut: J.L. Langer. Adelaide 1992–93 took its place as one of the greatest of all Test matches when Craig McDermott failed to get out of the way of a lifter from Courtney Walsh and gloved a catch to give West Indies victory by one run, the narrowest victory anyone has achieved in 116 years of Test cricket.

But it had been a game of fluctuating fortunes throughout. When Australia, needing 186 to win, lost their eighth second-innings wicket for 102, it appeared to have made its decisive shift. But then the 22-year-old debutant Justin Langer, who came in only when Martyn was injured at pre-match practice, added 42 with the No. 10 Tim May, who was playing his first Test in four years. After that May and the last man McDermott put on another 40 to get Australia within two of their target.

The unfolding drama lifted the TV cricket ratings in Australia to a new record. And, with the Adelaide Oval within walking distance of the city centre, new spectators rushed to the ground. Finally, a short ball from Walsh, pitched on off stump, lifted to brush McDermott's hand on its way through to Murray. Umpire Hair upheld the appeal. The West Indians on the field celebrated emotionally. The crowd who had been singing 'Waltzing Matilda' as Australia inched towards their goal were stunned into silence.

The Australian captain Border did not dispute Hair's decision, though he said that, like the result, it was a very close one. 'What can you say – one run? I was very confident of getting 186 at the start of the day.' His opposite number Richardson said: 'I knew Walshy would get a wicket with that very ball. I never lost hope.' Both leaders paid tribute to the man who made the result possible: Ambrose consolidated his reputation as the world's leading fast bowler with ten wickets in the match and a burst of three wickets in 19 balls after lunch to dismiss Steve Waugh, Border and Hughes. 'I have never seen a bowler like him,' said Richardson.

The pitch had been kept covered against unusually wet weather and was much fresher than is normal in Adelaide. But it was not only fast bowlers who prospered. The off-spinner May delighted his home crowd on his return to Test cricket by taking five wickets for five runs in 32 balls as the West Indians' second innings folded. West Indies' first-innings 252 was the highest total of the match, and that was disappointing after Haynes and Simmons had provided a comfortable start of 84. Hughes was rewarded for his persistence with five wickets but Australia had a foretaste of difficulties ahead as they lost Taylor in the second over and a stunning blow from Bishop split Langer's helmet shortly before the close.

Boon, hit on the forearm, was forced to retire hurt early on the rain-shortened second day. Returning when five wickets were down, he was left unbeaten as Australia conceded a lead of 39 on a remarkable third day which saw 17 wickets fall for 259 runs. An incisive opening spell by McDermott reduced West Indies to 65 for four and, after Richardson and Hooper added 59, the last six wickets collapsed for 22 in nine overs of spin, largely due to careless batting. May did most of the damage and took five of the wickets but the most crucial one belonged to Warne: Richardson for 72, having passed 5,000 Test runs.

On the fourth day, Australia started their quest for the victory that would have given them the Frank Worrell Trophy. They lost both openers cheaply and when four wickets fell for ten runs in the first half hour after lunch – three of them to Ambrose – it appeared certain that West Indies would square the series. Langer's determined resistance and his partnerships with Warne and May lifted Australian hopes, before May, batting with an injured hand, and McDermott brought them so close.

Man of the Match: C.E.L. Ambrose. *Attendance*: 57,573.

Close of play: First day, Australia 2-1 (D.C. Boon 1*, J.L. Langer 0*); Second day, Australia 100-3 (S.R. Waugh 35*, A.R. Border 18*); Third day, West Indies 146.

WEST INDIES

D.L. Haynes st Healy b May	.45 –	c Healy b McDermott .... .11
P.V. Simmons c Hughes b S.R. Waugh	.46 –	b McDermott .... .10
*R.B. Richardson lbw b Hughes	.2 –	c Healy b Warne .... .72
B.C. Lara c Healy b McDermott	.52 –	c S.R. Waugh b Hughes 7
K.L.T. Arthurton c S.R. Waugh b May	.0 –	c Healy b McDermott 0
C.L. Hooper c Healy b Hughes	.2 –	c Hughes b May .... .25
†J.R. Murray not out	.49 –	c M.E. Waugh b May 0
I.R. Bishop c M.E. Waugh b Hughes	.13 –	c M.E. Waugh b May 6
C.E.L. Ambrose c Healy b Hughes	.0 –	st Healy b May 1
K.C.G. Benjamin b M.E. Waugh	.15 –	c Warne b May 0
C.A. Walsh lbw b Hughes	.5 –	not out 0
L-b 11, n-b 12	.23	L-b 2, n-b 12 .... .14

1/84 (2) 2/99 (3) 3/129 (1) 4/130 (5)   **252**   1/14 (1) 2/49 (2) 3/63 (4) 4/65 (5)   **146**
5/134 (6) 6/189 (4) 7/206 (8)   5/124 (6) 6/137 (7) 7/145 (3)
8/206 (9) 9/247 (10) 10/252 (11)   8/146 (9) 9/146 (10) 10/146 (8)

Bowling: FIRST INNINGS – McDermott 16-1-85-1; Hughes 21.3-3-64-5; S.R. Waugh 13-4-37-1; May 14-1-41-2; Warne 2-0-11-0; M.E. Waugh 1-0-3-1. SECOND INNINGS – McDermott 11-0-66-3; Hughes 13-1-43-1; S.R. Waugh 5-1-8-0; May 6.5-3-9-5; Warne 6-2-18-1.

AUSTRALIA

M.A. Taylor c Hooper b Bishop	.1 –	(2) c Murray b Benjamin 7
D.C. Boon not out	.39 –	(1) lbw b Ambrose 0
J.L. Langer c Murray b Benjamin	.20 –	c Murray b Bishop .... .54
M.E. Waugh c Simmons b Ambrose	.0 –	c Hooper b Walsh .... .26
S.R. Waugh c Murray b Ambrose	.42 –	c Arthurton b Ambrose 4
*A.R. Border c Hooper b Ambrose	.19 –	c Haynes b Ambrose 1
†I.A. Healy c Hooper b Ambrose	.0 –	b Walsh 0
M.G. Hughes c Murray b Hooper	.43 –	lbw b Ambrose 1
S.K. Warne lbw b Hooper	.0 –	lbw b Bishop 9
T.B.A. May c Murray b Ambrose	.6 –	not out .... .42
C.J. McDermott b Ambrose	.14 –	c Murray b Walsh .... .18
B 7, l-b 3, n-b 19	.29	B 1, l-b 8, n-b 13 .... .22

1/1 (1) 2/16 (4) 3/46 (3) 4/108 (6)   **213**   1/5 (1) 2/16 (2) 3/54 (4) 4/64 (5)   **184**
5/108 (7) 6/112 (5) 7/181 (8)   5/72 (6) 6/73 (7) 7/74 (8)
8/181 (9) 9/197 (10) 10/213 (11)   8/102 (9) 9/144 (3) 10/184 (11)

In the first innings D.C. Boon, when 2, retired hurt at 16-1 and resumed at 108-5.

Bowling: FIRST INNINGS – Ambrose 28.2-6-74-6; Bishop 18-3-48-1; Benjamin 6-0-22-1; Walsh 10-3-34-0; Hooper 13-4-25-2. SECOND INNINGS – Ambrose 26-5-46-4; Bishop 17-3-41-2; Benjamin 12-2-32-1; Walsh 19-4-44-3; Hooper 5-1-12-0.

Umpires: D.B. Hair and L.J. King. Referee: D.B. Carr (England).

FOURTH TEST MATCH

At Kingston, April 29, 30, May 1, 3, 1995. Australia won by an innings and 53 runs. Toss: West Indies. Test debut: C.O. Browne. The final Test was settled by a partnership to be cherished in Australian history, the pinnacle of the cricketing lives of Steve and Mark Waugh. In a series featuring only one other century, Steve scored 200 and Mark 126. They added 231 in 57 overs to bankroll the innings victory that regained the Frank Worrell Trophy, surrendered by Simpson's team in 1977–78, and ended West Indies' 15 years without a series defeat.

Batting was meant to be easy on a shiny pitch of rolled mud, as polished as a danceroom floor. When Richardson won his fourth consecutive toss it looked like a decisive advantage: West Indies' first 100 whistled by in 20 overs, with Lara running up a scorching fifty. Quite unexpectedly, he fell for 65, caught behind. It was the first time Warne had dismissed him in eight Tests. Richardson remained, patiently crafting the first hundred of the series before he was eighth out at 251. A moderate total of 265 was West Indies' best in the four Tests and next day Australia were teetering at 73 for three when Steve Waugh joined Mark. From then on, the home side spiralled towards oblivion.

The Waughs hit their stride almost immediately, smacking 67 from 11 overs after lunch. One by one they repelled the pace brigade; the buoyant West Indians were suddenly under siege. Winston Benjamin sat weeping during the drinks break and had to be cajoled to continue; Ambrose bowled only 11 overs in the day, amid whispers of team disunity, and the underachieving Kenny Benjamin was hooted on arrival at the bowling crease. Sabina Park was stunned and some of the Waughs' best boundaries went unapplauded. They applauded each other's centuries (their eighth Test hundreds in both cases) reached by Mark in 146 balls and Steve in 183 – and shook hands, but no more. Mark had left behind his gambler's hat to play a low-risk game. His bravest stroke was a contemptuous laid-back dab off Walsh over the slips for four. He pulled and drove with great rhythm. As usual, Steve hit almost everything along the ground, displaying some attractive back-foot cover drives. He gave just one chance, on 42, when he was grassed by debutant wicket-keeper Courtney Browne (a late replacement for Murray, who was ill). Mark fell on the second evening but Steve was 110 at stumps. He retired to his room to get some sleep, after being woken the previous night by a thief. Next day, supported by Blewett and the tail, he advanced to a maiden double-hundred in Tests. He was last out after batting for close on ten hours and 425 balls, more than 150 short-pitched, and had 17 fours, one six and six aching bruises at the end of his greatest innings.

West Indies faced 14 overs that night; their doom was all but certain when Reiffel dismissed three. Their last chance was the weather, but rain restricted itself to the rest day. Only night-watchman Winston Benjamin and Browne passed 20 and Warne took the last four wickets – his best return of the tour – to complete the West Indians' shattering defeat.

Man of the Match: S.R. Waugh. *Man of the Series*: S.R. Waugh.

Close of play: First day, West Indies 265; Second day, Australia 321-4 (S.R. Waugh 110*, G.S. Blewett 6*); Third day, West Indies 63-3 (J.C. Adams 13*, W.K.M. Benjamin 1*).

WEST INDIES

S.C. Williams c Blewett b Reiffel . . . . .0 –	b Reiffel 20
*R.B. Richardson lbw b Reiffel . . . . .100 –	c and b Reiffel .14
B.C. Lara c Healy b Warne . . . . .65 –	lbw b Reiffel 0
J.C. Adams c Slater b Julian . . . . .20 –	c S.R. Waugh b McGrath 18
C.L. Hooper c M.E. Waugh b Julian . . . . .23 –	(6) run out 13
K.L.T. Arthurton c Healy b McGrath . . . . . .16 –	(7) lbw b Warne 14
†C.O. Browne c Boon b Warne . . . . .1 –	(8) not out 31
W.K.M. Benjamin lbw b S.R. Waugh . . . . .7 –	(5) lbw b Reiffel 51
C.E.L. Ambrose not out . . . . .6 –	st Healy b Warne 5
C.A. Walsh c Boon b S.R. Waugh . . . . .2 –	c Blewett b Warne 14
K.C.G. Benjamin c Healy b Reiffel . . . . .5 –	c Taylor b Warne 6
B 1, l-b 9, w 1, n-b 9 20	B 13, l-b 8, n-b 6 27

1/0 (1) 2/103 (3) 3/131 (4) 4/188 (5)   **265**   1/37 (2) 2/37 (3) 3/46 (1) 4/98 (4)   **213**
5/220 (6) 6/243 (7) 7/250 (8)   5/134 (5) 6/140 (6) 7/166 (7)
8/251 (2) 9/254 (10) 10/265 (11)   8/172 (9) 9/204 (10) 10/213 (11)

Bowling: FIRST INNINGS – Reiffel 13.4-2-48-3; Julian 12-3-31-2; McGrath 20-4-79-1; Warne 25-6-72-2; S.R. Waugh 11-5-14-2; M.E. Waugh 4-1-11-0. SECOND INNINGS – Reiffel 18-5-47-4; Julian 10-2-37-0; Warne 23.4-8-70-4; M.E. Waugh 1-0-1-0; McGrath 13-2-28-1; S.R. Waugh 4-0-9-0.

AUSTRALIA

*M.A. Taylor c Adams b Walsh 8	B.P. Julian c Adams b Walsh 8
M.J. Slater c Lara b Walsh 27	P.R. Reiffel b K.C.G. Benjamin 23
D.C. Boon c Browne b Ambrose 17	S.K. Warne c Lara
M.E. Waugh c Adams b Hooper 126	b K.C.G. Benjamin 0
S.R. Waugh c Lara	G.D. McGrath not out 3
b K.C.G. Benjamin 200	B 11, l-b 6, w 1, n-b 26 44
G.S. Blewett c W.K.M. Benjamin	
b Arthurton .69	1/17 (1) 2/50 (3) 3/73 (2) 4/304 (4) **531**
†I.A. Healy c Lara	5/417 (6) 6/423 (7) 7/449 (8)
b W.K.M. Benjamin 6	8/523 (9) 9/523 (10) 10/531 (5)

Bowling: Ambrose 21-4-76-1; Walsh 33-6-103-3; K.C.G. Benjamin 23.5-0-106-3; W.K.M. Benjamin 24-3-80-1; Hooper 43-9-94-1; Adams 11-0-38-0; Arthurton 5-1-17-1.

Umpires: K.E. Liebenberg (South Africa) and S.A. Bucknor.
Referee: Majid Khan (Pakistan).

SECOND TEST MATCH

At Kingston, March 13, 14, 15, 16, 1999. West Indies won by ten wickets. Toss: Australia. Test debuts: N.O. Perry, L.A. Roberts.

There can have been few more dramatic turnarounds in the history of Test cricket than this. Only Lara could have changed the course of the series after Trinidad, and he did so by defying odds and circumstances that would have crushed most men. On one fantastic, sunny, windy Sunday, Lara seduced the people of a bankrupt nation, resurrected his career as a batsman of rare gifts and reignited cricket throughout the

Caribbean. He did it with an unforgettable double-century, which enabled West Indies to reach an imposing 431 and a lead of 175. It was, by universal consent, one of the great Test innings: Tony Cozier, the distinguished Barbadian commentator, thought it was the most significant ever by a West Indian.

But for the steely determination of Steve Waugh on the opening day, Lara would have put the match out of the reach of the Australians much earlier. The most surprising aspect of Waugh's first hundred as Australian Test captain was that it took so long – two matches. Yet, while there was an inevitability about his run-gathering, the same could not be said for those around him. Only his brother Mark mustered the same spirited resistance. They added 112 for the fourth wicket, reviving memories of their epic stand of 231 on the same ground four years earlier. After Mark departed, Steve was compelled to manipulate the strike; he was the last out, for an even 100, against an attack again skilfully piloted by Walsh, on his way to another seven-wicket match return. But another West Indian disaster threatened when they closed on 37 for four.

Fourteen wickets had fallen on the first day and the same number would fall on the third. But on the second, there was not a solitary success for the Australians, despite the magnificent bowling of McGrath. Given the brittleness of the West Indian batting, this was a remarkable achievement, and Lara made special commendation of Adams for his selfless and highly intelligent support. Together, they put on 322, a West Indian record for the fifth wicket, but Adams replaced Collins, who retired hurt at 56 for four so, in all, 344 were added without loss. The previous record belonged to Garry Sobers and Seymour Nurse, with 265 against England at Headingley in 1966.

Lara was circumspect early on, but stepped up a gear to strike MacGill for two sixes in an over, and Blewett for four successive fours. He drove Warne for a third six, and hit 28 fours in all, batting for 469 minutes and 344 balls. It was his 11th century in Tests – but the first since June 1997 – and his third double. He gave a chance on 44, off McGrath, when Mark Waugh dropped him at slip, and could have been run out for 99 when Blewett demolished the stumps. The crowd decided he had safely completed a cheeky single before the third umpire delivered his verdict, which might have included an element of benefit of the doubt; only one camera was available. Lara had to be rescued by security men from the enveloping throng and then awaited the verdict on the boundary. No one knows how Sabina might have responded had he been given out. His double-century came without the same uncertainty but was greeted even more rapturously; one man ran on with a baby in his arms; another wore only a bandanna on his head. Lara sensibly retreated to the pavilion. He finally succumbed to McGrath early on the third morning, and the resolute Adams followed six short of his own century. McGrath finished with five in an innings for the third time running, but hardly anyone noticed.

Devastated at being put to the sword by Lara, the Australians offered no resistance in the second innings. Off-spinner Nehemiah Perry celebrated his debut in front of his home crowd by taking five for 70, with some assistance from a splendid pitch. The square had been impressively relaid after the highly embarrassing abandonment of the England Test the previous year. West Indies needed only three runs to complete an overwhelming victory, and level the series, early on the fourth morning.

Man of the Match: B.C. Lara.

Close of play: First day, West Indies 37-4 (Lara 7*, Collins 1*); Second day, West Indies 377-4 (Lara 212*, Adams 88*); Third day, Australia 157-8 (Gillespie 7*).

AUSTRALIA

M.J. Slater c Jacobs b Walsh	.22 –	(2) b Walsh 0
M.T.G. Elliott c Lara b Walsh	.0 –	(1) lbw b Perry 16
J.L. Langer c Jacobs b Walsh	.8 –	c Jacobs b Perry 24
M.E. Waugh b Perry	.67 –	c Walsh b Ambrose 21
*S.R. Waugh c Joseph b Collins	.100 –	c Jacobs b Perry 9
G.S. Blewett lbw b Walsh	.5 –	c Lara b Perry 30
†I.A. Healy run out	.6 –	run out 10
S.K. Warne c Joseph b Collins	.24 –	c Joseph b Walsh 23
J.N. Gillespie b Ambrose	.1 –	c Jacobs b Walsh 7
S.C.G. MacGill c Joseph b Collins	.0 –	c Joseph b Perry 7
G.D. McGrath not out	.2 –	not out 11
B 1, l-b 3, n-b 17	.21	L-b 3, n-b 16 19

1/8 (2) 2/28 (3) 3/46 (1) 4/158 (4)   **256**   1/4 (2) 2/36 (1) 3/51 (3) 4/63 (5)   **177**
5/171 (6) 6/179 (7) 7/227 (8)   5/86 (4) 6/107 (7) 7/137 (8)
8/242 (9) 9/248 (10) 10/256 (5)   8/157 (6) 9/159 (9) 10/177 (10)

Bowling: FIRST INNINGS – Ambrose 17-9-33-1; Walsh 20-6-55-4; Collins 16.3-2-79-3; Perry 17-1-79-1; Adams 1-0-6-0. SECOND INNINGS – Ambrose 14-4-28-1; Walsh 18-3-52-3; Perry 26-8-70-5; Collins 8-0-24-0.

WEST INDIES

S.L. Campbell b McGrath	.12 –	not out 1
S. Ragoonath lbw b Gillespie	.0 –	not out 2
L.A. Roberts c Warne b McGrath	.0	
*B.C. Lara c Healy b McGrath	.213	
D.R.E. Joseph c Blewett b McGrath	.14	
P.T. Collins c M.E. Waugh b MacGill	.13	
J.C. Adams c Elliott b McGrath	.94	
†R.D. Jacobs c Gillespie b Warne	.25	
N.O. Perry not out	.15	
C.E.L. Ambrose b MacGill	.3	
C.A. Walsh lbw b MacGill	.0	
B 12, l-b 8, n-b 22	.42	

1/4 (2) 2/5 (3) 3/17 (1) 4/34 (5)   **431**   (no wkts) **3**
5/378 (4) 6/398 (7) 7/420 (8)
8/427 (6) 9/431 (10) 10/431 (11)

In the first innings Collins, when 10, retired hurt at 56 and resumed at 420.

Bowling: FIRST INNINGS – McGrath 35-11-93-5; Gillespie 33-7-79-1; Warne 30-8-94-1; MacGill 22.3-3-84-3; Blewett 10-1-48-0; M.E. Waugh 2-0-13-0. SECOND INNINGS – McGrath 0.3-0-3-0.

Umpires: P. Willey (England) and S.A. Bucknor.
Referee: R. Subba Row (England).

THIRD TEST MATCH

At Bridgetown, March 26, 27, 28, 29, 30, 1999. West Indies won by one wicket. Toss: Australia.

Another transcendent innings by Lara saw West Indies touch the heights of glory just 22 days after they had hit rock bottom in Trinidad. Irrefutably, his undefeated 153 was the hand of a genius. Exhibiting the new awareness and maturity he discovered in Jamaica, he brilliantly orchestrated the conclusion to an unforgettable match. He guided his men to victory as though leading the infirm through a maze.

Two days earlier, West Indies had been 98 for six in response to Australia's imposing 490, and seemed destined to follow on. But they turned the game round so successfully that they found themselves needing 308 to take the lead in the series. It seemed improbable, but it was within Lara's reach. No one else scored more than 38, and the eighth wicket fell with 60 still wanted for victory. But Ambrose obdurately occupied the crease for 82 minutes to be followed by Walsh, who survived five balls, helped by a wide and a no-ball, before Lara crashed Gillespie to the cover boundary to complete a victory even more astonishing than the last one, giving West Indies a 2–1 lead in the series. It was only the fourth time West Indies had scored more than 300 to win a Test, the last occasion being at Lord's in 1984. Despite the result, Steve Waugh, who survived some extraordinary pace bowling from Ambrose to score a priceless 199, said he had never played in a better match – a telling observation, given that he had appeared in the tied Test against India in 1986–87.

While Lara and Steve Waugh manfully bore the brunt of the workload and responsibility, they did manage to elicit support at significant times against pace bowling of the highest class. On the pulsating final day, which left players and spectators emotionally spent, Adams again heard his captain's cries for help and occupied the crease for 170 minutes to complement the earlier efforts of the two Barbadians, Campbell and Griffith. And, earlier in the match, Campbell scored his most important Test century to help West Indies avoid the follow-on. He and Jacobs added 153 for the seventh wicket, blunting McGrath and Gillespie. After fraught beginnings against Gillespie, in particular, Campbell finished with 105, after six hours and ten minutes. His first 50 took 162 balls with five fours, his second 78 balls with ten fours.

Steve Waugh's assistance had come from Langer and Ponting. Langer played competently until he underestimated Hooper (returning from the sick-bed of his child in Australia). Ponting, who was recalled when Blewett withdrew with a hand injury, batted at No. 6, and made 104, adding 281 with Waugh – the highest fifth-wicket stand ever against West Indies, eclipsing 220, also for Australia, between Keith Miller and Ron Archer at Sabina Park in 1954–55. Waugh batted for nearly eight and a half hours, and struck 20 fours, a five and a six. He was philosophical at his dismissal one short of 200, saying he had never before played and missed so often – primarily against the rampant Ambrose. He was not as stoical, however, when Australia lost their last six wickets for 65, and he was even less pleased when they batted so limply and complacently against the relentless Walsh at their second attempt that they extended their 161-run first-innings lead by no more than a modest 146.

Yet again, the destiny of West Indies lay with Lara. He began the final day on two, having spent an awkward 28 minutes at the crease amid lengthening shadows the previous evening, when three of his colleagues were dismissed. When two more fell soon after the resumption, a scoreline of 105 for five seemingly spelled doom. Lara proceeded to play an innings of astonishing skill and daring. In full control of his emotions and meticulous in his shot selection, he dominated the minds of the Australian bowlers. One by one they were rendered impotent. Gillespie, bothered by back pain, spent critical time off the ground, compelling Steve Waugh to share the second new ball with McGrath, who hit Lara on the helmet, leading to an undignified altercation. Otherwise, it was an imperious innings – arguably greater than anything he had produced before because there was never any safety net. One mistake and the game was lost.

Actually, he made two, but Australia were too befuddled to take advantage: on 101, Warne failed to hold on to a very sharp return catch and, with just seven runs wanted, Healy put him down. These uncharacteristic lapses cost Australia the match. Though McGrath did bowl Adams with West Indies still 70 from victory, and followed up with two more wickets in two balls, Ambrose enabled Lara to advance the score to 302 before Walsh, the last man, was exposed. Then came the winning four and the stampede by the crowd. In all, Lara batted for 353 minutes and 256 balls, and struck 19 fours and a pulled six against Warne. The *Daily Nation* in Barbados headlined this as the Match of the Century, and its writer Haydn Gill said: 'It will go down in the history books as one of the most spirited ever revivals, the victory coming from the depths of despair.' Even an Australian could not argue with that.

Man of the Match: B.C. Lara.

Close of play: First day, Australia 322-4 (S.R. Waugh 141*, Ponting 65*); Second day, West Indies 80-4 (Campbell 23*, Hooper 13*); Third day, Australia 18-2 (Slater 14*, Gillespie 1*); Fourth day, West Indies 85-3 (Griffith 35*, Lara 2*).

AUSTRALIA

M.J. Slater c Lara b Ambrose	23	– (2) run out	26
M.T.G. Elliott b Jacobs b Walsh	9	– (1) c Jacobs b Walsh	0
J.L. Langer b Hooper	51	– lbw b Ambrose	1
M.E. Waugh b Ambrose	0	– (5) lbw b Walsh	3
S.R. Waugh lbw b Perry	199	– (6) b Collins	11
R.T. Ponting c Hooper b Perry	104	– (7) c Griffith b Walsh	22
†I.A. Healy lbw b Walsh	0	– (8) c Jacobs b Collins	3
S.K. Warne c Lara b Perry	13	– (9) lbw b Walsh	32
J.N. Gillespie not out	23	– (4) b Ambrose	14
S.C.G. MacGill run out	17	– c Campbell b Walsh	1
G.D. McGrath c Joseph b Hooper	3	– not out	8
B 4, l-b 10, n-b 34	48	L-b 5, w 1, n-b 19	25

1/31 (2) 2/36 (1) 3/36 (4) 4/144 (3)   **490**   1/0 (1) 2/12 (3) 3/35 (2) 4/46 (4)   **146**
5/425 (6) 6/427 (7) 7/429 (5)   5/48 (5) 6/73 (6) 7/81 (8)
8/446 (8) 9/483 (10) 10/490 (11)   8/134 (9) 9/137 (10) 10/146 (7)

Bowling: FIRST INNINGS – Ambrose 31.3-7-93-2; Walsh 38-8-121-2; Perry 33-5-102-3; Collins 35.5-7-110-0; Hooper 15.4-4-50-2. SECOND INNINGS – Walsh 17.1-3-39-5; Ambrose 20-2-60-2; Collins 9-0-31-2; Perry 4-0-11-0.

WEST INDIES

S.L. Campbell c S.R. Waugh b Gillespie	105	– lbw b McGrath	33
A.F.G. Griffith run out	0	– lbw b Gillespie	35
D.R.E. Joseph lbw b McGrath	26	– lbw b MacGill	1
P.T. Collins lbw b McGrath	0	– lbw b McGrath	0
*B.C. Lara c Healy b Gillespie	8	– not out	153
C.L. Hooper c Warne b McGrath	25	– c Healy b Gillespie	6
J.C. Adams c M.E. Waugh b McGrath	0	– b McGrath	38
†R.D. Jacobs c M.E. Waugh b Ponting	68	– lbw b McGrath	5
N.O. Perry lbw b Gillespie	24	– lbw b McGrath	0
C.E.L. Ambrose not out	28	– c Elliott b Gillespie	12
C.A. Walsh c Slater b Warne	12	– not out	0
B 10, l-b 3, n-b 20	33	B 8, l-b 13, w 2, n-b 5	28

1/1 (2) 2/50 (3) 3/50 (4) 4/64 (5)   **329**   1/72 (1) 2/77 (3) 3/78 (4)   **(9 wkts) 311**
5/98 (6) 6/98 (7) 7/251 (8)   4/91 (2) 5/105 (6) 6/238 (7)
8/265 (1) 9/291 (9) 10/329 (11)   7/248 (8) 8/248 (9) 9/302 (10)

Bowling: FIRST INNINGS – McGrath 33-5-128-4; Gillespie 28-14-48-3; Warne 15.5-2-70-1; MacGill 20-5-47-0; Ponting 4-1-12-1; Waugh 3-0-11-0. SECOND INNINGS – McGrath 44-13-92-5; Gillespie 26.1-8-62-3; Warne 24-4-69-0; MacGill 21-6-48-1; S.R. Waugh 5-0-19-0.

Umpires: D.L. Orchard (South Africa) and E.A. Nicholls.
Referee: R. Subba Row (England).

8

NEIGHBOURS:
AUSTRALIA v. NEW ZEALAND

'GO HOME LOSER. DON'T COME BACK.' When New Zealand's Roger Twose arrived at Hobart as a replacement on his country's 1997–98 Australian tour, he picked up his luggage at the airport to find this scrawl on his cricket coffin, apparently the judgement of an under-employed baggage handler. Now you know why those carousels take so long: your bags may be awaiting personal endorsement. You also have a sense of what New Zealanders hate – and love – about playing Australia.

Australian cricket hasn't exactly showered blessings on its nearest Test neighbour, declining to offer it a Test series until thirty years ago – 'a most belated act of recognition', commented Phil Wilkins in *Wisden* 1975. And even that did not mean the conferring of respect, which was a long time coming. 'Your basic Aussie is a winner … and second is a bag of horse manure,' wrote keeper Ian Smith of touring in 1989–90. 'Wherever we went it was basically a case of the Kiwi boys have come over to get their butts kicked and get them kicked they will.' Recognition required New Zealanders to do just that little bit extra: Dennis Lillee took 11 for 123 at Auckland in February 1977, Richard Hadlee 15 for 123 at Brisbane in November 1985.

'Australians are used to seeing New Zealanders as tough journeymen,' wrote Malcolm Knox in *Wisden Australia* 1998, 'colourless but miserly, short on natural ability but clever at exploiting their limited resources.' Certainly, New Zealanders have been involved in some of the most absorbing international draws of recent memory, including the Christchurch Test of February 1986, the Melbourne Test of December 1987 and the Perth Tests of November 1989 and November 2001. And it has as often been Australians doing the fending off as New Zealanders. *Pace* Australian baggage handlers, New Zealand's historical win/loss ratio against Australia is now actually superior to South Africa's, India's or Sri Lanka's.

—GH

SECOND TEST MATCH

At Auckland, February 25, 26, 27, March 1, 1977. Australia won by ten wickets. New Zealand competed with Australia for the first two days, and then were routed by Lillee on a surprisingly lively pitch. A grassy strip before the start, it was expected to yield uncomfortable bounce only for the first three hours or so. It was then thought likely to play quietly until it began to take spin on the fourth and fifth days. New Zealand shortened their batting to include two spinners; Australia played the First Test team. Unfortunately for New Zealand, the ball got up readily all through the first three days, and it was not even a consistent bounce.

New Zealand, sent in, spent nearly six hours scoring 229. Geoffrey Howarth, although slow, was very sound and stylish. The fireworks came from Edwards, who scored 51, with eleven 4's. He reached his fifty from only 45 balls, his first six scoring shots being boundaries. Richard Hadlee, in for over two hours, defended ably against a hostile Lillee, but once Edwards had gone, resistance was slight. Lillee had fine figures, but Walker deserved better ones.

On the second day Australia also struggled, even while McCosker and Chappell were adding 115 for the third wicket. Three chances were missed off them. Accurate bowling by the in-swinger, Cairns, started a recession and half an hour before stumps seven wickets were down for 245. Richard Hadlee bowled extremely well with the new ball, beating Gilmour repeatedly. Hadlee had five chances missed during the innings. On the third day Gilmour and O'Keeffe were hit by balls getting up sharply from a length, but they took their stand to 93 and Australia won a commanding lead. Chatfield bowled steadily but Hadlee's figures were grossly misleading.

New Zealand, 148 behind, began their second innings after lunch and in fifty-three minutes lost five men for 31. Lillee bowled at tremendous speed, and from near a full length he made the ball get up violently; the ones which dismissed Geoffrey Howarth and Congdon were almost unplayable. Edwards fell to a remarkable catch by Marsh, wide on the leg side.

Burgess, mixing desperate defence with fine forcing shots, helped in an astonishing stand of 105. Most of the runs came from Hadlee, who had the 18,000 crowd in a high state of excitement with his spectacular counter-attack. He on-drove Lillee magnificently for 6, and after thirty-eight minutes he had made 38 of a 50 partnership. He reached his own half-century from 43 balls in fifty-two minutes and at tea was 55 with the total 111. In the last period, Hadlee was not so convincing, although he played more strokes of splendid quality. He gave chances at 64 and 73 before he was bowled for 81, making a tired-looking attempt to drive. His innings of one and three-quarter hours contained one 6 and ten 4's. Australia had to wait until the fourth morning to make the 28 runs that were needed.

NEW ZEALAND

*G.M. Turner c Marsh b Walker	4	– c Walters b Lillee	23
G.P. Howarth c McCosker b Lillee	59	– c Turner b Lillee	2
B.E. Congdon c Marsh b Lillee	25	– c McCosker b Lillee	1
J.M. Parker c Cosier b Lillee	20	– c Turner b Walker	5
M.G. Burgess c Marsh b Walters	1	– b Walker	38
†G.N. Edwards c Lillee b Gilmour	51	– c Marsh b Lillee	0
R.J. Hadlee c McCosker b Lillee	44	– b Chappell	81
B.L. Cairns b Chappell	2	– c Lillee b Walker	7
H.J. Howarth b Walker	5	– lbw b Lillee	6
P.J. Petherick c Marsh b Lillee	4	– b Lillee	1
E.J. Chatfield not out	0	– not out	4
L-b 7, n-b 7	14	B 4, l-b 2, n-b 1	7

1/6 2/63 3/112 4/113 5/121 6/177   **229**   1/10 2/12 3/23 4/31 5/31 6/136   **175**
7/202 8/211 9/228   7/162 8/163 9/169

Bowling: FIRST INNINGS – Lillee 17.3-4-51-5; Walker 24-6-60-2; Gilmour 7-0-56-1; Chappell 13-4-28-1; Walters 4-1-20-1; O'Keeffe 1-1-0-0. SECOND INNINGS – Lillee 16.7-2-72-6; Walker 17-4-70-3; Gilmour 1-0-11-0; Chappell 9-4-15-l.

AUSTRALIA

I.C. Davis b Chatfield	13	– not out	6
A. Turner c Edwards b Cairns	30	– not out	20
R.B. McCosker c Edwards b Cairns	84		
*G.S. Chappell run out	58		
G.J. Cosier c and b Cairns	21		
K.D. Walters c Hadlee b Chatfield	16		
†R.W. Marsh lbw b Hadlee	4		
G.J. Gilmour b Chatfield	64		
K.J. O'Keeffe c Congdon b Hadlee	32		
D.K. Lillee not out	23		
M.H.N. Walker c Turner b Chatfield	9		
B 9, l-b 9, n-b 5	23	L-b 1, n-b 1	2

1/31 2/56 3/171 4/202 5/217 6/221   **377**   (No wkt) **28**
7/245 8/388 9/364

Bowling: FIRST INNINGS – Hadlee 28-2-147-2; Chatfield 27.1-3-100-4; Cairns 28-9-69-3; Congdon 5-1-8-0; H.J. Howarth 5-1-16-0; Petherick 4-2-14-0. SECOND INNINGS – Hadlee 2-0-11-0; Chatfield 1.6-0-15-0.

Umpires: D.E.A. Copps and R.W. Gardiner.

THIRD TEST MATCH

At Christchurch, March 19, 20, 21, 22, 1982. Australia won by eight wickets. Howarth again sent Australia in, and although Wood scored swiftly, New Zealand made good progress on a grassy pitch. Wood, with a diverting display, scored 64, reaching his half-century from only 58 balls. After an uncertain start on the first afternoon, Chappell was magnificent on the second morning when, in 106 minutes, he added 100 to his overnight 76. His 176 came from 218 balls in 260 minutes with two 6s and 23 4s.

If, with the exception of Hadlee's splendid bowling, New Zealand's performance in the field was disappointing, so was their batting. The Australians were all hostility, Thomson in particular bowling very fast, but New Zealand reached 50 with only one wicket down. Then six were lost in an hour, despite another knee injury to Lillee, whose last victim, caught by Marsh, gave the Australian wicket-keeper his 300th Test dismissal, 88 of them catches off Lillee.

At the close of the second day New Zealand were 98 for eight, needing another 56 runs to avoid the follow-on. Hadlee and Snedden scored all but 5 of them with some assertive batting, but both were out at 149 to give Australia a first-innings lead of 204. In Lillee's absence Chappell thought deeply before enforcing the follow-on. He opened the bowling himself, in order to rest Thomson, and when a stand of 93 between Wright and Howarth took New Zealand to 129 for two, a full recovery was in sight. Howarth was then given out caught at silly mid-on, a decision which caused considerable discussion, from which point New Zealand lost ground rapidly. Wright, driving beautifully, was 91 not out at the end of the day, with New Zealand 181 for seven. On the fourth morning he hit ten 4s in adding another 50, totalling seventeen 4s in his second Test century, but Australia, needing only 69 to win, had squared the series by mid-afternoon.

Attendance: 36,000. *Takings*: £41,000.

AUSTRALIA

B.M. Laird c Smith b Troup	12	– (2) c Edgar b Snedden	31
G.M. Wood c Crowe b Hadlee	64	– (1) c Coney b Hadlee	15
J. Dyson c Hadlee b Snedden	1	– not out	14
*G.S. Chappell c Smith b Coney	176	– not out	3
K.J. Hughes b Hadlee	12		
A.R. Border b Snedden	6		
†R.W. Marsh c Cairns b Hadlee	23		
B. Yardley c Cairns b Hadlee	8		
J.R. Thomson b Hadlee	25		
D.K. Lillee c and b Hadlee	7		
T.M. Alderman not out	1		
B 2, l-b 8, n-b 8	18	B 2, l-b 2, n-b 2	6

1/50 2/57 3/82 4/128 5/145 6/237   **353**   1/24 2/60   (2 wkts) **69**
7/256 8/340 9/352

Bowling: FIRST INNINGS – Hadlee 28.5-5-100-6; Troup 11-1-53-1; Snedden 18-2-89-2; Cairns 21-3-74-0; Coney 8-2-15-1; Morrison 3-0-4-0. SECOND INNINGS – Hadlee 8-2-10-1; Snedden 4-0-15-1; Cairns 9-1-28-0; Coney 1-0-2-0; Morrison 2-1-6-0; Wright 1-0-2-0; Crowe 0.3-0-0-0.

NEW ZEALAND

B.A. Edgar c Dyson b Alderman 22	– c Marsh b Alderman 11
J.G. Wright c Marsh b Lillee 13	– b Alderman 141
J.F.M. Morrison lbw b Thomson 8	– lbw b Chappell 4
*G.P. Howarth c Alderman b Thomson 9	– c Wood b Border 41
J.V. Coney b Lillee 0	– b Border 0
M.D. Crowe c Marsh b Lillee 0	– b Yardley 9
R.J. Hadlee c Marsh b Thomson 40	– c Alderman b Yardley 0
†I.D.S. Smith b Thomson 0	– c Wood b Yardley 0
B.L. Cairns run out 3	– lbw b Yardley 16
M.C. Snedden b Alderman 32	– b Border 20
G.B. Troup not out 0	– not out 8
B 8, l-b 2, w 1, n-b 11 22	B 4, l-b 7, w 2, n-b 9 22

1/33 2/57 3/57 4/57   **149** 1/21 2/36 3/129 4/133   **272**
5/67 6/82 7/82 8/87 9/149   5/162 6/166 7/166 8/215 9/249

Bowling: FIRST INNINGS – Thomson 21-5-51-4; Alderman 19.2-3-63-2; Lillee 12-6-13-3.
SECOND INNINGS – Alderman 23-5-66-2; Chappell 18-5-30-1; Thomson 19-5-54-0; Yardley 27-7-80-4; Border 10.3-4-20-3.

Umpires: D.A. Kinsella and F.R. Goodall.

FIRST TEST MATCH

At Brisbane, November 8, 9, 10, 11, 12, 1985. New Zealand won by an innings and 41 runs. When Coney sent Australia in to bat on a pitch which seemed to have some moisture in it, and with cloudy, humid weather aiding the faster bowlers, there was no early indication of the drama that this Test would provide. […] When bad light cut short the first day, Hadlee's fifteen overs had brought him four wickets for 35. […] He then demolished the Australian innings with one of the outstanding pieces of contemporary Test match bowling, having taken all eight by the time Australia were 175 for eight. He missed the chance of all ten wickets by taking a well-judged catch in the deep from Lawson to give Brown his first wicket in Test cricket, whereupon Brown returned the favour by catching Holland and Australia were all out for 179, with Hadlee returning figures of 23.4–4–52–9. […] The Australians had no bowler to match Hadlee's control and movement off the pitch, which had lost much of its spite, and staunch batting by Reid (71 not out) and Martin Crowe (58 not out) took New Zealand to 209 for two at stumps. On the third day they tightened New Zealand's grip on the match, reaching their centuries within five minutes of each other, Crowe from 197 balls with sixteen 4s, Reid 234 balls, fifteen 4s. It took a great diving catch by Border to remove Reid when the stand was worth 224, a New Zealand Test match record for the third wicket. Crowe, however, surged on, accompanied by free hitting from Coney and Jeff Crowe, hitting 26 4s in all before edging a delivery from Matthews into his stumps after 328 balls. Next Hadlee arrived to torment the Australians again – 50 from 41 balls with three 6s and four 4s – and New Zealand were 553 for seven at stumps, their highest score in Tests. Coney declared on the fourth morning with a lead of 374.

In a little more than two hours Hadlee, Chatfield and Snedden had Australia 67 for five, but Border found a stout ally in Matthews, who hit his first Test hundred from 171 balls and then saw Border to his fifteenth from 196 balls. However, when Hadlee took the second new ball fourteen minutes from stumps and had Matthews caught for 115, Border, 106 not out, was Australia's last hope as they went into the final day at 266 for six. He stood alone as Hadlee took three of the last four wickets to give him match figures of 52.3–13–123–15, the best match return by a New Zealand bowler. Border's undefeated 152, off 303 balls in just over seven and a half hours, included two 6s and twenty 4s. [...]

AUSTRALIA

K.C. Wessels lbw b Hadlee	.70	– (2) c Brown b Chatfield	3
A.M.J. Hilditch c Chatfield b Hadlee	.0	– (1) c Chatfield b Hadlee	12
D.C. Boon c Coney b Hadlee	.31	– c Smith b Chatfield	1
*A.R. Border c Edgar b Hadlee	.1	– not out	152
G.M. Ritchie c M.D. Crowe b Hadlee	.8	– c Coney b Snedden	20
†W.B. Phillips b Hadlee	.34	– b Hadlee	2
G.R.J. Matthews b Hadlee	.2	– c Coney b Hadlee	115
G.F. Lawson c Hadlee b Brown	.8	– (9) c Brown b Chatfield	7
C.J McDermott c Coney b Hadlee	.9	– (8) c and b Hadlee	5
D.R. Gilbert not out	.0	– c Chatfield b Hadlee	10
R.G. Holland c Brown b Hadlee	.0	– b Hadlee	0
B 9, l-b 5, n-b 2	16	L-b 3, n-b 3	6

1/1 2/70 3/72 4/82 5/148   **179**   1/14 2/16 3/16 4/47 5/67   **333**
6/150 7/159 8/175 9/179   6/264 7/272 8/291 9/333

Bowling: FIRST INNINGS – Hadlee 23.4-4-52-9; Chatfield 18-6-29-0; Snedden 11-1-45-0; M.D. Crowe 5-0-14-0; Brown 12-5-17-1; Coney 7-5-8-0. SECOND INNINGS – Hadlee 28.5-9-71-6; Chatfield 32-9-75-3; Snedden 19-3-66-1; M.D. Crowe 9-2-19-0; Brown 25-5-96-0; Coney 3-1-3-0.

NEW ZEALAND

B.A. Edgar c Phillips b Gilbert	17
J.G. Wright lbw b Matthews	46
J.F. Reid c Border b Gilbert	108
M.D. Crowe b Matthews	188
*J.V. Coney c Phillips b Lawson	22
J.J. Crowe c Holland b Matthews	35
V.R. Brown not out	36
R.J. Hadlee c Phillips b McDermott	54
†I.D.S. Smith not out	2
B 2, l-b 11, n-b 32	45

M.C. Snedden and E.J. Chatfield did not bat.

1/36 2/85 3/309   (7 wkts, dec.) **553**
4/362 5/427 6/471 7/549

Bowling: Lawson 36.5-8-96-1; McDermott 31-3-119-1; Gilbert 39-9-102-2; Matthews 31-5-110-3; Holland 22-3-106-0; Border 0.1-0-0-0; Wessels 1-0-7-0.

Umpires: A.R. Crafter and R.A. French.

THIRD TEST MATCH

At Melbourne, December 26, 27, 28, 29, 30, 1987. Drawn. The 24th Test between these two countries contained all the ingredients of a classic match, including not just exciting performances but also controversy and a heroic finish. The 127,184 spectators could not have wished for more. Put in to bat, the New Zealanders had reached 119 for one when, half an hour before tea, Jones edged a delivery from McDermott and watched as the Australian wicket-keeper, Dyer, rolled over then showed the ball in his raised right hand, indicating a clean catch. Umpire Crafter, sensing something was amiss, delayed his decision until umpire French at square leg indicated that the ball had carried. But television replays showed the ball bouncing out of Dyer's gloves and on to the ground, with the wicket-keeper scooping the ball back into his gloves before appealing. Wright, the New Zealand vice-captain, batted for 310 minutes before flashing outside off-stump, having hit ten fours in his 99. [...]

Continuing from their overnight 242 for five, the tourists soon lost Martin Crowe for 82, from 147 deliveries, and needed Smith's 44 to see them to 317. Then it was the turn of Hadlee to show his skills. He took four for 62 in three spells which left Australia precariously placed at 170 for five at the end of the second day. Waugh fell without addition on the third morning; but Sleep, with 90 in 310 minutes (256 balls) and Dodemaide, who was to follow his début half-century with six wickets, put on a record 61 for the ninth wicket to give Australia a first-innings lead of 40 runs. New Zealand's openers remained unbeaten for almost two hours, but once Dodemaide had effected a breakthrough, only Martin Crowe, with a fine 79 in just under two hours, including twelve fours, seemed able to guide his country's batting. When he reached 34, he became only the seventh player, and the first since L. Hutton in 1948, to score 4,000 first-class runs in a calendar year, while the catch that ended his innings was Border's 100th in Tests.

By dismissing New Zealand for 286 from the third ball of the final day, Australia had allowed themselves a minimum of 92 overs to score 247 for victory. At 176 for four, with Waugh and Veletta looking confident, they needed only 71 to win with 28 overs left. But at 5.17 p.m. when the score was 199 for five, Hadlee was brought back into the attack. Until the finish at 6.49 p.m., he gave his all for his country as 23,859 spectators watched in suspense. Elsewhere Australians were glued to their television sets; even the high-rating quiz shows were cancelled for the evening.

The wickets fell: Sleep at 209, Veletta at 209, Dyer at 216, and Dodemaide at 227. Hadlee had taken ten wickets in a Test match for a record eighth time, passing S.F. Barnes, C.V. Grimmett and D.K. Lillee, all with seven, and needed just one more wicket to pass I.T. Botham's record of 373 wickets in Tests. However, the last Australian pair, McDermott and Whitney, held out for 4.5 overs to claim a draw and give Australia the Trans-Tasman Trophy for the first time. When Whitney, playing in his first Test since 1981, dug out Hadlee's final ball of the match, the New Zealand fast bowler walked down the pitch to the exuberant batsman, put an arm around his shoulder and shook his hand. [...]

Close of play: First day, New Zealand 242-5 (M.D. Crowe 76*, J.G. Bracewell 4*); Second day, Australia 170-5 (S.R. Waugh 55*, P.R. Sleep 16*); Third day, New Zealand 0-0 (P.A. Horne 0*, J.G. Wright 0*); Fourth day, New Zealand 285-9 (I.D.S. Smith 12*, E.J. Chatfield 0*).

NEW ZEALAND

P.A. Horne c Dyer b Dodemaide	.7 – c Boon b Dodemaide	.27
J.G. Wright c Dyer b McDermott	.99 – b Sleep	.43
A.H. Jones c Dyer b McDermott	.40 – run out	.20
M.D. Crowe c Veletta b McDermott	.82 – c Border b Dodemaide	.79
*J.J. Crowe lbw b McDermott	.6 – c Boon b Sleep	.25
D.N. Patel b McDermott	.0 – c Dyer b Dodemaide	.38
J.G. Bracewell c Dyer b Whitney	.9 – (8) c Veletta b Dodemaide	.1
R.J. Hadlee c Dodemaide b Whitney	.11 – (7) lbw b Sleep	.29
†I.D.S. Smith c Jones b Whitney	.44 – c Dyer b Dodemaide	.12
D.K. Morrison c Border b Whitney	.0 – b Dodemaide	.0
E.J. Chatfield not out	.6 – not out	.1
B 1, l-b 4, n-b 8	.13	B 2, l-b 8, n-b 1	.11

1/32 2/119 3/187 4/221 5/223 **317** 1/73 2/76 3/158 4/178 5/220 **286**
6/254 7/254 8/280 9/294   6/272 7/272 8/281 9/285

Bowling: FIRST INNINGS – McDermott 35-8-97-5; Whitney 33.3-6-92-4; Dodemaide 20-4-48-1; Waugh 10-1-44-0; Sleep 12-1-31-0. SECOND INNINGS – McDermott 10-1-43-0; Whitney 20-5-45-0; Dodemaide 28.3-10-58-6; Sleep 26-5-107-3; Jones 8-3-23-0.

AUSTRALIA

D.C. Boon lbw b Hadlee	.10 – (2) c M.D. Crowe b Morrison	.54
G.R. Marsh c sub (K.R. Rutherford) b Hadlee 13 – (1) c Bracewell b Hadlee	.23
D.M. Jones c Smith b Hadlee	.4 – c M.D. Crowe b Chatfield	.8
*A.R. Border c J.J. Crowe b Bracewell	.31 – lbw b Hadlee	.43
M.R.J. Veletta lbw b Hadlee	.31 – c Patel b Bracewell	.39
S.R. Waugh c Jones b Bracewell	.55 – c Patel b Chatfield	.10
P.R. Sleep lbw b Hadlee	.90 – lbw b Hadlee	.20
†G.C. Dyer run out	.21 – c Smith b Hadlee	.4
A.I.C. Dodemaide c Smith b Morrison	.50 – lbw b Hadlee	.3
C.J. McDermott b Morrison	.33 – not out	.10
M.R. Whitney not out	.0 – not out	.2
L-b 8, n-b 11	.19	B 1, l-b 9, n-b 4	.14

1/24 2/30 3/31 4/78 5/121 **357** 1/45 2/59 3/103 4/147 **(9 wkts) 230**
6/170 7/213 8/293 9/354   5/176 6/209 7/209 8/216 9/227

Bowling: FIRST INNINGS – Hadlee 44-11-109-5; Morrison 27.4-5-93-2; Chatfield 30-10-55-0; Bracewell 32-8-69-2; Patel 12-6-23-0. SECOND INNINGS – Hadlee 31-9-67-5; Morrison 16-2-54-1; Chatfield 21-6-41-2; Bracewell 24-5-58-1.

Umpires: A.R. Crafter and R.A. French.

TEST MATCH

At Perth, November 24, 25, 26, 27, 28, 1989. Drawn. Toss: New Zealand. Wright had no hesitation in putting Australia in to bat on a good, bouncy pitch, but with the temperature near the century mark, his fast bowlers were made to toil by Australian batsmen determined to extend their record of first-innings totals over 400 to nine consecutive matches. After the early loss of Taylor, Boon and Moody, playing in his first Test, added 149 in 192 minutes for the second wicket. The next day saw Boon record his first Test double-hundred, and also the first in seventeen Test matches at Perth. Opening the innings again because Marsh had a broken toe, he batted for 7 hours 31 minutes, faced 327 balls and hit 28 fours. Jones continued the assault on the visiting attack, which never gave up despite being weakened by the absence of New Zealand's own newcomer, Cairns, with a back strain after the first day. Border declared on Jones's dismissal for 99 immediately after a drinks break late on the second day, giving his bowlers three days in which to dismiss New Zealand twice. They almost succeeded and were thwarted only by one of the most valiant rearguard actions in Test history.

Although Wright batted for two and a quarter hours when New Zealand began their reply, the only stand of substance in the first innings was between the left-handed Greatbatch and Martin Crowe, who put on 89 for the third wicket. Greatbatch was three and threequarter hours scoring 76 and Crowe slightly less over his 62, which included ten fours. Hughes, with four for 6 in 24 balls either side of tea, began New Zealand's slump, and from the relative security of 173 for two, they found themselves following on early on the fourth morning. Jeff Crowe had batted 90 minutes for his 7.

In their second innings, New Zealand lost two wickets for 11 runs, Border taking an excellent catch at gully to remove Wright, and at 107 for four a few minutes after the tea interval, they appeared to be heading for defeat. Instead, Greatbatch, in only his seventh Test, saved them. His battling, unbeaten 146 took five minutes under eleven hours, and his stands with Jeff Crowe (155 minutes), Cairns (93 minutes) and finally Snedden (202 minutes) ensured that New Zealand escaped without defeat from a match they had never looked likely to win. Greatbatch was 462 minutes reaching his second Test century, which at the time was the slowest first-class hundred in Australia, and his unbroken partnership of 88 with Snedden was a record for New Zealand's eighth wicket against Australia.

Man of the Match: M.J. Greatbatch. *Attendance*: 29,607.

Close of play: First day, Australia 296-2 (D.C. Boon 169*, A.R. Border 45*); Second day, New Zealand 25-0 (J.G. Wright 12*. R.H. Vance 4*); Third day, New Zealand 218-8 (M.C. Snedden 7*, D.K. Morrison 0*); Fourth day, New Zealand 168-4 (M.J. Greatbatch 69*, J.J. Crowe 42*).

AUSTRALIA

M.A. Taylor c Wright b Morrison	9	G.F. Lawson b Morrison 1
D.C. Boon c Wright b Snedden	200	C.G. Rackemann not out 15
T.M. Moody c Smith b Snedden	61	
*A.R. Border b Morrison 50		B 1, l-b 9, w 2, n-b 13 25
D.M. Jones lbw b Morrison 99		
S.R. Waugh c Greatbatch b Snedden 17		1/28 2/177 3/316 (9 wkts, dec.) **521**
†I.A. Healy c J.J. Crowe b Patel 28		4/361 5/365 6/449
M.G. Hughes c Wright b Snedden 16		7/489 8/490 9/521

T.M. Alderman did not bat.

Bowling: Morrison 39.1-8-145-4; Cairns 12-2-60-0; Snedden 42-10-108-4; Watson 37-7-118-0; Patel 28-5-80-1.

NEW ZEALAND

*J.G. Wright b Rackemann 34	– c Border b Lawson 3
R.H. Vance b Alderman 4	– c Alderman b Rackemann 8
M.J. Greatbatch c Healy b Hughes 76	– not out 146
M.D. Crowe lbw b Alderman 62	– c Taylor b Moody 30
D.N. Patel c Boon b Hughes 0	– lbw b Alderman 7
J.J. Crowe c Healy b Rackemann 7	– lbw b Hughes 49
†I.D.S. Smith c Lawson b Hughes 11	– c Border b Hughes 0
C.L. Cairns c Healy b Hughes 1	– lbw b Hughes 28
M.C. Snedden not out 13	– not out 33
D.K. Morrison c Border b Lawson 3	
W. Watson lbw b Alderman 4	
B 1, l-b 6, w 4, n-b 5 16	L-b 14, n-b 4 18
1/28 2/84 3/173 4/178 5/191 **231**	1/11 2/11 3/79 4/107 (7 wkts) **322**
6/204 7/206 8/212 9/226	5/189 6/189 7/234

Bowling: FIRST INNINGS – Alderman 25.4-7-73-3; Lawson 22-5-54-1; Rackemann 20-4-39-2; Hughes 20-7-51-4; Moody 4-1-6-0; Border 1-0-1-0. SECOND INNINGS – Alderman 32-14-59-1; Lawson 38-12-88-1; Rackemann 31-21-23-1; Hughes 36-8-92-3; Moody 17-6-23-1; Border 5-2-17-0; Jones 3-2-6-0.

Umpires: R.J. Evans and P.J. McConnell.

9

HOME AND AWAY:
AUSTRALIA v. INDIA

'A wonderful matter is the te-rain,' Kim was told by a fellow traveller. And Test matches between Australia and India have been all about terrain, both countries having been virtually unassailable on their own surfaces and in front of their home crowds. India has never won a rubber in Australia, and last claimed a Test on Australian soil more than twenty years ago; Australia won the last of its three away series in the 1960s.

At times, individuals have succeeded in alien environments and against the odds. Many recall India as the opponent when Donald Bradman registered his 100th first-class hundred in November 1947; not many that, thanks to 10 for 177 from the indefatigable Vinoo Mankad, India won the game by 47 runs. Vijay Hazare's twin hundreds at Adelaide two months later represent one of only two instances of such a feat in Australia coinciding with defeat. And you'd be hard-pressed to conceive of better performances in a beaten side than Matthew Hayden's 549 runs at 109.8 and Glenn McGrath's 17 wickets at 15.35 last year in India.

More often, though, matches between Australia and India have involved contestants making the most of home-ground advantages, from Ern Toshack's 11 for 31 on a Brisbane mudheap and Jasu Patel's 14 for 124 in a Kanpur dustbowl to Greg Chappell's merciless 204 at Sydney in January 1981 and V.V.S. Laxman's majestic 281 at Kolkata a little over twenty years later. Is it just an impression, or are there more often than usual in Australia–India matches periods where one team appears to achieve total subjection of its rival? Nine of 42 Tests between them have been decided by an innings, a further 15 by margins exceeding 150 runs or seven wickets.

The exception to these wide margins is the narrowest in cricket history: the second tie in the annals of Test cricket, at Madras in September 1986, featuring 18 more runs and played in temperatures vastly more hostile to cricket than the first a quarter of a century earlier. Most of the glory of this match tends to go to Dean Jones, whose 210 in just over 500 minutes is a candidate for the bravest innings in history. Usually forgotten is Allan Border's decision, little less brave, to declare overnight going into the final day, jeopardising his team's work over the four preceding days in order to press for victory. Border is nowadays dismissed as a rather unenterprising leader. Would that others were so unenterprising.

—GH

An Australian XI v. India

At Sydney, November 14, 15, 17, 18, 1947. India won by 47 runs, gaining their first victory of the tour over a side very little short of full Australian Test standard. The early stages went unfavourably, nine wickets falling for 229, but Kishenchand and Irani shared in a splendid partnership of 97. Bradman gave a glorious display in completing his hundredth hundred in first-class cricket, but, although he made 172 and Miller showed good form, the last six wickets fell for 38 and much of the home team's advantage was lost. Kishenchand again batted well for India and scored 138 in the match without losing his wicket. Set to get 251 in two and a half hours, the Australians accepted the challenge, but could not cope with the clever left-arm spin bowling of Mankad, who took eight for 84 for the innings.

India

V. Mankad c Miller b Johnston	3	– c Saggers b Dooland	34
C.T. Sarwate c Saggers b Miller	32	– c Bradman b Johnston	58
Gul Mahomed c Saggers b Loxton	85	– b Dooland	20
V.S. Hazare run out	38	– c Saggers b Miller	15
L. Amarnath b Loxton	10	– b Johnston	7
H.R. Adhikari c Saggers b Johnston	4	– c Loxton b Johnston	46
K.M. Rangnekar b Loxton	6	– c Harvey b Johnston	13
G. Kishenchand not out	75	– not out	63
W.S. Sohoni run out	14	– b Loxton	31
C.S. Nayudu c Hamence b Dooland	3	– not out	3
J.K. Irani lbw b Dooland	43	– run out	0
B 6, l-b 7	13	B 2, l-b 12	14
	326		**Nine wkts, dec. 304**

An Australian XI

R. Rogers run out	16	– b Mankad	31
W.A. Brown c Hazare b Sohoni	8	– run out	30
D.G. Bradman c Amarnath b Hazare	172	– c Sarwate b Mankad	26
K.R. Miller b Mankad	86	– st Irani b Mankad	13
R.A. Hamence c Hazare b Sohoni	27	– c Amarnath b Mankad	2
R.N. Harvey c Mankad b Hazare	32	– not out	56
S.J. Loxton c Irani b Sohoni	0	– lbw b Mankad	6
R.A. Saggers c Irani b Sohoni	1	– b Mankad	0
B. Dooland lbw b Mankad	5	– c Kishenchand b Mankad	31
M. Herbert not out	26	– c Gul Mahomed b Amarnath	1
W.A. Johnston c Irani b Amarnath	2	– c Sohoni b Mankad	2
B 3, l-b 2	5	B 5	5
	380		**201**

AN AUSTRALIAN XI BOWLING

	O	M	R	W	O	M	R	W
Loxton	22	3	70	3	25	9	43	1
Johnston	24	5	70	2	31	9	71	4
Dooland	15.1	0	58	2	26	4	76	2
Miller	13	0	36	1	9	1	24	1
Herbert	17	0	73	0	15	1	76	0
Hamence	2	0	6	0				

INDIA BOWLING

	O	M	R	W	O	M	R	W
Sohoni	17	2	89	4	4	0	31	0
Amarnath	15.1	2	53	1	11	0	54	1
Mankad	24	2	93	2	12	0	84	8
Sarwate	16	0	51	0	2	0	24	0
Nayudu	4	0	19	0				
Kishenchand	1	0	3	0				
Hazare	14	1	67	2				
Mahomed					1	0	5	0

FIRST TEST MATCH

At Brisbane, November 28, 29, December 1, 2, 3, 4, 1947. Australia won by an innings and 226 runs. [...] There was nothing wrong with the conditions when Australia batted first, and, after the early loss of Brown, Bradman gave one of his superb displays. He lost Morris at 97, but completely demoralised the bowlers by punishing methods which brought runs at a terrific rate. Not a ball could be bowled until five o'clock on the second day, but the surprising attendance of 11,000 watched the hour's cricket that took place. A further downpour saturated the pitch on the Sunday, but next day the sun appeared and India's task was hopeless. Realising the awkwardness of the conditions, the Australians soon declared. Bradman took four and three-quarter hours over 185, which contained twenty 4's.

With the ball doing all manner of unexpected tricks, India, used to the fast, hard pitches in their own country, were completely baffled. Mankad and Gul Mahomed fell in the first over from Lindwall, but the most successful bowler was Toshack, who, with left-arm slow-medium deliveries, dismissed five men in nineteen balls for two runs. All out 58, India followed-on 324 behind, and before the dismal day ended for them four second innings wickets fell for 41.

More rain restricted the fourth day to an hour, and nothing could be done next day, but conditions were not quite so difficult when play re-started on Thursday. Sarwate gave a stubborn defensive display for three hours, but few of his colleagues could cope with Toshack, who again made the most of the pitch. In the match he took eleven wickets for 31 runs. [...]

AUSTRALIA

W.A. Brown c Irani b Amarnath 11	R.R. Lindwall st Irani b Mankad 7
A.R. Morris hit wkt b Sarwate 47	D. Tallon not out 3
D.G. Bradman hit wkt b Amarnath .185	I.W. Johnson c Rangnekar b Mankad .6
A.L. Hassett c Gul Mahomed b Mankad 48	E.R.H. Toshack not out 0
K.R. Miller c Mankad b Amarnath 58	
C.L. McCool c Sohoni b Amarnath 10	B 5, l-b 1, w 1 7
W.A. Johnston did not bat.	Eight wkts, dec. **382**

INDIA

V. Mankad c Tallon b Lindwall 0	– b Lindwall 7
C.T. Sarwate c Johnston b Miller 12	– b Johnston 26
Gul Mahomed b Lindwall 0	– b Toshack 13
H.R. Adhikari c McCool b Johnston 8	– lbw b Toshack 13
G. Kishenchand c Tallon b Johnston 1	– c Bradman b Toshack 0
V.S. Hazare c Brown b Toshack 10	– c Morris b Toshack 18
K.M. Rangnekar c Miller b Toshack 1	– c Hassett b Toshack 0
S.W. Sohoni c Miller b Toshack 2	– c Brown b Miller 4
L. Amarnath c Bradman b Toshack 22	– b Toshack 5
C.S. Nayudu not out 0	– c Hassett b Lindwall 6
J.K. Irani c Hassett b Toshack 0	– not out 2
B 1, l-b 1 2	B 3, n-b 1 4
58	**98**

INDIA BOWLING

	O	M	R	W	O	M	R	W
Sohoni	23	4	81	0				
Amarnath	39	10	84	4				
Mankad	34	3	113	3				
Sarwate	5	1	16	1				
Hazare	11	1	63	0				
Nayudu	3	0	18	0				

AUSTRALIA BOWLING

	O	M	R	W	O	M	R	W
Lindwall	5	2	11	2	10.7	2	19	2
W. Johnston	8	4	17	2	9	6	11	1
Miller	6	1	26	1	10	2	30	1
Toshack	2.3	1	2	5	17	6	29	6
I. Johnson					3	1	5	0

FALL OF WICKETS

Australia – First Innings

1	2	3	4	5	6	7	8
38	97	198	318	344	373	373	380

India – First Innings

1	2	3	4	5	6	7	8	9
0	0	19	23	23	53	56	58	58

India – Second Innings

1	2	3	4	5	6	7	8	9
14	27	41	41	72	80	80	89	94

FOURTH TEST MATCH

At Adelaide, January 23, 24, 26, 27, 28, 1948. Australia won by an innings and 16 runs. Although they gained another overwhelming success, and in so doing won the rubber, the match was a personal triumph for Hazare, who followed Bradman's example in the Third Test and hit a hundred in each innings. Against such a powerful attack as that possessed by the Australians, this was a truly remarkable performance. To balance this, however, Bradman was once again in irresistible form, hitting a double hundred. Hassett fell only two short of that figure and Barnes also completed a century.

Bradman gave Australia a big advantage when he won the toss for the third time; on a perfect pitch bowlers were helpless to check the flow of runs. Morris fell early, but Barnes and Bradman shared in a second wicket stand of 236. Apart from a chance to second slip when 61, Barnes batted faultlessly. Bradman, always the complete master, scored 201 out of 341 before leaving towards the close of the first day. More free hitting came from Hassett and Miller during a fourth-wicket partnership of 142. An interesting race developed to see whether Hassett could complete two hundred, but he was just short, taking out his bat for an excellent 198. In reaching 674, Australia made the highest score ever recorded against India and also the biggest total for any Test match in Australia.

India made a shocking start, losing two wickets for six runs, but they fought back well. Half the side fell for 133, but Hazare found a capable partner in Phadkar, 188 runs being added. Hazare, always master of the situation, hit fourteen 4's and his partner fifteen 4's. Despite this gallant effort, India followed-on 293 behind, and this time their start was even worse, two wickets falling without a run on the board. Six men were out for 139 and it looked as though India would capitulate easily, but Hazare again refused to be disturbed by the situation; he received useful help from Adhikari and 132 runs were added. Then the end soon came, the last three wickets falling for six runs. Six men failed to score in this innings, most of the batsmen finding the pace of Lindwall too much for them. Accurate attacking bowling brought Lindwall seven wickets for 38 runs.

AUSTRALIA

S.G. Barnes lbw b Mankad 112
A.R. Morris b Phadkar 7
D.G. Bradman b Hazare 201
A.L. Hassett not out 198
K.R. Miller b Rangachari 67
R.N. Harvey lbw b Rangachari 13
C.L. McCool b Phadkar 27

I.W. Johnson b Rangachari 22
R.R. Lindwall b Rangachari 2
D. Tallon lbw b Mankad 1
E.R.H. Toshack lbw b Hazare 8
    B 8, l-b 6, n-b 2 16

674

INDIA

V. Mankad b McCool . . . . .49 – c Tallon b Lindwall 0
C.T. Sarwate b Miller . . . . .1 – b Toshack 11
P. Sen b Miller . . . . .0 – not out .0
L. Amarnath c Bradman b Johnson . . . . .46 – b Lindwall 0
V.S. Hazare lbw b Johnson . . . . .116 – b Lindwall 145
Gul Mahomed st Tallon b Johnson . . . . .4 – b Barnes 34
D.G. Phadkar lbw b Toshack . . . . .123 – lbw b Lindwall 14
G. Kishenchand b Lindwall . . . . .10 – b Lindwall 0
H.R. Adhikari run out . . . . .2 – lbw b Miller 51
K.M. Rangnekar st Tallon b Johnson . . . . .8 – b Lindwall 0
C.R. Rangachari not out . . . . .0 – c McCool b Lindwall 0
    B 18, l-b 3, n-b 1 .22   Extras .22

       381   **277**

INDIA BOWLING

	O	M	R	W	O	M	R	W
Phadkar	15	0	74	2				
Amarnath	9	0	42	0				
Rangachari	41	5	141	4				
Mankad	43	8	170	2				
Sarwate	22	1	121	0				
Hazare	21.3	1	110	2				

AUSTRALIA BOWLING

	O	M	R	W	O	M	R	W
Lindwall	21	5	61	1	16.5	4	38	7
Miller	9	1	39	2	9	3	13	1
McCool	28	2	102	1	4	0	26	0
Johnson	23.1	5	64	4	20	4	54	0
Toshack	18	2	66	1	25	8	73	1
Barnes	9	0	23	0	18	4	51	1
Bradman	1	0	4	0				

FALL OF THE WICKETS

Australia – First Innings

1	2	3	4	5	6	7	8	9
20	256	361	503	523	576	634	640	641

India – First Innings

1	2	3	4	5	6	7	8	9
1	6	69	124	133	321	353	359	375

India – Second Innings

1	2	3	4	5	6	7	8	9
0	0	33	99	139	139	271	273	273

AUSTRALIANS IN CEYLON AND INDIA, 1969–70

The two-month Australian tour of Ceylon and India, from October to December in 1969, provided keen cricket and stirred tremendous public interest. While big crowds watched every match, those for the five Tests far exceeded the gatherings that turned up to see the West Indies in 1966–67. The daily attendance for the Tests ranged from 35,000 to 50,000, only the limitation on accommodation keeping out many more. The composition of the touring party, which included Chappell, the heavy scoring batsman, and the glamorous Walters and Sheahan, and the fact that the team had beaten West Indies a season earlier in a home series, contributed to their tremendous attraction. India's victory in the third Test at Delhi also added fire to the enthusiasm of the fans. The tour was marred by disturbances – a riot at Bombay, an invasion of the crowd on to the field at Calcutta and stone-throwing at Bangalore – so much so that one heaved a sigh of relief when the programme was concluded. […]

FIRST TEST MATCH

At Brabourne Stadium, Bombay, November 4, 5, 6, 8, 9, 1969. Australia won by eight wickets, shortly after lunch on the fifth day. The match lacked neither drama nor good cricket. To boot there was also a riot on the evening of the fourth day. […] The Nawab of Pataudi won the toss and Sardesai and Engineer got off to a flashy start of 39. This was soon offset when McKenzie, in an admirable burst of speed, dismissed both the openers and Borde for 42 runs. He claimed them in six balls for two runs. Pataudi and Mankad retrieved the position with a stand of 146 runs, a fourth-wicket record against Australia. Pataudi was dropped by Mallett at square-leg off Gleeson when he was five, and Mankad escaped when 26, Redpath at leg-slip failing to catch a deflection off Mallett.

The pair then batted first with determination and later fluently. Mankad, promoted to number three, was content to jog along till he reached his fifty and then broke into confident strokes. He was out nine minutes after tea when McKenzie bowled him with the second new ball. Mankad scored 74 in four and a quarter hours, with seven 4's. Pataudi was not out with 73 and the score of 202 for four at close of play showed a splendid recovery. All four wickets had fallen to McKenzie. However, on the next day India were all out for 271. Pataudi fell five short of his hundred, when he skied a leg-break from Gleeson for an easy catch by Lawry at mid-on. He had batted for over six hours and hit fourteen 4's. McKenzie claimed one more wicket, that of Abid Ali, to finish with five for 69. Connolly and Gleeson shared the rest, the latter having an impressive analysis.

Australia finished the day with 93 for one wicket, that of Lawry to a fine delivery from Prasanna. They resumed after a rest day and went on to score 322 for seven wickets by the end of the third day. At tea, after Stackpole had hit a fine century, and with Walters and Redpath at the crease, they were 259 for three but the Indian spinners then struck and gained some quick wickets. [...] Australia were all out for 345 on the fourth morning. [...] India then collapsed in the second innings for 137, only Wadekar showing resistance to the clever spin of Gleeson and the cutters of Connolly. The last hour of play was marred by rioting from a section of the crowd, which did not approve of a decision against Venkataraghavan. The umpire upheld the catch behind the wicket by Taber off Connolly. Bottles were hurled on to the ground and chairs and canvas coverings were set on fire. But in din and smoke the play went on. India, 125 for nine at close of play were all out on the next morning. Australia, though they lost Stackpole and Lawry for only 13 runs, had no trouble in winning without further loss.

INDIA

D.N. Sardesai b McKenzie	20	– c Taber b Gleeson ... 3
†F.M. Engineer c Redpath b McKenzie	19	– c McKenzie b Mallett ... 28
A.V. Mankad b McKenzie	74	– b Redpath b Gleeson ... 8
*Nawab of Pataudi c Lawry b Gleeson	95	– c Stackpole b Gleeson ... 0
A.L. Wadekar lbw b Connolly	9	– c McKenzie b Stackpole ... 46
R.F. Surti st Taber b Gleeson	4	– lbw b Connolly ... 13
S. Abid Ali c Stackpole b McKenzie	3	– b Connolly ... 2
S. Venkataraghavan c Taber b Connolly	2	– c Taber b Connolly ... 9
E.A.S. Prasanna not out	12	– b Mallett ... 3
B.S. Bedi c McKenzie b Gleeson	7	– not out ... 1
B 15, l-b 4, n-b 5	24	L-b 4, n-b 2 ... 6

1/39 2/40 3/42 4/188 5/239   **271**   1/19 2/37 3/55 4/56 5/59   **137**
6/245 7/246 8/249 9/252   6/87 7/89 8/114 9/125

Bowling: FIRST INNINGS – McKenzie 29-7-69-5; Connolly 31-11-55-2; Gleeson 35.4-18-52-3; Walters 6-0-13-0; Mallett 30-19-43-0; Stackpole 3-1-8-0; Chappell 1-0-7-0. SECOND INNINGS – McKenzie 16-4-33-0; Connolly 20-10-20-3; Gleeson 32-17-56-4; Mallett 21-9-22-2; Stackpole 1.2-1-0-1.

AUSTRALIA

*W.M. Lawry b Prasanna 25	– b Surti 2
K.R. Stackpole c Surti b Prasanna 103	– lbw b Surti 11
I.M. Chappell b Prasanna 31	– not out 31
K.D. Walters c Venkataraghavan b Bedi 48	– not out 22
I.R. Redpath c Wadekar b Venkataraghavan .77	
A.P. Sheahan lbw b Venkataraghavan 14	
G.D. McKenzie c Borde b Prasanna 16	
†H.B. Taber c Surti b Bedi 5	
A.A. Mallett not out 10	
J.W. Gleeson c Borde b Prasanna 0	
A.N. Connolly c sub b Bedi 8	
B 4, n-b 4 8	B 1 1

1/81 2/164 3/167 4/285 5/297   **345**   1/8 2/13   (2 wkts) **67**
6/322 7/322 8/337 9/337

Bowling: FIRST INNINGS – Abid Ali 18-3-52-0; Surti 9-2-23-0; Venkataraghavan 31-11-67-2; Bedi 62.4-33-74-3; Prasanna 49-19-121-5. SECOND INNINGS – Abid Ali 3-0-14-0; Surti 4-1-9-2; Bedi 9-5-11-0; Prasanna 9-3-20-0; Venkataraghavan 1-0-2-0; Mankad 0.5-0-10-0.

Umpires: S. Pan and J. Gopalakrishnan.

FOURTH TEST MATCH

At Calcutta, December 12, 13, 14, 16, 1969. Australia won by ten wickets with more than a day to spare in spite of two and a half hours being lost through poor light on the first three days. The final day was marred by an invasion from a section of the crowd on to the field of play. The Eden Gardens pitch, which was not completely bereft of grass, was a bit soft on the first day but improved in the batsmen's favour from the second day. Lawry won the toss and had no hesitation in asking Pataudi to bat. Then McKenzie, with his best spell of bowling in the series, got to work in the heavy atmosphere and on the soft pitch and sent back Engineer and Wadekar without a run on the board. Viswanath attacked the bowling, especially McKenzie, with brilliant drives past point and through cover. He went on to score 54 runs with six 4's. His performance laid the basis for a fair recovery in which Venkataraghavan, Solkar and Prasanna played their part. McKenzie finished with six wickets for 67.

The Indian innings ended forty minutes before lunch on the second day and Australia had replied with 95 for two wickets at close of play. The visitors began brightly with a stand of 65, of which Stackpole scored a very competent 41 before he was run out. Lawry fell to the wiles of Bedi at the end of a fascinating duel with the Indian spinner. Then Chappell and Walters put on 101 for the third wicket. While Chappell was playing beautifully, Walters was in trouble with his timing. Just as he was getting his touch, Bedi beat him on the forward stroke, and as he lifted his foot Engineer stumped him. Sheahan was looking in his best form when he was run out for 32. All along Chappell was combining sterling defence with judicious aggression but after reaching 99 he edged a quicker ball from Bedi to slip. Chappell hit sixteen 4's in his faultless stay of five hours.

In spite of Chappell's domination Australia were contained to 335 runs. Prasanna was not in his best form and Bedi had to work single-handed – Venkataraghavan was not used as he should have been – and dismissed seven batsmen for 98 runs. Connolly enjoyed himself at the expense of Prasanna and hit him for three 6's, also hitting another six off Bedi. India were 12 for no wicket when the third day's play ended.

Next day McKenzie was as hostile as on the first day, though the pitch was now easy and the atmosphere clear. India collapsed for 161, Freeman and Connolly taking four wickets each. Freeman, who was playing his first Test in the series, bowled a good direction and kept the ball well up to the batsman; each success inspired him to a better effort. Wadekar alone batted well. Australia hit off the requisite 39 runs for victory without loss, but not before the crowd had provided some disturbance and excitement. In a part of the stands called the Ranji Stadium, with a flight of two decks, both uncovered, the spectators in the upper one started throwing stones and brickbats at those in the lower one, forcing the latter to rush on to the ground for safety. They were persuaded by the police to sit along the boundary and play was resumed after an interruption of about fifteen minutes.

INDIA

†F.M. Engineer c Stackpole b McKenzie	.....0 –	c Redpath b Freeman 10
A.V. Mankad c Stackpole b McKenzie	.......9 –	c Taber b McKenzie 20
A.L. Wadekar c Freeman b McKenzie	.......0 –	lbw b Freeman 62
G.R. Viswanath c Taber b Mallett	..........54 –	b Freeman 5
*Nawab of Pataudi c Chappell b Mallett	....15 –	c Connolly b Mallett 1
A. Roy c Taber b McKenzie	................18 –	c Sheahan b Connolly 19
E.D. Solkar c Taber b McKenzie	...........42 –	lbw b Connolly 21
S. Venkataraghavan c Stackpole b Mallett	...24 –	b Connolly 0
E.A.S. Prasanna run out	..................26 –	c Stackpole b Freeman 0
S. Guha b McKenzie	......................4 –	not out 1
B.S. Bedi not out	........................9 –	c Chappell b Connolly 7
B 5, l-b 1, w 1, n-b 4 11		B 6, l-b 4, n-b 5 15

1/0 2/0 3/22 4/64 5/103	**212**	1/29 2/31 3/40 4/90 5/93 **161**
6/103 7/154 8/178 9/184		6/141 7/141 8/142 9/159

Bowling: FIRST INNINGS – McKenzie 33.4-12-67-6; Freeman 17-6-43-0; Connolly 17-5-27-0; Mallett 27-9-55-3; Stackpole 2-0-9-0. SECOND INNINGS – McKenzie 18-4-34-1; Connolly 16.1-3-31-4; Freeman 26-7-54-4; Mallett 17-5-27-1.

AUSTRALIA

*W.M. Lawry c Solkar b Bedi	.35 – not out	.17
K.R. Stackpole run out	.41 – not out	.25
I.M. Chappell c Wadekar b Bedi	.99	
K.D. Walters st Engineer b Bedi	.56	
I.R. Redpath c Wadekar b Bedi	.0	
A.P. Sheahan run out	.32	
E.W. Freeman c Prasanna b Bedi	.29	
†H.B. Taber b Bedi	.2	
G.D. McKenzie c Pataudi b Bedi	.0	
A.A. Mallett not out	.2	
A.N. Connolly c Guha b Solkar	.31	
B 4, l-b 2, n-b 2	.8	

1/65 2/84 3/185 4/185 5/157   **335**   (No wkt.) **42**
6/279 8/302 9/302

Bowling: FIRST INNINGS – Guha 19-5-55-0; Solkar 9.1-1-28-1; Prasanna 49-15-116-0; Venkataraghavan 16-6-30-0; Bedi 50-19-98-7. SECOND INNINGS – Guha 3-1-25-0; Wadekar 2-0-17-0.

Umpires: S. Pan and J. Reuben.

FIRST TEST MATCH

At Sydney, January 2, 3, 4, 1981. Australia won by an innings and 4 runs, with two days to spare. Although ten years a Test player, this was Greg Chappell's first Test against India. He made up for the wait with a masterly 204, which ended a brave counter-offensive by India and softened them up for the kill. Chappell's score, for which he was voted Man of the Match, was the highest by an Australian against India, surpassing by 3 runs Don Bradman's record set up 33 years previously. His innings, occupying six and threequarter hours spread over two days, was the more notable as he was taken ill with a violent stomach upset during the night, when he was 41.

With the pitch still retaining much moisture from its preparation, Gavaskar's decision to bat was inconsistent with India's move of going into the match with only one spinner, Doshi, off-spinner Yadav being left out. Edging Lillee to Marsh, who took five catches in the innings, Gavaskar himself went without a run on the board and India were routed for 201, the Australian pace bowlers getting lift as well as movement from the pitch.

Chauhan, Vengsarkar and Viswanath all looked to have settled in, but none made more than 26. The only score of note was a handsome 65 by Patil, who drove with great power against anything overpitched until his vulnerability to the short-pitched ball got him into trouble. Hooking a bumper from Pascoe, Patil, who like most of his team-mates batted without protective headgear, was struck a vicious blow over the ear and had to retire.

When Australia batted, Kapil Dev harnessed the aid from the pitch obtained earlier by Lillee and Pascoe. He removed Dyson and Wood in his first two overs but Chappell was soon in command, if not as belligerent as on the next day, and he and a steadfast Hughes took Australia to 72 for two at the close. Hughes did not last long the following morning, but the indisposed Chappell quickly cut loose and Australia rapidly drew away. Border and Walters played well in supporting their captain. The second new ball was taken at 328 for four and the Indians must have feared the worst when Chappell took 12 runs in the first over from Kapil Dev, hitting the last three of his 27 4s. But, attempting a hook off Ghavri, he skied a catch – the stroke of a tired man. Walters had gone just before, edging a cut off Ghavri, who took five wickets in as many overs with the new ball.

Although the pitch had become quite tranquil, as was obvious from the fact that it took the Indians 35 minutes to take the last Australian wicket on the third morning, India were again bowled out in less than a day. Undisciplined batting was at the root of their collapse. The wind, blowing straight down the ground, was so strong that a fast bowler could operate from only one end. But that was of no help to India, who conceded wickets just as readily to Higgs, the leg-spinner, who thrived on a rare opportunity to bowl a long spell to take four for 45.

INDIA

*S.M. Gavaskar c Marsh b Lillee	.0	– (2) c Marsh b Hogg	.10
C.P.S. Chauhan c Border b Pascoe	.20	– (1) c Walters b Pascoe	.36
D.B. Vengsarkar c Marsh b Lillee	.22	– c Marsh b Pascoe	.34
G.R. Viswanath b Hogg	.26	– st Marsh b Higgs	.24
Yashpal Sharma c Marsh b Pascoe	.6	– c Walters b Lillee	.4
S.M. Patil retired hurt	.65	– (8) c Wood b Lillee	.4
Kapil Dev c Marsh b Pascoe	.22	– (6) c sub b Higgs	.19
†S.M.H. Kirmani c Walters b Lillee	.27	– (7) not out	.43
R.M. Binny c Marsh b Pascoe	.3	– lbw b Lillee	.0
K.D. Ghavri c Wood b Lillee	.7	– c Hogg b Higgs	.21
D.R. Doshi not out	.0	– c Lillee b Higgs	.0
L-b 1, n-b 2	.3	B 2, l-b 3, w 1	.6

1/0 2/36 3/62 4/70   **201**   1/21 2/74 3/92 4/110   **201**
5/78 6/145 7/183 8/186 9/201   5/120 6/140 7/144 8/144 9/201

Bowling: FIRST INNINGS – Lillee 20.2-3-86-4; Hogg 14-2-51-1; Pascoe 19-6-61-4. SECOND INNINGS – Lillee 18-2-79-3; Hogg 9-1-24-1; Pascoe 11-2-35-2; Higgs 18-8-45-4; Walters 6-3-12-0.

AUSTRALIA

G.M. Wood c Kirmani b Kapil Dev	.9	R.M. Hogg not out	.26
J. Dyson c Gavaskar b Kapil Dev	.0	L.S. Pascoe c Doshi b Ghavri	.7
*G.S. Chappell c Kapil Dev b Ghavri	.204	J.D. Higgs b Kapil Dev	.2
K.J. Hughes c Kirmani b Kapil Dev	.24		
A.R. Border c Kirmani b Kapil Dev	.31		
K.D. Walters c Viswanath b Ghavri	.67		
†R.W. Marsh c Binny b Ghavri	.12	B 4, l-b 3, w 3, n-b 9	.19
D.K. Lillee c Doshi b Ghavri	.5	1/3 2/14 3/95 4/164	**406**

5/341 6/355 7/363 8/365 9/376

Bowling: Kapil Dev 36.1-7-97-5; Ghavri 30-7-107-5; Binny 15-1-70-0; Doshi 27-0-103-0; Chauhan 1-0-10-0.

Umpires: M.W. Johnson and R.V. Whitehead.

THIRD TEST MATCH

At Melbourne, February 7, 8, 9, 10, 11, 1981. India won by 59 runs. This was a sen-sational match, not only for Australia's astonishing collapse in the second innings against an Indian attack that was badly handicapped by injuries. India had come near to forfeiting the match on the previous day when their captain, Gavaskar, so sharply disagreed with an lbw decision that he wanted to call off the contest. The incident took place in India's second innings, after an opening partnership of 165 between Gavaskar and Chauhan. When Gavaskar was given out by umpire Whitehead, he first indicated that he had edged the ball on to his pad, and then, as he walked past Chauhan he urged him to leave the field with him. Fortunately the manager of the Indian team, S.K. Durrani, intervened, meeting the in-coming pair at the gate and ordering Chauhan to continue his innings. [...]

The quality of pitches at the MCG had been a matter of criticism all season, with Greg Chappell leading the protest. On this occasion he elected to field, his decision being influenced by the extra grass the groundsman had left in the hope that it would hold the pitch together. The move was initially rewarding, Lillee and Pascoe seizing India's first six wickets for 115 runs, but the Indians were kept in the fight by Viswanath, who, coming in at 22 for two with the innings only eleven overs old, was ninth out four and a half hours later, having made 114 in his most accomplished manner. Patil supported him in a fourth-wicket stand of 48 in as many minutes, whereafter Kirmani, 25 in 85 minutes, and Yadav kept him company. Yadav, who resisted for 79 minutes, had his toe fractured by a yorker from Pascoe. Despite this, after taking a pain-killing injection he bowled throughout Australia's first innings. Doshi, although he did not know it at the time, toiled under a similar handicap, hav-ing been struck on the instep in the match against Victoria.

Australia also made a bad start, losing Dyson and Wood for 32 and Hughes at 81 before finding stability from a fourth-wicket partnership of 108 between Chappell and Border. Even on the second day, the pitch had lost most of what pace it had had, Chappell, who made 76, and Border, who was unbeaten that night with 95, hav-ing to graft for their runs. Batting until halfway through the third afternoon, Australia totalled 419. Border, staying just over another hour in the morning, made 124 off 265 balls, hitting twelve 4s and putting on 131 for the fifth wicket with Walters, who batted with much care for almost three and a half hours to score 78. Walters was sixth out at 356, but Australia continued to prosper through a fine innings by Marsh, who was partnered for 77 minutes by Lillee.

By the end of the third day, Gavaskar and Chauhan had reduced Australia's lead of 182 by 108, and on the fourth they added another 57 in 85 minutes before Gavaskar's contentious dismissal and dramatic walk-out. The incident disturbed the concentration of Chauhan, who, after batting in an agitated manner for another 8 runs, also succumbed to Lillee. With Vengsarkar, Viswanath and Patil helping towards rebuilding the innings, India at one stage were 296 for six, but the lower order surrendered quickly. When Australia batted again, with just over an hour left to the end of the fourth day, they needed 143 to win and India were without the bowling of Kapil Dev, who had strained a thigh muscle, and Yadav, whose injury had worsened from his efforts in the first innings. Doshi, too, was in great distress, but soldiered on. Nevertheless, the weakened attack made major inroads before the day was out, with Dyson, Wood and Chappell (out first ball, bowled behind his legs) all back in the dressing-room and only 24 runs on the board.

Kapil Dev, who had batted with a runner and had not appeared on the field on the previous day, joined the fray on the final morning and bowled unchanged to take five of the seven remaining Australian wickets that fell in just over two and a quarter hours. Following Lillee's lead, Kapil Dev bowled straight and to a length and let the pitch do the rest. The ball repeatedly kept low, but the Australians, as Chappell said afterwards, were 'lacking in the areas of application and determination'.

INDIA

*S.M. Gavaskar c Hughes b Pascoe	.10	– lbw b Lillee	.70
C.P.S. Chauhan c Yardley b Pascoe	.0	– c Yardley b Lillee	.85
D.B. Vengsarkar c Border b Lillee	.12	– c Marsh b Pascoe	.41
G.R. Viswanath c Chappell b Yardley	.114	– b Lillee	.30
S.M. Patil c Hughes b Lillee	.23	– c Chappell b Yardley	.36
Yashpal Sharma c Marsh b Lillee	.4	– b Pascoe	.9
Kapil Dev c Hughes b Pascoe	.5	– (8) b Yardley	.0
†S.M.H. Kirmani c Marsh b Lillee	.25	– (7) run out	.9
K.D. Ghavri run out	.0	– not out	.11
N.S. Yadav not out	.20	– absent hurt	.0
D.R. Doshi c Walters b Yardley	.0	– (10) b Lillee	.7
B 1, l-b 8, w 6, n-b 9	.24	B 11, l-b 8, n-b 7	.26

1/0 2/22 3/43 4/91   **237**   1/165 2/176 3/243 4/245   **324**
5/99 6/115 7/164 8/190 9/230   5/260 6/296 7/296 8/308 9/324

Bowling: FIRST INNINGS – Lillee 25-6-65-4; Pascoe 22-11-29-3; Chappell 5-2-9-0; Yardley 13-3-45-2; Higgs 19-2-65-0. SECOND INNINGS – Lillee 32.1-5-104-4; Pascoe 29-4-80-2; Yardley 31-11-65-2; Higgs 15-3-41-0; Border 2-0-8-0.

AUSTRALIA

J. Dyson c Kirmani b Kapil Dev	.16	– c Kirmani b Ghavri	.3
G.M. Wood c Doshi b Ghavri	.10	– st Kirmani b Doshi	.10
*G.S. Chappell c and b Ghavri	.76	– b Ghavri	.0
K.J. Hughes c Chauhan b Yadav	.24	– b Doshi	.16
A.R. Border b Yadav	.124	– (6) c Kirmani b Kapil Dev	.9
K.D. Walters st Kirmani b Doshi	.78	– (7) not out	.18
†R.W. Marsh c sub b Doshi	.45	– (8) b Kapil Dev	.3
B. Yardley lbw b Doshi	.0	– (5) b Kapil Dev	.7
D.K. Lillee c and b Patil	.19	– b Kapil Dev	.4
L.S. Pascoe lbw b Patil	.3	– run out	.6
J.D. Higgs not out	.1	– b Kapil Dev	.0
B 12, l-b 6, n-b 5	.23	L-b 5, n-b 2	.7

1/30 2/32 3/81 4/189   **419**   1/11 2/11 3/18 4/40   **83**
5/320 6/356 7/356 8/413 9/413   5/50 6/55 7/61 8/69 9/79

Bowling: FIRST INNINGS – Kapil Dev 19-7-41-1; Doshi 52-14-109-3; Ghavri 39-4-110-2; Yadav 32-6-100-2; Chauhan 2-0-8-0; Patil 12.3-4-28-2. SECOND INNINGS – Kapil Dev 16.4-4-28-5; Doshi 22-9-33-2; Ghavri 8-4-10-2; Patil 2-0-5-0.

Umpires: M.W. Johnson and R.V. Whitehead.

FIRST TEST MATCH

At Madras, September 18, 19, 20, 21, 22, 1986. Tied. On a hot and humid Monday, one of the most memorable Test match finishes was witnessed by some 30,000 spectators at Chepauk. For the second time in 1,052 Tests, the result was a tie, and coincidentally Australia had been involved each time. Yet there had been little hint of such a climax on the first four days; indeed, as India were being outplayed on the first three days, the thoughts of some Australians were possibly inclined to an innings victory. Only an inspired century against the odds by the Indian captain, Kapil Dev, precluded the possibility of India having to follow on after Australia had amassed their highest total in India – 574 in 742 minutes.

Border won the toss and Boon set the tone for positive Australian batting with his third Test hundred (331 minutes, 21 fours); all scored against India. On the second day, Jones cemented the solid start, first reaching his maiden Test hundred and then extending it to Australia's first double-hundred in a Test in India. Batting in all for 8 hours 23 minutes, facing 330 balls and hitting two sixes and 27 fours, Jones had to battle against the difficult weather conditions and overcome bouts of nausea and leg cramps. Yet he led the way in the partnership of 178 with Border, a record for Australia's fourth wicket against India. The Australian captain was dropped before scoring and twice more before reaching his nineteenth Test century in a little under four and a quarter hours.

Australia batted into the third day for 37 minutes; thereafter the Indians struggled against the workmanlike spin of Matthews and Bright. Srikkanth's aggressive 53 off 65 balls and a more chancy 50 off 59 balls by Azharuddin were entertaining but out of context, and by the close India still required 105 to make Australia bat again. Kapil Dev made sure they would with a free-flowing hundred off 109 balls. There were 21 fours in his 119, with 44 runs of his second fifty coming from boundaries. Matthews finished with five wickets in an innings for the first time.

Australia mustered 170 for five in the 49 overs available to them on the fourth day and Border declared first thing on the final morning, setting India 348 to win in a minimum of 87 overs. An opening stand of 55 announced what was assumed to be India's intention of a draw, but a century stand between Gavaskar, playing in his 100th consecutive Test match, and Amarnath pointed to different possibilities. When India went in to tea at 190 for two, a last-session chase (158 off 30 overs) was on the cards, and when the final twenty overs began, India were suitably placed with 118 needed and seven wickets in hand. However, at 251 Gavaskar mistimed a cover drive after 259 minutes' batting, and Kapil Dev, having promoted himself in the order, went 2 runs later. Azharuddin unsuccessfully tried to charge Bright, but Shastri took control with a clever mixture of outright offence and the safe picking of runs.

With 18 needed off the last 30 balls, the match seemed to be India's, but when Chetan Sharma, caught on the boundary, and More were dismissed in one over by Bright, a third possible result – an Australian victory – was sighted for the first time that day. Yadav, who had struck Matthews for six to take India within 7 runs of victory, was next out, bowled off his pads by Bright, leaving India 344 for nine with eight balls remaining. Maninder Singh defended the last two balls from Bright, which gave Shastri the strike for the last over, from Matthews. He blocked the first ball and, scenting victory off the second, hit a shade too eagerly: the ball went in front of deep square leg off a thick inside edge and a misfield enabled 2 runs to be taken safely. The next ball he placed calmly towards mid-wicket for the single which eliminated the possibility of an Australian win. Maninder defended the fourth ball, with some difficulty, and at 5.18 p.m. was leg-before to Matthews's penultimate delivery. The Australians were jubilant, none more so than a tiring Matthews, who had been bowling since the ninth over and had taken his second five-wicket return, giving him ten in a match for the first time. With Bright also taking five wickets, all ten wickets in India's second innings had fallen to spin.

Close of play: First day, Australia 211-2 (D.M. Jones 56*, R.J. Bright 1*); Second day, Australia 556-6 (G.R.J. Matthews 34*, S.R. Waugh 5*); Third day, India 270-7 (Kapil Dev 33*, Chetan Sharma 14*); Fourth day, Australia 170-5 (G.R.J. Matthews 27*, S.R. Waugh 2*).

AUSTRALIA

D.C. Boon c Kapil Dev b Chetan	122	– (2) lbw b Maninder	49
G.R. Marsh c Kapil Dev b Yadav	22	– (1) b Shastri	11
D.M. Jones b Yadav	210	– c Azharuddin b Maninder	24
R.J. Bright c Shastri b Yadav	30		
*A.R. Border c Gavaskar b Shastri	106	– (4) b Maninder	27
G.M. Ritchie run out	13	– (5) c Pandit b Shastri	28
G.R.J. Matthews c Pandit b Yadav	44	– (6) not out	27
S.R. Waugh not out	12	– (7) not out	2
B 1, l-b 7, w 1, n-b 6	15	L-b 1, n-b 1	2

1/48 2/206 3/282   (7 wkts, dec.) **574**   1/31 2/81 3/94   (5 wkts, dec.) **170**
4/460 5/481 6/544 7/574   4/125 5/165

†T.J. Zoehrer, C.J. McDermott and B.A. Reid did not bat.

Bowling: FIRST INNINGS – Kapil Dev 18-5-52-0; Chetan 16-1-70-1; Maninder 39-8-135-0; Yadav 49.5-9-142-4; Shastri 47-8-161-1; Srikkanth 1-0-6-0. SECOND INNINGS – Chetan 6-0-19-0; Kapil Dev 1-0-5-0; Shastri 14-2-50-2; Maninder 19-2-60-3; Yadav 9-0-35-0.

INDIA

S.M. Gavaskar c and b Matthews	8	– c Jones b Bright	90
K. Srikkanth c Ritchie b Matthews	53	– c Waugh b Matthews	39
M. Amarnath run out	1	– c Boon b Matthews	51
M. Azharuddin c and b Bright	50	– c Ritchie b Bright	42
R.J. Shastri c Zoehrer b Matthews	62	– (7) not out	48
C.S. Pandit c Waugh b Matthews	35	– (5) b Matthews	39
*Kapil Dev c Border b Matthews	119	– (6) c Bright b Matthews	1
†K.S. More c Zoehrer b Waugh	4	– (9) lbw b Bright	0
Chetan Sharma c Zoehrer b Reid	30	– (8) c McDermott b Bright	23
N.S. Yadav c Border b Bright	19	– b Bright	8
Maninder Singh not out	0	– lbw b Matthews	0
B 1, l-b 9, n-b 6	16	B 1, l-b 3, n-b 2	6

1/62 2/65 3/65 4/142 5/206   **397**   1/55 2/158 3/204 4/251 5/253   **347**
6/220 7/245 8/330 9/387   6/291 7/331 8/334 9/344

Bowling: FIRST INNINGS – McDermott 14-2-59-0; Reid 18-4-93-1; Matthews 28.2-3-103-5; Bright 23-3-88-2; Waugh 11-2-44-1. SECOND INNINGS – McDermott 5-0-27-0; Reid 10-2-48-0; Matthews 39.5-7-146-5; Bright 25-3-94-5; Border 3-0-12-0; Waugh 4-1-16-0.

Umpires: D.N. Dotiwala and V. Vikramraju.

SECOND TEST MATCH

At Eden Gardens, Kolkata, March 11, 12, 13, 14, 15, 2001. India won by 171 runs. Toss: Australia. A peripheral player best known by his initials single-handedly engineered one of the most remarkable victories in Test cricket. V.V.S. (Vangipurappu Venkat Sai) Laxman hit India's highest individual Test score as he converted a massive first innings deficit of 274 into a head-spinning advantage of 383. Such was his achievement that other heroic deeds that would normally have demanded attention paled by comparison. The young off-spinner Harbhajan Singh became the first Indian to take a Test hat-trick (dismissing Ricky Ponting, Adam Gilchrist and Shane Warne) on his way to a match haul of 13 wickets, Rahul Dravid silenced his critics with a timely innings of immense character, and Steve Waugh crafted a thrilling century before a crowd that embraced him as one of their own. [...]

Dropped catches and fielding lapses enabled the Australians to recover after the loss of six wickets for 76 had squandered the splendid start provided by Matthew Hayden, Michael Slater and Justin Langer. Once again it was Steve Waugh who led the fight-back, with his 25th Test century, and one he marked with an unusually open display of emotion – a run in an arc beyond the wicket and a series of joyful punches at the dusty sky. Jason Gillespie supported him in a ninth-wicket partnership of 133 in 190 minutes before Glenn McGrath enabled Waugh to reach his century as the pair added a breezy 43 in only 37 minutes for the last wicket. It seemed the final humiliation for India. They batted as though they were collectively beyond therapy, with only Laxman offering any resistance to an Australian attack superbly directed by McGrath.

Criticism later directed at Waugh for enforcing the follow-on was unwarranted. The decision was in keeping with his attacking philosophy, which had brought the team success in the previous 16 Tests and changed the mood of Test cricket the world over. Furthermore, India's first innings had occupied just 58.1 overs. There was no questioning of Waugh's judgment when Gillespie accounted for Tendulkar for 10 with a pearl of a delivery and India were three for 115 and still a colossal 159 runs in arrears. Indeed, such was the frustration of spectators that a water pouch was thrown at Tendulkar as he departed. A sense of frustration and despair was palpable as Saurav Ganguly joined Laxman.

It says much for Laxman's temperament that he was unaffected by the chaos which surrounded him. Before Laxman had removed his pads in the first innings Ganguly told him he would be granted his long-held wish to bat at No. 3 in the second innings [...] First he elicited support from the struggling Ganguly, adding 117 in 128 minutes for the fourth wicket, before he was joined by Dravid, who set about rebuilding his reputation as a world-class player. So effective was his rehabilitation that he stayed with Laxman throughout the fourth day, a day many thought would not have been required, adding a colossal 335 runs off the regulation 90 overs. [...] Ganguly's greatest challenge in the end was the timing of his declaration. He left it late, batting on even after Laxman failed to reach the triple century so fervently anticipated by the vast crowd. But the Australians, unused to being so aggressively challenged, capitulated before the guileful Harbhajan and Tendulkar, losing their last nine wickets for 106 after Hayden and Slater had again provided a sound foundation [...] In the end India won easily, inflicting Australia's first defeat since Kandy in September 1999. It was only the third time a team had followed on and won a Test match. Each time the losing side has been Australia.

Man of the Match: V.V.S. Laxman.

Close of play: First day, Australia (1) 8-291 (S.R. Waugh 29, Gillespie 6); Second day,India (1) 8-128 (Laxman 26, Raju 3): Third day, India (2) 4-254 (Laxman 109, Dravid 7); Fourth day, India (2) 4-589 (Laxman 275, Dravid 165).

AUSTRALIA

M.J. Slater c Mongia b Zaheer Khan ....42 –	(2) c Ganguly b Harbhajan Singh 43
M.L. Hayden c (sub) Badani	
b Harbhajan Singh ....97 –	(1) lbw b Tendulkar 67
J.L. Langer c Mongia b Zaheere Khan ......58 –	c Ramesh b Harbhajan Singh 28
M.E. Waugh c Mongia b Harbhajan Singh ..22 –	lbw b Venkatapathy Raju 0
*S.R. Waugh lbw b Harbhajan Singh ......110 –	c (sub) Badani b Harbhajan Singh ...24
R.T. Ponting lbw b Harbhajan Singh ....6 –	c Das b Harbhajan Singh 0
†A.C. Gilchrist lbw b Harbhajan Singh ......0 –	lbw b Tendulkar 0
S.K. Warne c Ramesh b Harbhajan Singh ....0 –	(9) lbw b Tendulkar 0
M.S. Kasprowicz lbw b Ganguly ....7 –	(10) not out 13
J.N. Gillespie c Ramesh b Harbhajan Singh .46 –	(8) c Das b Harbhajan Singh 6
G.D. McGrath not out ....21 –	lbw b Harbhajan Singh 12
B 19, l-b 10, n-b 7 36	B 6, n-b 8, penalty 5 19

(131.5 overs, 575 mins)   **445**   (68.3 overs, 272 mins)   **212**

Fall: 103 193 214 236 252 252 252   Fall: 74 106 116 166 166 167 173
269 402 445   174 191 212

Bowling: FIRST INNINGS – Zaheer Khan28.4-6-89-2; Venkatesh Prasad 30-5-95-0; Ganguly 13.2-3-44-1; Venkatapathy Raju 20-2-58-0; Harbhajan Singh 37.5-7-123-7; Tendulkar 2-0-7-0. SECOND INNINGS – Zaheer Khan 8-4-30-0; Venkatesh Prasad 3-1-7-0; Harbhajan Singh 30.3-8-73-6; Venkatapathy Raju 15-3-58-1; Tendulkar 11-3-31-3; Ganguly 1-0-2-0.

INDIA

S.S. Das c Gilchrist b McGrath ....20 –	hit wicket b Gillespie 39
S. Ramesh c Ponting b Gillespie ....0 –	c M.E. Waugh b Warne 30
R.S. Dravid b Warne ....25 –	(6) run out (S.R. Waugh/Kasprowicz) 180
S.R. Tendulkar lbw b McGrath ....10 –	c Gilchrist b Gillespie 10
*S.C. Ganguly c S.R. Waugh b Kasprowicz ..23 –	c Gilchrist b McGrath 48
V.V.S. Laxman c Hayden b Warne ....59 –	(3) c Ponting b McGrath 281
†N.R. Mongia c Gilchrist b Kasprowicz .....2 –	b McGrath 4
Harbhajan Singh c Ponting b Gillespie ....4 –	(9) not out 8
Zaheer Khan b McGrath ....3 –	(8) not out 23
S.L. Venkatapathy Raju lbw b McGrath 4	
B.K. Venkatesh Prasad not out 7	
L-b 2, n-b 12 14	B 4, l-b 14, w 2, n-b 14 34

(58.1 overs, 258 mins)   **171**   (178 overs, 737 mins)   (7 wkts, dec.) **657**

Fall: 0 34 48 88 88 92 97 113 129 171   Fall: 52 97 115 232 606 624 629

Bowling: FIRST INNINGS – McGrath 14-8-18-4; Gillespie 11-0-47-2; Kasprowicz 13-2-39-2; Warne 20.1-3-65-2. SECOND INNINGS – McGrath 39-12-103-3; Gillespie 31-6-115-2; Warne 34-3-152-1; M.E. Waugh 18-1-58-0; Kasprowicz 35-6-139-0; Ponting 12-1-41-0; Hayden 6-0-24-0; Slater 2-1-4-0; Langer 1-0-3-0.

Umpires: P. Willey (England) and S.K. Bansal. TV Umpire: S.N. Bandekar.
Referee: C.W. Smith (West Indies).

THIRD TEST MATCH

At M.A. Chidambaram Stadium (Chepauk), Chennai, March 18, 19, 20, 21, 22, 2001. India won by two wickets. Toss: Australia. Test debuts: S.V. Bahutule, S.S. Dighe. Memories of the 1986–87 tied Test at this ground were vividly evoked in a tense, hard-fought conclusion to the series. India managed to maintain its imposing home record against Australia and inflict the first series defeat on Steve Waugh's team since Sri Lanka's victory in 1999–2000.

In the end, the Australians did not have enough runs with which to manoeuvre, despite more remarkable batting by Matthew Hayden on the first two days. He carried all before him, this time compiling a consummate double-century to take his aggregate of runs for the series beyond 500. Hayden, who again swept spectacularly, provided his team-mates with the opportunity to bat India out of the game but they lacked the nous or the ability to do it. Australian batsmen have a history of insecurity against the best off-spin bowling, but on this occasion the middle and lower order were guilty of impulsive, thoughtless batting after a first day that had realised a handsome stumps score of three for 326. Hayden was the ninth batsman dismissed after almost eight hours at the crease in the enervating conditions for which the cement cauldron at Chennai is renowned. He faced 320 balls and struck 15 fours and six sixes in a thrilling assault on the Indian spinners. After taking 1/100 off 26 unusually nervous overs Harbhajan Singh again tormented the Australian batsmen with his turn, bounce and subtle variations in line, finishing the innings with 7/133 on his way to becoming only the 12th bowler and the second Indian to take 15 wickets in a Test.

Hayden's only substantial support came from the Waugh brothers. Not for the first time Mark Waugh again regained touch when he most needed it, surviving a stumping chance on nine to score 70 and follow it with the only half-century of the second innings. Steve Waugh, customarily the most vigilant and calculating of batsmen, had a rare lapse in concentration and became just the sixth player in 1,539 Tests to be out handled the ball. He had survived a leg before wicket appeal from Harbhajan, but as the ball bounced back towards him, he reflexively fended it away from the stumps with the palm of his right hand. [...]

After failing to impose himself on the first two Tests, Sachin Tendulkar scored his 25th Test century a month in advance of his 28th birthday. [...] There was an inevitability about his hundred, although Michael Slater at mid-wicket should have held the straightforward catch Tendulkar offered at 82 off the bowling of Colin Miller. The marauding Harbhajan never allowed Australia to take control of their second innings, taking 8/84 and finishing the series with 32 wickets (the next-best Indian bowler took three) and a richly deserved Man of the Series triumph. Then, in pursuit of a seemingly modest 155 on a pitch that, despite its appearance, remained hard and true, India were three for 101 when they collectively lost their nerve to plunge to seven for 135 and then eight for 151. As ever, the Australian bowlers, most notably the indefatigable Glenn McGrath and Jason Gillespie, endeavoured to atone for the deficiencies of their batting colleagues, and with the help of Miller went perilously close to defying extraordinary odds. But at the end, fittingly, Harbhajan struck the winning runs, and the Indian team, ridiculed just 10 days earlier, held aloft the glittering prize – the Border–Gavaskar Trophy.

Man of the Match: M.L. Hayden and Harbhajan Singh.

Close of play: First day, Australia (1) 3-326 (Hayden 147, S.R. Waugh 43); Second day, India (1) 1-211 (Das 84, Laxman 59); Third day, India (2) 4-480 (Bahutule 4, Kulkarni 0); Fourth day, Australia (2) 7-241 (S.R. Waugh 43).

AUSTRALIA

M.J. Slater c Laxman b Zaheer Khan	4	– (2) c Laxman b Harbhajan Singh	48
M.L. Hayden c Ganguly			
b Harbhajan Singh	203	– (1) c Zaheer b Kulkarni	35
J.L. Langer c Dravid b Harbhajan Singh	35	– (4) c Laxman b Bahutule	21
M.E. Waugh c (sub) Badani b Bahutule	70	– (5) c Dravid b Harbhajan Singh	57
*S.R. Waugh handled ball	47	– (6) c Das b Harbhajan Singh	47
R.T. Ponting st Dighe b Harbhajan Singh	0	– (7) c Dravid b Harbhajan Singh	11
†A.C. Gilchrist lbw b Harbhajan Singh	1	– (3) lbw b Harbhajan Singh	1
S.K. Warne c Das b Harbhajan Singh	0	– lbw b Harbhajan Singh	11
J.N. Gillespie c Ganguly b Harbhajan Singh	0	– c Dravid b Harbhajan Singh	2
C.R. Miller c Bahutule b Harbhajan Singh	0	– lbw b Harbhajan Singh	2
G.D. McGrath not out	3	– not out	11
B 8, l-b 10, n-b 10	28	B 8, l-b 6, n-b 4	18

(115.2 overs, 474 mins)   **391**   (97.5 overs, 373 mins)   **264**

Fall: 4 67 217 340 340 344 374
376 385 391

Fall: 82 84 93 141 193 211 241
246 251 264

Bowling: FIRST INNINGS – Zaheer Khan 15-5-57-1; Ganguly 2-1-11-0; Harbhajan Singh 38.2-6-133-7; Kulkarni 23-5-67-0; Bahutule 21-3-70-1; Tendulkar 16-1-35-0. SECOND INNINGS – Zaheer Khan 4-0-13-0; Ganguly 1-0-8-0; Harbhajan Singh 41.5-20-84-8; Kulkarni 30-11-70-1; Tendulkar 12-0-43-0; Bahutule 9-0-32-1.

INDIA

S.S. Das lbw b McGrath	84	– c and b McGrath	9
S. Ramesh c Ponting b Warne	61	– run out (Ponting/Gilchrist)	25
V.V.S. Laxman c M.E. Waugh b McGrath	65	– c M.E. Waugh b Miller	66
S.R. Tendulkar c Gilchrist b Gillespie	126	– c M.E. Waugh b Gillespie	17
*S.C. Ganguly c Gilchrist b McGrath	22	– c M.E. Waugh b Gillespie	4
R.S. Dravid c Gilchrist b Gillespie	81	– c S.R. Waugh b Miller	4
†S.S. Dighe lbw b Warne	4	– not out	22
S.V. Bahutule not out	21	– c Warne b Miller	0
Zaheer Khan c and b Miller	4	– c M.E. Waugh b McGrath	0
Harbhajan Singh c M.E. Waugh b Miller	2	– not out	3
N.M. Kulkarni lbw b Miller	4		
B 19, l-b 2, w 1, n-b 5	27	L-b 3, n-b 2	5

(165 overs, 697 mins)   **501**   (41.1 overs, 217 mins) (8 wkts)   **155**

Fall: 123 211 237 284 453 468 470 475 477 501   Fall: 18 76 101 117 122 135 135 151

Bowling: FIRST INNINGS – McGrath 36-15-75-3; Gillespie 35-11-88-2; Miller 46-6-160-3; Warne 42-7-140-2; Ponting 2-1-2-0; M.E. Waugh 3-0-8-0; Hayden 1-0-7-0. SECOND INNINGS – McGrath 11.1-3-21-2; Gillespie 15-2-49-2; Miller 9-1-41-3; Warne 6-0-41-0.

Umpires: R.E. Koertzen (South Africa) and A.V. Jayaprakash.
TV Umpire: C.R. Vijayaraghavan. Referee: C.W. Smith (West Indies).

1 0

NEW FRONTIERS: AUSTRALIA v. PAKISTAN AND SRI LANKA

Pakistan is the only country to have beaten Australia at their first meeting, albeit in a one-off Test played on mats at Karachi in October 1956 without the benefit of any preparatory matches. The game set a trend in matches between the two countries for the unforeseen, sometimes unfortunately so. Salim Malik remains the only international captain to try and suborn Australian cricketers, something not known when *Wisden* reported the Test in question at Karachi in September 1994, but infamous by the time the teams met again at Brisbane in November 1995.

This was not the first time *Wisden* had joined others in trying to work out what might be happening under the surface and behind the scenes in Pakistani cricket. Consider Phil Wilkins' puzzled study of Majid Khan on tour in Australia thirty years ago: 'His behaviour in Sydney was most strange for he adopted an inattentive attitude and occasionally sat down between deliveries at first slip.' Perhaps nobody should have been surprised when Majid's team, chasing 158 for their first victory in Australia, lost eight wickets for 54 and lost the game by 52 runs.

This section encompasses some unusual feats. Few stranger bowling analyses have featured in *Wisden* than Ken Mackay's on the mats of Dacca in November 1959: his 64–38–58–7 now reads like the specifications of a supermodel with IQ appended. It also contains its share of ugliness. No more repellent image has appeared in *Wisden* than that of Javed Miandad and Dennis Lillee shaping up to one another in Perth in November 1981 as if in a martial arts movie. Brian Osborne's description of the episode as 'one of the most undignified incidents in Test history' hardly does it justice; nor did the token suspension of Lillee from two one-day games imposed by Bob Merriman. Not that it checked the progress of either: Lillee is an inductee of the Australian Cricket Hall of Fame, Merriman the chairman of the Australian Cricket Board.

Australia's history with Sri Lanka is a brief one, spanning only thirteen Tests, though at least one of these, at the Sinhalese Sports Club's ground in September 1992, merits the status of a classic. Sri Lanka's collapse, losing 8 for 37 in incurring a 16-run defeat, delayed what should have been their first Test victory against Australia by seven years. *Wisden*'s report included Allan Border's excited comment: 'It must be the greatest heist since the Great Train Robbery.' Little did anyone know at the time how close were the relations between cricket and crime.

—GH

FIRST TEST MATCH

At Dacca, November 13, 14, 15, 17, 18, 1959. Australia won by eight wickets. Heavy rain prior to the match ruled out the possibility of it being played on grass and Pakistan, sent in by Benaud, soon lost Ijaz Butt on the matting pitch. Hanif Mohammad and Saeed Ahmed improved the position with a second-wicket stand of 72 and after the fall of the third wicket at 82, Hanif received notable assistance from Sharpe, who was making his Test debut. Mackay struck an important blow for Australia by dismissing Hanif, who had batted stolidly for 66, a quarter of an hour before the close of play on the first day. Sharpe batted attractively until he was splendidly run out by O'Neill from cover-point. Mackay proved too good for the tail and Pakistan were all out for 200.

Australia, too, found scoring difficult and despite an excellent innings of 96 by Harvey, they only secured first innings lead through Grout, whose spirited 66 not out, including seven 4's, came in an hour and twenty-five minutes. Fazal Mahmood was the most successful bowler for Pakistan with five wickets for 71. Mackay, bowling off-spinners on a perfect length, severely troubled Pakistan when they batted a second time and he finished with six for 42. Sharpe, alone, defied him for any length of time and Australia, needing 110 for victory, scored the runs for the loss of Favell and Harvey.

PAKISTAN

Hanif Mohammad b Mackay	66	– b Benaud	19
Ijaz Butt c Grout b Davidson	0	– b Mackay	20
Saeed Ahmed c Harvey b Davidson	37	– b Mackay	15
W. Mathias c and b Benaud	4	– lbw b Mackay	1
D. Sharpe run out	56	– lbw b Mackay	35
Wazir Mohammad c Meckiff b Benaud	0	– lbw b Benaud	5
Imtiaz Ahmad b Davidson	13	– b Mackay	4
Shuja-ud-din not out	2	– not out	16
Israr Ali st Grout b Benaud	7	– b Benaud	1
Fazal Mahmood b Benaud	1	– c and b Mackay	4
Nasim-ul-Ghani b Davidson	5	– c McDonald b Benaud	0
B 5, l-b 1, n-b 3	9	B 8, l-b 5, n-b 1	14

1/3 2/75 3/82 4/145 5/146 6/170 **200** 1/32 2/57 3/62 4/68 5/81 **134**
7/184 8/191 9/193   6/94 7/117 8/128 9/133

Bowling: FIRST INNINGS – Davidson 24.5-7-42-4; Meckiff 10-2-33-0; Lindwall 15.1-1-31-0; Benaud 35-10-69-4; Mackay 19-12-16-1. SECOND INNINGS – Davidson 11-3-23-0; Meckiff 3-1-8-0; Lindwall 2-0-5-0; Benaud 39.3-26-42-4; Mackay 45-26-42-6.

AUSTRALIA

C.C. McDonald lbw b Fazal	.19	– not out	.44
L. Favell b Israr Ali	.0	– c and b Israr Ali	.4
R.N. Harvey b Fazal	.96	– b Fazal	.30
N. O'Neill b Nasim	.2	– not out	.26
P. Burge c Imtiaz b Nasim	.0		
R. Benaud lbw b Nasim	.16		
K. Mackay b Fazal	.7		
A.K. Davidson b Israr Ali	.4		
W. Grout not out	.66		
R.R. Lindwall lbw b Fazal	.4		
I. Meckiff b Fazal	.2		
L-b 9	.9	B 3, l-b 3, n-b 2	.8
1/0 2/50 3/53 4/53 5/112 6/134	**225**	1/12 2/65	(2 wkts) **112**
7/143 8/151 9/189			

Bowling: FIRST INNINGS – Fazal 35.5-11-71-5; Israr 23-5-85-2; Nasim 17-4-51-3; Shuja 3-0-9-0. SECOND INNINGS – Fazal 20.1-4-52-1; Israr 9-0-20-1; Nasim 10-2-16-0; Shuja 8-4-12-0; Saeed Ahmed 1-0-4-0.

THIRD TEST MATCH

At Sydney, January 6, 7, 8, 10, 11, 1973. Australia won by 52 runs. Victory stared Pakistan in the face but their batsmen were overwhelmed by the occasion. On a green and responsive wicket, the Pakistan pace bowlers Saleem Altaf and Sarfraz Nawaz gave their side the chance to regain prestige only to see their batsmen fall to a remarkable piece of swing bowling by Walker who took six for 15 from 16 overs.

Australia had Stackpole, Edwards, Walters and Massie back in the team, but the selectors continued their experimentation for the West Indies tour by playing the Newcastle leg-spinner Watkins after only five first-class games. [...] Australia struggled hard throughout this game and that they won reflected no small credit on Ian Chappell and his team. With Lillee hampered by a back injury all seemed lost, especially when Pakistan gained a vital breakthrough in the Australian second innings.

Pakistan won the toss, a happy event in the circumstances, and had their trio of pace men used the new ball as skilfully on the first day as they did later, Australia would almost certainly have lost. Redpath survived for four hours for his 79, valuable runs painfully achieved after being dropped off Sarfraz at nine; Edwards made a neat 69.

Nasim had some good fortune, but played a number of splendid drives in his 64, prompting again the question why greater use was not made of this accomplished all-rounder. Mushtaq had had meagre success for a batsman of his repute but he made his first century against Australia in 28 Tests, and his fourth century in all. He played some fine cover drives in an innings of just under five hours, aided by Saleem Altaf in a stand of 56 when it appeared Mushtaq might be denied his hundred by lack of partners. Lillee delivered only 10 overs before he withdrew with a slight back strain and G.S. Chappell, who took the new ball with Massie, earned five wickets with his lively medium-pace.

In the last session of the third day, Saleem and Sarfraz seamed the ball dangerously to have Australia in a critical position at seven for 94, a lead of only 68 runs. Watkins and Massie shared a record ninth wicket partnership of 83 runs but with a lead of only 158, defeat for Australia seemed inevitable. Edwards brought off a superlative diving one-handed catch at point to dismiss Sadiq and this proved a major setback for the tourists. The following day, with Lillee returning to aid his team at reduced pace, Walker's swing and accuracy demoralised Pakistan, his six for 15 including a period of 30 deliveries in which he took five wickets for three runs. Lillee bowled splendidly as his support.

AUSTRALIA

K.R. Stackpole c Wasim b Sarfraz	28	– c Intikhab b Saleem ...9
I.R. Redpath run out	79	– c Nasim b Sarfraz ...18
*I.M. Chappell lbw b Sarfraz	43	– c Wasim b Sarfraz ...27
G.S. Chappell b Majid	30	– lbw b Sarfraz ...6
R. Edwards c Wasim b Saleem	69	– lbw b Saleem ...3
K.D. Walters b Asif Iqbal	19	– lbw b Saleem ...6
†R.W. Marsh c Wasim b Saleem	15	– c Zaheer b Saleem ...0
M.H.N. Walker c Majid b Sarfraz	5	– c Mushtaq b Sarfraz ...16
J.R. Watkins not out	3	– c Zaheer b Intikhab ...36
D.K. Lillee b Sarfraz	2	– not out ...0
R.A.L. Massie b Saleem	2	– c Sadiq b Mushtaq ...42
B 18, l-b 8, w 4, n-b 9	39	B 10, l-b 3, n-b 8 ...21

1/56 2/138 3/196 4/220   **334**   1/29 2/31 3/34 4/44   **184**
5/271 6/315 7/324 8/327 9/329   5/70 6/73 7/94 8/101 9/184

Bowling: FIRST INNINGS – Asif Masood 18-1-81-0; Saleem 21.5-3-71-3; Sarfraz 19-3-53-4; Majid 18-1-66-1; Intikhab 2-0-13-0; Asif Aqbal 2-0-11-1. SECOND INNINGS – Asif Masood 3-0-15-0; Saleem 20-5-60-4; Sarfraz 21-7-56-4; Intikhab 4-2-9-2; Asif Iqbal 2-0-10-0; Mushtaq 3.1-0-13-1.

PAKISTAN

Sadiq Mohammad c G.S. Chappell b Lillee	30	– c Edwards b Massie ...6
Nasim-ul-Ghani c Redpath b G.S. Chappell	64	– b Lillee ...5
Zaheer Abbas c Marsh b Massie	14	– c Redpath b Lillee ...47
Majid Khan b Massie	0	– lbw b Walker ...12
Mushtaq Mohammad c Walker b G.S. Chappell	121	– c Marsh b Lillee ...15
Asif Iqbal c Marsh b G.S. Chappell	65	– c Marsh b Walker ...5
*Intikhab Alam c Marsh b Massie	9	– c Watkins b Walker ...8
†Wasim Bari b G.S. Chappell	1	– c Edwards b Walker ...0
Saleem Altaf c Marsh b Walker	12	– c Massie b Walker ...0
Sarfraz Nawaz b G.S. Chappell	12	– c Redpath b Walker ...1
Asif Masood not out	1	– not out ...3
B 12, l-b 10, w 6, n-b 3	31	L-b 2, w1, n-b 1 ...4

1/56 2/79 3/83 4/131   **360**   1/7 2/11 3/52 4/83   **106**
5/270 6/279 7/280 8/336 9/349   5/88 6/93 7/95 8/95 9/103

Bowling: FIRST INNINGS – Lillee 10-2-34-1; Massie 28-6-123-3; Walker 16-2-65-1; G.S. Chappell 18.6-5-61-5; Walters 9-3-25-0; Watkins 6-1-21-0; I.M. Chappell 1-1-0-0. SECOND INNINGS – Lillee 23-5-68-3; Massie 7-4-19-1; Walker 16-8-15-6.

Umpires: T.F. Brooks and J.R. Collins.

PAKISTAN IN AUSTRALIA, 1978–79

By Brian Osborne

[...] Derogatory comments by Asif Iqbal on the eve of the Melbourne Test on the standards of the Australian and England teams in their series created ill-feeling that manifested itself in several incidents during the two Tests. These can only be described as unsportsmanlike and completely opposed to the best traditions of the game, even if they technically complied with the Laws of Cricket. In Melbourne, Hogg was run out by Miandad, who moved from silly point to break the wicket after the batsman, having played a defensive stroke a short distance down the wicket, left his crease to inspect the wicket. Although Hogg was recalled by Mushtaq, umpire Harvey confirmed his earlier decision. Hogg promptly struck down the stumps before leaving the wicket. At Perth, fast bowler Hurst ran out Sikander when he was 'backing up' ahead of the delivery – thus breaking a troublesome last wicket partnership with Asif who, in turn, wrecked his own wicket in the same style as Hogg. Then in the final Australian innings, the acting captain, Hilditch, at the non-striker's end, picked up the ball after a return from a fieldsman, handed it in a helpful manner to bowler Sarfraz, and was immediately the victim of an appeal and dismissal for 'handled the ball'. All three incidents were much to be deprecated. [...]

FIRST TEST MATCH

At Melbourne, March 10, 11, 12, 14, 15, 1979. [...] Yallop took advantage of winning his sixth toss in the seventh Test of the summer and so gave his pace battery the opportunity to use what little early life existed in the wicket. Both openers, Majid and Mohsin, were caught as they attempted to drive – Majid by the wicket-keeper and Mohsin in the slips – and when Zaheer was bowled at 28, Hogg had completed a fiery opening spell of six overs with three wickets for a personal cost of only nine runs. The recalled Clark then removed Asif Iqbal with a sharp, lifting delivery that carried from glove to Wright and only 40 runs were on the board. The captain, Mushtaq, set about a recovery and he received solid support from Imran and Sarfraz. Although earlier erratic, Hurst later played his part with three wickets when it appeared Australia had let their advantage slip from six wickets for 99 to the eventual Pakistan total of 196.

Australia, one for no wicket at the close and having included an additional batsman, appeared set for a big score. However, next morning, a between-wickets collision between openers Wood and Hilditch forced the former to retire with a sprained wrist and he did not return till the fall of the ninth wicket. Hilditch was quickly removed by Imran, and Yallop was twice dropped as he struggled to 20 in a brief partnership with Border. Both were bowled by Imran. Hughes became the eleventh Australian run out in the season's Test matches when Whatmore did not respond to a call. Nevertheless, the burly new Test batsman applied himself well for nearly three and a half hours to top score with 43 in a poor total that fell 28 runs short of Pakistan's. Hogg displayed his annoyance and enlivened proceedings by knocking down the stumps with his bat when he was given run out after walking from his crease before the ball was 'dead'. Although Hogg was recalled by the Pakistan captain, umpire Harvey refused to permit a reversal of the decision.

Pakistan used the third day to consolidate their position with aggressive batting. Mohsin cover-drove and hooked Hogg for boundaries before another fierce drive was brilliantly held by the bowler – his first catch in Test cricket. Majid and Zaheer then played glorious strokes all round the ground as they added 135 for the second wicket, taking particular toll of the new leg-spinner, Sleep. Starting the day with a delightful straight driven boundary off Hogg, Majid altogether hit sixteen 4s in his seventh Test century – 108 in three hours forty minutes. Zaheer's similarly positive approach was followed by Asif once he settled down, and Pakistan were 307 runs ahead when bad light stopped play twenty minutes early.

After rain delayed the resumption on the fourth day for an hour, Pakistan added a further 74 runs before declaring. Whatmore, substituting for Wood as opener, batted solidly for eighty minutes and shared a partnership of 49 with Hilditch, who – although dropped at 26 and 59 – batted steadfastly until he became Sarfraz's second victim of the innings. At the close, Australia, at 117 for two, needed 265 to win.

Within half an hour on the final morning, Yallop was foolishly run out, changing his call. This brought together Border and Hughes for a new Australia–Pakistan Tests fourth-wicket partnership which eclipsed by 2 runs the 175 of Ian Chappell and Ross Edwards in 1972–73. Combining concentration with tempered aggression, and unruffled by several dropped catches, the pair carried on steadily through the second new ball and until half an hour after tea, when Sarfraz bowled Border off a deflection with a beautiful ball that cut back sharply. Border batted six and a quarter hours and hit seven boundaries in an innings notable for his footwork.

The remainder of the innings is history. The injured Wood jabbed a catch to the wicket-keeper off the first ball, Sleep was yorked without scoring, and Hughes – attempting to resume the run-getting – lofted a catch to mid-off. Sarfraz then removed the remaining three batsmen without scoring to complete the dismissal of all wickets except Yallop (run out) and finish with nine wickets for 86. His match figures of eleven wickets for 125 comfortably won him the Man of the Match award. The aggregate match attendance was 37,495.

PAKISTAN

Majid J. Khan c Wright b Hogg	1	– b Border	108
Mohsin Khan c Hilditch b Hogg	14	– c and b Hogg	14
Zaheer Abbas b Hogg	11	– b Hogg	59
Javed Miandad b Hogg	19	– c Wright b Border	16
Asif Iqbal c Wright b Clark	9	– lbw b Hogg	44
*Mushtaq Mohammad c Wright b Hurst	36	– c sub b Sleep	28
Wasim Raja b Hurst	13	– c Wright b Hurst	28
Imran Khan c Wright b Hurst	33	– c Clark b Hurst	28
Sarfraz Nawaz c Wright b Sleep	35	– lbw b Hurst	1
†Wasim Bari run out	0	– not out	8
Sikander Bakht not out	5		
B 2, l-b 7, w 1, n-b 10	20	B 4, l-b 6, n-b 9	19

1/2 2/22 3/28 4/40	**196**	1/30 2/165 3/204	(9 wkts dec.) **353**
5/83 6/99 7/122 8/173 9/177		4/209 5/261 6/299 7/330 8/332 9/353	

Bowling: FIRST INNINGS – Hogg 17-4-49-4; Hurst 20-4-55-3; Clark 17-4-56-1; Sleep 7.7-2-16-1. SECOND INNINGS – Hogg 19-2-75-3; Hurst 19.5-1-115-3; Clark 21-6-47-0; Sleep 8-0-62-1; Border 14-5-35-2.

AUSTRALIA

G.M. Wood not out . . . . .5 –(6) c Bari b Sarfraz 0
A.M.J. Hilditch c Miandad b Imran . . . . .3 – b Sarfraz 62
A.R. Border b Imran . . . . .20 – b Sarfraz 105
*G.N. Yallop b Imran . . . . .25 – run out 8
K.J. Hughes run out .19 – c Mohsin b Sarfraz 84
D.F. Whatmore lbw b Sarfraz . . . . .43 – (1) b Sarfraz 15
P.R. Sleep c Bari b Imran . . . . .10 – b Sarfraz 0
†K.J. Wright c Imran b Raja . . . . .9 – not out 1
W.M. Clark c Mushtaq b Raja . . . . .9 – b Sarfraz 0
R.M. Hogg run out . . . . .9 – lbw b Sarfraz 0
A.G. Hurst c and b Sarfraz . . . . .0 – c Bari b Sarfraz 0
    B 1, l-b 5, w 2, n-b 8 16   B 13, l-b 13, n-b 9 35

1/11 2/53 3/63 4/97   **168**   1/49 2/109 3/128 4/305   **310**
5/109 6/140 7/152 8/167 9/167   5/305 6/306 7/308 8/309 9/310

Bowling: FIRST INNINGS – Imran 18-8-26-4; Sarfraz 21.6-6-39-2; Sikander 10-1-29-0; Mushtaq 7-0-35-0; Raja 5-0-23-2. SECOND INNINGS – Imran 27-9-73-0; Sarfraz 35.4-7-86-9; Sikander 7-0-29-0; Mushtaq 11-0-42-0; Raja 3-0-11-0; Majid 9-1-34-0.

Umpires: R.C. Bailhache and C.E. Harvey.

SECOND TEST MATCH

At Perth, March 24, 25, 26, 28, 29, 1979. Australia won by seven wickets. Pakistan never really recovered from the loss of half the side for 90 runs in the opening session of play after being sent in to bat. Australia, on the other hand, were much encouraged by brilliant batting and fielding from the recalled Darling, the Man of the Match, and achieved a comfortable win within the last hour of play. The withdrawal of Yallop because of injury gave Hughes the opportunity of becoming the first Western Australian to lead the national team, and it also enabled the season's leading scorer, Moss, to move into the Test arena at last.

A small attendance of 8,550 saw Majid steer Hogg's second ball of the innings most comfortably to fourth slip; and when Hurst, erratic at first, changed to Hogg's end, he soon reduced the innings to 49 for four. Mudassar was caught behind from a ball which appeared to touch pad rather than bat, Haroon followed quickly, and Wright brilliantly rose high to gather a top edge from the aggressive Zaheer. Miandad and Asif then added 41 in a determined stand that was broken in the last over before lunch when Darling raced from cover to throw down Asif's wicket as he attempted a sharp single. Despite a painful finger injury, Mushtaq defended stoutly as Miandad monopolised a stand of 86, only to be run out by another brilliant throw from Darling. Imran observed care as Miandad – capitalising on being dropped twice in Hogg's tenth over – progressed to his sixth Test century, scored in four hours with thirteen boundaries. [...] When the Pakistan innings folded before lunch on the second day, Miandad was unbeaten on 129 after a useful eighth-wicket partnership of 52 with Sarfraz. In the afternoon, Australia proceeded to 180 for three. [...] When Darling, on 75, surprisingly missed a drive and was leg before to Mudassar, he had hit eight boundaries in his entertaining stay of nearly three and a half hours.

Australia eventually went 50 runs ahead on the third day, but their highest Test score of the season had occupied nearly nine and a half hours against an attack weakened throughout by the absence of Mushtaq. Border top-scored with 85 but, after opening brightly on the previous evening, he was at the crease for thirteen minutes short of six hours and altogether failed to take advantage of the favourable conditions. Moss and Whatmore also disappointed in the light of their normal propensity for attractive cricket. Imran was the most dangerous of a very limited, defensive attack.

From 19 for one overnight, Pakistan's position deteriorated to an overall lead of only 103 runs when Yardley ended Haroon's invaluable innings of 47 with a brilliant catch at square leg off the fiercest of hook shots and then, 1 run later, trapped Mushtaq leg before as the sixth dismissal. Through all this, Asif had played with his customary style, and he now added all his skill and experience to monopolise a partnership of 92 with Imran. Showing the same capable defence as in the first innings, Imran contributed 15 of the runs before becoming Wright's seventh victim of the match – brilliantly taken by a diving leg-side catch near the end of the day's play.

Asif completed his century in three hours, fifty minutes with fourteen choice boundaries and on the final day he scored 33 of the 39 runs added as the last four wickets fell. Australia – with almost four and threequarter hours to achieve their objective – again received a good start with 87 runs on before Hilditch was given out to the controversial 'handled ball' decision. Darling wasted no time reaching his second fifty of the match and he was still in complete charge when brilliantly run out by substitute fieldsman Mohsin Khan. Border, in company with Moss – now showing much more command – kept up the momentum, and success duly came in the closing stages of the match to square the series. The aggregate match attendance was 21,847.

PAKISTAN

Majid J. Khan c Hilditch b Hogg	0	– c sub b Hogg	0
Mudassar Nazar c Wright b Hurst	5	– c Hilditch b Hurst	25
Zaheer Abbas c Wright b Hurst	29	– c Wright b Hogg	18
Javed Miandad not out	129	– c Wright b Hurst	19
Haroon Rashid c Border b Hurst	4	– c Yardley b Dymock	47
Asif Iqbal run out	35	– not out	134
*Mushtaq Mohammad run out	23	– lbw b Yardley	1
Imran Khan c Wright b Dymock	14	– c Wright b Hurst	15
Sarfraz Nawaz c Wright b Hurst	27	– c Yardley b Hurst	3
†Wasim Bari c Hilditch b Dymock	0	– c Whatmore b Hurst	0
Sikander Bakht b Dymock	0	– run out	0
L-b 3, w 3, n-b 5	11	B 3, l-b 8, n-b 12	23

1/0 2/27 3/41 4/49   **277** 1/0 2/35 3/68 4/86   **285**
5/90 6/176 7/224 8/276 9/277   5/152 6/153 7/245 8/263 9/263

Bowling: FIRST INNINGS – Hogg 19-2-88-1; Hurst 23-4-61-4; Dymock 21.6-3-65-3; Yardley 14-2-52-0. SECOND INNINGS – Hogg 20-5-45-2; Hurst 24.7-2-94-5; Dymock 23-5-72-1; Yardley 14-3-42-1; Border 4-0-9-0.

AUSTRALIA

W.M. Darling lbw b Mudassar	.75	– run out	.79
A.M.J. Hilditch c Zaheer b Imran	.41	– handled the ball	.29
A.R. Border c Majid b Miandad	.85	– not out	.66
*K.J. Hughes lbw b Sikander	.9		
J.K. Moss c Bari b Mudassar	.22	– not out	.38
D.F. Whatmore c Iqbal b Imran	.15		
†K.J. Wright c Bari b Mudassar	.16		
B. Yardley b Sarfraz	.19	– run out	.1
G. Dymock not out	.5		
R.M. Hogg b Imran	.3		
A.G. Hurst c Bari b Sarfraz	.16		
B 3, l-b 4, w 1, n-b 13	.21	L-b 13, n-b 10	.23

1/96 2/143 3/161 4/219   **327**   1/87 2/153 3/155   (3 wkts) **236**
5/246 6/273 7/297 8/301 9/304

Bowling: FIRST INNINGS – Imran 32-5-105-3; Sarfraz 35.1-7-112-2; Sikander 11-1-33-1; Mudassar 16-2-48-3; Miandad 2-0-8-1. SECOND INNINGS – Imran 17-1-81-0; Sarfraz 19-1-85-0; Mudassar 10.1-2-35-0; Miandad 2-0-12-0.

Umpires: A.R. Crafter and M.G. O'Connell.

THE PAKISTANIS IN AUSTRALIA, 1981–82

By Brian Osborne

[...] The confrontation between Miandad and Lillee was one of the most undignified incidents in Test history. Miandad, batting to Lillee, had turned a ball to the on side and was in the course of completing a comfortable single when he was obstructed by Lillee. In the ensuing fracas Lillee kicked Miandad, who responded by shaping to strike him with his bat. The Australian team imposed a $200 fine (£120 approx.) on Lillee and sought an apology from Miandad for his part in the affair. However, the umpires, who had assisted in quelling the incident, objected to the penalty as being too lenient and the matter was dealt with at a Melbourne hearing before Mr R. Merriman, the coordinator of the Australian Cricket Board's cricket sub-committee. His ruling was that Lillee's penalty, set by the players, was not sufficient and he imposed a suspension from Australia's two ensuing one-day internationals – against Pakistan and West Indies. No apology was forthcoming from Miandad, whose participation in the incident was also referred to in the umpires' report. [...]

FIRST TEST MATCH

At Perth, November 13, 14, 15, 16, 17, 1981. Australia won by 286 runs. Australia won the first Test effortlessly after being sent in to bat by Miandad. But the match was marred by a lamentable confrontation between fast bowler Lillee and the Pakistan captain. In reasonable batting conditions Australia scored only 154 for seven on the first day, off a miserly 74 overs. The Australian innings finished quickly on the second morning preparatory to a sensational batting collapse by Pakistan before the pace of Lillee and Alderman, who reduced them to 26 for eight wickets. Sarfraz, batting at No. 8, made 26, but the innings petered out at 62 – Pakistan's lowest total in a Test match. Lillee took five for 18, Alderman four for 36 including the first-ball dismissal of Rizwan-uz-Zaman, making his début. At the close of the second day Australia led by 288 with eight second-innings wickets standing, Chappell having gone cheaply.

Laird batted 298 minutes for 85 and Hughes 271 minutes for 106. Yallop batted with assurance for 38 and Border for 37 before being brilliantly caught low down at square leg by Mudassar Nazar. Marsh made an aggressive 47. Set to score 543 to win, Pakistan lost two early batsmen before Mansoor and Miandad took the score to 96, when Mansoor was dismissed by Thomson. There then followed the Lillee–Miandad fracas, after which Yardley's clever off-spin removed six batsmen in a row, including Miandad, top-scorer with 79, Wasim Raja and Imran Khan, to bring Australia a sweeping victory. [...]

AUSTRALIA

B.M. Laird c Bari b Imran	.27	– (2) c Bari b Imran ... .85
G.M. Wood lbw b Sikander	.33	– (1) b Qasim ... .49
*G.S. Chappell lbw b Imran	.22	– b Imran 6
K.J. Hughes b Sarfraz	.14	– c Majid b Imran ... .106
G.N. Yallop c and b Qasim	.20	– c Imran b Sikander ... .38
A.R. Border c Bari b Sarfraz	.3	– c Mudassar b Sikander ... .37
†R.W. Marsh c Qasim b Sikander	.16	– c Mansoor b Raja ... .47
B. Yardley c Bari b Imran	.9	– st Bari b Qasim ... .22
D.K. Lillee c Bari b Raja	.16	– not out 4
J.R. Thomson b Imran	.2	– not out 5
T.M. Alderman not out	.0	
L-b 5, w 1, n-b 12	.18	B 1, l-b 9, w 1, n-b 14 ... .25

1/45 2/81 3/89 4/113 5/119   **180**   1/92 2/105 3/192   (8 wkts dec.) **424**
6/136 7/154 8/165 9/180   4/262 5/327 6/360 7/412 8/416

Bowling: FIRST INNINGS – Imran 31.4-8-66-4; Sarfraz 27-10-43-2; Sikander 21-4-47-2; Qasim 3-1-6-1; Raja 1-1-0-1. SECOND INNINGS – Imran 39-12-90-3; Sarfraz 27-5-88-0; Sikander 23-3-79-2; Qasim 26-4-81-2; Raja 20-3-58-1; Miandad 1-0-2-0; Mudassar 2-1-1-0.

PAKISTAN

Mudassar Nazar c Marsh b Lillee	0	– lbw b Alderman	5
Rizwan-uz-Zaman lbw b Alderman	0	– c Marsh b Alderman	8
Mansoor Akhtar c Marsh b Alderman	6	– c Hughes b Thomson	36
*Javed Miandad c Hughes b Alderman	6	– b Yardley	79
Majid J. Khan c Marsh b Lillee	3	– c Marsh b Yardley	0
Wasim Raja c Thomson b Lillee	4	– c Hughes b Yardley	48
Imran Khan c Yardley b Lillee	4	– c Alderman b Yardley	31
Sarfraz Nawaz c Marsh b Alderman	26	– c and b Yardley	9
†Wasim Bari c Marsh b Lillee	1	– c Border b Yardley	20
Iqbal Qasim c Alderman b Thomson	5	– c Alderman b Lillee	4
Sikander Bakht not out	3	– not out	0
N-b 4	4	L-b 1, n-b 15	16

1/1 2/1 3/14 4/17 5/21   62   1/8 2/27 3/96 4/99 5/174   256
6/25 7/25 8/26 9/57   6/198 7/229 8/236 9/254

Bowling: FIRST INNINGS – Lillee 9-3-18-5; Alderman 10.2-2-36-4; Thomson 2-1-4-1. SECOND INNINGS – Lillee 20-3-78-1; Alderman 16-4-43-2; Thomson 12-4-35-1; Yardley 25.5-5-84-6.

Umpires: A.R. Crafter and M.W. Johnson.

FIRST TEST MATCH

At Sinhalese Sports Club, Colombo, August 17, 18, 19, 21, 22, 1992. Australia won by 16 runs. Toss: Sri Lanka. Test debut: R.S. Kaluwitharana.

The carelessness of Aravinda de Silva cost Sri Lanka what would have been their third and most famous victory since entering the Test arena in February 1982. With 54 runs needed from nearly 25 overs, de Silva, who had taken 37 from 32 balls with seven fours, attempted to strike McDermott for the second time over Border at mid-on. Border, at full stretch, ran 25 metres with the flight of the ball and held a magnificent catch over his shoulder.

From that moment Sri Lanka collapsed utterly, losing their last eight wickets for 37 runs. A crowd of 10,000, the biggest of the match, jeered them at the presentation ceremony. In just 17.4 overs they had squandered the impressive gains of the first three days, after Ranatunga had compelled the Australians to bat first on a damp pitch under overcast skies. The occasional seamer, Hathurusinghe, exploited the conditions with sharp and late movement to claim the wickets of Boon, Jones, Border and Waugh in just 24 balls as Australia were dismissed for 256 on the first day.

On a more docile pitch and beneath comparatively clear skies next day, the stylish Mahanama laid the foundations for Sri Lanka's first total of 500, in their 38th Test. Breaking further new ground, three of their number scored centuries in one innings. Gurusinha, wearing new contact lenses, played the anchor role, and batted eight hours 45 minutes for 137. With Ranatunga he added 230 for the fourth wicket – the second-highest partnership for Sri Lanka. Ranatunga and Kaluwitharana, on his debut, changed the tempo with audacious hundreds. Ranatunga took 127 from 192 balls, with 15 fours and three sixes; at the height of his assault, he thumped 29 off three overs from the leg-spinner, Warne. Meanwhile, Kaluwitharana, supposedly chosen as a specialist wicket-keeper, batted with breathtaking arrogance for an unbeaten 132 from 158 balls with 26 boundaries – nine against Warne and seven off McDermott.

[...] Though they lost five batsmen in clearing a deficit of 291, Australia entered the final morning 102 ahead with three wickets in hand. Matthews's responsible 64, which took Australia from 269 for five to 431 for nine, was one of four fifties from the seven top-order batsmen, who could not muster 100 runs between them in the first innings, and gallant resistance from tailenders McDermott, Warne and Whitney proved the ideal complement. A final total of 471 set Sri Lanka 181 in 58 overs and gave the visitors just a little optimism. Then, after de Silva's fateful error, Matthews returned four for 76 and with Warne, who claimed three in 13 balls without conceding a run, he engineered an improbable victory. It was a fine comeback for Matthews, ignored by the Australian selectors for the past year; it was also one of Australia's greatest fightbacks. Only once before had they won a Test after trailing by more than 200 on the first innings: in Durban in 1949–50 they beat South Africa by five wickets despite being bowled out for 75 in response to 311.

Man of the Match: G.R.J. Matthews.

Close of play: First day, Sri Lanka 9-0 (R.S. Mahanama 6*, U.C. Hathurusinghe 3*); Second day, Sri Lanka 265-3 (A.P. Gurusinha 87*, A. Ranatunga 69*); Third day, Australia 26-0 (T.M. Moody 8*, M.A. Taylor 9*); Fourth day, Australia 393-7 (G.R.J. Matthews 51*, C.J. McDermott 28*).

AUSTRALIA

M.A. Taylor lbw b Wickremasinghe 42	– (2) c Gurusinha b Anurasiri 43	
T.M. Moody lbw b Ramanayake 1	– (1) b Ramanayake 13	
D.C. Boon c Ramanayake b Hathurusinghe . .32	– c Ranatunga b Anurasiri 68	
D.M. Jones lbw b Hathurusinghe 10	– run out 57	
M.E. Waugh c Kaluwitharana		
b Hathurusinghe 5	– c Kaluwitharana b Wickremasinghe . .56	
*A.R. Border b Hathurusinghe 3	– c Gurusinha b Anurasiri 15	
G.R.J. Matthews lbw b Ramanayake 6	– c Kaluwitharana b Ramanayake 64	
†I.A. Healy not out 66	– lbw b Hathurusinghe 12	
C.J. McDermott c Ranatunga b Ramanayake . .22	– lbw b Ramanayake 40	
S.K. Warne c and b Anurasiri 24	– b Anurasiri 35	
M.R. Whitney c and b Wickremasinghe 13	– not out 10	
L-b 10, w 3, n-b 19 32	L-b 23, w 1, n-b 34 58	

1/8 (2) 2/84 (3) 3/94 (1) 4/96 (4)   **256**   1/41 (1) 2/107 (2) 3/195 (3)   **471**
5/109 (6) 6/118 (5) 7/124 (7)   4/233 (4) 5/269 (6) 6/319 (5)
8/162 (9) 9/207 (10) 10/256 (11)   7/361 (8) 8/417 (9) 9/431 (7) 10/471 (10)

Bowling: FIRST INNINGS – Ramanayake 20-4-51-3; Wickremasinghe 18-4-69-2; Hathurusinghe 22-5-66-4; Madurasinghe 10-1-21-0; Gurusinha 2-0-17-0; Anurasiri 12-2-22-1. SECOND INNINGS – Ramanayake 37-10-113-3; Wickremasinghe 19-0-79-1; Hathurusinghe 27-7-79-1; Anurasiri 35-3-127-4; Madurasinghe 14-1-50-0.

Sri Lanka

R.S. Mahanama c Healy b Waugh ....78 – c Boon b Matthews 39
U.C. Hathurusinghe c Taylor b Waugh .....18 – run out 36
A.P. Gurusinha c Jones b Whitney ....137 – not out 31
P.A. de Silva lbw b Matthews ....6 – c Border b McDermott 37
*A. Ranatunga c Warne b Matthews ......127 – c Border b McDermott 0
M.S. Atapattu b Matthews ....0 – b Matthews 1
†R.S. Kaluwitharana not out ....132 – b Matthews 4
C.P.H. Ramanayake c Healy b McDermott ...0 – lbw b Matthews 6
G.P. Wickremasinghe c Matthews
   b McDermott ....21 – c Waugh b Warne 2
A.W.R. Madurasinghe not out ....5 – (11) c Matthews b Warne 0
S.D. Anurasiri (did not bat)   – (10) c Waugh b Warne 1
   B 2, l-b 7, w 1, n-b 13 23   B 2, l-b 3, n-b 2 7

1/36 (2) 2/128 (1) 3/137 (4)   (8 wkts dec.) 547   1/76 (1) 2/79 (2) 3/127 (4)   **164**
4/367 (5) 5/367 (6) 6/463 (3)   4/132 (5) 5/133 (6) 6/137 (7)
7/472 (8) 8/503 (9)   7/147 (8) 8/150 (9) 9/156 (10) 10/164 (11)

Bowling: First Innings – McDermott 40-9-125-2; Whitney 32-10-84-1; Moody 17-3-44-0; Waugh 17-3-77-2; Warne 22-2-107-0; Matthews 38-11-93-3; Border 4-1-8-0. Second Innings – McDermott 14-4-43-2; Whitney 5-2-13-0; Moody 5-0-10-0; Matthews 20-2-76-4; Waugh 2-0-6-0; Warne 5.1-3-11-3.

Umpires: K.T. Francis and T.M. Samarasinghe. Referee: F.J. Cameron (New Zealand).

First Test Match

At National Stadium, Karachi, September 28, 29, 30, October 1, 2, 1994. Pakistan won by one wicket. Toss: Australia. Test debut: M.G. Bevan. Australia's new era, after the end of Allan Border's decade of captaincy, began with an epic encounter. What looked like Australia's first Test victory in Pakistan for 35 years was turned into a home triumph by the bold batting of Inzamam-ul-Haq and Mushtaq Ahmed on a slow, low pitch. Coming together at 258 for nine with the awesome task of averting Pakistan's first ever defeat at the National Stadium, Inzamam and Mushtaq added 57 on a worn pitch against the redoubtable leg-spin of Warne. To the unrestrained delight of a crowd chanting 'Allah-O-Akbar' (God is great), they accomplished their goal in 8.1 overs, against an attack weakened by the withdrawal of McDermott, with an infected toe, and then by injuries to McGrath and May. In the end, Warne and Angel, in his second Test, were the only front-line bowlers still standing. Pakistan had never scored as much as 314 in a fourth innings to win. […] It was especially deflating for Taylor, the first man to score a pair of spectacles in his first Test as captain. He had decided to take the new ball at 229 for seven, when Warne was in full cry. The final result was disappointing for both Warne, who gave another command performance – eight for 150 from 63.1 overs – and Michael Bevan, who announced his arrival in the Test arena with a composed 82. It was especially dispiriting for the vice-captain and wicket-keeper, Healy, who blamed himself for the defeat: Pakistan gained the winning runs from four leg-byes when Inzamam was out of his ground attacking Warne.

The Australians had converted a useful first-innings lead of 81 into a handsome overall advantage of 313, thanks principally to Boon, who scored his 19th century in 90 Tests, and added 122 in 174 minutes with Mark Waugh. Waugh's dismissal precipitated a collapse of eight wickets for 61 runs, the last five for just 19 in 9.2 overs, against the irresistible fast bowling of Wasim Akram and Waqar Younis. Wasim finished with a match analysis of eight for 138 and Waqar seven for 144. They were responsible for six ducks over Australia's two innings. Flamboyant opener Saeed Anwar was inspired to play two wonderfully expressive hands of 85 and 77.

Just when it seemed Australia's ensign might finally be raised again in Pakistan, his efforts were backed up by Inzamam, who was undefeated over two hours and 35 minutes, Rashid Latif, with a daring 35 from 56 balls at No. 9, and Mushtaq. Pakistan's famous victory was only the seventh by one wicket in Tests. It was Australia's third wafer-thin failure in successive seasons, following the defeat by one run against West Indies at Adelaide in 1992–93 and by five runs against South Africa at Sydney in 1993–94.

Man of the Match: S.K. Warne.

Close of play: First day, Australia 325-7 (I.A. Healy 54*); Second day, Pakistan 209-7 (Wasim Akram 12*, Akram Raza 1*); Third day, Australia 181-5 (D.C. Boon 85*, I.A. Healy 3*); Fourth day, Pakistan 155-3 (Saeed Anwar 67*, Akram Raza 1*).

AUSTRALIA

M.J. Slater lbw b Wasim Akram 36	– (2) lbw b Mushtaq Ahmed 23	
*M.A. Taylor c and b Wasim Akram 0	– (1) c Rashid Latif b Waqar Younis 0	
D.C. Boon b Mushtaq Ahmed 19	– not out 114	
M.E. Waugh c Zahid Fazal		
b Mushtaq Ahmed 20	– b Waqar Younis 61	
M.G. Bevan c Aamir Sohail		
b Mushtaq Ahmed 82	– b Wasim Akram 0	
S.R. Waugh b Waqar Younis 73	– lbw b Wasim Akram 0	
†I.A. Healy c Rashid Latif b Waqar Younis ..57	– c Rashid Latif b Wasim Akram 8	
S.K. Warne c Rashid Latif b Aamir Sohail ...22	– lbw b Waqar Younis 0	
J. Angel b Wasim Akram 5	– c Rashid Latif b Wasim Akram 8	
T.B.A. May not out 1	– b Wasim Akram 1	
G.D. McGrath b Waqar Younis 0	– b Waqar Younis 1	
B 2, l-b 12, n-b 8 22	B 7, l-b 4, n-b 5 16	

1/12,(2) 2/41 (3) 3/75 (4) 4/95 (1)   **337**   1/1 (1) 2/49 (2) 3/171 (4) 4/174 (5)   **232**
5/216 (6) 6/281 (5) 7/325 (8)   5/174 (6) 6/213 (7) 7/218 (8)
8/335 (7) 9/335 (9) 1337 (11)   8/227 (9) 9/229 (10) 10/232 (11)

Bowling: FIRST INNINGS – Wasim Akram 25-4-75-3; Waqar Younis 19.2-2-75-3; Mushtaq Ahmed 24-2-97-3; Akram Raza 14-1-50-0; Aamir Sohail 5-0-19-1; Salim Malik 1-0-7-0. SECOND INNINGS – Wasim Akram 22-3-63-5; Waqar Younis 18-2-69-4; Mushtaq Ahmed 21-3-51-1; Akram Raza 10-1-19-0; Aamir Sohail 7-0-19-0.

PAKISTAN

Saeed Anwar c M.E. Waugh b May	.85	– c and b Angel	.77
Aamir Sohail c Bevan b Warne	.36	– run out	.34
Zahid Fazal c Boon b May	.27	– c Boon b Warne	.3
*Salim Malik lbw b Angel	.26	– c Taylor b Angel	.43
Basit Ali c Bevan b McGrath	.0	– (6) lbw b Warne	.12
Inzamam-ul-Haq c Taylor b Warne	.9	– (8) not out	.58
†Rashid Latif c Taylor b Warne	.2	– (9) lbw b S.R. Waugh	.35
Wasim Akram c Healy b Angel	.39	– (7) c and b Warne	.4
Akram Raza b McGrath	.13	– (5) lbw b Warne	.2
Waqar Younis c Healy b Angel	.6	– c Healy b Warne	.7
Mushtaq Ahmed not out	.2	– not out	.20
L-b 7, n-b 4	.11	B 4, l-b 13, n-b 3	.20

1/90 (2) 2/153 (1) 3/154 (3) 4/157 (5)   **256**   1/45 (2) 2/64 (3) 3/148 (4)   **(9 wkts) 315**
5/175 (6) 6/181 (7) 7/200 (4)   4/157 (5) 5/174 (1) 6/179 (7)
8/234 (9) 9/253 (10) 10/256 (8)   7/184 (6) 8/236 (9) 9/258 (10)

Bowling: FIRST INNINGS – McGrath 25-6-70-2; Angel 13.1-0-54-3; May 20-5-55-2; Warne 27-10-61-3; S.R. Waugh 2-0-9-0. SECOND INNINGS – McGrath 6-2-18-0; Angel 28-10-92-2; S.R. Waugh 15-3-28-1; Warne 36.1-12-89-5; May 18-4-67-0; M.E. Waugh 3-1-4-0.

Umpires: H.D. Bird (England) and Khizar Hayat. Referee: J.R. Reid (New Zealand).

FIRST TEST MATCH

At Brisbane, November 9, 10, 11, 13, 1995. Australia won by an innings and 126 runs. Toss: Australia. Test debut: Salim Elahi. After Warne's match-rigging allegations against Salim Malik, dramatic necessity dictated that the pair should confront each other at the Gabba. Warne dismissed Malik for nought, fourth ball, which was as satisfying in itself for Australia as the entire lop-sided result, achieved with more than five sessions to spare. On the first day Malik had made a splendid diving catch at midwicket to dismiss Australia's captain, Taylor, and had needed six stitches in split webbing on his left hand. By the time he walked out to bat at No. 8 in Pakistan's second innings, to sporadic abuse, with overwhelming defeat beckoning and his hand heavily strapped, all Australia had cast Warne in the role of avenging angel. Malik offered a hesitant leading edge against a slightly turning top-spinner and McDermott plunged to hold a low catch at mid-off.

The fielders' temperate reaction was testimony to Taylor's positive influence, but Warne, understandably, could not resist commenting after the match. 'It showed that there is justice in the game,' he said. Warne's match figures of 44–19–77–11 took his record in three Tests at the Gabba, a traditional haven for seam bowling, to 30 wickets at 10.40. Brisbane's extra bounce enabled him to make full use of flight and dip as well as turn. At times, by his own high standards, he did not bowl uncommonly well, but he did not need to, such was his psychological hold over the batsmen.

Australia spent the best part of two days making 463. [...] Steve Waugh scored an unbeaten six-hour 112, characterised by his singular method against short balls, jumping up and nudging where others would prefer to hook or avoid. He himself called it an ugly innings and he was missed twice in the eighties off Aamir Sohail's left-arm spin. Pakistan, 40 for three on the second evening, capitulated to 97 all out, with Warne's morning's work amounting to six for 16 in 12.1 overs. Though temporarily denied Malik, his dominance was otherwise complete. Sohail – the only one to reach 20 – was stumped trying to sweep; Basit Ali was deceived by flight, Wasim by bounce; Moin misguidedly heaved to leg. The greatest culprit was Inzamam, who scooped suicidally to short mid-wicket as he sought to lift Warne out of the ground.

Sohail's indignation fuelled a dynamic 99 when Pakistan followed on, and they had regained some respect at 217 for three on the fourth morning. Then Mark Waugh, brought on simply to allow Warne to switch ends, tempted Inzamam to spoon him to mid-off, and Pakistan's last seven wickets – Malik among them – duly fell for 23, with Australia securing victory after only 88 minutes cricket.

Man of the Match: S.K. Warne. *Attendance*: 23,639.

Close of play: First day, Australia 262-4 (S.R. Waugh 24*, G.S. Blewett 0*); Second day, Pakistan 40-3 (Aamir Sohail 17*); Third day, Pakistan 197-3 (Inzamam-ul-Haq 56*, Basit Ali 11*).

AUSTRALIA

*M.A. Taylor c Salim Malik	P.R. Reiffel lbw b Waqar Younis 9
b Saqlain Mushtaq 69	S.K. Warne c Moin Khan
M.J. Slater c Mohammad Akram	b Aamir Sohail 5
b Wasim Akram 42	C.J. McDermott b Waqar Younis 8
D.C. Boon c Inzamam-ul-Haq	G.D. McGrath st Moin Khan
b Aamir Sohail .5	b Wasim Adram 5
M.E. Waugh c Salim Elahi	B 2, l-b 6, w 4, n-b 13 25
b Saqlain Mushtaq 59	
S.R. Waugh not out 112	1/107 (1) 2/119 (2) 3/213 (4) **463**
G.S. Blewett lbw b Waqar Younis 57	4/250 (3) 5/385 (6) 6/411 (7)
†I.A. Healy c sub (Mushtaq Ahmed)	7/434 (8) 8/441 (9)
b Mohammad Akram 18	9/452 (10) 10/463 (11)

Bowling: Wasim Akram 38-9-84-2; Waqar Younis 29.5-7-101-3; Mohammad Akram 33.1-4-97-1; Saqlain Mushtaq 44-12-130-2; Aamir Sohail 16.5-2-43-2.

PAKISTAN

Aamir Sohail st Healy b Warne	.32	– b McGrath	.99
Salim Elahi c Taylor b McDermott	.11	– c Healy b McGrath	.2
Ramiz Raja c Taylor b Warne	.8	– c Healy b McGrath	.16
Saqlain Mushtaq lbw b McGrath	.0	– (9) not out	.2
Inzamam-ul-Haq c S.R. Waugh b Warne	.5	– (4) c McDermott b M.E. Waugh	.62
Basit Ali c Taylor b Warne	.1	– (5) lbw b McGrath	.26
†Moin Khan c McDermott b Warne	.4	– (6) c Healy b Reiffel	.9
*Wasim Akram c Boon b Warne	.1	– (7) c Slater b Warne	.6
Waqar Younis not out	.19	– (10) lbw b Warne	.0
Mohammad Akram c Blewett b Warne	.1	– (11) lbw b Warne	.0
Salim Malik absent hurt	–	(8) c McDermott b Warne	.0
B 4, l-b 5, n-b 6	.15	B 7, n-b 11	.18

1/20 (2) 2/37 (3) 3/40 (4) 4/62 (1)   **97**   1/30 (2) 2/88 (3) 3/167 (1) 4/217 (4)   **240**
5/66 (5) 6/70 (7) 7/70 (6)   5/218 (5) 6/233 (7) 7/233 (8)
8/80 (8) 9/97 (10)   8/239 (6) 9/240 (10) 10/240 (11)

Bowling: FIRST INNINGS – McDermott 11-4-32-1; McGrath 14-3-33-1; Warne 16.1-9-23-7. SECOND INNINGS – McDermott 11-0-47-0; Reiffel 15-4-47-1; McGrath 25-7-76-4; Warne 27.5-10-54-4; S.R. Waugh 2-1-3-0; M.E. Waugh 5-2-6-1.

Umpires: K.E. Liebenberg (South Africa) and S.G. Randell.
Referee: R. Subba Row (England).

SECOND TEST MATCH

At Peshawar, October 15, 16, 17, 18, 19, 1998. Drawn. Toss: Australia.

If ever a sound typified a Test then it was the mellow thwack of the ball meeting the middle of Mark Taylor's bat during his undefeated 334 in this game. On a flat, evenly grassed yellow pitch, which hardly changed appearance over five days, Taylor played as well as he ever had in his ten-year Test career. After a less than perfect start against some very fast bowling from Shoaib Akhtar, Taylor made barely an error, hitting the ball with the sweet spot of his bat hour after hour. His pulling was brutal, his cutting precise. […]

After Shoaib's first spectacular spell, which removed Slater with the score at 16, Taylor and Langer settled into a 279-run stand for the second wicket, asserting a dominance of bat over ball which never faltered. Their partnership became the highest for any wicket in Australia–Pakistan Tests, eclipsing 259, also for the second wicket, by another pair of left-handers, Wayne Phillips and Graham Yallop, at Perth in 1983–84. On the second day, Australia added 375 for the loss of three wickets. At stumps, they were 599 for four, with Taylor unbeaten on 334 and level with Bradman's Australian record at Headingley in 1930. He clipped the final ball of the day, from Aamir Sohail, towards square leg, but Ijaz, who had hardly excelled in the field before then, threw down a hand and managed to stop what would have been a record-breaking single.

Taylor had batted for exactly 12 hours and 564 balls, hitting 32 fours and a six. His innings was the seventh-highest score in Test history, the 15th triple-century and the fifth by an Australian. He also became the fourth Australian to pass 7,000 Test runs. Yet more drama followed next morning as the news spread around the ground – and the world – that Taylor had sacrificed the chance of breaking both Bradman's mark and Brian Lara's world record 375 by declaring. Immediately the theorising and myth-making began. One explanation which quickly gained currency was that he had refused to pass the record of Bradman, the greatest batsman the game has produced. The simplest explanation was the correct one: Taylor thought 599 in two days was more than enough runs, and he wanted to try to win by giving his bowlers a chance at Pakistan's batsmen from the start of the third day. There were a number of team meetings that evening, and several players urged Taylor to bat on and beat Lara. But it was typical of his approach to the game that he should be aware of the record without being obsessed by it.

The declaration did not help. As the Pakistanis came to the crease, it became more and more obvious that this pitch would have been more suitable for a timeless Test than one scheduled for a mere five days. Pakistan were able to declare 19 behind, at 580 for nine, with Saeed Anwar making a polished 126, Ijaz a typically brutal 155 and Inzamam-ul-Haq a patchy 97. It was the third time Inzamam had passed 90 without reaching a century in Tests at Peshawar. Australia resumed on the fourth evening and reached 289 for five before the match was called off. Taylor led the way again with 92, bringing his match tally to 426 for once out; only Graham Gooch, with 456 against India in 1990, had scored more runs in a single Test. And he had stamped his name forever on a game that would otherwise have seemed wholly pointless.

The postscript to the game came weeks later when Taylor visited Bradman at his home in Adelaide, and the Don thanked him – as he had in a letter – for not exceeding his record. The thanks might have been better directed at Ijaz.

Man of the Match: M.A. Taylor.

Close of the play: First day, Australia 224-1 (Taylor 112*, Langer 97*); Second day, Australia 599-4 (Taylor 334*, Ponting 76*); Third day, Pakistan 329-2 (Ijaz Ahmed 125*, Inzamam-ul-Haq 31*); Fourth day, Australia 21-0 (Slater 7*, Taylor 13*).

AUSTRALIA

*M.A. Taylor not out	334	– (2) b Aamir Sohail	92
M.J. Slater c Azhar Mahmood			
b Shoaib Akhtar	2	– (1) lbw b Mushtaq Ahmed	21
J.L. Langer c Moin Khan			
b Azhar Mahmood	116	– c Yousuf Youhana b Mushtaq Ahmed	14
M.E. Waugh c Salim Malik b Aamir Sohail	42	– b Shoaib Akhtar	43
S.R. Waugh c Moin Khan b Shoaib Akhtar	1	– not out	49
R.T. Ponting not out	76	– lbw b Ijaz Ahmed	43
†I.A. Healy (did not bat)		– not out	14
L-b 9, w 3, n-b 16	28	L-b 4, n-b 9	13

1/16 (2) 2/295 (3) (4 wkts dec.) **599** 1/39 (1) 2/67 (3) 3/170 (2) (5 wkts) **289**
3/418 (4) 4/431 (5) 4/179 (4) 5/269 (6)

D.W. Fleming, C.R. Miller, S.C.G. MacGill and G.D. McGrath did not bat.

Bowling: FIRST INNINGS – Shoaib Akhtar 31-6-107-2; Mohammad Zahid 16-0-74-0; Mushtaq Ahmed 46-3-153-0; Azhar Mahmood 23-2-82-1; Aamir Sohail 42-8-111-1; Salim Malik 16-0-63-0. SECOND INNINGS – Shoaib Akhtar 16-2-68-1; Azhar Mahmood 3-0-18-0; Mushtaq Ahmed 20-1-59-2; Mohammad Zahid 10-2-42-0; Aamir Sohail 10-1-35-1; Salim Malik 15-1-30-0; Ijaz Ahmed 14-1-33-1.

PAKISTAN

Saeed Anwar c Healy b Miller 126
*Aamir Sohail c Fleming b McGrath 31
Ijaz Ahmed sen. c Healy b MacGill 155
Inzamam-ul-Haq c Healy b S.R. Waugh ..97
Salim Malik c Taylor b McGrath 49
Yousuf Youhana c S.R. Waugh
    b MacGill 28
†Moin Khan c Healy b Ponting 0
Azhar Mahmood c Langer b McGrath ...26

Shoaib Akhtar did not bat.

Mushtaq Ahmed not out 48
Mohammad Zahid lbw b Fleming 1
    B 5, l-b 9, n-b 4 19

1/45 (2) 2/256 (1)   (9 wkts dec.) **580**
3/371 (3) 4/454 (4)
5/500 (5) 6/501 (7)
7/521 (6) 8/571 (8) 9/580 (10)

Bowling: McGrath 36-8-131-3; Fleming 35.1-6-103-1; MacGill 42-5-169-2; Miller 38-12-99-1; M.E. Waugh 8-0-32-0; S.R. Waugh 8-1-19-1; Ponting 5-1-13-1.

Umpires: S.A. Bucknor (West Indies) and Mohammad Nazir.
Referee: P.L. van der Merwe (South Africa).

SECOND TEST MATCH

At Bellerive Oval, Hobart, November 18, 19, 20, 21, 22, 1999. Australia won by four wickets. Toss: Australia.

Australia's cricketers often talk about the importance of winning the big moments in matches, and the Hobart Test was an example of how the theory works. Pakistan crafted themselves a winning position on the fourth day at Bellerive Oval, but could not close the deal on the fifth. Set a formidable 369 to win the match and seal another series victory, Australia were a precarious five for 126 late on the fourth day. But Adam Gilchrist, playing in only his second Test match, was accosted by Justin Langer when he walked to the wicket. 'You never know,' said the more experienced left-hander of the pair. Their union yielded 238 runs, the third-highest ever by an Australian pair for the sixth wicket, and took Australia to the cusp of a famous victory. The climax came at three o'clock on the final day when Gilchrist hoisted Saqlain Mushtaq into the deep for the winning run. In the excitement of the moment, clear-headed Gilchrist had to remind his partner, Shane Warne, to complete the run. With a chanceless 149 not out in such circumstances against a high-quality quartet of bowlers, Gilchrist had announced himself as a player of considerable stature.

Langer contributed 127, a cathartic innings after his place in the team had been questioned. That he top-edged Saqlain to be caught when just five more runs were needed only served to show that there are few fairytales in cricket. Langer was embraced by his father, Colin, at the gate, for the job was all but complete. Three balls later, Gilchrist, who had played what his captain called 'one of the great Test match innings', clinched Australia's four-wicket victory. It was a match with numerous twists and sub-plots, punctuated with breathtaking cricket. The Australians drew in several members of Sir Donald Bradman's 'Invincibles' for their team gathering on the eve of the match; they could not have known how appropriate the appearance of the likes of Arthur Morris would become. In 1948, Bradman's team chased and extracted three for 404 at Headingley to defeat England, and the chase inspired by Gilchrist and Langer was second only to that among Australian fourth-innings journeys. [...]

Pakistan were rolled for a poor 222, with only Mohammad Wasim going past 30. His 91 was laced with speculative shots, and three times in one over from Warne he lofted boundaries. But on the notoriously batsman-friendly Bellerive, Pakistan did not look to have enough runs. It was a notion that carried more weight when Australia reached one for 191 after lunch on the second day. Michael Slater had been dropped four times, and the slipshod Pakistanis threatened to unravel. But having plumbed the depths, Pakistan suddenly surged behind Waqar Younis' brief, furious spell, ripping his patented yorker through Mark Waugh and bowling Ricky Ponting with a ball that the Tasmanian did not deign to play. Slater fell three runs short of another century, and Saqlain's fabled 'doosra', the ball that goes on with the arm, bamboozled the Australians. He took 6/46 as the last nine Australian wickets tumbled for only 55 runs.

Australia's lead had been kept to only 24, and Saeed Anwar helped himself to 78 before he was bowled by Warne's massive leg-break out of the bowlers' footmarks. A trimmer Inzamam-ul-Haq celebrated his loss of seven kilograms of flab, due to a fitness campaign, by compiling a delightful 118. By the time Warne had prised out the Pakistanis early on the fourth day, they had set Australia 369. Time was not an issue, but early wickets tipped the balance Pakistan's way, and though Gilchrist and Langer engaged in a counter-attack, Australia's position at stumps on the fourth evening seemed precarious to say the least.

When play resumed on the final day, Gilchrist showed a remarkable knack of playing his natural game regardless of the circumstances, so that Steve Waugh would observe that he performed 'as if he's playing in his own backyard'. His century, raised with a sublime off-drive just before lunch, took only 110 balls, the second 50 in just 38 deliveries. Langer had survived a confident shout for caught behind from Wasim Akram's bowling when he was 76, and umpire Peter Parker's shake of the head proved to be the final straw for Pakistan. [...] The Australians had watched super slow-motion videotape of Saqlain between innings, such was their concern, but in the end it was left-handedness that helped them most. [...] (*Martin Blake*)

Man of the Match: J.L. Langer. *Attendance*: 20, 730

Close of play: First day, Australia (12) 0-29 (Slater 16, Blewett (9); Second day, Pakistan (2) 1-61 (Saeed Anwar 36, Saqlain Mushtaq 0); Third day, Pakistan (2) 7-351 (Inzamam-ul-Haq 116, Wasim Akram 1); Fourth day, Australia (2) 5-188 (Langer 52, Gilchrist 45).

PAKISTAN

Saeed Anwar c Warne b McGrath	.0 –	b Warne	.78
Mohammad Wasim c Gilchrist b Muller	.91 –	c McGrath b Muller	.20
Ijaz Ahmed c Slater b McGrath	.6 –	(4) c S.R. Waugh b McGrath	.82
Inzamam-ul-Haq b Muller	.12 –	(5) c M.E. Waugh b Warne	118
Yousuf Youhana c M.E. Waugh			
b Fleming	.17 –	(6) c Ponting b Fleming	.2
Azhar Mahmood b Warne	.27 –	(7) lbw b Warne	.28
†Moin Khan c McGrath b Muller	.1 –	(8) c Gilchrist b Fleming	.6
*Wasim Akram c Gilchrist b Warne	.29 –	(9) c Blewett b Warne	.31
Saqlain Mushtaq lbw b Warne	.3 –	(3) lbw b Warne	.8
Waqar Younis not out	.12 –	run out (Gilchrist)	.0
Shoaib Akhtar c Gilchrist b Fleming	.5 –	run out	.5
B 10, l-b 6, w 3	.19	L-b 6, w1, n-b 7	.14

(72.5 overs, 283 mins)   **222**   (128.5 overs, 521 mins)   **392**

Fall: 4 18 71 120 148 153 188 198 217 222   Fall: 50 100 122 258 263 320 345
                                                   357 358 392

Bowling: FIRST INNINGS – McGrath 18-8-34-2; Fleming 24.5-7-54-2; Muller 12-0-68-3; Warne 16-6-45-3; Blewett 2-1-5-0. SECOND INNINGS – McGrath 27-8-87-1; Fleming 29-5-89-2; Warne 45.5-11-110-5; Muller 17-3-63-1; S.R. Waugh 4-1-19-0; M.E. Waugh 2-0-6-0; Ponting 2-1-7-0; Blewett 2-0-5-0.

AUSTRALIA

M.J. Slater c Ijaz Ahmed b Saqlain Mushtaq	.97 –	(2) c Azhar Mahmood b Shoaib Akhtar	.27
G.S. Blewett c Moin Khan			
b Azhar Mahmood	.35 –	(1) c Moin Khan b Azhar Mahmood	.29
J.L. Langer c Mohammad Wasim			
b Saqlain Mushtaq	.59 –	c Inzamam-ul-Haq b Saqlain Mushtaq	127
M.E. Waugh lbw b Waqar Younis	.5 –	lbw b Azhar Mahmood	.0
*S.R. Waugh c Ijaz Ahmed b Wasim Akram	24 –	c and b Saqlain Mushtaq	.28
R.T. Ponting b Waqar Younis	.0 –	lbw b Wasim Akram	.0
†A.C. Gilchrist st Moin Khan			
b Saqlain Mushtaq	.6 –	not out	149
S.K. Warne b Saqlain Mushtaq	.0 –	not out	.0
D.W. Fleming lbw b Saqlain Mushtaq	.0		
G.D. McGrath st Moin Khan			
b Saqlain Mushtaq	.7		
S.A. Muller not out	.0		
B 2, l-b 6, n-b 5	.13	B 1, l-b 4, n-b 4	.9

(80 overs, 355 mins)   **246**   (113.5 overs, 503 mins)   (6 wkts) **369**

Fall: 76 191 206 206 213 236 236 246 246   Fall: 39 81 81 125 126 364

Bowling: FIRST INNINGS – Wasim Akram 20-4-51-1; Shoaib Akhtar 17-2-69-0; Waqar Younis 21-1-42-2; Saqlain Mushtaq 24-8-46-6; Azhar Mahmood 7-1-30-1. SECOND INNINGS – Wasim Akram 18-1-68-1; Waqar Younis 11-2-38-0; Shoaib Akhtar 23-5-85-1; Saqlain Mushtaq 44.5-9-130-2; Azhar Mahmood 17-3-43-2.

Umpires: P. Willey (England) and P.D. Parker. TV Umpire: S.J. Davis.
Referee: J.R. Reid (New Zealand).

BOUNDARIES AND LIMITS: ONE-DAY CRICKET

No-one foresaw how one-day cricket would sweep the world when the English counties introduced the domestic Gillette Cup in 1963. And had they done so, there might have been greater resistance to the idea. At times since, cricket has seemed in danger of choking on cheap thrills, becoming like every other form of mass-market entertainment – a threat that remains.

Australians were not long before sampling cricket's new variant. Australia's 1964 Ashes tour concluded with a 50-over-a-side match against the Gillette Cup's first winners, Sussex, while the Australians recruited as county imports after 1968 soon became adept in the short-form game: Greg Chappell was the first centurion in the new Sunday League in June 1969. But it took time for Australians to assimilate the customs of containment that are intrinsic to limited-over cricket. Though the first international one-day match was an Australian occasion, at the MCG in January 1971, and the proliferation of one-day cricket was an Australian concept, promoted by Kerry Packer during his breakaway World Series Cricket between 1977 and 1979, the notion of cramping and curtailing cricket sat ill with Australian players. Dennis Lillee reflected his countrymen's ambivalence when he wrote in *One-Day Cricket* in 1980: 'I know it sounds un-Australian, and I almost find the idea offensive, but in limited-over cricket we must learn to think negatively.' Of Australia's performance in the 1979–80 World Series Cup, *Wisden* noted: 'Greg Chappell made it clear he disliked this defensive form of cricket. He attempted to win his matches without resorting to negative bowling or spreading his fielders round the boundary.' In a sense, the notorious underarm conclusion to the third World Series Cup final of February 1981 was as much a reflection of Chappell's contempt for one-day cricket as of the shortcomings of his sportsmanship, a sort of *reductio ad absurdum* of its principles. That contempt showed again when, in a decision costly for Australia, Chappell opted out of the 1983 World Cup – something that seems unthinkable twenty years later.

The turning point in Australia's one-day fortunes was the next World Cup, fifteen years ago in India. Allan Border's team worked within the form, stressing skills such as fitness, fielding, full-length bowling and running between wickets that the truncated game brings to the fore. 'They worked and worked as a team,' commented Scyld Berry in *Wisden*. 'And every follower of the game had to be pleased in some measure when, at the end of the Australians' victory lap around Eden Gardens, Allan Border was raised on the shoulders of his team-mates and the gold Reliance Cup placed in his hands.' There have been some setbacks since but few lookbacks: an Australian win/loss ratio of poorer than 50 per cent has since edged near 60 per cent.

Quite how memorable much of the one-day cricket has been over the last fifteen years is a harder question to answer. To compile this section was to be reminded, paradoxically, how forgettable limited-overs internationals can be. At the same time, this is partly a function of the sheer profusion of tournaments, and it would be perverse to blame the one-day game for its popularity. When two good teams meet with plenty at stake, as in Australia's spellbinding skirmishes with South Africa in the 1999 World Cup, the result is cricket that would satisfy the most astringent judge. It's merely a pity that those circumstances aren't replicated more often.

—GH

SUSSEX V. AUSTRALIANS

At Hove, September 14, 1964. Sussex, the Knock-out Champions for the past two years, met their masters in a 50-overs-a-side game. Burge and Booth, dominated the Australian innings which produced 282 for three in three hours. They shared an unbroken partnership of 193, with Burge, driving, cutting and hooking powerfully. He hit seventeen 4's and two 6's in his 124. The successful snatching of sharp singles was a feature of the Australian batting. Sussex, without Dexter who did not play because of a strained groin, were dismissed in just over two and a half hours. Parks stood almost alone. He drove forcefully and hit 84 in as many minutes with two 6's and eleven 4's among his attractive strokes. Credit went to McKenzie for breaking the back of the Sussex innings by taking the wickets of Suttle, Lenham and Pountain. O'Neill made a brilliant one-hand catch at square-leg to dispose of Langridge. The game produced the rarity of two Sussex bowlers sharing one over. Snow, after bowling three balls, went off for attention to a split boot, and the umpires allowed Pountain to bowl the remaining three balls. Burge was declared the man of the match by Frank Woolley.

AUSTRALIANS

W.M. Lawry b Thomson 34	B.C. Booth not out 79
*R.B. Simpson c Suttle b Snow 34	L-b 8, n-b 3 11
N.C. O'Neill c Langridge b Thomson 0	1/48 2/48 3/89 (3 wkts after 50 overs) **282**
P.J. Burge not out .124	

T.R. Veivers, †A.T.W. Grout, G.D. McKenzie, N.J.N. Hawke, A.N. Connolly and G.E. Corling did not bat.

Bowling: Thomson 11-0-49-2; Buss 11-1-57-0; Bates 8-0-40-0; Snow 10.3-1-56-1; Pountain 9.3-0-69-0.

SUSSEX

K.G. Suttle b McKenzie 28	J.A. Snow b Corling 14
L.J. Lenham b McKenzie 3	A. Buss c Lawry b Corling 11
F.R. Pountain b McKenzie 1	N.I. Thomson b Veivers 31
*†J.M. Parks c O'Neill b Connolly 84	D.L. Bates not out 0
R.J. Langridge c O'Neill b Connolly 15	B 1, l-b 9, n-b 1 11
M.G. Griffith c Booth b Connolly 7	1/13 2/17 3/92 4/135 5/140 **216**
P.R.V. Ledden c Booth b Veivers 11	6/154 7/163 8/175 9/212

Bowling: McKenzie 11-0-40-3; Corling 11-1-31-2; Connolly 7-0-35-3; Hawke 6-0-32-0; Veivers 9.4-1-67-2.

Umpires: John Langridge and J.H. Parks.

WORLD CUP

SEMI-FINAL

ENGLAND V. AUSTRALIA

At Leeds, June 18, 1975. Australia won by four wickets. In recent years the Headingley pitch has often been criticised as unsuitable for the big match occasion. This surface was strongly criticised by both captains and in that a game, supposedly, between some of the finest batsmen in the world could be finished in 65 overs, there was much to be said for their opinion. Yet, there was no feeling of being cheated by anyone in the capacity crowd. There was tremendous excitement, especially when Australia, in search of 94 runs needed to win, lost six wickets for 39 runs. Gasps, groans, or cheers, followed every ball.

The pitch was the same strip as that used ten days earlier in the Pakistan–Australia game but, of course, the groundsman had watered it and it looked green and damp. Australia had no hesitation about putting England in to bat after winning the toss and, from the way fieldsmen ran to change round at the end of each over they were obviously trying to get as many overs as possible bowled before the greenness went, or, if things went badly, they were concerned about batting in the faint light of late evening. They need not have worried for things went gloriously right for them. Their fast-medium, left-arm bowler Gilmour ripped through the England batting. Bowling a full length, over the wicket, he not only swung the ball in the heavy atmosphere, but he moved it both ways after pitching. Bringing the ball back after pitching on the off stump he had Amiss, Fletcher, Hayes and Knott lbw – Fletcher without playing a shot – and all played back. He bowled Wood with a perfect yorker and had Greig caught one-handed by Marsh. In his 12 overs, bowled in one spell, Gilmour took six wickets for 14 runs. England came in for lunch at 52 for eight. Denness and the tail took the score to 93.

Not until the eighth over with the new ball did England meet success and then Snow and Old ripped into the Australian batsmen as dramatically as Gilmour had treated England. Then came Gilmour as a batsman. With Walters he shared an unbroken partnership adding 55 vital runs. The huge crowd rose to him and the former West Indies captain, Jeffery Stollmeyer, had no difficulty in naming him Man of the Match.

ENGLAND

D.L. Amiss lbw b Gilmour	.2	J.A. Snow c Marsh b Lillee	.2
B. Wood b Gilmour	.6	G.G. Arnold not out	18
K.W.R. Fletcher lbw b Gilmour	.8	P. Lever lbw b Walker	5
A.W. Greig c Marsh b Gilmour	.7		
F.C. Hayes lbw b Gilmour	.4	L-b 5, w 7, n-b 2	14
*M.H. Denness b Walker	27		
†A.P.E. Knott lbw b Gilmour	.0	1/2 2/11 3/26 4/33 5/35 (36.2 overs) **93**	
C.M. Old c G.S. Chappell b Walker	.0	6/36 7/37 8/52 9/73	

Bowling: Lillee 9-3-26-1; Gilmour 12-6-14-6; Walker 9.2-3-22-3; Thomson 6-0-17-0.

AUSTRALIA

A. Turner lbw b Arnold	.7	†R.W. Marsh b Old	5
R.B. McCosker b Old	15	G.J. Gilmour not out	28
*I.M. Chappell lbw b Snow	.2	B 1, l-b 6, n-b 6	13
G.S. Chappell lbw b Snow	.4		
K.D. Walters not out	20	1/17 2/24 3/32 (6 wkts, 28.4 overs) **94**	
R. Edwards b Old	.0	4/32 5/32 6/39	

M.H.N. Walker, D.K. Lillee and J.R. Thomson did not bat.

Bowling: Arnold 7.4-2-15-1; Snow 12-0-30-2; Old 7-2-29-3; Lever 2-0-7-0.

Umpires: W.E. Alley and D.J. Constant.

THE FINAL

AUSTRALIA V. WEST INDIES

At Lord's, June 21, 1975. West Indies won by 17 runs and Prince Philip presented the Cup amidst hilarious scenes to their talented captain, the Man of the Match, Clive Lloyd, just before nine o'clock on a glorious summer's evening. From 11 a.m. till 8.43 p.m. the cricketers from the Caribbean had been locked in a succession of thrills with the cricketers from the Southern Cross. It might not be termed first-class cricket, but the game has never produced better entertainment in one day.

The deciding factor was the wonderful hundred by Clive Lloyd after Ian Chappell had won the toss and invited the West Indies to bat. Until Lloyd arrived at 50 for three, Chappell had set a fairly tight field and his battery of quick seam bowlers had kept the West Indies under subjection. Australia gained the initiative when Fredericks hooked a bouncer high over fine leg for 6 only to lose his balance and tread on his wicket. Greenidge spent eighty minutes crawling to 13 and a rash cut by Kallicharran ended in a flick to the wicket-keeper.

Then came Lloyd and at once he showed himself master of the situation. He hooked Lillee in majestic style, square for 6, and then put Walker off the back foot past cover with disdainful ease. At the other end Lloyd had the dependable Kanhai as a willing anchor man – he did not score for 11 overs – and so the pair put on 149 together in 36 overs. Lloyd hit two 6's and twelve 4's and was at the crease only one hour and forty-eight minutes while making his scintillating hundred off 82 balls. More powerful hitting came from Boyce and Julien so that Australia required 292 to lift the Cup.

Although they challenged to the very end and might have won had they shown some discretion when trying to steal precious runs, they contributed to their own destruction, for as many as five men were run out by the brilliant West Indies fielders. The amazing Kallicharran, who had begun their troubles with a dazzling slip catch which removed McCosker, threw down the stumps twice from backward square leg and he also enabled Lloyd to break the wicket at the bowler's end when Ian Chappell hesitated and then set off for the third impossible run.

Nevertheless, Turner and particularly Ian Chappell played extremely well before their mishaps, but West Indies always had the edge until near the end when Thomson and Lillee threw their bats, adding 41 in their attempt to win a lost cause. It was the longest day of the year; the longest day in cricket history and one that those who were there and the millions who watched it on television will never forget. The full attendance was 26,000 and the paying crowd produced receipts of £66,950, a record for a one-day match in England. (*Norman Preston*)

WEST INDIES

R.C. Fredericks hit wkt b Lillee 7	B.D. Julien not out 26
C.G. Greenidge c Marsh b Thomson 13	†D.L. Murray c and b Gilmour 14
A.I. Kallicharran c Marsh b Gilmour 12	V.A. Holder not out 6
R.B. Kanhai b Gilmour 55	L-b 6, n-b 11 17
*C.H. Lloyd c Marsh b Gilmour 102	
I.V.A. Richards b Gilmour 5	1/12 2/27 (8 wkts, 60 overs) **291**
K.D. Boyce c G.S. Chappell b Thomson ..34	3/50 4/199 5/206 6/209
	7/261 8/285

A.M.E. Roberts did not bat.

Bowling: Lillee 12-1-55-1; Gilmour 12-2-48-5; Thomson 12-1-44-2; Walker 12-1-71-0; G.S. Chappell 7-0-33-0; Walters 5-0-23-0.

AUSTRALIA

A. Turner run out 40	M.H.N. Walker run out 7
R.B. McCosker c Kallicharran b Boyce 7	J.R. Thomson run out 21
*I.M. Chappell run out 62	D.K. Lillee not out 16
G.S. Chappell run out 15	B 2, l-b 9, n-b 7 18
K.D. Walters b Lloyd 35	
†R.W. Marsh b Boyce 11	1/25 2/81 3/115 (58.4 overs) **274**
R. Edwards c Fredericks b Boyce 28	4/162 5/170 6/195
G.J. Gilmour c Kanhai b Boyce 14	7/221 8/231 9/233

Bowling: Julien 12-0-58-0; Roberts 11-1-45-0; Boyce 12-0-50-4; Holder 11.4-1-65-0; Lloyd 12-1-38-1.

Umpires: H.D. Bird and T.W. Spencer.

WORLD SERIES CUP

AUSTRALIA V. WEST INDIES

At Melbourne, December 9, 1979. West Indies won by 80 runs. This match will remain in the memory of a crowd of almost 40,000 and thousands of others who watched it on television for Richards's exceptional batsmanship. Given pain-killing injections to ease a back injury, and hobbling throughout his innings, he launched a furious assault on every bowler, scoring 153 not out from 131 balls with one 6 and sixteen 4s. Haynes, who played his best innings of the season, was completely overshadowed in their partnership of 205. Australia, left with a virtually impossible task, never looked likely to get on terms.

WEST INDIES

C.G. Greenidge c Marsh b Lillee 11
D.L. Haynes c Marsh b Thomson 80
I.V.A. Richards not out 153
A.I. Kallicharran not out 16
    B 1, l-b 10 11

1/28 2/233   (2 wkts, 48 overs) **271**

L.G. Rowe, C.L. King, *†D.L. Murray, A.M.E. Roberts, M.A. Holding, J. Garner and D.R. Parry did not bat.

Bowling: Lillee 10-1-48-1; Hogg 10-1-50-0; Chappell 4-0-24-0; Thomson 8-0-43-1; Bright 6-0-29-0; Hookes 1-0-10-0; Border 7-0-40-0; Wiener 2-0-16-0.

AUSTRALIA

B.M. Laird b Holding 7	D.K. Lillee b King 19	
J.M. Wiener c and b Parry 27	R.M. Hogg not out 3	
A.R. Border run out 44		
*G.S. Chappell c Richards b King 31	B 1, l-b 6 7	
K.J. Hughes b Holding 12		
D.W. Hookes c Murray b Roberts 9	1/16 2/54 3/102	(8 wkts, 48 overs) **191**
†R.W. Marsh c Rowe b Roberts 13	4/119 5/128 6/147	
R.J. Bright not out 19	7/151 8/185	

J.R. Thomson did not bat.

Bowling: Roberts 8-1-33-2; Holding 10-2-29-2; Garner 10-1-26-0; King 10-0-40-2; Parry 10-0-56-1.

Umpires: K. Carmody and R. Whitehead.

THIRD FINAL MATCH

AUSTRALIA V. NEW ZEALAND

At Melbourne, February 1, 1981. Australia won by six runs. With New Zealand need-ing 6 runs to tie the match off the last ball, Trevor Chappell, instructed to do so by his brother and captain, Greg, bowled McKechnie an underarm ball, which caused a furore that could haunt Australian–New Zealand cricket for a long time. Earlier in the day Greg Chappell, when 52, had refused to walk when Snedden, at deep mid-wicket, claimed what appeared to be a low but fair catch off Cairns; as neither umpire was watching the incident – they said they were looking for short runs – New Zealand's impassioned appeals for a catch were in vain. After quickly losing Border, Wood and Greg Chappell added 145 for Australia's second wicket in 34 overs, Chappell again being in his best form. When he was finally out, caught by Edgar diving forward at deep mid-wicket, it was to a similar catch to that which was earlier held by Snedden and confirmed by the television replays. This time Chappell went without hesitation. Late in the innings Kent and Marsh both made useful runs. Although Wright and Edgar gave New Zealand another excellent start, putting on 85 in 24 overs, and runs continued to come at a rate which made a New Zealand victory possible, such a result always seemed just against the odds. Edgar, with a splendid hundred to his name, was not out at the end. After some good blows by Parker, Trevor Chappell came on to bowl the last over with 15 still needed and four wickets left. Hadlee straight drove the first ball for 4 and was lbw to the second. Smith then hit two 2s before being bowled, swinging at the fifth ball, leaving New Zealand with 6 to tie off the now infamous underarm delivery.

AUSTRALIA

A.R. Border c Parker b Hadlee 5	K.D. Walters not out 6	
G.M. Wood b McEwan 72	B 8, l-b 3 .11	
*G.S. Chappell c Edgar b Snedden 90		
M.F. Kent c Edgar b Snedden 33	1/8 2/153 3/199	(4 wkts, 50 overs) **235**
†R.W. Marsh not out 18	4/215	

K.J. Hughes, T.M. Chappell, G.R. Beard, D.K. Lillee and M.H.N. Walker did not bat.

Bowling: Hadlee 10-0-41-1; Snedden 10-0-52-2; Cairns 10-0-34-0; McKechnie 10-0-54-0; McEwan 7-1-31-0; Howarth 3-0-12-0.

NEW ZEALAND

J.G. Wright c Kent b G.S. Chappell 42	R.J. Hadlee lbw b T.M. Chappell 4	
B.A. Edgar not out 102	†I.D.S. Smith b T.M. Chappell 4	
*G.P. Howarth c Marsh b G.S. Chappell . .18	B.J. McKechnie not out 0	
B.L. Cairns b Beard 12	L-b 10 10	
M.G. Burgess c T.M. Chappell		
b G.S. Chappell 2	1/85 2/117 3/136	(8 wkts, 50 overs) **229**
P.E. McEwan c Wood b Beard 11	4/139 5/172 6/221 7/225 8/229	
J.M. Parker c T.M. Chappell b Lillee 24		

M.C. Snedden did not bat.

Bowling: Lillee 10-1-34-1; Walker 10-0-35-0; Beard 10-0-50-2; G.S. Chappell 10-0-43-3; T.M. Chappell 10-0-57-2.

Umpires: P.M. Cronin and D.G. Weser.

from NOTES BY THE EDITOR

SHARP PRACTICE IN MELBOURNE

[...] *Wisden* 1981 carried a picture of Michael Holding kicking a stump out of the ground, during a Test match, to show his disapproval of an umpire's decision. This year, in the same disreputable category, is one of Trevor Chappell bowling a sneak in Melbourne, at his brother's behest, to prevent New Zealand from making the 6 runs they needed to tie a one-day match. Some say it is money that has caused this collapse in the ethics of the game, others that it is the reflection of a graceless age.

In Australia, I am afraid, it is partly the result of weak government. For too long the Australian Cricket Board have been over-tolerant of indiscipline and actions of dubious intent. True cricket-lovers have been as sickened by Lillee's antics as they have been spell-bound by his bowling. The latest precept, that Australian players shall penalise each other for misconduct, hardly seems a step in the right direction. [...] (*1982*)

WORLD CUP

AUSTRALIA V. ZIMBABWE

At Nottingham, June 9, 1983. Zimbabwe won by 13 runs. In their first appearance in the competition, the amateurs of Zimbabwe brought off a bigger surprise than any in the previous two World Cups. The Australian captain described his side as being 'out-played'. Having been put in, Zimbabwe made no more than a steady start, but from 94 for five their captain, Duncan Fletcher, who was once a professional with Rishton in the Lancashire League, led an acceleration, adding 70 in fifteen overs with Curran and 75 in twelve overs with Butchart. Australia missed five catches, bowled moderately and, though Wood and Wessels gave their innings an adequate start, they slipped behind the required rate against Fletcher's four for 42 and some fine fielding and catching.

Man of the Match: D.A.G. Fletcher.

ZIMBABWE

A.H. Shah c Marsh b Lillee 16	K.M. Curran c Hookes b Hogg 27
G.A. Paterson c Hookes b Lillee 27	I.P. Butchart not out 34
J.G. Heron c Marsh b Yallop 14	L-b 18, w 7, n-b 6 31
A.J. Pycroft b Border 21	
†D.L. Houghton c Marsh b Yallop 0	1/55 2/55 3/86 (6 wkts, 60 overs) **239**
*D.A.G. Fletcher not out 69	4/86 5/94 6/164

P.W.E. Rawson, A.J. Traicos and V.R. Hogg did not bat.

Bowling: Lawson 11-2-33-0; Hogg 12-3-43-1; Lillee 12-1-47-2; Thomson 11-1-46-0; Yallop 9-0-28-2; Border 5-0-11-1.

AUSTRALIA

G.M. Wood c Houghton b Fletcher 31	G.F. Lawson b Butchart 0
K.D. Wessels run out 76	R.M. Hogg not out 19
*K.J. Hughes c Shah b Fletcher 0	B 2, l-b 7, w 2 11
D.W. Hookes c Traicos b Fletcher 20	
G.N. Yallop c Pycroft b Fletcher 2	1/61 2/63 3/114 (7 wkts, 60 overs) **226**
A.R. Border c Pycroft b Curran 17	4/133 5/138 6/168 7/176
†R.W. Marsh not out 50	

D.K. Lillee and J.R. Thomson did not bat.

Bowling: Hogg 6-2-15-0; Rawson 12-1-54-0; Butchart 10-0-39-1; Fletcher 11-1-42-4; Traicos 12-2-27-0; Curran 9-0-38-1.

Umpires: D.J. Constant and M.J. Kitchen.

WORLD SERIES CUP

AUSTRALIA V. ENGLAND

At Sydney, January 22, 1987 (day/night). England won by three wickets. Lamb struck Reid for 2, 4, 6, 2, 4 in the final over to blast England to a tremendous win with a ball to spare. Although the pitch lacked pace, Australia, who chose to bat first, should have scored more than 233 for eight after passing 150 in the 33rd over. Wellham played deftly (154 balls, five fours), but Australia lost momentum, adding only 43 in the last ten overs. England's innings followed a similar pattern, Broad's 45 coming off 58 balls and Gower and Lamb adding 86 off twenty overs. However, a clever spell by Matthews, supported by good fielding, left England needing 32 off three, 25 off two and 18 off the final over. Lamb, who until then had been at loggerheads with his timing and had not hit a boundary, was equal to the task, hauling Reid twice to square leg and once over deep mid-wicket.

AUSTRALIA

G.R. Marsh c Richards b Edmonds 47	†T.J. Zoehrer not out 9
D.M. Wellham c Athey b Emburey 97	P.L. Taylor st Richards b Emburey 0
D.M. Jones c Athey b DeFreitas 34	
*A.R. Border c Dilley b Edmonds 13	B 2, l-b 5, n-b 2 9
S.R. Waugh c Athey b Dilley 10	
G.R.J. Matthews c DeFreitas	1/109 2/156 3/189 (8 wkts, 50 overs) **233**
b Emburey 2	4/205 5/208 6/208
K.H. MacLeay b Dilley 12	7/230 8/233

S.P. O'Donnell and B.A. Reid did not bat.

Bowling: Dilley 9-2-28-2; DeFreitas 10-0-46-1; Gatting 2-0-11-0; Botham 10-0-51-0; Emburey 9-0-42-3; Edmonds 10-0-48-2.

ENGLAND

B.C. Broad c Matthews
   b Taylor 45
C.W.J. Athey c Zoehrer b Reid 2
D.I. Gower c Wellham b O'Donnell 50
A.J. Lamb not out 77
*M.W. Gatting b O'Donnell 1
I.T. Botham b Waugh 27

J.E. Emburey run out 4
†C.J. Richards c Waugh b O'Donnell 3
P.A.J. DeFreitas not out 6
   L-b 16, w 2, n-b 1 19

1/33 2/51 3/137   (7 wkts, 49.5 overs) **234**
4/143 5/186 6/191 7/202

P.H. Edmonds and G.R. Dilley did not bat.

Bowling: MacLeay 4-0-22-0; Reid 9.5-3-44-1; Taylor 10-0-42-1; Waugh 5-0-22-1; Matthews 10-1-36-0; Border 3-0-13-0; O'Donnell 8-0-39-3.

Umpires: A.R. Crafter and R.A. French.

THE RELIANCE WORLD CUP

INDIA V. AUSTRALIA

At Madras, October 9, 1987. Australia won by 1 run. Toss: India. Kapil Dev's sportsmanship proved the deciding factor in a close-run match. One of Jones's two sixes, in his 39 from 35 balls, had been signalled as four; but between innings Kapil concurred with the Australians' insistence that the ball cleared the boundary. That India's target was increased by 2 seemed insignificant when Gavaskar (32 balls, one six, six fours), Srikkanth (83 balls, seven fours) and Sidhu (79 balls, five sixes, four fours) sent them racing past 200 for the loss of only two wickets. McDermott's first four overs went for 31 runs, but he came back strongly to whip out the middle order. Even so, India, with four wickets in hand, needed just 15 from the last four overs; when the last over began, the requirement was 6, with the last man, Maninder Singh, taking strike. He managed two 2s, but along with his sang-froid went his off stump. Australia's innings, like India's, had been built around the top-order batsmen. On a pitch of little pace or bounce, Marsh and Boon put on 100 at almost 5 an over. Jones played quite beautifully, but the middle order lost the initiative. Marsh, in 95-degree heat and high humidity, batted more than three hours and hit a six and seven fours in 141 balls.

AUSTRALIA

D.C. Boon lbw b Shastri 49
G.R. Marsh c Azharuddin b Prabhakar . .110
D.M. Jones c Sidhu b Maninder 39
*A.R. Border b Binny 16
T.M. Moody c Kapil Dev b Prabhakar 8

S.R. Waugh not out 19
S.P. O'Donnell run out 7
   L-b 18, w 2, n-b 2 22
1/110 2/174 3/228   (6 wkts, 50 overs) **270**
4/237 5/251 6/270

†G.C. Dyer, P.L. Taylor, C.J. McDermott and B.A. Reid did not bat.

Bowling: Kapil Dev 10-0-41-0; Prabhakar 10-0-47-2; Binny 7-0-46-1; Maninder 10-0-48-1; Shastri 10-0-50-1; Azharuddin 3-0-20-0.

INDIA

S.M. Gavaskar c Reid b Taylor 37	R.M.H. Binny run out 0
K. Srikkanth lbw b Waugh 70	M. Prabhakar run out 5
N.S. Sidhu b McDermott 73	Maninder Singh b Waugh 4
D.B. Vengsarkar c Jones b McDermott . . .29	B 2, l-b 7, w 2 11
M. Azharuddin b McDermott 10	
*Kapil Dev c Boon b O'Donnell 6	1/69 2/131 3/207 (49.5 overs) **269**
R.J. Shastri c and b McDermott 12	4/229 5/232 6/246
†K.S. More not out 12	7/256 8/256 9/265

Bowling: McDermott 10-0-56-4; Reid 10-2-35-0; O'Donnell 9-1-32-1; Taylor 5-0-46-1; Waugh 9.5-0-52-2; Border 6-0-39-0.

Umpires: D.M. Archer and H.D. Bird.

FINAL

AUSTRALIA V. ENGLAND

At Calcutta, November 8, 1987. Australia won by 7 runs. Toss: Australia. Batting first suited Australia; and when they took the field to defend a total of 253, it was in the knowledge that no side batting second had scored 254 to win in this World Cup. England, 135 for two after 31 overs, and with Australia beginning to show signs of disarray in the field, were then almost on target. But in a moment too crass to contemplate, Gatting handed back the initiative. To Border's first ball, bowled on the line of his leg stump, the England captain attempted to play a reverse sweep. Having in the semi-final swept the ball on to his leg stump, he now contrived to hit it on to his shoulder, whence it looped into Dyer's gloves. The Australians' joy was unconcealed.

England had conceded points from the start, an erratic opening spell from DeFreitas and Small helping Marsh and Boon post 52 in ten overs. Foster and the two spinners repaired the damage, with Foster's eight overs costing just 16 runs and bringing the wicket of Marsh in the eighteenth over. Gooch, too, was economical until coming under fire as Border and Veletta (31 balls, six fours) added 73 in the ten overs following Boon's dismissal. Boon's 75 (125 balls, seven fours) was his fifth score of 50 or more in six innings. DeFreitas, brought back to bowl the last over, went for 11 to bring to 65 the runs scored from England's last six overs.

Robinson, undone by pace to no-one's great surprise, was out first ball to McDermott's fourth. Gooch (57 balls) and Athey put on 65 in seventeen overs, Athey and Gatting (45 balls) 69 in thirteen, Athey (104 balls) and Lamb 35 in just over eight. It was Waugh whose throw ran out Athey as he went for a third run; and with England slipping farther behind the run-rate (75 from ten overs had drifted to 46 from five), he bowled Lamb (55 balls) in the 47th over. DeFreitas gave England renewed hope with 14 (464) in McDermott's penultimate over, but Waugh conceded just 2 runs, as well as having DeFreitas caught, in the 49th. That left 17 runs needed from the final over, and there was no way McDermott was going to allow that.

Man of the Match: D.C. Boon. *Attendance*: 70,000 approx.

AUSTRALIA

D.C. Boon c Downton b Hemmings 75
G.R. Marsh b Foster 24
D.M. Jones c Athey b Hemmings 33
C.J. McDermott b Gooch 14
*A.R. Border run out 31
M.R.J. Veletta not out 45

S.R. Waugh not out 5
    B 1, l-b 13, w 5, n-b 7 26

1/75 (2) 2/151 (3)   (5 wkts, 50 overs) **253**
3/166 (4) 4/168 (1)
5/241 (5)

S.P. O'Donnell, †G.C. Dyer, T.B.A. May and B.A. Reid did not bat.

Bowling: DeFreitas 6-1-34-0; Small 6-0-33-0; Foster 10-0-38-1; Hemmings 10-1-48-2; Emburey 10-0-44-0; Gooch 8-1-42-1.

ENGLAND

G.A Gooch lbw b O'Donnell 35
R.T. Robinson lbw b McDermott 0
C.W.J. Athey run out 58
*M.W. Gatting c Dyer b Border 41
A.J. Lamb b Waugh 45
†P.R. Downton c O'Donnell b Border 9
J.E. Emburey run out 10
P.A.J. DeFreitas c Reid b Waugh 17

N.A. Foster not out 7
G.C. Small not out 3
    B 1, l-b 14, w 2, n-b 4 21

1/1 (2) 2/66 (1)   (8 wkts, 50 overs) **246**
3/135 (4) 4/170 (3)
5/188 (6) 6/218 (5)
7/220 (7) 8/235 (8)

E.E. Hemmings did not bat.

Bowling: McDermott 10-1-51-1; Reid 10-0-43-0; Waugh 9-0-37-2; O'Donnell 10-1-35-1; May 4-0-27-0; Border 7-0-38-2.

Umpires: R.B. Gupta and Mahboob Shah.

WORLD SERIES CUP

AUSTRALIA V. WEST INDIES

At Sydney, January 1, 1996 (day/night). Australia won by one wicket. Toss: West Indies.

[...] With the last man in, Bevan lofted the final ball straight to the boundary to extend Australia's winning streak to four, while West Indies completed their fourth straight defeat. The bowler, Harper, shared a high-five with Bevan; given that he had claimed a catch against him earlier, which the umpires correctly decreed had hit the ground, it was pleasant to see them dispel any tension. Bevan had scored 78 from 89 balls to rescue Australia from 38 for six, and Bobby Simpson, who had witnessed most of his country's 337 one-day internationals as player, commentator or coach, called it the best chasing innings he had seen. Hooper's role was not dissimilar in rallying West Indies from 54 for five. It was Reiffel, however, who took the match award, having helped Bevan to double the score in a critical eighth-wicket stand after bagging four for 29.

Man of the Match: P.R. Reiffel. *Attendance*: 37,562.

WEST INDIES

S.C. Williams c Healy b Reiffel 5	†C.O. Browne c Warne b Reiffel 2	
S.L. Campbell lbw b Warne 15	C.E.L. Ambrose b Warne 0	
P.V. Simmons c Warne b Reiffel 4	*C.A. Walsh not out 3	
S. Chanderpaul c Taylor b Reiffel 3	L-b 6, w 7, n-b 2 15	
C.L. Hooper not out 93		
J.C. Adams c Waugh b Warne 0	1/13 2/21 3/28 ....(9 wkts, 43 overs) 172	
R.A. Harper run out 28	4/54 5/54 6/135	
O.D. Gibson b McGrath 4	7/150 8/164 9/168	

Bowling: McGrath 9-2-22-1; Reiffel 9-2-29-4; Law 6-0-34-0; Lee 6-0-20-0; Warne 9-2-30-3; Bevan 4-0-31-0.

AUSTRALIA

M.J. Slater c Simmons b Ambrose 5	P.R. Reiffel c Hooper b Simmons 34	
*M.A. Taylor run out 1	S.K. Warne run out 3	
M.E. Waugh c Harper b Gibson 16	G.D. McGrath not out 1	
R.T. Ponting b Ambrose 0	L-b 2, w 3, n-b 4 9	
S.G. Law c Browne b Ambrose 10		
M.G. Bevan not out 78	1/4 2/15 3/15	(9 wkts, 43 overs) 173
S. Lee c Browne b Gibson 0	4/32 5/38 6/38	
†I.A. Healy b Harper 16	7/74 8/157 9/167	

Bowling: Ambrose 9-3-20-3; Walsh 9-2-22-0; Gibson 9-2-40-2; Harper 8-0-38-1; Simmons 5-0-31-1; Hooper 3-0-20-0.

Umpires: A.J. McQuillan and P.D. Parker.

WORLD CUP, 1999

By Matthew Engel

With about five playable hours of daylight remaining on the longest Sunday of the year, Darren Lehmann struck the ball towards the Lord's Grand Stand for the boundary that gave the seventh World Cup to Australia. This concluded a final so one-sided that it descended from anticlimax into bathos. A match that had started at 11.15, half an hour late, was all over by 4.35 because Pakistan, the most exciting side in the tournament, had gone to pieces when it mattered most.

The first World Cup final, at Lord's 24 years earlier almost to the day, had lasted nearly ten hours. This one was over shortly after it started. The nature of one-day cricket is such that two evenly matched teams can easily produce a lop-sided match, simply because of the breaks of the game. It was, however, true to the uniquely perverse nature of Pakistani cricket that it should happen to them on such an occasion.

Thus the best Test team in the world became the world one-day champions, uniting the two forms of cricket into one undisputed title for the first time since West Indies lost their invincibility in the last Lord's final 16 years before. Hindsight made it seem like manifest destiny. It was obvious all along, wasn't it? But it was nothing of the kind.

When Australia had gone to Old Trafford three Sundays earlier for their final group match, they were in severe danger of the earliest possible exit; two Sundays after that, during the last Super Six match, Australian journalists and officials had been making calls to check on airline seat availability, which would have been firmed up had Herschelle Gibbs not celebrated too soon and literally thrown away a catch offered by Steve Waugh.

In the semi-final four days later, as Damien Fleming prepared to bowl to Lance Klusener – the player of the tournament – with South Africa needing one to win, Australia were effectively goners. But that game, arguably the greatest in the history of one-day cricket, produced a final twist that no one could have foreseen or invented. Klusener and Allan Donald had a horrendous running mix-up, the match was tied, and Australia went through on 'net run-rate'. [...]

Australia's improbable lurch into the final was in complete contrast to their opponents' confident strut. The Pakistanis lost three successive games which did not matter, but returned to form in time to earn their place at Lord's by blowing Zimbabwe and New Zealand away by huge margins. But it has been noticed before that the way to win World Cups – and not just in cricket – is to fiddle quietly through the early matches and peak at the end. This is a lesson South Africa, who blazed their way through the early stages of all three World Cups in the 1990s without ever reaching the final, urgently need to learn. It is, however, rather difficult to convert this observation into a strategy. Steve Waugh's diamond-hardness, and the bowling gifts of Glenn McGrath and Shane Warne, seem in retrospect like the determining factors of the 1999 World Cup. [...]

AUSTRALIA V. SOUTH AFRICA

At Leeds, June 13, 1999. Australia won by five wickets. Toss: South Africa.

This was do or die for Australia. So, in a thriller, they duly did – leapfrogging over South Africa in the process, and loading the dice for the semi-final. South Africa batted first on a bouncy Headingley pitch and rattled up 271, despite the return to form of Warne, who snared his old foe Cullinan and Cronje in one over. Gibbs, with a mixture of steadiness and flair, made South Africa's only century of the tournament, and the second of his short one-day international career. Then Klusener, back to his best, masterminded a swashbuckling 47 from the final five overs.

At 48 for three in reply, Australia faced meltdown. But no one had told Steve Waugh, that iciest of icemen. He and Ponting, slogging adeptly, added 77 between overs 22 and 29. They were particularly harsh on Cronje and Boje who, in the absence of Kallis with an abdominal strain, had to muddle through ten overs, which yielded 79. Then Waugh, on 56, was unfathomably dropped by a prematurely celebrating Gibbs at mid-wicket. Waugh reportedly told him: 'Hersh, you've just dropped the World Cup.' Hindsight suggests he did. Waugh raced to 120 in 110 balls, only his second century in 266 one-day internationals. Though Donald and Pollock returned with some ferocious stuff at the end, Australia's momentum carried them through; the exhausted teams headed for Edgbaston and a rematch.

Man of the Match: S.R. Waugh. *Attendance*: 15,479.

SOUTH AFRICA

G. Kirsten c Ponting b Reiffel 21	†M.V. Boucher not out 0
H.H. Gibbs b McGrath 101	L-b 7, w 8, n-b 6 21
D.J. Cullinan b Warne 50	
*W.J. Cronje lbw b Warne 0	1/45 (1) 2/140 (3)　　(7 wkts, 50 overs) **271**
J.N. Rhodes c M.E. Waugh b Fleming 39	3/141 (4) 4/219 (2) 5/250 (5)
L. Klusener c Warne b Fleming 36	6/271 (6) 7/271 (7)
S.M. Pollock b Fleming 3	Score at 15 overs: 56-1

S. Elworthy, N. Boje and A.A. Donald did not bat.

Bowling: McGrath 10-0-49-1; Fleming 10-0-57-3; Reiffel 9-0-47-1; Moody 8-1-56-0; Warne 10-1-33-2; Bevan 3-0-22-0.

AUSTRALIA

M.E. Waugh run out 5	T.M. Moody not out 15
†A.C. Gilchrist b Elworthy 5	L-b 6, w 7, n-b 7 20
R.T. Ponting c Donald b Klusener 69	
D.R. Martyn c Boje b Elworthy 11	1/6 (2) 2/20 (1)　　(5 wkts, 49.4 overs) **272**
*S.R. Waugh not out 120	3/48 (4) 4/174 (3)
M.G. Bevan c Cullinan b Cronje 27	5/247 (6)
	Score at 15 overs: 54-3

S.K. Warne, P.R. Reiffel, D.W. Fleming and G.D. McGrath did not bat.

Bowling: Pollock 9.4-0-45-0; Elworthy 10-1-46-2; Donald 10-0-43-0; Klusener 10-0-53-1; Cronje 7-0-50-1; Boje 3-0-29-0.

Umpires: S. Venkataraghavan and P. Willey. Referee: J.R. Reid.

SEMI-FINAL

AUSTRALIA V. SOUTH AFRICA

At Birmingham, June 17, 1999. Tied. Toss: South Africa. This was not merely the match of the tournament: it must have been the best one-day international of the 1,483 so far played. The essence of the one-day game is a close finish, and this was by far the most significant to finish in the closest way of all – with both teams all out for the same score. But it was a compressed epic all the way through, and it ended in a savage twist. The tie meant that South Africa, for the third World Cup in a row, failed to reach the final despite making much of the early running. The crucial fact was that Australia finished higher than them in the Super Six table, and that was determined by the obscurity of net run-rate. Many spectators were left baffled.

Klusener's brawn had powered South Africa to the brink of the final but, when he got there, his brain short-circuited. Only he could have smashed and grabbed 31 runs off 14 balls, cutting a daunting target down to a doddle: one needed off four balls, Klusener himself on strike, and a decent, experienced tailender at the other end in Donald. The bowler, Fleming, had only one thing going for him: he had bowled the final over that beat West Indies in the 1996 World Cup semi-final. Having let Klusener pummel consecutive fours to level the scores, he tightened up. Steve Waugh, knowing a tie would be enough, set a field that gave new meaning to the phrase 'a ring saving one'. Klusener thumped the ball straight, and Donald, backing up too far, would have been run out if Lehmann had hit the stumps. The scare should have been a warning. But Klusener then repeated his straight biff and charged. Donald grounded his bat, dropped it, and finally set off, while the Australians were demonstrating the benefits of a recent visit to a bowling alley: Mark Waugh, at mid-on, flicked the ball to Fleming, who rolled it to Gilchrist, who broke the wicket, and South African hearts.

The rest of the match was studded with outstanding performances. When Australia batted, Pollock, finally finding the edge, was magnificently incisive. Donald twice took two wickets in an over. Steve Waugh and Bevan performed a repair job which showed first self-control, then controlled aggression. Kallis, carrying a stomach injury, bowled fast and tight, and held the batting together with a cool fifty. Above all, there was Shane Warne. The ball that bowled Gibbs was a miraculous replay of his most famous delivery, to Mike Gatting six years earlier. His first spell of eight overs went for only 12 runs. He pocketed three more wickets, and the match award. The game was the last as South Africa's coach for Bob Woolmer, whose blend of science and imagination had produced a 73 per cent success rate in one-day internationals. He deserved better than to go out on a technicality. (*Tim de Lisle*)

Man of the Match: S.K. Warne. *Attendance*: 19,639.

AUSTRALIA

A.C. Gilchrist c Donald b Kallis 20	D.W. Fleming b Donald 0
M.E. Waugh c Boucher b Pollock 0	G.D. McGrath not out 0
R.T. Ponting c Kirsten b Donald 37	B 1, l-b 6, w 3, n-b 6 16
D.S. Lehmann c Boucher b Donald 1	
*S.R. Waugh c Boucher b Pollock 56	1/3 (2) 2/54 (3) (49.2 overs) **213**
M.G. Bevan c Boucher b Pollock 65	3/58 (4) 4/68 (1) 5/158 (5)
T.M. Moody lbw b Pollock 0	6/158 (7) 7/207 (8)
S.K. Warne c Cronje b Pollock 18	8/207 (9) 9/207 (10)
P.R. Reiffel b Donald 0	10/213 (6) Score at 15 overs: 61-3

Bowling: Pollock 9.2-1-36-5; Elworthy 10-0-59-0; Kallis 10-2-27-1; Donald 10-1-32-4; Klusener 9-1-50-0; Cronje 1-0-2-0.

SOUTH AFRICA

G. Kirsten b Warne 18	S. Elworthy run out 1
H.H. Gibbs b Warne 30	A.A. Donald run out 0
D.J. Cullinan run out 6	L-b 1, w 5 6
*W.J. Cronje c M.E. Waugh b Warne 0	1/48 (2) 2/53 (1) (49.4 overs) **213**
J.N. Rhodes c Bevan b Reiffel 43	3/53 (4) 4/61 (3) 5/145 (6)
S.M. Pollock b Fleming 20	6/175 (5) 7/183 (7) 8/196 (9)
L. Klusener not out 31	9/198 (10) 10/213 (11)
M.V. Boucher b McGrath 5	Score at 15 overs: 53-3

Bowling: McGrath 10-0-51-1; Fleming 8.4-1-40-1; Reiffel 8-0-28-1; Warne 10-4-29-4; M.E. Waugh 8-0-37-0; Moody 5-0-27-0.

Umpires: D.R. Shepherd and S. Venkataraghavan. Referee: R. Subba Row.

AUSTRALIA V. PAKISTAN

At Lord's, June 20, 1999. Australia won by eight wickets. Toss: Pakistan.

Australia won the seventh World Cup with such single-minded ruthlessness that even an eight-wicket victory failed to do them justice. Pakistan, the most exciting team in the tournament, were totally outplayed and outwitted at the crucial moment. There were barely four and a half hours of cricket, most of it one-sided. For all but the most fervent Australian, it was not a pretty sight.

It was a sight, though, spared many Pakistanis by a controversial ticketing policy. This favoured not the fans of the competing teams but those who had ostensibly proved their loyalty to the game – and the depth of their pocket – by buying a package of tickets long before. So Lord's was awash with disinterested observers, while from outside came the klaxon, whistle and bugle of fanatical Pakistan support. About a hundred fans clambered up a building site overlooking the ground. As the police moved in, a game of cat and mouse ensued, providing an alternative spectacle for the Grand Stand opposite. Eventually, the fans, like their team, were unceremoniously bundled out of St John's Wood.

On a pitch that Steve Waugh believed was good for 260 or so, Wasim Akram chose to bat. Saeed Anwar cut the third ball of the day for four and added two more boundaries in the fourth over as Fleming struggled for consistency. For Pakistan, this was as good as it got. Next over, Wajahatullah Wasti followed a ball from McGrath that bounced and left him. Mark Waugh, at second slip, flew to his right and clung on with both hands. It set the tone for the match.

After Anwar had played on, Abdur Razzaq and Ijaz Ahmed briefly looked more at home. Razzaq benefited from Australia's one false move – McGrath dropped a comfortable catch at long-off – but minutes later was smartly caught by Steve Waugh, lunging forward at extra cover. With Pakistan faltering at 69 for three after 21 overs, Waugh brought on Warne. It was, literally, the turning point of the match.

Warne produced an astounding delivery to dismiss Ijaz, who had hung around doggedly for 22. The ball pitched on or just outside leg and hit off. It was not quite the famous Gatting ball, nor even the one that dismissed Gibbs in the semi-final, but it sent shockwaves through the lower order. Pakistan tried to get out of trouble with all guns blazing. But for every ball that ricocheted off the boards, another landed in Australian hands. Luck was against them, too: a ball from Reiffel clipped Inzamam's pad on its way to Gilchrist. The Australians went up in appeal; umpire Shepherd's finger in judgment. An incredulous Inzamam plodded off at funereal pace. When Wasim holed out, Warne had claimed four wickets for the second game running, taking his tally to 20, a World Cup record shared with Geoff Allott of New Zealand. McGrath brought the innings to a swift end when Ponting held a superlative catch at third slip in the 39th over. The target was just 133.

Wasim later claimed he could have defended 180 but the way Gilchrist began, 300 would have been within reach. Shoaib Akhtar was desperately unlucky when his first ball was edged by Gilchrist and fell agonisingly short of long leg. Thereafter, boundaries came thick, fast and off the middle of the bat. Gilchrist's fifty took 33 balls. When he fell to the first ball of the 11th over, the broadcasters felt the end was close enough to remove the stump cameras.

In fact, it took another ten overs, in which time Mark Waugh passed 1,000 World Cup runs. Australia needed a mere 121 balls to win, and the game was over at 4.32 p.m. – despite a heavy shower which had delayed the start by half an hour and a half-hearted pitch invasion moments after an announcement in Urdu had requested restraint. This, the 200th World Cup match, spanned less than 60 overs. The people who reportedly paid touts £5,000 for a pair of £100 tickets might have felt short-changed. Or maybe not: they were Australians. (*Hugh Chevallier*)

Man of the Match: S.K. Warne. *Man of the Tournament*: L. Klusener. *Attendance*: 27,835.

PAKISTAN

Saeed Anwar b Fleming 15	Saqlain Mushtaq c Ponting b McGrath ..0
Wajahatullah Wasti c M.E. Waugh	Shoaib Akhtar not out 2
b McGrath 1	
Abdur Razzaq c S.R. Waugh b Moody ...17	L-b 10, w 13, n-b 2 25
Ijaz Ahmed, sen. b Warne 22	
Inzamam-ul-Haq c Gilchrist b Reiffel 15	1/21 (2) 2/21 (1) 3/68 (3) (39 overs) **132**
†Moin Khan c Gilchrist b Warne 6	4/77 (4) 5/91 (6) 6/104 (5)
Shahid Afridi lbw b Warne 13	7/113 (7) 8/129 (8) 9/129 (9)
Azhar Mahmood c and b Moody 8	10/132 Score at 15 overs: 53-2
*Wasim Akram c S.R. Waugh b Warne ...8	

Bowling: McGrath 9-3-13-2; Fleming 6-0-30-1; Reiffel 10-1-29-1; Moody 5-0-17-2; Warne 9-1-33-4.

AUSTRALIA

M.E. Waugh not out 37	D.S. Lehmann not out 13
†A.C. Gilchrist c Inzamam-ul-Haq	
b Saqlain Mushtaq 54	L-b 1, w 1, n-b 3 5
R.T. Ponting c Moin Khan	1/75 (2) 2/112 (3) (2 wkts, 20.1 overs) **133**
b Wasim Akram 24	Score at 15 overs: 103-1

S.R. Waugh, M.G. Bevan, T.M. Moody, S.K. Warne, P.R. Reiffel, D.W. Fleming and G.D. McGrath did not bat.

Bowling: Wasim Akram 8-1-41-1; Shoaib Aktar 4-0-37-0; Abdur Razzaq 2-0-13-0; Azhar Mahmood 2-0-20-0; Saqlain Mushtaq 4.1-0-21-1.

Umpires: S.A. Bucknor and D.R. Shepherd. Referee: R.S. Madugalle.

1 2

THE STATES' RITES:
SHEFFIELD SHIELD

Wisden can claim to have been on the scene early with Australian first-class cricket. When the almanack first documented the Australian domestic game, reporting some matches from the 1887–88 season, the contests were still known as inter-colonials, and were played with no specific trophy in mind. Thus its coverage was already up and running when the Australasian Cricket Council minted a shield in honour of benefactor Lord Sheffield, and over the next century encompassed more than 1,500 games played in that trophy's pursuit.

In the early years of *Wisden*'s reporting, South Australian George Giffen was the dominant force, almost a one-man team. In consecutive matches against Victoria in 1891, he accumulated runs and wickets with the avidity of a land boomer buying subdivisions: 237, 271, and 28 wickets at 12.8. Huge team totals subsequently became a pattern, reflecting both the improving quality of pitches and the timeless basis of matches. The volume and vigour of scoring in the Sheffield Shield before World War I, in fact, stands comparison with that in any era, even Bradman's. Few matches have been harder fought than New South Wales' six-day dogfight with South Australia in December 1907, involving 1,716 runs and a margin of only 20. And few milestones in Australian cricket have been less likely than the 53 in that game by South Australian leggie Albert Wright, after twenty previous innings worth 42 runs.

Warwick Armstrong's successor as Victoria's champion, Bill Ponsford, quickly became a favourite at *Wisden*, delighting both statisticians and salesmen. *Wisden* 1926 included the advertising boast that 'W.H. Ponsford of Melbourne scored 2,500 runs with an ordinary quality *Wisden* 'Exceller', included in which was the world's record score of 429'.

When Ponsford subsequently broke his own record in December 1927 with 437 against Queensland, batting seemed to have reached a new pitch of perfection. In fact, the next generation was already in waiting. Bradman's debut hundred in the same few days became the first stage in an arithmetic progression towards seizing the record himself: two hundreds in a match, a triple century, and finally a four-decker in the span of little over two years.

Were a Bradman to arise today, sadly, he'd be little seen in interstate cricket. And to revisit the games in this section is to be reminded how international cricket has steadily impoverished the domestic game. You don't find Richie Benaud and Alan Davidson pitted against Garry Sobers nowadays, or anything like it. The era when Barry Richards peeled a run-a-minute off a West Australian attack including five Test bowlers is long gone. So, for that matter, is the Sheffield Shield, buried hugger-mugger in December 1999: a decision that *Wisden* rightly condemned, before seeing the responsible ACB executive promoted to run the International Cricket Council. Funny game, cricket.

—GH

VICTORIA V. SOUTH AUSTRALIA

Played at Melbourne, January 1, 2, 3, 5, 1891. – In this match South Australia beat Victoria by an innings and 62 runs. The victory was mainly the work of George Giffen, who has never displayed in a more conspicuous light his pre-eminent qualities as an all-round cricketer. He played an innings of 237, and took in all twelve of the Victorian wickets – five for 89 runs and seven for 103. His magnificent display dwarfed everything else in the game, but several other players showed good batting, notably Trott with a second innings of 81 for Victoria. Phillips again bowled well, taking in an innings of 472 six wickets for 91 runs.

SOUTH AUSTRALIA

J.J. Lyons, b M'Leod	53	J.Noel, b Morris	49
A.H. Jarvis, c Houston, b Phillips	29	L. Evan, c Morris, b Trott	3
G. Giffen, c Blackham, b Phillips	237	F. Jarvis, c Blackham, b Phillips	9
J.E. Gooden, c M'Leod, b Phillips	1	E. Scrymgour, not out	6
J. Reedman, b Trumble	7	B 11, w 12	23
H. Blinman, c M'Leod, b Phillips	50		
E.J. Hiscock, c Trumble, b Phillips	11		**472**

VICTORIA

R. Houston, run out	54	– c Evan, b Giffen	8
W. Bruce, c and b Giffen	58	– b Giffen	13
H. Trott, c Blinman, b Lyons	0	– c Gooden, b Giffen	81
S. Morris, l-b-w, b Giffen	3	– b F. Jarvis	0
R. M'Leod, b Giffen	24	– st A.H. Jarvis, b Giffen	14
C. Ross, not out	29	– c Scrymgour, b Giffen	6
J. M'C. Blackham, b F. Jarvis	0	– c Hiscock, b Giffen	0
J.Worrall, c Scrymgour, b F. Jarvis	20	– run out	1
H. Trumble, b Giffen	20	– st A.H. Jarvis, b Reedman	48
S. Donahoo, run out	0	– st A.H. Jarvis, b Giffen	0
J. Phillips, c Scrymgour, b Giffen	0	– not out	17
B 5, l-b 7	12	W 1, n-b 1	2
	220		**190**

VICTORIAN BOWLING

	Balls	Mdns	Runs	Wkts
Trumble	234	13	104	1
Phillips	334	20	91	6
M'Leod	156	7	66	1
Trott	60	2	38	1
Bruce	162	9	58	0
Ross	42	1	18	0
Morris	72	4	39	1
Worrall	144	5	35	0

Trumble bowled one wide, Bruce eight, and Ross two.

SOUTH AUSTRALIAN BOWLING

	Balls	Mdns	Runs	Wkts	Balls	Mdns	Runs	Wkts
Giffen	308	21	89	5	150	5	103	7
F. Jarvis	180	10	74	2	108	2	54	1
Lyons	138	10	42	1	36	1	25	0
Reedman	6	0	3	0	9	0	6	0

SOUTH AUSTRALIA v. VICTORIA

Played at Adelaide, November 7, 9, 10, 11, 1891. – Victoria did not send by any means a representative team to Adelaide, and the result of the match was a single innings victory for South Australia with 164 runs to spare. This decisive issue was clearly due to the two great South Australian cricketers, George Giffen and J.J. Lyons. George Giffen was batting seven hours for his splendid innings of 271, and afterwards followed up his success by taking sixteen wickets for 166 runs. Including this 271, Giffen has during the past five years scored 921 runs against Victoria in seven innings. Lyons's 104 was a fine display, but he gave a couple of chances.

SOUTH AUSTRALIA

J.J. Lyons, c Laver, b Phillips 104
A.H. Jarvis, b McLeod 2
G. Giffen, c McLean, b Phillips 271
H. Le Haldane, c Harry, b Phillips 9
H. Blinman, c Harry, b Phillips 32
W.F. Giffen, retired hurt 65
J. Reedman, c McLeod, b Marshall 11

J. Noel, c Harry, b Phillips 10
C.W. Hayward, lbw, b Marshall 27
H. Moore, c McLeod, b Phillips 0
F. Jarvis, not out .19
    B 8, l-b 4 .12

562

VICTORIA

F.H. Walters, b G. Giffen ....50 – c and b G. Giffen 0
A.N.A. Bowman, lbw, b G. Giffen ....52 – b G. Giffen 0
R. McLeod, c Noel, b G. Giffen ....27 – b G. Giffen 0
J. Harry, c and b Lyons ....17 – b G. Giffen 19
J. M'C. Blackham, b G. Giffen ....22 – b Lyons 31
H. Stuckey, b G. Giffen ....7 – st Haldane, b G. Giffen 22
H. McLean, b G. Giffen ....12 – st Haldane, b Lyons 33
J. Carlton, c Reedman, b G. Giffen ....16 – c and b G. Giffen 16
F. Laver, c Reedman, b G. Giffen ....5 – c Scrymgour, b Moore 1
J. Phillips, c Hayward, b G. Giffen ....13 – not out 39
H. Marshall, not out ....5 – c Noel, b G. Giffen 0
Byes, &c. ....9 — L-b 2

	235		163

VICTORIA BOWLING

	Balls	Mdns	Runs	Wkts	Balls	Mdns	Runs	Wkts
McLeod	240	11	116	1				
Laver	168	4	64	0				
Marshall	225	6	96	2				
Phillips	360	7	156	6				
Carlton	132	1	72	0				
Blackham	12	1	4	0				
Harry	78	5	31	0				
McLean	24	0	11	0				

SOUTH AUSTRALIAN BOWLING

	Balls	Mdns	Runs	Wkts	Balls	Mdns	Runs	Wkts
F. Jarvis	132	11	30	0	78	3	29	0
Lyons	198	12	59	1	48	0	51	2
G. Giffen	301	12	96	9	155	4	70	7
Noel	96	4	26	0				
Moore	36	2	13	0	24	1	11	1
Reedman	24	1	2	0				

Noel bowled a wide and Reedman a no-ball.

SOUTH AUSTRALIA v. NEW SOUTH WALES

Played at Adelaide, Monday, Tuesday, Wednesday, Thursday, December 17, 18, 19, 20, 1900. – In this match, the South Australians found consolation for their severe defeat a month before at the hands of Victoria, beating New South Wales by an innings and 35 runs. This decisive victory was due to a truly magnificent display of batting by Clement Hill, who, with a score of 365 not out, beat the record in Australia in first-class matches. He was at the wickets eight hours and thirty-five minutes, and his only mistake was a chance when he had made nineteen. Among his hits were one eight (four for an over-throw), and thirty-five 4's. He had a tremendous reception, and was presented to Lord and Lady Tennyson. In the second innings of New South Wales the two young bowlers, Travers and Matthews, did excellent work on a pitch that was beginning to wear.

NEW SOUTH WALES

V. Trumper b F. Jarvis	32	– lbw, b Travers	53
H. Donnan c Matthews b Giffen	19	– b Travers	13
F.A. Iredale c Leak b F. Jarvis	37	– b Matthews	9
M.A. Noble b Travers	28	– b Travers	46
A.J. Hopkins st A. Jarvis b Travers	65	– not out	17
S.E. Gregory st A. Jarvis b Reedman	51	– lbw, b Matthews	31
R.A. Duff c Stuart b Reedman	5	– b Matthews	16
C. Gregory b Travers	16	– c Hill b Travers	5
J.J. Kelly c and b Reedman	11	– b Travers	0
W.P. Howell b Reedman	5	– c Leak b Matthews	19
J.J. Marsh not out	3	– c Reedman b Travers	1
B 5, l-b 2	7	L-b	2
	279		**261**

SOUTH AUSTRALIA

E.H. Leak b Marsh	4	J. Matthews b Marsh	12
F.T. Hack b Marsh	12	A.H. Jarvis b Marsh	0
C. Hill not out	365	E. Walkley b Marsh	53
G. Giffen c and b Howell	7	J. Travers b Howell	0
F. Jarvis c Howell b Hopkins	9	B 23, l-b 10, w 9	42
J.C. Reedman c Howell b Hopkins	71		
P. Stuart b Hopkins	0		**575**

SOUTH AUSTRALIA BOWLING

	Overs	Mdns	Runs	Wkts	Overs	Mdns	Runs	Wkts
Travers	35	7	85	3	31.1	10	74	6
Matthews	9	1	29	0	24	6	61	4
F. Jarvis	18	2	50	2	11	1	29	0
Giffen	12	0	49	1	18	1	67	0
Walkley	7	0	27	0	5	0	18	0
Reedman	12.3	3	32	4	4	1	10	0

NEW SOUTH WALES BOWLING

	Overs	Mdns	Runs	Wkts
Noble	26	7	57	0
Marsh	53	12	181	5
Howell	34	3	100	2
Hopkins	34	8	116	3
Trumper	15	1	67	0
Gregory	2	0	12	0

NEW SOUTH WALES V. SOUTH AUSTRALIA

Played at Sydney, Saturday, Monday, Tuesday, Wednesday, January 5, 7, 8, 9, 1901. –
In this match New South Wales set up a new record in first-class cricket, their total
beating the 887 obtained by Yorkshire against Warwickshire in May, 1896. In another
particular their innings was unique, five individual scores of over 100 being obtained.
Perhaps the feature of the batting was the success gained by Poidevin in his first big

match. The huge score of 918 was obtained very rapidly, the innings only lasting nine hours and twenty minutes. New South Wales had the game in their hands all the way through and won by an innings and 605 runs – one of the most overwhelming victories in the history of cricket.

SOUTH AUSTRALIA

F.T. Hack c Kelly b Noble	2	– c Kelly b Trumper	12
B.T. Bailey b Marsh	57	– b Marsh	0
C. Hill c Howard b Marsh	55	– c Noble b Marsh	20
G. Giffen b Marsh	6	– absent hurt	0
J.C. Reedman lbw, b Marsh	1	– b Marsh	6
F. Jarvis b Trumper	7	– c Duff b Marsh	9
E. Walkley b Trumper	0	– b Marsh	17
A.H. Pellew b Marsh	7	– c Kelly b Hopkins	14
J. Matthews b Hopkins	12	– not out	24
A.H. Jarvis c Gregory b Hopkins	3	– b Noble	0
J. Travers not out	0	– lbw, b Noble	11
Byes, &c.	7	Byes, &c.	3
	157		**156**

NEW SOUTH WALES

F.A. Iredale c A. Jarvis b Travers	118	L.S. Poidevin not out	140
V. Trumper b Jarvis	70	J.J. Kelly c Hill b Hack	34
A.J. Hopkins c A. Jarvis b Travers	27	A. McBeth c Matthews b Bailey	7
M.A. Noble c Giffen b Matthews	153	J. Marsh lbw, b Travers	1
S.E. Gregory b F. Jarvis	168	Byes, &c.	17
R.A. Duff st A. Jarvis b Travers	119		
T. Howard c Bailey b Matthews	64		**918**

NEW SOUTH WALES BOWLING

	Overs	Mdns	Runs	Wkts	Overs	Mdns	Runs	Wkts
Noble	4	1	7	1	6.2	1	7	2
McBeth	6	0	36	0	1	1	0	0
Marsh	16	7	34	5	20	3	59	5
Howard	2	0	5	0	9	1	38	0
Trumper	8	2	23	2	8	1	39	1
Hopkins	10	0	45	2	3	1	10	1

SOUTH AUSTRALIA BOWLING

Travers	69	15	197	4
Matthews	27	2	162	2
Giffen	23	0	119	0
Jarvis	49	7	225	2
Reedman	17	1	70	0
Walkley	6	0	43	0
Hack	10	1	44	1
Hill	1	0	18	0
Bailey	6	1	23	1

NEW SOUTH WALES v. SOUTH AUSTRALIA

Played at Sydney, Friday, Saturday, Monday, Tuesday, Wednesday, Thursday, December 6, 7, 9, 10, 11, 12, 1907. – This was one of the most remarkable matches ever played. In the course of six days 1,716 runs were scored, and yet in the end South Australia only won the game by 20 runs. Though they were beaten, New South Wales gave a display in the fourth innings comparable to that of the Players against the Gentlemen at Lord's in 1900. They were set the tremendous task of getting 593 and actually made 572. At the end of the fifth day they had a wicket to fall but Whiddon was caught off the third ball next morning. New South Wales sadly missed Macartney and Cotter, who were playing against the English team at Brisbane. There was some wonderful batting in the match, Trumper, Noble, Clem Hill, Dolling, and Carter, being all seen at their best.

SOUTH AUSTRALIA

D.R.A. Gehrs b Kelleway	18 – not out	8
E.R. Mayne c Carter b Whiddon	91 – b Whiddon	17
C. Hill b Kelleway	92 – st Carter b Kelleway	94
C.E. Dolling st Carter b Whiddon	2 – c Duff b Whiddon	113
C.B. Jennings lbw, b Hopkins	56 – c Blaxland b Hopkins	52
J.H. Pellew b Noble	17 – b Whiddon	10
N. Claxton st Carter b Whiddon	15 – lbw, b Kelleway	75
L.R. Hill not out	50 – b Kelleway	28
L.W. Chamberlain b Hopkins	0 – b Johnson	36
J.A. O'Connor b Whiddon	0 – b Whiddon	6
A.W. Wright run out	1 – b Hopkins	53
B 3, w 3, n-b 1	7 B 13, l-b 7, w 4, n-b 3	27
	349	**519**

NEW SOUTH WALES

V. Trumper b Claxton	44 – c Chamberlain b Wright	135
A. Diamond b Wright	22 – c Chamberlain b O'Connor	8
M.A. Noble c Jennings b L.R. Hill	93 – b O'Connor	51
M.H. Blaxland b L.R. Hill	6 – c Pellew b L.R. Hill	29
R.A. Duff b L.R. Hill	7 – b Claxton	37
E.L. Waddy c L.R. Hill b O'Connor	39 – b O'Connor	49
A.J. Hopkins c Jennings b L.R. Hill	5 – c C. Hill b Claxton	62
H. Carter st Jennings b Wright	46 – c Wright b O'Connor	125
C. Kelleway b L.R. Hill	1 – not out	31
H. Whiddon b Wright	10 – c Chamberlain b Wright	11
F.B. Johnson not out	1 – b O'Connor	19
B	2 B 4, l-b 4, w 3, n-b 4	15
	276	**572**

NEW SOUTH WALES BOWLING

	Overs	Mdns	Runs	Wkts	Overs	Mdns	Runs	Wkts
Kelleway	25	8	78	2	46	9	114	3
Johnson	19	4	52	0	23.5	2	62	1
Noble	20	2	74	1	26	4	58	0
Hopkins	13	3	65	2	23	1	70	2
Whiddon	21	3	73	4	38	6	140	4
Duff					11	3	48	0

SOUTH AUSTRALIA BOWLING

	Overs	Mdns	Runs	Wkts	Overs	Mdns	Runs	Wkts
O'Connor	30	4	80	1	57	11	172	5
L.R. Hill	21	3	82	5	28	3	79	1
Wright	18.1	2	54	3	27.3	1	123	2
Claxton	11	1	34	1	27	4	104	2
Chamberlain	2	0	13	0	16	0	79	0
Pellew	5	1	11	0	16	0	79	0

VICTORIA v. NEW SOUTH WALES

Played at Melbourne, December 24, 27, 28, 29, 1926. – In this match Victoria set up a new record in first-class cricket, their total of 1,107 beating that of 1,059 obtained by the same State against Tasmania in the 1922–23 season. Throughout the innings which lasted ten hours and a half, runs came at a great pace. A brilliant opening partnership between Ponsford and Woodfull produced 375 runs in three hours and three-quarters and the former player and Hendry added a further 219 for the second wicket in just under two hours. Ponsford hit thirty-six 4's in a memorable display. The brightest of some wonderful batting was that of Ryder, who, by powerful driving, obtained six 6's and thirty-three 4's and scored 295 out of 449 in rather more than four hours. New South Wales, with a weak team, were outplayed from the start and suffered defeat by an innings and 656 runs.

NEW SOUTH WALES

N.E. Phillips c Blackie b Liddicut	52	– lbw, b Hartkopf	36
G. Morgan c Love b Liddicut	13	– c King b Liddicut	26
T.J.E. Andrews st Ellis b Hartkopf	42	– b Liddicut	0
A.F. Kippax b Liddicut	36	– b Hartkopf	26
A.D. Ratcliffe c Ryder b Liddicut	2	– c Morton b Hartkopf	44
A. Jackson c Ellis b Blackie	4	– not out	59
J.R. Hogg not out	40	– c Hendry b Liddicut	13
A.A. Mailey b Ryder	20	– c Morton b Hartkopf	3
N. Campbell lbw, b Blackie	0	– c Ryder b Hartkopf	8
R. McNamee b Ryder	8	– b Liddicut	7
H. McGuirk b Ryder	0	– b Hartkopf	0
Byes, &c.	4	Byes, &c.	8
	221		**230**

VICTORIA

W.M. Woodfull c Ratcliffe b Andrews . . .133
W.H. Ponsford b Morgan 352
H.L. Hendry c Morgan b Mailey 100
J. Ryder c Kippax b Andrews 295
F.L. Morton run out 0
H.S.B. Love st Ratcliffe b Mailey 6
S. King st Ratcliffe b Mailey 7

A.E.V. Hartkopf c McGuirk b Mailey . .61
A.E. Liddicut b McGuirk 36
J.L. Ellis run out 63
D.D.J. Blackie not out 27
 Byes, &c. 27

1107

VICTORIA BOWLING

	Overs	Mdns	Runs	Wkts	Overs	Mdns	Runs	Wkts
Morton	15	4	45	0	11	0	42	0
Liddicut	21	7	50	4	19	2	66	4
Ryder	9	1	32	3				
Blackie	16	3	34	2	5	1	16	0
Hendry	3	2	1	0				
Hartkopf	17	1	57	1	16.3	0	98	6

NEW SOUTH WALES BOWLING

McNamee	24	2	124	0
McGuirk	26	1	130	1
Mailey	64	0	362	4
Campbell	11	0	89	0
Phillips	11.7	0	64	0
Morgan	26	0	137	1
Andrews	21	2	148	2
Kippax	7	0	26	0

NEW SOUTH WALES V. VICTORIA

Played at Sydney, January 26, 27, 28, 1927. – Taking the field without Ponsford, Woodfull, Ryder, Love and Hartkopf, Victoria suffered defeat by an innings and 253 runs. On a tricky wicket their batsmen collapsed completely before McNamee and Macartney [...] McNamee, right hand medium pace, bowled with such deadly effect that, during one period, he took five wickets without a run being scored from him. The delightful batting of Kippax stood out prominently among many failures. His 217, obtained in less than four hours, included twenty-four 4's.

NEW SOUTH WALES

N.E. Phillips c Ellis b Morton 12
G. Morgan lbw, b Blackie 29
C.G. Macartney lbw, b Blackie 41
A.F. Kippax not out 217
J.M. Taylor c Salvana b Mullett 28
A. Jackson b Morton 42
W.A. Oldfield b Millar 56

S.C. Everett lbw, b Blackie 10
E. O'Brien c Baring b Hendry 5
N. Fox c Ellis b Mullett 8
R. McNamee c Ellis b Liddicut 8
 Byes, &c. 13

469

VICTORIA

S. Salvana c Morgan b McNamee	6	– b Macartney	0
F. Baring c Oldfield b McNamee	0	– c Fox b Everett	35
H.L. Hendry c Morgan b Macartney	7	– c Fox b Everett	28
A.E. Liddicut lbw, b Macartney	1	– c Everett b Fox	55
K. Rigg c Everett b McNamee	1	– run out	17
K. Millar b McNamee	0	– c Oldfield b McNamee	7
J.L. Ellis b McNamee	1	– b McNamee	4
B.J. Davie not out	10	– c Oldfield b Macartney	15
L. Mullett b McNamee	0	– b McNamee	0
F.L. Morton b Macartney	4	– b Fox	5
D.D.J. Blackie st Oldfield b McNamee	1	– not out	0
Byes, &c.	4	Byes, &c.	15
	35		**181**

VICTORIA BOWLING

	Overs	Mdns	Runs	Wkts	Overs	Mdns	Runs	Wkts
Morton	24	0	129	2				
Liddicut	21	3	78	1				
Blackie	37	6	126	3				
Mullett	11	0	45	2				
Hendry	7	0	29	1				
Davie	3	0	23	0				
Millar	4	0	26	1				

NEW SOUTH WALES BOWLING

	Overs	Mdns	Runs	Wkts	Overs	Mdns	Runs	Wkts
McNamee	8.4	3	21	7	16	2	49	3
Macartney	9	3	10	3	9	4	14	2
Morgan	1	1	0	0				
Everett					11	0	45	2
O'Brien					8.3	0	41	0
Fox					5.2	0	17	2

VICTORIA V. QUEENSLAND

Played at Melbourne, December 16, 17, 19, 20, 1927. – This match, which Victoria won by an innings and 197 runs, was the most noteworthy of the series. O'Connor, the Queensland captain, won the toss and sent Victoria in but at the end of the first day's play only two men were out with 400 runs on the board and ultimately Victoria completed their innings for the huge total of 793. Scoring 437, Ponsford established a new World's record, beating his 429 against Tasmania in 1922 – the previous record for an individual innings in first-class cricket. At the crease for ten hours and twenty-one minutes, Ponsford gave two chances – both difficult ones. He might have been caught off a return to Bensted when 162 and offered a chance of stumping with his score 239. Using a bat weighing 2 lb. 10 oz., he placed his shots with rare judgment, and was practically always master of the situation throughout his long stay. Victoria forced their opponents to follow-on in a minority of 604. Oxenham, although making only 19, kept his end up for an hour and a half, but Nothling alone showed real ability to cope with the slow deliveries of Blackie, who took six wickets for less than 8 runs each. In the Queensland second innings, Blackie and Ryder, owing to injury, could not bowl, and Thompson took advantage of the weakened attack to score a faultless hundred but occupied more than four hours in so doing.

VICTORIA

W.M. Woodfull run out 31	J.L. Ellis c Nothling b Thompson 15
W.H. Ponsford c and b Amos 437	D.D.J. Blackie b Amos 35
H.L. Hendry b Gough 129	F.L. Morton c O'Connor b Amos 0
J. Ryder c Rowe b Nothling 70	H. Ironmonger not out 1
J. Scaife b Amos .18	B 6, l-b 3, w 6 15
A.E.V. Hartkopf b Amos 15	
C. Sindrey c Bensted b Rowe 27	**793**

QUEENSLAND

L.P.D. O'Connor c Ellis b Blackie 11	– c sub b Ironmonger 66
L.E. Oxenham lbw, b Ryder 19	– lbw, b Morton 3
F. Gough b Blackie 0	– b Ironmonger 54
F.C. Thompson lbw, b Blackie 8	– c Ellis b Ironmonger 118
W. Rowe b Morton 34	– b Ryder 9
O.E. Nothling lbw, b Ironmonger 66	– b Morton 18
L. Litster c Hendry b Ironmonger 10	– b Ironmonger .43
E. Bensted not out 11	– run out 14
L.L. Gill b Blackie 0	– c Ellis b Ironmonger 27
A.C. Hurwood lbw, b Blackie 1	– b Morton 1
G.S. Amos st Ellis b Blackie 0	– not out 27
B 15, l-b 9, w 2, n-b 3 29	B 16, l-b 8, n-b 3 27
189	**407**

QUEENSLAND BOWLING

	Overs	Mdns	Runs	Wkts	Overs	Mdns	Runs	Wkts
Amos	29	0	148	5				
Hurwood	28	3	133	0				
Gill	19	0	91	0				
Nothling	26	6	101	1				
Bensted	20	0	95	0				
Rowe	13	1	65	1				
Thompson	22	2	74	1				
Gough	10	1	56	1				
Litster	2	0	15	0				

VICTORIA BOWLING

Morton	13	3	34	1	32	6	103	3
Ironmonger	17	5	26	2	40.6	12	88	5
Blackie	23.5	5	46	6	3	2	2	0
Ryder	5	1	17	1	5.6	0	12	1
Hartkopf	7	0	37	0	22	1	128	0
Hendry					16	4	47	0

Umpires: J. Richards and P.E. Smith.

FROM NOTES BY THE EDITOR

[…] Cricket records, as given in *Wisden*, do not deal with any of those established after the close of the English season. The achievements of W.H. Ponsford during the past two or three months, however, have been so remarkable that I must find room for a list of some of that player's performances that has been supplied to me by my friend Mr Ashley-Cooper. In the first place, Ponsford, making 437 for Victoria against Queensland at Melbourne, has beaten the previous record for an individual score – his own 429 for Victoria against Tasmania at Melbourne put together in the winter of 1922–23. In eleven consecutive matches up to the end of 1927, he always reached three-figures in one innings or another. Four times he has made three consecutive hundreds: 162, 429 and 108 (these were registered in his second, third and fourth matches in first class cricket) – 159, 110 and 110 not out – 151, 352, and 108 – and 133, 437 and 202. On four occasions he has put together innings of more than three hundred – 429, 352, 437 and 336. One of the few things he has not done is to equal W.G. Grace's aggregate of 839 in three successive innings – 344, 177 and 318 not out – but he came desperately near that achievement last December when he scored 437, 202 and 336 in following matches but broke the run of centuries with a score of 38 in the second innings of the match in which he obtained 202. Up to the end of last year he had played sixty innings in first-class cricket, twice not out, making 5,582 runs and averaging 96.24. […] (*1928*)

SOUTH AUSTRALIA v. NEW SOUTH WALES

Played at Adelaide, December 16, 17, 19, 20, 1927. – A keenly-fought match ended in exciting fashion, South Australia, despite some splendid bowling by McNamee, getting home by one wicket. Bradman joined the select band of cricketers who have made a century in their first Sheffield Shield match and Kippax – twice compelled to retire owing to illness – and Phillips also put together three-figure scores for New South Wales. Owing much to the sound cricket of their early batsmen, South Australia made a creditable response, Schneider, the diminutive left-hander, batting attractively in partnerships with Harris and Richardson which realised 140 and 128 for the first and second wicket respectively. The rest of the game saw the bowlers with the upper hand. Grimmett, taking eight wickets for 57, had chief share in the cheap dismissal of New South Wales in the visitors' second innings. Set 189 to win, South Australia had seven men out for 131 but Lee and Grimmett batted steadily when the issue hung in the balance.

New South Wales

N.E. Phillips b Whitfield	112	– lbw, b Grimmett	11
G. Morgan b Scott	11	– b Grimmett	34
T.J.E. Andrews c Williams b Grimmett	58	– b Scott	20
A.F. Kippax c Alexander b Williams	143	– c and b Grimmett	0
A. Scanes c Williams b Schneider	44	– c Whitfield b Grimmett	26
W.A. Oldfield c Hack b Grimmett	12	– c Richardson b Grimmett	4
D. Bradman c Williams b Scott	118	– b Grimmett	33
F. Jordan lbw, b Scott	1	– lbw, b Grimmett	0
S.C. Everett st Hack b Grimmett	5	– c Harris b Scott	8
A.A. Mailey b Scott	0	– c Schneider b Grimmett	5
R.L.A. McNamee not out	1	– not out	1
B 2, l-b 5, w 1, n-b 6	14	B 1, l-b 1, w 1, n-b 5	8
	519		**150**

South Australia

K.J. Schneider c and b Mailey	108	– lbw, b McNamee	11
G.W. Harris c and b Andrews	77	– b McNamee	18
V.Y. Richardson b Jordan	80	– b McNamee	0
W.C. Alexander st Oldfield b Mailey	42	– b Andrews	49
E.A. Johnson st Oldfield b Andrews	0	– b Mailey	0
H.E.P. Whitfield b Jordan	15	– run out	17
A. Hack c Morgan b Everett	45	– b McNamee	6
P.K. Lee st Oldfield b Mailey	28	– not out	27
C.V. Grimmett not out	43	– c Oldfield b McNamee	32
J.D. Scott c Phillips b Everett	0	– c Phillips b Mailey	14
N.L. Williams b Everett	21	– not out	0
B 8, l-b 12, n-b 2	22	B 4, l-b 11	15
	481		**189**

South Australia Bowling

	Overs	Mdns	Runs	Wkts	Overs	Mdns	Runs	Wkts
Scott	19.6	1	99	4	17	3	46	2
Whitfield	17	3	43	1	7	1	26	0
Grimmett	31	1	160	3	21.7	5	57	8
Williams	11	0	70	1	2	0	13	0
Lee	17	1	76	0				
Schneider	6	0	39	1				
Alexander	3	0	14	0				
Johnson	1	0	4	0				

New South Wales Bowling

	Overs	Mdns	Runs	Wkts	Overs	Mdns	Runs	Wkts
Everett	26.7	4	92	3	3	0	16	0
McNamee	22	11	34	0	29.2	12	53	5
Jordan	21	1	65	2	4	0	13	0
Mailey	50	9	143	3	28	2	79	2
Andrews	18	0	86	2	6	1	13	1
Phillips	7	0	22	0				
Morgan	3	0	17	0				

Umpires: G.A. Hele and J.J. Quinn.

QUEENSLAND V. NEW SOUTH WALES

Played at Brisbane, October 27, 29, 30, 31, November 1, 1928. – If failing to justify expectations in the Test Trial, Bradman batted so brilliantly in the first of the Sheffield Shield matches that he scored a hundred in each innings. In winning by six wickets, after being 76 behind on the first innings, New South Wales owed nearly everything to Bradman and Hooker, the former making 264 for once out and the latter taking ten wickets for less than 12 runs each. O'Connor and Gough, sharing in a second wicket stand of 129, carried off the honours in Queensland's first innings. Thurlow, a new fast bowler, brought about a sensational collapse, the last seven New South Wales wickets actually falling for 11 runs. Thompson afterwards showing great form, Queensland set their opponents 399 to get to win. The task was tackled with fine determination. An opening partnership of 121 by Jackson and Loder and a third wicket stand of 185 by Bradman and Kippax brought victory with plenty of time to spare.

QUEENSLAND

R.K. Oxenham b McNamee	1	– b Morgan	7
L.P. O'Connor c Love b Hooker	72	– b Hooker	2
F.J. Gough b Hooker	67	– c and b Carter	39
W. Rowe c Nicholls b Morgan	15	– b Nicholls	22
F.C. Thompson lbw, b Hooker	29	– not out	158
R. Higgins c Morgan b Hooker	58	– b McNamee	33
Dr O.E. Nothling b Morgan	18	– c Nicholls b Hooker	3
E. Knowles c Love b Morgan	2	– b Campbell	30
E.C. Bensted not out	36	– b McNamee	0
P.M. Hornibrook c Love b Hooker	0	– c Nicholls b Hooker	16
H.M. Thurlow b Hooker	1	– c Morgan b Hooker	1
B 11, l-b 10, n-b 4	25	L-b 7, n-b 4	11
	324		**322**

NEW SOUTH WALES

A. Jackson c Hornibrook b Nothling	50	– c Nothling b Rowe	71
R. Loder b Thurlow	1	– run out	49
D.G. Bradman c O'Connor b Thurlow	131	– not out	133
A.F. Kippax b Thurlow	47	– c Hornibrook b Rowe	96
G. Morgan lbw, b Thurlow	4	– b Thurlow	6
H.S.B. Love c O'Connor b Thurlow	5	– not out	31
C.O. Nicholls b Thurlow	2		
H. Hooker b Oxenham	0		
J. Carter lbw, b Oxenham	0		
N. Campbell b Oxenham	0		
R. McNamee not out	0		
L-b 4, n-b 4	8	B 11, l-b 3, n-b 1	15
	248		**401**

New South Wales Bowling

	Overs	Mdns	Runs	Wkts	Overs	Mdns	Runs	Wkts
Nicholls	17	1	64	0	9	2	50	1
Hooker	24.3	9	46	6	31.6	5	72	4
McNamee	29	7	85	1	27	5	93	2
Carter	11	0	47	0	7	1	31	1
Morgan	11	1	36	3	9	3	28	1
Campbell	5	0	21	0	6	0	37	1

Queensland Bowling

	Overs	Mdns	Runs	Wkts	Overs	Mdns	Runs	Wkts
Hornibrook	12	2	52	0	20.4	3	62	0
Thurlow	15	3	59	6	21	2	94	1
Oxenham	18.2	3	56	3	29	2	77	0
Nothling	8	1	22	1	13	0	52	0
Rowe	5	0	15	0	11	3	45	2
Bensted	6	0	30	0	9	0	35	0
Thompson	1	0	6	0	8	3	21	0

Umpires: J.P. Orr and J.A. Scott.

New South Wales v. Victoria

Played at Sydney, January, 24, 25, 26, 28, 29, 1929. – This proved to be the key match of the competition and New South Wales, taking first innings points, made sure of the Sheffield Shield. Of absorbing interest, the cricket was especially notable for the feat of Bradman who made 340 not out – the highest score by a New South Wales player in Sheffield Shield games and the highest in a first-class match on the Sydney ground. Bradman batted for roughly eight hours and did not give a chance. Fairfax also making a hundred, New South Wales, having established themselves in an impregnable position, were able to declare with six wickets down. Hooker and Bettington – the latter recently returned from England – bowled with such success that Victoria had to follow on 448 behind. Hooker actually took four wickets with four balls, his victims being Ebeling, Gamble and Ironmonger in one over, and Austen, with his next ball – his first in the second innings. Onyons in the follow-on batted with skill for four hours and a half. Scaife assisted him to add 187 and Darling, a left-hander, hit hard in a third wicket stand realising 143. Lansdown and Bird also showed confidence at the crisis of the game, and New South Wales had to be content with the honours of a drawn match.

NEW SOUTH WALES

A. Jackson b Ironmonger 41
A. Fairfax b Gamble 104
D.G. Bradman not out 340
T.J.E. Andrews lbw, b Ironmonger 19
S. McCabe b Gamble 60
A. Marks c Lansdown b Darling 56

R.H. Bettington c Austen b Darling 40
J. Fingleton not out 25

B 11, l-b 15, n-b 2 28

*713

L. Davidson, C.O. Nicholls, H. Hooker did not bat.

*Innings declared closed.

VICTORIA

B.A. Onyons st Davidson b Bettington ......61 – c Fingleton b Hooker 131
E.T. Austen b Hooker ....19 – b Hooker 5
J. Scaife c Fingleton b Bettington ....42 – run out 91
L. Darling c Davidson b Hooker ....37 – c McCabe b Fairfax 96
W. Reddrop b Hooker ....33 – b McCabe 14
H.C. Lansdown b Bettington ....4 – not out 48
T. Bird c and b Nicholls ....22 – c Fingleton c Marks 63
J.L. Ellis not out ....19 – not out 7
H.I. Ebeling b Hooker ....4 – b Fairfax 14
H.S. Gamble b Hooker 0
H. Ironmonger c and b Hooker 0
B 14, l-b 2, n-b 8 24   B 27, l-b 7, w 1, n-b 6 41

265   **510**

VICTORIA BOWLING

	Overs	Mdns	Runs	Wkts	Overs	Mdns	Runs	Wkts
Gamble	29	1	193	2				
Ebeling	39	3	142	0				
Ironmonger	56	7	220	2				
Darling	18	1	77	2				
Scaife	2	0	14	0				
Austen	1	0	17	0				
Onyons	1	0	22	0				

NEW SOUTH WALES BOWLING

	Overs	Mdns	Runs	Wkts	Overs	Mdns	Runs	Wkts
Nicholls	23	7	52	1	18	3	88	0
Hooker	28	11	42	6	27	3	94	2
Bettington	27	3	92	3	25	3	96	0
Fairfax	19	4	35	0	19	4	54	2
McCabe	5	3	10	0	16	2	44	1
Andrews	1	0	10	0	6	0	33	0
Fingleton					2	1	1	0
Marks					15	4	59	1

Umpires: A.C. Jones and W.H. Bayfield.

NEW SOUTH WALES V. QUEENSLAND

Played at Sydney, January 3, 4, 6, 7, 1930. – Everything else in this game paled before the phenomenal performance of Bradman who, in scoring 452 not out – a feat that occupied him 415 minutes – played the highest individual innings recorded in first-class cricket. That splendid exhibition led the way to a victory for New South Wales by 685 runs. Displaying a wider range of strokes than usual, Bradman batted without a trace of error during his long stay and hit no fewer than forty-nine 4's. His prolific scoring followed upon comparatively low totals in the first innings of each side. Against Hurwood, who kept an admirable length, New South Wales found run-getting hard and Queensland fared no better, only Bensted and Goodwin appearing to advantage. New South Wales, going in again eight runs ahead, gained a complete mastery over the bowling. Bradman, batting with such brilliancy, made matters easy for his colleagues. Kippax put together a hundred and McCabe and Allsopp also scored readily. Faced with the appalling task of getting 770 runs, Queensland offered scarcely any resistance. Half the wickets actually fell for 23 and on the last morning Everett finished off the innings. In the two spells of bowling he disposed of six batsmen at a cost of less than four runs each.

NEW SOUTH WALES

C. Andrews st Leeson b Hurwood	56	– c Levy b Hurwood	16
D.G. Bradman c Leeson b Hurwood	3	– not out	452
A. Marks c Hurwood b Thurlow	40	– c Bensted b Hurwood	5
A.F. Kippax lbw, b Thurlow	15	– lbw, b Rowe	115
S. McCabe c Leeson b Thurlow	15	– c Leeson b Hurwood	60
A. Allsopp c and b Hurwood	9	– b Hurwood	66
A. Fairfax b Brew	20	– st Leeson b Hurwood	10
S.C. Everett c Bensted b Brew	41	– c Goodwin b Hurwood	4
H.L. Davidson lbw, b Hurwood	14	– c and b Goodwin	22
S. Burt b Thurlow	10		
H. Chilvers not out	6		
B 3, l-b 3	6	B 6, l-b 1, w 2, n-b 2	11
	235		***761**

*Innings declared closed.

QUEENSLAND

R.M. Levy c Everett b Fairfax	6	– b Everett	0
L.P. O'Connor c Andrews b Fairfax	21	– b McCabe	17
F.C. Thompson lbw, b Chilvers	1	– lbw, b Everett	0
W. Rowe b McCabe	11	– c Bradman b Chilvers	1
F.J. Gough c Marks b McCabe	14	– c Allsopp b Chilvers	20
E.C. Bensted c Davidson b McCabe	51	– b Everett	3
V. Goodwin c Marks b Fairfax	67	– run out	4
A. Hurwood b Chilvers	4	– b Everett	6
F.M. Brew b McCabe	20	– c Davidson b Everett	26
H. Leesen c Davidson b McCabe	14	– not out	2
H.M. Thurlow not out	3	– b Everett	0
B 9, l-b 3, n-b 3	15	B 1, l-b 1, w 1, n-b 2	5
	227		**84**

QUEENSLAND BOWLING

	Overs	Mdns	Runs	Wkts	Overs	Mdns	Runs	Wkts
Thurlow	18.1	0	83	4	25	0	147	0
Hurwood	22	6	57	4	34	1	179	6
Bensted	6	0	39	0	12	0	70	0
Brew	8	0	50	2	6	0	61	0
Rowe					19	0	143	1
Thompson					15	0	90	0
Gough					4	0	40	0
Levy					2	0	20	0
Goodwin					0.1	0	0	1

NEW SOUTH WALES BOWLING

	Overs	Mdns	Runs	Wkts	Overs	Mdns	Runs	Wkts
Everett	10	1	46	0	8.5	1	23	6
Fairfax	15	1	53	3	7	3	12	0
Chilvers	20	5	52	2	8	0	22	2
McCabe	15.1	5	36	5	5	3	15	1
Burt	8	1	25	0	2	0	7	0

Umpires: G. Borwick and E.J. Shaw.

NEW SOUTH WALES V. VICTORIA

At Melbourne, December 22, 24, 26, 27, 1956. Tied. Craig, suffering from tonsillitis, and Burke, with a broken finger, batted for New South Wales in their second innings and helped in the first tie in the 100 years' history of inter-State cricket. On a drying pitch New South Wales needed 161 runs for victory. When seven wickets fell for 70 they seemed sure to be beaten, but Craig and Benaud shared a stand of 75 for the eighth wicket. Craig, pale and weak, batted for thirty minutes. Victoria's heroes were the 22-year-old Kline, slow left-arm bowler, and Meckiff, tall and fast, who also played a valuable first innings. For New South Wales, Burke carried his bat through the first innings and was well supported by the 19-year-old O'Neill.

VICTORIA

C.C. McDonald b Benaud ....50 – c Lambert b Wyatt 8
W. Lawry c Lambert b Davidson ....1 – lbw b Wyatt 7
R.N. Harvey c Lambert b Treanor ....46 – b Burke 22
J. Shaw lbw b Martin ....26 – st Lambert b Treanor 52
K. Kendall c Watson b Benaud ....8 – lbw b Treanor 21
S.J. Loxton b Benaud ....26 – c sub b Treanor 0
L. Maddocks c Craig b Martin ....16 – b Benaud 33
A. Dick b Benaud ....0 – b Benaud 29
I. Meckiff b Wyatt ....55 – b Treanor 8
L. Kline b Davidson ....11 – not out 9
J. Salmon not out ....0 – b Treanor 0
    Extras 5   Extras 8
          244   197

NEW SOUTH WALES

S. Carroll c Dick b Meckiff	11	– b Kline	14
J.W. Burke not out	132	– c Maddocks b Meckiff	8
J. Treanor c Maddocks b Salmon	14	– c Maddocks b Meckiff	0
N. O'Neill st Maddocks b Kline	69	– c and b Kline	11
I.D. Craig lbw b Dick	3	– c Lawry b Kline	24
W. Watson c Harvey b Meckiff	16	– lbw b Kline	15
R. Benaud c Harvey b Meckiff	8	– c Shaw b Kline	63
J. Martin b Loxton	1	– c Maddocks b Meckiff	6
A.K. Davidson lbw b Kline	22	– b Meckiff	0
O. Lambert b Kline	0	– lbw b Kline	5
A. Wyatt run out	0	– not out	2
Extras	5	Extras	12
	281		**160**

NEW SOUTH WALES BOWLING

	Overs	Mdns	Runs	Wkts	Overs	Mdns	Runs	Wkts
Wyatt	9.3	0	38	1	4	2	14	2
Davidson	14	3	50	2	17	1	65	0
Treanor	16	5	50	1	10.4	2	36	5
Benaud	26	2	67	4	21	9	34	2
Martin	7	0	34	2				
Burke					13	1	40	1

VICTORIA BOWLING

	Overs	Mdns	Runs	Wkts	Overs	Mdns	Runs	Wkts
Meckiff	21	6	65	3	21.1	6	56	4
Salmon	13	4	41	1				
Loxton	9	0	56	1	5	2	10	0
Kline	20	0	72	3	19	3	57	6
Dick	14	2	42	1	13	1	25	0

NEW SOUTH WALES V. VICTORIA

At Sydney, January 26, 27, 29, 30, 1962. New South Wales won by ten wickets. Simpson and Craig shared a century opening stand in each New South Wales innings; they put on 161 runs in the first innings, despite fiery bowling by the fast left-hander Meckiff, and made 139 in the second innings, without being separated. The first innings had produced a memorable last-wicket partnership in which Davidson (106) completed his first century in first class cricket on the Sydney ground, and with wicket-keeper Ford added 59 runs. Davidson, in an innings of massive power and shrewd judgment, actually made 58 of these runs, the remaining single being a leg-bye. Ford faced only three balls. The left-handers, Lawry and Furlong, put on 169 for Victoria's second wicket but they were sometimes painfully slow. Lawry (67) again showed his toughness in the second innings under difficult conditions.

VICTORIA

*W. Lawry c Misson b Simpson	.97	– b Benaud	.67
D. Anderson b Davidson	.0	– c Craig b Davidson	.0
R. Furlong c and b Martin	.82	– c O'Neill b Simpson	.26
J. Potter c Benaud b Davidson	.53	– c Ford b Martin	.12
R. Cowper not out	.64	– c O'Neill b Simpson	.18
N. Crompton c Ford b Simpson	.2	– b Benaud	.27
†R. Jordon c Ford b Martin	.3	– b Martin	.3
C. Guest st Ford b Martin	.5	– c O'Neill b Benaud	.27
L. Kline c Davidson b Simpson	.5	– c Booth b Simpson	.2
I. Meckiff run out	.6	– b Benaud	.0
R. Gaunt c and b Martin	.0	– not out	.0
B 3, l-b 1	.4	B 13, l-b 2, n-b 1	.16

1/3 2/172 3/190 4/266 5/279   **321**   1/3 2/33 3/66 4/112 5/125   **198**
6/279 7/293 8/302 9/319   6/161 7/186 8/195 9/198

Bowling: FIRST INNINGS – Davidson 16-1-63-2; Misson 23-4-72-0; Booth 4-1-10-0; Martin 30.1-8-80-4; Benaud 9-1-24-0; Simpson 27-7-66-3; O'Neill 1-0-2-0. SECOND INNINGS – Davidson 3-0-8-1; Misson 3-0-9-0; Martin 24-4-85-2; Benaud 19.3-5-49-4; Simpson 19-5-31-3.

NEW SOUTH WALES

R. Simpson b Meckiff	.95	– not out	.67
I. Craig lbw b Guest	.80	– not out	.65
N. O'Neill c Jordon b Meckiff	.0		
F. Misson c Crompton b Guest	.21		
B. Booth c Cowper b Gaunt	.7		
N. Harvey c Cowper b Guest	.46		
G. Thomas b Meckiff	.0		
A. Davidson c Anderson b Guest	.106		
*R. Benaud c Cowper b Kline	.7		
J. Martin run out	.0		
†D. Ford not out	.0		
B 9, l-b 9, w 3, n-b 1	.22	B 3, l-b 3, n-b 1	.7

1/161 2/164 3/208 4/212 5/227   **384**   (No wkt) **139**
6/230 7/306 8/325 9/325

Bowling: FIRST INNINGS – Meckiff 26-4-97-3; Gaunt 10-2-37-1; Guest 22.7-0-103-4; Kline 16-1-98-1; Crompton 3-0-27-0. SECOND INNINGS – Meckiff 5-1-15-0; Gaunt 2-0-16-0; Guest 7-0-35-0; Kline 9-0-25-0; Cowper 5-0-37-0; Anderson 1-0-4-0.

Umpires: E.F. Wykes and F. Tilley.

SOUTH AUSTRALIA V. NEW SOUTH WALES

At Adelaide, February 9, 10, 12, 13, 1962. South Australia won by 130 runs. In an animated game, South Australia repeated their previous season's Adelaide victory over New South Wales, who led on the first innings. It was a great match for Sobers, who in a brilliant innings for 251 made the highest score at Adelaide Oval since the war, and in the last innings of the match took six New South Wales wickets for 72 runs, having switched from swing to spin on the last day. Sobers began his splendid innings uncomfortably against Davidson and Benaud, but later thrashed the bowling. Sellers and Sincock hit freely in a ninth-wicket stand in South Australia's first innings, and Martin and Misson performed similarly for New South Wales after the young left-hander Sincock had O'Neill caught in his first over and Sobers had taken three wickets in 10 balls.

SOUTH AUSTRALIA

*L. Favell c Craig b Davidson 28	– c O'Neill b Davidson 8
J. Lill c Martin b Misson 8	– b Benaud 51
G. Sobers c Ford b Davidson 2	– b Davidson 251
I. McLachlan c Ford b Davidson 7	– b Martin 5
N. Dansie c Simpson b Davidson 40	– b Benaud 71
R. Lloyd c Ford b Davidson 1	– c Booth b Benaud 35
N. Hawke c Thomas b Misson 0	– not out 6
†B. Jarman c Benaud b Misson 15	– c Martin b Benaud 12
R. Sellers c Craig b Booth 33	– c Martin b Benaud 9
D. Sincock not out 52	
G. Brooks b Benaud 1	
L-b 1, n-b 2 3	B 4, l-b 5, w 1, n-b 1 11

1/36 2/36 3/45 4/46 5/48   **190**   1/11 2/112 3/294 4/323   (8 wkts, dec.) **459**
6/51 7/83 8/104 9/172   5/420 6/444 7/444 8/459

Bowling: FIRST INNINGS – Davidson 17-5-40-5; Misson 12-2-38-3; Simpson 13-0-52-0; Martin 5-0-37-0; Booth 8-2-12-1; Benaud 6.6-0-8-1. SECOND INNINGS – Davidson 25-0-99-2; Misson 9-1-39-0; Simpson 11-3-43-0; Martin 18-0-121-1; Benaud 34.3-6-121-5; O'Neill 5-0-25-0.

NEW SOUTH WALES

R. Simpson c Jarman b Brooks 19	– st Jarman b Sobers 1
I. Craig lbw b Sobers 32	– c Jarman b Sobers 56
N. O'Neill c Brooks b Sincock 1	– c Brooks b Sobers 43
B. Booth lbw b Brooks 9	– st Jarman b Sincock 28
N. Harvey st Jarman b Sincock 39	– b Sobers 22
G. Thomas c Lill b Sobers 6	– c Favell b Sincock 28
A. Davidson c Jarman b Sobers 0	– c Favell b Sincock 9
*R. Benaud c Jarman b Brooks 19	– not out 38
J. Martin c Jarman b Hawke 63	– b Sobers 9
F. Misson not out 51	– c Jarman b Sobers 4
†D. Ford c Jarman b Hawke 6	– lbw b Hawke 27
L-b 4 4	B 2, l-b 1, w 1, n-b 1 5

1/30 2/33 3/54 4/89 5/97 6/97   **249**   1/68 2/122 3/127 4/130 5/180   **270**
7/109 8/137 9/231   6/184 7/189 8/204 9/212

Bowling: FIRST INNINGS – Brooks 18-0-53-3; Hawke 11.4-2-41-2; Sincock 17-0-78-2; Sobers 14-1-51-3; Sellers 3-0-22-0. SECOND INNINGS – Brooke 11-1-52-0; Hawke 7.4-2-20-1; Sincock 18-2-96-3; Sobers 23-3-72-6; Sellers 4-0-17-0; Dansie 3-0-8-0.

Umpires: C.J. Egar and A.F. Godson.

NEW SOUTH WALES V. WESTERN AUSTRALIA

At Sydney, November 8, 9, 11, 12, 1963. New South Wales won by nine wickets. Although Western Australia lost four wickets for 69, Shepherd batted strongly for his first Sydney century. However, the total of 420 was passed by New South Wales with only one wicket down and in the second innings they lost only one for 262. Simpson, 247 not out in five and a quarter hours, and Thomas enjoyed a mammoth opening stand of 308 runs. Booth, who opened in the second innings hit a century in ninety-four minutes between lunch and tea and had reached 169 not out in two and three-quarter hours when his team won with an hour to spare.

WESTERN AUSTRALIA

A. Jones st Ford b Martin 18	– c Corling b O'Neill	.34
†G. Becker b Misson 27	– lbw b Misson	.1
H. Joynt c Misson b Martin 16	– c O'Neill b Benaud	.11
*B. Shepherd lbw b Martin 149	– c Simpson b Martin	.29
J. Inverarity b Corling 4	– run out	.50
R. Waugh c and b Benaud 87	– c Corling b Misson	.1
T. Jenner b Corling 2	– c Lee b Philpott	.13
G.D. McKenzie c Corling b Lee 50	– b Benaud	.31
K. Slater not out 49	– b Misson	.58
H. Bevan b Martin 2	– b Corling	.5
I. Gallash b Martin 1	– not out	.4
B 3, l-b 9, w 1, n-b 2 15	B 21, l-b 8	.29

1/36 2/50 3/62 4/69 5/249   **420**   1/13 2/15 3/57 4/122 5/131   **266**
6/255 7/339 8/386 9/418   6/182 7/184 8/230 9/254

Bowling: FIRST INNINGS – Misson 13-2-48-1; Corling 23-3-46-2; Martin 24.6-3-104-5; Philpott 8-0-32-0; O'Neill 2-0-19-0; Lee 19-2-59-1; Benaud 25-5-71-1; Simpson 9-0-26-0. SECOND INNINGS – Misson 12.6-4-26-3; Corling 5-0-23-1; Martin 12-1-54-1; Philpott 7-0-39-1; O'Neill 12-1-52-1; Lee 12-4-25-0; Benaud 16-10-18-2.

NEW SOUTH WALES

G. Thomas c and b Slater 127		
R. Simpson not out 247		
P. Philpott not out 38	– not out	.37
N.C. O'Neill (did not bat) ....–	b Gallash	.43
B.C. Booth (did not bat) ....–	not out	.169
L-b 5, n-b 8 13	B 5, l-b 5, n-b 3	.13

1/308   (1 wkt, dec.) **425**   1/127   (1 wkt) **262**

*R. Benaud, T. Lee, J.W. Martin, F.M. Misson, †D. Ford and G.E. Corling did not bat.

Bowling: FIRST INNINGS – McKenzie 14-0-73-0; Bevan 10-0-68-0; Gallash 21-1-86-0; Slater 21-1-101-1; Jenner 9-0-76-0; Waugh 1-0-8-0. SECOND INNINGS – McKenzie 12-3-40-0; Bevan 4-0-29-0; Gallash 5-0-36-1; Slater 6-0-62-0; Jenner 9-0-53-0; Waugh 4-0-25-0; Shepherd 0.3-0-4-0.

Umpires: E.F. Wykes and W.E. Hicks.

WESTERN AUSTRALIA v. SOUTH AUSTRALIA

At Perth, November 20, 21, 22, 23, 1970. South Australia won by an innings and 111 runs. The match was dominated by Richards with his great innings of 356; he was with I.M. Chappell in a second-wicket partnership for 308 runs in two hours fifty minutes. Richards missed by three runs equalling the highest score in Australian first-class cricket since the war, R.B. Simpson's 359 for New South Wales against Queensland in Brisbane in 1963–4. Richards, who hit one 6 and forty-eight 4's, batted in all for six hours and 12 minutes. Against a well-balanced attack, supported by keen fielding, he scored 325 runs on the first day, in five and a half hours: 79 before lunch, 137 from lunch to tea, and 109 from tea to 'stumps'. His first 100 runs came in 125 minutes, and 200 in 208 minutes and 300 in 317 minutes. He was out lbw to a full toss next morning. Irvine and Inverarity showed defiance in both innings for Western Australia. Hammond bowled effectively, taking nine for 79.

SOUTH AUSTRALIA

B.A. Richards lbw b Mann 356	†R.P. Blundell b Mann 0
J.J. Causby c Chadwick b Lock 38	A.A. Mallett not out 6
*I.M. Chappell st Marsh b Lock 129	T.J. Jenner c McKenzie b Mann 5
G.S. Chappell c Marsh b McKenzie 11	
K.G. Cunningham c Inverarity b Lock ...13	N-b 4 4
K. Langley run out 7	
E.W. Freeman c Irvine b Lock 6	1/109 2/417 3/447 4/551 (9 wkts, dec.) **575**
	5/553 6/563 7/563 8/564 9/575

J.R. Hammond did not bat.

Bowling: McKenzie 19-2-101-1; Lillee 18-1-117-0; Brayshaw 12-1-69-0; Mann 20.6-1-120-3; Lock 16-1-108-4; Inverarity 8-0-56-0.

WESTERN AUSTRALIA

D. Chadwick c Blundell b Jenner 49	– c and b Hammond 2
C. Scarff c Blundell b Hammond 11	– b Cunningham 7
J.T. Irvine b Jenner 33	– c and b G.S. Chappell 57
R.J. Inverarity c G.S. Chappell b Hammond .85	– c and b G.S. Chappell 35
R.D. Meuleman retired hurt 28	– absent hurt 0
I.J. Brayshaw lbw b Freeman 22	– c Richards b Mallett 13
†R.W. Marsh c I.M. Chappell b Hammond ...9	– c I.M. Chappell b Richards 19
A.L. Mann c Blundell b Hammond 2	– c I.M. Chappell b Hammond 1
D.K. Lillee c Cunningham b Hammond 12	– b Hammond 6
G.D. McKenzie b Hammond 10	– not out 18
*G.A.R. Lock not out 2	– c Hammond b Mallett 8
L-b 7, w 2, n-b 17 26	B 1, n-b 8 9

1/33 2/88 3/110 4/239 5/256   **289**   1/3 2/15 3/102 4/110 5/137   **175**
6/261 7/270 8/285 9/289   6/141 7/142 8/161 9/175

Bowling: FIRST INNINGS – Freeman 15-1-53-1; Hammond 12.3-1-54-6; G.S. Chappell 8-1-23-0; Jenner 22-4-78-2; Mallett 18-5-37-0; Cunningham 9-2-18-0. SECOND INNINGS – Freeman 4-0-16-0; Hammond 9-2-25-3; G.S. Chappell 12-1-41-2; Jenner 8-0-25-0; Mallett 12.5-2-43-2; Cunningham 4-0-12-1; Richards 1-0-4-1.

Umpires: W. Carter and N. Townsend.

SOUTH AUSTRALIA V. VICTORIA

At Adelaide, October 22, 23, 24, 25, 1982. Drawn. South Australia 4 pts. Despite Yallop's batting for Victoria, and the Inverarity/Hookes partnership in the first South Australian innings, the climax to the game overshadowed all else. An ungenerous declaration had left South Australia needing 272 from approximately 30 overs. Opening the innings, Hookes scored the fastest century ever made by an Australian in first-class cricket. It took him 43 minutes (34 balls), and contained three 6's and seventeen 4's. When dismissed, he had batted for 55 minutes, and after ten overs the score was 128. But it was too good to last, and another five wickets having fallen in failing light, the chase was called off and play halted with six overs remaining and Victoria only three wickets from victory.

VICTORIA

J.M. Wiener c Hookes b Garner	.2 –	b Garner	.73
G.M. Watts c Hilditch b Garner	.0 –	c Wright b Hogg	.0
*G.N. Yallop c Darling b Sincock	.28 –	c and b Sincock	.151
P.J. Davies c Garner b Hookes	.29 –	b Garner	.27
B.C. Green c Wright b Garner	.14 –	c Harris b Inverarity	.70
P.J. Cox c Hogg b Garner	.20 –	c and b Harms	.47
S.F. Graf c Garner b Harms	.48 –	c Wright b Inverarity	.18
†P.G. Sacristani c Garner b Sincock	.55 –	lbw b Harms	.2
P.D. King c Wright b Hogg	.54 –	not out	.15
R.J. McCurdy not out	.5 –	lbw b Inverarity	.9
J.D. Higgs b Hogg	.0 –	not out	.1
B 1, l-b 1, n-b 3	.5	L-b 3, n-b 4	.7

1/1 2/2 3/39 4/63 5/95   **260**   1/0 2/141 3/220 4/261   (9 wkts, dec.) **420**
6/109 7/168 8/248 9/256   5/373 6/373 7/380 8/404 9/418

Bowling: FIRST INNINGS – Garner 28-5-73-4; Hogg 20.1-4-38-2; Sincock 18-9-50-2; Harms 14-4-38-1; Hookes 3-1-8-1; Inverarity 14-5-48-0. SECOND INNINGS – Garner 30-9-81-2; Hogg 21-6-62-1; Sincock 18-3-77-1; Harms 29-9-71-2; Hookes 2-1-6-0; Inverarity 41-7-116-3.

SOUTH AUSTRALIA

W.M. Darling c McCurdy b King	10	– c Sacristani b McCurdy	11
K.P. Harris c Sacristani b McCurdy	9	– (8) lbw b Graf	0
A.M.J. Hilditch b Graf	42	– (9) not out	0
R.J. Inverarity lbw b McCurdy	126	– (7) not out	15
*D.W. Hookes c Sacristani b Cox	137	– (2) c Green b McCurdy	107
R.J. Zadow c Wiener b King	5	– lbw b McCurdy	8
†K.J. Wright c Davies b King	33	– (3) b McCurdy	30
C.L. Harms c Wiener b Green	21	– (5) c Sacristani b McCurdy	3
J. Garner c Sacristani b King	7	– (4) b Graf	19
R.M. Hogg c Wiener b King	0		
A.T. Sincock not out	8		
L-b 6, w 1, n-b 4	11	B 5, l-b 7, w 1	13

1/16 2/28 3/76 4/288 5/301   **409**   1/122 2/128 3/154 4/159   (7 wkts) **206**
6/367 7/373 8/386 9/390   5/184 6/203 7/204

Bowling: FIRST INNINGS – McCurdy 23-2-95-2; King 28-5-88-5; Graf 23-5-74-1; Cox 25-3-69-1; Higgs 10-1-46-0; Green 4.3-1-16-1; Yallop 5-2-10-0. SECOND INNINGS – McCurdy 12-0-88-5; King 2-0-38-0; Graf 10-0-67-2.

Umpires: A.R. Crafter and B.E. Martin.

SHEFFELD SHIELD FINAL

NEW SOUTH WALES V. QUEENSLAND

At Sydney, March 15, 16, 17, 18, 19, 1985. New South Wales won by one wicket. Queensland had Hohns to thank – he made his second century of the season – for reaching a satisfactory first-innings total. Imran was New South Wales's best bowler, Holland's leg-spin being ineffective. When New South Wales batted, Smith hit out well, but in spite of a marathon effort by Dyson they were in trouble at 226 for seven. Waugh then showed his attacking flair in taking his side to within 56 of Queensland. In their second innings Queensland collapsed first to the pace of Imran, then to the spin of Bennett, their last five wickets falling for 20 runs as the pitch showed signs of wear. Needing 220 to win New South Wales looked on the verge of defeat, and Queensland of their first-ever Sheffield Shield, at 175 for eight. But Clifford, dropped when 37, kept his head, and first Holland, then Gilbert, helped him take New South Wales to a thrilling victory, a cover drive by Gilbert producing the winning runs. The aggregate attendance was 24,000 and Queensland's fears of a pitch heavily weighted in favour of the spinners proved groundless.

QUEENSLAND

R.B. Kerr b Imran	9	– (2) lbw b Imran	3
B.A. Courtice b Gilbert	5	– (1) b Imran	0
K.C. Wessels c Dyson b Gilbert	49	– c Dyson b Holland	22
*A.R. Border c Dyson b Bennett	64	– (5) c Dyson b Imran	45
G.M. Ritchie c Waugh b Imran	20	– (6) c and b Bennett	12
G.S. Trimble c Wellham b Bennett	38	– (7) c Waugh b Bennett	16
T.V. Hohns st Rixon b Holland	103	– (8) c Clifford b Bennett	2
†R.B. Phillips c Smith b Waugh	53	– (4) c Wellham b Imran	47
J.N. Maguire b Imran	19	– b Imran	4
C.G. Rackemann b Imran	1	– c Imran b Bennett	3
J.R. Thomson not out	0	– not out	1
B 3, l-b 5, n-b 5	13	B 3, l-b 2, w 1, n-b 2	8

1/12 2/18 3/99 4/141 5/159   **374**   1/0 2/3 3/41 4/116 5/129   **163**
6/224 7/321 8/370 9/374   6/143 7/154 8/154 9/160

Bowling: FIRST INNINGS – Imran 27.3-6-66-4; Gilbert 27-6-67-2; Matthews 27-10-53-0; Waugh 12-6-15-1; Bennett 34-16-54-2; Holland 43-12-111-1. SECOND INNINGS – Imran 19-6-34-5; Gilbert 15-5-24-0; Bennett 20-4-32-4; Waugh 6-1-21-0; Holland 15-5-39-1; Matthews 2-0-8-0.

NEW SOUTH WALES

J. Dyson c Ritchie b Rackemann	66	– c Phillips b Thomson	19
S.B. Smith c Phillips b Maguire	76	– hit wkt b Rackemann	7
†S.J. Rixon c Phillips b Maguire	0	– (4) c and b Thomson	2
*D.M. Wellham lbw b Thomson	31	– (3) b Thomson	39
P.S. Clifford c Phillips b Thomson	13	– not out	83
G.R.J. Matthews lbw b Maguire	16	– c Phillips b Rackemann	8
Imran Khan c Phillips b Rackemann	7	– c Border b Rackemann	18
S.R. Waugh c Maguire b Thomson	71	– c Phillips b Rackemann	21
M.J. Bennett c Phillips b Border	10	– c Border b Rackemann	1
R.G. Holland c Trimble b Border	0	– c Kerr b Rackemann	10
D.R. Gilbert not out	8	– not out	8
L-b 1, n-b 19	20	B 3, l-b 2, n-b 2	7

1/98 2/98 3/167 4/185 5/219   **318**   1/13 2/53 3/59 4/76 5/100   (9 wkts) **223**
6/223 7/226 8/281 9/283   6/140 7/173 8/175 9/209

Bowling: FIRST INNINGS – Thomson 27.3-6-83-3; Rackemann 30-9-80-2; Maguire 33-6-90-3; Border 7-2-27-2; Hohns 24-7-37-0. SECOND INNINGS – Rackemann 30.2-8-54-6; Thomson 20-4-81-3; Maguire 14-2-27-0; Hohns 20-4-56-0.

Umpires: M.W. Johnson and R.A. French.

WESTERN AUSTRALIA V. NEW SOUTH WALES

At Perth, December 20, 21, 22, 23, 1990. Drawn. New South Wales 2 pts. Toss: Western Australia. Marsh's decision to field brought a sensational reaction from the Waugh twins, who became the first brothers in first-class cricket to score double-hundreds in the same innings. They joined forces with New South Wales struggling at 137 for four and Reid enjoying a fruitful spell of three for 25. More than a day later they were still batting, and Lawson declared immediately the scoreboard showed that they had broken every Australian partnership record. Their 464, occupying 407 minutes, was also a world record for the fifth wicket. Both Mark (446 minutes, 343 balls, one six, 35 fours) and Steve (339 balls, 24 fours) reached their highest scores, and they so dominated the vaunted Western Australian pace attack that Zoehrer had to discard his wicket-keeping duties to bowl leg-breaks. The pitch was without blemish, but Western Australia's batsmen made little impression on bowling that was at least steady, and wickets fell regularly until late on the fourth day. It was then that MacLeay and Zoehrer, both of whom survived chances early on, put on 242 in 139 minutes, setting an eighth-wicket partnership record for Western Australia and denying New South Wales the opportunity of winning outright. Both hit nineteen fours in their unbeaten hundreds. Western Australia also owed much to Matthews, who curbed his big-hitting method to hold up New South Wales for three and a half hours.

Close of play: First day, New South Wales 375-4 (M.E. Waugh 128*, S.R. Waugh 112*); Second day, Western Australia 131-2 (M.R.J. Veletta 59*, G.M. Wood 15*); Third day, Western Australia 92-3 (T.M. Moody 27*, C.D. Matthews 1*).

NEW SOUTH WALES

S.M. Small c Wood b Reid 26	S.R. Waugh not out 216
M.A. Taylor b Reid 57	L-b 18, n-b 26 44
T.H. Bayliss c Zoehrer b Reid 20	
M.D. O'Neill c Zoehrer b MacLeay 9	1/37 2/106 3/111	(4 wkts, dec.) **601**
M.E. Waugh not out 229	4/137

G.R.J. Matthews, †P.A. Emery, *G.F. Lawson, M.R. Whitney and W.J. Holdsworth did not bat.

Bowling: Alderman 30-9-91-0; Reid 33-3-147-3; Matthews 17-0-95-0; Moody 14-0-63-0; MacLeay 34.2-6-109-1; Andrews 12-2-54-0; Zoehrer 5-0-24-0.

WESTERN AUSTRALIA

*G.R. Marsh c Matthews b Lawson 4	– (2) c Matthews b S.R. Waugh 5
M.R.J. Veletta run out 64	– (1) b Matthews 33
T.M. Moody c Whitney b Holdsworth 38	– c Emery b Holdsworth 56
G.M. Wood c M.E. Waugh b Whitney 54	– b Matthews 12
W.S. Andrews b Whitney 23	– (6) c Small b Whitney 4
M.W. McPhee c O'Neill b Matthews 11	– (7) c Taylor b Matthews 16
†T.J. Zoehrer c Small b Matthews 17	– (8) not out 133
K.H. MacLeay not out 46	– (9) not out 102
C.D. Matthews c S.R. Waugh b Lawson 8	– (5) c Lawson b Holdsworth 71
B.A. Reid b Holdsworth 2	
T.M. Alderman c M.E. Waugh b Lawson ...15	
B 5, l-b 2, w 1, n-b 24 32	B 12, l-b 14, w 1, n-b 16 43

1/4 2/80 3/156 4/186 5/215	**314**	1/21 2/62 3/88 4/134	(7 wkts) **475**
6/227 7/243 8/272 9/277		5/172 6/199 7/233

Bowling: FIRST INNINGS – Lawson 24.1-5-71-3; S.R. Waugh 5-1-18-0; Matthews 31-6-68-2; Holdsworth 20-2-74-2; Whitney 17-4-68-2; M.E. Waugh 1-0-8-0. SECOND INNINGS – Lawson 16-5-43-0; S.R. Waugh 10-1-43-1; Matthews 39-8-119-3; Holdsworth 25-7-92-2; Whitney 19-5-70-1; M.E. Waugh 4-0-41-0; O'Neill 3-0-27-0; Small 1-0-14-0; Bayliss 1-1-0-0.

Umpires: R.J. Evans and T.A. Prue.

SOUTH AUSTRALIA V. QUEENSLAND

At Adelaide, February 7, 8, 9, 10, 1992. South Australia won by four wickets. South Australia 6 pts, Queensland 2 pts. Toss: South Australia. South Australia became the first Australian team to score more than 500 in the fourth innings to win a first-class match. Their 506 has been exceeded only by Cambridge University's 507 for seven against MCC and Ground at Lord's in 1896. Coming in when Queensland declared soon after lunch on the third day, Hilditch and Blewett put their heads down and scored 204 by stumps. Blewett was out early next morning, and when McDermott took three more quick wickets Queensland looked home and dry. However, Siddons and Sleep took advantage of the tired bowlers to add 152, and when the last over began, the scores were level. The first three balls evaded Sleep's bat, but the fourth took an inside edge and the batsmen scampered through. Queensland established a first-innings lead of 204 having been put in to bat, thanks to some inferior bowling and batting by South Australia. Rackemann did not enforce the follow-on, as he was nursing a leg injury and McDermott had put in 18 superlative overs unchanged. With the weather set fair, it seemed that only a miracle could thwart Queensland when they added another 301. But with hindsight, it can be seen that the match turned when Border missed a return catch off Hilditch, then 69. Hilditch went on to bat for nearly six hours, and Blewett, Siddons and Sleep all responded brilliantly to his example.

Close of play: First day, Queensland 313-9 (G.J. Rowell 30*, C.G. Rackemann 3*); Second day, Queensland 149-1 (M.L. Hayden 71*, D.M. Wellham 1*); Third day, South Australia 204-0 (G.S. Blewett 97*, A.M.J. Hilditch 93*).

QUEENSLAND

T.J. Barsby c Owen b Hickey	.6	– lbw b Scuderi	.67
M.L. Hayden run out	.79	– c Owen b May	.80
D.M. Wellham lbw b Hickey	.34	– c Nielsen b Hickey	.28
A.R. Border c Hookes b Hickey	.0	– (5) c Nielsen b Scuderi	.46
S.G. Law c Siddons b Hickey	.12	– (4) not out	.35
G.M. Ritchie run out	.58	– not out	.23
†I.A. Healy c Nielsen b Scuderi	.31		
P.L. Taylor c Brayshaw b Sleep	.29		
C.J. McDermott lbw b Scuderi	.5		
G.J. Rowell not out	.45		
*C.G. Rackemann run out	.9		
L-b 7, w 3, n-b 16	.26	B 5, l-b 3, n-b 14	.22

1/13 2/80 3/80 4/92 5/208 **334** 1/143 2/184 (4 wkts, dec.) **301**
6/212 7/264 8/277 9/282 3/194 4/271

Bowling: FIRST INNINGS – Hickey 23-2-96-4; Scuderi 30.1-5-96-2; Owen 14-3-49-0; May 24-8-52-0; Blewett 5-1-10-0; Sleep 6-0-24-1. SECOND INNINGS – Hickey 14-1-81-1; Scuderi 17-5-62-2; Owen 11-5-40-0; May 14-3-45-1; Blewett 7-0-31-0; Sleep 12-6-34-0.

SOUTH AUSTRALIA

G.S. Blewett c Barsby b McDermott	34	– c Healy b McDermott	98
A.M.J. Hilditch c Rowell b Rackemann	5	– c Healy b McDermott	137
J.A. Brayshaw c Rowell b McDermott	1	– b Rowell	39
*J.D. Siddons c Barsby b McDermott	0	– b Rackemann	87
D.W. Hookes c Taylor b McDermott	5	– c Border b McDermott	3
J.C. Scuderi c sub b Rowell	10	– lbw b McDermott	0
P.R. Sleep c Rackemann b McDermott	16	– not out	97
†T.J. Nielsen lbw b McDermott	1	– not out	14
T.B.A. May not out	20		
D.J. Hickey c Law b Rackemann	12		
C.J. Owen c Border b Rackemann	0		
L-b 6, n-b 20	26	L-b 11, n-b 20	31

1/8 2/15 3/19 4/27 5/44	**130**	1/209 2/283 3/307	(6 wkts) **506**
6/86 7/90 8/95 9/130		4/314 5/316 6/468	

Bowling: FIRST INNINGS – McDermott 18-2-58-6; Rackemann 10.4-3-22-3; Rowell 7-0-44-1. SECOND INNINGS – McDermott 37-6-124-4; Rackemann 32.4-6-117-1; Rowell 18-1-64-1; Taylor 42-6-126-0; Law 1-0-1-0; Border 23-4-63-0.

Umpires: S.J. Davis and D.J. Harper.

FINAL

QUEENSLAND V. SOUTH AUSTRALIA

At Brisbane, March 24, 25, 26, 27, 28, 1995. Queensland won by an innings and 101 runs. Toss: South Australia.

Queensland's victory was virtually settled from the moment Siddons chose to bat. South Australia's innings fell apart: they were 30 for four in just over an hour, and a total of 214 on a good pitch was quite inadequate. For the next three days, only spasmodic rain breaks held up Queensland's batting orgy. Hayden and Barsby were untroubled in opening with 144, then Love joined Barsby to add 192. Barsby showed rare restraint early on, but then reverted to his flamboyant style, batting in all for six hours and 151 runs and bringing the best out of his younger partners. Love responded with an emphatic hundred of his own and Border looked certain to follow suit, in what he had hinted might be his last match, until he dragged a wide ball on to his stumps. Queensland's 664 was the highest score in a Shield final and their highest at the Gabba. Resuming 450 behind, South Australia's second innings was little more than academic although Nobes and Webber showed some spirit. Near-capacity crowds attended the match and there was plenty of emotion when Law took the trophy to end Queensland's 68-year-long wait.

Close of play: First day, Queensland 36-0 (T.J. Barsby 11*, M.L. Hayden 14*); Second day, Queensland 409-3 (M.L. Love 114*, A.R. Border 18*); Third day, Queensland 501-4 (A.R. Border 76*, J.P. Maher 6*); Fourth day, South Australia 59-2 (P.C. Nobes 24*, D.S. Lehmann 14*).

SOUTH AUSTRALIA

B.A. Johnson c Hayden b Bichel ....4 – c Hayden b Jackson 10
P.C. Nobes c Law b Tazelaar ....0 – b Tazelaar 100
*J.D. Siddons c Border b Rackemann ....8 – c Seccombe b Rackemann 3
D.S. Lehmann c Seccombe b Tazelaar ......12 – c Tazelaar b Bichel 62
J.A. Brayshaw run out ....53 – c Seccombe b Rackemann 16
D.S. Webber c Seccombe b Bichel ....33 – c and b Law 91
†T.J. Nielsen b Jackson ....53 – lbw b Tazelaar 0
J.N. Gillespie c Seccombe b Rackemann .....18 – c Rackemann b Jackson 39
P.E. McIntyre c Rackemann b Jackson ......9 – c Law b Bichel 2
S.P. George b Rackemann ....15 – c Bichel b Jackson 4
M.A. Harrity not out ....0 – not out 0
   B 1, n-b 8 9   B 4, l-b 8, n-b 10 22

1/4 2/6 3/26 4/30 5/93   **214** 1/31 2/34 3/142 4/194 5/253   **349**
6/126 7/179 8/189 9/210   6/253 7/314 8/335 9/347

Bowling: FIRST INNINGS – Bichel 19-4-54-2; Tazelaar 20-3-45-2; Rackemann 18-6-54-3; Law 10-3-26-0; Jackson 14.4-5-34-2. SECOND INNINGS – Bichel 29-6-90-2; Tazelaar 21-6-65-2; Rackemann 30-10-86-2; Jackson 37.2-9-81-3; Border 1-0-1-0; Law 3-1-14-1.

QUEENSLAND

T.J. Barsby c Gillespie b Johnson 151   P.W. Jackson not out 11
M.L. Hayden c Nielsen b Harrity 74   D. Tazelaar b McIntyre 22
M.L. Love c Nielsen b Brayshaw 146   C.G. Rackemann lbw b McIntyre 7
*S.G. Law c Webber b George 11   B 1, l-b 14, w 3, n-b 34 52
A.R. Border b Johnson 98
J.P. Maher c Nielsen b Gillespie 36   1/144 2/336 3/376   **664**
†W.A. Seccombe c Harrity b Gillespie 18   4/479 5/553 6/565
A.J. Bichel c Nielsen b Gillespie 38   7/618 8/618 9/652

Bowling: Harrity 46-12-129-1; George 33-8-102-1; Gillespie 35-10-112-3; McIntyre 49.5-10-176-2; Johnson 22-1-96-2; Brayshaw 14-5-34-1.

Umpires: D.B. Hair and P.D. Parker.

MIRACLE IN QUEENSLAND (SOMEWHAT BELATED)

By Gideon Haigh

It behoves the young players of the present day to prove themselves throughout the cricket struggles that are ahead of them, to be worthy in every way of the honour conferred on their association by the conference of the Sheffield Shield States in the year 1926. – E.H. Hutcheon, Queensland cricketer and historian.

It took 68 years and nearly 500 matches before Queensland cricketers proved equal to their behoving: at 3.52 p.m. precisely, Tuesday March 28, 1995, was transformed into VQ Day, when the state beat South Australia by an innings and 101 runs and finally took custody of Australia's symbol of interstate cricket supremacy.

To make himself audible above the celebratory din of his Banana Army of supporters, and to adjust to the sensation of victory, captain Stuart Law enunciated his post-match remarks carefully: 'We have won the Shield. It does sound strange saying it. It's just a fantastic feeling to finally have that thing in our room, to hold it up above our heads and feel really proud. It's been the longest week ever. We've won it. Now we can get on with enjoying life again.' Law's team was still encircled by 1,000 revellers at midnight. Nobody the next day would have pissed a fatness test.

Given the 14 occasions the state have been runners-up in the Shield, Queensland have always been wary of the Ides of March. They have traditionally been sombre and self-recriminatory times: Where did we go wrong this time? Whom should we sack this time? Is our state cursed? Should the captain/ coach/groundsman/Premier go?

The last time Queensland were in possession of the Shield was before their opening match in 1926, when it was borrowed from New South Wales for a shop window display. In the meantime, the nearest they had come was winning the Bougainville Sheffield Shield, contested by Australian soldiers in the South Pacific who were awaiting repatriation after VJ Day. This Shield was actually the casing of a military shell.

In 1995, however, the real Shield arrived. The players took it on a three-day tour in a Government plane round the state's vast hinterland. There was a ticker-tape parade in Brisbane itself, a vintage car cavalcade in Mackay, an escort by Harley-Davidson bikers in Mount Isa, and a quick trip to Kynuna (population: 25). It was all such a novelty that in one town they left it behind.

Fortune toyed with Queensland from their admission to join New South Wales, Victoria and South Australia in the Shield in 1926–27. Set 400 to win in their first match by NSW's Alan Kippax, local captain Leo O'Connor was run out by debutant Gordon Amos for 196, only 19 short of victory, and he saw his side lose by a paltry eight runs. O'Connor was presented with engraved gold cufflinks in honour of his resistance, but there were precious few other spoils before the Second World War: Queensland won only a dozen Shield matches and lost 53.

Having established a tradition of wretched defeat for Queensland, it was fitting that Amos should establish another: he crossed the border to play for Queensland in 1927–28. (Poignantly, Amos died, aged 90, ten days after the final.) In that first match, ten of the Queensland team had been born in the state. But an amazing squad could be assembled from Queensland's VIPs (Very Imported Players): extra-colonials Colin McCool, Ray Lindwall, Greg Chappell, Jeff Thomson, Dirk Wellham, Ian Davis, Ray Phillips, Allan Border and Paul Jackson; extra-continentals Kepler Wessels, Majid Khan, Vivian Richards, Tom Graveney, Graeme Hick, Alvin Kallicharran, Rusi Surti, Ian Botham and Wes Hall.

It is a squad to beat the world, but not the rest of Australia. While a few gave their all, others gave only some and at least a handful provided precious little. Queensland seemed in some seasons likelier to win the FA Cup than the Sheffield Shield. And that the most consciously patriotic and occasionally separatist Australian state should acquire such a dependency struck many as eccentric. The Olympic swimming coach Laurie Lawrence wrote, after Queensland crumbled again a couple of years ago: 'Imports are not the answer, or at least they are not the answer that will give any Queenslander any satisfaction.'

Year after year, John Morton, the sports editor of the now defunct Brisbane *Telegraph*, used to run the same headline at the start of the season: 'This is the Year'. And people were intoning the words this time. But otherwise Queensland's 1994–95 campaign had an altogether different feel, derived from its investment in homespun talent. Law's squad were, if not native, at least long resident in the state: Border's career with NSW and left-arm spinner Jackson's prior duties in Victoria are now some yellow books back.

Blown in from such outposts as Toowoomba, Wondai, Bileola, Kingaroy, Innisfail and Mundubberra, and mingling the born-again Border and the indestructible Carl Rackemann with the supple skills of tyros like Martin Love, Jim Maher, Wade Seccombe and Andrew Symonds, they played with resource and without regret.

The Gabba was being refurbished and the schedule proved too inflexible to allow the Sir Leslie Wilson Stand a few days' grace for the final, though spectators enlisted the debris in their visions of victory. The Brisbane bard, 'Rupert' McCall – a modern-day Albert Craig – wrote this pre-match doggerel for the Brisbane *Courier-Mail*:

> Let's get out there and win 'cos we're the best team in the land,
> Let's demolish South Australia like the Leslie Wilson Stand.

Which Queensland did. Their 664 was more than enough to overwhelm South Australia and, since a draw was going to be enough anyway, locals were able to savour the prospect of victory for at least three days before its arrival. Grown men – as they do in all the best sports stories – wept. John Maclean, chairman of the Queensland Cricket Association, greeted century-maker and player-of-the-season Trevor Barsby with tears of joy running down his face saying: 'You don't know what you've done.' He probably didn't. And that may have been why he and his team-mates were able to do it. (*1996*)

from NOTES BY THE EDITOR

IMPURE MILK

[...] With the 1999–2000 competition already under way, the Sheffield Shield, Australian cricket's inter-state Championship for the last 107 years, suddenly ceased to exist. The competition had acquired a sponsor and, as part of the deal, the trophy itself was immediately retired, as were both parts of the name. Inter-state first-class cricket was henceforth to be contested for – one can hardly bring oneself to write it – the Pura Milk Cup. The very phrases that have been part of the fabric of the Australian language for generations were effectively banned: Shield cricket, Shield records, Shield player.

This is not sponsorship. It is an act of vandalism against both cricket's past and its future: an attempt to blank out future generations from any understanding of the game's history. Tradition is harder to come by in Australia than in England, and therefore more highly valued. *The Age* in Melbourne rightly called the decision 'abhorrent'.

Domestic first-class cricket is hard to sell and the game has to make a living. But this time cricket has sold its dignity as well as its advertising space. Tim Lamb, chief executive of the ECB, once said, in perhaps his happiest piece of phrase-making, that professional cricket was a business inside a game not a game inside a business. He should have that drawn up as a motto in appliqué work and distributed at the next ICC meeting to be stuck up in every chief executive's office around the globe. [...] (*2000*)

13

PORTRAIT GALLERY

Australia has had an official Cricket Hall of Fame since December 1996, but an un-official one far longer, and part of its creation has been in the pages of *Wisden*. Through the institution of its Five Cricketers of the Year section, the almanack has played a significant role in deciding which cricketers matter in the histories of the various Test nations. Although the garland has traditionally been awarded on the basis of performances in England, it has seldom in the last century eluded a cricketer of note.

Wisden began the practice of profiling cricketers in 1889, with its toasts to Six Great Bowlers of the Year, followed by 1890's Nine Great Batsmen of the Year and 1891's Five Great Wicket-keepers. The tributes were mostly workmanlike, and usually short, word count not being thought a measure of eminence: in the less-is-more spirit, for example, it was said of John Blackham that he 'does not need a lengthy notice, his name being a household word with all who take any interest in the game of cricket'.

The format of Five Cricketers of the Year was settled on for the 1897 almanack, after another Australian visit, and became enshrined by repetition. Other comple-mentary forms of tribute have also evolved, such as the retirement portrait, and the special obituary. This chapter groups a range of profiles, predominantly elevations to the Five, but also end-of-career farewells such as R.C. Robertson-Glasgow's to Sir Donald Bradman and Mike Coward's to Allan Border, and fond obsequies such as Neville Cardus's to Jack Gregory.

Not that *Wisden* has ever felt writers to have a monopoly on wisdom. One trend in the almanack that emerged early was for the assessment of individuals by contempo-rary or like-minded cricketers, often resulting in the sort of technical insights to which only players are usually privy. An early example here is the collection of posthumous tributes to Frederick Spofforth in *Wisden* 1927, as fresh today as the day of their composition. Lord Harris recalls the length and straightness of Spofforth's follow-through, and the 'high' heels with which he so cunningly gouged the narrower pitches of his day; the Earl of Darnley, formerly the Hon. Ivo Bligh, remembered the need to watch Spofforth's hand for the bent wrist that signified the slower breakback. We're also richer for knowing, thanks to Darnley, that one of Spofforth's feats of strength 'was to support [George] Bonnor, weighing over 16 stone, on the calf of his right leg, held horizontally backwards at right angles to the upright leg'. Mind you, neither expert dispelled the mystery of the speed at which Spofforth bowled. Harris didn't think him quick ('It is a common misconception, amongst those who did not see or play him, that he was a very fast bowler'), Darnley did ('In some accounts recently published of Spofforth's bowling it was said that he was never a really fast bowler. I believe this statement to be quite incorrect'), and editor Sydney Pardon let them prolong their civilised disagreement into eternity.

Cricketers, though, know what matters. Nobody could have had a tighter view of Clarrie Grimmett than that of Bill O'Reilly, and the warmth is heartfelt: 'With 'Grum' at the other end to pick me up and dust me down, I feared no batsman.' Richie Benaud draws on a long friendship to enumerate the virtues of Ian Chappell; John Benaud writes from the vantage points of manager and selector in toasting Mark Taylor; Paul Sheahan, having put career before cricket in the early 1970s, looks back ten years later on three erstwhile team-mates who turned cricket into career: Greg Chappell, Dennis Lillee and Rod Marsh. There are all species of cricketer here, all styles of writing, and all kinds of musings on how talent expresses itself in the sporting arena.

—GH

R. BENAUD

If one player, more than any other, has deserved well of cricket for lifting the game out of the doldrums, that man is RICHARD BENAUD. Captain of Australia in four successive and triumphant series to the end of 1961, he has demonstrated to enthusiasts all over the world that the intention to make cricket, particularly Test cricket, attractive and absorbing is every bit as important as skilled technique in batting, bowling and fielding. He has succeeded in his aim to re-create interest in cricket because he loves playing it.

That was, of course, why Benaud junior – to distinguish him from his cricketer father, Louis Richard Benaud – took up the sport which brought him fame as a crusading captain and high commendation as a spin bowler, batsman and close fielder. No wonder that Richie – born Richard – at Penrith, thirty-odd miles from Sydney, on October 6, 1930, showed a fondness for cricket at an early age. He had his father, a first-grade player for twenty years with the unique feat to his credit of twenty wickets in a match, as instructor and mentor. Benaud senior, a third generation Australian of Huguenot extraction, and a schoolteacher, bowled leg-breaks during a long career for the Cumberland club and so it was natural that he imparted the art of delivering them with the appropriate variations the googly and top-spinner to his son.

A small bat and tennis ball, then a bigger bat and hard ball, were the implements used by the eager boy in his formative years as a cricketer under his father's expert eye. When the Benaud family after living for a while in Jugiong moved to Sydney, Richie went to Parramatta High School and here he had his first experience of captaincy. At 16, he followed in his father's footsteps by playing for Cumberland's first-grade team and, eventually, captained them. The New South Wales State selectors, ever on the look-out for rising talent, first picked him when 18 as a batsman and this was still his primary role when promotion to international status came his way at the age of 21 in the fifth Test Match against West Indies at Sydney in January 1951.

Thus far, his ambition had been realised, but he had no means of knowing that almost ten years later, against the same country, he would lead Australia in the first Test Match tie in history. Meantime, Richie Benaud came to England in 1953 and 1956 and he also earned representative honours against South Africa, India and Pakistan. His gradually mounting bowling skill was evident on his first two English trips, but he is remembered chiefly during those ventures for the dashing 97 he hit off the England attack in the second Test at Lord's in 1956.

The 1957–58 tour to South Africa at length established him as an all-rounder of top-class, for he took 106 wickets, which surpassed the previous record of 104 by S.F. Barnes, and scored 817 runs including four centuries, two of them in Test matches. Ian Craig led Australia in this series, but the following year slow recovery from illness precluded his choice for the captaincy against England when they toured 'Down Under'. So Benaud, somewhat to his surprise, but very keen to put his many theories into practice, was appointed to the task of recovering the Ashes which England had held since Hutton wrested them from Hassett in 1953. Benaud duly completed his mission and fully justified the selectors' faith in him despite fears that the burden of captaincy might affect his form. His fine bowling, which yielded him 31 wickets for 18.83 runs apiece, proved a major factor in Australia's triumph of winning four Tests and drawing the other. Shrewd and inspiring captaincy transformed an ordinary side into an invincible combination bent on revenge – and gaining it. Eight Test appearances in India and Pakistan a year later and five more during the memorable visit of West Indies to Australia in 1960–61 – all as captain – brought Benaud's total of caps to fifty. In India and Pakistan he excelled by taking 47 wickets (average 20.19) in the Tests and in the ensuing exciting rubber against Worrell's West Indies team he was second in the wicket-taking list with 23 to the evergreen Davidson's 33. […]

When Benaud arrived in England with his team he pledged them to play attractive cricket – winning or losing. He also promised more overs to the hour as an antidote to defensively-minded batsman or bowlers. He promised quicker field-changing and fewer time-wasting tactical conferences during play. He and his men did their best to carry out his positive policy, and their faster scoring alone proved a telling reason for the success of the tour. When unable to lead his team, Benaud planned strategy with Neil Harvey, his able and wise vice-captain.

Pain from a shoulder injury, for which he had injections, did not deaden Benaud's intense desire to conquer on an English visit. That his playing share was limited to 32 innings for 627 runs and 61 wickets for 23.54 apiece spoke eloquently of his influence and worth in other directions. Nevertheless, his contribution of six wickets for 70 in the second innings of the fourth Test at Manchester when the issue of the match and series lay in the balance, was a traditional captain's effort made at a crucial time. He explained the achievements of his side by declaring that they had risen to the occasion, but, modestly, sought no credit for his part in them.

It was a great pity that, because of his shoulder injury, Benaud could not give his admirers last summer other than rare glimpses of his best form, but he had already done enough to make sure of a high place in cricket history. He came with the reputation of being one of the finest close-fielders in the world – either at gully or in a silly position – and appreciative of the hazards thus entailed he would never ask a man to take up a dangerous post he would not himself occupy.

As a forcing batsman, Benaud, tall and lithe, has always been worth watching. His drives, powerfully hit and beautifully followed through, are strokes of especial joy to those whose day is made if they see a ball sent hurtling over the sightscreen. At Scarborough in 1953 Benaud hit eleven 6's and nine 4's while making 135. Still it is as a bowler that Benaud, in recent years, has touched the heights. An advocate of practice and yet more practice, the erstwhile youngster from the backwoods has long had a bulging quiver of arrows for attack. The leg-break, the googly and the top-spinner have been used most often, and lately Benaud has added the 'flipper' to his armoury. This is a ball, spun out of the finger-tips, which flashes across from off to leg – in effect an off-spinning top-spinner. For his discovery of this unusual and effective delivery, Benaud thanks Bruce Dooland who perfected it while assisting Nottinghamshire after making his name in Australian cricket. [...]

A fighter, indeed, he has been all through his cricket career which nearly came to a tragic end almost before it had begun when, as a youngster playing for New South Wales Second XI, he suffered a fractured skull in failing to connect with a hook stroke. Fortunately, he recovered to bring pleasure to cricket followers all over the world and to attain a place among the great players, a distinction earned by his tak-ing of 219 wickets and scoring 1,744 runs in fifty-four Test matches to the end of 1961. Only three other Australians – M.A. Noble, Keith Miller and Ray Lindwall – have scored 1,500 runs and taken 100 wickets in Tests, and Lindwall alone (228) has captured more wickets for Australia.

By profession, Benaud, who is married and has two sons, is a newspaper reporter on the *Sydney Sun*. He writes as well as he plays and his self-written book *Ways of Cricket* will act as a spur to aspiring young players to tread the road which leads to Test fame. (*1962*)

ALLAN BORDER – 11,174 TEST RUNS

By Mike Coward

Allan Border, who retired in May 1994 as Test cricket's highest run-scorer, commit-ted the greater part of a long and distinguished career to re-establishing the credibil-ity and image of Australian cricket. A self-effacing man of simple tastes and pleas-ures, Border served at the most tempestuous time in cricket history and came to rep-resent the indomitable spirit of the Australian game. As it grappled with two schisms, the first over World Series Cricket, the second over the provocative actions of the mercenaries in South Africa, it was debilitated and destabilised as never before and cried out for a figure of Bradmanesque dimensions to return it to its rightful and influential position on the world stage.

Into the breach strode earnest Allan Robert Border, a working-class boy, born at Cremorne on the north shore of Sydney Harbour, who grew up over the road from the Mosman Oval that now bears his name. At one time he was a beach bum, who was cajoled from his indolence and indifference by the noted coach and former England Test player, Barry Knight. But Border, standing just 5 ft 9 in, bestrode the Test match arena like a colossus for more than 15 years. When he retired 11 weeks before his 39th birthday, Border was entitled to be ranked alongside Sir Donald Bradman as the great-est of Australian cricketers. Certainly no one since Sir Donald has done more to advance Australian cricket throughout the world – particularly in developing countries.

Border's batting cannot really stand comparison with Bradman but many of his achievements go far beyond the Bradmanesque – 156 Test matches, 153 of them con-secutive, on 36 grounds in eight different Test-playing countries (Sir Donald played 52 Tests on ten grounds, all in Australia and England); 11,174 runs at 50.56 with 27 centuries and 63 fifties; 93 consecutive Test matches as captain; 156 catches; 273 lim-ited-overs appearances, 178 as captain, including Australia's victory in the 1987 World Cup final. All of these accomplishments are in a league of their own and some may remain so: Sunil Gavaskar, the only other scorer of more than 10,000 Test runs, doubts that Border's run record will ever be broken. Yet only in the twilight of his career did Border become even faintly interested in his statistical achievements. Essentially he was an unromantic, uncomplicated but uncompromising workman-cricketer. It is problematical whether Border, unlike Bradman, has ever understood his place in history. He reinvigorated Australian cricket and provided it with stabil-ity, direction and enthusiasm; this was the most significant of his many contributions and the one which gave him the greatest satisfaction. There is a remarkable set of fig-ures to underscore the extent of the stability Border provided. From the time he suc-ceeded his fragile friend Kim Hughes on December 7, 1984, until his captaincy ended on March 29, 1994, opposing countries commissioned 38 captains – 21 of them against Australia. From his first Test, at Melbourne, on December 29, 1978, he played with and against 361 different players.

To gain a true appreciation of Border, it is necessary to examine his formative years in the leadership when his team was scorned and he was disturbingly close to a breakdown. In 1985 when Australian cricket reached its nadir and a collection of leading players defected to South Africa, Border, the least political of men, was dragged into a black hole of depression. He was barely four months into his term of office – while he forgave them, he never forgot the hurt caused by those team-mates who pursued the dollar rather than the dream, and opted to play in South Africa. For a man who placed such store in team loyalty, it was a cruel lesson. When he retired, Border reflected: 'I felt very let down. We were playing in Sharjah and everyone was having a beer and saying that the team was starting to get it together. There was that sort of talk. You feel such a fool when you then read in the paper that blokes you have trusted, who have told you how great the future looks, are going to South Africa.'

Many of his attitudes were formed and much of his philosophy as a captain for-mulated at this time when Australia were not expected to win and, in the main, did not. The dire circumstances of the day compelled him to think defensively, and it was not until 1989 when he engineered a memorable 4-0 eclipse of a dispirited England that there was a measure of optimism and aggression about his leadership. But while his entitlement to the job was hardly ever questioned, the negativism of his captain-cy was the area that most occupied the attention of his critics. In mitigation he insist-ed that the circumstances of his time had made it impossible for him to develop a totally positive philosophy. He evolved into an enterprising captain when he was finally in charge of able and ambitious men, as was evidenced by his thoughtful and often bold use of the leg-spinner Shane Warne. In this period, some English critics felt that Australia's approach was getting too hard: that might say more about them than about Border. [...] With few, if any, exceptions, his team-mates and employers indulged his contrariness; it was infrequent and irritating rather than damaging. Indeed, the fact that his actions and reactions were always so commonplace, so human, made him an endearing as well as an enduring champion. Essentially, he was an ordinary soul who accomplished extraordinary deeds. For a suburban family man, with an unselfconscious hankering for a beer around a backyard barbecue, Border became an exceptionally worldly cricketer. That he was able to expunge many of the prejudices and preconceptions amongst his team-mates about playing cricket in the Third World was another of the outstanding legacies of his captaincy.

The fact that his technique and temperament allowed him to play productively in the most extreme conditions and situations was perhaps the true gauge of his greatness. Indeed, the tougher the predicament the more resolute and more resourceful was his batting. He averaged 56.57 in 70 overseas Tests. In Australia, he averaged 45.94 in 86 Tests. And he averaged fractionally more as captain (50.94) than as non-captain (50.01) – further confirmation of his red-blooded response to challenge.

While he was never numbered among the poetic left-handers, it is erroneous to categorise him as just an accumulator of runs. In his pomp, he hooked and pulled as well as he square cut and drove in front of point. For many years he was bracketed with Javed Miandad, another eminent and indefatigable scrapper, as the foremost player of slow bowling in the world. Furthermore, Border was blessed with all-round skills. He was a sure catch anywhere, but especially at slip, and in the limited-overs game earned an impressive reputation for his ability to throw down the stumps from any angle within the circle. And while he was self-deprecating about his left-arm orthodox spin bowling, he once took 11 wickets in a Sydney Test against West Indies. But that was no balm for his disappointment at being unable to defeat West Indies in a Test series and so legitimately claim for Australia the unofficial title of world champion. At Adelaide in 1992–93 he went within two runs of attaining the goal.

His retirement from the captaincy and Test cricket was messy, an unfortunate situation caused, more than anything, by a misunderstanding between Border and the Australian Cricket Board. It should have been done with style. But he handed to Mark Taylor the most precious gift of all – a stable, committed, educated, enterprising and hard-edged elite cricket team. Australian cricket will forever be in the debt of AB, the cricketer's cricketer, the people's cricketer and a bloody good bloke with it. (1995)

SIR DONALD BRADMAN

By R.C. Robertson-Glasgow

Don Bradman will bat no more against England, and two contrary feelings dispute within us: relief, that our bowlers will no longer be oppressed by this phenomenon; regret, that a miracle has been removed from among us. So must ancient Italy have felt when she heard of the death of Hannibal.

For sheer fame, Dr. W.G. Grace and Don Bradman stand apart from all other cricketers – apart, indeed, from all other games-players. The villagers used to crowd to their doors when 'W.G.' and his beard drove through their little main street. Bradman, on his visits to England, could never live the life of a private citizen. He couldn't stroll from his hotel to post a letter or buy a collar-stud. The mob wouldn't let him. There had to be a car waiting with engine running, and he would plunge into it, like a cork from a bottle. When cricket was on, Bradman had no private life. He paid for his greatness, and the payment left some mark. The informal occasion, the casual conversation, the chance and happy acquaintance, these were very rarely for him, and his life was that of something between an Emperor and an Ambassador. Yet, for all that, there remained something of that boy who, thirty years before, had knocked a ball or ball-like object about in the backyard of a small house in New South Wales. He never lost a certain primitive and elemental 'cheekiness', and mingled, as it were, with his exact and scientific calculations, there was the immortal impudence of the *gamin*.

But, above all, Bradman was a business-cricketer. About his batting there was to be no style for style's sake. If there was to be any charm, that was for the spectator to find or miss. It was not Bradman's concern. His aim was the making of runs, and he made them in staggering and ceaseless profusion. He seemed to have eliminated error, to have perfected the mechanism of stroke. Others before him had come near to doing this; but Bradman did it without abating the temperature of his attack. No other batsman, surely, has ever been able to score so fast while at the same time avoiding risk. He was, as near as a man batting may be, the flawless engine. There were critics who found surfeit in watching him. Man, by his nature, cannot bear perfection in his fellow. The very fact that something is being done which had been believed to be impossible goads and irritates. It is but a short step from annoyance to envy, and Bradman has never been free from envy's attacks. So, when, first in 1930, he reeled off the centuries, single, double and treble, there were not wanting those who compared him unfavourably with other great ones – Trumper, Ranjitsinhji, Hobbs, Macartney. And Bradman's answer was more runs. Others, perhaps, *could* have made them, but they didn't. No one before had ever been quite so fit, quite so ruthless.

It was a coolly considered policy. Cricket was not to be his hobby, his off-hours delight. It was to be his life and his living. A few hundreds here and there for Australia and State – what use in that? Others had done it, would do it again. He did not mean to be just one of the stars, but the sun itself. Never was such ambition achieved and sustained. Never was the limelight directed so unwaveringly on one man in one game. To set such a standard was unique. To keep it was a miracle.

But the sun itself has degrees of splendour; and, whatever the numbers may say, Bradman was never again quite so incredible as in England in the summer of 1930. Like all great artists, he knew how to begin. So he made 236 at Worcester and 185 not out at Leicester. Then, with a mere trifle of 78 against Yorkshire he relented into rest. At Nottingham, in the first Test, he was set fair to win the match for Australia when R.W.V. Robins bowled him with a googly. It is a freak of chance that in both his first and last Test matches in England he should have fatally mistaken a googly for a leg-break. It is also reassuring to mere mortality. In that first Test he scored 131. This was a hors d'œuvre of the feast to follow. At Lord's, in the second Test, he made 254, and the innings only ended with one of those catches that set A.P.F. Chapman apart from the other England fieldsmen. Then, at Leeds, he scored 334.

George Duckworth, who was keeping wicket for England, rates this innings as the greatest he ever saw. Archie Jackson, that glorious and ill-fated batsman, had opened the Australian innings with W.M. Woodfull. Off the fifth ball of the second over from Maurice Tate, Jackson was caught at short-leg. Bradman joined his captain. The first ball that he received from Tate whizzed just over his off-stump, and Duckworth, believing that Bradman must be bowled, let it go for byes. Then the show began. Bradman never hit in the air. Boundaries sprang from his bat with murderous precision and calculated profusion. Larwood, Tate and Geary – no mean trio – were helpless. A new machine was at work. A new standard of ambition had been set. At Manchester, Ian Peebles induced Bradman into error to the leg-break. But Bradman returned to himself with 232 at the Oval in the fifth Test. In the five Tests he had scored 974 runs at an average of 139. Statistics cannot record the number of runs he carried with him to each innings. But, in a country of great fieldsmen, he stood out pre-eminent. His gathering and throwing approached perfection. Only in catching, probably owing to the smallness of his hands, he was no better than the next man.

Then, after he had taken his pleasure of the South African bowling in Australia, came the first eclipse. A new style of attack, popularly known as 'Body-Line', with the great fast bowler Larwood as its spearhead, was launched on the Australians in Australia by D.R. Jardine. This is no place for discussing the ethics of the matter. Technically, Bradman found no satisfactory answer. He met it, certainly, with a virtuosity of footwork possible to him alone. But his average in eight Test innings sank to a mere trifle of 57, including a score of 103 not out.

When Bradman next came to England, in 1934, there was no Larwood against him, and no Voce. He resumed his mastery. In the Leeds Test he scored 304; at The Oval 244. But, whereas in 1930 he had annihilated doubt, there were now certain qualifications. He was found to be incomplete against that great left-hand bowler, Hedley Verity, on a sticky wicket. At Lord's, in the second Test, he lost his head, if one may use such a phrase of such a master of calculation and coolness. Perhaps it was attributable to his uncertain health. But too much emphasis has been laid on this failure. Verity himself did not agree with the popular generalisation that Bradman couldn't play on the bad ones. And he knew. But it should be said that, with the exception of Larwood in Australia during the 1932–33 tour, Verity was the one bowler who battled with Bradman on something like level terms, even on the truest of pitches. Besides this failure at Lord's in 1934, another man, one of his own team, contributed to some dimming of the Bradman glory. That was W.H. Ponsford, of Victoria. He was playing in his last Test series against England. Most of his records, once seemingly unassailable, had been stolen by Bradman; but now Ponsford, one of the greatest players of spin bowling that ever batted, ran level with his rival, and actually beat him in the matter of Test average by a decimal point.

Already Bradman had proved his power to live on a pinnacle of success. Now, against G.O. Allen's team in Australia, 1936–37, he was to show that he could return from failure. He started downright badly, and the vultures that await the fall of the great hovered expectantly. But he disappointed them, and, by the end of the tour, he was once more the authentic Bradman. In 1938, his third visit to England, he came as captain. Henceforward, in Tests, except for one innings of 234 at Sydney, he was to deal in single centuries only. It was a concession to old man Time.

Where does Bradman stand as a captain? Such a question opens the way to opinions which, even when gathered from those who played with him from day to day, cannot be reduced to any certain conclusion. On the field he was superb. He had seen and weighed it all. Shrewd and tough, he was not likely to waste anything in dreams or mercy. No one ever saw Bradman not attending. Cricket, to one who made and kept his way from hard beginnings, was a business, not a pastime.

He made mistakes. He took only three regular bowlers on to the field for the last Test at The Oval in 1938. For him, as for Australia, the match was a disaster. Bradman, when bowling, fell and injured his leg. England scored 903 for seven wickets; Hutton 364. Both these totals are Test records. Bradman was unable to bat, and Australia lost by the record margin of an innings and 579. How different from the scene of ten years later, when Lindwall went through the England batting like a steam drill. But, all in all, Bradman was the supreme tactician.

On the personal side, his success was more doubtful. Great captaincy begins off the field. True leadership springs from affection even more than from respect. Bradman certainly earned the respect. But, by his very nature, he was bound to have admirers rather than friends. Stripped to the truth, he was a solitary man with a solitary aim. It was what the man did rather than what he was that invited obedience. There are humorously affectionate stories about most great cricketers; intimate, if somewhat apocryphal tales about them; of what Dr. Grace said when Ernest Jones bowled a ball through his beard; of Patsy Hendren's reply to a criticism from the Sydney Hill; of what Johnny Douglas uttered when second slip floored a catch. But there are no funny stories about the Don. No one ever laughed about Bradman. He was no laughing matter.

During the War, disturbing rumours reached England about his health; and, whatever truth there may have been in them, certainly the England team under W.R. Hammond found Bradman uncommonly near to being a sick man. But, happily, he recovered. So did his batting. Not without luck, surely earned, he first groped, then rushed, his way back to normal. Enough of the old skill returned for him to score 187 at Brisbane and 234 at Sydney.

There followed his last visit as a Test cricketer to England. As a batsman he no longer flamed high above his fellows. He was now no more than a very fine player, and it was arguable that both S.G. Barnes and A.R. Morris were stronger factors in the quelling of bowlers. But Bradman's fame, if possible, increased. Next to Mr Winston Churchill, he was the most celebrated man in England during the summer of 1948. His appearances throughout the country were like one continuous farewell matinée. At last his batting showed human fallibility. Often, especially at the start of the innings, he played where the ball wasn't, and spectators rubbed their eyes. But such a treasury of skill could spare some gold and still be rich. He scored 138 against England at Nottingham, and, when it much mattered, 173 not out at Leeds.

Most important of all, he steered Australia through some troubled waters and never grounded on the rocks. Returning home, he received the first Knighthood ever given to a playing cricketer.

Bradman's place as a batsman is among the few who have been blessed with genius. He was the most wonderful run-scorer that the game has yet known, and no batsman in our own time has so highly excited expectation and so rarely disappointed it. (*1949*)

I.M. CHAPPELL

Australian cricket was going through a disastrous period when IAN MICHAEL CHAPPELL was thrust into the captaincy in the final Test of the 1970–71 series against England. He lost his first Test by 62 runs, his second by 89 runs and then was never beaten in a Test series against any country. When Chappell took over, the national team had not won a Test in the previous nine times of asking. To make room for him at the top, the Australian selectors removed W.M. Lawry in a step that had all the subtlety of the guillotine in the French Revolution. Not only was Lawry dropped from the captaincy but from the team as well, at a time when he had made 324 runs, average 40.50 against Snow and Company.

An unjust reward perhaps for a man who made over 5,000 runs for Australia and often had to make do with a bowling attack better recognised for its fighting heart than any ability to blast out the opposition. Any Test team needs two top class bowlers to win a series. Three is a wonderful bonus. When Chappell took over as captain the bowling attack was an inexperienced Lillee, Dell from Queensland, Walters, G.S. Chappell, Jenner and O'Keeffe. It was not until the Second Test in England at Lord's in 1972 that the Lillee–Massie combination came together and they squared the series there, with Massie making a dream début in Test cricket.

Back in Australia two names were on the selectors' short list for the future; J.R. Thomson and M.H.N. Walker, the first an unorthodox but very fast bowler and the second a promising medium pacer. It was on those two, plus Lillee and the reliable Ashley Mallett, that Chappell based his on the field strategy and Australia have not had many better combinations over the years with the ball, particularly when allied to the brilliant close to the wicket catching produced by the team. The fast bowlers' skills were blunted a little by the dry summer in England in 1975 but Chappell still won that series and, in the final Test at The Oval, announced his decision not to be available again to captain Australia.

Chappell captained Australia 30 times, won 15 of those games and lost only five, two of the latter being his first two efforts. By the time he retired from the leadership to be a Test player only he had lifted Australia right back to the top in world cricket. His brother Greg took over the captaincy and celebrated his appointment by becoming only the fourth Australian to hit a century in his first innings as skipper – 123 against the West Indies in Brisbane.

Ian left him a legacy of a very good cricket team with a wonderful team spirit and a burning ambition to stay on top. He did more than that however for his players. Ian Chappell is and was very definitely a players' man. He has had more brushes with officialdom than any other players since K.R. Miller and S.G. Barnes just after the end of the war and most of those brushes have been because of his unwillingness to compromise.

Nothing is a shade of grey to Chappell and, although his candid speech and honesty can be refreshing, the same attributes also have landed him in trouble with administrators on several occasions. In the summer of 1975 in Australia he was carpeted by the South Australian Cricket Association and warned that a recurrence of complaints from umpires concerning the bowling of 'protest' head high full tosses and further excessive use of bad language on the field would bring suspension.

Three weeks later in Brisbane he wore Adidas cricket boots with three blue stripes instead of the three white stripes and was warned of the Australian Cricket Board's insistence on white gear being worn on the field. Chappell's reply appeared in an Australian newspaper the next day, wherein he said he supposed if he wanted to play in the remaining Tests in the series against the West Indies he had better put his boots back in the cupboard. He also made some typically candid and accurate remarks about the administrators' attitudes to advertising on Test match ground fences and advertising used by players.

By his players and others of the same era Chappell will be remembered as much for his bid to improve the players' lot as he will for his run-getting and captaincy. He became the first captain to be invited to the Australian Cricket Board's annual meeting, where he put up several suggestions to the Board concerning possible improvements for players and changes in the Laws.

He was instrumental from the team's point of view in negotiating the bonus from the 1974–75 series and there followed an increase in players' payments and allowances. The Australian Cricket Board contains many youngish administrators nowadays and they too have been keen to see that the players are looked after as well as possible. Chappell himself would disclaim any suggestion of militant shop steward style thinking but he has certainly livened things up in four years of captaincy, in a game where the top players have always been ridiculously underpaid.

At the same time, he has batted brilliantly for Australia on many occasions and is approaching 5,000 runs in Tests. The man he succeeded as captain, W.M. Lawry, classes him as Australia's best player on all types of pitches, a rating that is disputed by those who see his brother Greg as one of the great players for Australia since the war. As batsmen they are different types, as different as they are in personality. Greg is the more elegant strokeplayer of the pair, Ian the more rugged and ebullient in his shot-making.

Ian was born on September 29, 1943 at Unley, South Australia and played first for South Australia against Tasmania in the 1961–62 season, hit a splendid century against New South Wales a little later and played in the only Test against Pakistan in Melbourne in 1964. In 1965–66 in Australia, he played in the final two Tests when Australia squared the series but his Test batting results were moderate until he played against India in Melbourne in December 1967 and hit a magnificent 151 against an attack based on spin.

In 1968 in England, he finished second in the Test averages to Lawry, averaging 43 for 348 runs, and he topped the tour batting figures with 1,261 runs at 48.50 per innings – I.R. Redpath was the only other batsman to reach 1,000 runs for the tour. After being made captain he played some splendid fighting innings for Australia, notably in the opening Test in Brisbane in 1975 when, on a pitch of decidedly variable bounce, he made 90 and allowed Australia to finish with a first innings score of 309. In England in 1975, he had a great series, scoring 429 runs at 71.50 and making 192 at The Oval, as well as three other half centuries.

He has been a most reliable number three for his country – never backward in taking on the fast bowlers with the hook shot, though in recent times he has been more careful to pull in front of square leg rather than hook in the area behind the umpire. His batting technique has been carefully planned to provide the best possible returns against pace bowling and he is always concentrating on getting behind the line of the ball, too much so on occasions when England's fast bowlers have been able to take advantage of a sight of the leg stump.

He hit a century in his final match as captain of Australia, and his brother Greg, who was one of the *Wisden* Five in 1973, hit a century in his first Test as Australian captain. A unique record. The statistics will not unduly delight Ian ... he is interested more in winning cricket matches than the figures produced by those who do the winning. (*Richie Benaud*) (*1976*)

CHAPPELL, LILLEE AND MARSH

By Paul Sheahan

For centuries the magical qualities of the number three have fascinated mathematicians. Even the Almighty moves in threes – Father, Son and Holy Ghost – and without any disrespect, there would be many Australians who believe that the deeds of their revered trio, Greg Chappell, Dennis Lillee and Rodney Marsh, approach divine proportions!

The mere mention of their names evokes the complete gamut of emotions from cricket followers round the world. All three lived through the most turbulent period in modern-day cricket – the schism caused by the creation of World Series Cricket. They were regarded, in many eyes, as prime movers in the establishment of Mr Kerry Packer's brand of cricketing entertainment, and, as a consequence, they incurred the wrath of the Establishment. As well, each one has been involved in incidents which have brought little credit upon themselves and of which, given the luxury of hindsight, they may not be particularly proud.

In assessing their careers, both individually and collectively, it is difficult not to be at least partially influenced by the controversy that surrounded the latter parts of their playing days. However, each of them holds a world Test record: Chappell, the number of catches by a fieldsman, Lillee, the number of wickets by a bowler, and Marsh, the number of catches and dismissals by a wicket-keeper. They have performed miraculous cricketing deeds. I feel honoured to have been asked to write this article, in which I hope that I can do justice to them and to posterity.

Greg Chappell and I had first-class careers that began at almost the same time, preceded, in each case, by fairly successful schoolboy days. We first played against each other in an inter-state Colts fixture in Melbourne. Greg bowled what I thought were rather tempting leg-breaks. Subsequently, under the wily guidance of Somerset's Australian ex-patriate, Bill Alley, he developed into a very useful slow-medium swerve bowler. His basic grounding with Somerset, in the mill of English county cricket, lasted for long enough to play a significant part in moulding a near-perfect defensive batting technique without stultifying his creative and attacking flair.

We Victorians felt that Greg, early in his career, gave us a real chance outside the off stump, and to some extent that was true. A relative weakness on the leg stump was also exposed in the series against England in which he made a wonderful début; but it was a measure of his strength and intelligence that in the long run he made opponents pay dearly for blind adherence to outdated strategy. Against England, the most respected of Australia's foes, he gathered 2,619 runs in the most elegant of styles, averaging 45.94 and making nine centuries. In all, he amassed 7,110 Test runs, an Australian record, at 53.86, with 24 centuries.

His first innings in Test cricket, against the Englishmen in Perth in December 1970, sounded a warning to those from the 'Old Country' that here was a true artist in the making. England implemented a leg-stump attack which was to bring considerable success later in the series on the slower eastern-state pitches; but Perth's true and predictable bounce allowed him to plunder an attack that was spearheaded by one of the great, if slightly unpredictable, fast bowlers, John Snow. Those with any perception realised that Greg possessed extraordinary talent and grace. By honing these qualities, he delighted Australian cricket followers and, I suspect, international ones as well for the next decade and a half. But genius often bears the cross of fragility, and illness struck Chappell at times when he strove for the highest peaks. The 1980–81 summer was an example: West Indies were touring Australia and Chappell had a wretched season. Whatever one's allegiances, though, he will be remembered as one of the most graceful of all batsmen, whose on-side play will be discussed for years.

My first memory of Dennis Lillee is from late 1968 when Western Australia were visiting Victoria. I had become friendly with John Inverarity, who was to become Western Australia's skipper and guiding light in what was a remarkable run of success for them, through our similar interests of schoolmastering and mathematics. When the 'Sandgropers' arrived, I went to their hotel to see 'Invers' who was full of news about their new fast bowler. Having read various whimsical pieces of prose about the demon fast bowler, I was somewhat sceptical of his captain's claims. In the bar of the hotel Inverarity called over a skinny, hairy lad with a wild look in his eye and a fiendish grin, introducing him to me as the next 'fastest bowler in the world'. I lived to regret my scepticism, as a bump on my head bore witness. It is history now that the 'stripling' developed into a strapping man who eventually established a world Test record.

As with most fast blowers, Dennis had his fair share of injury, and his career was not without controversy. When the Australians toured England in 1972, he was diagnosed as suffering stress-fractures to three vertebrae, which saw him break down subsequently in the West Indies. It was a testament to the man's courage and his devotion to his country, as well as to Ian Chappell, that he fought on to complete that series in England (the most thrilling in which I played) with a record 31-wicket haul. In the four short years since I had met him, he had blossomed from a tearaway into one of the most athletic sights one is likely to see.

During that period I had the fortune to see one of the most destructive pieces of speed bowling imaginable. For political reasons, the South Africans did not undertake their planned tour of Australia in 1971–72 and a World XI was hastily assembled to fill the void. In the first innings of the match against Australia in Perth, Lillee destroyed them to the tune of eight for 29. From the covers, it was plainly visible how his awesome pace either exposed weaknesses in the techniques of some of the world's best batsmen or had them so terrified that they capitulated. That remains for me the most sensational example of the devastating effect of sheer speed.

It is history now that he secured 355 Test victims in a career that humbled the greatest of batsmen as it matured from out-and-out pace to swing and deviation off the pitch. Dennis is an extraordinary athlete, possessed of strength and subtlety. He served his captains with courage and devotion. It was a shame, therefore, to find him involved in shabby incidents later in his career, prompted, in my opinion, by a growing belief in some of the commercial publicity that surrounded cricketers in the late 1970s. It seemed so out of character for him to behave in that way, for off the field he was a delightful man and an excellent tourist. Happily, his skill lives uppermost in my memory.

My early memories of Rod Marsh are not so clear, though I did play with him in Perth for a Combined XI against the touring West Indians late in 1968. I was introduced to a rather untidy and very stocky young man who was to do the wicket-keeping. Visions of his leaping around behind the stumps raised fears of seismic disturbances in the west of the continent. I recall that his keeping was vigorous and energetic, with no thought spared for the 'uprights' in a stumping; but there was no doubting the spirit or the desire.

He and Lillee were largely instrumental in Western Australia's emergence as a Sheffield Shield power, so it is understandable that both were imbued with a fierce and unquenchable desire to succeed. 'Bacchus' Marsh, so named because of the Victorian township of Bacchus Marsh rather than his penchant for food and wine, rode the storm that surrounded his elevation to the Test team, at the expense of Brian Taber; but he became quietly obsessed with making those who dubbed him 'Iron Gloves' eat humble pie. While there are those who make much of his being blessed with having Lillee and Jeff Thomson to feed him, there can be no denying his great record – 343 catches and twelve stumpings in 96 Tests with five victims in an innings twelve times.

But it was not only his ability behind the stumps that made him a redoubtable opponent. Three Test centuries and four scores in the nineties bear eloquent testimony to his additional skill with the bat. In fact my happiest memory of Test cricket came during the second innings of the fifth Test of the 1972 tour of England when he and I put on 71 at The Oval and were still at the crease when victory was Australia's. It was a stirring sight to see him, with forearms like a coalminer's and legs like bollards, dealing body-blow after body-blow to the venomous cutters of Derek Underwood. That was the essence of the man. Never one to cower meekly, always prepared to bite off more than most men could chew. His ebullience and power turned the course of some critical Tests. It was disappointing that he made only two fifties in his last 48 Test innings, but I suspect he was overpowered in the end by the philosophy of limited-overs cricket. To be fair, though, he was trying to play by then with a knee injury that would have crippled many others. My abiding memory of Rod is of the archetypal Australian: strong, disrespectful of most authority yet fiercely loyal to those he admired.

To speak of the three of them individually is one thing, but their collective influence must also be recognised: the idea of Trinity and Unity springs to mind, again with no sacrilege intended. Their Test-playing days began in the same series, 1970–71 against England in Australia, and they retired simultaneously, after the final Test against Pakistan in Australia in January 1984, having played together 64 times. Their débuts came at a time when Australia were floundering after a mauling at the hands of South Africa. After such a disastrous series the Australian selectors decided to chart a new course with a group of talented youngsters who were to become the champions of the world but who came to be resented in certain quarters for their arrogance and boorishness.

Any mention of their collective deeds should not be made in isolation from Australia's captain at the time, Greg's brother, Ian. He it was who welded a group of relative novices into a powerful combination by his example and unswerving loyalty to his players. This loyalty had to be experienced first-hand to be understood. Many critics did not understand it, with the result that there was open warfare between a closely knit team and certain other individuals and organisations who were not prepared to compromise. The Australian side were involved at that time in incidents which, as a schoolmaster, I found difficult to forgive and would not have been proud to be a part of. By implication they encouraged youngsters to follow their examples. But their defiance and truculence have to be tempered by the tension that existed between the players and the administrators, who had lost contact with each other. How galling and how sad that just as the latter were preening themselves, justifiably, at the success of the Centenary Test in Melbourne in March 1977, the players were negotiating to leave the scene! Homerian treachery? Perhaps. Yet the secrecy merely served to underline the gulf that existed. That said, Greg Chappell, Dennis Lillee and Rod Marsh performed with great distinction and wonderful success for Australia, and the effect of their absence has already been felt dramatically. (*1985*)

JACK GREGORY, CRICKETER IN EXCELSIS

By Sir Neville Cardus

JACK MORRISON GREGORY, of a famous Australian cricket family, had a comparatively brief Test Match career, for although he played in twenty-four representative games, his skill and his power were as unpredictable as a thunderstorm or a nuclear explosion. He was known mainly as a fearsome right-arm fast bowler but, also, in Test Matches he scored 1,146 runs, averaging 36.96 with two centuries. He batted left-handed and gloveless.

As a fast bowler, people of today who never saw him will get a fair idea of his presence and method if they have seen Wes Hall, the West Indian. Gregory, a giant of superb physique, ran some twenty yards to release the ball with a high step at gallop, then, at the moment of delivery, a huge leap, a great wave of energy breaking at the crest, and a follow-through nearly to the batsman's door-step. He lacked the silent rhythmic motion over the earth of E.A. (Ted) McDonald, his colleague in destruction. Gregory bowled as though against a gale of wind. It was as though he *willed* himself to bowl fast at the risk of muscular dislocation. Alas, he did suffer physical dislocation, at Brisbane, in November 1928, putting an end to his active cricket when his age was thirty-three.

My earliest vivid impression of his fast bowling was at the beginning of the first game of the England v. Australia rubber, at Trent Bridge, in 1921. The England XI had just returned from Australia after losing five Tests out of five (all played to a finish). Now, in 1921, England lost the first three encounters, taking long to recover from Gregory's onslaught at Trent Bridge. He knocked out Ernest Tyldesley in the second innings with a bouncer which sped from cranium to stumps. Ernest's more famous brother J.T. had no sympathy; he bluntly told his brother, 'Get to the off side of the ball whenever you hook, then, if you miss it, it passes harmlessly over the left shoulder.' At Trent Bridge, that May morning in 1921, 'Patsy' Hendren arrived with runs in plenty to his credit, largesse of runs in county matches. Gregory wrecked his wicket with an atom bomb of a breakback. Yes; it *was* a ball which came back at horrific velocity, not achieved, of course, by finger-spin, but by action.

Gregory, like Tom Richardson, perhaps the greatest of all fast bowlers ever, flung the upper part of his body over the front left leg to the offside as the arm came over, the fingers sweeping under the ball. Herbert Strudwick once told me that in the first over or two he took from Richardson he moved to the offside to 'take' the ball. It broke back, shaving the leg stump, and went for four byes. Gregory, at Trent Bridge, took six wickets for 58, in England's first innings of 112; next innings McDonald took five for 52. Only once, at Lord's, in 1921, did Gregory recapture the Trent Bridge explosive rapture.

In the South African summer of 1921–22 he renewed his batteries and regained combustion. Next, in Australia 1924–25, he was able to take 22 wickets in the Tests against England at 37.09 runs each. But the giant was already casting a shadow; in 1926, in England, his three Test wickets cost him 298 runs. He was not a subtle fast bowler, with the beautiful changes of pace, nuance and rhythmical deceptions of Lindwall or McDonald (at his best). But as an announcement of young dynamic physical power and gusto for life and fast bowling, there has seldom been seen on any cricket field a cricketer as exciting as Jack Gregory.

In 1921 certain English critics made too much ungenerous palaver about Gregory's 'bouncers'. These 'bouncers', no doubt, were awesome but not let loose with the regularity of, say, a Hall. In fact, no less an acute judge of the game as A.C. MacLaren declared, in 1921, that Gregory's bowling during the first deadly half hour at Trent Bridge was compact of half-volleys. [...]

He was a generous and likeable Australian. He gave himself to cricket with enthusiasm and relish. He enjoyed himself and was the cause of enjoyment in others. At Johannesburg in 1921 Gregory scored a century in seventy minutes v. South Africa – the fastest hundred in the long history of Test cricket. He was a slip fielder of quite unfair reach and alacrity, a Wally Hammond in enlargement, so to say, though not as graceful, effortless, and terpsichorean. Gregory was young manhood in excelsis. All who ever saw him and met him will remember and cherish him. (*1974*)

CLARRIE GRIMMETT

By Bill O'Reilly

Born in Dunedin in the South Island of New Zealand on Christmas Day, Clarence Victor Grimmett must have been the best Christmas present Australia ever received from that country. Going to Australia in 1914, on a 'short working holiday' which lasted for 66 years, he joined the Sydney club, which had its headquarters at

Rushcutters Bay. Three years in Sydney District cricket were sufficient to warn him
that Arthur Mailey, another great spinner, had literally been given the green light
towards the New South Wales team and all fields beyond. This, and marriage to a
Victorian girl, took Grimmett to Melbourne, where he played with the South
Melbourne club. During his six years in Melbourne he was given only three invitations to play for Victoria, the third of which was against South Australia when, prov-
identially, he collected eight wickets.

It was after his visit to Sydney with the Victorians, for the first Shield match after the
Great War, that I managed to see him for the first time. In Sydney, in the match against
New South Wales, Ted McDonald had performed outstandingly for Victoria and was
consequently the cynosure of all eyes when the Victorian team, on its way home to
Melbourne, played an up-country match in the mountain city of Goulburn. Not quite
all eyes, however. The attention of one pair, belonging to a thirteen-year-old boy named
O'Reilly, was rivetted on a wiry little leg-spinner whose name on the local score-board
was 'Grummett'. To me, from that day onward, Grummett he remained, and my own
endearing name for him throughout our later long association was 'Grum'.

We played together for the first time in an Australian team at Adelaide against
Herbie Cameron's South Africans in 1931, and for the last time in the Durban Test
of 1936 when Vic Richardson's Australian side became the first ever to go through a
tour undefeated – a feat paralleled by Bradman's 1948 team in England. On that
1935–36 South African tour, 'Grum' set an Australian record for a Test series with
44 wickets, yet he came home to be dropped forever from the Australian side. He
was shoved aside like a worn-out boot for each of the five Tests against Gubby
Allen's English team in Australia in 1936–37 and he failed to gain a place in the 1938
team to England, led by Bradman.

It was illogical to assume that age was the reason for his discard. He was 47, it is
true, when the touring side was chosen, yet two years later, at the age of 49, he established an Australian record of 73 wickets for a domestic first-class season. Which
raises, rather pointedly, the question of 'why the hell was he dropped?' By now Don
Bradman was Grimmett's captain for South Australia, and also Australia's captain.
As such he was an Australian selector, and Bradman, it seemed, had become inordi-
nately impressed with the spin ability of Frank Ward, a former clubmate of his in
Sydney. It was Ward who was chosen for the first three Tests against Allen's side in
1936–37 and who caught the boat for England in 1938. Bradman, it seemed, had lost
faith in the best spin bowler the world has seen. 'Grum's' departure was a punishing
blow to me and to my plans of attack. His diagnostic type of probing spin buttressed
my own methods to such a degree that my reaction to his dismissal was one of infi-
nite loss and loneliness.

Unlike Arthur Mailey, the first of the Australian spin trilogy of the inter-wars era,
Grimmett never insisted on spin as his chief means of destruction. To him it was no
more than an important adjunct to unerring length and tantalising direction.
Grimmett seldom beat a batsman by spin alone. Mailey often did. I cannot remember Grimmett bowling a long-hop, whereas Mailey averaged one an over. So much,
in fact, did inaccuracy become a feature of Mailey's success that he himself came to

believe that it was an essential ingredient. Such wantonness was anathema to Grimmett, who believed that a bowler should bowl as well as he possibly could every time he turned his arm over. And Grimmett was perhaps the best and most consistently active cricket thinker I ever met.

He loved to tell his listeners that it was he who taught Stan McCabe how to use his left hand correctly on the bat handle – and I never heard Stan deny it. The 'flipper' was originated by 'Grum' during that Babylonian Captivity of his, and he used it to good effect in his record-breaking last season before the Second World War. He passed it on to men like Bruce Dooland and Cecil Pepper. He seldom bowled the 'wrong 'un', because he preferred not to toss the ball high. On hard, true pitches he would bowl faster than his usual pace, taunting good batsmen to get to him on the half-volley. He was a genius on direction, and his talent for preying on a batsman's weakness was unequalled. He never let a batsman off the hook; once you were under his spell you were there to stay.

Grimmett joined South Australia from Victoria in 1923, just in time to bowl his way into the final Test in Sydney against Arthur Gilligan's 1924–25 England team. In his baptismal effort he took eleven wickets. In 79 Sheffield Shield games he tallied 513 wickets, an Australian record that will probably last for ever. The most successful Shield spinner in modern times, Richie Benaud, totalled 266 wickets in 73 matches, a relatively insignificant performance. Of Grimmett's 106 Test wickets against England, nearly 70 were collected on English pitches in a land where savants say leg-spinners are ineffective. One wonders what colossal figures he would have amassed had he played all his first-class cricket in England. Had he done so, you can be sure there would not be half the present insistence on pacier finger-cutting.

It was lucky for me that I preferred to bowl downwind, an unusual trait in a spinner's character. It allowed our partnership to develop and prosper. No captain ever had to worry which bowling end was whose. We competed strongly with each other and kept a critical eye on one another's performances. In Johannesburg in 1936, all-rounder 'Chud' Langton hit me clean over the top of the square-leg grandstand of the old Wanderers ground. Cackling gleefully, 'Grum' left no doubt in my mind that it was the biggest hit he had ever seen. Silently I was inclined to agree. In Clarrie's next over, 'Chud' clouted him straight over the sightscreen and so far into the railway marshalling yards that the ball was never returned. From that delivery, until hostilities ceased for the afternoon, I never managed to get within earshot of my bowling mate.

Social life meant little to 'Grum'. Not until late in his career did he discover that it was not a bad idea to relax between matches. In England in 1934 I bought him a beer in the Star Hotel in Worcester to celebrate his first ten wickets of the tour. It took him so long to sink it that I decided to wait for his return gesture till some other time on the tour. Later he told me, with obvious regret, that on previous tours he had been keeping the wrong company and had never really enjoyed a touring trip. That I thought was sad, but not half as sad as I felt when, at the very zenith of his glorious career, he was tipped out of business altogether. With 'Grum' at the other end, prepared to pick me up and dust me down, I feared no batsman. Our association must have been one of cricket's greatest success stories of the twentieth century. (*1981*)

A.L. HASSETT: A BORN CRICKETER

By Neville Cardus

One of cricket's rare fascinations is the way it responds to atmosphere, and is quick to express scene or character and even a national spirit. After all, a great game is an organism in an environment, so we need not be surprised if players change according to the pressure of circumstances in which they find themselves, technical and psychological. By no accident did men such as A.C. MacLaren, F.S. Jackson, C.B. Fry, K.S. Ranjitsinhji, R.H. Spooner and G.L. Jessop lord the green earth of our cricket fields in the opulent years of the Edwardian high noon and the glowing Victorian sunset.

Two wars have altered the economy of living, have altered the attitude to living. MacLaren and 'Ranji' and others of that breed played the game, even in a Test match, much in the same mood in which they went to Ascot or Goodwood; it was for them a summer pastime. They set the tempo of cricket, and it moved to the same rhythm as that of the privileged world they dwelt in. The professionals had to go with them at the same pace – and how admirably they emulated the amateur tradition! Johnny Tyldesley, George Hirst, David Denton, Ernest Hayes, Frank Woolley, Jack Hobbs before 1914 – no batsman, not MacLaren himself, made strokes more splendid, more daring, more intensely infused with the true blood and spirit of cricket, than the strokes of these, all of them cricketers for a livelihood, in a period when sport was by no means the paying proposition it is to-day.

I once saw MacLaren drive the fifth ball in a Test match straight for four; an over or so later he was caught near the sight-screen, trying to repeat the hit, only aiming higher and farther. Such an extravagant gesture would scarcely meet the approval of the modern policies; indeed, I am certain that if MacLaren were playing nowadays he would be called 'ham' by the present generation, just as they would call Henry Irving 'ham'. (I find it ironical that in a half-starved rationed time of the troubled history of the world, the term 'ham' should have been used as a term of contempt to apply to any excessive sign of a generous and romantic nature!)

It is bad criticism to set the masters of one period against those of another and to blame, say, a Hutton or a Hassett for not indulging the gestures and points of view of a MacLaren or a Jackson. MacLaren and Jackson were representative men in a particular national scene and atmosphere; Hutton and Hassett each are, in relation to the contemporary environment, equally as representative. The style is the man himself. Nobody by evidence of statistics or by aesthetic argument can *prove* that Jackson was greater as a batsman than Hutton. All that a critic as seasoned as myself is entitled to say is that he preferred the richer and 'hammier' sorts of cricket to the scientifically-rationed products of later origin.

Lindsay Hassett might serve as a perfect example to point our moral: that cricket reacts to the social and economic pressure of life, and that inborn skill is very much swayed by external compulsion. Hassett, in his first seasons, promised to join the ranks of the quicksilver rapier-like users of the bat, kindred with Macartney, Tyldesley, Hendren, 'a little terror', five feet six of aggression, pertinacity and brilliance. I have seen Hassett 'lay into' W.J. O'Reilly even as Johnny Tyldesley once 'laid into' Colin Blythe and Warwick Armstrong.

When Hassett arrived fresh to England in 1938, he at once became renowned for combined consistency and beautifully-poised swiftness of stroke-play, an enchanting late-cutter and a vehement hooker. Following 43 at Worcester, he scored 146, 148 run out and 220 not out in consecutive innings. At the crisis of the Leeds Test match the same summer, Australia in their second innings had lost four wickets for 61, needing 105 to win on an unpleasant pitch, in a dreadful light. Douglas Wright, bowling then with nothing less than genius, overwhelmed Bradman and McCabe. With thunder in the air and in a tension unbearable, Hassett drove and pulled with the ease and confidence of nature. He won the match, plucked the brand from the burning – though as a matter of course, all in the afternoon's work.

Hassett was born in 1913, and therefore the foundations of his technique and approach to cricket were laid during a time still enlivened and ennobled by traditions and memories of Australia's greatest stroke players. Not yet had Test matches lost the fresh impulse of pleasure and sport from the first ball bowled. The idea never occurred to Trumper, Macartney, McCabe, MacLaren, Tyldesley, Woolley to play in a Test match extending over several days 'a different game' from the one they played in three-day matches. It is generally forgotten that all Test matches in Australia, until the second war, were played to a finish. But because there was no time-limit Victor Trumper did not dawdle at the wicket; it was not in his nature to do so.

No great cricketer compromises his true character or his instinctive technical capacity. And if his technique doesn't work by instinct, he isn't a master. Hassett was born to natural elegance and boldness as a batsman; he found himself caught after 1939 in a tremendous transition, both in cricket and world environment. Nothing could have signified more emphatically his resources, as man of character and cricketer of innate flexible skill, than his adaptation to an altered scheme of things, a changed and less individually enterprising view of Test cricket, a view putting value primarily on security and team-work. He never lost lightness of touch, though, no matter how for the cause's sake, he controlled himself, bat in hand, often seeming to hide himself behind it, over after over.

There was no sullenness about his slow scoring; we could get the flavour of a humourous principle behind it all; it wasn't himself that was bearing the cross of long patience stonewalling but the crowd! And he knew it! I once stopped him in North Terrace, Adelaide, after he had batted all day on a perfect wicket, scoring about twenty runs an hour, mostly in singles, and, weary in my soul I asked him: 'Good gracious, what's the matter, Lindsay?...' With a twinkle he replied: 'Wore out. Just wore out!'

In his career he scored 16,890 runs, average 58.24. Against England, here and in Australia, his figures are 42 innings, 1,572 runs, average 38.34. But to discuss Hassett statistically is a waste of time and sense. He played cricket with the wit of his mind. At Melbourne in 1951, when England won a Test match after years in the wilderness, Hassett went on to bowl at the finish, just to provide generously the winning-hit in a kissing-cup, so to say. With eight wickets in hand England wanted only another three or four. But Hassett set his field very mathematically, moving men about to an inch. Then he solemnly measured out his run. And then, before bowling – an old ball, of course – comic inspiration visited him; he rubbed it vigorously on the right side of his stomach.

Australia has sent to these shores no captain of cricket who shared Hassett's secret into our English ways – knowing it without any surrender of Australia's own related yet not entirely similar ways. He could be open-hearted, apparently casual, even complying. But, at the pinch, he would put on his poker face – and now – not Armstrong himself could have been more obstinate. It is because of Hassett's influence that Test matches between England and Australia are emerging from the mechanically stupid to a condition not unconnected with volatile sport as conceived by the present generations.

An Australian of Hassett's vintage likes to win, we may be sure, and, moreover, does his damndest to win. But should the luck go the wrong way, well, there's always the consoling thought that, come to think of it, we've been playing a game; and none of us is the worse for it and some of us much the better. And there are friends as well as runs to be got out of it. Lindsay Hassett goes into retirement to the good wishes of far more friends all over the globe than all the 16,000-odd runs he accumulated, at his leisure and according to his own sweet will, at the wicket. (*1954*)

W.M. LAWRY

A comparatively unknown 24-year-old cricketer who came to England with Richie Benaud's 1961 team made the strongest impact of any post-war Australian batsman on his initial tour. He was WILLIAM MORRIS LAWRY, a member of the Northcote Cricket Club in Melbourne and of the Victoria State eleven. As a Test left-handed opener he established himself as successor to Arthur Morris.

It was ironical that this tall, lean young man with the sharp jaw, who stood six feet two inches, bore the nickname 'The Phantom' bestowed upon him when he first joined the Victoria team and his colleagues discovered his youthful addiction to a comic strip character of that name. As he went from one triumph to another Lawry, with his slight crouch at the wicket, his long reach to kill the spin was very much there in the flesh in the eyes of the England bowlers. Presenting a really straight bat, he combined a well-organised defence with a satisfying, if not very wide, range of strokes, showing readiness to hit the loose ball and extraordinary facility in placing it. Admirable composure and power of intense concentration supplemented these assets. He was stout hearted, stubborn or pugnacious as circumstances prescribed, and had the temperament of being able to carry on unruffled by error.

One of eleven newcomers to England in the Australian party, Lawry topped the batting with 2,019 runs, average 61.18 in first-class matches and 420 runs at 52.50 an innings in the five Tests. Also he hit most centuries, nine. Only Don Bradman, 2,428 runs in 1948, and Neil Harvey, 2,040 in 1953, among Australians also made over two thousand runs in England since the war. That the summer was mostly fine after the first week did not detract from the left-hander's glory. He hit a century in each of the two Tests that Australia won: 130 on the exacting ridge at Lord's and 102 in the Test which decided the Ashes at Old Trafford after 74 in the first innings.

Lawry, the raw recruit, soon adapted himself to English pitches which he found slower than those at home but with more pronounced spin and cut. He had been sent to England as a promising opener – solid and with strokes developing. His sole major achievement had been 266 – after being dropped at 12 – in a punishing innings for Victoria against New South Wales in Sydney shortly before the Australian selectors chose the team for the tour.

Born in the Melbourne suburb of Thornbury on February 11, 1937, Bill Lawry had no family background in big cricket. At the age of nine he took part in his first competition with Thornbury Presbyterian Church team; he spent three years in church cricket and also played for Preston Technical School. The Australian district clubs set out to 'catch 'em young' and when he was 12 Northcote claimed him in their fourth grade side where he stayed two seasons, then one in the third, one in the second and at 16 he was promoted to the first. Thus he had eight summers in the senior grade before he toured England.

His first-class career had one serious check. A few months before his nineteenth birthday he made his debut for Victoria, against Western Australia in 1955–56. He appeared in all the Victoria State matches in 1956–57, but was dropped completely in 1957–58 and for half the next season. Restoration came in Victoria's return game against M.C.C. in 1958–59; he scored 24 and 22 and since then has played continuously.

Lawry acknowledges the help he received from Jack Baggott, coach of the Northcote club whose first eleven he now captains. He greatly admires Australia's post-war left-handers, Morris and Harvey, although he did not try to copy their methods. Lawry is also a left-hander at winter baseball which has given him a splendid throwing arm. He also finds time to breed racing pigeons.

During the early days of the tour, O'Neill, Harvey and Burge each scored a century for the Australians before Lawry got his first in England at The Oval. It was a dominating innings against Surrey on a Saturday in May; also it was one of the most significant of the whole season. It was a flowering of technique and temperament and it opened many English eyes and many Australian eyes, too.

In four and a half hours, Lawry scored 165 out of 286. He produced powerful drives beautifully placed past cover or mid-off; he hooked hard and he pulled hard. He pounced on anything loose offered by Test spinner, Tony Lock. Denis Compton said he had not seen such ferocious hooking since the days of Bradman. Lawry had arrived. As at The Oval, he hit a century on his first appearance at Lord's, 104 against M.C.C.; and was shaping for a second, 84 not out, when the closure was applied. [...]

Lawry was Australia's spinal column in the second Test at Lord's. This was an indomitable effort of sheer graft under severe pressure with the ball flying about and he was tenacious, painstaking and wonderfully cool. He took bruising blows. True, he made some 'passes' at fiery Trueman and Statham, but he stuck it out for six hours, hitting the loose ball cleanly and placing it well. That innings of 130, his fifth hundred of the tour, gave Lawry one thousand runs inside two months.

After the Old Trafford Test, W.E. Bowes, a former England pace bowler, wrote that Lawry was 'one of the best players against fast bowling I have ever seen'. In the later stages of the tour some staleness was evident and his batting lacked previous composure and colour, but the fact remained that the tall one's batting did expand on his baptismal tour. Returning to his own country, Lawry promptly became the Victoria captain. A popular character, modest, staunch and intelligent, he is a splendid team man. (*1962*)

TWO ERAS OF AUSTRALIAN PACE

By I.A.R. Peebles

Barring mishaps, it does seem certain that once again England will see the old firm of Lindwall and Miller in action. In the past there have been premature reports of their impending retirement, and even at the moment of writing when Sheffield Shield cricket in Australia is well under way and the selectors are doubtless studying the individual form of the players with anxious eyes, both have been troubled by injury. Whatever the future may bring, a comparison between Lindwall and Miller and their only rivals as a pair in the present century of Australian cricket, Gregory and McDonald, is fascinating as it is inevitable.

In making any such comparison it is necessary to recognise that fashions and techniques in cricket, as in other matters, have changed with the passing of the generation which separates two distinct eras. It is a wide subject and, as space will allow only the study of certain aspects, these few reflections are perforce confined to the bowlers' point of view, and again largely to that of the pace bowler.

This will be the third Australian team to visit England since the war, and it will embark on the sixth series since that major interruption. In the number of matches and in actual years this period is almost the exact counterpart of that between the end of the first war and the eve of the 1930 tour. There is also a close parallel in the trend of events. In both cases England were outplayed in the reopening tour and the return visit, achieved a solitary victory in the third series and won the fourth in each case by a final deciding match at The Oval. The succeeding series, those of 1928–29 and 1954–55, saw England once more in the ascendancy by a good margin.

The similarity in result during these decades was reflected by a close resemblance in the actual play. A period of Australian supremacy, achieved by a combination of powerful batting, devastating fast bowling and much superior fielding, was followed by a gradual English resurgence led by an outstanding fast-medium bowler. Finally, there comes a complete reversal of the balance, largely brought about by a counterblast of fast bowling. Certainly there were many other factors which contributed to the ebb and flow of the tide, some alike and some totally dissimilar, but few cricket cycles can have been so alike in broad outline.

BRADMAN INTERVENES

They were divided by the era of Bradman who made his first appearance in the 1928–29 series and led the triumphant teams of 1946–47 and 1948. Despite the overlap, the division may be regarded as fairly clear, for on the one hand, despite early success, he was still something of an unknown quantity and, on the other, although still a tremendous force, he was scarcely the man who changed the character of international cricket in the 'thirties. In comparing the two eras, it is possible to identify several elements which affected tactics and techniques; but to say for how many of these Bradman was directly or indirectly accountable or to estimate his total influence on the game as a whole is very difficult. What is plain is that the game as played in the post second war years differed considerably in form from that of 1921.

To start with cold, impersonal figures – if indeed cricket figures can ever be cold or impersonal – surely the most pertinent item amongst Mr Roy Webber's exhaustive figures dealing with these years is the fact that in the 1920–21 and 1921 series England, a well-beaten side, scored forty-nine and fifty runs per hundred balls bowled. Australia were naturally rather more expeditious scoring fifty-three and fifty-six. In the first two post second war series the rates dropped to thirty-seven and thirty-eight for England and fifty and forty-six for Australia. Thereafter the Australian rate dropped farther back. The trend in the intervening years had been a steady decline in the pace of scoring despite a large proportion of runs supplied by Bradman at an exceptionally high personal rate. Even if the 1920–21 and 1921 seasons were abnormal, it hardly calls for the mass of additional evidence available to demonstrate that the play of thirty-five years ago was of a considerably freer character. Whether it was as efficient is another matter.

What is the main reason for this change or deceleration? The broad answer must surely be the transference of the bowlers' focus from the region of the off-stump to that of the leg and the consequent throttling of off-side play but, equally importantly, the denial of the safe deflecting stroke to leg. The causes of this transference are several and complex, and the credit or responsibility must be shared between groundsman, bowler and batsman in what proportion we may later determine. Somewhat unfashionably I am inclined to exculpate the legislators.

In 1921 the spearhead of the Australian attack, the speed of Gregory and McDonald, was directed at the stumps and supported by three slips. The good length ball aimed at the stumps pitched regularly to the off and it was desirable that any error should be further in that direction. If the error was to drop the ball outside the leg-stump the batsman could play boldly in the knowledge that he had free passage to a distant fine-leg who could, at most, rob him of three runs.

When Lindwall and Miller bowled the slips had increased in number and some of them had now migrated to the hitherto uninhabited regions on the leg-side. For England, Bedser, with his sharp in-swerver, had perfected the same technique and the impact on batsmanship must have been as profound as the introduction of the googly. What had been a safe and attractive scoring shot had now elements of suicide, for if the ball 'moved' a little to the on a mishit was almost certain to result in a catch. Indeed, a correctly executed stroke was often fatal, owing to the difficulty of placing and keeping the ball down in this sector. The dangers of this situation were clear when Bradman, who seldom repeated a serious mistake, fell three times in succession to the backward short-leg position during the 1948 series. [...]

The highlights of each era, Gregory and McDonald attacking Hobbs and Woolley or Lindwall and Miller in action against Compton and Hutton obviously transcended the differences in character to which I have referred and even the one-sided nature of the matches. The chief point in common amongst the batsmen is that they formed a first line of defence with little reserve behind them. The bowlers have much similarity in circumstance and in performance. They reigned supreme at a time when there was a world shortage of fast bowling and batsmen were ill-equipped to meet it.

Which was the finer pair and which the greatest individual must ever be open to argument and is much a matter of opinion. Certainly in span and in the matter of statistics the moderns have a much more impressive record. Gregory and McDonald appeared together in but eleven Test matches, eight against England and three against South Africa. The latter then left the international field at the height of his powers but his senior partner played for another seven years, a total of 24 matches. There is no doubt, however, that his powers declined greatly after the dissolution of the partnership.

COMPARISON OF FIGURES

Up to the present Lindwall and Miller have appeared together on 46 occasions and have played 49 and 47 Test matches respectively. In his Test career Gregory took 75 wickets at 35.30 runs apiece and McDonald 43 at 35.60 each. So far Lindwall has taken 192 wickets for 21.88 apiece and Miller 147 at 22.99 runs each.

There can be little doubt that McDonald was the most graceful of the quartette and possibly the most perfect cricket machine of all time. In the opinion of many well-qualified judges he could produce a faster ball than anyone within living memory. In his county days he seldom exerted himself to the full; only recently I was given an enthralling eye-witness account of one of his latter bursts of speed, occasioned by the appearance of an amateur who had treated him roughly in a previous match. This apparently irritated him out of his customary impassive calm and the results were spectacular. My informant, who has played most of the fast bowlers of the last thirty years, says it was the fastest bowling he has ever seen and only approached by Lindwall's stupendous three-over burst at Manchester in 1948. It was interesting to hear that the only perceptible increase in effort was that he accelerated in the last five yards of the impeccable run up to a swift gallop. His point established he reverted to the normal cruising speed which carried him through many strenuous seasons.

Gregory was to my mind the most inspiring. One might apply to him the words of a motoring critic who said of a famous make of sports car that others might have gone faster but none had achieved the glorious frenzy of its progress. Estimates as to his maximum speed vary, but it must have been extremely swift especially in the opening overs, and his height and very high arm added greatly to the general hostility of the performance. It might also be said of both Gregory and Miller that, in contrast to the polished craftsmanship of their partners, they were both children of nature.

LINDWALL COMES FIRST

A large mass of opinion places Lindwall first of all fast bowlers, a judgement based on pace, variation, control and consummate technique of seam and swerve. In addition he is a wonderfully shrewd and discerning tactician. I have already dwelt on the modern emphasis on the leg stump and the close surrounding field. Lindwall has retained the classical off-side attack but has added to it the cramping assault on the region of the batsman's pads. The so-called 'Carmody field', which consists of a cover-point and a short-leg to the fore and the rest of the field spread on either side of the wicket-keeper like the horns of a Zulu Impi, would doubtless appear monstrous and absurd to an eye reopened after thirty years. In the hands of the master it is in fact a formidable instrument. When it is new, the bowler pitches the ball well up, almost to half-volley length, and invites the batsman to drive him into the untenanted foreground. But swinging bat and very late swinging ball are ill met and the mis-hit from either edge means almost certain disaster with the Australian in-field to hand.

Batsmen have told me that Lindwall's low arm gives the ball an awkward angle of flight in addition to the complication of his late and unpredicted dip in either direction. When, as in the last series, the ball came at varying heights from the pitch the skill demanded of the modern opener is such that it is not surprising that few regularly succeed in such circumstances. It may be observed that doped, paceless wickets kill these dangers just as effectively as they obliterate any other point of interest.

Of Miller it might be said that he is the most mercurial but, in the mood, as deadly as any. His careless, almost casual air bears no relation to the power and fire of his action which seems to develop its maximum effort and weight as the arm comes to the downward sector of its swing so that the ball hits the pitch with a resounding thump. Although it may be with less design than in the case of Lindwall, he makes the ball move sharply in either direction.

MILLER THE MENACE

After the splendid performances of our own fast bowlers in Australia in 1954–55 it may seem almost ungrateful to say so but, with Lindwall in at least a temporary decline, Miller was the most menacing bowler of the series with the new ball. He may have lost something of his stamina but his opening assaults at Brisbane, Melbourne and Adelaide were positively hair-raising as seen through the eyes of a visiting supporter. Three balls at the start of the crucial second innings at Adelaide all but wrecked English hopes and remain vividly in the imagination. First there was a ferocious 'in-dipper', which appeared to affect Edrich's nervous system as violently as it did his middle and leg stumps. This was followed at uncomfortably short intervals by two very fast balls to Hutton and Cowdrey which left the pitch like leg-breaks and resulted in bullet-like catches, both beautifully picked up in the slips. The challenge was met by magnificent batting by May and Compton, but until the first welcome signs of fatigue appeared the final target of 94 runs seemed immeasurably distant.

Miller has the additional virtue of being a most entertaining bowler, and his impish delight in loosing off googlies and round armers without previous notice must be highly disconcerting, if it does not seem to meet with any great material success.

THE COMBINED EFFORT

But when all is said and done, which of these great pairs will be given premier place in Australian cricket history in the years to come is a very open question. Gregory and McDonald have one very special niche in all cricket history. At least so far as international cricket is concerned they were the pioneers of all fast opening attack. Since then it has been regarded as the most effective use that can be made of the new ball, and it can well be argued that two fast bowlers, provided they are of quality, have had more influence on the result of a given series than any other factor, with the possible exception of the phenomenal Bradman. In support of this view I would cite Larwood and Voce; Martindale and Constantine in their own country, Lindwall and Miller and finally Statham and Tyson. There have been many fine individual performers during the same time, but it seems that the combined effort is necessary to derive the fullest service from the individual. (*1956*)

A.R. MORRIS

Whatever relief English bowlers may have felt at the knowledge that they were pitting their wits against D.G. Bradman for the last time in 1948 must have been largely counter-balanced by the realisation that, given normal continuation of form and luck, another record-breaking Australian batsman had arisen in the person of ARTHUR ROBERT MORRIS, the New South Wales left-hander whose Test performances during the series surpassed even those of his captain. Eighteen months earlier Morris hit three centuries in successive Test innings against W.R. Hammond's team and, though he maintained his form when India toured Australia in 1947–48, his feats in England provided the final qualifications which led to his assessment as one of the world's best left-hand batsmen. Yet, Morris made his entry into Australian grade cricket as a left-hand slow bowler whose batting ability was so little regarded that he went in last.

Morris was born on January 19, 1922, at Sydney, New South Wales, where his father, a schoolmaster who bowled fast for the Waverley club, taught him the rudiments of the game and moulded his love for it. When his family moved to Newcastle, Morris attended the High School there and, at the age of 13, gained a place in the school eleven for his slow bowling. Thence, back again to Sydney, Morris figured in the Canterbury High School team for the next three years. He was chosen each season to represent Combined High Schools at cricket and Rugby football and in the last two years he captained both his own school cricket team and the Combined High School side. Even when at school Morris began to receive cricket honours. He joined the St. George District club which, captained by W.J. O'Reilly, won the First Grade premiership three years running. Though Morris started with St. George's as a bowler and continued to go in last observant critics noticed his growing skill with the bat and more opportunities arose till, after hitting a century against Sydney University when 16, he was promoted to open the innings. [...]

Before reaching his 19th birthday Morris set the cricket world talking when hescored a century in each innings of his first inter-state match for New South Wales against Queensland at Christmas 1940, a feat without parallel at the time of writing. Morris, whose scores were 148 and 111, shared in a second wicket stand of 261 with S.G. Barnes in the first innings and in the second he and M.B. Cohen (118) opened with another three-figure partnership. No man could wish for finer inspiration at the start of his cricket life, but Morris was, of course, made of mortal clay and there followed a run of less startling innings, though he finished the season with an average of 55.14 for his State. During the six war years which followed Morris played scarcely any cricket and he spent a long time in Australian Army Movement Control in New Guinea. Not until the 1946–47 season when the M.C.C. team arrived could he take part in serious cricket again. Then, in his first State game, he hit 27 and 98, he and D.K. Carmody making 153 off the Queensland bowlers for the first wicket in the second innings. Two weeks later Morris scored 115 for an Australian XI against the touring team in what was regarded as a Trial Match for Australian Test candidates and the same week he obtained 81 not out for New South Wales against Hammond's side.

His choice for the Tests followed as a matter of course. He made only two and five in the first two matches, but the continued faith of the Selectors was not misplaced, for in the Third Test, at Melbourne, he hit 21 and 155 and in the next Test 122 and 124 not out during terrific heat at Adelaide, where Compton also scored a century in each innings. This was the first time a batsman on each side had performed the feat in a Test. The only other Australian with a Test century in each innings against England was Warren Bardsley, a left-hand opening batsmen to whom Morris had been compared, though good judges who saw both declared that Bardsley did not possess the same fluency of stroke-play as Morris. That season Morris played in all five Tests and finished with an aggregate of 503 runs, average 71.85. The following season, 1947–48, Morris played in the first four Tests against India, getting one century and averaging 52.25. He missed the fifth because the Selectors wished to see the form of other probable choices for the English tour. Appointed captain of New South Wales he hit another century against India and was a certainty for England. Although he began the tour with 138 in the first match, he found difficulty for a few weeks in adapting himself to the new conditions, and reached 50 only twice in nine innings. During this period Morris sometimes made the mistake of trying to drive the ball pitched just short of a length. When it lifted suddenly he was liable to give a catch. He adjusted his methods and success followed immediately. Morris hit 184 against Sussex and scored five more centuries before the end of the season, including the highest innings of his career, 290 against Gloucestershire.

In these 1948 Tests Morris was the most consistent batsman on either side with 696 runs in nine innings – 31, 9, 105, 62, 51, 54 not out, 6, 182, and 196 – average 87.00. No other batsman scored three centuries in the series and Morris finished the summer with an aggregate of 1,922 – average 71.18 in first-class games; and this despite for most of the tour being troubled by a split between the first and second fingers of his left hand caused by constant jarring from the bat as he played the ball. Usually after Morris had been batting a few overs the wound opened again and bled; towards the end of the season the affected part became swollen and he underwent a minor operation which kept him out of a few games.

Although Morris acquired most of his cricket prowess by contact with other good players whose methods he watched closely during his early days, he also acknowledged the debt he owed to W.J. O'Reilly. Morris is at once imposing to opponents and impressive to spectators by his air of complete composure at the wicket. Possessed of an ideal temperament, he combines unusual defensive qualities with the ability to decide early in the ball's flight what his stroke shall be. Often he may walk right in front of the stumps to get well behind the ball when making a defensive stroke and looks likely to be out leg-before but rarely errs as he watches the ball off the pitch on to the bat. He compares well with Bradman in placing his strokes clear of fieldsmen and in keeping the ball along the ground. Seldom does the hittable ball find him unprepared and rarely is it allowed to go without full punishment. Like most left-handers, Morris is specially good at driving through the covers, hitting to leg and in powerful square-cutting, and few excel him in on-driving. Fair-haired Morris, who is five feet nine inches tall, is an executive in a motor tyre distributor's business in Sydney. Of quiet disposition he is unmarried. (*1949*)

THE TIGER

O'REILLY, WILLIAM JOSEPH, OBE, who died in a Sydney hospital on October 6, 1992, aged 86, was probably the greatest spin bowler the game has ever produced. Bill 'Tiger' O'Reilly was unquestionably one of cricket's great figures: as a player, as a character and later as a writer on the game. His cricket was proof that spin bowling was not necessarily a gentle art. He was 6ft 2in tall, gripped the ball in his enormous right hand and released it at a pace that could be almost fast-medium. It would then bounce ferociously on the hard pitches of his time and, on occasion, knock wicket-keepers off their feet. He bowled leg-breaks and, especially, top-spinners and googlies, backed up by an intimidating manner. Jack Fingleton said he was 'a flurry of limbs, fire and steel-edged temper'. It has been suggested that his action and the general commotion before delivery were born of a deep sense of frustration at not being able to bowl fast enough to knock the batsman down. Off the field, his gruffness was mitigated by his intelligence, erudition, wit and twinkling eyes.

He played 27 Test matches and took 144 wickets – 102 of them Englishmen and the vital wicket of Walter Hammond ten times – averaging 22.59. But his figures have to be judged by the fact that all but one of his Tests came in the 1930s, when other bowlers were dominated by batsmen to an unprecedented extent. No one ever dominated O'Reilly. Even when England made 903 at The Oval in 1938, he bowled 85 overs and finished with figures of three for 178. And before that, he had secured the Ashes by taking five for 66 and five for 56 at Headingley,

O'Reilly was born in White Cliffs in the New South Wales bush into a large Irish family on December 20, 1905. His father was a small-town schoolmaster and young Bill was above average at several sports, including tennis, athletics and rugby. Cricket was harder to arrange. According to Jack Fingleton in *Cricket Crisis*, the four O'Reilly brothers played with a gum-wood bat and a piece of banksia root chiselled down to make a ball. Since the others were older, Bill inevitably bowled more than he batted. The brothers also cuffed him a lot, possibly because he was starting to show them up. In 1917 the family moved to Wingello. When he played his first match for Wingello Juniors, the team walked to the opposition's ground seven miles away in Tallong, with their dogs chasing rabbits along the way. In 1919, he went to the high school in the larger town of Goulburn, where he concentrated on his athletics as much as his cricket. And when he went to the teachers' college at Sydney University in his late teens he was more interested in such events as the hop, step and jump, in which he held the state record. According to Fingleton's account he would probably have been lost to cricket had he not been asked to make up the numbers in a Sydney junior match and, with a method that at first made everyone giggle, whipped out the opposition.

In the summer of 1925–26, the young O'Reilly, by now an undergraduate at the teachers' college in Sydney University, met the man whose destiny was to be linked with his for ever. O'Reilly's own account of this remains a classic. He was passing through Bowral Station on his way home to Wingello for his summer holiday when he heard his name being called down the platform. He put his head out of the carriage window and was told to get out at once: Wingello were playing at Bowral and needed him.

'How was I to know that I was about to cross swords with the greatest cricketer that ever set foot on a cricket field? He didn't have it all his own way, let me tell you. Well, not for the first couple of overs, anyway.' By the close of play, 17-year-old Don Bradman was 234 not out. The match resumed a week later, according to the local custom. 'The sun shone, the birds sang sweetly and the flowers bloomed as never before. I bowled him first ball with a leg-break which came from the leg stump to hit the off bail. Suddenly cricket was the best game in the whole wide world.'

In 1926–27 O'Reilly was chosen for the New South Wales state practice squad on the strength of one match for North Sydney. A year later he made his first-class debut against the New Zealanders. But teachers in New South Wales work for the state rather than an individual school and the newly-qualified O'Reilly was despatched to three different bush towns. This may have cost him the chance of a Test against England in 1928–29 and, very probably, a tour in 1930. He was transferred back to Sydney in time for the 1931–32 season and after four more matches made his debut for Australia. He performed quietly in a match in which Bradman scored 299 not out and Grimmett took 14 wickets, but he had arrived.

In the 1932–33 Bodyline series he took 27 wickets, without anyone noticing much, given what else was happening. In the series in England in 1934 he took 28 wickets, including seven in an innings twice. At Trent Bridge he won the match with seven for 54, achieved by what *Wisden* called 'clever variation in flight and pace combined with spin off the worn turf'. In blazing heat at Old Trafford, he transformed the game in an over which England began at 68 for no wicket. Walters was caught at forward short leg off the first ball, Wyatt bowled middle stump by the second and Hammond, after glancing a four off the third, was bowled by the fourth. Hendren and Leyland recaptured the initiative and England declared at 627 for nine but O'Reilly finished with seven for 189. He took 109 wickets on the tour, including nine for 38 against Somerset. He went back to Australia and suddenly announced his retirement. He had married in 1933, had a daughter and was anxious about his teaching career. However, Sydney Grammar School offered him a job that enabled him to play on. He toured South Africa in 1935–36 and took 27 wickets again, 25 in the great series against England in 1936–37 and 22 back in England in 1938, despite the unforgiving wickets ('dosed up to the eyeballs', said O'Reilly) of Trent Bridge and The Oval.

He played only one more Test, the one-off game against New Zealand at Wellington in March 1946 when he was already 40. The opposition barely beat his age: they were bowled out for 42 and 54 and O'Reilly took five for 14 and three for 19. It was the 11th time he had taken five in an innings in Tests. O'Reilly then began writing on cricket for the *Sydney Morning Herald* with a muscular, very Australian prose style flavoured with wit and imagery ('You can smell the gum leaves off him', he wrote of one country boy just starting with Queensland). Until he finally retired in 1988, he was as revered in Australian press boxes as he had been on the field. His opinions often came more from the heart than the head especially if it was a question of attacking the selectors for playing safe and ignoring a young player, most especially a young leg-spinner. But he was consistent, loved quality and hated one-day cricket ('hit-and-giggle') which he generally refused to watch. He was hot-blooded and humorous which perhaps explains why his relationship with the cooler Bradman is believed to have been based on intense mutual respect rather than the profoundest form of Australian mateship. While Sir Donald walked the corridors of cricketing power O'Reilly was the rumbustious backbencher.

His last few years were rendered miserable by illness, including the loss of a leg. But he was blessed with a marriage to Molly that lasted 59 years. In his career he took 774 wickets at 16.60 and was successful at every level: playing for North Sydney and St George, he topped the Sydney Grade averages 12 times and took 962 wickets at 9.44. He took a wicket every 49 balls in his first-class career and it was said he never bowled a wide. His batting was left-handed, hard-hitting and occasionally stubborn (1,655 runs at 13.13); he never quite forgave himself for getting out at Lord's in 1934 when he might have saved the follow-on, in which case he rather than Verity would have had use of a rain-affected wicket. He did save the follow-on by making 30 not out at Old Trafford in the next Test. Future generations will have to judge the greatness of his bowling on the fragments of film that survive and the written descriptions, of which R.C. Robertson-Glasgow's may stand as definitive:

> As with those more florid opponents of legendary heroes, there seemed to be more arms than Nature or the rules allow. During the run-up, a sort of fierce galumph, the right forearm worked like a piston; at delivery the head was ducked low as if to butt the batsman on to his stumps. But it didn't take long to see the greatness; the control of leg-break, top-spinner and googly; the change of pace and trajectory without apparent change in action; the scrupulous length; the vitality; and, informing and rounding all, the brain to diagnose what patient required what treatment.

When O'Reilly died, Bradman said he was the greatest bowler he had ever faced or watched. (*1993*)

RECOLLECTIONS OF MR F.R. SPOFFORTH

By Lord Harris

I was talking to Mr Noble early in the season at the Oval, and he told me that Spofforth was seriously ill, and then put to me the astonishing question, 'Was he a great bowler?' It was about equivalent to asking if W.G. was a great bat. 'About the best I ever played,' was my reply; 'but did you never see him?' It was another shock to find that Noble, with whom I had never played, had never seen him bowl. Later on I went down to see Spofforth, and we had a chat about old times; he was keenly interested in past as well as present times, but as I left the room he said, 'The doctors say I shall see the First Test Match; but I made my reputation in May; you knocked me out in May; and I shall go out in May'. He actually passed away in the first days of June.

Now what he described as my knocking him out, was a very curious coincidence. If anyone cares to look at the Cricket Records of 1885 and 1887, he will find in Australians v. Gentlemen of England, at Lord's, in 1884: F.R. Spofforth absent 0, and absent 0, and in 1886, F.R. Spofforth retired hurt 0, and that he did not bowl at all in the second innings.

I have recorded in 'A Few Short Runs', and I can but repeat that on each occasion I hit a ball back which injured his right hand; and he always said that he was never the same bowler after the second injury. He followed up his ball very far, and as I probably jumped in, he was very close, too close to put his hand in exactly the right place; else he was ordinarily a very good field to his own bowling, but so full of nerves, that a hard blow made more difference to him than to many.

An amusing illustration of this sensitiveness occurred at Canterbury, in 1886, in Kent v. Australians. I was in with G.G. Hearne, who would always run at a nod from me. Old Spof had been rather upset about the wicket keeping; a ball was thrown in badly from long field, which hurt him; he went dancing about wringing his hand, at last danced on the opposite side of the wicket to where the ball was lying close to the wicket, and we ran, much to the amusement of the crowd.

It is a common misconception, amongst those who did not see or play him, that he was a very fast bowler. He may have been in Australia before his first visit to England, in 1878, but he was far too knowledgeable on our slower wickets, and 1878 was little better than a mud lark, to depend on pace. He could bowl a very fast ball, and did, as often perhaps as once an over; but what he depended on was what he termed the 'judgment' ball; medium pace, but with great variety of pace, and therefore of flight, and a strong break from the off. He could break slightly from leg, I believe, though I cannot remember his doing so; and the rumour went round amongst us who had to face him for the first time, that if he was going to break from the off, he held the ball at the tips of his fingers; if from leg, in the palm of his hand. In my opinion what deceived the batsman, was that he came up at a great pace and then bowled a much slower ball than his pace up to the wicket led one to expect. Consequently the batsman played rather too quickly, cocked the ball up a bit, and he was so close up, and judged the direction the ball would come off the bat so well, that he brought off the catch and bowl very frequently; and if it did not come off in his direction, the break would take it round to silly mid-on, where Boyle was waiting for and seldom missed it. Indeed, with Spof bowling, Blackham at the wicket, and Boyle at short leg, the forward type of play on slow wickets almost certainly led to disaster. That he was a great bowler cannot be disputed, his performances on the tours he took part in were astonishing, as shown elsewhere in this volume.

There were two signs which pretty clearly indicate what the public thought of him; his title 'The Demon' Bowler; and that he was singled out amongst cricketers for a cartoon in *Vanity Fair*. In after years there were quite a number of cricketers similarly honoured by that paper, but in his day it was a rarity.

I have said that he came up to the wicket very fast, and he followed up straight down the wicket, thus, left foot on or about the popping crease, right foot well on to the half volley pitch, and then both feet plump on the awkward pitch; and when wickets were soft, he undoubtedly made a mess of the pitch. In those days we were not so particular as cricketers are now; we took such happenings as the 'rubs' of the game; but in his case we used to remonstrate, and Spof's indignation was deep seated and high voiced. 'Look at my heels, no spikes,' was his retort; which was true, but the heels were high.

At Sydney in 1878–79, we had made a very good start. I was in, and could not imagine why they did not put Evans, a most accurate bowler, on to bowl at the hole Spof had made. At last they did, and I said to Murdoch, who was keeping wicket, 'This innings is over,' and we were out for some 40 more. Evans kept on finding the broken spot. He was much more thought of than Spofforth in Australia, and was a much better cricketer all round; but was not successful when he came home, partly due to ill-health. Spofforth was of no great worth as a bat, and was never conspicuous in the field; he seemed to concentrate on his bowling, and I think did really study his opponents' weak points, and work at them; and in after years it was interesting to get him to talk about his performances, which, when we met at Lord's, he was quite ready to do.

I was playing for ten years abroad and at home against those great medium pace Australian bowlers, Allan, Garrett, Palmer, Giffen, Turner, and Ferris, as well as Spofforth, and I have of course also played such great English medium pace bowlers as Alfred Shaw, Watson, Jim Lillywhite, Lohmann, C.T. Studd and W.G. Grace, and I am quite satisfied and always have been, that Spofforth was the most difficult of them all, because he concealed so well the pace of the ball. What he could have done on the easy wickets of the present day, no one can say, but I am sure he could have adapted his bowling to them; and does it matter? What we must judge performances by are the circumstances and conditions of the time when they were done, and taking those as the criteria, I do not see how any bowler can be held to be better than was F.R. Spofforth.

By The Earl of Darnley

I well remember the first time that I encountered the Demon Bowler – in the Cambridge v. Australian match, at Lord's, in 1878. We had all been warned by our captain, the Hon. Edward Lyttelton who had, I think, recently made a big score against the Australians, to watch Spofforth's bowling hand as he came to the wicket. If the wrist was bent, one was to expect a slower ball with break back; if the wrist was straight, a very fast ball, and not improbably a 'yorker'.

In some of the accounts recently published of Spofforth's bowling it was said that he was never a really fast bowler. I believe this statement to be quite incorrect. If my memory does not deceive me, there were two very distinct stages in his bowling. When he first came to England in 1878, his bowling was very fast indeed, almost as fast as the fastest we have seen, with occasional very well disguised slower ones, which were very deceiving to the batsman and caused many a premature forward stroke and retirement of the batsman – caught and bowled.

After 1878 he greatly moderated his pace, and relied more on the fast-medium ball of wonderfully good length and considerable break back, with the occasional variation of the very fast one, including a particularly deadly 'yorker'.

I should imagine that the nickname of 'Demon' arose from the terrifying aspect of his final bound at the wicket when delivering the ball – long lean arms whirling through the air from a commanding height, and a long stride coming down with great force and damaging effect on a very awkward spot for a breaking-back ball bowled from the other end. The long arms seemed to be whirling round at much the same speed whether the ball was coming fast or slow, and he had practised these disguises of pace to great perfection.

Some of his bowling success may be traced to certain physical attributes of an unusual character – very tall, 6ft. 3in., broad shouldered, but unusually lean and sinewy and carrying very little weight. A year or two ago, he told me that at his best he only weighed 11 stone 7 lbs. His early life on horse-back in the Australian bush gave to him the lasting power which made him incomparably the best stayer of any fast or medium pace bowler that I can remember. Though of so comparatively light build, he was exceptionally strong, and one of his feats was to support Bonnor, weighing over 16 stone, on the calf of his leg, held horizontally backwards at right angles to the upright leg – no mean feat. He and Bonnor were the two fastest hundred yards runners in the Australian elevens of those days, one weighing some 5 stone more than the other.

In addition to these physical features, no bowler that I ever saw had a more graceful, spacious sweep of the arm, and his delivery gave a most satisfactory sensation of perfection of pace and power combined. Unlike most of the modern fast bowlers, his run up to the wicket was only of average length, and his pace and power owed nothing to the impetus of an abnormally long run.

One of the very best bowlers that the last 50 years have seen, unquestionably; possibly the best of all. A cheery and amusing companion, withal, amongst his fellow cricketers. Fond of a good story, and, like many of his compatriots, not inclined to understatement. His old cricketing friends will cherish a very kindly recollection of his unique personality.

By Mr C.I. Thorton

I first met F.R. Spofforth on the Orleans Club ground at Twickenham where the Australians of 1878 met a team which I had got together. My side included I.D. Walker, W. Yardley, W N. Powys, D.Q. Steel and three professionals – Fred Wild, the Notts wicket-keeper, Arnold Rylott of Leicestershire, and Ted Barratt of Surrey. Barrett took twelve wickets and when the game was left drawn we wanted only 75 to win and had eight wickets to fall. In the 'seventies' and 'eighties' I knew Spofforth well and played a lot of cricket with him. He was a first-rate judge of the game and certainly the best bowler of the 'dodgy' class I ever saw, as he varied his run up to the wicket and you could never tell what paced ball was coming along. Still he never stuck me up as much as did Ferris and Giffen. To get Spofforth and E.M. Grace on a side was to ensure a pleasant day's cricket if not necessarily a successful one. Spofforth was at his happiest at country matches where his stories – always told with an air of sincerity – used to amuse people immensely. One special one that never failed to please used to be given in the following circumstances. I would say to him at lunch 'How did you learn to be such a fine short-slip, Spoff?' And he would reply 'When I was quite young I made a boy, when out for a walk, throw stones into a hedge, and as the sparrows flew out, I caught 'em. (1927)

FIRST AMONG EQUALS

By John Benaud

Even before candles at Mark Taylor's birthday celebrations reached double figures there were notable signs of spirit and staying power from the boy who by his 34th birthday had patiently and forthrightly shaped an era full of some of Australian cricket's most pleasure-giving moments.

In the 1960s, young Mark's father Tony was a property valuer on a rising career path with the Rural Bank of New South Wales and, three times in seven years, the talent spotters at head office sent orders down the line asking the Taylor family to pack up and criss-cross the vast Riverina district of south-western New South Wales. For a small boy these domestic upheavals were adventures, but they were also long journeys made longer by the gun-barrel straightness of the highways, the dry, thirst-inducing heat and the featureless landscape stretching to the horizon.

Mark Taylor was born in 1964 in Leeton, a fruit-growing town. There, on a notable occasion not long after the outbreak of World War II, the labourers were motivated enough to pack 419,609 cans of peaches in a day, a record that stands as tall among the townspeople in 1999 as Taylor's and Bradman's shared 334 does among cricket fans. Of course, a record set in the packing sheds at Leeton hardly deserves to stand with one grafted out in the heat and dust of Peshawar in Pakistan. At first glance it is incongruous nonsense, but the link does sharpen the focus on a particularly Australian way of advancement: wealth from toil.

In the era when Don Bradman was turning the best any bowler could produce into fodder, Leeton was enjoying a prosperous farming and grazing culture, but by the 1960s the area had embraced intensive cropping with irrigation. The change in traditional land usage meant values changed too, and rapidly. A rural valuer had to know good country from bad, had to identify potential when he saw it, because landholders needed to borrow against guaranteed crops. And a valuer had to know people: he had to identify the good, diligent managers and cull the dreamers. Tony Taylor's returns made the Rural Bank think he was head office material.

When Mark was barely 18 months old the bank moved Tony 320 kilometres due west to Dareton, just a speck on the map, and located on the mighty Murray River. In the next five years Taylor senior was posted 400 kilometres north-east to West Wyalong, then sent 100 kilometres due south to Wagga. Then there were seven years with no further moves, plenty of time for a banker to spend valuable time with a boy who was developing an interest in most sports. Mark's soccer career was brief: 'I got sick of it. I played centre-half, I think because I was the only one gutsy enough to head the ball ... or silly enough!' He preferred Australian Rules: 'My best mate played it.' But mostly Mark enjoyed cricket.

Tony's district cricket bowling averages were always more pleasing to the eye than his batting ones but he knew enough about willow wielding to educate Mark: 'Foot forward, always watch the ball closely: he was thorough about the basics. We used to play on the concrete in the carport at Wagga ... any part of the house on the full was out.' First lesson: don't slog.

When Mark was the ripe old age of 13. Tony went halves with him in his first senior cricket bat, a Rod Marsh autograph: 'Rod was a bit of a hero. I gave it the works, oiled it, rolled it, knocked it in with the ball in the stocking … I didn't use it for two weeks!' This was an early display of discipline, certainly patience. Determination was not long in announcing itself.

If another left-hander was a hero to Taylor then Rod Marsh's team-mate Doug Walters left a rather different impression, an occasion recalled with a good-natured guffaw by Taylor: 'Mr Walters came to Wagga to pick promising young cricketers to go up to Sydney to Cranbrook School for coaching. He gave the nod to two other kids. I was shattered. After I got over it I thought, "I'll just have to do better."' When Mark was 14 the family moved to Sydney – Tony Taylor had made it to head office. In all the years the father had traced his bush learning curve it is improbable that he ever once imagined that the most valuable property to come under his gaze would turn out to be his sports-interested son.

In 1991 Mark Taylor, by then one of world cricket's most highly regarded opening batsmen (25 Tests, 2,272 runs, average 52.84) was offered his own career path to head office: the national selectors made him captain of an Australian B team to tour Zimbabwe. Zimbabwe was something of a booby-trap for a young captain because the selectors had structured the B combination in such a way that two rookie leg-spinners, Shane Warne and Peter McIntyre, had to play in every game – and three of the games were one-dayers. And in those days, wrist-spinners were regarded as poison in a limited-overs line-up.

Taylor's leadership was impressive. Team meetings pursued clear objectives and encouraged discussion. He never forgot the experimental nature of the tour and offered every player a chance to fulfil his potential. Long plane trips, hot, dry conditions, slow pitches and a couple of tight finishes invited an outpouring of frustration – but the whinge never came. Taylor had seized the moment: 'I realised that if I continued to do well then one day I could captain Australia. After Zimbabwe I became more tactically aware, thinking a lot more about where a game was headed rather than just about how I was hitting them.'

Historically. the Australian captaincy-elect has been something of a banana skin: just a dozen Tests later, at the end of a scratchy series against the West Indies, Taylor was demoted to drinks waiter and, distressed by this vote of no confidence, it is possible his mind flashed back to that grey day with Doug Walters. But the rest is history: 104 Tests, 50 as captain, 26 wins, 7,525 runs, 19 centuries, 157 catches. The statistical mountain does, however, camouflage the captain's bat-dead state in the mid-90s when merely 'hitting them' became his chief challenge.

Taylor recalls the darkest moment during the 1997 tour of South Africa: 'I wasn't depressed, but flabbergasted – how was I going to make any bloody runs? The chairman of selectors, Trevor Hohns, came over after the Tests, before the one-dayers, and asked me how I was going and I said, "I'm playing like an A-grade drunk!" He said: "Do you want to have the one-dayers off, go home and get ready for England? We want you to captain the Ashes tour." I said, "Thanks for the offer, but I'd like to stay even if I don't play them all. I'm the captain of the tour and I want to stay." He said, "No problem." End of story.'

The bluntness inherent in his concluding remark – 'end of story' – is a reminder that even in the laid-back state of retirement he has the grits about those who spread rumours about the Cricket Board wanting to sack him. It was not shorthand for 'I'm contemplating the final curtain'. A month or two after South Africa, the cricketer they call Tubby offered for critical acclaim his own version of 'It ain't over till the fat lady sings': 129 at Edgbaston.

'A miracle', some said, but Taylor's 334 at Peshawar was the miracle. Long before the captain made those runs Australia's unquestionable Test world champion status had properly won Taylor favourable comparison with Richie Benaud and Ian Chappell, the high priests of Australia's captaincy church.

Whatever it was that denied Taylor the one run he needed to beat Bradman – good luck or bad management, call it what you will – the chances are it was fate which saw more benefit to cricket in Taylor forever sharing a line with the almighty rather than his just occasionally peeping from under the creamy cassocks of Benaud and Chappell.

Now, future generations will be more likely to dust off his file and try to understand the impact his style and character had on the game. They'll be able to decide if sacking one of our greatest opening batsmen and finest captains from the one-day game was a reasonable manoeuvre or the catalyst for compromising cricket's traditional values. For the stone has been cast: any future Australian captain must be limited-overs-friendly. A clear message has been sent to budding young cricketers: opening batsmen will no longer require the good technique that enables them to hang around when the going is tough. They'll be expected to take the shine off the new ball by slogging it over the fence.

In limited-overs exile Mark Taylor sought to resolve his predicament, which he conceded had at times affected his overall game: 'I had a strike-rate of 60, an average of 33 … I asked myself, 'What can I do differently?' My only options were not to worry or to get back in the team by doing something different. But if I had done things differently then I might never have played 100 Test matches. 'Taylor thinks one Test batsman did implode, New Zealand's Mark Greatbatch: 'He was encouraged to become a one-day hitter and all of a sudden this bloke who was a fine Test batsman couldn't bat. He could only slog.'

Is this really the future of the Australian game? Taylor: 'In 2010 I hope our cricket is not too much different from now. Of course the players will be faster and fitter, and every game improves over the years. But administrators, and cricket people like myself, have to decide by how much we want to change the game. If we take away the four-day or five-day cricket it will eventually affect one-day cricket because techniques will be affected. Do we want to change the game completely; do we want to make it almost like baseball? I think there'll be more one-day cricket. Schedules are getting tighter and if we want the game to progress we may have to shorten a Test to four days of say 110 overs. Why do we have to start at 11 and finish at six …? Maybe cricket should become a nine-to-five job.'

His 334 ruffled Taylor and, for a mad moment, he thought he had been blessed with the elixir of youth: 'I'd said to a few people that Sydney [Fifth Ashes Test, 1999] would be "it", but after Pakistan I began to wonder, "Maybe I'm retiring a fraction early here. I'm 34, that's not old. Maybe I've still got a couple of years in me if I really want them." But after winning the Ashes I kept asking myself one question: "Do I really want to keep playing?" Every time the answer was the same: "No!"' Common sense, but only after due consideration, a constant theme in Taylor's cricket.

In his last limited-overs game, an interstate final against Victoria at the MCG, Taylor made a duck. In his last Sheffield Shield match at the SCG he made 61. He struggled for timing on a slow pitch, but survived, until the first one he did sweetly time, a hearty pull shot, was caught by mid-wicket leaping up and sideways like a soccer goalkeeper. His ugly three-hour fight for survival was a valuable lesson in temperament and teamwork for any young batsman, especially the No. 4 who followed Taylor to the crease. The lad ignored it, as if he'd been hiding behind the dressing-room door. He was out within half a dozen balls, aiming a limited-overs hack at a riser just outside off. Taylor would have let it go through to the 'keeper.

So rapid is the intrusion of the dollar and glamour into cricket's image that impatient young cricketers think traditional toil is about as useful as Coke without bourbon. Bush blokes like Bradman and Taylor are not so sentimental as to decry the game's modern thinkers, but each would quietly hope that their chosen method of advancement is never forgotten. (*1999–2000*)

VICTOR TRUMPER

By Neville Cardus

It is futile to ask 'who was the greatest batsman?' There are different orders of greatness. Talent, even genius, is conditioned by the material circumstances in which it is developed. Victor Trumper was the embodiment of gallantry as he made his runs. He was a chivalrous batsman, nothing mean or discourteous in any of his movements or intentions at the wicket. 'He had no style,' wrote C.B. Fry of him, 'but he was all style.' But the most handsome compliment ever made to him, or to any other cricketer, was A.C. MacLaren's: 'I was supposed to be a batsman of the Grand Manner. Compared to Victor I was a cab-horse to a Derby winner.'

His stance was relaxed, but watchful, a panther ready to spring. Yet this panther simile suggests a certain cruelty and hungriness. Trumper scored his runs generously, as though out of an abundance of them in his possession. He, so to say, *donated* runs over the field, bestowing them like precious jewels to us, to the crowd, to the bowlers even. He wasn't, as Bradman was, a 'killer'. His strokes didn't stun or insult a bowler. I have seen bowlers applaud the glory of Trumper's strokes; he put them, with the rest of us, under an enchantment. Do I exaggerate? I confess that whenever I write about Trumper I am in danger of exhausting a store of superlatives. So I'll be content for the moment to quote from the formal restrained prose of the 'M.C.C.'s *Cricket Scores and Biographies*':

> For Trumper the English season of 1902 was a triumphal progress, and those who were fortunate to witness his amazing brilliance will never be able to forget the unrivalled skill and resource he displayed. On "sticky" wickets he hit with freedom, whilst everybody else

were puddling about the crease, unable to make headway and content if they could keep up their wickets.

The season of 1902 was the spin-bowler's dream of heaven. Rain and hot sun day by day. Wickets uncovered. When the pitch dried the ball whipped in, whipped away, reared and kept low, changing direction and pace, sometimes startling the bowlers themselves. And in 1902 Trumper had to cope with the greatest spinners the game had so far evolved – Rhodes, Blythe, Haigh, Wass (fast from leg stump to the off), Walter Mead, J.T. Hearne, S.F. Barnes, to name a few. In this year of 1902 Trumper scored 2,570 runs, average 48.49, with eleven centuries. His rate of scoring was round about 40 an hour, and 1902 was his first experience of vicious English wickets, for in 1899, his first visit to this country, the summer had been dry.

In the upstairs tea-room at Kennington Oval hangs a photo of Victor showing him jumping out to drive, yards from the crease, bat aloft behind him, the left leg prancing like a charger's in the Bayeux tapestry. A certain England batsman, vintage 1950, looked at this picture in my company and said, 'Was he really any good?' 'Why do you ask?' was my natural question. 'Well,' said this International, 'just look where he is – stumped by yards if he misses.' This sceptical England batsman had never in his life been so far out of his crease. But Trumper was stumped only once in all the 89 Test innings of his career. And only five times was he lbw.

Like Hobbs, he led the way to the counter-attack of the googly bowling, a new problem to harass batsmen of his period. In Australia, 1910–11, against the superb South African back-of-the-hand bowlers, such as Vogler, Schwarz, Pegler and Faulkner, his Test scores in the rubber were 27 (run out), 34, 159, 214 (not out), 28, 7, 87, 31 and 74 not out – 661 runs, average 94.42. Let me quote Jack Fingleton: 'He teased Percy Sherwell, the South African captain. When a fieldsman was shifted, Trumper deliberately hit the next ball where the man had been ... Later, somebody commiserated with Sherwell at having his captaincy and his fieldsmen torn to tatters while Trumper made 214. Whereupon Sherwell said, "Ah, don't talk about it. We have seen batting today."'

For six balls apparently alike in pitch, or pace or spin, Trumper could produce six different strokes. His footwork was quick, graceful and effortless. With the easiest swing of the bat he could drive an extraordinary distance. His cutting and his leg glancing were performed by wrists of rare flexibility. 'He played a defensive stroke,' wrote C.B. Fry, 'as a last resort.'

At Old Trafford, in 1902, A.C. MacLaren lost the toss for England on a slow wicket which, he knew, would turn difficult by mid-afternoon. Lockwood was unable to get a sure foothold until shortly before lunch. So MacLaren's plan was, as he himself put it, 'to keep Victor quiet for an hour or two'. Then, with the pitch developing tantrums, Australia could be disposed of at ease. MacLaren's reserve bowlers were Rhodes, F.S. Jackson, Tate and Braund, and they were ordered to operate defensively. 'I set my field with the inner and outer ring,' said MacLaren. Some of the best cricket brains and skill in England concentrated to 'keep Victor quiet'. At lunch Australia's score was 173 for one, Trumper a century.

So easily did Trumper bat, though his rate of scoring frequently equalled Jessop's, never for a moment did he make an impression of violence or hurry. His every movement was lovely to see. Against Victoria for New South Wales at Sydney, in 1905, on a bowler's wicket, he scored 101 out of 139 in fifty-seven minutes. On a Melbourne 'gluepot', in 1904, he scored 74 out of Australia's all out total of 122 v. England – England's bowlers being Rhodes (who took 15 wickets in the match for 124), Hirst, Relf and Braund.

In 1913, playing in a match at Goulburn for the benefit of J.A. O'Connor, Australian Test cricketer, Victor scored 231 in ninety minutes. In 1899 he scored 300 not out v. Sussex in five hours. In 1902 he scored 62 out of 80 in fifty minutes v. England at Sheffield. His achievements in high-class Grade cricket in Sydney have become historic. For his team, Paddington, in 1897 and 1898, he averaged 204, with 1,021 runs, when he was only twenty years old.

These statistics, chosen at random, tell their tale. But not by counting Victor's runs, not by looking at any records, will you get the slightest idea of Trumper's glorious cricket. You might as well count the notes of the music of Mozart. He was sadly on his way to a fatal illness when he came to England in 1909, for the last time, but a flash of the dauntless Victor came out at The Oval in an innings for Australia of 73, scored against D.W. Carr (googly), Barnes, Woolley, Rhodes, and Sharp. And, as we have noted, his genius burnt in wonderful flame and colour against South Africa in Australia in 1910–11. But it was burning itself out. He died, only 37 years old, in June 1915; and the Sydney streets were packed with sorrowing crowds as the funeral passed by.

He was good-looking, clean-shaven (a rare and boyish thing in those days), weighing 12 stones, and 5 feet 10 inches of height. He was, as everybody vowed who came his way, even the bowlers, a quiet but delightful companion. The gods of cricket loved him, so he died young. (*1963*)

SHANE WARNE

There are three elements to Shane Warne's greatness – skill, novelty and drama – and all were manifest in the one great delivery that made his name, at Old Trafford in 1993.

The delivery was exceptionally skilful. It began its flight innocently so as to lull Mike Gatting, drifted to leg, pitched in the batsman's blind spot, then rounded on him fiercely and bent back off stump. It was at once pinpoint in its accuracy and prodigious in its spin, qualities that had always been thought to be irreconcilable. Later that summer, John Woodcock would write that it was doubtful if there had ever been a bowler who could aim the ball as precisely and turn it as far as Warne. This is a sentiment that has echoed down the seasons.

The delivery was something different. West Indies and their battery of pace bowlers had set the agenda for 20 years; spin, particularly wrist-spin, had become nearly defunct, but suddenly here it was again in more irresistible form than ever before.

Most of all, the Gatting ball was not just early in his spell, but his very first delivery – in the match, in the series, in Ashes cricket. That gave the ball a sense of theatre, and Warne a name for showmanship, that has grown at each new threshold of his startling career, and at its peak made him nearly mystical. In the modern era, only Ian Botham could compare.

The triumph of SHANE KEITH WARNE is of the rarest kind, of both substance and style together. At his best, he has the ruthlessness of a clinician and the flourish of a performer, and his bowling is simultaneously a technical and dramatic masterpiece. It was not enough for him to take a hat-trick; it had to be in an Ashes Test on the MCG. It was not enough for him to take 300 wickets; the 300th had to be accompanied by lightning and apocalyptic thunderclaps at the climax of another consummate and match-winning performance against South Africa at the SCG.

Thus in 1993 a theme was established for Warne's career: extraordinary performances, extraordinary production values. He was the cricketer of and for his times. Australia's finest moments, but also their worst, their most controversial, most splendid, most dramatic, most sordid, have all revolved around Warne. From the wretchedness of the bookmakers' scandal to the glory of the World Cup triumph, from the agony of a one-wicket defeat in Pakistan in 1994–95 to the ecstasy of a come-from-behind Ashes win in 1997, he was always the central character.

By cold statistics, Warne has not had such a profound influence on Australian cricket in his time as Dennis Lillee in his. Australia were already on the rise when Warne joined the team and, when they had their crowning moment, in the Caribbean in 1994–95, he was good, but not dominant. He takes fewer wickets per match than Lillee at a more profligate average. Moreover, Australia can and do win matches without him. But Warne's impact can never be understated. When he was first picked, cricket was under the tyranny of fast bowling and aching for another dimension. Soon enough, the world came to know that a man could take Test wickets by seduction as well as extortion.

And the legend grew, moment by moment, coup by coup, performance by performance. He made fools of good players, short work of fools. Australia's method was indestructibly simple: bat first, bowl last, win quickly. Always it was the stage that invigorated him as much as the challenge. For Victoria, who play in empty stadia, he averages more than 40. But for Australia, he has taken more than 350 wickets and, although projections for him to take 600 now seem fanciful, he is already by some margin the most successful spinner in Test history.

At length, intimations came of Warne's mortality. Wear, tear and public glare took a toll. Variously, the fitness of his finger, shoulder, stomach, ethics and manners for Test cricket were called into question, but not until recently, when he returned too hastily from shoulder surgery, was his capability doubted.

Physically, undoubtedly, his powers have declined, but not his hold on opponents. So it was that on the biggest stage of all, at the climax of the World Cup, at a moment when Australia looked impossibly behind, he came again. The only caveat on making him one of the cricketers of the 20th century is that he may yet figure in deliberations for the 21st. —(*Greg Baum*) (*2000*)

STEVE WAUGH

By John Birmingham

He seems fated, or maybe doomed, to martial allusions. It is partly tabloid sloth, an easy play on an adaptable name leading to such sub-editorial infantilism as 'Waugh Zone' and 'Waugh Declared'. It is partly the increasing aggression of professional sport, where ugly and bone-headed nationalism serves the ends of multinational media companies. And partly it is providence of his own creation. For if ever a man was born to embody the howl of Shakespeare's Henry before the half-achieved walls of Harfleur it was Stephen Rodger Waugh, his competitive spirit lending the eye a terrible aspect, and stiffening the sinews of a band of men who were already formidable before he ascended to their leadership.

The corollary of Henry's call to arms, however, that in peace nothing so becomes a man as modest stillness and humility, is often forgotten. And so it is with Waugh. The most unyielding of foes on the field, he is simply a warrior for that working day, a ferocious competitor, but with the fairest of natures away from the field. With the pall of match-fixing hanging over the highest levels of the game this last year, it is refreshing to ponder the public and private actions of one who regularly travels to the subcontinent – not to engage with the game's gambling underworld – but to tend to Nivedita House, a home for destitute girls, the daughters of parents with leprosy, which he has made his own personal responsibility. Waugh gave up part of last Easter with his family – from whom he is separated at least eight months a year – to travel to India to support Nivedita, auctioning off cricket memorabilia, of which he is an avid collector, and organising the delivery of 300 beds from Australia, which he donated to his 'second family'.

In the first flush of international success, after Australia's initial World Cup win at Calcutta in 1987-88, and the first of a long run of Ashes victories in 1989, Waugh expressed some discomfort with the rewards of playing cricket at the highest levels, given the awful poverty in which most of the game's fans lived. He was referring to the lives of those millions of devotees in the Third World. But nor have Stephen and brother Mark, from Bankstown, a tough working-class suburb of Sydney, forgotten the relative deprivation of their own hometown strugglers. Attending the dedication of a new pavilion in their honour at the Bankstown Oval, Steve praised the character of his local community and was overwhelmed by the generosity of 'people who haven't got a lot out of cricket like we have'. And in contrast to some international players who eschew their country's domestic first-class competitions when not required by Australia, both brothers are known to carve out time for the odd precious game of club cricket with awestruck 16-year-olds and time-worn veterans of western Sydney's hard-baked suburban grounds. It is said that to encounter Steve in one of these matches is no less intimidating than having him put the evil eye on you at the MCG or Sabina Park.

Herschelle Gibbs would know the feeling. In a rush of youthful *brio*, at a crucial juncture in the World Cup Super Six match at Headingley in June 1999, Gibbs intercepted a chance from Waugh's bat and made to toss it heavenwards. Gibbs instead lost control of the ball, spilling it to the turf. After the match a story circulated that Waugh had asked the distraught youngster how it felt to 'drop the World Cup'. Having broken the Proteas' spirit, he then set about their systematic destruction with an innings of astonishing but calculated violence, clubbing the republic's bowlers for 120 off only 110 balls, his bat wielded more like a highlander's claymore than a gentleman's rapier.

The Gibbs story is untrue, but gained currency because it rings so true of the on-field Waugh. No matter how dire the situation the Australians found themselves in during their World Cup campaign, their captain simply refused to countenance any outcome but victory. And in the search for victory no quarter was expected and none would be given. When asked at Lord's by a West Indian journalist whether he would temper the Australians' ruthlessness, their fierce sledging and bullying of their opponents, Waugh was both frank and brief: 'No.' After a controversial win over the West Indies at Old Trafford, he shrugged off criticism by rumbling: 'We're not here to win friends, mate.'

Waugh is here to cement an era of Australian domination that rivals West Indies' 15-year reign of terror. Accepting the Ceat Cricket Award in Mumbai at the end of 1998, a few months before assuming Mark Taylor's office, Waugh said that the team had set themselves this goal after winning in the West Indies, South Africa and Pakistan. Long suspect when touring or chasing small totals, the Australians seem to have transmuted into something much harder and forbidding under Waugh's direction. Justin Langer, whose batting has grown in stature and force as Waugh's tenure has progressed, testified that the veteran's confidence and tactical acumen inspired the team's younger players, erasing their doubts and producing 'a feeling of invincibility'.

Also banished has been the corrosive effect of Mark Taylor's intermittent form lapses. In Waugh, at last, the Australians once more have a leader who has not needed the selectors' faith as a batsman. During the record-breaking series of wins in the Australians' golden summer of 1999–2000, Waugh peeled off three handsome hundreds to become the first batsman to take a century off every attack in the modern Test-playing world. At the end of March he polished that little bauble with some unexpected help from the dubious batting talents of Glenn McGrath. During the Second Test against New Zealand in Wellington the fast bowler meandered out to the centre with Waugh on 132. McGrath then kept watch while his boss stole eighteen runs to make 150, becoming the first man to make 150 against all eight Test opponents.

All three of Waugh's 1999–2000 hundreds proved timely contributions to the Australians' unbroken sequence of success over the southern summer, Waugh's personal investment in the business of building an era. A brawling, unconquered 151 punched Zimbabwe out of their inaugural match with Australia in Harare. Another 150 in Adelaide at the start of the three-match rubber against India rescued the home side after their plans for world domination had gone a little pear-shaped at four for 52. This century, Waugh's 21st, saw him draw level with Sachin Tendulkar, and also pass 8,000 Test runs. In the meantime, Pakistan's challenge had been swatted aside with imperious disdain. When Waugh's men picked off the third-highest Test winning total, 369, to wrap up the series, they also buried a decade's legacy of soft last-innings collapses; testimony to the complete negation of a nagging self-doubt which had haunted the dressing-room under Allan Border and, to a lesser extent, Mark Taylor.

A good deal of the credit for this aggressive self-esteem goes to the new captain. Ian Chappell, the last truly assured and pitiless Australian captain, identified the re-emergence of Waugh's youthful belligerence late in 1998, during the Fourth Ashes Test, when he unleashed a savage barrage of cover drives and cross-bat swats at a rampant Darren Gough, snatching the initiative from a temporarily ascendant old enemy. Seven months later, Chappell affirmed that a newly focused combativeness in Waugh's batting and game tactics was a return to first principles for the man who had once bounced Viv Richards three times in one over. After losing his berth in the national side to brother Mark in January 1991, Steve had returned as a circumspect, risk-averse droid, programmed to collect runs without a care for style or artistry. Only after his place had been long secured, and the captaincy of the one-day side delivered into his hands, were the Byronic flourishes of his early career seen again.

Steve Waugh has been lucky, in the way that Clive Lloyd was lucky, to be blessed with a crop of freakishly talented players. Adam Gilchrist succeeded the old campaigner Healy in fine style, precociously establishing himself as the best wicket-keeper/batsman in the world. McGrath and Warne continue to carry all before them, while Brett Lee simply turned up one day and started bowling faster than mere flesh and blood beings have any right to. Justin Langer decided to become one of the most reliable bats in the world and Ricky Ponting delivered on his promise to break the hearts and minds of bowlers from all points of the compass. It is almost as though Waugh, the last survivor of Australia's darkest hours in the 1980s, has been rewarded by the gods for his implacable resolve. (*2000– 01*)

1 4

ISSUE OF THE DAY

'Personally, I am all for a little bit of controversy in Test cricket,' observed Richie Benaud in *Wisden* 1973, and he could have been speaking on *Wisden*'s behalf. Much as it has deprecated ill-feeling and deplored sharp practice, it has been around such issues that *Wisden* has often thrived.

In its early days, *Wisden* tended to stand aloof from debate. When it was nearly the case that two English teams toured Australia in 1886–87, editor Charles Pardon elected to 'say very little about this matter because there was a good deal of ill-feeling displayed at the time'. When two English teams actually did tour Australia a year later, Pardon again decided that it 'would serve no purpose now to go into the causes of the blunder'. When the financial arrangements of the 1888 Australian team occasioned acute public interest, Pardon also made clear that gentlemen did not enquire about other gentlemen's personal affairs: 'The men were, we believe, banded together in a commonwealth, though we do not profess to know, nor should we put on record if we did know, the private and financial relations that existed among the members of the XI.'

Wisden did not baulk, however, at reporting controversies as they emerged elsewhere, and Australians in some fashion have often been part of them. One such was at the Marylebone Cricket Club's 1891 annual meeting, where secretary Henry Perkins informed members of 'wholesale complaints of bad umpiring' the previous year: 'The Australians, who were the chief grumblers, told him at the end of the match played for the benefit of the cricketers' fund [in September 1890] that the umpiring was the worst they had seen, though quite as many decisions had been given in their favour as against them. That was not complimentary to umpires.' When *Wisden* surveyed opinion in the 1895 edition, one of the more creative suggestions came from the Australian Billy Murdoch, by then representing Sussex: 'He had a strong opinion … that it was desirable to provide a room for umpires. At present they went into the players' room and were subjected to all sorts of remarks and sometimes abuse; and no matter how honest an umpire might be – and he believed they were all honest – they could hardly fail to be affected. If umpires were kept apart from cricketers a great deal of good would be done.'

Murdoch also dilated on the subject of illegal bowling actions: 'To my mind the remedy for throwing is very simple; the rule says "if the umpire be not satisfied of the absolute fairness of the delivery of any ball he shall call 'no ball'." Now if the MCC were to instruct all umpires that it was absolutely necessary to carry out this rule without respect to persons, I think it would have the desired effect.' Editor Sydney Pardon decided to make the issue his own, and the editorial commentaries he wrote between 1896 and 1900 are among the toughest and most explicit that *Wisden* has published. He was harshest at first on visiting colonials, describing Ernie Jones as 'radically unfair' and claiming that Tom McKibbin 'continually threw', but soon found his strongest support coming from an Australian, umpire Jim Phillips, whose interdiction against bowlers with illegal actions in county and Test cricket was swiftly effective.

Pardon's crusade had enormous implications for *Wisden*, establishing its credentials as a force for reform; and inaugurating the tradition of 'Notes' by the editor. Throwing has remained a controversy of interest to the almanack, too: outbreaks in the late 1950s, early 1960s and mid-1990s are reported extensively. And if anything, this sampling of cricket's crises bears out their cyclicality. The Sydney riot of February 1879 was widely ascribed to gambling on the match between Lord Harris' Englishmen and New South Wales, while the players' strike of 1884–85 was all about what proportion of revenues the game's players should justifiably command. The late 1990s returned us to both issues: match fixing and player payments. About the only controversy documented here that has not recurred is the very first: W.G. Grace's abduction of Billy Midwinter in June 1878. But then, there's never been another W.G. Grace.

—GH

THE AUSTRALIANS' SECOND MATCH AT LORD'S

Middlesex v. The Australians. – Played at Lord's, June 20, 21, 22, 1878. – The Australians' second appearance at Lord's was favoured with glorious weather of true English summer form, bright and burning hot, weather that was the more welcome because, up to that time, it had been so rare. [...] Midwinter was to have played for the Australians, and just before noon on the first day he was duly flannelled and practising at Lord's ready for play, but shortly after W.G. Grace arrived in hot haste from Kennington, claiming and obtaining Midwinter to play for Gloucestershire v. Surrey, which match was commenced that day on the Oval. It was rumoured W.G. Grace acted on a prior made agreement; be that as it may Midwinter played that day for Gloucestershire, and never again played for the Australians. [...]

FROM NOTES BY THE EDITOR

VARYING STRENGTH

The rise and decline of great players affected the strength of the sides to such an extent that Gloucestershire have not once finished first since 1877. That was the season when Midwinter, who was born at Cirencester and had come back from Australia, appeared as the first professional in the Gloucestershire ranks. He returned to Australia in the winter, played in the two matches against J. Lillywhite's England team and started the next summer with the Australians captained by David Gregory. He took part in five matches, but he was induced to resume playing for Gloucestershire 'in dramatic fashion', as Sydney Pardon used to describe. The Australians were at Lord's for the match with Middlesex; Gloucestershire, on arriving at The Oval for their game with Surrey, decided that they must have Midwinter. In order to impress a man nearly 6 feet 3 inches in height and weighing about 15 stones, W.G. Grace, the Gloucestershire captain, himself a heavyweight, and E.M. Grace, the Coroner, took with them J.A. Bush, comparable to Midwinter as a giant. In a four-wheeled cab they drove to Lord's and brought back Midwinter. Weighty argument had the desired effect! Midwinter went to and from Australia for several consecutive seasons. He considered himself an Australian and once said: 'I made a mistake in deserting the first Australian eleven of 1878.' He played for Alfred Shaw's team in the four matches against Australia in 1881 and 1882, and appeared for W.L. Murdoch's 1884 team against England at Manchester, Lord's and the Oval, so representing both these countries in matches against each other – a unique distinction. (*1942*)

THE ENGLISH ELEVEN V. THE NEW SOUTH WALES ELEVEN

Played on the Association Ground, at Sydney, February 7, 8, 10, 1879. – The weather was splendid. On the first day it was recorded there were 4000 persons present, including Lady Robinson and party. On the second day, a Saturday and the day of disturbance, it was reported there were fully 10,000 persons present; but on the third day (Monday) there were not more than 1,500 on the ground. [...] On the Saturday the not outs resumed their innings about noon, to the bowling of Lucas and Emmett, the former being subsequently succeeded by Ulyett, and he by Hornby, who, later on, clean bowled Massie for 38 – an innings that included four 4's. The score was at 130 when Massie was bowled. Then Emmett's bowling had a good time, inasmuch as it captured the remaining seven wickets, the innings closing for 177 runs, *Murdoch having triumphantly played all through the innings, taking his bat out for 82* – described 'a grand innings.' Murdoch's hits were eleven 4's, three 3's, nine 2's, and 11 singles. Emmett's bowling in that innings summed up 52 overs (less one ball) for 47 runs and 8 wickets. Being in a minority of 90 runs, the N.S.W. men, in due course, 'followed on,' Murdoch and A. Bannerman commencing their second innings. 19 runs had been made, 10 of them by Murdoch, when an appeal to Coulthard, the Umpire, resulted in Murdoch being run out, then arose

THE DISTURBANCE
that *The Australasian* remarked would 'for ever make the match memorable in the annals of New South Wales cricket.' It appears that on the decision being given Murdoch (like a true cricketer) retired; whereupon arose cries of 'Not Out!' – 'Go back, Murdoch!' – 'Another Umpire!' and so on. The crowds rushed to the wickets, and, stated *The Australasian*, 'rowdyism became rampant for the rest of the afternoon.'

The Eleven Englishmen were surrounded by a rough and excited mob, who prevented further cricket being played that day. Much was said and written on this deplorably disgraceful affair; but it is gratifying to record that all respectable portions of Australian society, and all the leading journals in the Colonies strongly condemned this outrage. The *South Australian Register* stated 'The scene was a disgrace to the people,' and 'profound regret is expressed at the occurrence.' *The Sydney Mail* remarked, 'The English team soon found themselves in the centre of a surging, gesticulating, and shouting mob, and one rowdy struck Lord Harris across the body with a whip or stick.' *The Australasian* stated 'His Excellency, Lady Robinson, and party were present, and were pained witnesses of all that occurred;' and 'The disgraceful affair was the talk of the town,' furthermore, *The Australasian* headed a report with 'What will they say in England?' *The South Australian Chronicle* chronicled the remark that 'Such a scene had never before been witnessed on a cricket field.' And in a subsequent edition, *The Australasian* added – 'Before the game was resumed on the Monday, Mr R. Driver (President of the Cricket Association), Mr F.H. Dangar, and others, waited upon Lord Harris, and on behalf of the cricketers of Sydney expressed their extreme regret at the disgraceful scene that took place on the Saturday. The Captain of the English team, in reply, said, 'he did not place any blame on the Association, or the cricketers of Sydney, but it was an occurrence which it was impossible he could forget.'

The Sydney Morning Herald of February 27, said: – 'Our English readers will be glad to learn that steps have been taken to wipe out the disgrace of the discreditable attack on Lord Harris and his cricketers. William Rigney and John Richards were recently charged at the Water Police Court with having participated in the disorder arising in consequence of Murdoch being declared out by the Umpire for the English team. Both men expressed deep regret for what had occurred, and pleaded guilty and it was in consideration of this rather tardy contrition, and the good character given them by the police that the Bench fined them 40s, and to pay 21s. professional costs, and 5s. costs of Court. Mr Driver, who appeared for the prosecution, stated that inmates of the pavilion who had initiated the disturbance, including a well-known book-maker of Victoria who was at the time ejected, had had their fees of membership returned to them, and they would never again be admitted to the ground. The Bench referring to the kindly hospitable treatment the Australian cricketers received in England, expressed deep regret that Lord Harris and his team should have met such a disagreeable experience. [...]

Any notice of this match would be inexcusably incomplete that left out two important documents subsequently published, *i.e.*, – Lord Harris's letter to a friend that appeared in the London newspapers early in April, and The New South Wales Cricket Association's reply to that letter, published in the London newspapers the last week of July. Space in this little book can ill be spared for these letters, but they are deemed of such import that the compiler has no choice but to chronicle them. Here follows a copy of

LORD HARRIS'S LETTER

'I am not certain whether you will be astonished or not at what I have to tell you, but I know you will be distressed that your friends, a party of gentlemen travelling through these Colonies for the purpose of playing a few friendly games of cricket, should have been insulted and subjected to indignities it distresses us to look back upon. We began the return match with the N.S.W. Eleven on Friday, February 7, scored 267, and got our opponents out for 177 by 3.30 on the Saturday afternoon. Murdoch, who had carried his bat out in the first, and A. Bannerman went to the wickets to commence the second innings. At 19 on the telegraph the former was run out. Before he got back to the pavilion I heard shouts of "not out," "go back," &c., arise from that quarter, and saw the occupants of it rise almost *en masse*. I at once saw what was the matter, and instead of waiting for D. Gregory (the captain) to come out to me, perhaps unwisely walked to the pavilion to meet him at the gate. He, I found, in the name of the N.S.W. Eleven, objected to Coulthard, the umpire. I must here diverge to explain certain facts connected with umpires in these Colonies which are not known or understood at home. Contrary to *our* custom, it is here the exception to employ professional umpires. This I was not told until *after* the disturbance. As you know, we brought no umpire, and on arrival at Adelaide I asked the representatives of the Melbourne C.C. if they could recommend anyone to us whom we could take about with us throughout our tour. They mentioned this man Coulthard, a professional on their ground, whom they had constantly tried and found competent, and added that if we *on trial* also considered him competent the M.C.C. would be very glad to give him leave of absence so long as we wanted his services. I considered him on trial a good and trustworthy umpire, and arranged with the M.C.C. that he should accompany us to N.S.W. Had we known on our arrival that a feeling existed in these Colonies against the employment of professional umpires, it is possible we might have acted differently; but, understand, at the same time, that I have seen no reason as yet to change my opinion of Coulthard's qualities, or to regret his engagement, in which opinion I am joined by the whole team. To resume my account of the disturbance on the ground on the Saturday. I asked Gregory on what grounds the objection was raised, and he said at first general incompetence, but afterwards admitted that the objection was raised on account of the decision in Murdoch's case. I implored Gregory, as a friend, and for the sake of the N.S.W. Cricket Association which I warned him would be the sufferer by it, not to raise the objection, but he refused to take my view of the case. Looking back in the midst of this conversation, I found the ground had been rushed by the mob, and our team was being surrounded. I at once returned to the wickets, and in defending Coulthard from being attacked was struck by some "larrikin" with a stick. Hornby immediately seized this fellow, and in taking him to the pavilion was struck in the face by a would-be deliverer of the "larrikin", and had his shirt nearly torn off his back.

He, however, conveyed his prisoner to the pavilion in triumph. For some thirty minutes or so I was surrounded by a howling mob, resisting the entreaties of partisans and friends to return to the pavilion until the field was cleared, on the grounds that if our side left the field the other eleven could claim the match. I don't suppose that they would have done so, but I determined to obey the laws of cricket, and may add that for one hour and a half I never left the ground, surrounded during the whole time, with two short intervals, by some hundreds of people. At about five o'clock the crowd was cleared off somehow. I then took the opinion of the Eleven as to changing the umpire, and it was decided *nem. con.* that there were no grounds for the objection, and that we should decline to change him. I informed Gregory of the decision, whereupon he said, "Then the game is at end." On Coulthard appearing from the pavilion groans arose from the crowd, and at the same moment it began to break the ring again. The two batsmen who had been standing at the wickets returned to the pavilion, re-called, I afterwards found, by Gregory, but at the time I thought possibly because of the threatened irruption of the crowd. I turned to Mr Barton, the N.S.W Eleven umpire, and asked if I could not claim the match according to the laws of cricket. His answer was "I shall give it you in two minutes' time if the batsmen do not return." I said to him, "I won't claim it yet. I'll give the other side every chance of reconsidering a decision arrived at, I believe, unadvisedly, and in a moment of passion. Please ask Gregory what he means to do." On returning Mr Barton informed me that Gregory would send two men to the wickets – a curiously sudden change of mind I think you will allow. However, before the batsmen could appear the crowd had covered the ground for the second time. After some twenty minutes it was cleared for the second time also. A. Bannerman and Thomson then took their places at the wickets, but before a ball could be bowled the crowd broke in for the third and last time. I remained on the ground until the time for drawing the stumps, surrounded as before. Beyond slyly kicking me once or twice the mob behaved very well, their one cry being, "Change your umpire." And now for the cause of this disturbance, not expected, I may say, by us, for we have heard accounts of former matches played by English teams. It was started and fomented by professional betting men in the pavilion, members of the association. The disgraceful part of the business is that other members of the association – one a member of the legislative assembly – aided and abetted the bookmakers in raising the cry. I blame the N.S.W. eleven for not objecting to Coulthard before the match began, *if* they had reason to suppose him incompetent to fulfil his duties. I blame the members of the association (many, of course, must be excepted) for their discourtesy and uncricket like behaviour to their guests; and I blame the committee and officers of the association for ever permitting betting, but this last does not, of course, apply to our match only. I am bound to say that they did all in their power to quell the disturbance. I don't think anything would have happened if A. Bannerman had been run out instead of Murdoch, but the latter, besides being a great favourite, deservedly I think, was the popular idol off the moment through having carried his bat out in the first innings. As a contrast to the reception the Australian Eleven met with after beating the M.C.C. at Lord's, I may say that when we won the match on Monday, hardly a cheer was given us by the ring. The occupants of the pavilion acknowledged our victory. They are capital winners out there, but I am afraid I can't apply the same adjective to them as losers. To conclude, I cannot describe to you the horror we felt that such an insult should have been passed on us, and that the game we love so well, and wish to see honoured, supported, and played in an honest and manly way everywhere, should receive such desecration. I can use no milder word. The game was finished on Monday with no interruption. Coulthard had made two mistakes in our first innings, one favouring us, the other the opposite. Murdoch's decision was considered by cover-point and point to be a good one, and I repeat that the N.S.W. Eleven had no grounds whatever for raising an objection. We never expect to see such a scene of disorder again – we can never forget this one.

'I remain,

'Yours sincerely,

'February 11, 1879.'   'HARRIS.

THE NEW SOUTH WALES CRICKET ASSOCIATION'S REPLY
(Contributed to The Daily Telegraph by Mr J.M. Gibson,
the hon. secretary to the Association).

'A few days ago a letter from Lord Harris, published in your issue of April 1, appeared in the Colonial Press. That letter dilated upon a lamentable disturbance which occurred at Moore Park, near this city, during a match played between his lordship's eleven and an eleven of New South Wales, on February 7, 8 and 10 last. Upon the appearance of the letter in our newspapers a feeling of indignation was generally expressed, and within a few hours a requisition influentially signed was presented, calling on me to convene a special general meeting of the New South Wales Cricket Association for the purpose of considering the letter and comments made upon it in some of the London papers. A meeting was accordingly convened and took place this evening. The President, Mr Richard Driver, M.P., occupied the chair, in the presence of an unusually large attendance of members. The letter referred to having been read, and the President, Sir George Innes, M.L.C., Mr M.H. Stephen, Q.C., Mr G.H. Reid, and Mr Richard Teece having addressed the meeting, it was unanimously resolved that I should ask to publish the following statement, in correction of the account transmitted by Lord Harris, which, principally upon the following grounds, is universally regarded here as both inaccurate and ungenerous.

'When Lord Harris prepared his letter of February 11, he was fully aware of the following facts:

'1. That on the previous day a deputation from the association, consisting of our president, some of the vice-presidents, officers, and members waited upon him, and expressed profound sorrow and regret for the conduct of the unruly portion of the crowd, and Lord Harris was pleased to assure the deputation that he did not hold the association in any way responsible for what had occurred.

'2. That immediately after the disorder on the cricket ground the public and the press were loud in their indignation at the occurrence, and assured our visitors of their utmost sympathy; and the team received similar marks of good feeling from all quarters.

'3. That betting on cricket matches is strictly prohibited by the trustees of the ground, so far as it can be so prohibited, and large placards to that effect have always been kept posted throughout the pavilion and its inclosures.

'Lord Harris, by what we feel to be a most ungenerous suppression of these facts and others, has led the British public to suppose that in New South Wales, to quote his own words, "a party of gentlemen travelling through these colonies for the purpose of playing a few friendly games of cricket should have been insulted and subjected to indignities," whilst the press and inhabitants of Sydney neither showed surprise, indignation, nor regret. We cannot allow a libel upon the people of New South Wales so utterly unfounded as this to pass without challenge. The country upon which such a reproach could be fastened would be unworthy of a place among civilised communities, and in the imputation is especially odious to Australians, who claim to have maintained the manly, generous, and hospitable characteristics of the British race.

'Having shown that for what actually occurred the fullest acknowledgements were made, it is now right to point out that the misconduct of those who took possession of the wickets has been exaggerated. So popular amongst our people is the game of cricket that multitudes of all ages and classes flock to a great match. They watch these contests with an interest as intense as any felt in England over a great political question. Lord Harris is, we believe, the first English cricketer who failed to observe that they applaud good cricket on either side, and, so far from our crowds being the bad losers he represents, the English Elevens who have visited New South Wales were never made more of than when they defeated the local team. Previous decisions of the professional brought from Melbourne to act as umpire for the English Eleven had created real, though suppressed dissatisfaction, and one, giving Lord Harris a second "life", was openly admitted by his lordship to be a mistake; and when Mr Murdoch, the hero of the hour, who had carried his bat through in the first innings, was at the crisis of the game given "run out" by what a large proportion of the spectators, both in the pavilion and round the enclosure, as well as the batsman himself, whether rightly or wrongly, took to be a most unfair decision, the excitement and indignation of a section of the spectators, led by the juvenile element, unhappily broke through restraint. Only once before in New South Wales was a cricket ground rushed, and then, as in the present instance, the crowd was seized with a conviction of foul play. But the present demonstration was entirely against the umpire, whom Lord Harris still considers competent, whilst admitting "he had made two mistakes in our innings." It certainly was not against our gallant visitors. The only cry was "Change your umpire!" and the mob voluntarily left the ground more than once in the hope that that would be done. The betting men to whom Lord Harris alludes, and of whom only one or two were present, were not members of this association at all, and it was completely unjust to assign the demonstration to any such agency. Bad as it was, it sprang from no mercenary motive.

'Sydney, June 4th, 1879.'

SHAW'S TEAM IN AUSTRALIA, 1884—85

At 2 p.m. on Tuesday, October 7th 1884, the cricketers reached Aden, and at 11.15 on the same day, sailed for Port Adelaide, where they arrived early on the morning of Wednesday, October the 29th. The voyage had been a very pleasant one, and at Adelaide they were met by the leading members of the South Australian Cricketing Association Committee, who conducted them to the city, where the Mayor accorded them an official reception of a very cordial character, remarking that he was sure their visit would be a very pleasant one. Similar kindly greetings were extended to them wherever they went, but from the moment the members of Murdoch's team landed from the *Mirzapore* prior to the commencement of the third match, it became evident they were animated by a feeling of bitter hostility towards Shaw and his party. As a commencement, the Victoria contingent of the team declined to play for their Colony against the Englishmen, urging as an excuse their want of practice, while it afterwards transpired that Murdoch's Eleven had endeavoured to arrange a match with New South Wales on the same days as those fixed for the contest between Shaw's Team and Victoria. Next, Murdoch and A. Bannerman refused to take part in the match New South Wales v. Shaw's Eleven, and after the South Australian Cricket Association had succeeded in bringing about a meeting between Shaw's Team and Murdoch's Eleven at Adelaide, each side receiving 450 pounds, the climax of the quarrel was reached when Murdoch's men declined to play for Combined Australia against the Englishmen on New Year's Day. This unpatriotic conduct was severely condemned by the public and press of Australia, as the following will show:

'At a luncheon given at Adelaide during a cricket match on New Year's Day the Attorney-General of South Australia (the Hon. C.C. Kingston) said that he could not let the occasion pass, as a lover of the game for itself, without referring to the conduct of the Australian Eleven, who appeared to sink everything for monetary considerations. If the cricketing public of Australia were to allow the game to be sacrificed for money it would be a national calamity from a cricket point of view. (Applause.) One of the effects of this was that on that day there was a match proceeding in which the full strength of Australia should have been pitted against a worthy representative team of all England, but Australia was not represented in its full strength because of the existence of the Australian Eleven. It did not matter what was the reason why the Australian Eleven refrained from participating in the match – some said it was a difference between their manager and the Englishmen – but the cricketing public of Australia should show their disapproval of this line of conduct when the national cricketing honour was concerned. He hoped that the Australian team would win. (Applause.) He was certain, however that the combined team who took part in the contest would not be disgraced, but the Australian Eleven would have the reputation of having sacrificed the cricketing honour of their nation to monetary considerations. He would not have referred to this matter, but as an earnest supporter and upholder of manly sports he consider it his duty, in common with others, to protest against cricket being reduced to a mere money-making matter. The fourth Australian Eleven had received a large share of Australian sympathy, but he trusted a repetition of their conduct would never be witnessed in any Australian team.'

Commenting on the above, the *South Australian Register* states: 'The pungent criticism of the conduct of the Australian Eleven indulged in by the Attorney-General will be endorsed by most of those who are acquainted with the facts. Very hard things indeed have been said of the team in the other colonies. The spirit they have displayed since their return from their successful and financially profitable trip in the mother country has been most illiberal. Instead of going out of their way to advance the interests of the company of English players now on a visit to Australia thay have assumed an attitude of antagonism towards them which can only be attributed to mercenary motives altogether unworthy of them and Australian cricketers in general. Remembering that they claim to rank as gentlemen players, and not as professional, and that they met with the most liberal treatment in Great Britain, they owed it to themselves as well as to the visiting players to do all in their power to make the tour of the latter successful. At the same time they owed it to Australia to put their services as cricketers at the disposal of the country in order to maintain its cricketing reputation against the formidable team who have come to gather laurels, as well as gate-money, in these colonies. How little their action has been influenced by a regard for the interests of Australia, and how much by monetary considerations, is illustrated by the nature of the terms they demanded from the South Australian Cricketing Association before agreeing to play on the Adelaide Oval. They insisted upon being placed upon the same footing as the professionals, and thus practically shut out the Association from all chance of realising any profit out of the match. It cannot be doubted that the grasping policy of the Eleven tended to estrange public sympathy here, and caused the victory of the Englishmen to be rather popular than otherwise. The latest grievance against the team is that they have been so tenacious of their financial rights that not one of them has taken part in the match Players v. All Australia now proceeding in Melbourne. In one sense it is an advantage that they should be thus excluded, as it has given an opportunity for the bringing together of an independent eleven not ill-qualified to do battle for Australia, but it is, of course, anomalous that from a match against all Australia the redoubtable members of Murdoch's Eleven should all be shut out. It is greatly to be regretted that the Australian team proper should have made such a shabby ending to an otherwise brilliant career.'

The Cricket Association of Victoria called upon the Victorian section of the team for an explanation of their refusal to play, and at an adjourned meeting, held on the 13th of January, 1885, the following motion was carried unanimously: 'That the replies received from the Victorian contingent of the Australian Eleven who have been asked for an explanation in refusing to play in the combined match, Australia v. England, are unsatisfactory to this Association, and that the selector of teams be instructed not to select any one of this team to play in any match played under the auspices of the Association.'

This ban was not removed until the 11th of November of the same year, and one of the results of the antagonism of the Fourth Australian Team, and of the action of the Victorian Association, was that Shaw's men had to play two matches against New South Wales, and one each against Victoria and a combined eleven at Melbourne without a single member of Murdoch's Team being opposed to them. Peace however, was partially restored towards the close of the tour, and in the last three matches against representative elevens of Australia, A.C. Bannerman was opposed to the English team on each occasion, Bonnor and Giffen appeared in two matches, and Scott, Palmer, M'Donnell and Blackham each played once. Spofforth, it must be stated, was not in accord with the other members of the Australian Team. He did not arrive in Australia until some time after all the others had landed, and was always favourably disposed towards the Englishmen, playing against them whenever circumstances permitted. [...]

from The Australians in England 1896

[…] There is one thing left to be said and that unfortunately is not of a pleasant nature. Up to last season one of the special virtues of Australian bowling was its unimpeachable fairness. Despite the evil example set by many English throwers, team after team came over to this country without a bowler to whose delivery exception could have been taken, but unhappily things are no longer as they once were. We have not the least hesitation in saying that a fast bowler with the action of Jones, or a slow bowler with a delivery so open to question as McKibbin, would have found no place in the earlier elevens that came to England. Jones's bowling is, to our mind, radically unfair, as we cannot conceive a ball being fairly bowled at the pace of an express train with a bent arm. The faults of our own bowlers with regard to throwing have been so many and grievous that we are extremely glad Jones was allowed to go through the season unchallenged, but now that the tour is a thing of the past it is only a duty to speak plainly on the matter. We do so with the more confidence as we know that our opinion is shared by a great many of the best English players. As was only natural in the case of a slow bowler McKibbin's action was less talked about, but there can be little doubt that he continually threw when putting on his off break. It is no new matter for McKibbin's delivery to be called in question, as we believe Blackham once went to the length of saying that he would probably be no-balled if he ever went to England. Now that the evil effects of our own laxity with regard to unfair bowling have spread to Australia, it is to be hoped that the M.C.C. will at last be moved to action in the matter. […]

Throwing

A Note by the Editor

In reviewing in last year's *Wisden* the tour of the Australian team of 1896, I ventured to condemn as unfair the bowling of both Jones and McKibbin. I had no wish to say anything disagreeable, but while closely watching all the matches played in London by the team, I was so struck by the deplorable change that had come over the methods of Australian bowlers, that I did not see how the question could be ignored. The criticism has, I think, been more than justified by subsequent events. On the 26th of January, a letter condemning McKibbin's action in most uncompromising terms was addressed by Mr Spofforth to the *Sporting Life*, and at Adelaide at the end of October in the first match played in Australia by Mr Stoddart's Team, Jones was no-balled by James Phillips for throwing.

The significance of Mr Spofforth's letter, which is quoted in full further on, and of Phillips's action at Adelaide seems to me very great. It is certain that Mr Spofforth would not, unless he had felt very strongly indeed on the matter, have gone to the length of denouncing a brother Australian as an unfair bowler, and no one who knows James Phillips can think it possible that he would have no-balled Jones without adequate cause. From what Phillips has done nothing but good can come. If years ago any representative English umpire had shown the same courage many scandals would have been avoided. As regards both McKibbin and Jones the point to bear in mind is that the fault lies primarily with English bowlers and English umpires. Australian bowlers never threw in England till we had shown them over and over again that Law X could be broken with impunity. The following is Mr Spofforth's letter:

CONCERNING 'THROWING' AND THE 'FOLLOW-ON' RULE
TO THE EDITOR OF THE *SPORTING LIFE*.

SIR, – The all-absorbing topic among cricketers seems to be altering of the 'follow on' rule; but I scarcely think, no matter how this rule is changed, it will have much effect on the game, seeing that in the annals of first-class cricket it has only been 'infringed' twice, and that by a body of cricketers anyone would have least expected it from.

In the first instance there may have been an excuse, but when a conservative body like the M.C.C. thought it so serious as to alter the rule, it showed the worst possible taste to breathe it again.

But what I consider a far more serious consideration for the authorities is, Are they going to legalise throwing? There is scarcely a first class county which does not include a 'thrower' amongst its cricketers many of them men who would scorn to cheat an opponent out, and who, if a wicket-keeper were in the habit of kicking down the stumps or knocking off the bails with his hands and appealing for a bowl out, would not hesitate to bring him before his committee, or refuse to play with him again. Still, they will not only employ a man to throw, but will actually throw themselves, and acknowledge it, their only excuse being that 'others do it', and they will name many.

This practice of throwing is growing rapidly, and many young cricketers are now adopting it who a year or so back were quite above suspicion. Australia has now taken it up, and with the last eleven there was one who hardly ever delivered a 'fair' ball, and although I am quite aware I may raise a 'hornet's nest' about my head by mentioning names, I allude to McKibbin who, I shall always maintain, should never be allowed to play under the existing rule. Now, I think it is only fair I should mention an Englishman, and although I could name many I am anxious not to injure any one. So I will take Bobby Peel, one of England's best bowlers, and one who has no need to resort to throwing. I acknowledge he does not often take to it, still it is well known to cricketers that at times he does 'shy'. Again, there are many who, while not exactly throwing, do not bowl fairly according to the existing rule. They 'put' the ball, which is they throw only from one point, mostly the elbow. The remedy for this unfair play is rather hard to find, especially as there is no umpire in England who dare no-ball a cricketer, while should a fair bowler even touch the bowler's crease when delivering a ball he is at once 'called'.

I am of opinion the best way to put down throwing is to form a committee of all the captains of the first class counties with Lord Harris as chairman, and on anyone being reported for throwing, a vote be taken, and if unfavourable the cricketer be suspended for a week, if brought up a second time fined and suspended, a third time he should be disqualified for the season. Both jockeys and footballers are suspended and fined for unfairness, and why should cricketers be exempt? In conclusion, if nothing is to be done in the matter, the best way is to legalise throwing, and in one season it would bring about its own cure.

Yours, etc.,
January 25, 1897
FRED. R. SPOFFORTH (*1898*)

THROWING

A NOTE BY THE EDITOR

A twelvemonth ago I ventured to say that nothing but good could come from James Phillips's action in no-balling Jones, the Australian fast bowler, for throwing. I did not imagine, however, that the result would be either so speedy or so satisfactory. Throwing on English cricket grounds had for such a long time been allowed to go on unchecked – the umpires taking no heed of even the most flagrant offenders – that I was not prepared to see any steps taken last season. When once a man has done a courageous thing, however, he is very apt to find imitators, and such was James Phillips's case last season. For the first time within my experience – with one trifling exception – bowlers were no-balled in first class matches in England for throwing, Mr C.B. Fry being no-balled by West at Trent Bridge, by Phillips himself at Brighton and by Sherwin at Lord's; and the new Warwickshire bowler, Hopkins, coming under the ban of Titchmarsh at Tonbridge. More than that there were, I believe, one or two cases of no-balling in matches played by the smaller counties. The no-balling of Mr Fry was only a case of long-delayed justice. As a matter of fact he ought never, after his caricature of bowling in the M.C.C. and Oxford match at Lord's in 1892, to have been allowed to bowl at all. As he had enjoyed immunity for six years I cannot regard him as an object of sympathy, but he could fairly urge that during that time many bowlers far more formidable than he had been permitted to throw without protest. However, in nearly all cases of reform some one has to suffer and so far from Mr Fry's fame as a cricketer declining, he proceeded as soon as he gave up bowling to bat as he had never batted before. Personally, I regard the no-balling of Hopkins as even more significant than that of Mr Fry. While the latter might be looked upon as an old offender, Hopkins was a new man, just at the outset of his career. In this point lay the importance of what Titchmarsh did at Tonbridge. Let it once be understood that new bowlers who do not deliver the ball with strict fairness will be no-balled, and throwing will strictly disappear from first-class cricket. To the contention that it is difficult for umpire to distinguish between throwing and fair bowling I have never attached the slightest importance. An umpire who is fit for his post can always tell and, moreover, it is important to bear in mind that a rule was specially framed to help him, Law 48A reading: 'If the umpire at the bowler's end be not satisfied of the absolute fairness of the delivery of any ball, he shall call "no ball".' Inasmuch as this rule deprives the offender of the benefit of the doubt, it may be rather dubious law, but it immensely strengthens the hands of the umpire. (*1899*)

FROM NOTES BY THE EDITOR

[...] Last summer in England, and later on in Australia, there arose two questions that caused considerable comment. Towards the end of our cricket season a statement appeared that a bowler had been reported to the M.C.C. for having, in the Worcestershire and Middlesex match, lifted the seam of the ball. Whether this is correct or not is immaterial, but it is significant that the Marylebone Club subsequently issued to the first-class umpires a circular that contained among other memoranda of importance, the following: 'That the practice of lifting the seam by a bowler is illegal and comes within Law 43.' If umpires had previously been in doubt, this ruling clearly pointed the way to them, as to the action they are to take in the future. Viewed from any angle the practice – happily, I think, very rare – is indefensible.

The other point did not come quite within the same category, but admitted of discussion. It cropped up over a statement by Mailey, the Australian googly bowler, that it was quite in order for a bowler to use resin on his fingers as a means of imparting additional spin to the ball. From inquiries made I found that resin had, in fact, been used at various times by some of our own bowlers. If not actually contrary to the laws, this is quite foreign to the spirit of cricket, and, for that reason alone, it should not be countenanced by the captain of a side. The use of an outside agent such as resin was never contemplated by those who framed the rules. It has been urged that if sawdust is permissible in order to obtain a proper grip, no exception should be taken to resin. There is no analogy. Sawdust is allowed after rain to restore the condition of the ball to normal; resin clearly brings about a condition that is abnormal.

Where a reasonable argument exists is in the fact that wicket-keepers smear the palms of their gloves with an adhesive solution. This practice began some forty years ago when manufacturers produced wicket-keeping gloves with a thin coating of india rubber outside the padding which protected the palms of the hands. It has continued ever since without, I believe, any protest. If this is allowed then, in fairness, resin must be also. There is danger in both, for to the introduction of adventitious aids there may be no end. Better will it be for the matter to be settled forthwith than wait until much greater issues, perhaps, are involved. [...] (1926)

CRICKET REFORM

The following letter from Mr J.W. Trumble, a member of the Australian team that visited England in 1886, appeared in *The Times* on October 16, 1926. At a time of outcry against the artificial preparation of wickets in this country, it is of special interest in showing to what lengths that process has gone in Australia.

SIR, – May I, before returning to Australia, avail myself of the medium of your paper to supplement my remarks in my previous letter on the subject of cricket reform? I would like also to say that I am pleased to learn, on the announcement of Lord Harris, that the

Advisory Committee of the M.C.C. is now giving attention to this matter. There is no doubt that the conditions in which the game is now played unduly favour the batsman as against the bowler, and as a consequence rob the game to a great extent of that attractiveness which was formerly its great charm. Only those of us who had experience of first-class cricket some 40 or 50 years ago and have since kept in touch with the game can fully appreciate this. We know that the groundsman now holds sway over the game, and that he has been encouraged by cricket committees in recent years, largely for financial reasons, to secure a wicket which, mainly by the introduction of binding soils and the use of the heavy roller, is little short of the condition of concrete.

As regards the composition of turf, I may here say that it is possible for the soil expert to produce almost any class of turf, and as indicative of this it may be of interest if I say something of the M.C.C. (Australia) wicket, and its preparation for Test match play. A short time ago the groundsman, at my request, broke open the ground at the wicket, and went down to a depth of over one foot, and, as I suspected from its non-draining condition, I found the soil all the way down similar to what it was at the surface. This represented an accumulation of the heavy black clay top dressing which had been put on yearly over a period of 40 years. In preparing our wicket, after nursing it for some time, the groundsman, for about 12 days before play, proceeds with its more immediate preparation. He then floods the area, and, the flooding gradually soaks in, leaving the surface of the consistency of putty, he knows he has the required moisture content to carry the wicket through the period of play, however long that may be. The surface is then worked up daily by the heavy roller, until at last it becomes of the hardness of a marble slab. After the cutter has done its work, an expert scytheman takes off most of what remains of the grass, and the heavy roller then grinds out the substance of what is left. The final rolling puts a polished face on the wicket, preventing the spin ball from getting a grip of the ground, and the surface of the wicket assumes a coconut matting appearance.

Can one picture a more absurd representation of a turf wicket than this? It might be just as sensible to cut out all this toil of preparation and put down a permanent concrete bed. In the matter of spin on this class of wicket I might instance the bowling of Howell, one of the greatest of Australian medium-pace spin bowlers. The condition of the wicket often beat him in the early stages of a game, but so accurate was his bowling that in time he wore off a patch of the polished face and then succeeded in getting on terms with the batsmen. I question, however, whether on the wickets as now prepared it would be possible for a medium-pace bowler to get in on our wickets as Howell did even at a later stage of play.

This all goes to show to what lengths groundsmen can get in the preparation of present-day wickets. The position in Australia is rapidly becoming farcical, and should have immediate attention. You are interested in this country because you are concerned in Test cricket over there. The first move, however, should be made here. I have given to Sir John Russell, Director of Rothamsted Experimental Station, samples of the Melbourne and Adelaide wickets. He was much surprised at their appearance, and a member of his staff suggested that they resembled a substance with commercial possibilities unearthed in Scotland from which oil was extracted.

It is contended that the ball now used is to a large extent responsible for the non-success of our bowlers. While admitting that bowlers are to some extent handicapped by this ball, I cannot agree that the return to the smaller ball will improve matters very much. The wicket will still beat the bowler. One has only to bring to mind the great medium-pace bowlers of the past, and look for their class now, to realize the change, gradual though it has been, that has come over the game.

Assuredly the secret of what is wrong with cricket lies in the wicket. Let us discard the binding soils and the heavy roller and get back to the old-time natural springy turf, and with batsman and bowler on equal terms matches will end in a reasonable time, and, instead of being tests of patience and endurance, they will bring out those qualities of initiative and resource and the ability to rise superior to surroundings which so characterized the play of many of our great cricketers of the past.

Yours, etc.,
J.W. TRUMBLE (*1927*)

CRICKET AT THE CROSSROADS

By D.G. Bradman

The Editor of *Wisden* has honoured me by asking for a contribution from my pen. He has left the subject of the article to me, but in doing so has helpfully made suggestions regarding various phases of cricket which are today the cause of much discussion. As I looked through those suggestions, I conceived the title of this article. It is intended to convey a meaning but not to be misunderstood.

No matter how much we love cricket and desire to regard it as a friendly pastime we cannot possibly disassociate its future, at least in the first-class category, from the cold, hard facts of finance. Nor can we blind ourselves to the fact that at this very moment public support for cricket (possibly excepting Test cricket, around which there is special glamour) suggests either that cricket is becoming less attractive or other forms of entertainment are gaining ground. It is a state of affairs calling for very serious consideration from player and legislator alike.

I am all in favour of hastening slowly and have admired the peaceful but purposeful way in which cricket has for so long been administered in England. Nevertheless, I cannot help feeling that with the quickening of modern tempo, the more Americanised trend which is demanding speed, action and entertainment value, it behoves all of us to realise we are the custodians of the welfare of cricket and must guard its future even more zealously than its present.

No matter what we may desire individually, we cannot arrest nor impede the tenor of everyday life whether it be in business or sport. With such thoughts uppermost in my mind, my reflections are intended to convey the impressions gleaned by an Australian who will naturally view things from a slightly different angle to the average Englishman. Also my opinions are based upon experience in the middle allied to contact with administrative officers and the public.

DURATION OF TEST MATCHES

One of the most debated subjects at the moment is whether Test Matches should be limited or played out. Considerable colour has been lent to this particular aspect of cricket because of the remarkable happenings at The Oval last August. I have always held the opinion that it is futile to expect Australian teams to travel many thousands of miles to compete in a series of matches for The Ashes, and yet play under conditions which allow quite a big possibility of one match deciding the rubber, especially when that result may depend entirely on the weather and be inconsistent with the degree of skill otherwise displayed. But I rather doubt whether the big issue is limited or played-out Tests. I think the first consideration is the mental outlook of the individual who can, if he chooses, spoil any game by his interpretation of its character. And secondly, would it not be a better game if, by virtue of rules and conditions, the possibility of a match extending beyond three or four days became extremely improbable?

If these problems were attended to, maybe the other one would disappear. At least, I think it very largely would. There can be no doubt that in recent years changes have taken place in the methods adopted for preparing certain English wickets. The popular term used for the latest and questionable method is 'doping the wicket'. From my experience on this tour and discussions with people who are in a position to know, I am satisfied that some groundsmen can, and do dope their wickets. The effect is to produce an absolutely dead and lifeless wicket, useless to any type of bowler and not conducive to stroke-play by the batsman.

It is imperative that we should have wickets which are true and not dangerous (fiery wickets produce a crop of accidents, rob batsmen of confidence and drive them into less dangerous sports), but let them be reasonably natural and amenable to some fair degree of wear, not the sort upon which the world's best spin-bowlers can't turn the ball an inch until the pitch is three days' old. This difficulty with wickets mainly applies to Test matches. County matches are usually played on wickets offering some degree of equality, whilst practice wickets on most English grounds receive so little consideration that one has virtually no chance of getting real practice except in the middle. The scales are not evenly balanced, and the question of wickets needs serious consideration.

A prominent English International, writing in the daily press, declared: 'Give me another half hour of Leeds and let me forget The Oval.' He probably conveys in that statement the innermost thoughts of the majority of the players and the public. I agree with him, if I may add 1934 and 1938 after The Oval. I do that to ensure that my concurrence will not be misconstrued. At The Oval in 1934 we Australians accomplished approximately what England did in 1938, so that I have experienced both winning and losing under those conditions. People left The Oval tired of watching the unequal fight. They did it when Ponsford and I were batting in 1934. They did it when Hutton and Hardstaff were batting in 1938. Not so at Leeds. The match was one succession of thrills. People fought to get into the ground, not out of it. Their hearts beat frantically with excitement, mine along with the rest of them. Did anyone think of that curse of modern cricket – batting averages? No! It was the game which mattered. Australia won. She nearly lost and if she had it would have been a greater game still. It was stirring, exhilarating cricket. There wasn't time to think of timeless Tests at Leeds.

VIEWS ON L.B.W.

I believe the time is imminent when another change in the lbw law should be made. When our forefathers devised this beautiful game, I have no doubt they intended it to remain a contest between bat and ball. But evidently, to use the words of an eminent politician, they didn't make it clear, and the practice of pad obstruction eventually reached such proportions that it became necessary to legislate against the use of pads.

Irrespective of where the batsman's pads or feet are, I believe that if a ball is pitched in a line between wicket and wicket or on the off-side of the wicket and would have hit the stumps but is prevented from doing so by part of the batsman's person (providing the ball has not first touched his bat or hand) the bowler is entitled to be rewarded. Under the existing law, that part of the batsman's person which is struck by the ball must be between wicket and wicket. Those last six words afford the batsman too much latitude.

An experiment could be tried with my suggestion similar to the experiment tried before the last alteration. I am confident that it would result in further reducing huge scores, increasing off-side shots, brightening the play and reducing the effectiveness of the purely defensive rabbit. The leg-side may have to be considered in later years, but it would possibly be too drastic a step to alter both sides at once. Just prior to the introduction of the last alteration in the lbw rule, there was a great deal of adverse comment about it. I then stated that these hypothetical ills would be found to disappear in practice. They did – and they would do so again.

Even if we assume a reasonably severe result and found county matches ending in two days, and the leading batting average dropping from 70 to 50, what would it matter? All figures would alter correspondingly and the gates for two days would exceed what they now are for three.

An experiment is going to be made with the eight-ball over. It has been used in Australia for years, has proved a great success and saved a tremendous amount of time. The only people who can reasonably object to it are the fast bowlers. Whilst their claims may be reasonable, we must consider the welfare of the game itself before any of its component parts. And in any event, if the authorities consider that fast bowlers are going to be unjustly handicapped, there may be other ways of assisting them, such as by allowing a new ball earlier than after the scoring of 200 runs as at present.

We very frequently hear a suggestion that the old method of tossing should be dispensed with. If any person has grounds for objection, surely it is I, after my 1938 experiences, but, on the contrary, I favour retention of the present method. To enable one captain to know in advance which team would have the choice of batting would pave the way to so many undesirable possibilities that I do not think it worth while discussing.

A PLEA FOR MODERN SCORE BOARDS

I do, however, counsel very urgently the need of up-to-date scoring boards of the Australian type at your principal grounds. I have just been reading an article in a leading English cricket publication by a very well-known writer. He was describing the happenings in an important match at Lord's. After telling of a glorious innings by a young player, he wrote: 'I had no idea of his identity – there were no score-cards about at the time.' Subsequently, he told how he discovered the player's name.

Such a state of affairs to an Australian enthusiast is hard to comprehend. I am well aware of the forceful argument regarding the revenue produced from selling score-cards, but I submit that 10,000 spectators who do not need score-cards to tell them what is happening are going to be a happier and more virile advertisement for the game than 8,000 who do. Cricket needs to retain its present followers and to gain new ones. Modern scoring-boards would be a big help, and any temporary loss would be recouped eventually through the turnstiles.

There are many other factors upon which I could enlarge, such as playing hours, the number of matches, and so on. They are sure to form a basis for future debate and argument, but their importance is, for the present at any rate, subservient to other problems.

Whether my suggestions prove practicable or otherwise, time alone will tell. They are at least submitted in an honest endeavour to assist in ensuring that the game we all cherish so much will be enjoyed by future generations no less than our own.

I doubt if a happier series of Test matches than the 1938 series has been played and I am quite sure the administrators of England and Australia are more closely united now than ever before. To me, therefore, it seems an appropriate time to try and achieve a greater measure of uniformity of opinion about current cricket problems. (*1939*)

FROM NOTES BY THE EDITOR

'NO BALL'

The remarkable film pictures showing how Ray Lindwall, the New South Wales fast bowler, brought his back foot almost up to the 'popping crease' before delivering the ball indicates the necessity of a more drastic change in the laws than the deletion of the word 'grounded'. To judge the position of the back foot, whether in the air or on the turf, as regards the crease, at the time of delivering the ball must be extremely difficult, if not impossible. The remedy required to remove all doubt as to the fair delivery of the ball seems to depend on the position of the front foot when the bowler lets the ball from his hand. I do not think that anyone could deliver the ball with his front foot in the air except by throwing. If the law insisted that the front foot must be grounded between the two creases the trouble would be removed. A third line, some twelve inches behind the popping crease, would simplify matters, the law being that the front foot must not be grounded beyond this line. That should suffice. Touching the line with the foot would not matter, and the umpire would be relieved of judging the slightest of margins. Chief importance attaches to the position of the front foot, because its encroachment can reduce the actual length the ball travels before getting within reach of the batsman's stroke. This point will exercise the minds of the astute M.C.C. Committee still considering the working of the laws as re-framed for use this year. (*1948*)

FROM NOTES BY THE EDITOR

DEFNING THROW

After all the controversy over throw and drag during the last M.C.C. visit to Australia, it is most satisfactory to know that these matters are being considered at such a high level as the Imperial Cricket Conference. All countries are searching for common solutions so that in future the Laws framed by M.C.C. can be interpreted uniformly in various parts of the world. If any uncertainty existed in the past umpires now know they will receive the fullest support from M.C.C. when they 'call' bowlers with illegal actions. At various times during the last eighty years Wisden has drawn attention to the evils of throwing. It is a menace which crops up from time to time and must be stamped out. The legislators in both England and Australia are to be congratulated on having the courage during recent months to define a throw. Never before had this been attempted by cricket bodies. Whether it was wise to remove the word "jerk" from the dictionary definition, only time will tell; but one must remember that the decisions, as set forth in the special article on 'Throw and Drag', are experimental and will not become permanent unless they prove satisfactory. [...] (*1960*)

THE THROWING CONTROVERSY

IMPERIAL CONFERENCE TACKLE MANY PROBLEMS

By Leslie Smith

November 3, 1960, will go down as a momentous day in cricket. It was the day when England and Australia announced details of the agreement on throwing for 1961; a day on which the Laws were partially amended to permit throwing without penalty for a period of five weeks; a day on which the very small number of offenders temporarily gained the upper hand over the vast majority and the day on which English umpires were instructed to hold in abeyance their interpretation of what constituted fair and unfair bowling. A day, in fact, which, to my mind, reflected no credit on the authorities of the two senior cricketing countries.

For years throwing had become an increasing menace to the game and it was obvious that firm action had to be taken. In 1959 English umpires received a definite assurance that they would be given support in their efforts to stamp out the evil of throwing. This came in the statement issued by M.C.C. on March 17, following a meeting of the Advisory County Cricket Committee: '*The part of Law 26 which deals with throwing and jerking has been under discussion between M.C.C., the county committees and captains, and the first-class umpires since the winter of 1957–58. In the autumn of last year, it was unanimously agreed by the umpires that the action of certain bowlers in this country was, on occasion, suspect. The counties concerned have undertaken to warn these bowlers. The umpires have again been assured of the fullest support of M.C.C., the counties and the county captains in any action they may feel it necessary to take.*'

Taking M.C.C. at their word, the umpires set about their task, reluctantly but, in most cases, fearlessly. This led last season to the no-balling of Geoff Griffin, the South African, and several English bowlers. Instead of continuing with their policy, which unpleasant though it may have been, would certainly have put a quick end to throwing, at least in England, M.C.C., at the suggestion of Australia, partially relaxed their determination and reached the following compromise:

M.C.C. and the English counties have agreed with the Australian Board of Control for International Cricket to the following application of Law 26 during the Australian Tour to the United Kingdom in 1961:– English umpires will be instructed not to call on the field for a suspect delivery (throwing) any Australian bowler on the 1961 tour prior to June 7, 1961. Up to that date every umpire who officiates in an Australian match and who is not entirely satisfied of the absolute fairness of a delivery of any Australian bowler will, as soon as possible after the conclusion of each match, complete a confidential report on a form to be provided and send it to the President of M.C.C. – a duplicate copy to be sent through the Secretary of M.C.C. to the Manager of the Australian team. From June 7, 1961, the umpires will be instructed to implement Law 26 on the field in the normal way, according to their own judgment; and the Australian bowlers will become liable to be called for any infringement. At no stage of the tour will a bowler be, as it were, declared illegal and he will be free to play as and when chosen at Australia's discretion.

In view of the new definition of a throw and the agreement referred to above, the M.C.C. and the English counties will consider whether or not to adopt the same procedure in all first-class matches prior to June 7, 1961.

The Umpire's Report is set out thus:

CONFIDENTIAL   *UMPIRE'S REPORT*   *FORM 'A'*

To the President,
M.C.C.

I beg to report that I officiated at the match Australia v. .... played on .... (date) at ....
In my opinion the Australian bowler .... (name) infringed Law 26 (Throwing) in this match to the following degree:–
❑   *Basically – that is every ball.*
❑   *Frequently.*
❑   *Occasionally.*
❑   *Very rarely.*

(Please mark category thus [X] and make any comments you may wish and especially any which you think may help the bowler concerned.)
Yours faithfully,

At the Advisory County Cricket Committee on November 16, it was agreed that the same truce period should apply to English bowlers in matches against the Australians. At the same time the counties stated that they did not intend to have anything to do with it for Championship matches. They were quite happy with the position as it stood.

It was difficult to see what benefits either side could derive from a five-week truce period. […] On the other hand, should an umpire believe that the action of any bowler was doubtful he would, in all honesty, have to call him in June, irrespective of what happened in May unless his action had been changed in the meantime. The Australians, whether they had adverse written reports in front of them or whether umpires had taken action on the field, had the same amount of time to consider what move they would make, if any were necessary.

Let me make it clear that I am not for a moment suggesting that English umpires are always right or that the English interpretation of the Laws is necessarily correct. Indeed, to do so would be to condone the very thing which is helping to damage cricket – the increasing Nationalism and the win-at-all-costs attitude which has developed. Indeed, all around us we can see examples of such Nationalism and the bad feeling it causes. Almost every International sporting occasion is riddled with it and the public must be getting heartily sick and tired of the perpetual squabbles on and off the field. Dwindling gates in practically every major sport reflects the public reaction. First-class cricket, confined as it is to a handful of countries within the Commonwealth, ought to rise above such pettiness.

I can well see the point of view of the Australian Board of Control. The man most concerned was Ian Meckiff, the left-arm fast bowler. Now, I have not seen Meckiff in the flesh although I have watched him on film, both at normal speed and in slow motion. Therefore I must reserve my final opinion although I felt that there was, at the very least, a doubt about his action. Many of those who have seen him and whose views are not those of hot-headed sensationalists (the favourite term used by people who see no wrong in Meckiff) are convinced that on occasion he has thrown. They include several past and present Australian cricketers. Meckiff was not alone in having a suspect action and one of Australia's greatest cricketers has gone on record as claiming, cynically, that he was the last of the fast straight-arm bowlers in that country. Keith Miller stated many times that Meckiff's action was definitely questionable and so did Jack Fingleton, the former Test player and a respected journalist. These were only two of the several.

But the point remained that Meckiff had not been no-balled by any umpire in Australia, nor in South Africa, New Zealand, India and Pakistan, where he has toured. So what could the Australian Board do? Should they not select him, purely on account of his action, they would be condemning the umpires of five countries. On the other hand, by choosing him they stood the risk of losing a valuable man if English umpires thought otherwise. This was their dilemma and they saw the problem long before they had to tackle it. This may well have led to the compromise agreement, but personally I cannot approve of it. As it happened, Meckiff lost form during the West Indies' tour and he was not chosen for the visit to England. Nor was any other bowler whose action had been queried. So the compromise, after all, should be proved unnecessary. Surely, the sensible thing for the authorities of any country to do would be to free from all possible doubt in their own minds that a bowler's action was absolutely fair before sending him on tour and placing the onus on the home country. It could be that one or two bowlers in various parts of the world would have to be sacrificed, but would that not be better than ruining the entire game? Is the winning or losing of a Test series so much more important than cricket itself? […] (1961)

AUSTRALIAN
INTERSTATE MATCHES 1962–63

[…] The fast left-hander Meckiff took most wickets in first-class cricket, 58, with Benaud 55, G. McKenzie and Sobers each 51. Meckiff bowled with zest; but this former Test bowler for long a controversial figure, was twice 'no-balled' from square-leg for unfair delivery. The first occasion was by Umpire J. Kierse in the Shield game in Adelaide; the second by Umpire W. Priem in Brisbane. Meckiff sometimes reverted to his 'old' style of delivery. Before the start of 1963–64 season, the State Associations, at the instance of the Australian Board of Control, urged umpires to tighten up on the matter of bowling action and promised them complete support in any action they took to stamp out irregularity. The experimental front-foot 'no-ball' rule came into operation for that season. […] (*1964*)

AUSTRALIA V. SOUTH AFRICA

FIRST TEST

At Brisbane, December 6, 7, 9, 10, 11, 1963. Drawn. There was never much hope of a definite result with one day lost through rain, but the match was made memorable by the no-balling of Meckiff for throwing and his subsequent retirement from first-class cricket. Australia made a shaky start, Simpson, Lawry and Burge being out for 88, but Booth rallied them. O'Neill, although struggling to find form, helped Booth add 120 and Benaud also shared a century stand with Booth. The bowling wilted towards the end of the day and with 153 coming in the last two hours, Australia reached 337 for five by the close. Booth went on to make 169 and the innings closed for 435.

Then came the dramatic over by Meckiff who was no-balled by Egar on his second, third, fifth and ninth deliveries. That was his only over. Egar was booed and Meckiff was carried shoulder high by a section of the crowd at the close. South Africa made a promising start, but ran into trouble against Benaud and were 157 for four at the end of the second day.

No play was possible on Monday and on the fourth day extra police were sent to the ground because of fears that the umpires, selectors and Benaud might be molested because of the Meckiff incident. There were no scenes. With little hope of victory, South Africa concentrated on saving the game. Barlow hit his first Test century, batting nearly six hours for 114. Waite also batted carefully and the Australian lead was restricted to 89. Lawry hit briskly for 87 outscoring O'Neill and Benaud declared, setting South Africa to score 234 in four hours. A little later a violent storm flooded the ground and ended the match. Afterwards Goddard entered hospital for a nasal operation. Booth suffered two chips on a knuckle while fielding.

AUSTRALIA

W.M. Lawry c G. Pollock b Barlow ....43 – not out 87
R.B. Simpson c Waite b P. Pollock ....12 – c sub b Partridge 34
N.C. O'Neill c Barlow b P. Pollock ....82 – not out 19
P.J. Burge run out 13
B.C. Booth c Barlow b P. Pollock 169
*R. Benaud lbw b Goddard 39
T. Veivers c Goddard b P. Pollock 14
†A.T.W. Grout c Seymour b P. Pollock 6
I. Meckiff b P. Pollock 7
A. Connolly not out 1

| B1, l-b 5 ....6 | L-b 4 ....4 |

1/39 2/73 3/88 4/208 5/310   **435**   1/83   (1 wkt., dec.) **144**
6/394 7/415 8/427 9/434

Bowling: FIRST INNINGS – P. Pollock 22.6-0-95-6; Partridge 24-3-87-0; Goddard 24-6-52-1; Barlow 9-0-71-1; Seymour 11-0-39-0; D. Pithey 23-6-85-0; SECOND INNINGS – P. Pollock 6-0-26-0; Partridge 17-1-50-1; Goddard 7-0-34-0; D. Pithey 5-0-30-0.

SOUTH AFRICA

*T.L. Goddard c Meckiff b Benaud ....52 – not out 8
E.J. Barlow b Benaud ....114 – c Simpson b McKenzie 0
P.R. Carlstein c and b Benaud ....0 – not out 1
R.G. Pollock b McKenzie 25
D. Lindsay lbw b Benaud 17
†J.H.B. Waite lbw b Connolly 66
P.L. Van der Merwe b O'Neill 17
D.B. Pithey c Meckiff b Veivers 18
P.M. Pollock lbw b Benaud 8
M.A. Seymour b Simpson 10
J.T. Partridge not out 3

| B 3, l-b 5, n-b 8 ....16 | B 4 ....4 |

1/74 2/78 3/120 4/157 5/239   **346**   1/1   (1 wkt.) **13**
6/272 7/321 8/325 9/335

Bowling: FIRST INNINGS – McKenzie 23-1-88-1; Meckiff 1-0-8-0; Connolly 19-4-46-1; Veivers 34-15-48-1; Benaud 33-10-68-5; Simpson 18.5-5-52-1; O'Neill 7-0-20-1; SECOND INNINGS – McKenzie 3.3-1-3-1; Connolly 1-0-2-0; Benaud 2-1-4-0.

Umpires: C. Egar and L. Rowan.

FROM NOTES BY THE EDITOR

DISCIPLINE

[...] Alarmed at the growing incidence of bad behaviour by players in all levels of grade cricket – which includes Test players – the New South Wales Cricket Association held a discussion at Cricket House, Sydney, and requested that the following message be printed in a prominent place in each club's annual report. I make no excuse for bringing it forward to wider spheres in the cricket world because the issues raised appertain not solely to Australia, but to most parts of the world where cricket is played. The advent of big prize-money may well be the cause of the spread of excessive bad manners.

IT HAS TO STOP

The game of cricket has long been known to epitomise the highest levels of conduct and sportsmanship. It is a competitive game to be played in an atmosphere of comradeship and enjoyed by players, umpires and spectators alike.

Bad behaviour by players is bringing the game into disrepute. It is alienating public support and making it almost impossible to recruit and hold umpires.

The following examples give rise to concern:

- Fieldsmen making ridiculous appeals in the hope of intimidating umpires into giving a favourable decision.
- Fieldsmen making disparaging remarks about umpires.
- Fieldsmen swearing at a batsman in an attempt to break his concentration.
- Fieldsmen directing a dismissed batsmen to the pavilion with a torrent of abuse.
- Batsmen disputing an umpire's decision by remaining at the crease and making disparaging remarks to the umpire.
- Batsmen making offensive remarks to fieldsmen attempting to field a ball or take a catch.
- Batsmen on the way back to the pavilion banging the bat on the ground, swearing, and throwing the bat on reaching the dressing-room.

Players must be capable of exercising self-discipline without the need for club administrators or the Association itself enforcing codes of behaviour. Captains have a special responsibility to exercise control over their players in these matters.

Let it be quite clear – the Association will not hesitate to impose severe penalties on any player reported for bad behaviour in the future.

If you are a player reported by an umpire, then be prepared to watch your team from the sidelines.

The NSWCA believes in the adage 'the game is bigger than the player'.

So, players, let's get the game back to where it should be. [...] (*1980*)

WHITHER CRICKET NOW?

By Sir Donald Bradman

At the request of the Editor I wrote a short piece for the 1939 *Wisden*. My main theme then was a plea for cricket to adapt itself to the quickening tempo of modern life, for administrators to consider ways of speeding up the game, to provide more modern scoreboards (especially in England), to face up to financial problems, and so on. Little did I appreciate at the time what a revolution would engulf cricket before another 50 years had passed.

The great stadiums of Sydney and Melbourne now display huge electronic score-boards costing millions of dollars and giving a wealth of information to the spectators. The enormous electric light towers turn night into day at the flick of a switch. That, in turn, demands the use of a white ball, and to satisfy the television and marketing moguls the players turn out in a variety of coloured outfits.

The whole scene stirs up human emotions ranging from those of a largely new and young audience (more liberally sprinkled with females than of yore), who yell and scream their support, to those of the dyed-in-the-wool lovers of Test cricket, who yearn for more peaceful, bygone days. As with so many things, it becomes well-nigh impossible to bring about a reconciliation between the opposing attitudes. But where does the truth lie and what about the future?

Despite my deep feeling for the traditional game, and my conviction that a vast majority of players and the public still regard Test cricket as the supreme contest, we must accept that we live in a new era. If Sir Neville Cardus were alive today, I can well imagine how eloquently he would bemoan the huge attendances at pop concerts compared with the lack of support for opera or a Beethoven evening. But I am sure he would also admit that, irrespective of the quality of the music or the musicians, the public are primarily interested in entertainment. Perhaps he would throw in his well-known reference to an eagle, no matter how beautiful in flight, being no match for the Concorde. I am satisfied that one-day cricket, especially day/night cricket, is here to stay. If there is a threat to the survival of the game of cricket, that threat lies in the first-class arena, and it behoves the administrators to understand the challenge and face up to it.

I confess to a love for both types of game. Nothing can match the continuous cut and thrust of a Test match, where the advantage see-saws and the result is unpre-dictable to the last ball. I can't imagine any sporting event being more exciting than the tied Test between West Indies and Australia. It wasn't only the finish. Here you had two teams of great players, led by imaginative and intelligent captains deter-mined from the first ball to pursue victory by adhering to the principles upon which the game was founded. The match had spin and speed, superb batting and fielding; every facet of the game was manifested as both sides strove for victory.

It starkly revealed the Achilles' heel of the limited-overs match, namely the pre-mium placed on defensive bowling and negative and defensive field-placing. One can get bored to death watching countless singles being taken when even the world's fastest bowler may be operating with no slips and five men on the boundary.

But let me turn to the good thing about one-day cricket. It rids the game of the unutterable bore who thinks occupancy of the crease and his own personal aggrand-isement are all that matter. It demands fieldsmen of great speed and agility with good throwing arms. The standard of fielding at all levels of cricket has undoubtedly been lifted. Running between the wickets, too, has taken on a new dimension. Risks must be taken to maintain the essential run-rate. Umpires are put under enormous pres-sure, having to adjudicate frequently on split-second issues: to their credit, I believe they have responded in a very positive manner and improved their standards.

Inevitably one sees the odd umpiring mistake, graphically portrayed by the mod-ern marvel of the instant replay on television. With this new aid available, I should see no loss of face or pride if umpires were to agree, when in doubt about a decision, to seek arbitration from the box. This could never apply to LBW, but for run-outs, and on odd occasions, for stumpings or a disputed catch, it would seem logical.

My first-class playing career began in 1927, and I remain a Trustee of the Adelaide Oval and a member of the main South Australian Cricket Association committee. Having watched first-class cricket in 1921, I have seen as observer, player or administrator, all the great players of the last 65 years. Indeed, I can probably claim to span 75 years because many of the 1920–21 players also played before the Great War. It is still absolutely fascinating to me to watch and compare players of different generations.

How often I was asked in 1985 whether Clive Lloyd's West Indians were the best team of all time! Unhesitatingly I replied that they were the best fielding combination I have seen. But no matter how competent their batting, bowling and fielding, they were so reliant on fast bowlers that they became out of balance on a slow, turning pitch. In addition, their batting became vulnerable, which was proved in Sydney when Australia's two spinners, Bennett and Holland, tore the heart out of the West Indian batting to win a convincing victory for Australia. And without detracting from the skill of Bennett and Holland, it was clear to any knowledgeable observer that they were not of the quality of O'Reilly and Grimmett. To me these facts are indisputable and tend to place matters in their proper perspective. Australia's victory confirmed my view that my 1948 side was the best I ever saw, with Lloyd's 1984–85 team and Armstrong's 1920–21 Australian side not far behind. And my reading of history causes me to think Joe Darling's 1902 Australians were perhaps equal to any. How lovely to be able to speculate without having to prove the answer!

Many cricket enthusiasts claim that the one-day game has brought in its wake a decline in batting technique. This may have some validity, but it is not necessarily true. People get confused between a normal mode of play and the essential improvisation needed to circumvent defensive fields. Vivian Richards and Clive Lloyd are marvellous examples of batsmen capable of coping quite adequately in both types of cricket without sacrificing any basic soundness of technique. The main difference in their one-day attitude has been a willingness to take the risk of lofting the ball over fieldsmen's heads. I doubt if modern players in general cut or pull quite as well as some of their forbears did, but I attribute this largely to the ultra-heavy bats they use. These hinder shots other than those of the perpendicular kind, such as the drive.

Undeniably the limited-overs game caters for a plethora of fast and medium-pace bowlers who tend to bowl just short of a length. In general it discourages, in fact it almost tolls the knell of, the slow leg-spinner. But here again one must acclaim the marvellous leg-spin bowling of the young Indian, Sivaramakrishnan, who proved against the best batting in the world in Sydney and Melbourne early in 1985 that he could bowl his ten-overs stint, get wickets, and still be economical. I don't doubt that O'Reilly, Grimmett, Benaud, Verity and others would have done the same. So perhaps, after all, the game is highlighting the fact that top-quality spinners can and will survive any challenge.

An interesting facet of the limited-overs game is the general rule governing bouncers. It unquestionably controls them in a sensible and practical way, and is a rule which I believe should be adopted in all grades of cricket without delay. It clearly reveals the way experimental laws could be used in one-day games to ascertain their effectiveness and/or desirability in first-class matches.

I also believe we have now reached the stage when some limitation in the length of a bowler's run-up is warranted. It would be the first and most logical step towards speeding up the over-rate. In Australia that magnificent player Malcolm Marshall (excluding Frank Tyson, the fastest bowler I have seen since Larwood) has repeatedly shown us that a short run-up is sufficient to generate maximum speed.

The money now being paid to players has spawned professionalism beyond anything dreamed of 50 years ago. With so much money at stake I doubt if the modern professionals enjoy their cricket as much as did the players who were financially independent of the game and played purely for the love of it. Perhaps, too, monetary reward is responsible for some of the theatrical performances and even bad manners occasionally portrayed in recent years on the field. Happily I feel this unhealthy phase is on the wane, as players understand that good sportsmanship and keen competitiveness are not incompatible.

Most people agree that too much cricket was played during the Australian summer of 1984–85, owing to the Melbourne anniversary tournament being added to the schedule. It highlighted the need to strike a proper balance between one-day games and normal first-class matches. The attendances at Sheffield Shield matches were adversely affected. Indeed, the mounting losses on Shield games, now amounting to hundreds of thousands of dollars annually, constitute the most seemingly intractable problem confronting Australian cricket today. We need the Shield to produce Test cricketers, but can receipts from sponsorship, television rights etc, continue to make up the losses? The current threat to the legality of certain sponsorships compounds the problem. Looking on the bright side, 1984–85 produced the best Indian and Pakistan teams of my lifetime, and that is a great gain for the future of cricket in the international sphere. The advance of these two coincided with some lack-lustre efforts from England and Australia.

Lovers of cricket will find in the pages of *Wisden* plenty of evidence that cricket has had its problems for a century past. Things have not changed much. Problems are still there – they are just different. It remains for players and administrators to accept the challenge to keep cricket alive and vibrant, and not to shrink from the decisions needed to ensure that end. (*1986*)

THE SRI LANKANS IN AUSTRALIA, 1995–96

By Trent Bouts

Sri Lanka arrived in November to provide the second and, according to most forecasts, the subsidiary act of the Australian summer, following Pakistan and the reincarnated Salim Malik. On their departure ten weeks later, Arjuna Ranatunga's men were so much the main event that the two countries' political leaders were forced to take note.

Sadly, government interest had less to do with the cricket than with the drama it generated. The three Tests barely qualified as contests. Mark Taylor's Australians were both professional and ruthless, winning by an innings and 36 runs in Perth, ten wickets in Melbourne and then by 148 runs in Adelaide. They landed another sweep, although Sri Lanka would argue just how clean it was, in the finals of the one-day World Series, which they won 2–0. But Sri Lanka's very presence in the finals was significant; West Indies, minus Brian Lara, failed to qualify.

Despite the lop-sided scorelines, public interest remained high and ultimately exceeded expectations. In Melbourne, the 55,239 who attended on Boxing Day bettered the equivalent crowd for England 12 months earlier, and a staggering 72,614 watched the first World Series final. The incendiary nature of the summer may have helped: there was certainly no lack of publicity, although it was overwhelmingly at Sri Lanka's expense. They were briefly convicted of doctoring the ball in the First Test, had their leading wicket-taker branded a chucker in the Second and played the Third under a thinly veiled threat to behave if Australia were not to pull out of their upcoming World Cup match in Colombo.

All the while, the Sri Lankans and their supporters, including a significant expatriate population, simmered over umpiring. The players' patience ran out in the one-day decider at Sydney in January, though by then they may have been itching for a dust-up. Several verbal and physical brushes, and probably the disappointment of defeat in a rain-shortened affair, led many Sri Lankans to snub Taylor's outstretched hand at the presentation in full public view. Although competition was stiff, it was probably the least savoury incident of the summer. Earlier that day, Shane Warne had talked about his fears as one of several Australians who had received a death threat. Craig McDermott was told to expect a diet of hand-grenades when he arrived in Colombo. Small wonder the Australian Cricket Board sought advice from the Department of Foreign Affairs and that Sri Lanka mobilised diplomatic resources in an attempt to quell Australian alarm. Though it was a terrorist bomb unconnected with cricket that eventually persuaded the Australians not to go to Colombo, many players were pretty happy to have found an excuse.

Remarkably, up to and after the Sydney final, relations between the players on both sides were no more strained than in most international competition. But as the series wore on, the home team found themselves subject to increasing criticism from their own public. This was partly due to Australians' traditional support for the underdog, though Taylor, a staunch advocate of improved on-field behaviour, was hurt by the backlash. While his players were by no means perfect – Glenn McGrath, for one, needed to calm down a little – the street-smart Ranatunga was no angel either. Still, the players had less to answer for than some officers of the game.

The officials got things seriously wrong in the Perth Test. Umpires Khizar Hayat of Pakistan and Peter Parker of Queensland failed to impound the ball when they suspected interference and referee Graham Dowling, the former New Zealand captain, gave the impression that he had made his mind up that the Sri Lankans were guilty even before the post-match hearing began. ICC overturned his verdict.

When Muttiah Muralitharan was called for throwing by Australian umpire Darrell Hair on the first day of the Melbourne Test, both had a right to ask why the bowler had been able to negotiate 22 Tests, indeed his entire first-class career, in safety until then. Either Hair was wrong or some, if not all, of those who had not called Muralitharan in the past six years were. ICC divulged that umpires, via match referees, had expressed doubts about his legitimacy for more than two years. But Sri Lanka produced an array of doctors and biomechanists who declared the off-spinner in the clear.

None said Muralitharan could not throw, but they argued that the elbow he had been unable to straighten completely since birth could create the visual illusion of a throw, a contention lost on most observers. It was certainly lost on Ross Emerson who, umpiring his first international ten days later, also no-balled Muralitharan repeatedly, even after the distraught bowler resorted to leg-spin. Instead of the intended celebration of the 25th anniversary of one-day internationals, the first such match under lights in Brisbane provided one of the short game's darkest hours. The umpires were booed from the field under police escort and Muralitharan did not play again on tour. [...]

STRUCK OUT – AN APPRAISAL OF THE PLAYERS' DISPUTE

By Malcolm Knox

In the early 1990s, when Australia's cricketers were establishing themselves as the game's most successful and profitable, their individual incomes came to the attention of Kerry Packer. Still the most powerful person in Australian cricket, through his Nine Network's 18-year hold over free-to-air television broadcast rights, Packer was perturbed by how little the senior players were earning.

The salaries, well below those of sportsmen in the more parochial fields of Australian rules football and rugby league, indicated a weakness in Packer's commercial hold over cricket. Throughout the world, entrepreneurial corporations were bidding to organise cricket tournaments independently of national authorities. So far, as in the case of the International Management Group's (IMG) limited-overs tournament between India and Pakistan in Canada, and the 1996 World Cup, also run by IMG, the new entrepreneur had worked in tandem with the existing powers. But this need not continue to be so, as Packer knew. He, of course, had taken a large chunk of international cricket out of the national bodies' hands in 1977, and was able to do so because the players, disaffected by their meagre payments, wanted to play for him.

So Packer urged the Australian Cricket Board (ACB) to increase the payments to Test players, negotiated under common-law contracts between the Board and each individual. Packer further locked in the loyalty of the elite, signing Shane Warne, Mark Taylor, Ian Healy and Michael Slater to lucrative Channel Nine contracts requiring token television work for unheard-of bonuses.

Steve Waugh was added to the Nine roster at the beginning of the 1997–98 season, and Packer's expensive blocking manoeuvre bore immediate fruit. The loyalty of key players to the television broadcaster was a significant factor in averting Australia's first full-scale cricket strike. Cricketers' guilds have had a tenuous hold in Australia, partly because of the workforce's transience, and largely because of cricketers' innate distaste for industrial action.

Accordingly, many of the player-welfare concerns raised by the Australian Cricketers' Association (ACA) since its birth in 1995 were identical to issues raised in 1977, and even during the player revolt in 1911, when Test cricketers refused to tour England because an ACB member, rather than a professional manager, was supervising the tour.

Into the 1990s, pay was the key issue. Most Sheffield Shield players earn less than $40,000 a year despite the game's professional requirements, making a second job untenable for most. The ACA lobbied State Associations and the Board for increased and secured payments, greater financial accountability, consultation on programming, superannuation, and a range of welfare issues left to fester for a century. The Board, satisfied that it was buying off the senior Test players with contracts worth more than $400,000 a year, argued that it could not afford to pay more to State cricketers, whose competition ran at a loss of more than $6 million a season.

The dispute remained unresolved for the 1997–98 season, due equally to the Board's intransigence and the ACA's provocations. A straightforward industrial matter became combustible in mid-1997 when the ACA hired Graham Halbish as its adviser. Halbish had been an ACB official and chief executive for 15 years until he was dismissed by chairman Denis Rogers early in 1997.

Rogers and Halbish were implacably opposed on many matters. The ACB launched legal action to bar Halbish's appointment to the players' body, but failed. Halbish proceeded to step off the ACA's payroll, and into business with IMG's former Australian head, James Erskine. Erskine became the cricketers' key negotiator, and the paymaster of their union, contributing $250,000 a year on a five-year contract to run the ACA. Erskine's payoff would be approximately 15 per cent of any financial increase he could negotiate on the players' behalf.

Meetings between the abrasive Erskine and equally stubborn Board representatives broke down continually in October and November 1997, and the matter came to a head during the Second Test between Australia and New Zealand in Perth, when the Board released a letter leaked from the players, asking all of the 120 ACA members to approve a strike during the coming one-day international series.

Nearly all of the Sheffield Shield players approved the strike. But on the night before the Test players were to vote, the Channel Nine employees – Warne, Waugh, Taylor and Healy – met Nine's director of sport, Gary Burns, with whom they discussed the proposed action. Nine, whose coverage of one-day internationals sustained its summer programming, would be the entity most affected by a strike.

Next evening, the Test players voted to back away from industrial action. Taylor tried to negotiate a personal solution with Rogers, but this, too, was rejected. The players had done what they saw as the honourable thing – public sympathy had weighed more heavily with employer than workers – and disavowed strike action as a way of forcing the Board to negotiate seriously.

An undisclosed settlement was reached in March 1998. Whatever its terms, it has left Erskine with a position of some influence over the game. The extent of his influence will become apparent in 1999 when the television broadcast rights are again contested. Erskine's most favourable outcome would be to open the rights to a competitive auction when Nine's present contract expires. Packer, of course, would prefer a continuation of his comfortable arrangement with the ACB. To these interests, Erskine is a nuisance and a threat.

Whether Australia's State cricketers are paid enough is a moot point. They argue that their sport is more important than rugby league or Australian football, and they should be paid commensurately. But those sports have been subject to raids by Rupert Murdoch and all manner of commercial turbulence which has led to salary explosions. There is no normative scale of fairness. Compared to rugby league players, 200 of whom earn more than $100,000 a year, cricketers are paupers. Compared to members of the entertainment and arts industries, such as actors or sculptors, cricketers are doing quite nicely. (*1998–99*)

THE CORRUPTION OF CRICKET

By Mihir Bose

It had been obvious for some time that cricket's great bribery saga was far from over. The wholly unexpected twist of December 1998 was that the goodies threatened to change places with the baddies. The original accusation was that the Australians Shane Warne, Tim May and Mark Waugh had been approached by Salim Malik, who allegedly offered them $200,000 bribes to throw matches in October 1994. This first alerted a dozing cricket world to the heavy illegal betting going on in the subcontinent and Sharjah, and to the possibility that players were being bribed to rig matches. More than four years later, it finally emerged that Warne and Waugh had their own involvement with subcontinental bookmakers and that the Australian Cricket Board knew about this and had covered it up all that time. Suddenly, the rights and wrongs seemed a great deal muddier.

Until the new Australian revelations, the affair had followed a predictable pattern. The Pakistanis had held three inquiries into the allegations, the Indians had held one, Malik had denied everything, nothing had been proven and in four years the only victim had been a journalist. This was Ramaswamy Mohan, for 18 years the cricket correspondent of *The Hindu*, one of India's leading newspapers. The paper has never officially commented on Mohan's departure, although one source there said: 'The *Hindu* had to think of the credibility of the paper.'

But everyone's credibility was at stake. In 1997 the Delhi-based magazine *Outlook* published claims by the former Indian Test cricketer Manoj Prabhakar that he was offered 2.5 million rupees (about £40,000) by a team-mate 'to play below my usual standards'. Prabhakar said the incident happened just before the India–Pakistan fixture (which was rained off anyway) in the Singer World Series in Sri Lanka in September 1994. 'I told him to get out of my room,' Prabhakar said.

Until then, the Indian Board had been looking on Pakistan's difficulties on this issue with a slightly smug and superior air. Now it asked Mr Justice Chandrachud, a former Chief Justice of India, to examine the Prabhakar story. But Prabhakar refused to name the player concerned, so Chandrachud concluded in December 1997 that there was nothing to report. This limp-wristed conclusion pleased no one. The general feeling by now was that betting and match-throwing were part of the subcontinent's cricket culture, and that nothing could be done about it. People began to accept the resigned comment of a Bombay police investigator: 'Every side with the exception of Australia and England can be purchased.'

This remained the accepted wisdom for another year. In the meantime, the Pakistanis did begin a far more serious inquiry into the issue. Justice Malik Mohammad Qayyum sat in Lahore while Pakistan's cricketing elite made depositions.

Inexorably, a picture of casual corruption built up. The International Cricket Council privately promised that, once Qayyum had finished, it would take action. But it was, the rest of the cricketing world thought, primarily Pakistan's problem.

Then, on December 8, 1998, the former Australian cricketer David Hookes mentioned to a Melbourne radio station that two Australians had given information to an Indian bookmaker. This turned the whole story on its head. The new revelation was that, during the same tournament in Sri Lanka in 1994, Waugh and Warne had been approached by an Indian bookmaker identified only as 'John', who had asked them to begin giving him apparently innocent information about the weather and the state of the pitch – less, said the players, than they might routinely give free to journalists. For this, Waugh was paid $A6,000 (about £2,500) and Warne $A5,000.

The players had admitted this after making their original allegations about Malik to the Australian Cricket Board, which then fined them slightly more than John paid them ($A10,000 for Waugh and $A8,000 for Warne). But the ACB had said nothing about this publicly for almost four years. However, it informed ICC at the time, telling Sir Clyde Walcott, the then chairman, and David Richards, the chief executive, to keep it secret, which they did. The news incensed the Australian public, and Waugh was booed during the Adelaide Test against England. Warne escaped this because he was injured. But letter-writers to Australian papers demanded that both be drummed out of the game. Warne and Waugh admitted being 'naive and stupid' but insisted they had not been involved in match-fixing in any way.

The news also incensed the Pakistanis. Justice Qayyum's inquiry was just nearing its end. Two months earlier, Waugh and Mark Taylor (representing Warne) had given evidence to him during Australia's tour of Pakistan. The Pakistanis had made special arrangements to accommodate their wishes, assembling a special court in a private house. Waugh and Taylor promised to tell the truth, the whole truth and nothing but the truth. They were not asked about John and (though Taylor was in on the secret) neither said anything. They did speak loftily about their cricketing ideals, and Justice Qayyum was much impressed by Waugh's testimony – until the news broke. 'If he did not have a legal obligation, he had a moral duty to bring it to our notice, and it casts doubt on his credibility,' Qayyum said.

Pakistani officials were also angered by ICC's connivance in the Australian cover-up. 'We felt the way ICC was constituted, we could not inform Pakistan,' said Richards. 'We were of the view that the onus was on the ACB to disseminate the information.' Yet when the first Pakistan inquiry, under Justice Fakhruddin G. Ebrahim, suggested that the Australians had concocted their complaints against Malik, the Australians had demanded that ICC hold its own inquiry under Rule 2 of the Code of Conduct.

Now it was the Pakistanis who were making demands. They wanted Waugh and Warne to return to Pakistan to give further evidence. The compromise was that the Pakistani court travelled instead, at the Australian Board's expense. A hearing was arranged in Melbourne; it was in effect a Pakistani court, sitting under Pakistani law. Ali Sibtain Fazli, the Pakistan Board's lawyer, closely questioned Warne and Waugh about the match that was now felt to be the key to the whole affair. This was the one-day international in Colombo on September 7, 1994, eight days before the washed-out India–Pakistan match, and immediately preceding the Australian Test tour when

Malik allegedly made his approach. Australia had scored just 179 for seven; Pakistan, captained by Malik and going well until Saeed Anwar retired with a hamstring injury, had lost by 28 runs. The Singer World Series involved India, who went on to win it, and Sri Lanka as well. It was rapidly becoming the centre of the many allegations; and it was after this tournament that the Pakistani Board banned mobile telephones from the dressing-room. A Pakistani bookmaker had previously told the commission in secret that he had given money to two players to fix this game. Both denied it.

When Warne and Waugh were given a grilling by the Pakistani investigators, no new information emerged. And the sense of anticlimax was heightened two days later when ICC held its much-heralded executive meeting. This was billed as the occasion when the organisation would finally come of age and take some of the powers of policing invested in similar international sporting organisations. Instead, ICC announced a three-man commission to supervise the investigation of such allegations but left the initial responsibility with the domestic boards.

The belief that this is a Pakistani issue remains deeply ingrained. Yet in the month before the meeting, one Australian – Ricky Ponting – and two England players – Adam Hollioake and Dougie Brown – said they had received approaches from bookmakers. The approach to Ponting was made at a Sydney dog track, a long way from Pakistan. In 1817, it was easy for MCC to ban the miscreant William Lambert and expel the bookmakers from Lord's. The world is a more complex place in 1999. There seemed little sign of this sorry story ever ending, let alone soon. (*1999*)

A DISGRACEFUL EXHIBITION

In *Wisden* 1891, the almanack passed judgement on the game between the visiting Australians and Oxford University in May 1890. The colonials had subsided to 8 for 96 at one point before rallying to 234 through the agency of Charlie Turner and prevailing by an innings and 61 runs, and *Wisden* felt that the real villain of the piece was a young university fieldsman: 'Had Jardine accepted a chance of running Turner out before the Australian had scored, the colonial side might have been out for less than 110.' The whole report, in fact, turns on 'the mistake by Jardine', as indeed did the match.

The Jardine involved was Malcolm, of Scottish extraction and Indian birth. A little over forty years later, his son Douglas, a less accomplished lawyer but a far better cricketer, embarked for Australia at the head of an MCC party to play a series bound for history. Seventy summers have elapsed since, but the five 'Bodyline' Tests can still boil tempers. Whether you see the summer of 1932–33 as another 'mistake by Jardine' usually depends on where you're standing.

Wisden's version of the series will surprise Australian readers grown up to regard 'Bodyline' as of a piece with English betrayal at Gallipoli and Singapore, and Bradman as a Gary Sweet lookalike. The almanack actually wasn't as tough on Douglas as it had been on Malcolm; Sydney Southerton's view was that Jardine 'captained the side superbly', and 'generally, despite the rancour he aroused by the manner in which he exploited fast leg-theory bowling, earned unstinted praise from all the critics for his able management of the team in the field'.

Southerton, nonetheless, was still capable of observing that the Adelaide Test was 'probably the most unpleasant ever played'. And the phrases in *Wisden*'s editorial 'The Bowling Controversy' are among the most carefully weighed in its history. Southerton declined to use the word 'Bodyline', regarding it as 'an objectionable term, utterly foreign to cricket'. But, without quite abandoning Jardine altogether, he had begun to see things the Australian way: 'I hold no brief either for Jardine or Larwood, or for Richardson, Woodfull and Bradman; but while some of the Australians may have exaggerated the supposed danger of this form of bowling I cling to the opinion that they cannot all be wrong.'

How much of this was heartfelt, and how much expedient, is hard to say. Certainly, Southerton felt genuine distress at the rupture 'Bodyline' had obviously caused, and was continuing to cause. *Wisden* discountenanced bad blood even more than it did bad cricket; Southerton applauded the condemnation of 'direct attack' by the meeting of county captains at Lord's in November 1933 that cleared the way for the following year's Ashes tour. And he reserved his harshest words for the infamous recrudescence of 'Bodyline' at Trent Bridge in August 1934. 'The thought of the glorious traditions of Nottinghamshire cricket,' said Southerton, 'makes it hard to believe that such a state of affairs could have been brought about by a few men who placed their own individual conception of what they imagined was right and above-board in the spirit of cricket, against the considered opinion of practically the whole of the cricketers of England.' In this, *Wisden* helped soften the bruise that 'Bodyline' left on Anglo-Australian cricket relations, which came at the cost of Jardine and Larwood's careers.

There remains, however, a school of thought in England that finds it difficult to comprehend Australian stridency where 'Bodyline' is concerned and it has made its presence felt from time to time in *Wisden*. In Malcolm Jardine's obituary, *Wisden* 1948 referred to Douglas setting fields in Australia 'in a manner since copied by Australian teams without objection by England or adverse criticism'. Its farewell to Jardine himself a decade later could hardly be more laudatory, and David Frith's elegy for Harold Larwood and Bob Wyatt in *Wisden* 1996 saw Jardine's last two comrades off to eternity in fine style. International sport surely is an admirable avenue to mutual misunderstanding.

—GH

THE MCC TEAM IN AUSTRALASIA 1932–33

While in some of the early tours to Australia strong differences of opinion on various points arose to cause trouble it is very doubtful if ever a team from England travelled through the Commonwealth and met with such openly expressed hostility as that visiting Australia in the winter of 1932–33. The members of it were successful in their mission, and, winning four of the five Test matches, recovered the Ashes which had been lost at the Oval to the men who came to England under the command of W.M. Woodfull in 1930. [...] One must always be a little chary of instituting comparisons, but it would be idle to pretend that anything like the same cordial feelings between our players and those of Australia existed during the more recent tour as they did on the occasion of the preceding visit. [...] Suffice it to say here that a method of bowling was evolved – mainly with the idea of curbing the scoring propensities of Bradman – which met with almost general condemnation among Australian cricketers and spectators and which, when something of the real truth was ultimately known in this country, caused people at home – many of them famous in the game – to wonder if the winning of the rubber was, after all, worth this strife. [...]

The tour was rather lavishly arranged. To begin with seventeen playing members was, to our mind, rather too heavy a load to carry, for admitting the strain imposed by long and tiring railway journeys, the fact that five players, in addition to the one acting as twelfth man, had to kick their heels about and look on, could not possibly be regarded as a good thing for the general well-being of the side. Into the question as to the desirability of taking two managers, there is no need to enter very deeply, but it made the whole party rather unwieldy, with the ever-present danger of a body of young fellows having too many masters. [...] As a touring side they were not too strong in all-rounders, for both Wyatt and Hammond, if proving successful in batting, did nothing of consequence in bowling. Still, that is a small point, which, having regard to the successful issue of the tour, need not be stressed. Jardine had under his command a fine array of batsmen, twelve of whom in first-class matches in Australia, earned averages of over 21, while of the regular bowlers nine finished with averages of under 29. In the Test match averages the batting figures were very impressive, ranging from 61 by Paynter to 22 by Jardine, with eight players coming in between these two. Larwood, taking 49 wickets in all first-class matches, stood only a little below Verity who obtained 44 wickets for less than sixteen runs apiece. In the Test matches Larwood actually took 33 for less than 20 runs apiece, falling only three short of Tate's record. The next most successful bowler in Tests was G.O. Allen with 21 wickets, while in all first-class matches, he obtained 39. [...]

Jardine, while nothing like the batsman in Australia of four years earlier, captained the side superbly. Fortunate in having four fast bowlers at command in Larwood, Allen, Voce and Bowes, he rang the changes on them in most astute fashion; placed his field very judiciously and generally, despite the rancour he aroused by the manner in which he exploited fast leg-theory bowling, earned unstinted praise from all the critics for his able management of the team in the field. He had one great difficulty which he never successfully overcame. That was to find a suitable partner for Sutcliffe as opening batsman. In the course of the tour he tried several experiments and while on occasions some of these seemed sound no real successor to Hobbs was discovered. It may be taken for granted that, so much depending upon a satisfactory start to the innings, this caused him a good deal of anxiety. He sought in match after match for a solution to the problem, but not even by the time the team sailed from Auckland on their journey home, did he discover one. [...]

Successfully as at times Allen, Voce and Verity acquitted themselves, it was the opinion on all hands that to Larwood belonged chief credit for England winning the rubber. Sharply divergent views will probably always be held as to the desirability of the method of attack he employed. This, however, is not the place to discuss that somewhat thorny subject. Suffice it to say that his fast leg-theory bowling, with three or four fieldsmen close in and others deeper on the leg-side, enabled him to establish an ascendancy over practically all the leading Australian batsmen that continued until the end of the tour. Whatever may be thought of this type of bowling, no possible doubt existed that Larwood proved himself the ideal exponent of it. Stronger probably than on the occasion of his previous visit to Australia, and very judiciously nursed during the matches by Jardine, he not only maintained an extraordinarily accurate length necessary for this form of attack but kept up a tremendous pace. In his own way Larwood obviously must have bowled magnificently. His record of wickets and the standing of his victims proves this, and in match after match Australian batsmen clearly gave the impression of being overawed. [...] (*Sydney J. Southerton*)

FIRST TEST MATCH

Played at Sydney, December 2, 3, 5, 6, 7, 1932. – Leading off in fine style in the series of Test Matches, England won this, the first, early on the fifth day by ten wickets. The bowling of Larwood, who in the two innings dismissed ten men at a cost of 124 runs – five of them in the second innings for less than six runs apiece – and the batting of Sutcliffe, Hammond and Pataudi stood out as the prominent successes of the match from the English point of view.

At the same time the encounter brought great fame to McCabe, the young Australian cricketer, who, with an innings of 187, obtained his first century in Test Matches and scored off Larwood's bowling in a style which for daring and brilliance was not approached by any other Australian during the tour. Later in the game the displays of the three Englishmen discounted considerably the fine work done by McCabe. Sutcliffe gave a typical exhibition, being wonderfully sure in defence and certain in his off-driving; Hammond, if not quite so dashing as a little time previously at Melbourne, was eminently good, but Pataudi – like two other famous Indians, Ranjitsinhji and Duleepsinhji, reaching three figures in his first Test match – was, for the most part, plodding and rather wearisome to watch. He did not show the Sydney public anything like the great array of strokes of which he is known to be capable of executing and seemed on the whole disinclined to take the slightest risk with balls which apparently were quite safe to hit. Still, it was a great performance on the part of England that their first three wickets should each have produced over a hundred runs and for Sutcliffe to have taken part in all three stands.

Woodfull won the toss for Australia who, before lunch on the first day, scored 63 for the loss of their captain at 22. Following the interval Larwood, bowling at a great pace, met with astonishing success for in his first, third and fifth overs he sent back Ponsford, Fingleton and Kippax, the score in the meantime being advanced only to 87. Larwood obtained these three wickets for 15 runs. Then came another dramatic change, McCabe finding a valuable partner in Richardson who in just over two hours, helped to add 129 runs. Both men took chances against the high-rising balls delivered at them, but everything came off, McCabe's hitting on the on-side being marvellous. Later on Grimmett gave trouble so that in the last three-quarters of an hour, 59 runs were put on.

Australia finished up with six men out for 290 and all things considered they had no great reason to be dissatisfied, but England, having on the next day polished off the innings for 360, proceeded to place themselves in a strong position. McCabe took out his bat, scoring 60 of the 70 runs added by the last four Australian wickets. Altogether he and Grimmett put on 68, and when Wall was in with him 55 runs came in about half an hour. Except that he was nearly caught by Larwood at 159, McCabe gave a faultless display; in just over four hours he hit no fewer than twenty-five 4's.

England batted for the rest of the day, scoring 252 for the loss of one wicket – that of Wyatt. Sutcliffe and Wyatt made 112 together and then Hammond stayed with Sutcliffe for the rest of the afternoon, both men batting gloriously. England remained at the wickets the whole of Monday and, adding 227 runs for the loss of five more wickets, wound up 119 runs ahead with four men to be disposed of. The Australian bowling, and especially that of O'Reilly, remained very steady, but the Englishmen did not attempt to force the pace, being more concerned in consolidating a sound position already gained. Hammond was second out at 300 after helping to add 188, but he did not quite approach the brilliance he had shown on Saturday. Still, his innings was a very fine one and then, shortly after tea, Sutcliffe was third to leave at 423, when he and Pataudi had increased the score by 123. In his highest Test innings against Australia Sutcliffe batted seven hours and a quarter, but he hit only thirteen 4's. He had one great piece of luck when he was 43, playing a ball on to his wicket without, however, removing the bails. Otherwise his defensive strokes were perfect. For the rest of the time Pataudi dominated the proceedings and when on the fourth day the innings closed for 524, or 164 ahead, he was last out. He stayed for five hours and a quarter, scoring chiefly by leg glances and strokes on the off-side, but he hit only six 4's.

Going in a second time, Australia collapsed badly. Larwood, again bowling at a great pace, and well backed up by Voce, carried everything before him and when play ceased Australia had lost nine wickets for 164 runs. Thus they had exactly cleared off the arrears. Larwood's speed was tremendous and nobody faced him with any confidence, but after eight men were out for 113 there came unexpected resistance from Nagel and Wall. Of the previous batsmen only Fingleton and McCabe stayed any time. The match being as good as over, there were less than a hundred people present to see the finish the next morning. Wall was out without addition and, going in again with Wyatt, Sutcliffe at once obtained the one run necessary to win. Reference to the fact that Bradman, owing to illness, was unable to play in the match must not be omitted, although in view of subsequent events it is, to say the least, questionable, if his presence would have staved off disaster.

AUSTRALIA

W.M. Woodfull c Ames b Voce	7	– b Larwood	0
W.H. Ponsford b Larwood	32	– b Voce	2
J.H. Fingleton c Allen b Larwood	26	– c Voce b Larwood	40
A.F. Kippax lbw, b Larwood	8	– b Larwood	19
S.J. McCabe not out	187	– lbw, b Hammond	32
V.Y. Richardson c Hammond b Voce	49	– c Voce b Hammond	0
W.A. Oldfield c Ames b Larwood	4	– c Leyland b Larwood	1
C.V. Grimmett c Ames b Voce	19	– c Allen b Larwood	5
L.E. Nagel b Larwood	0	– not out	21
W.J. O'Reilly b Voce	4	– b Voce	7
T.W. Wall c Allen b Hammond	4	– c Ames b Allen	20
B 12, l-b 4, n-b 4	20	B 12, l-b 2, w 1, n-b 2	17
	360		**164**

ENGLAND

H. Sutcliffe lbw, b Wall ....194 – not out 1
Mr R.E.S. Wyatt lbw, b Grimmett ....38 – not out 0
W.R. Hammond c Grimmett b Nagel 112
Nawab of Pataudi b Nagel 102
M. Leyland c Oldfield b Wall 0
Mr D.R. Jardine c Oldfield b McCabe 27
H. Verity lbw, b Wall 2
Mr G.O. Allen c and b O'Reilly 19
L.E.G. Ames c McCabe b O'Reilly 0
H. Larwood lbw, b O'Reilly 0
W. Voce not out 0
    B 7, l-b 17, n-b 6 30

524

1

ENGLAND BOWLING

	Overs	Mdns.	Runs	Wkts	Overs	Mdns.	Runs	Wkts
Larwood	31	5	96	5	18	4	28	5
Voce	20	4	110	4	17.3	5	54	2
Allen	15	1	65	0	9	5	13	1
Verity	13	4	35	0	4	1	15	0
Hammond	14.2	0	34	1	15	6	37	2

AUSTRALIA BOWLING

	Overs	Mdns.	Runs	Wkts	Overs	Mdns.	Runs	Wkts
Wall	38	4	104	3				
Nagel	43.4	9	110	2				
O'Reilly	67	32	117	3				
Grimmett	64	22	118	1				
McCabe	15	2	42	1	0.1	0	1	0
Kippax	2	1	3	0				

Umpires: G. Hele and G. Borwick.

SECOND TEST MATCH

Played at Melbourne, December 30, 31, 1932, January 2, 3, 1933. – Jardine again lost the toss, but England started even better than they had done at Sydney and, at the end of the first day, Australia had seven men out for 194. This splendid work was not followed up at all well when it came England's turn to bat and the match – over in four days – resulted in a victory for Australia by 111 runs.

Larwood did not take a wicket on the first afternoon and, so far from repeating his success of the earlier Test match, he dismissed only four men in the two innings at a cost of 102 runs. Having recovered from his indisposition, Bradman was able to play for Australia, whose bowling was strengthened by the inclusion of Ironmonger. Bradman, dismissed for nought on the opening day, afterwards scored a brilliant 103 not out, but O'Reilly had most to do with the success of Australia by getting rid of ten of the

Englishmen for less than 13 runs apiece. Wall, too, helped materially when England batted a first time and Ironmonger later on completed the discomfiture of the visitors.

For a Test Match in Australia, this was a game of small scores, the highest innings being 228 by Australia, and it can be said at once that the pitch proved quite different from any experienced in former tours by English cricketers. For some reason or other it lacked the usual firmness associated with wickets at the Victorian capital and Jardine, playing all his pace bowlers by including Bowes for Verity, was completely misled in his assumption that fast bowling would be likely to win the match. Apart from Wall, spin bowlers carried off the honours and of these England had only Hammond in their team.

To begin with Fingleton, going in first, made 83 out of 156 before being fifth to leave. His defence throughout was wonderfully sound and his patience unlimited to withstand for nearly four hours an attack composed of Larwood, Voce, Allen, Bowes and Hammond. At times he made poor strokes, but generally he timed those on the leg side well and his cutting was excellent. McCabe occupied an hour and a quarter over 32 and Richardson hit up 34 in about the same time. Australia had their worst shock when Bradman was out first ball to Bowes. He tried to hook it, but edged it down on to the stumps. Previously Woodfull had also been cheaply dismissed. At times the ball bounced a good deal, Woodfull on one occasion being struck over the heart.

On the second day the last three wickets went down for another 34 runs but then against O'Reilly and Wall the Englishmen gave such a poor display that at the drawing of stumps nine wickets were down for 161 and with only Bowes to go in they were still 67 runs behind. Sutcliffe scored 52 but enjoyed unusual luck in getting them. All things considered the Australians were to be congratulated on fighting back so well. Wyatt and Hammond were quickly dismissed near lunch time and, although the score at tea was 91 for three wickets, six men were got rid of during the hour and a half afterwards for 70 runs, only some plucky hitting by Allen retrieving the situation to some extent. Actually five wickets fell after tea for 47 before Allen and Voce added 23 in the last half hour.

On the third day there was a record crowd of nearly 70,000 people present. The England innings was finished off for 169 which gave Australia a lead of 59 runs. At their second attempt Australia, thanks almost entirely to Bradman, made 191 and towards the end of the day England, left to get 251 in the last innings had forty-five minutes' batting. Jardine changed the batting order, sending in Leyland with Sutcliffe and so well did this move turn out that the two men scored 43 together without being separated. In the whole match that was the most momentous period for England and, after what had gone before, it said worlds for the skill of the two Yorkshiremen that they should have kept their wickets intact through a most anxious time. The day's cricket really was dominated by Bradman who, after a succession of failures, simply took his courage in both hands and played a wonderful innings. In a way his batting was masterly. He went in when two wickets had fallen for 27 runs; resisted a lot of good bowling for over three hours and a half to complete his hundred when Ironmonger, the last man, was in with him. While Wall and O'Reilly were his partners he sacrificed many runs in order to keep the bowling. To few other Australian batsmen could such an innings as Bradman played have been possible. The England bowling was very good all the time, Hammond doing excellent work.

So, on the last day, England, with all their wickets in hand, required 208 runs, but O'Reilly and Ironmonger proved too much for them on a pitch which by this time took the spin of the ball to a pronounced degree and England were all out for 139. Sutcliffe and Leyland were soon separated and of the rest only Wyatt, Hammond and Allen stayed any time. For Australia the victory was a triumph of team work and they were to be congratulated on pulling the match out of the fire after their poor show on the first day. [...] The fact that in fine weather forty wickets went down in four days for an aggregate of 727 runs clearly suggested that at no time was the pitch all that it should have been.

AUSTRALIA

J.H. Fingleton b Allen	83	– c Ames b Allen	1
W.M. Woodfull b Allen	10	– c Allen b Larwood	26
L.P. O'Brien run out	10	– b Larwood	11
D.G. Bradman b Bowes	0	– not out	103
S.J. McCabe c Jardine b Voce	32	– b Allen	0
V.Y. Richardson c Hammond b Voce	34	– lbw, b Hammond	32
W.A. Oldfield not out	27	– b Voce	6
C.V. Grimmett c Sutcliffe b Voce	2	– b Voce	0
T.W. Wall run out	1	– lbw, b Hammond	3
W.J. O'Reilly b Larwood	15	– c Ames b Hammond	0
H. Ironmonger b Larwood	4	– run out	0
B 5, l-b 1, w 2, n-b 2	10	B 3, l-b 1, w 4, n-b 1	9
	228		**191**

ENGLAND

H. Sutcliffe c Richardson b Wall	52	– b O'Reilly	33
Mr R.E.S. Wyatt lbw, b O'Reilly	13	– lbw, b O'Reilly	25
W.R. Hammond b Wall	8	– c O'Brien b O'Reilly	23
Nawab of Pataudi b O'Reilly	15	– c Fingleton b Ironmonger	5
M. Leyland b O'Reilly	22	– b Wall	19
Mr D.R. Jardine c Oldfield b Wall	1	– c McCabe b Ironmonger	0
L.E.G. Ames b Wall	4	– c Fingleton b O'Reilly	2
Mr G.O. Allen c Richardson b O'Reilly	20	– st Oldfield b Ironmonger	23
H. Larwood b O'Reilly	9	– c Wall b Ironmonger	4
W. Voce c McCabe b Grimmett	6	– c O'Brien b O'Reilly	0
W.E. Bowes not out	4	– not out	0
B 1, l-b 2, n-b 2	5	L-b 4, n-b 1	5
	169		**139**

ENGLAND BOWLING

	Overs	Mdns	Runs	Wkts	Overs	Mdns	Runs	Wkts
Larwood	20.3	2	52	2	15	2	50	2
Voce	20	3	54	3	15	2	47	2
Allen	17	3	41	2	12	1	44	2
Hammond	10	3	21	0	10.5	2	21	3
Bowes	19	2	50	1	4	0	20	0

AUSTRALIA BOWLING

Wall	21	4	52	4	8	2	23	1
O'Reilly	34.3	17	63	5	24	5	66	5
Grimmett	16	4	21	1	4	0	19	0
Ironmonger	14	4	28	0	19.1	8	26	4

Umpires: G. Hele and G. Borwick.

THIRD TEST MATCH

Played at Adelaide, January 13, 14, 16, 17, 18, 19, 1933. – The Third Test Match of the tour, in which England were victorious by no fewer than 338 runs, will go down to history as probably the most unpleasant ever played. So hostile was the feeling against Jardine that on the days before the game started people were excluded from the ground when the Englishmen were practising. As Jardine won the toss and England batted first nothing out of the common occurred to begin with, but later on, when Australia went in and Woodfull was hit over the heart while Oldfield had to retire owing to a blow he received on the head, the majority of the spectators completely lost all hold on their feelings. Insulting remarks were hurled at Jardine, and when Larwood started to bowl his leg-theory he came in for his share of the storm of abuse. Not to put too fine a point on it, pandemonium reigned.

A passage of words between P.F. Warner and Woodfull in the dressing-room increased the bitter feeling prevalent in the crowd, and the dispatch of the cablegram protesting against 'body-line' bowling served no purpose in whatever endeavours were made to appease tempers already badly frayed by the various happenings. Altogether the whole atmosphere was a disgrace to cricket. One must pay a tribute to Jardine. He did not shrink from the line of action he had taken up; he showed great pluck in often fielding near to the boundary where he became an easy target for offensive and sometimes filthy remarks; and above all he captained his team in this particular match like a genius. Much as they disliked the method of attack he controlled, Australian critics were unanimous in their praise of his skill as a leader.

England made a dreadful start, four wickets going down in an hour for 30 runs, but then came a stand which put England on the road to ultimate success. Leyland and Wyatt batted, in the circumstances, uncommonly well while adding 156 in about two and a half hours. Leyland hit thirteen 4's in an innings which included many fine off-drives. Wyatt, whose hitting to square-leg brought him two or three 6's, left soon afterwards, but Paynter and Allen added a useful 32 runs, so that at the end of the day England had 236 on the board with seven men out. On the next morning Paynter continued to bat marvellously well, and Verity, who took Bowes's place in the England team, defended so manfully that the stand for the eighth wicket realised 96 runs in about two and a quarter hours.

England were all out soon after three o'clock for 341 and followed this up by getting down the first four Australian wickets for 51. It was during this time that Woodfull, ducking to avoid what he thought would be a rising ball, was hit on the body. Later, Ponsford and Richardson added 58 in the last seventy minutes, but Australia wound up 232 behind with six wickets to fall. Ponsford played a fine fighting innings, cutting very well and meeting the leg-theory form of attack in able style. He and Richardson put on 80 runs and Oldfield stayed for just over two hours when his active participation in the match was closed by a blow on the head by a ball from Larwood.

Australia finished their innings 119 behind, and although with one wicket down for 85 England lost Sutcliffe cheaply they stood, at the close of play, 204 runs ahead. On the fourth day, England placed themselves in such a position that they could not very well lose, and realising that their team was going to be beaten the Adelaide public who went to the ground were not nearly so noisy and insulting. Both Leyland and Wyatt made useful scores; Verity supplemented his 45 in the first innings with 40, while Jardine, Hammond and Ames by first-rate cricket all played important parts in carrying England towards victory. […] England in the end put together a total of 412 so that Australia were left to get 532 to win.

Before the fifth day's play ended, the home side lost four of their best batsmen for 120 runs and to all intents and purposes the game was as good as over. Australia in their last innings had Fingleton and Ponsford out with only 12 runs on the board, but then came an excellent stand by Woodfull and Bradman, 88 being put on in an hour and a quarter. Bradman was in first-rate form, hitting a six and ten 4's, but just when he was becoming dangerous Verity caught him from a hard return.

On the last day of the match Richardson and Woodfull defended stubbornly for a time, but they were separated at 171, and then Allen and Larwood quickly finished off the innings for 193. The greatest praise is due to Woodfull who for the second time in his career in a Test match carried his bat through the innings. He was in for nearly four hours, making most of his runs from strokes on the leg-side. Throughout the match the Englishmen fielded well, while Allen bowled splendidly.

ENGLAND

H. Sutcliffe c Wall b O'Reilly	9	c sub., b Wall ... 7
Mr D.R. Jardine b Wall	3	lbw, b Ironmonger ... 56
W.R. Hammond c Oldfield b Wall	2	b Bradman ... 85
L.E.G. Ames b Ironmonger	3	b O'Reilly ... 69
M. Leyland b O'Reilly	83	c Wall b Ironmonger ... 42
Mr R.E.S. Wyatt c Richardson b Grimmett	78	c Wall b O'Reilly ... 49
E. Paynter c Fingleton b Wall	77	not out ... 1
Mr G.O. Allen lbw, b Grimmett	15	lbw, b Grimmett ... 15
H. Verity c Richardson b Wall	45	lbw, b O'Reilly ... 40
W. Voce b Wall	8	b O'Reilly ... 8
H. Larwood not out	3	c Bradman b Ironmonger ... 8
B 1, l-b 7, n-b 7	15	B 17, l-b 11, n-b 4 ... 32
	341	**412**

AUSTRALIA

J.H. Fingleton c Ames b Allen 0	– b Larwood 0
W.M. Woodfull b Allen 22	– not out 73
D.G. Bradman c Allen b Larwood 8	– c and b Verity 66
S.J. McCabe c Jardine b Larwood 8	– c Leyland b Allen 7
W.H. Ponsford b Voce 85	– c Jardine b Larwood 3
V.Y. Richardson b Allen 28	– c Allen b Larwood 21
W.A. Oldfield retired hurt 41	– absent hurt 0
C.V. Grimmett c Voce b Allen 10	– b Allen 6
T.W. Wall b Hammond 6	– b Allen 0
W.J. O'Reilly b Larwood 0	– b Larwood 5
H. Ironmonger not out 0	– b Allen 0
B 2, l-b 11, n-b 1 .14	B 4, l-b 2, w 1, n-b 5 12
	222		**193**

AUSTRALIA BOWLING

	Overs	Mdns	Runs	Wkts	Overs	Mdns	Runs	Wkts
Wall	34.1	10	72	5	20	6	75	1
O'Reilly	50	19	82	2	50.3	21	79	1
Ironmonger	20	6	50	1	57	21	87	3
Grimmett	28	6	94	2	35	9	74	1
McCabe	14	3	28	0	16	0	42	0
Bradman					4	0	23	1

ENGLAND BOWLING

	Overs	Mdns	Runs	Wkts	Overs	Mdns	Runs	Wkts
Larwood	25	6	55	3	19	3	71	4
Allen	23	4	71	4	17.1	5	50	4
Hammond	17.4	4	30	1	9	3	27	0
Voce	14	5	21	1	4	1	7	0
Verity	16	7	31	0	20	12	26	1

Umpires: G. Hele and G. Borwick.

FOURTH TEST MATCH

Played at Brisbane, February 10, 11, 13, 14, 15, 16, 1933. – England won the Fourth Test Match by six wickets, so being successful in the rubber and regaining The Ashes. [...] Once more Jardine captained his side with remarkable skill, his management of his bowlers and his placing of the field being worthy of great praise. In this respect he certainly outshone Woodfull, who had under his command three new men, while in the England side Voce, who was unwell, stood down for Mitchell. Bromley and Darling were brought into the Australian eleven as left-handers likely to counteract the effect of Larwood's leg-theory bowling, and Love kept wicket as Oldfield was not well enough to take his usual place behind the stumps.

The Australians at times seemed to have more than a reasonable chance, but they failed to drive home a temporary advantage, and generally speaking they did not appear to be a well-balanced side, while there is no doubt that nearly all of them were overawed by Larwood. The match will always be memorable for the great part played in the victory of England by Paynter. Suffering from an affection of the throat, he left a sick-bed to bat, and put together a splendid innings of 83, while he enjoyed the additional satisfaction later on of making the winning hit with a six.

Woodfull again won the toss, and this time took in with him to open the Australian innings Victor Richardson. This move proved highly successful, for both men left the balls on the leg-side severely alone and thanks to their opening partnership of 133 Australia on the first day stayed in all the afternoon to make 251 for the loss of three wickets. This was indeed a good beginning for Australia. The English fielding was not so smart as in former matches, but Jardine made a fine catch to dismiss McCabe, while Mitchell justified his inclusion by bowling Woodfull late in the day. Richardson after lunch made some splendid hits and Bradman carried on the good work, being not out 71 when stumps were pulled up. Larwood did not take a wicket, but Verity kept an uncommonly good length while having only 32 runs hit off twenty-two overs. Woodfull played a characteristic innings, being in four hours for his 67. On the second day, the Australian innings closed a little after lunch time for 340, the last seven wickets thus falling for the addition of 89. In getting rid of Australia for less than 400 runs, the Englishmen could congratulate themselves. Larwood did great work in taking four wickets, bowling Bradman at 264 and Ponsford at 267. The quick dismissal of these two renowned batsmen meant a great deal to the visiting team. Bradman did not play at all well in the closing stages of his innings, drawing away more than once from Larwood's bowling. After that there was little of note in the batting. Darling and Bromley each made a few runs, the latter hitting out in rather care-free style. For the rest of the afternoon, Jardine and Sutcliffe occupied themselves in scoring 99 runs together without being separated. The third day did not go quite so well for England, for at the close England had eight men out for 271 and thus were still 69 runs behind. Everyone who went in reached double figures, but the batting of the Englishmen generally was timorous and many balls which looked to be perfectly safe to hit were allowed to escape. This negative kind of batting following the opening partnership of 114 runs, was disappointing. Hammond took an hour and a half to get 20; Wyatt was forty-seven minutes over 12; Leyland forty-five minutes for a similar number; Allen twenty-six minutes for 13, and Ames an hour and twenty-two minutes for 17. Against this Larwood hit up 23 out of 39 in thirty-three minutes. Paynter, ill and weak, obviously could not force matters, but he was 24 not out at the close of the day, and on the next morning he gave a superb exhibition. He scored the runs by a variety of splendid strokes while Verity kept up his end in manly fashion. Paynter was not dismissed until England were in front, and in the end England gained an advantage of 16 runs.

At Adelaide, Paynter and Verity put on 96 at a critical period; at Brisbane they added 92 runs in about two hours and thirty-five minutes. Paynter's display of patient and skilful batting was certainly one of the greatest examples of pluck and fortitude in the history of Test cricket. He was in for nearly four hours, and sent the ball ten times to the boundary. As near as possible England were batting ten hours for their total of 356, which on the face of it seemed absurd.

In the last two and a half hours of the day, however, they atoned for this by some splendid bowling and fielding so that Australia lost four wickets in their second innings for 108 and wound up only 92 runs in front. Richardson led off in rare style, and Bradman batted brightly before falling once more to Larwood at 79. For the second time in the match Mitchell dismissed Woodfull. Apart from Darling, who at a very critical point lost his wicket through a misunderstanding with Bromley, nobody did anything of consequence on the fifth day and soon after lunch Australia were all out for 175. Once more, the Australians showed what a long tail they had to their team, the last five men scoring between them only 16 runs.

England were thus left with only 160 to get, but with five scored Sutcliffe was out. Leyland then joined his captain and the two men stolidly played themselves in. There was one period of over an hour when Jardine did not score, playing in this time no less than eighty-two deliveries. Altogether he was in for two hours and ten minutes, he and Leyland adding 73 runs, and play ceased with the score at 107 for two wickets. On the last day the flags all round the ground were at half-mast owing to the death that morning of Archie Jackson. Hammond left at 118 and Leyland 20 runs later, but then Paynter and Ames hit off the balance and soon after the match was won rain came on and poured steadily for twelve hours. Nothing could have been finer than Leyland's batting. He only hit when it was safe to do so and by his strong defence and watchful methods he prevented the Australian bowlers from getting on top at what was after all a crucial period.

AUSTRALIA

W.M. Woodfull b Mitchell	67	– c Hammond b Mitchell	19
V.Y. Richardson st Ames b Hammond	83	– c Jardine b Verity	32
D.G. Bradman b Larwood	76	– c Mitchell b Larwood	24
S.J. McCabe c Jardine b Allen	20	– b Verity	22
W.H. Ponsford b Larwood	19	– c Larwood b Allen	0
L. Darling c Ames b Allen	17	– run out	39
E.H. Bromley c Verity b Larwood	26	– c Hammond b Allen	7
H.S. Love lbw, b Mitchell	5	– lbw, b Larwood	3
T. Wall not out	6	– c Jardine b Allen	2
W.J. O'Reilly c Hammond b Larwood	6	– b Larwood	4
H. Ironmonger st Ames b Hammond	8	– not out	0
B 5, l-b 1, n-b 1	7	B 13, l-b 9, n-b 1	23
	340		**175**

ENGLAND

Mr D.R. Jardine c Love b O'Reilly	46	– lbw, b Ironmonger	24
H. Sutcliffe lbw, b O'Reilly	86	– c Darling b Wall	2
W.R. Hammond b McCabe	20	– c Bromley b Ironmonger	14
Mr R.E.S. Wyatt c Love b Ironmonger	12		
M. Leyland c Bradman b O'Reilly	12	– c McCabe b O'Reilly	86
L.E.G. Ames c Darling b Ironmonger	17	– not out	14
Mr G.O. Allen c Love b Wall	13		
E. Paynter c Richardson b Ironmonger	83	– not out	14
H. Larwood b McCabe	23		
H. Verity not out	23		
T.B. Mitchell lbw, b O'Reilly	0		
B 6, l-b 12, n-b 3	21	B 2, l-b 4, n-b 2	8
	356		**162**

ENGLAND BOWLING

	Overs	Mdns	Runs	Wkts	Overs	Mdns	Runs	Wkts
Larwood	31	7	101	4	17.3	3	49	3
Allen	24	7	83	2	17	3	44	3
Hammond	23	5	61	2	10	4	18	0
Mitchell	16	5	49	2	5	0	11	1
Verity	27	12	39	0	19	6	30	2

AUSTRALIA BOWLING

	Overs	Mdns	Runs	Wkts	Overs	Mdns	Runs	Wkts
Wall	23	6	66	1	7	1	17	1
O'Reilly	67.4	27	120	4	30	11	65	1
Ironmonger	43	19	69	3	35	13	47	2
McCabe	23	7	40	2	7.4	2	25	0
Bromley	10	4	19	0				
Bradman	7	1	17	0				
Darling	2	0	4	0				

Umpires: G. Hele and G.E. Borwick.

FIFTH TEST MATCH

Played at Sydney, February 23, 24, 25, 27, 28, 1933. – The rubber having been won by England, the batting of both sides in their first innings in the last Test Match was generally much brighter than that which previously had been seen. The strain was lifted from both sides, but Australia gave a poor display in the second innings and England demonstrated their superiority over their opponents in no uncertain fashion in winning by eight wickets.

Unfortunately the match was marred by bad catching, each side being at fault, and to Victor Richardson in particular it must have proved a dismal memory, for going in first again with Woodfull he was dismissed without scoring in each innings. On the other hand, Verity had joyful recollections, bowling so well as to take eight wickets for 95 runs, five of them in the second innings for less than seven runs apiece, while Larwood, although damaging his foot when bowling, came out as a batsman with a splendid innings of 98. What a pity he could not have capped his great bowling successes by obtaining a hundred in a Test Match! Voce came back to the England team in place of Mitchell; Oldfield again kept wicket for Australia, while P.K. Lee, the South Australian all-rounder, and Alexander, the Victorian fast bowler, were included, Wall having to withdraw owing to an injured heel.

For the fourth time Jardine lost the toss, and in the first over Richardson was out. Woodfull and Bradman carried the score to 59, but then Woodfull played-on and in the next over Bradman left at 64. Thenceforward, matters went well for Australia. The score was 67 for three wickets at lunch, and O'Brien and McCabe afterwards played finely, although O'Brien was twice missed in the slips. Altogether the two batsmen added 99 runs at the rate of about one a minute. At the tea interval Australia had 183 on the board with four men out, and then Darling followed the success of his colleagues by playing a very bright innings. The fifth partnership realised 81 runs,

McCabe having been in nearly three hours. Darling and Oldfield next added 84, and when play ceased for the day the score stood at 296 for five wickets, this being the highest number of runs scored on the first day of any of the Tests. Darling, Oldfield and Lee all batting well on the second day, Australia added another 139 runs to their overnight score, the total of 435 being better than anything they had previously accomplished. Lee hit up 42 out of 57 in thirty-five minutes.

The success of the younger members of the side was, from the Australian point of view, very gratifying. It was, however, estimated that England missed no fewer than fourteen catches. Australia were also at fault when England went in, Jardine giving two chances in scoring less than 20. He left at 31, but then came some brilliant batting, Sutcliffe and Hammond being in their very best form while adding 122 runs. Sutcliffe played well, but was overshadowed by his partner who drove and turned the ball to leg in wonderful style. But like several of the others he was let off. When the partnership ended Larwood was sent in to play out time, England, with 159 runs on the board and two men out, finishing up 276 behind. During the afternoon, protests were made by the Englishmen about Alexander scratching up the pitch after he had delivered the ball, a fault which had been noticed during the previous tour.

On the Saturday, England batted all day and finished up only 17 runs behind with two wickets to fall. Continuing his innings, Hammond did not play in quite the same brilliant style, and most of the applause was earned by Larwood who drove in glorious fashion and treated the spectators to a great display. He and Hammond put on 92 runs, Hammond, after being in nearly three hours and a half for his second hundred of the tour in Test Matches, being dismissed just before lunch. England at that point were in a comfortable position, and Larwood and Leyland, after playing themselves in, added 65 in as many minutes. Then Larwood, trying to place the ball to the on for a two to reach three figures, did not time his stroke properly and was caught by Ironmonger, a notoriously bad fieldsman. Larwood treated the bowling as no other of the Englishmen had previously done. He made his runs in two hours and a quarter, hitting a six, a five and nine 4's, and being fourth out at 310. He was loudly cheered. Bad judgment in running cost the wickets of Leyland and Ames, while Wyatt played a dull, colourless innings. He was out in the last over of the day, having been in two hours and forty minutes for 51.

Monday was full of sensation. England increasing their score to 454 gained a lead of 19 runs, Allen who batted well for nearly an hour and threequarters having a lot to do with this towards the end. When Australia went in again the first wicket once more fell before a run had been scored, but then Woodfull and Bradman put on 115. Bradman was in his most daring mood, often stepping back to the leg-theory bowling of Voce and Larwood and forcing the ball to the off. Verity, however, bowled Bradman when the batsman misjudged the flight of the ball, and with his dismissal a breakdown occurred. At tea-time the score was 139 for four, and Woodfull's fine innings came to an end at 177 when he was seventh out, playing-on to Allen. He batted just over three hours in his usual watchful style. Subsequently, Verity dismissed O'Reilly and Alexander with consecutive balls and as Ironmonger was next in the Yorkshireman had a good chance of doing the 'hat trick'. This he did not accomplish, Lee, who had swung the bat a good deal at the bowling, being dismissed by Allen and the innings closing for 182.

England were thus left with 164 to get to win, half an hour remaining for play. Jardine, who took Wyatt in with him, complained about Alexander running down the pitch after his delivery, and the crowd booed and hooted. Alexander then bumped several balls down to Jardine, and when the England captain was struck on the thigh sections of the crowd cheered. A disgraceful exhibition. Eleven runs were scored without loss and on the last day Jardine and Leyland were out at 43. Ironmonger was making the ball turn off the scratched-up turf and Hammond and Wyatt took some pains to play themselves in. Steadily the bowling was worn down and then Hammond surprised everyone by on-driving O'Reilly for six – one of the biggest hits ever seen on the Sydney ground. Hammond, after that, played in brilliant fashion and finished the match in dramatic style with another big six. Actually Hammond and Wyatt hit off the 125 runs after Leyland left in just over two hours, the concluding cricket of the last Test Match being thus very brilliant.

AUSTRALIA

V.Y. Richardson c Jardine b Larwood	.0 –	c Allen b Larwood .0
W.M. Woodfull b Larwood	.14 –	b Allen .67
D.G. Bradman b Larwood	.48 –	b Verity .71
L.P. O'Brien c Larwood b Voce	.61 –	c Verity b Voce .5
S.J. McCabe c Hammond b Verity	.73 –	c Jardine b Voce .4
L.S. Darling b Verity	.85 –	c Wyatt b Verity .7
W.A. Oldfield run out	.52 –	c Wyatt b Verity .5
P.K. Lee c Jardine b Verity	.42 –	b Allen .15
W.J. O'Reilly b Allen	.19 –	b Verity .1
H.H. Alexander not out	.17 –	lbw, b Verity .0
H. Ironmonger b Larwood	.1 –	not out .0
B 13, l-b 9, w 1	.23	B 4, n-b 3 .7
	435	**182**

ENGLAND

H. Sutcliffe c Richardson b O'Reilly	.56	
Mr D.R. Jardine c Oldfield b O'Reilly	.18 –	c Richardson b Ironmonger .24
W.R. Hammond lbw, b Lee	.101 –	not out .75
H. Larwood c Ironmonger b Lee	.98	
M. Leyland run out	.42 –	b Ironmonger .0
Mr R.E.S. Wyatt c Ironmonger b O'Reilly	.51 –	not out .61
L.E.G. Ames run out	.4	
E. Paynter b Lee	.9	
Mr G.O. Allen c Bradman b Lee	.48	
H. Verity c Oldfield b Alexander	.4	
W. Voce not out	.7	
B 7, l-b 7, n-b 2	.16	B 6, l-b 1, n-b 1 .8
	454	**168**

ENGLAND BOWLING

	Overs	Mdns	Runs	Wkts	Overs	Mdns	Runs	Wkts
Larwood	32.2	10	98	4	11	0	44	1
Voce	24	3	80	1	10	0	34	2
Allen	25	1	128	1	11.4	2	54	2
Hammond	8	0	32	0	3	0	10	0
Verity	17	3	62	3	19	9	33	5
Wyatt	2	0	12	0				

AUSTRALIA BOWLING

	Overs	Mdns	Runs	Wkts	Overs	Mdns	Runs	Wkts
Alexander	35	1	129	1	11	2	25	0
McCabe	12	1	27	0	5	2	10	0
O'Reilly	45	7	100	3	15	5	32	0
Ironmonger	31	13	64	0	26	12	34	2
Lee	40.2	10	111	4	12.2	3	52	0
Darling	7	5	3	0	2	0	7	0
Bradman	1	0	4	0				

Umpires: G. Hele and G. Borwick.

THE BOWLING CONTROVERSY:
TEXT OF THE CABLES

During the tour of the M.C.C. team in Australia in 1932–33, exception was taken in that country to the methods adopted by certain of the visiting bowlers, and long correspondence by cable between the M.C.C. and the Australian Board of Control followed. Below will be found, in chronological order, the text of these cables together with – in proper sequence – a short report of meetings bearing upon the subject.

FROM AUSTRALIAN BOARD OF CONTROL TO M.C.C., JAN. 18, 1933

'Bodyline bowling has assumed such proportions as to menace the best interests of the game, making protection of the body by the batsmen the main consideration.

'This is causing intensely bitter feeling between the players as well as injury. In our opinion it is unsportsmanlike.

'Unless stopped at once it is likely to upset the friendly relations existing between Australia and England.'

FROM M.C.C. TO AUSTRALIAN BOARD OF CONTROL, JAN. 23, 1933

'We, Marylebone Cricket Club, deplore your cable. We deprecate your opinion that there has been unsportsmanlike play. We have fullest confidence in captain, team and managers and are convinced that they would do nothing to infringe either the Laws of Cricket or the spirit of the game. We have no evidence that our confidence has been misplaced. Much as we regret accidents to Woodfull and Oldfield, we understand that in neither case was the bowler to blame. If the Australian Board of Control wish to propose a new Law or Rule, it shall receive our careful consideration in due course.

'We hope the situation is not as serious as your cable would seem to indicate, but if it is such as to jeopardize the good relations between English and Australian cricketers and you consider it desirable to cancel remainder of programme we would consent, but with great reluctance.'

FROM AUSTRALIAN BOARD OF CONTROL TO M.C.C., JAN. 30, 1933

'We, Australian Board of Control, appreciate your difficulty in dealing with the matter raised in our cable without having seen the actual play. We unanimously regard body-line bowling, as adopted in some of the games in the present tour, as being opposed to the spirit of cricket, and unnecessarily dangerous to the players.

'We are deeply concerned that the ideals of the game shall be protected and have, therefore, appointed a committee to report on the action necessary to eliminate such bowling from Australian cricket as from beginning of the 1933–34 season.

'We will forward a copy of the committee's recommendations for your consideration, and it is hoped co-operation as to its application to all cricket. We do not consider it necessary to cancel remainder of programme.'

The committee appointed consisted of Messrs. R.J. Hartigan (Queensland) representing the Board of Control; W.M.Woodfull, V.Y. Richardson and M.A. Noble.

FROM M.C.C. TO AUSTRALIAN BOARD OF CONTROL, FEB. 2, 1933

'We, the Committee of the Marylebone Cricket Club note with pleasure that you do not consider it necessary to cancel the remainder of programme, and that you are postponing the whole issue involved until after the present tour is completed. May we accept this as a clear indication that the good sportsmanship of our team is not in question?

'We are sure you will appreciate how impossible it would be to play any Test Match in the spirit we all desire unless both sides were satisfied there was no reflection upon their sportsmanship.

'When your recommendation reaches us it shall receive our most careful consideration and will be submitted to the Imperial Cricket Conference.'

FROM AUSTRALIAN BOARD OF CONTROL TO M.C.C., FEB. 8, 1933

'We do not regard the sportsmanship of your team as being in question.

'Our position was fully considered at the recent meeting in Sydney and is as indicated in our cable of January 30.

'It is the particular class of bowling referred to therein which we consider is not in the best interests of cricket, and in this view we understand we are supported by many eminent English cricketers.

'We join heartily with you in hoping that the remaining Tests will be played with the traditional good feeling.'

The Australian Board of Control, meeting on April 21, 1933, considered a proposal submitted to them by the special sub-committee set up to consider the question of 'body-line' bowling and cabled M.C.C. asking that body to give the proposal their consideration. The cable read as follows: 'Australian Board adopted following addition to Laws of Cricket in Australia, namely:

'Any ball delivered which, in the opinion of the umpire at the bowler's end is bowled at the batsman with the intent to intimidate or injure him shall be considered unfair and "No-ball" shall be called. The bowler shall be notified of the reason. If the offence be repeated by the same bowler in the same innings he shall be immediately instructed by the umpire to cease bowling and the over shall be regarded as completed. Such bowler shall not again be permitted to bowl during the course of the innings then in progress.'

'Law 48a shall not apply to this Law. Foregoing submitted for your consideration and it is hoped co-operation by application to all cricket.'

FROM M.C.C. TO AUSTRALIAN BOARD OF CONTROL, JUNE 12, 1933

'The M.C.C. Committee have received and carefully considered the cable of the Australian Board of Control of April 28th last. They have also received and considered the reports of the Captain and Manager of the cricket team which visited Australia 1932–1933.

'With regard to the cable of the Australian Board of Control of April 28th last, the Committee presume that the class of bowling to which the proposed new law would apply is that referred to as "body-line" bowling in the Australian Board of Control's cable of January 18th. The Committee consider that the term "body-line" bowling is misleading and improper. It has led to much inaccuracy of thought by confusing the short bumping ball, whether directed on the off, middle or leg stump, with what is known as "leg-theory".'

'The term "body-line" would appear to imply a direct attack by the bowler on the batsman. The Committee consider that such an implication applied to any English bowling in Australia is improper and incorrect. Such action on the part of any bowler would be an offence against the spirit of the game and would be immediately condemned. The practice of bowling on the leg stump with a fielder placed on the leg side necessary for such bowling is legitimate, and has been in force for many years. It has generally been referred to as "leg-theory". The present habit of batsmen who move in front of their wicket with the object of gliding straight balls to leg tends to give the impression that the bowler is bowling at the batsman, especially in the case of a fast bowler when the batsman mistimes the ball and is hit.

'The new Law recommended by the Australian Board of Control does not appear to the Committee to be practicable. Firstly, it would place an impossible task on the umpire, and secondly, it would place in the hands of the umpire power over the game which would be more than dangerous, and which any umpire might well fear to exercise.

'The Committee have had no reason to give special attention to "leg-theory" as practised by fast bowlers. They will, however, watch carefully during the present season for anything which might be regarded as unfair or prejudicial to the best interests of the game. They propose to invite opinions and suggestions from County Clubs and Captains at the end of the season, with a view to enabling them to express an opinion on this matter at a Special Meeting of the Imperial Cricket Conference.

'With regard to the reports of the Captain and Managers, the Committee while deeply appreciative of the private and public hospitality shown to the English Team, are much concerned with regard to barracking, which is referred to in all the reports, and against which there is unanimous deprecation. Barracking has, unfortunately, always been indulged in by spectators in Australia to a degree quite unknown in this Country. During the late tour, however, it would appear to have exceeded all previous experience, and on occasions to have become thoroughly objectionable. There appears to have been little or no effort on the part of those responsible for the administration of the game in Australia to interfere, or to control this exhibition. This was naturally regarded by members of the team as a serious lack of consideration for them. The Committee are of opinion that cricket played under such conditions is robbed of much of its value as a game, and that unless barracking is stopped, or is greatly moderated in Australia it is difficult to see how the continuance of representative matches can serve the best interest of the game.

'The Committee regret that these matters have to be dealt with by correspondence and not by personal conference. If at any time duly accredited representatives of Australian Cricket could meet the Committee in conference, such conference would be welcomed by M.C.C.'

FROM AUSTRALIAN BOARD OF CONTROL TO M.C.C., SEPT. 22, 1933

'We note that you consider that a form of bowling which amounted to a direct attack by the bowler on the batsman would be against the spirit of the game. We agree with you that Leg-theory Bowling as it has been generally practised for many years is not open to objection. On these matters there does not appear to be any real difference between our respective views.

'We feel that while the type of bowling to which exception was taken in Australia, strictly was not in conflict with the Laws of Cricket, yet its continued practice would not be in the best interests of the game. May we assume that you concur in this point of view and that the teams may thus take the field in 1934 with that knowledge?

'We are giving consideration to the question of barracking and you may rely upon our using our best endeavours to have it controlled in future tours.

'We are most anxious that the cordial relations which have so long existed between English and Australian cricket shall continue.'

FROM M.C.C. TO AUSTRALIAN BOARD OF CONTROL, OCT. 9, 1933

'The M.C.C. Committee appreciate the friendly tone of your cable and they heartily reciprocate your desire for the continuance of cordial relations.

'In their view the difference between us seems to be rather on the question of fact than on any point of interpretation of the Laws of Cricket or of the spirit of the game. They agree and have always agreed that a form of bowling which is obviously a direct attack by the bowler upon the batsman would be an offence against the spirit of the game.

'Your team can certainly take the field with the knowledge and with the full assurance that cricket will be played here in the same spirit as in the past and with the single desire to promote the best interests of the game in both countries.

'The Committee much appreciate your promise to take the question of barracking into consideration with a view to ensuring that it shall be kept within reasonable bounds.

'Your team can rely on a warm welcome from M.C.C., and every effort will be made to make their visit enjoyable.'

FROM AUSTRALIAN BOARD OF CONTROL TO M.C.C., Nov. 16, 1933

'We appreciate the terms of your cablegram of October 9 and assume that such cable is intended to give the assurance asked for in our cablegram of September 22.

'It is on this understanding that we are sending a team in 1934.'

A joint meeting of the Advisory County Cricket Committee and the Board of Control of Test Matches at Home, at which the county captains were present, was held at Lord's on Thursday, November 23, 1933, to consider the replies received from the counties to the M.C.C.'s circular letter in regard to fast leg-theory bowling.

A decision was reached that no alteration of the Law was desirable. It was agreed that any form of bowling which is obviously a direct attack by the bowler upon the batsman would be an offence against the spirit of the game.

It was decided to leave the matter to the captains in complete confidence that they would not permit or countenance bowling of such type.

FROM M.C.C. TO AUSTRALIAN BOARD OF CONTROL, DEC. 12, 1933

'Reference your cable of November 16th, you must please accept our cable of October 9th, which speaks for itself, as final.

'We cannot go beyond the assurance therein given. We shall welcome Australian cricketers who come to play cricket with us next year. If, however, your Board of Control decide that such games be deferred, we shall regret their decision.

'Please let us know your Board's final decision as soon as possible and in any event before the end of the year.'

FROM AUSTRALIAN BOARD OF CONTROL TO M.C.C., DEC. 14, 1933

'With further reference to your cable of October 9 and your confirmatory cable of December 12 in reply to ours of November 16, we, too, now regard the position finalised. Our team will leave Australia on March 9.'

FROM M.C.C. TO AUSTRALIAN BOARD OF CONTROL, DEC. 14, 1933

'Thank you for your cable. We are very glad to know we may look forward to welcoming the Australians next summer. We shall do all in our power to make their visit enjoyable.'

BY THE EDITOR

Had the foregoing cables been the medical history sheets of a person suddenly afflicted by some mental or physical trouble a doctor would have experienced little difficulty in tracing and analysing the disease from its onset to its cure. In like manner cricketers can gather from the cables almost the whole course of the disturbance brought about between the M.C.C. and the Australian Board of Control over the question of fast leg-theory bowling. I have purposely omitted to use the expression 'body-line bowling'. It may have conveyed to those to whom it was presented at the outset the meaning the inventor of it wished to infer, but to my mind it was an objectionable term, utterly foreign to cricket, and calculated to stir up strife when the obvious aim of everybody should have been directed towards the prevention of any breach.

Happily the controversy is now at an end, and little reason exists, therefore, to flog what we can regard as a 'dead horse'. But, obviously from the historical point of view, something on the subject must be said. I hope and believe that the ventilation of their grievances by the Australians, and the placatory replies of the M.C.C. will have done much towards imparting a better spirit to Test Matches which of recent years have become battles rather than pleasurable struggles. A false atmosphere has pervaded them. During the last few tours of M.C.C. teams in Australia, and the visits of the Australians to this country one could not fail to detect a subtle change taking place in the conduct of Test Matches – reflected unfortunately in the style of play of the cricketers themselves. The *result* of the contests was given a prominence out of keeping even with the importance of Test Matches, and the true sense of perspective stood in danger of disappearing altogether.

There is no need to enter into some of the reasons for the hostility with which D.R. Jardine in particular and certain of his team were received by the huge crowds in Australia. Animosity existed and was fanned into flame largely by the use of the term 'body-line' when Larwood and others met with such success against the leading Australian batsmen. To such an extent had real bitterness grown that the storm burst during the Third Test Match at Adelaide. The dispatch of the petulant cablegram by the Australian Board of Control even placed the completion of the tour in jeopardy. Saner counsels prevailed, and, although tension existed for months afterwards, the M.C.C. for their part never lost their grip of the situation and, what was even more important, refused to be stampeded into any panic legislation. Whatever individual opinions were held at the time the M.C.C. Committee, as a whole, naturally stood by the captain of their Team in Australia. They had heard only one side of the question.

And now, what of this fast leg-theory method of bowling to which not only the Australian players themselves, but a vast majority of the people of Australia took such grave exception? With the dictum of the M.C.C. that any form of bowling which constitutes a direct attack by the bowler on the batsman is contrary to the spirit of the game everyone must unquestionably concur. D.R. Jardine, on his return to England, stated definitely in his book that the bowling against which the Australians demurred was not of this description, and Larwood, the chief exponent of it, said with equal directness that he had never intentionally bowled at a man. On the other hand, there are numerous statements by responsible Australians to the effect that the type of bowling adopted was calculated to intimidate batsmen, pitched as the ball was so short as to cause it to fly shoulder and head high and make batsmen, with the leg-side studded with fieldsmen, use the bat as a protection for their bodies or their heads rather than in defence of the wicket or to make a scoring stroke. Victor Richardson, the South Australian batsman, has said that when he took his ordinary stance at the wicket he found the ball coming on to his body; when he took guard slightly more to the leg-side he still had the ball coming at him; and with a still wider guard the ball continued to follow him. I hold no brief either for Jardine or Larwood or for Richardson, Woodfull or Bradman; but while some of the Australians may have exaggerated the supposed danger of this form of bowling I cling to the opinion that they cannot all be wrong. When the first mutterings of the storm were heard many people in this country were inclined to the belief that the Australians, seeing themselves in danger of losing the rubber, were not taking defeat in the proper spirit always expected from honourable opponents. I will confess that I thought they did not relish what seemed to me at that stage to be a continuous good length bombardment by our fast bowlers on to their leg-stump. This idea I afterwards found was not quite correct.

There is nothing new in leg-theory bowling. The most notable exponent of it in recent years was Root, of Worcestershire; to go back to just before the War A. Jaques, of Hampshire, often exploited it with success; and to delve deeper into the past an Australian – no less than the famous Spofforth himself – would at times bowl on the leg-stump with an off-break and two fieldsmen close in on the leg-side. […] That type of bowling, however, is very different from the kind sent down at top-speed with the ball flying past the shoulders or head of the batsman who has only a split second in which to make up his mind as to whether he will duck, move away, or attempt to play it with the bat high in the air. Against one sort a perfectly legitimate and reasonable stroke could be played without any apprehension of physical damage; against the other it seems to me that by touching the ball in defence of the upper part of his body or his head a batsman would be almost bound to be out. One would not accuse Hammond or Hendren of being slow on their feet, yet Hendren at Lord's on one occasion was not quick enough to get out of the way and received a crashing blow on his head, while last season at Manchester Hammond, in the Test Match against the West Indies, had his chin laid open, and on resuming his innings was caught off a similar kind of ball. We saw in that particular match at Old Trafford what I should conceive to be a somewhat pale – but no less disturbing – imitation of Larwood in Australia, when Martindale and Constantine on the one hand, and Clark, of Northamptonshire, on the other were giving a demonstration of fast leg-theory bowling. Not one of the three had the pace, accuracy of pitch, or deadliness of Larwood, but what they did was sufficient to convince many people with open minds on the subject that it was a noxious form of attack not to be encouraged in any way. […]

Fast bowlers of all periods have delivered the ball short of a length on occasions – sometimes by accident, and sometimes by intention to keep batsmen on the *qui-vive* – but in modern days some of our bowlers of pace have become obsessed with the idea that it is necessary to do this three or four times in an over. I desire none of my readers to get the impression that I am against fast bowling. Nothing is further from my thoughts. I like to see fast bowling, the faster the better, but I do like to see it of good length and directed at the stumps. The Australians without any doubt thought that during the last tour they were being bowled at, and small wonder that edging away as some of them unquestionably did they found themselves bowled when, instead of the expected short-pitched 'bouncer', occasional good-length straight balls came along and beat them before they were in a proper position to defend their wickets. It is, to say the least, significant that G.O. Allen, whom nobody would place quite in the same class as Larwood, enjoyed many successes and for the most part obtained his wickets by bowling with which we in England are familiar. Surely, with his extra pace, Larwood could have done as well as Allen and so have prevented that bitter ill-feeling which led a good many people in this country to the belief that the winning of The Ashes had been gained at too great a cost to the relations hitherto existing between England and Australia.

For myself, I hope that we shall never see fast leg-theory bowling as used during the last tour in Australia exploited in this country. I think that (1) it is definitely dangerous; (2) it creates ill-feeling between the rival teams; (3) it invites reprisals; (4) it has a bad influence on our great game of cricket; and (5) it eliminates practically all the best strokes in batting. Mainly because it makes cricket a battle instead of a game I deplore its introduction and pray for its abolition, not by any legislative measures, but by the influence which our captains can bring to bear and by avoiding use of the objectionable form of attack take a great part in wiping away a blot. Early last season I heard Mr Weigall, the Recorder of Gravesend, deliver a great speech at dinner to the West Indies team, in which in beautifully chosen phrases he exhorted them always to look upon cricket with the idea that the game is of far greater importance than the result. If that lesson is driven home to all our cricketers we shall hear no more of the kind of bowling which so nearly brought about a severance of the cricket relations between England and Australia. (*1934*)

THE SETTLEMENT OF
THE BOWLING CONTROVERSY

The following communication was issued by the M.C.C. Committee from Lord's Cricket Ground on Wednesday, November 21, 1934, after the meetings of the Advisory County Cricket Committee and the Board of Control of Test Matches at Home:

FAST SHORT BOWLING ON THE LEG SIDE.

In 1933 the M.C.C. Committee passed the following resolution:

'That any form of bowling which is obviously a direct attack by the bowler upon the batsman would be an offence against the spirit of the game.'

On November 23rd, 1933, at a joint meeting of the Board of Control of Test Matches at Home and the Advisory County Cricket Committee, at which 14 of the 17 Captains of the first-class cricketing Counties were present and the remaining three represented, this resolution was accepted and an 'understanding' was arrived at to the effect that the County Captains would not permit or countenance bowling of such type.

This principle was also affirmed by the Imperial Cricket Conference on July 26th, 1934, and it was urged that the controlling bodies of cricket should not permit or countenance such form of bowling.

In June 1933 the M.C.C. Committee cabled to the Australian Board of Control to say that they would watch carefully for anything which might be regarded as unfair or prejudicial to the best interests of the game.

As a result of their own observations and from the reports received the M.C.C. Committee consider that there is evidence that cases of the bowler making a direct attack upon the batsman have on occasions taken place during the past cricket season. Bowling of this kind was not unknown in the past, but has developed and may continue to develop if left unchecked.

In order to eliminate this type of bowling from the game and to ensure in future that there shall be no misunderstanding as to what exactly constitutes 'a direct attack by the bowler upon the batsman,' the M.C.C. Committee have ruled:

> 'That the type of bowling regarded as a direct attack by the bowler upon the batsman and therefore unfair consists in persistent and systematic bowling of fast short-pitched balls at the batsman standing clear of his wicket.'

The M.C.C. Committee have further ruled that Umpires in the 1st and 2nd Class County Competitions be instructed that they will be strongly supported by the M.C.C. Committee in any action which they may take under Law 43 to prevent this type of bowling as now defined being practised.

At a meeting of the Advisory County Cricket Committee held to-day the Counties represented endorsed the above definition of 'a direct attack by the bowler on the batsman' and it was resolved that the County Committees and the County Captains would take the strongest possible steps to see that the type of bowling as now defined be in future eliminated from the game.

The M.C.C. Committee hope that these steps will suffice and that it will not be found necessary to take further action. (*1935*)

FROM NOTES BY THE EDITOR

No matter the angle from which it may be viewed it is next to impossible to regard the cricket season of 1934 as other than unpleasant. In using this word I am not referring to the fact that England lost the rubber in the Test Matches with Australia. That, after we had won four matches out of five in Australia in the winter of 1932–33, was a hard enough blow to our self-esteem; but the whole atmosphere of cricket in England was utterly foreign to the great traditions of the game. As a journalist, born and bred in cricket and in mature years coming under the influence of that great lover and writer of the game, Sydney Pardon, I deplored the attitude of a certain section of the Press in what seemed to me an insane desire constantly to stir up strife. […] One outcome of this was that the Australians themselves, who had come here perfectly prepared and hoping to go through the season without any bother or recurrence of the arguments surging around 'direct attack' bowling, proceeded through their programme of matches constantly on the look out for something which might occur to give them just cause for complaint. Happily the season was nearing its close before anything happened to rouse their feelings, but at Nottingham in August they were subjected to a form of attack in bowling which not only they themselves, but the majority of people in England, fondly imagined had been 'scotched'.

While, therefore, fourteen of the seventeen first-class county captains – the other three being represented – at a joint meeting of the Board of Control and the Advisory County Cricket Committee in November, 1933, came to an 'understanding' that they would not permit or countenance any form of bowling which was obviously a direct attack on the batsman, Mr A.W. Carr, the Nottinghamshire captain, whether he agreed with the 'understanding' or not, stated that not only was he opposed to 'direct attack' bowling but that neither Larwood nor Voce practised it. Consequently it was not in the least degree surprising that, influenced by his opinions, Voce and Larwood felt that they were justified in continuing to bowl on many occasions during the summer fast bumping leg-theory deliveries with the leg-side packed with fieldsmen. Larwood escaped censure; Voce, on the definite evidence of the umpires, exploited direct attack methods against both the Australians at Trent Bridge and Middlesex at Lord's, but it is important to note that Carr did not captain Nottinghamshire in either of these games. In each case complaint was made; the allegation was found proved and the Nottinghamshire Committee, as they were bound to do, apologised. Later on this Committee appointed two young amateurs G.F. Heane and S.D. Rhodes joint captains of the Nottinghamshire eleven for next season in place of A.W. Carr. This sequence of events led to a storm of protest in Nottingham and the county. A special general meeting was held at which a resolution of 'no confidence' in the Committee was passed. The Committee thereupon resigned en bloc.

I do not intend here to go into the question of what may happen – or by the time these lines appear in print what has happened – if the new Nottinghamshire Committee disavows the action of their predecessors, first in apologising and later on dispensing with the services of A.W. Carr. The effects may be far-reaching but, in any case, Nottinghamshire, unless they conform strictly to the agreement arrived at during the meeting in November, 1933, will have fewer friends among the other counties than they now possess. The thought of the glorious traditions of Nottinghamshire cricket, the history of which extends back for so many years, makes it hard to believe that such a state of affairs could have been brought about by a few men who placed their own individual conception of what they imagined was right and above-board in the spirit of cricket, against the considered opinion of practically the whole of the cricketers of England.

At the same time I do not hold the former Nottinghamshire Committee entirely blameless for the position in which they found themselves. With some feeling of confidence in their members I feel sure a statement could have been put forward, which, without betraying any secrets that should not have been made known generally, would have convinced those who clamoured for the heads of the Committee on a charger that the course taken was in the best interests of the County club. I would even go as far as to commend this paragraph with my suggestion to the attention of other County clubs and even to the M.C.C. They perhaps may not know it but they have many friends besides myself on the Press and a little well-judged confidence at times has before now smoothed over difficult situations. Even statesmen and politicians do not forever remain silent on important questions. Secrecy carried to excess begets mistrust. [...]

Perhaps, after all, it was as well. Possibly greater complications than those which arose in Nottinghamshire were avoided. After deep consideration, and carefully weighing up the effects of the disruption in English cricket together with contributory causes, I incline to the opinion that it would in the long run have been better if the Australians had postponed their visit until the echoes of the cable fencing between the M.C.C. and the Australian Board of Control died away. Test cricket then could have been resumed when both sides were in the mood to meet in the traditional sporting spirit which characterised the struggles of thirty or forty years ago. One little sentence more: let us get back to cricket as a game; compose our internal differences and, above all, go on to the field against Australia with the knowledge that we intend to 'play the game'. [...] (*1935*)

NOTTINGHAMSHIRE V. AUSTRALIANS

Played at Nottingham, Saturday, Monday, Tuesday, August 11, 13, 14, 1934. – A match rendered unpleasant by the antagonistic attitude of the spectators towards the visitors ended in a draw. The Australians, encountering 'direct attack' bowling for the first time during the tour, fared none too well. Woodfull and Brown began with a stand of 70, but afterwards only Woodfull and Chipperfield gave much trouble. During Voce's various spells of bowling, the Australian batsmen were obviously uncomfortable with short-pitched deliveries, and found themselves subjected to considerable barracking. Voce placed five men on the leg-side, four of them close to the batsman, and of his eight victims, five fell to catches in this 'leg-trap'. Although Wall, suffering from leg strain, retired from the game early in Nottinghamshire's innings, the county batted indifferently, the tourists gaining a lead of 54. The absence of Voce – stated to be suffering from sore shins – on Tuesday began a series of rumours, the crowd apparently attributing his withdrawal from the match to an Australian protest. Consequently, the atmosphere grew increasingly hostile, and when the Australians took the field for the last innings, they were greeted by a storm of booing. A fine partnership of 164 between Brown and Kippax enabled the tourists to declare, and Nottinghamshire, set 285 to get, never looked like succeeding.

AUSTRALIANS

W.M. Woodfull c Harris b Voce	81	– b Butler	1
W.A. Brown c Gunn b Voce	27	– not out	100
S.J. McCabe c Harris b Voce	10	– b Butler	43
A.F. Kippax c Hardstaff b Voce	7	– not out	75
L.S. Darling c Lilley b Voce	11		
A.G. Chipperfield c Harris b Voce	57		
E.H. Bromley b Butler	13		
B.A. Barnett c Lilley b Voce	1		
C.V. Grimmett c Hardstaff b Butler	0		
T.W. Wall c and b Voce	13		
L.O'B. Fleetwood-Smith not out	7		
B 6, l-b 3, n-b 1	10	B 5, w 2, n-b 4	11
	237		(Two wkts, dec.) **230**

NOTTINGHAMSHIRE

W.W. Keeton c Bromley b Wall 24	– b Fleetwood-Smith 17
C.B. Harris lbw, b Fleetwood-Smith 14	– c Darling b Grimmett 9
W. Walker lbw, b Grimmett 25	– c Grimmett b Fleetwood-Smith 8
J. Hardstaff lbw, b Grimmett 38	– c and b Grimmett 13
A. Staples lbw, b Grimmett 0	– c Bromley b Grimmett 9
R. Taylor b McCabe 1	– not out 16
G.V. Gunn run out 26	– c Grimmett b Fleetwood-Smith 29
B. Lilley b Grimmett 25	– not out 18
W. Voce c Bromley b McCabe 22	
F.G. Woodhead b McCabe 1	
H.J. Butler not out 1	
B 3, l-b 3 6	B 8, l-b 1 9
183	**(Six wkts) 128**

NOTTINGHAMSHIRE BOWLING

	Overs	Mdns	Runs	Wkts	Overs	Mdns	Runs	Wkts
Voce	23	6	66	8	2	0	2	0
Butler	16	4	43	2	15	3	50	2
Woodhead	7	3	23	0	7	1	31	0
Staples	10	0	43	0	17	2	54	0
Gunn	12	3	38	0	11	0	44	0
Harris	3	0	14	0	6	0	38	0

AUSTRALIANS BOWLING

	Overs	Mdns	Runs	Wkts	Overs	Mdns	Runs	Wkts
Wall	9	0	31	1				
McCabe	19.3	2	42	3	4	1	6	0
Grimmett	36	16	70	4	14	5	35	3
Fleetwood.Smith	14	6	34	1	20	0	47	3
Darling					6	2	8	0
Chipperfield					5	0	21	0
Bromley					3	1	2	0

Umpires: W.A. Buswell and J.W. Hitch.

JARDINE, MR DOUGLAS ROBERT, who died in Switzerland on June 18, 1958, aged 57, was one of England's best captains and a leading amateur batsman of his time. He caught tick fever while visiting Southern Rhodesia in 1957 and thenceforward had been in poor health.

Son of M.R. Jardine, himself an Oxford Blue, Douglas Jardine was born at Bombay and educated at Winchester, where he was in the XI for three years, being captain in the last, 1919, when he headed the batting figures with 997 runs, average 66.46. Going up to New College, Oxford, he got his Blue as a Freshman and played against Cambridge in 1920, 1921 and 1923 without achieving anything out of the ordinary. He missed the 1922 University match because of a damaged knee. In 1923 he began to play for Surrey and in 1932 took over the captaincy from P.G.H. Fender.

He went to Australia in 1928–29 with the M.C.C. team under A.P.F. Chapman, taking part in all five Test matches. To England's success by 12 runs in the fourth Test he made a big contribution when scoring 98 and sharing with W.R. Hammond in the third-wicket partnership of 262. He also enjoyed the distinction of hitting three centuries in successive innings, against Western Australia, Victoria and New South Wales.

Four years later he captained the M.C.C. side in Australia in what was probably the most controversial tour in history. England won four of the five Tests, but it was the methods they employed rather than the results which caused so much discussion and acrimony. H. Larwood and W. Voce, the Nottinghamshire fast bowlers, exploited 'leg-theory', or what came to be known as 'body-line' bowling to a packed leg-side field. The Australians and others considered this means of attack placed batsmen at a grave disadvantage because they had either to risk being struck on the head or body by persistently short-pitched balls or, if they attempted to play them, were virtually certain to be caught by the close-set field.

Strongly-worded cables passed between the Australian Board of Control, who asserted that 'body-line bowling has assumed such proportions as to menace the best interests of the game, making protection of the body the main consideration', and the M.C.C. The Australians threatened to call off the projected tour of England in 1934. M.C.C. at length agreed that 'a form of bowling which is obviously a direct attack by the bowler upon the batsman would be an offence against the spirit of the game.' Jardine always defended his tactics and in a book he wrote about the tour described allegations that the England bowlers directed their attack with the intention of causing physical harm as 'stupid and patently untruthful'. [...]

Meanwhile in 1933, however, fast leg-theory had been employed by both England and the West Indies in the second Test match at Old Trafford. Jardine, who always held that this type of attack could be successfully countered by a resolute batsman, set out to prove the accuracy of his contention. For nearly five hours he faced the hostile pace of L.N. Constantine and E.A. Martindale and he hit 127, his first and only century in a Test match. In the process, he took much physical punishment, but 'The Iron Duke', as he was sometimes called, had proved his point to his own satisfaction.

Jardine captained the M.C.C. team in India the following winter, but thereafter his appearances on the field became fewer till in 1937 he dropped out of first-class cricket altogether. At the same time he maintained his interest in the game, being President of the Oxford University C.C. from 1955 to 1957 and making occasional contributions to the Press. In 1953 he became the first President of the Association of Cricket Umpires.

Six feet tall, he possessed a very strong defence and was specially skilful in on-side strokes. In 22 Test match appearances he hit 1,296 runs, average 48, and held 26 catches. During his career his runs numbered 14,821, average 46.90, the highest of his 35 centuries being 214 not out against Tasmania in 1928–29. Extremely proud of his Oxford associations, he always wore a Harlequin cap.

Tributes included:

Sir Pelham Warner: 'In my humble opinion, Jardine was a very fine captain, both on and off the field, and in the committee-room he was also extremely good. If ever there was a cricket match between England and the rest of the world and the fate of England depended upon its result, I would pick Jardine as England captain every time.'

Sir Jack Hobbs: 'I played with him a lot in the Surrey side and I feel that he will be chiefly remembered as a splendid skipper. As a captain, I would rank him second only to P.G.H. Fender. He was a great batsman – how great I do not think we quite appreciated at the time. I remember that he was the first man to refer to me as "The Master".'

W.E. Bowes: 'To me and every member of the 1932–33 M.C.C. side in Australia, Douglas Jardine was the greatest captain England ever had. A great fighter, a grand friend and an unforgiving enemy.'

R. Aird: 'Jardine was a great player and captain and a man of character who, like all men of character, was not liked by everybody. He did what he set out to do, as when his side won the "Ashes" in Australia in 1932–33, even if the method he adopted did not meet with general approval. His sound, solid batting inspired confidence in his colleagues.'

THE LAST OF THE LINE

By David Frith

The generations slip gently away. All the Edwardian Golden Age cricketers are gone. And in 1995, within 93 days, the last two truly eminent English survivors of the 1920s and 1930s died. R.E.S. Wyatt and Harold Larwood were not the last living pre-war Test cricketers, but they were clearly the most outstanding of the oldest soldiers, and symbolic of the two English divisions, the two castes: amateur and professional, Gentleman and Player.

All about them was contrast: their backgrounds, their speech, their education, their financial standing. Yet united they stood as two of the toughest and most resilient cricketers ever to have represented England: Larwood (H.), the Nottinghamshire express bowler, and Mr R.E.S. Wyatt, the very serious Warwickshire and later Worcestershire captain, who was vice-captain during England's notorious 1932–33 'Body-line' tour of Australia.

The former miner finished that explosive venture with a broken foot, which might have been coupled with a broken heart had he been made of lesser stuff, for he was expected to shoulder all the blame when those who ran English cricket finally came to comprehend the malodorous nature of D.R. Jardine's strategy.

Larwood was accessible in his Sydney home, where he spent more than half his life after emigrating in 1950 with his wife Lois and their five daughters. In short-sleeved shirt, braces and slippers, liberated from the drudgery of a sweet-shop in Blackpool, he would tell visitors of his pride in his achievements as a cricketer, of his respect for his vilified skipper, of his undying love for his homeland and his gratitude to Australia, where he had once been hated and abused during that acrimonious 1932–33 tour, when his bumpers crashed into Australian flesh. He never lost that sense of wonder at the warmth of welcome extended to him by his former adversaries, though in truth Australia was proud to accommodate a sporting icon of such dimension and vintage. England had been the losers, not just in their refusal to open the way for Larwood's return to the Test side later in the 1930s.

In a faintly anachronistic panama hat, and latterly in need of sturdy walking-sticks, Mr Wyatt was also accessible whenever he left his remote home in Cornwall to watch cricket or attend functions in the metropolis. In spite of his physical discomfort he journeyed till the end with his wife Mollie – South Africa in 1989, Lord's summer after summer, at ease in Paul Getty's box in the new Mound Stand. From that vantage-point, the action out in the middle gradually became a blur, though the memory – of olden days if not of last week – never failed. Didn't Percy Chapman make a century here against Australia in 1930 when Bob Wyatt was not playing? Yes – missed before he'd scored a run!

The nonagenarian with the basset-hound eyes and slightly glottal voice, in common with the old fast bowler who now lived on the other side of the world, was firm in his opinions. Mr Wyatt loved theory. He would talk at length and with passionate conviction on the iniquities of the lbw law (among other things, he believed it discouraged backplay).

Larwood, for his part, was good on whether a batsman stood up to fast bowling or revealed a shortfall in courage. At his most animated he could still be scathing in the matter of Australian heart in that particular Test series with which, alas, he will always be linked. Always, though, he referred to his old captain as Mr Jardine (or 'the Skipper') and to the MCC vice-captain as Mr Wyatt. Decades in Australia's egalitarian environment came too late for him to throw off the code of etiquette into which he had been born in 1904.

These two old cricketers were characteristic of the two classes of pre-war English life which coalesced into an often formidable Test team, rather as a horse and jockey become one for the purpose of their challenge. Those who made the acquaintance of Larwood and Mr Wyatt over the past half-century could only study photographs or close their eyes to imagine what they were like all those years ago.

For Mr Wyatt, one would fancy a bright blazer, an upturned shirt collar, a period cottage adorned with climbing roses, a pair of red setters reclining on the lawn, and a fairly fine motor-car in the garage. There might also, among the mail on his hall carpet, have been some sort of medical report following the latest of his countless injuries. And a disputatious letter from a club committeeman.

For Larwood, picture a foaming tankard of beer and a cigarette, a respectable suit and a respectable trilby hat, and a virile ease among his fellow professionals which might quickly tense up when any of the officer class came by. It would take little imagination to discern for which political party each of them might have voted.

Mr Wyatt and Larwood, at opposite ends of the social and economic scales in the 1920s, when both were first chosen to play for England, could scarcely have been further apart physically from 1950 onwards, with the Larwood family resident 12,000 miles away, where so many of the disillusioned have thrown off their shackles.

That they held each other in deep respect is beyond question. Visualise cricket's 1995 Legion of the Departed as they shuffled up the steps of the Greatest Pavilion: 'After you, Lol …' 'Naw, after you, Mr Wyatt …'

If there was any final imbalance, it was that Prime Minister John Major, he who wished to create a classless society, gave Harold Larwood an MBE by way of long-overdue atonement. Bob Wyatt was never thus recognised. It was as illogical and unjust as Larwood's ostracism by Lord's following Bodyline. (*1996*)

1 6

THE PACKER CASE

Sometimes, upheaval is nearer than you think. Just as 1977 yielded both the Queen's Silver Jubilee and the Sex Pistols' 'God Save the Queen', so did it feature not only the Centenary Test but Kerry Packer's World Series Cricket: a celebration of the old and a shock of the new. Indeed, it was in the course of Test cricket marking its first century that Packer's agents were most active in what remains the most extraordinary recruiting drive in the game's history.

The chain of events begins in May 1977, when it was revealed that Packer had recruited the thirty-five best international cricketers money could buy for a series of matches to be screened by his Channel Nine television network. 'The Packer Case', as *Wisden* called it, whose unprecedented consequence was two seasons in which official and unofficial versions of the game competed for the Australian public's attention, dominated the pages of the almanack for the next three years, while its after-effects have since been endlessly debated.

For an essentially conservative enterprise, *Wisden* was not as resistant to WSC as it might have been. Editor Norman Preston twigged immediately that 'the public will pronounce the verdict' – something overlooked by many who assumed they knew the verdict in advance. He also gave the first floodlit game, one of WSC's most influential innovations, a cordial reception: 'It is possible that night cricket has come to stay in Australia.' And, given that WSC fixtures were not classified first-class and had been officially 'disapproved' by the International Cricket Conference at Lord's, Preston's decision to report their scores, if not to report the matches themselves, was a pretty fair one.

In that first summer, 1977–78, official cricket prospered in Australia. The national team, rebuilt from young talent that Packer had not recruited, was led to a 3–2 win against India by Bob Simpson, who for many assumed the role of a sporting Cincinnatus. WSC, meantime, struggled to find an audience, despite its galaxy of talent and grandeur of design. But Simpson's colts found the going harder in the West Indies, both politically and professionally, and the summer of 1978–79 found roles reversed: while an inexperienced Test side was routed by England, WSC went from strength to strength. Packer's strategy, embodied in the advertising jingle 'C'mon Aussie C'mon', was to make WSC look more like official cricket rather than less, to present the WSC Australian XI as more truly the representative team of the nation than its Australian Cricket Board equivalent. The Chappells, Dennis Lillee and Rod Marsh were a persuasive unit. As Gordon Ross put it in his third instalment of 'The Packer Case': 'The Australian public (and who can blame them?) have no stomach for the second best in sport, and this to a measurable degree was reflected in attendances.'

The board, without the wherewithal to withstand its barren summer, was left to sue for peace with Packer. In May 1979, in return for him disbanding WSC, it agreed to extend to Channel Nine the exclusive broadcasting and promotional rights for international cricket in this country – Ross compared the board to 'a very small dog, with Packer as a very large tail'. Despite ACB chairman Bob Parish's spirited self-defence in *Wisden* 1984, the remark now seems prescient.

—GH

FROM NOTES BY THE EDITOR

ASHES FOR ENGLAND IN JUBILEE YEAR

The summer of 1977 will be remembered by most people for the Queen's Silver Jubilee. For lovers of cricket there were two other important topics. First, England won back The Ashes and secondly, there came the announcement in May that Kerry Packer, the Australian newspaper and television magnate, had secretly signed up at fabulous fees thirty-five Test stars from England, Australia, the West Indies, South Africa and Pakistan.

THE CENTENARY TEST

Earlier in the year at Melbourne, Australia and England had celebrated the centenary of the first Test Match in that city in 1877. It was a wonderful occasion with 200 former Test players present and it produced some splendid cricket. Many Australians had by then made up their minds to break with tradition to earn as much as they could from the game whatever the consequences. Mr Packer's eyes may have been opened wider to the amount which big cricket itself could attract by the happenings at Melbourne, but this could not be put forward as the reason for his determination to skim the game of its cream. The lack of response from the Australian Cricket Board to his overtures for TV rights for his Channel Nine Commercial Station was clearly at the root of the trouble, and this was further illustrated both during Mr Packer's visit to Lord's to meet the International Cricket Conference and the protracted High Court case in London in which Mr Justice Slade came down heavily against the cricket authorities. By then the world of cricket outside Australia had been drawn into an intricate and complicated web of other people's making.

THE PUBLIC WILL DECIDE

No one can be positive for the time being about the success or failure of Mr Packer's venture. It is said that he would be willing to spend as much as nine million Australian dollars to put his World Series Cricket firmly on the map, but in the end it will be the public who will pronounce the verdict, mainly by their attendance at his matches and the time they devote to his TV presentations. The big test will come at the end of the year when England visit Australia for cricket of the traditional kind in another struggle for the Ashes.

Moreover the England selectors will have to bear this tour in mind when picking the teams to face Pakistan and New Zealand in the dual tours this summer. I cannot see how room can be made for the Packer men like Greig, Underwood, Knott, Woolmer and Amiss when they will not be available later to play in Australia, unless before then there is a compromise, which is possible.

As things stand at the time of writing at the New Year no solution would appear to be in sight and the cricket authorities, particularly those in England, who spend thousands of pounds raising young talent to the top level, run the risk of losing players to any rich entrepreneur, for Packer could only be the first in the line. I feel that those who signed for Packer were placed in a dilemma – loyalty to those that nurtured them or the attraction of financial reward for playing another kind of cricket that excludes them from first-class recognition because it is outside the bounds of the International Cricket Conference. [...] (1978)

THE PACKER CASE

By Gordon Ross

First news of what was to become, virtually, 'The Packer Explosion', came from South Africa towards the end of April 1977 when South Africa's *Sunday Times* broke the news that four South African cricketers had signed lucrative contracts to play an eight-week series of matches throughout the world. It was said that when the team visited South Africa and played local teams it would have immeasurable benefits for the game there.

In the middle of May, *The Bulletin*, Australia's 97-year-old magazine owned by The Australian Consolidated Press Limited (chairman, Kerry Packer) announced the completion of a huge sporting deal in which thirty-five top cricketers had been signed for three years to play specially arranged matches, beginning with a series of six five-day Test matches, six one-day games, and six three-day round robin tournaments in Australia in 1977–78. Prize money would be $100,000. The deal had been put together by JP Sports and Television Corporation Limited, proprietors of Channel 9 in Sydney (Chairman, Kerry Packer).

The thirty-five players signed up were:

Eighteen Australian and seventeen from Overseas, chosen by Ian Chappell and Tony Greig; I.M. Chappell (Captain), R.J. Bright, G.S. Chappell, I.C. Davis, R. Edwards, G.J. Gilmour, D.W. Hookes, D.K. Lillee, M.F. Malone, R.W. Marsh, R.B. McCosker, K.J. O'Keeffe, L.S. Pascoe, I.R. Redpath, R.D. Robinson, J.R. Thomson, M. H.N. Walker, K.D. Walters.

A.W. Greig (Captain), Asif Iqbal, E.J. Barlow, D.L. Hobson, M.A. Holding, Imran Khan, A.P.E. Knott, C.H. Lloyd, Majid Khan, Mushtaq Mohammad, R.G. Pollock, M.J. Procter, B.A. Richards, I.V.A. Richards, A.M.E. Roberts, J.A. Snow, D.L. Underwood.

G. Boycott was invited to take part in the scheme but declined. Richie Benaud and his Sports Consultancy Company were engaged in the management of the series. Many of the signings were carried out during the Centenary Test match in Melbourne, and the New Zealand–Australia series. Austin Robertson and John Kitto (Secretary and Attorney of the Television Corporation Group) flew to West Indies where West Indies were playing Pakistan, and then to Britain to finalise the arrangements with the English and South African players.

The Australian team was already in England. The Manager, Len Maddocks, was quoted as having said: 'I do not envisage the present development having a detrimental effect upon this tour. But if any of them play for a side contrary to the jurisdiction of the Australian Board, they will place their careers in jeopardy.'

On May 13 the Cricket Council issued a statement at the end of an emergency meeting to the effect that Greig was not to be considered as England's captain in the forthcoming series against Australia. The statement went on: 'His action has inevitably impaired the trust which existed between the cricket authorities and the Captain of the England side.' F.R. Brown, Chairman of the Council, added: 'The captaincy of the England team involves close liaison with the selectors in the management, selection and development of England players for the future and clearly Greig is unlikely to be able to do this as his stated intention is to be contracted elsewhere during the next three winters.'

On May 25 it was announced from Lord's that a special meeting of full and foundation members of the International Cricket Conference would be held at Lord's on June 14 to discuss the situation, and the next day the Test and County Cricket Board said that the selection committee should pick England sides this summer strictly on merit, which obviously meant that Greig, Knott and Underwood could play.

At the end of May, Packer arrived in England, and at a Press Conference, said: 'It is not a pirate series but a Super-Test Series. I have sent telegrams to all the cricketing bodies but they don't reply. I am willing to compromise but time is running out.' He referred to cricket as the easiest sport in the world to take over, as nobody had bothered to pay the players what they were worth.

At this point the only cricket subject being discussed from the highest Committee Room in the land to the Saloon Bar of the tiniest inn, was 'Packer', and from all the multifarious points raised, one was likely to be proved the dominant factor in the end. In this age of extreme partisanship, had non-partisanship cricket any future? Does the world not want to see England beat Australia, or Arsenal beat Tottenham, or England beat Wales at Twickenham – or vice versa, according to particular loyalties? Could a collection of players, however great, stimulate public interest, when there was nothing on the end of it, except a considerable amount of money for the participants? The fact that tennis players and golfers are a constant attraction was irrelevant; they are individuals playing for no-one but themselves. And moreover, the whole crux of this matter was linked to big business – the business of television, and not so much to the furtherance of cricket or cricketers.

Mr Packer, as Chairman of Channel 9 of Australia, was bitterly disappointed that an offer he had made to the Australian Board of Control for television rights for conventional test cricket had not been given the due consideration which Mr Packer felt the offer had merited. Out of this frustration, his scheme was born and nurtured.

Meanwhile, unanimous agreement on their attitude to Packer's television circus was reached at the emergency meeting of the International Cricket Conference on June 14. Mr Packer, who left Heathrow that evening for the United States, was to be invited to discuss his plans with representatives of the ICC at the earliest possible moment. This meeting was arranged for June 23, but negotiation was not found possible on one salient point – Mr Packer demanded exclusive television rights from the Australian Board of Control from 1981 when their present contract with the Australian Broadcasting Commission ended. The ICC representatives told him that it would be totally wrong in principle if this were taken as a condition of agreement. The representatives of all the countries present were unanimous that no member country should be asked to submit to such a demand. The ICC's five conditions were:

1. Programme and venues of the circus to be acceptable to the home authority, and the length of programme not to exceed six weeks. Matches under home authority and the laws of cricket.
2. No player to participate without the permission of his home authority, who would not withhold it unreasonably.
3. No teams to be represented as national. That is, not Australia, possibly 'an Australian XI'.
4. Players contracted to Mr Packer to be available for Tests, first-class fixtures and other home-authority sponsored matches.
5. The home authority must be able to honour all contractual commitments to existing sponsors and advertisers.

Afterwards, Packer said: 'I will take no steps at all to help anyone. It isn't 40 players, it's 51.' It seemed clear that his purpose in signing up the players was essentially as a bargaining weapon to help him to secure the exclusive television rights he so badly wanted. Names of other players to have joined Packer were being announced from day to day – D.L. Amiss, A.I. Kallicharran, C.L. King, B.D. Julien, C.G. Greenidge. At the crucial meeting at Lord's on July 26 the ICC tabled three principal resolutions:

1. No player, who after Oct. 1, 1977, has played or has made himself available to play in a match previously disapproved by the Conference, shall thereafter be eligible to play in any Test match without the express consent of the Conference, to be given only on the application of the governing body for cricket of his country.
2. Any match arranged or to be arranged by J.P. Sports (PTY) Ltd., Mr Kerry Packer, Mr Richie Benaud or associated companies or persons, to take place in Australia or elsewhere between Oct. 1, 1977 and March 31, 1979 is disapproved.
3. Matches are liable to be disapproved if so arranged as to have the probable result that invitations to play in such matches will conflict with invitations which have been or may be received to play in first-class matches.

Zaheer Abbas was yet another to defect from cricketing authority, making the known total at that time forty-one, except that it was announced that Jeff Thomson had withdrawn, as indeed had Kallicharran, according to Mr David Lord, the Australian agent for them both. Packer swiftly answered this possible damage to his cause by setting out for England to talk to them. Lord, who also acted for Vivian Richards, said: 'I shall be offering them the same advice that I have given to Jeff. I am going to make it my job to see as many players as I can to try and persuade them to follow this example.'

Mr Packer then announced that he would apply for an injunction and damages in the High Court against the International Cricket Conference and Test and County

Cricket Board, and a similar action was to be started against Mr David Lord, claiming that Mr Lord had wrongfully induced players to break their contracts with the company. A temporary injunction was granted against Lord, but the TCCB gave an undertaking that no Packer player would be banned until the Court hearing.

The meeting at Lord's on August 10 produced the following conditions:

The TCCB's new sub-rules to meet the ICC request concerning players who are members of the Packer group are:

1. No player who, after October 1, 1977, has played or made himself available to play in a match previously disapproved by the Conference shall thereafter be eligible to play in any Test match without the express consent of the Conference.

2. No county shall be entitled to play in any competitive county cricket match, any cricketer who is and remains precluded from playing in a Test match on the above grounds before the expiration of a period of two years immediately following the date of the last day of the last match previously disapproved by the ICC in which he has played or made himself available to play.

This, of course, was subject to any High Court ruling which might follow. The name of Bob Woolmer was added to the list of Packer players. On Monday September 26 the High Court hearing began, and it lasted 31 days, the judgment, occupying 221 foolscap pages, took five and a half hours to deliver. Herewith are extracts from this massive document, summarised from *The Times*:

THE JUDGEMENT

Mr Justice Slade granted three English cricketers who had contracted to play for Mr Kerry Packer's World Series Cricket Pty Ltd. declarations that all the changes of the rules of the International Cricket Conference and all their resolutions banning them from Test cricket are *ultra vires* and void as being in unreasonable restraint of trade. So, too, are the Test and County Cricket Board's proposed rules governing qualification and registration of cricketers in Test and competitive and county cricket.

His Lordship also granted similar declarations to World Series Cricket.

The three cricketers, the individual plaintiffs, were Mr Tony Greig, Mr John Snow and Mr Michael Procter.

His Lordship said that as a result of the entry of World Series Cricket into cricket promotion, the International Cricket Conference in July, 1977, changed its rules in a manner which, if implemented, was likely effectively to disqualify any of the individual plaintiffs from playing in official international Test cricket for an indefinite time if he played in any cricket match organized by WSC The TCCB proposed, subject to the court's decision, to change its rules in a manner which was likely to disqualify any of the plaintiffs from playing in English county cricket for at least several years if he played WSC cricket.

In both actions the plaintiffs claimed that the new or proposed new rules would be legally invalid, and sought orders which would effectively prevent the ICC and TCCB from implementing them. WSC further claimed that those rules were or would be an unlawful inducement to a number of players who had entered into contracts to break them.

His Lordship considered that there were nine principal questions for ultimate decision.

(A)   Are the contracts between WSC and its players void?

(B)   Has WSC established that, as at August 3, and subject to any statutory immunity conferred by the 1974 Act, it has a good cause of action in tort against the ICC based on inducement of breach of contract?

(C)   Has WSC established that as at August 3 and subject as aforesaid, it had a good cause of action in tort against the TCCB based on the same grounds?

(D)   Subject to the provisions of the 1974 Act, are the new ICC rules void as being in restraint of trade?

(E)   Subject to aforesaid, are the proposed new TCCB rules void as being in restraint of trade?

(F)   Is the ICC an 'employers' association' within the 1974 Act?

(G)   Is the TCCB an 'employers' association'?

(H)   If either the ICC or TCCB or both be 'employers' associations', does this itself bar any cause of action that would otherwise exist?

(I)   In the light of the answers, what relief (if any) should be given to (i) the individual plaintiffs and (ii) WSC?

Summarizing the evidence, his Lordship commented that the evidence relating to the conditions under which cricketers worked, particularly in the United Kingdom, would have filled a book and would doubtless provide useful raw material for cricket historians of the future.

His Lordship could see the possible force of criticism directed against Mr Greig, who, when he signed his contract with WSC and recruited others to do so, had just completed a tour of Australia as captain of the England team, was still generally regarded as its captain and could have looked forward with reasonable confidence to his formal reappointment as such. There was obviously a case for saying that his responsibilities to the TCCB were of a rather special nature.

However, two points had to be borne in mind in regard to him and all the other United Kingdom players. (1) Neither the Cricket Council (the governing body of cricket in England recognized by the ICC) nor the TCCB had themselves entered into any kind of commitment, legal or otherwise, ever to offer employment to any of those players again. (2) The players themselves had entered into no contractual commitment with the Cricket Council or the TCCB precluding them from playing cricket for a private promoter.

In conclusion his Lordship said that Mr Michael Kempster, in his opening speech for the defendants, generously but correctly, acknowledged five positive beneficial effects which, on the evidence, had already been produced by the emergence of WSC as a promoter of cricket. First it had offered the promise of much greater rewards for star cricketers. Indeed, it had gone farther – it had offered secure, regular, remunerative employment in cricket to more than 50 cricketers, in most cases for three English winter seasons, at a time when most of them would otherwise have no guarantee of regular employment in the game. Secondly, it had already stimulated new sponsors for traditional cricket. Thirdly, it has brought back to the game in Australia several talented players. Fourthly, it, or the group of companies of which it formed part, had initiated a useful coaching scheme for young players in New South Wales. Fifthly, it had increased public interest in the game.

For all those acknowledged benefits, the defendants had held the strong opinion that ICC's effective monopoly in the promotion of first-class cricket at international level had been good for the game and that the emergence of WSC into the promotion field was bad for it. However, whether or not that opinion was correct had not been the question for the court. The question for decision had been whether the particular steps which the ICC and the TCCB took to combat what they regarded as the threat from WSC were legally justified. The long investigation had satisfied his Lordship that the positive demonstrable benefits that might be achieved by introducing the ICC and TCCB bans and applying them to players who had already committed themselves to contracts with WSC were at best somewhat speculative.

On the other hand there were demonstrable disadvantages if the bans were to be applied in that way. They would preclude the players concerned from entry into important fields of professional livelihood. They would subject them to the hardships and injustice of essentially retrospective legislation. They would deprive the public of any opportunity of seeing the players concerned playing in conventional cricket, either at Test or at English county level; for at least a number of years. By so depriving the public they would carry with them an appreciable risk of diminishing both public enthusiasm for conventional cricket and the receipts to be derived from it. Furthermore, the defendants by imposing the bans, in the form which they took and with the intentions which prompted them, acted without adequate regard to the fact that WSC had contractual rights with the players concerned, which were entitled to the protection of the law. The defendants acted in good faith and in what they considered to be the best interests of cricket. That, however, was not enough to justify in law the course which they had taken.

Judgment was given for the plaintiffs in both actions with costs.

BEARING THE COSTS

It was estimated that the costs to the defendants were likely to be about £200,000, and whilst this sort of figure was a severe blow to any organisation – certainly to the game of cricket, there were three cardinal factors to be borne in mind in connection with the financial administration of Test and County Cricket in this country. First, since the International Cricket Conference were co-defendants, it is assumed that they would bear some of the costs. Secondly, as a result of the Packer intervention, Cornhill moved in to sponsor Test cricket in England, a sum of one million pounds spread over five years was mentioned, and not, apparently, being far from the mark, and thirdly, the Test and County Cricket Board received £150,000 from Mr Packer for the television rights for his Channel 9 coverage of the England v. Australia Test matches during the 1977 summer.

Whatever the net loss to the TCCB, it would be spread over the various beneficiaries from the TCCB's income for 1977 such as the seventeen first-class counties, the Minor Counties, Universities, and so on. Admittedly, the county budgets could not readily accommodate any deduction from their share, but overall the blow divided by at least twenty was brought down to more bearable proportions.

The defendants were given six weeks from the date of entering of the order to consider the possibility of an appeal. They no doubt took account of three important factors – the total lack of crowds at Packer's early matches in his series, and, although Packer brushed this aside as having no consequence because he was only interested in television reaction and ratings, one must take the ramifications of a lack of interest on the part of paying customers as being important. Secondly, that Australia beat a very good Indian side in three Tests without their Packer players, and thirdly that the England side held their own in Pakistan where both sides were without their Packer players. A good deal of water will have to flow under the bridge before a total clarification of all the implications, short, and long-term, is possible.

Early in February 1978, the International Cricket Conference and the TCCB decided not to appeal and agreed to share their burden of the costs.

WSC World XI v. WSC Australian XI

At Gloucester Park, Perth, January 27, 28, 29, 30, 1978. World XI won by an innings and 73 runs.

World XI

B.A. Richards c G. Chappell b Bright ...207	A.M.E. Roberts c G. Chappell
C.G. Greenidge c Marsh b Bright 140	b Gilmour 1
I.V.A. Richards c Walker b Lillee 177	W.W. Daniel b Bright 1
C.H. Lloyd c G. Chappell b Lillee 37	D.L. Underwood not out 0
Asif Iqbal c G. Chappell b Lillee 1	B 4, l-b 4, n-b 4 12
*A.W. Greig c Edwards b Lillee 14	
Imran Khan c Walker b Bright 15	1/369 2/461 3/481 4/552 **625**
†A.P.E. Knott c Walker b Bright 20	5/571 6/587 7/613 8/622 9/624

Note: Greenidge retired hurt at 234 for no wkt and resumed his innings at 481 for three.

Bowling: Lillee 27-1-149-4; Gilmour 33-3-141-1; Walker 14-1-115-0; Bright 30.3-3-149-5; I. Chappell 3-0-22-0; G. Chappell 6-0-37-0.

Australian XI

B.M. Laird c Knott b Imran 6	– b Imran 20
I.C. Davis c Knott b Roberts 2	– b Daniel 7
*I.M. Chappell c sub b Underwood 62	– not out 13
M.F. Kent c Knott b Imran 0	– c Greig b Imran 0
R. Edwards b Roberts 34	– c Roberts b Underwood 39
G.S. Chappell c Knott b Imran 174	– c I. Richards b Greig 26
†R.W. Marsh lbw b Roberts 27	– c Roberts b Underwood 23
G.J. Gilmour c Roberts b Underwood 9	– c I. Richards b Greig 13
R.J. Bright not out 41	– b Greig 0
D.K. Lillee lbw b Greig 1	– b Imran 8
M.H.N. Walker c Asif b Greig 10	– b Imran 4
B 10, l-b 3, w 2, n-b 12 27	B 3, n-b 3 6
1/3 2/19 3/19 4/73 5/150 **393**	1/18 2/23 3/30 4/91 **159**
6/209 7/251 8/367 9/368	5/102 6/126 7/136 8/136 9/155

Bowling: First Innings – Roberts 17-2-65-3; Imran 19-1-79-3; Daniel 10-1-59-0; Underwood 24-5-79-2; Greig 20.4- 1-75-2; Asif 2-0-9-0. Second Innings – Roberts 8-2-18-0; Imran 7-1-24-4; Daniel 7-1-30-1; Underwood 15-3-54-2; Greig 10-2-27-3.

INDIA IN AUSTRALIA, 1977–78

By D.J. Rutnagur

India's third tour of Australia was not seen to suffer from competition by the newly-established World Series Cricket. The Australian public soon gave its vote to the traditional game and, overall, the Test matches drew bigger attendances than on the Indians' previous visit, in 1967–68. Only in Perth, the newest of Australia's Test venues, were the crowds of disappointing size. Both Australia and India responded magnificently to the challenge of WSC and to the enthusiasm of those who watched and followed the Test matches. The tourists kindled the flame of public interest by winning every State game leading up to the first Test.

In what turned out to be a fascinating series, Australia won the first two Tests, but both in desperately close finishes. In each of them, also, fortunes ebbed and flowed intriguingly from day to day, sometimes from session to session. Moreover, both sides batted attractively and bowled positively. Hence, the series was made. Then India won the third and fourth Tests, both more decisively than Australia had won the two preceding encounters. The two-all situation set up the series for a glorious finish, and the finale was indeed dramatic and exciting. Australia won the six-day final Test on the last day after India, in an heroic second-innings recovery, had made a record losing score of 445.

Even before it was dismembered by Packer, the Australian side had looked a poor collection during the tour of England in the summer of 1977. Obviously, the hurriedly rebuilt teams that Australia fielded were of moderate class, and much credit for Australia winning the series under these circumstances is due to the inspiring leadership and personal achievement of Bobby Simpson who, at 41, came out of a ten-year retirement to aid Australian cricket in its worst crisis ever. His experienced and able captaincy was not Simpson's only contribution to Australia's success. His proven expertise in playing spin bowling made him the pillar of Australia's batting. [...] Simpson's influence on the series extended beyond his tactical success and the accumulation of runs. He instilled in his young team a feeling of pride in wearing the baggy green cap and also re-introduced all the decent, old-fashioned values traditionally associated with the game. Under Simpson, the Australian side conducted themselves on and off the field with impressive dignity, were smartly dressed, and were courteous to all. The Indians, also, were admirable in this respect. [...]

AUSTRALIA IN THE WEST INDIES, 1977–78

By Tony Cozier

Australia's fourth tour of the West Indies was depressingly dominated more by events off the field than on them. The inauguration of Kerry Packer's World Series Cricket, which had created such chaos throughout the cricket world, had considerable influence over the series.

The Australian Cricket Board of Control adamantly refused to select any of the Packer players, with the result that they sent a young and inexperienced party under the captaincy of the veteran Bobby Simpson, recalled from retirement to lead his country in the earlier series against India. The West Indies Board, on the other hand, decided they would choose players contracted to WSC on the grounds that they had never refused to play for their country and had now made themselves available.

With the two teams thus constituted, West Indies proved far superior in the first two Tests, which they won by large margins inside three days. By the end of the Second Test, however, it was clear that relations between the Board and the Packer players were becoming strained.

The Board was 'to say the least, extremely disappointed' when three young players – Austin, Croft, and Haynes – signed contracts with WSC despite an earlier, verbal assurance not to do so. The West Indies Board felt the Packer representatives were militant in their financial negotiations, seeking substantial increases just before the First Test. For their part, the players were irritated by the decision to relieve Deryck Murray, their spokesman, of the vice-captaincy in mysterious circumstances on the opening day of the series. They detected a coldness in the Board's attitude towards them and, when they were handed a March 23 deadline to state whether they would be available for the tour of India and Sri Lanka later in the year, saw it as unwarranted pressure because of their Packer associations.

The Board, however, simply stated that they wanted to be prepared for the India and Sri Lanka trip. When they received no definite response by the date set, the selectors decided to replace three WSC signees – Austin, Haynes, and Deryck Murray – with three who had no such ties – Gomes, David Murray, and Williams – for the third Test. Clive Lloyd made an almost immediate protest, announcing his resignation from the captaincy he had held for 29 successive Tests since 1974. It was time the West Indies Board made 'very clear the principles underlying the selection of the present team,' he said. Within two days, other West Indian players contracted to WSC also withdrew from the team in solidarity with Lloyd. Although a meeting between Lloyd, some of the players involved, and the West Indies Board – headed by the president, Mr J.B. Stollmeyer – was held on the eve of the third Test, nothing was resolved. The West Indies then named a new team, appointing Alvin Kallicharran captain for the remaining three Tests.

The impasse caused an emotional explosion throughout the Caribbean with heated arguments raging everywhere. Kerry Packer himself flew to the West Indies to meet with his players and state his case. Groups in Trinidad and Jamaica called for the public to boycott the fourth and fifth Tests; the Board and the selectors were widely criticised and urged to resign. In response, the Board declared that they had bent over backwards to accommodate the Packer players and charged that they were 'vacillating' and 'were under the domination of WSC'. With the teams more evenly matched as a result of the dispute, the final three Tests produced far keener cricket. [...]

THE PACKER CASE

By Gordon Ross

[...] It was announced from Lord's on Thursday, February 2, 1978 that an appeal against the High Court ruling by Mr Justice Slade the previous November in favour of Mr Kerry Packer and some of his players would not be in the best interests of international cricket. Mr Jack Bailey, secretary of the International Cricket Conference, said that once the delegates had agreed there should be no appeal – the first item on the agenda – all discussions that followed were in the light of the High Court judgment. No pressure could be brought to bear upon member countries about whom they should select to play; the ICC could not make stipulations concerning this aspect. Mr Bailey told a Press conference that, though it was felt that both the ICC and the TCCB had reasonable grounds for appeal, there was no guarantee of success, and to appeal just for the sake of appeal would be churlish:

The selectors of individual countries will, as now, be responsible for making their own decisions and there may be different criteria used – consideration of the short-term or long-term requirements of that particular country.

As far as the TCCB were concerned, Peter Lush, the spokesman on their behalf, said that the selection by counties of World Series Cricket players was a matter for individual members; just as, in the case of the ICC, the TCCB was not in a position to make recommendations. At this moment, six England players were under contract to WSC – Greig, who had just been relieved of the Sussex captaincy because of derogatory remarks made about Boycott – Amiss, Snow, Knott, Underwood, and Woolmer. The ICC meeting, which lasted two days, agreed that the costs of the High Court hearing would be divided between the ICC and the TCCB. The question of making contractual arrangements with players had been aired, but no collective decision was taken. If individual countries were approached by WSC, any discussion would have to be with the ICC as a whole.

Meanwhile, WSC were continuing to sign up players; or rumour had it that they were. On February 3 *The Sydney Sun* claimed that Sunil Gavaskar and Bishan Bedi were to be offered lucrative contracts for the next season, though Bedi said he knew of no such offer, and was loathe to comment further until he did. On February 7 it was revealed that Greig and Sydney promoter David Lord had had lengthy discussions with a view of effecting a compromise between WSC and the ICC, with a new international series, under the auspices of the ICC, to be played in addition to scheduled Test series. In what struck observers as a most curious finale to their discussions, it was stated that Greig had not signed the joint statement because it did not constitute a perfectly true expression of his views. The Australian Board's view has never wavered from its original course; that if WSC wished to re-open talks with the Board, it should do so through the ICC in London. On this they stood firm.

In any event, a joint statement not signed by the second party hardly constituted the basis for serious discussion. On the same day, in England, a meeting of Kent's full committee decided to have back all their four Packer players should they wish to return. Hampshire announced at the same time that Greenidge, Richards, and Roberts would again be playing for them in the summer. Inevitably, all shades of opinion were being expressed. A letter to *The Times* from Surrey's chairman, Raman Subba Row, advocated a genuine discussion between the ICC and the rival system; two days later, Oliver Popplewell, QC, in a letter to the same newspaper, stated that the authorities should stand firm and beware the siren song of compromise until such time as Kerry Packer notified them that players signed by him would be released for the whole of the England tour of Australia in 1978–79.

During these diverse expressions of opinion, the WSC Packer matches were taking place in Australia to attendances considerably smaller than Packer would have hoped for. The exceptions were matches played in floodlight, which obviously had a novelty attraction and were well patronised. Before a crowd of 2,716 WSC Australia prevented a run of three defeats at the hands of the WSC World XI by winning by 41 runs. Comparative failure by Australia, in any sport, is something that appeals less to Australian crowds than to those in most other cricketing countries, and the Australian team's performance clearly could not have aided the Packer cause.

The true financial picture of this first series may not emerge for some time – if ever – but estimates put the loss in excess of £2,000,000; derived from an outlay of some three and a half million, with receipts from advertising revenue about a million, and gate receipts of a shade under half a million. Packer's comment was: 'We are still amateurs, but we are more professional than we were, and will become even more professional.' It was said that the prize-money, worth $A201,500, had gone into a provident fund for three years, after which it would be paid out with interest. Still on the question of finance, it was apparently agreed, at a meeting between the Victorian Football League and Kerry Packer, that the mobile pitches at VFL Park would stay in place throughout the football season at an additional cost to WSC, who paid VFL $A850,000 for the use of the ground for three summers, with an original agreement to remove the pitches before the start of each football season.

When the dust was allowed to settle on this first adventure, followers of traditional cricket throughout the world had some comfort that this adventurer, Mr Kerry Packer, had clearly not met with the resounding success for which he had hoped. On the other hand, any new enterprise is subject to teething troubles. Moreover, Mr Packer's make-up is such that he was most unlikely to throw in the towel after a disastrous first round, and suffer a loss of pride as well as of money. In the end, of course, he may have to decide how much money he can afford to spend on pride. At a much later date a new managing director, Andrew Caro, emerged, clearly with the brief to make WSC pay, and to fight what, at that stage, appeared to be a battle with authority.

In Australia, one factor in the whole affair had remained constant – the unwavering line pursued by the Australian Board. Any opinion suggesting that the Australian Board might have taken a more conciliatory view of this rather ugly menace thrust upon them, holds little water when it is accepted that the Board, even if somewhat reluctantly, were party to the working arrangement proposed at the ICC meeting, which Packer turned down, out of hand. The Board knew well enough, after this, that they had a fight on their hands, and they prepared for the fray. Who could blame them? Australia's point of view was fairly and comprehensively put by Mr E.W. Swanton, in an article in *The Cricketer* of May 1978 entitled 'Bob Parish pumps home the facts.' Mr Parish, chairman of the Australian Cricket Board, was at great pains to point out, in a speech in his home state of Victoria, the enormous improvements in payments made to their players in recent years; long before Packer's arrival. […] Mr Parish, with a touch of irony, substantiated the improvement in the lot of the Australian cricketer by quoting from a book recently published by Greg Chappell, in which the former captain of Australia wrote: 'Cricketers' rewards have increased dramatically in a comparatively short time. In a matter of just two seasons the base Test payment doubled from $A200 to $A400. Sizeable bonuses have been handed out at the end of the past two series, provident fund money has been increased, cash endorsements are flowing as never before, and the Test team is now sponsored for three years. It's hardly surprising that Australia leads the way in providing a far better deal for cricketers.' Chappell's words seem to make a mockery of the well-worn cry that Establishments do little to improve the lot of the first-class cricketer. However, it is only fair to say that the advent of Packer was clearly instrumental in substantially improving the lot of the England Test player. Not, of course, from the purse of Mr Packer, but in the way the surrounding controversy brought into the public gaze the fact that perhaps the England Test player was inadequately rewarded for his labours on behalf of his country. So in one way, Greig's cry that what he was doing was for the good of all cricketers, and not just the élite, had a ring of truth about it; but possibly not in the precise way that Greig had contemplated.

Just as Australia was firm, Pakistan, too, was doing its best to follow the hard-line. When the Board of Control for Cricket in Pakistan announced the names of about 30 players to attend the training camp in preparation for the tour of England, Majid, Imran, Mushtaq, and Zaheer were omitted. The Board stated they were prepared to consider the Packer players, provided they could guarantee their availability to play for Pakistan, not only on the tour of England but for all future commitments. This, they could not give; and there followed a raging controversy, the result of which was a meeting called on March 26 under the chairmanship of the Chief Martial Law Administrator and attended by former Pakistan captains, prominent cricket organisers, and representatives from every province. At the end of it, the Administrator ruled that Packer players would not be included in the Pakistan team. There, it seemed, the matter was closed, but shortly before the team were due to leave, rumours spread that Miandad, Haroon, and Sarfraz had signed Packer contracts. This was at once denied by the Board, but suspicion lingered on. In the end, the air was cleared when a Packer representative announced that neither Miandad nor Haroon had signed any form of contract, and Sarfraz, in due course, announced that neither had he. The poor showing of the Pakistan team, deprived of the Packer players, was later to generate some re-thinking.

West Indies, perhaps the most vulnerable of all ICC members in the matter of cricket finance, was placed in an increasingly difficult position. The distance between the islands – 1,200 miles, for instance, between Jamaica and Barbados – and multifarious other problems have made it an intense struggle for any treasurer of the West Indies Board to make ends meet; and a West Indies team that was virtually a second team would impair this rickety financial structure even more. It is not surprising, therefore, that West Indies had taken the most moderate line with Packer players. The Board were against the original ICC ban, although subsequently voting for it in the interests of unity, and they decided to continue to play their Packer men, provided they made themselves available. Anyone with first-hand knowledge of West Indies cricket will readily understand their thinking. […] The international position at this moment was that Australia, England, and Pakistan were not playing Packer players, West Indies, though having done so, were now in line with the others; India, New Zealand and South Africa were not specifically concerned, though India and New Zealand could conceivably be in the future. South Africa, not playing Test cricket, would not.

An important factor was to affect the thinking of both the West Indies and Pakistan Boards; the opinion of cricket followers in both countries. Clearly, through-out the Caribbean, sympathy was with the Packer players; or more precisely with West Indies always fielding the best available side in Test cricket. The same applied in Pakistan; if anything, feeling was heightened by the palpably poor performance of the Pakistan side in England. Attempts were made by Pakistan's supporters to make martyrs out of the discarded Packer players and ridicule the team, at a time when it needed firm support. Clearly, something had to be done, especially by the West Indies Board who faced the stark reality of a huge financial loss on the series with Australia; it was rumoured to be in the region of £100,000.

It was not so much a turn-about, therefore, as facing reality when the West Indies Board recommended that dialogue between the International Cricket Conference and World Series Cricket be re-opened at the earliest opportunity; and, if necessary, on the initiative of the ICC. The second resolution offered the Board's services to initiate such discussions. Meanwhile, WSC, which had named Deryck Murray as its Caribbean representative, was writing to the clubs responsible for the major grounds in West Indies, plus Antigua and St Lucia, to set up a West Indies v. Australia WSC series in 1978–79. The West Indies Board were to have the enemy on their doorstep – if enemy they were to be – doing irreparable damage to the future of organised cricket in West Indies. It left the Board with virtually no option but to seek a peaceful solution.

World opinion and interest was now focussed on the International Cricket Conference meeting that was to begin at Lord's on Tuesday, July 25 1978. […] It sub-sequently transpired that David Clark and Jack Bailey had, prior to the meeting, gone to the United States to hear the WSC proposals for an amicable solution, both parties being particularly anxious that the meeting should be a matter of great secrecy. These proposals, given in detail below, are so ludicrous, as to evoke intense speculation as to what WSC hoped to achieve by them. Was it that Packer had no wish for an agree-ment, and was confident of his own future without any need to placate anyone in cricket? If he was looking for a middle-of-the-road settlement, then these absurd pro-posals would generate contempt rather than stimulate a mood of reconciliation and lead to sensible discussion. The Packer package was as follows.

WSC ask for fully representative teams (to be selected by WSC) to be available for WSC matches on the following basis:

(A) October-November: India, New Zealand and Pakistan to play a preliminary knockout competition in one of these countries to provide a winner to participate in the one-day internationals and 'super Test' series in Australia later in the season.

(B) December 22–January 24: Australia, England, West Indies and Pakistan (or whoever may be the winners of the preliminary competition) and a World XI to play in a series of one-day internationals, avoiding actual dates of official Test matches in Australia.

(C) February 2–March 12: Australia, England, West Indies and Pakistan (or whoever may be the winners of the preliminary competition) to play in a WSC 'super Test' series. These teams, plus a World XI, would also play further one-day internationals.

(D) Assuming Australia were winners, for approximately three weeks in March-April, May-June, September-October and October-November, the winners of the WSC Super-Test series to play in West Indies, England, India and Pakistan respectively.

The ICC gave their reasons for finding these proposals totally unacceptable, though elaboration was hardly necessary. [...]

Despite the two sides being poles apart, it was agreed that the dialogue should be continued, and that WSC be asked to reconsider their proposals. [...]

In England, at the end of the summer, attention was focused on two players at the opposite ends of the earth; Dennis Amiss in Warwickshire and Jeff Thomson in Australia. Amiss was told by Warwickshire that, as a Packer player, he would not be retained by the county in 1979. Thomson, despite being under contract to the official Australian Cricket Board, signed a three-year contract with World Series Cricket. It was announced that the Board would be seeking legal advice. [...]

Thomson's move represented yet another twist in his topsyturvy relationship with Packer. First he signed; then he withdrew on the advice of his agent, who was taken to court by Packer. Now, on the eve of an Ashes series, he has defected again in breach of another contract. The Australian Board are particularly unfortunate, because obviously Thomson was Australia's principal drawing-card in the series against England. Packer knew this well, and countered with a contract and a cheque book; in 1978, the two together seem to be a passport to anywhere.

Swiftly on the heels of Thomson's defection, the Australian Cricket Board issued the following statement:

'It was announced last Friday, September 29 that World Series Cricket had entered into a three-year contract with Mr Jeff Thomson despite its awareness that Mr Thomson had agreed to play only in matches controlled by the Board and state associations during the 1978–79 Australian season, and despite the publicity given to the fact that the Board had refused Mr Thomson's request that he be released from his contractual obligations to the Board.'

'The Board would naturally have preferred to resolve this matter without resort to the courts and, in order that Mr Thomson's contractual obligations to the Board should be respected, the Board sought an assurance from World Series Cricket that it would not select Mr Thomson to play cricket in any of its teams until after the conclusion of the Australian cricket season on March 31, 1979. World Series Cricket has declined to give such an assurance.'

In the subsequent court action, Mr Justice Kearney decided, after a twelve-day hearing, that Thomson, who has said he will never play Test cricket for Australia again, was bound by a contract he signed with the Australian Cricket Board earlier in the year. He could not, therefore, play for Packer until April. Judge Kearney said that some of Thomson's evidence before the court had been quite unreliable. He awarded costs against Thomson and World Series Cricket. Thomson replied by saying that he would probably spend the summer as a professional fisherman off the Queensland coast rather than play grade cricket; in the words of the famous Bing Crosby song – 'Gone Fishin'. [...] (1979)

WSC AUSTRALIA V. WSC WORLD XI

At Sydney, February 2, 3, 4, 1979. WSC World XI won by five wickets.

WSC AUSTRALIA

K.C. Wessels c Richards b Procter	.27	– c Greig b Procter	.1
B.M. Laird c Zaheer b le Roux	.2	– c Knott b Imran	.58
*I.M. Chappell c Imran b le Roux	.3	– b Imran	.19
I.R. Redpath c Knott b Rice	.4	– c Knott b Rice	.3
D.W. Hookes c Knott b Procter	.33	– b le Roux	.96
M.F. Kent c Greig b le Roux	.2	– run out	.4
†R.W. Marsh c Knott b le Roux	.6	– c Knott b Imran	.6
R.J. Bright not out	.27	– c Barlow b le Roux	.10
G.J. Gilmour c Greig b Procter	.27	– c sub b le Roux	.0
D.K. Lillee c Procter b Rice	.8	– not out	.9
L.S. Pascoe b le Roux	.25	– b le Roux	.2
L-b 7, w 1	.8	B 2, l-b 9	.11

1/7 2/11 3/25 4/66   **172**   1/8 2/29 3/32 4/166   **219**
5/70 6/74 7/80 8/119 9/135   5/172 6/179 7/203 8/203 9/211

Bowling: FIRST INNINGS – le Roux 18.4-3-57-5; Imran 9-2-35-0; Rice 13-2-38-2; Procter 7-2-33-3; Underwood 3-2-1-0. SECOND INNINGS – le Roux 17.3-4-44-4; Imran 22-5-60-3; Rice 12-2-26-1; Procter 18-2-45-1; Underwood 17-7-26-0; Greig 1-0-7-0.

WSC WORLD XI

B.A. Richards c Wessels b Pascoe	.28	– not out	.101
E.J. Barlow lbw b Lillee	.0	– c Gilmour b Lillee	.0
Zaheer Abbas c Laird b Gilmour	.18	– c Wessels b Gilmour	.37
C.E.B. Rice c Marsh b Gilmour	.18	– c Marsh b Pascoe	.4
Asif Iqbal c Bright b Gilmour	.8	– lbw b Gilmour	.3
M.J. Procter lbw b Lillee	.1	– b Bright	.44
*A.W. Greig c Marsh b Lillee	.0		
Imran Khan lbw b Lillee	.6	– not out	.17
†A.P.E. Knott b Gilmour	.9		
G.S. le Roux not out	.33		
D.L. Underwood b Lillee	.32		
L-b 9, n-b 6	.15	L-b 3, w 4, n-b 13	.20

1/8 2/39 3/69 4/71   **168**   1/3 2/57   (5 wkts) **226**
5/80 6/80 7/85 8/86 9/104   3/70 4/84 5/175

Bowling: FIRST INNINGS – Lillee 18.5-6-51-5; Gilmour 25-6-53-4; Pascoe 13-3-29-1; Bright 5-1-10-0; Hookes 3-1-10-0. SECOND INNINGS – Lillee 17-4-57-1; Gilmour 22-6-75-2; Pascoe 12-2-49-1; Bright 6-1-25-1; Chappell 0.1-0-0-0.

ENGLAND IN AUSTRALIA, 1978—79

[...] The competition from World Series Cricket put heavy demands on the Australian authorities, and the game at large suffered from an over-heavy pro-gramme and too much exposure on television. The well-oiled and professional WSC publicity machine often distracted attention from the Ashes series, and the public grew tired of supporting a losing team. An original error was perhaps made in play-ing two Tests on the over-worked ground at Sydney, where Packer was strongly established. A brave effort was made to stimulate interest with skydivers arriving with the match ball, or the coin, marching displays and athletic events during the intervals. But the essential factor of a winning Australian team was missing and atten-dances dropped to alarming levels by the final Test.

The public longed for better results and new heroes. One emerged in Rodney Hogg, the 27-year-old fast bowler, whose 41 wickets passed the record 36 taken by Arthur Mailey in the five-Test series against England in 1920–21. Fittingly Hogg broke the old record in front of his home crowd at Adelaide in the fifth Test, and he went to Sydney with a chance of beating C.V. Grimmett's Australian record of 44 wickets in a series, set up in South Africa in 1935–36. But Hogg, who had averaged eight a match for five Tests, could manage only one in conditions not suited to him.

Australia's euphoria, both after the victory in the third Test at Melbourne, and in Hogg's achievement, was short-lived. For the most part England had greater all-round strength, bowlers of genuine quality to make the fullest use of the varied pitches, were better led and more experienced, and always found a man for a crisis. The character of the team was shown in the way they fought out of desperate posi-tions in the fourth and fifth Tests, and their refusal to panic when Australia reduced the lead to 2–1. [...]

THE PACKER CASE

By Gordon Ross

[...] The supreme test for Packer's brand of jet-age razzamatazz cricket was to come in the winter of 1978–79 when an official Ashes series would take place in Australia at the same time. To seasoned and ardent followers of the game, Packer's offering was almost a masquerade of the game of cricket; to young Australians, however, especially when it was staged at night with the right sort of refreshment available, WSC was certainly having appeal. To them, whether or not it conformed to the accepted stan-dards of the game of cricket was immaterial, as long as it provided dramatic enter-tainment. So it seemed likely that as well as two separate series being played, they would be watched by two quite diverse species of Australian life.

Tony Lewis, reporting from Sydney, in January 1979, had this to say of the World Series Cricket game in a feature in the *Sunday Telegraph*:

> The most dangerous act in the entertainment business these days is not balancing on the high wire nor even putting a head in the lion's mouth. It is, without doubt, batting in Kerry Packer's Flying Circus. Fast bowling and repeated bouncers are destroying some of the best

batsmen we have ever seen. I have never seen so many bouncers bowled in a session as by the World team against the West Indies in a one-day game last week.

Tony Greig, in the *Sun Herald*, gave the true flavour of WSC cricket when he wrote:

The competition in WSC is so intense, teams can no longer afford to allow the opposition tailenders to hang around. Consequently the pace bowlers are dishing out an unprecedented amount of bouncers to the 'rabbits'. So it is pleasing to see that cricketers like Dennis Lillee and Garth le Roux have got the message, swallowed their pride, and are wearing helmets.

Are these cricketers, or mercenaries risking their skin for a sizeable bag of gold? *The Australian* reported the conclusion of one game as follows:

Last night's game ended dramatically when number 11 batsman, Joel Garner, playing with a broken left middle finger from an accident only nine days previously, was struck on the finger by a short ball from World XI all-rounder Clive Rice. Garner was in considerable pain and walked from the field, giving the World XI a win by 35 runs.

While the circus moved from place to place for one-day stands, the Ashes series was taking the course the Australian Cricket Board had reason to fear most. Their team, without the cream of its talent who had defected to Packer, were no match for a competent England side, except for a little splutter in the middle of the series when Australia won the third Test at Melbourne by 103 runs. England won the series by five Tests to that solitary one. The Australian public (and who can blame them?) have little stomach for the second best in sport, and this, to a measurable degree, was reflected in attendances. On the other hand, Packer gave the public free parking at Sydney, free transport out to the Waverley ground in Melbourne, and played his matches when spectators have time to watch – at night, and with a white ball which they can see better. In addition, with his television network, he promoted his stars as Hollywood used to theirs in the thirties. They became household names, and faces. It was all a personality cult.

There had been many estimates as to how much the Packer organisation had lost in its first season of WSC cricket. But much of the enormous outlay of capital expenditure would not apply a second time round. Although the figures were not available until March 1979, the Group's figures up to December 23, for the half-year, suggested that Packer cricket would open its account in the coming months of 1979 as follows.

'The holding company and operators of TCN Channel 9, Publishing and Broadcasting Holdings Ltd., yesterday confirmed the improvement with a solid 26 per cent profit rise from \$A6,657,000 to \$A8,407,000 in the half-year to December 23. While no figures for WSC are published in the interim report, if the rising attendances and substantially lower costs are any criteria, Mr Packer would have been laughing at the end of the six-month period. After losing at least \$A3.5 million in its first season WSC would now be close to breaking even and may even chalk up a maiden profit for the full year to June 30. But this depends largely on the financial success of the current WSC Australian tour of the West Indies.

'During the 1978–79 Australian season, WSC is said to have drawn about 730,000 people through the gates over 85 days of cricket. An estimated 580,000 people went through the turnstiles up to the end of Publishing and Broadcasting's interim period – December 23 – although it is not known how many of these were paying customers. But it is known that

WSC costs that season were substantially lower than the start-up costs of the previous year. Publishing and Broadcasting would also have benefited from better advertising response during the cricket coverage on Channel 9 and inter-state stations.'

So, at this stage, Packer seemed to have the edge over the Australian Cricket Board on the question of balancing budgets. The official Test series in what was once the greatest of sporting series – the Fight for The Ashes – had done financially worse than any series before it; much worse.

As far as Packer's next move was concerned, the spotlight switched to England, where there was considerable conjecture as to what might happen at the next Cricketers' Association meeting. Would the players in English domestic cricket, especially those who constituted the present England team, vote for a ban on Packer players? If they did, Packer had always threatened to bring his circus to England, and no-one ever doubted that Packer meant what he said. When Ian Davis, a bank employee, was refused leave to join Packer's tour to the West Indies, Packer sharpened his teeth and promptly withdrew two very substantial accounts.

From the start, there had been a strong feeling in cricket's higher echelon that Packer would never be able to find suitable grounds in Britain. But there was an equally strong body of confident opinion that he would. A great number of cricket grounds are not owned by the county which plays on them. Take, as an example, St Helen's, Swansea, which belongs to the City Corporation. Could they possibly refuse a glittering cash guarantee from Packer if he wanted to play there? Glamorgan could reply by refusing to play there again if the Corporation sold out to Packer, but would that matter as much to the Corporation as it might to Glamorgan.

Packer had always claimed that his first season of WSC was a disappointment, mainly because, to quote him, 'People had been so heavily indoctrinated against the idea.' The reprisal this time was to indoctrinate people in favour of the idea in preference to orthodox cricket. Almost every Australian newspaper had a former player who was on the Packer payroll banging the drum, and Packer's own television network remorselessly did the same. Still, not everyone was taken in. In a letter to an Australian newspaper, D.M. Elliston of Tasmania wrote: 'Are these posturing gum-chewing yahoos who participate in that rather poor standard television production could or perhaps mis-called World Series Cricket members of actors equity? With sadness I remember back to the days when some of them were cricketers.'

Packer admitted that he was fading himself into the background. 'I spent a disproportionate amount of time on cricket at first – it's only three or five per cent of the business.' He told Alan Lee in an interview on February that, if he had been asked 'Would you do it all over again?' he would probably have said 'No'. He was 'still prepared to compromise for the good of cricket, but the longer it goes on the less eager I shall be.' Alan Lee, writing of this interview in the *Sunday Telegraph*, concluded: 'World Series Cricket has grown beyond being a temporary intrusion on the game, and its threat to England adds completely new pressures to every county player at their crucial April meeting. Packer is awaiting their decision with something more than indifference.'

It was reported, however, that a group of England players who toured Australia were stepping up their campaign against players affiliated to World Series Cricket. They were proposing to the annual meeting of the Cricketers' Association in April

1979 that no county should be allowed to sign a player dismissed by another county because of his links with Kerry Packer. Additionally, they said that no county should recruit any further players on the WSC payroll, or known to be about to sign for the organisation. They would reserve the right to refuse to play against them.

Some England players, however, were hoping for an encouraging statement before the Association's meeting from the International Cricket Conference about talks held with Packer representatives in Australia. If these gave some hint of compromise, then their proposals could be dropped. But there were still proposals on the table which could seriously affect the coming Prudential World Cup, calling, as they did, for English players to refuse to play with or against any of the Packer men. Certainly, West Indies and Pakistan would select their Packer players, so confrontation and disruption of the World Cup was, at that stage, a serious possibility.

Packer, in the meantime, was turning his attention to the West Indies. It will be remembered that the half-year financial report had suggested that a possible profit on the cricket operation depended largely on the financial success of the current WSC Australian tour of the West Indies. There must be considerable sympathy for the West Indies Board who, by the nature of events in the Caribbean, operate within the framework of the most slender financial resources at the best of times. Their position had worsened considerably since the arrival of Packer. The 1977–78 series against Bobby Simpson's Australians, virtually a second team, was diluted still further when Clive Lloyd and his Packer players withdrew from the Test in Georgetown. The series, having become totally unrepresentative, resulted in heavy financial loss.

For season 1978–79, with the absence of the Packer men – a team and a half of them – and with West Indies committed to sending a team to India and Sri Lanka, there was not a single first-class match in any of the territories until the end of March. Then within a few weeks, because a large number of their players would be due back in England, the Shell Shield matches – once the backbone of cricket in the West Indies – would have to be rushed through. Meanwhile, the Packer circus was on the road in the Caribbean; and as it contained all the top players of both countries, the attraction was inevitable and immediate.

In the desperate necessity to stay afloat financially, the West Indies Board had only one option – to seek some stability, regardless of where it came from. Of course, it came from Packer. E.W. Swanton wrote:

> There is, however, one consolation at the moment for West Indies cricket. The various territories are getting from WSC both rentals for grounds and a portion of the gate over an agreed figure; also – let us give the devil his due – the Board itself is to receive an *ex-gratia* payment which will at least do something to compensate for the inevitable diminution of interest in its own Shell Shield and the absence of opportunity of discovering new talent until the tail-end of the season.

Mr Swanton went on:

> So, although the International Cricket Conference has done all possible from the start to accommodate any reasonable proposals put forward by the opposition – and I gather, by the way, that the January talks at Sydney, between the ICC representatives and Kerry Packer were decorously conducted – the Boards of individual countries can only proceed on the basis that, in the foreseeable future, the two systems may co-exist.

With Packer in the West Indies, the cricket world had by now accepted condition-
ally that his influence on the game was likely to be of a permanent nature. It was not a
pie in the sky that would go as it came, simply because of the established business
principle that he could now negotiate from strength.

Packer's tour of the West Indies will be remembered, not for its cricket but for violent crowd scenes almost unprecedented in an area where crowd disturbances have
become almost routine. Tony Cozier, writing in *The Cricketer* of the fourth Supertest
in Georgetown, gave this dramatic account of the proceedings:

> After a sunny Saturday, Guyana's lone Sunday newspaper quoted a WSC official as giving
> the assurance that play would commence on time on Sunday provided no more rain fell. Far
> from there being rain, the weather remained fine and a capacity crowd of 13,000 packed the
> tiny ground from as early as 7.00 a.m. to watch the much-heralded superstars in action.
>
> Gradually it became clear to everyone that the optimistic predictions of a prompt start
> were unfounded. The public-address system announced that the umpires had inspected
> and would inspect again at 12 noon. In the interim, players, dressed in civvies, appeared on
> the ground, prodding it dubiously with much shrugging of shoulders. The noon inspection
> led to a further announcement of a 2.00 p.m. inspection. As the alcohol flowed and the tem-
> perature became less bearable, spectators' patience became shorter and shorter. A good forty
> minutes after the 2.00 p.m. survey by the umpires it was announced that play would com-
> mence at 3.30 p.m.
>
> Too late. The hurricane was already blowing and could not now be curbed. By the time
> it was over, the ground was in shambles, fences torn down, benches and chairs hurled on to
> the outfield, broken bottles all over the place. The pavilion had been stormed and ransacked
> and the two teams trapped in their dressing-rooms where they remained huddled in cor-
> ners, most using their helmets as protection against drink bottles, not cricket balls. Two
> West Indies were slightly cut but the riot police, with their tear gas, arrived before the ram-
> pant mob could do any further damage. The prior disturbances in Barbados and Trinidad
> were minor by comparison. Apart from the embarrassment of the various disturbances,
> WSC also had its image tarnished by an incident involving Ian Chappell who was charged,
> convicted and fined $G150 in a Georgetown magistrate's court for assaulting a local WSC
> official and using indecent language.

Financially, however, WSC reported favourably. There were excellent crowds and
substantial input by sponsors, the Board was a beneficiary, and a coaching programme
by former West Indies Test cricketers was apparently highly successful. Whether the
product is good, bad or indifferent, much of its success or failure lies in marketing
techniques, and in this respect Packer has clearly shown the way to success. The West
Indies Board, having seen the size and nature of the sponsorships, would obviously be
looking at this source of revenue for their own future advantage. [...]

Towards the end of April there came the Australian Cricket Board's long-
expected granting to Kerry Packer's Channel 9 of exclusive television rights for Test
and other matches in Australia. What Packer had tried to achieve in 1976 he had
achieved in 1979, at a damaging cost all round. It will be remembered that the Board
had said throughout that they would put this contract out to tender when the time
came for its renewal. Opinion at this latest news was cautious, to say the least. Much
more detail was needed, but the agreement apparently was for three years and the
Board would benefit by an estimated £600,000. As to the future of World Series

Cricket, it was reported that this would be disbanded from January 31, 1980. It need never have started had Packer accepted that the Australian Cricket Board was bound by a contract to the Australian Broadcasting Commission until 1979, and that his money was likely to win the prize he so dearly sought when the time came.

This news of Packer winning the television contract was largely expected and was nothing like the bombshell which exploded upon the cricket world a month later when, from the outside, it appeared that from being arch-enemies with no compromise possible in any set of circumstances, the parties had wed and were now hand in hand for, as they said, the future good of cricket. Whether the rest of the world thought so was quite another matter. The feeling in many quarters was that when the Australian Board first found Packer at their throats, the rest of the cricket world had supported them to the hilt; even to the extent of highly expensive court cases which cricket could ill afford. Now, when it suited Australia, they had brushed their friends aside to meet their own ends. Let us, first of all, look at the full text of the statement made by the chairman of the Australian Cricket Board, Bob Parish.

> I am pleased to announce that the agreement between the Australian Cricket Board and PBL Sports Pty Ltd has been signed and will be lodged with the Trade Practices Commissioner.
>
> Under the agreement the Board has granted PBL Sports Pty Ltd the exclusive right, for a term of ten years, to promote the programme of cricket organised by the Board and to arrange the televising and merchandising in respect of that programme. For the first three years of the agreement the Board has agreed that PBL Sports Pty Ltd may arrange a contract for the televising of the programme with the Channel 9 network.
>
> World Series Cricket Pty Ltd will cease to promote cricket matches in Australia or elsewhere during the term of the agreement. However, under the programme the World Series logo will continue to be worn in international one-day matches by Australian players.
>
> The Australian Board will have the exclusive responsibility for the selection of Australian teams and has agreed that no player will be excluded from selection by reason only of that player having participated prior to the commencement of the 1979–80 cricket season in any match not authorised by the Board. There will be no change in Board policy that Australian teams will be selected only from those players who participate in Sheffield Shield cricket.
>
> It is envisaged that the programme each season will comprise five or six Test matches and an international one-day series, to be known as the Benson and Hedges World Series Cup, of fifteen matches plus a final which will be the best of five matches. These international matches will involve two overseas teams and the Australian team. The programme will also include the Sheffield Shield competition and a one-day series of nine matches between the states.
>
> Playing conditions of all matches will be under the control of the Board and the Board has agreed to consider favourably the introduction of the 30-yard circle in limited-overs matches, day/night matches and, on an experimental basis, the use of coloured clothing in Benson and Hedges World Series one-day limited-overs international matches.
>
> The programme for the 1979–80 season will not be finally determined for some weeks. England and India have accepted invitations to come to Australia in 1979–80. The Board has agreed to ask the Indian board to defer their visit until next season, 1980–81, and will invite the West Indian Board to send an official team to participate in the 1979–80 programme.
>
> A basic programme of matches has been prepared by the Board programme committee. All matches will be played on venues as determined by the Board.

The following prize-money will be provided: for each Test – $A10,000 comprising $A6,000 to the winner, $A3,000 to the loser, $A1,000 to the player of the match. For each one-day match – $A5,000 comprising $A3,000 to the winner, $A1,500 to the loser, $A500 to the player of the match. For the one-day final – $A50,000 comprising $A32,000 to the winner, $A16,000 to the loser, $A2,000 to the player of the match.

The Board is pleased to advise that the Benson and Hedges company will continue to be the sole and official sponsor of international cricket in Australia, of the Sheffield Shield competition and the Australian team. [...] The Board is unanimously of the opinion that its decision to accept the proposal from PBL is in the best interests of Australian and international cricket.

[...] Throughout the debate, the sixty-four thousand dollar question was 'Why has the Australian Board done this?', and the sixty-four thousand dollar answer can be succinctly given in one word – Money. For the first time in the history of the Ashes, an Australia v. England series had lost money. Faced with nothing in the kitty, and a tour by India – and this was bound to lose money – the Australian Board could see the spectre of bankruptcy close round the corner. It was left with precious little bargaining power. Packer had all the cards in his hand. It could be said that, in the circumstances, Australia had come out of it pretty well. Financially, of course, they may have, but time alone will tell whether the Australian Board – a very small dog, with Packer as a very large tail – will find that the tail wags the dog on any issue of divided opinion. It easily could. [...] (*1980*)

FROM NOTES BY THE EDITOR

THE PASSING OF WSC

[...] On the surface, the end of traditional cricket's acrimonious dispute with Mr Kerry Packer brought a reasonably harmonious return to normality. But at what cost to the game? Cricketers who were previously paid too little are now, in some cases, being paid more than the game can afford or they themselves are worth. Money has become the talk of the first-class dressing-rooms, with the average county cricketer feeling that Test players are getting a disproportionately large slice of the cake.

In Australia, one worrying aspect of the settlement which led to the running-down of World Series Cricket is the new structure of the first-class game there, this now being devised to accommodate commercial television. When England were in Australia in the winter of 1979–80, a tour they shared with West Indies, such was the confusion of fixtures that attendances and authenticity both suffered. The public seemed not to know what to expect next, or indeed for what trophy any given match was being played. As for the players, they were given little chance to settle down to any one type of cricket, whether one-day, four-day or five-day, all of which call for different tactics and not necessarily the same skills. It is important that before England tour Australia next, in 1982–83, they should negotiate resolutely for the itinerary they consider to be in the best interests of both countries. [...] (*1981*)

THE GREATER GAME

'At the moment of writing, one hears nothing but War! War! War!' wrote A.G. Steel in *Wisden* 1900. 'What numbers of gallant young soldier cricketers have gone to the front, eager for the chance; well the true wishes of all cricketers and readers of *Wisden* will go with them.' Steel was referring to the Boer War, but beginning a long acquaintanceship between the almanack and armed conflict. *Wisden* has kept going through both world wars, when there was precious little cricket but many cricketer casualties to report. In doing so, it not only gained the trust of its readers, but more generally sustained faith in the future.

The Boer War resulted in the first Australian cricket casualty, J.J. Ferris, a report of whose death from enteric fever opens this *Wisden*'s eye view of Australians at war. Ferris prefaces a selection of twenty further obituaries for casualties of World Wars I and II. *Wisden*'s listings of the Australian fallen were not comprehensive: they overlooked the death of Norman Callaway during World War I, for example, and Ken Ridings in World War II. But they were pleasingly accessible to cricketers of relatively minor distinction, unconsciously enriching the sense of a rich, living, lived game. When Balmain team-mates saw their pals Grant Ward and R.J. Woolcott off to war, who would have anticipated their memorialising on the same page of *Wisden* 1917?

In between the cricketers at war is cricket at war. Keeping the game going was about more than protecting a pastime – it was considered a contribution to the general psychological welfare of the empire. Sixty years ago, *Wisden* quoted a speech by Marylebone Cricket Club president Stanley Christopherson at the Club Cricket Conference: 'An officer came to my box at Lord's haggard and tired, and he remarked, "To see this green grass and the bat and ball is heaven!" When that officer left the ground, his face had quite a different appearance.' In a warm essay included here from *Wisden* 1944, 'Australians in English Club Cricket', RAAF flight lieutenant Bruce Andrew recalls a Australian bomber pilot in the MCC pavilion after recording a duck: 'Well, I have had the honour of playing at Lord's. They can send me home now if they want to.'

In reading wartime *Wisden*s, one obtains a sense of how much joy there is to cricket during times of hardship. This section documents cricket in all its wartime forms, from festive matches for charity to 'Test' matches in POW camps in Germany and Malaya. The pleasure is palpable. 'It is strange, perhaps, but true, how many of us agreed on this,' wrote Major E.W. Swanton in his essay for *Wisden* 1946, 'Cricket Under the Japs'. 'That we were never so thankful for having been cricketers as we were when we were guests of the Japanese.' Thus, perhaps, the unconfined exuberance of the military fixtures celebrating victory: the AIF XI tour of England, South Africa and Australia in 1919 and the Victory Test series pitting the Australian Services Team against England in 1945. Like *Wisden*'s unbroken sequence, they represented faith rewarded.

—GH

MR J.J. FERRIS, died on November 17, 1900, at Durban, where he was serving with the British forces. Mr Ferris, though only in his thirty-fourth year, had for some time dropped out of first-class cricket, and had to a certain extent outlived his fame. Still, though his career ended early, he will always be remembered as one of the finest left-handed bowlers – either English or Australian – that ever appeared. Having in the two previous winters done great things against English teams in the Colonies, Ferris first came to this country in 1888 as a member of the Australian eleven captained by the late Percy McDonnell. Much was expected of him, and he more than fulfilled the most sanguine anticipations. No one who can recall the cricket season of 1888 – one of the wettest on record – will need to be told what a sensation he and Charles Turner created. They were the mainstays of a team which, after a brilliant start, suffered many defeats, but the shortcomings were not in any way due to the two bowlers, who made their names famous wherever cricket is played. The eleven being deficient in change bowling, they had far too much to do, but they never seemed to tire, keeping up their form in a really wonderful way. Turner was the more successful of the two, taking in the whole tour 314 wickets for little more than 11 runs each. Ferris, however, also has a splendid record, 220 wickets falling to him for something over 14 runs apiece. The two men formed a perfect contrast, Turner being right hand, with an off-break perhaps never equalled at his speed, and Ferris left hand, with great accuracy, fine variety of pace, and a lot of spin. The weather flattered them, the wickets day after day giving them immense assistance, but it may be questioned if two finer bowlers ever played on the same side. One would not say that they were better than Spofforth and Palmer in 1882, but by reason of one being right-handed and the other left they were a more effective combination. As to the relative merits of Spofforth and Turner, cricketers have always been divided in opinion, the balance – among English players, at any rate – being in Spofforth's favour on account of his better head and more varied resources. In Ferris's case no question of comparison arose, as he was the first great left-handed bowler produced by Australia since the days of Frank Allan and Tom Kendall. Ferris and Turner came to England for the second time in 1890, and though associated with the least successful of all the Australian elevens, they fully sustained their reputations. This time Turner could only show a fractional superiority over his comrade. In the whole tour each man took 215 wickets, and there was a difference of less than a run a wicket in their averages. The summer was very wet, but there were more hard wickets to bowl on than in 1888, and under conditions favourable to run-getting Ferris perhaps did better work than Turner. That, at least, was the general opinion while the tour was in progress. With the tour of 1890 Ferris's career as a representative Australian cricketer came to an end. He agreed to qualify for Gloucestershire, and when the Australians came here in 1893 he played for the county against his old friends. For Gloucestershire, however, he proved as a bowler – not to mince matters – an utter failure. It was thought that he would be invaluable to the eleven, but he rarely showed a trace of the skill that had made him so famous, and when we last saw him bowl in a Gloucestershire match – in 1895 – he had lost his pace, his spin, his action, and everything. In the autumn of 1895 he returned to Australia, but his efforts to recover his old position in Colonial cricket met with no success, and little was heard of him till it was announced that he had gone to South Africa to try his fortune at the war with the Imperial Light Horse. We must not forget to add that he went out to South Africa with Mr W.W. Read's team in the winter of 1891–2. He had a brilliant tour, taking 235 wickets, but he never bowled in the same form afterwards.

2ND LIEUT. J.O. ATCHISON (5th Yorkshire Light Infantry), killed in Flanders on July 14, 1915, aged 30, was born in Australia and educated at the Oratory, Birmingham, where he was captain of the school and of the cricket and football elevens. He kept up the game subsequently in Australia and Upper Burma.

CAPT. HAROLD VERNON BROWNE (1st Queen's Own Dorset Yeomanry) was born at Buckland Park, South Australia, and died on September 7, 1915 of wounds received at the Dardanelles. In 1901 and 1902 he was in the Wellington Eleven, without, however, performing anything of note.

ERNEST CAPP (Australian Expeditionary Force), who died of wounds in Cairo in May 1915, aged 34, was a strong defensive batsman of the Singleton C.C., of New South Wales. In November, 1901, when playing for Northern Districts XVIII against England at West Maitland, he contributed 114 to the locals' total of 558 for fifteen wickets.

COLLINS, LIEUT. FRED BISSET, born February 25, 1881; killed October, 1917. Scotch Coll. (Melbourne) XI. East Melbourne C.C. XI from 1898–9 onwards, his bowling summary for the Club being 15,039 balls, 5,896 runs, 422 wickets, average 13. Played for Victoria 1899–00 to 1908–9. In inter-State games took 122 wickets for 3,267 runs, and against English sides 20 wickets for 420. Gave up cricket early owing to a strain. Excellent slip, useful bat, and bowled medium pace, with big off-break and a deceptive flight. Could bowl a really fast ball. Height 6 ft 1 in.

COTTER, ALBERT B., killed at Beersheba, October 20, 1917. New South Wales and Australia.

Albert Cotter was the successor to Ernest Jones as Australia's fast bowler, coming to England with the teams of 1905 and 1909. His first trip was not an unqualified success. It is true that in all matches he took 124 wickets for less than 20 runs apiece, but up to a certain point of the tour he had so little command over his length that his bowling was a quaint mixture of long hops and full pitches. Still, irregular as he was, his extreme pace often made him dangerous. He gained greatly in command over the ball when he shortened his run and in the last Test Match, at the Oval, he bowled splendidly on a perfect wicket, his pace being terrific. In 1909 his bowling came out very badly for the whole tour, but he had a big share in winning the Test Match at Leeds, taking five wickets in England's second innings at a cost of only 38 runs. For several seasons Cotter was the fast bowler of the New South Wales XI. He will never be ranked among the great Australian bowlers, but on his day he was deadly. (*Sydney Pardon*).

Some of his best performances were:

4 wickets for 5 runs, NSW v. Queensland, at Brisbane, 1903–4.

7 for 15 and 12 for 34, Australia v. Worcestershire, at Worcester, 1905.

Took four wickets in four balls for Glebe v. Sydney, at Wentworth Park, April 29, 1911.

ELTHAM, LIEUT. KEITH (Australian Expeditionary Force), born at Hobart, October 10, 1886, killed December 31, 1916. Representative Tasmanian player. Scored 78 v. New South Wales, at Sydney, 1910–11; 58 v. Victoria, at Melbourne, 1912–13; 51 v. South Africans, at Hobart, 1910–11. Played in district cricket for Wellington and (later) West Hobart, scoring 2,589 runs with an average of 33.62, his highest innings being 146 for West Hobart v. New Town, in 1905–6. A useful bowler.

KNOX, CAPT. WM. JOHNSTONE, M.C. (Australian Field Artillery), born 1887; died of wounds, August 20, 1917. Scotch College, Melbourne; in the XI.

LUGTON, LANCE-CORPORAL FRANK (Australian Expeditionary Force), killed July 29, 1916, aged 22. Northcote C.C., of Melbourne; for Victoria v. Tasmania, at Launceston, in March 1914 he scored 94 not out and 20. For Victoria that season his batting figures gave him an aggregate of 218 runs and an average of 31; and he took nine wickets for 34.11 runs each.

ALAN MARSHAL (15th Battalion Australian Imperial Forces), who was born at Warwick, in Queensland, on June 12, 1883, died of enteric at Imtarfa Military Hospital, Malta, on July 23, 1915, after serving in Gallipoli. He was a cricketer of unfulfilled promise. He had it in him to be great, but somehow he missed the position that at one time seemed to be within his reach. A hitter of greater natural powers has seldom been seen. The son of a Lincolnshire man who had emigrated to Australia, he took to cricket while quite young, playing both at the South Brisbane State School and the Brisbane Grammar School. He learned much through watching Boyle, McDonnell, S.P. Jones, and others, and at the early age of fourteen began to play in Grade cricket. Later he played for a time in Grade matches in Sydney and had represented Queensland a few times before coming to England. He always showed distinct talent, his batting improving rapidly from the time he had the advantage of playing on turf wickets. On arriving in England he soon made his mark, his form being so good that before he had been here long he was asked to qualify for Surrey. For London County in 1905 he made 2,752 runs with an average of 56.16 and took 118 wickets at a cost of 16.41 runs each, and in the corresponding fixtures of the following year his aggregates were 3,578 (average 76.12) and 167 (average 14.10) respectively. In all matches in 1906 he scored 4,350 runs, making fourteen hundreds, and took 210 wickets. Against Croydon he made 300 not out at the Crystal Palace, and 171 in the return: he also scored 246 v. Egypt at the Crystal Palace, 219 v. Norbury at Norbury, and 204 not out v. Cyphers at the Palace. Having qualified by the necessary two years' residence, he duly appeared for the county. Everything suggested that Surrey had found a prize. At first, however, Marshal did not do himself full justice in his new surroundings. In 1908 he showed all that he could do. He had a splendid season for Surrey scoring 1,884 runs with an average of 40 in all matches for the county and finishing second only to Hayward. Five times he exceeded the hundred, an innings of 108 against Middlesex at the Oval being a marvel of powerful driving. When the season ended his place among the great players of the day seemed assured. The future looked bright indeed for him, but he never again reached the same level. At the height of the season of 1909 the Surrey committee suspended him for a time and in the following year they terminated his engagement. Marshal returned to Queensland and played cricket there, but without doing anything exceptional. He sailed for Australia on September 12th, 1910, and on the day before his departure played a magnificent innings of 259 not out for Whitcomb Wanderers v. W. Jones' XI, at Acton, hitting thirteen 6's and thirty-six 4's. Earlier in the season – at Ashford (Middlesex) on July 7 – he had taken all ten wickets in an innings for 28 runs for A.H. Marriott's XI v. Ashford. [...]

MOULE, CAPT. FRED G. (Australian Imperial Force), died of wounds in October, 1917. Melbourne Church of England Grammar School XI; played for St. Kilda C.C., and headed the club's bowling in season 1914–15. Bowled left-hand. Nephew of W.H. Moule of the second Australian team in England.

MUIR, LIEUT. A.R. (Australian Imperial Force). Military Cross. Killed October 13, 1917. Newington College, Sydney, XI; Sydney University XI. A fine bat.

PARKER, GUNNER ERNEST F. (Australian Expeditionary Force), killed May 2, 1918, aged 33. Perth High School XI; St. Peter's Coll., Adelaide, XI. For some years the 'star' batsman of Western Australia. Scored 76 and 116 v. South Australia at Fremantle in 1905–6; 26 and 69 v. New South Wales at Perth in 1906–7; and 1 and 117 v. Victoria at Perth in 1909–10. For Rest of Australia v. Australian XI, at Melbourne, in 1908–9, he made 65 and 8. In club cricket he made many hundreds, and in 1902–3 made 1,003 runs, fourteen complete innings for the East Perth C.C., including 246, 199, 172 and 105. He also scored 204 not out for St. Peter's Coll. Old Boys v. Prince Alfred College Old Boys in 1904–5; and 222 not out for Wanderers v. North Perth in 1906–7. He was a great lawn-tennis player, and gave up cricket on account of failing eye-sight.

WALKER, SERGT. JOHN P. (Australian Imperial Force), killed at Battle of Pozieres, July 29, 1916, aged 25. A first-class wicket-keeper and a forcible batsman of great promise. Headed the East Melbourne averages in 1911-12 with 52.66. Played for Victorian Colts.

SERGT. GRANT WARD (Australian Expeditionary Force), killed on August 27, 1915, was a promising First-Grade batsman in Sydney cricket. He played for Balmain.

SERGT. R.J. WOOLCOTT, D.S.O. (Australian Expeditionary Force), killed on September 28, 1915, played for the Balmain C.C., of Sydney.

THE AUSTRALIAN IMPERIAL FORCES TEAM

When the proposed tour of an Australian Service Team was given up, it being found impossible to get a representative side together, few people expected that a band of Australian cricketers would be seen in the field last summer. However, the Military Authorities stepped in, made themselves wholly responsible in the all important matter of finance, and arranged a tour on amateur lines. Apart from the proposed Test matches – very properly dropped – they took over with little or no alteration the list of fixtures that had been provisionally drawn up. The success that, in a cricket sense, attended the enterprise, exceeded all expectation. Such an abundance of talent was available that no difficulty was found in building up an all round team of remarkable strength. In the early part of the season, C. Kelleway was captain, but owing to some disagreement he dropped out, the leadership being given to H.L. Collins – also a member before the war of the New South Wales eleven. Collins proved quite the right man for the post, and was also, as batsman and bowler, one of the mainstays of the side. Twenty-eight first-class matches were played, and in addition some minor games. Of the twenty-eight matches the Australians won twelve, lost only four, and left twelve unfinished. [...] Collins, though Willis beat him both in aggregate of runs and average, was probably the best batsman after Kelleway had dropped out. Very steady and resourceful he made many big scores. The great asset so far as individual players were concerned was the possession of a really fast bowler. Gregory finished up with a very good record, but he was far more valuable than his average would suggest. Many batsmen who revel in ordinary fast bowling are uncomfortable against abnormal pace and that is what they got when they faced Gregory. He was very fast indeed – quicker than anyone else who bowled last summer – and helped by his great height and high delivery he often made the ball get up on the hard wickets in a way that reminded one of Knox in 1906. If he can resist the fascination of batting – he made two hundreds in one game when the team reached home after their victories in South Africa – he may be a great force in the Test matches of the future.

NORTHAMPTONSHIRE V. AUSTRALIANS

Played at Northampton, Thursday, Friday, Saturday, June 26, 27, 28, 1919. – Following their defeat at Lord's, the Australians beat Northamptonshire by 196 runs, but it was not till the third morning that they gained an overwhelming advantage. With four wickets to fall they were 228 ahead. Fine hitting carried their score from 177 to 314, and they set Northamptonshire 366 to get. Three of the county's best wickets were down for 28, and a useful stand by Woolley and Walden only delayed the end. Gregory had a wonderfully successful match, scoring 164 runs and taking eight wickets.

AUSTRALIANS

Mr J.M. Taylor run out	17	– b Thomas	35
Mr J.M. Gregory c Beasley b Woolley	115	– c Seymour b Davies	49
Mr J.T. Murray c Seymour b Wright	12	– b Seymour	7
Mr W.L. Trennery run out	1	– b Walden	58
Mr H.L. Collins c Hawes b Holland	1	– b Woolley	12
Mr A.W. Lampard b Woolley	11	– c Haywood b Walden	51
Mr C.E. Pellew b Wright	70	– b Seymour	10
Mr C.B. Willis c Wright b Seymour	12	– c Wright b Beasley	36
Mr E.A. Bull lbw, b Woolley	0	– b Walden	34
Mr C.T. Docker b Woolley	0	– not out	10
Mr E. Long not out	13	– c Holland b Walden	4
B 1, l-b 3, w 1	15	B 5, l-b 3	8
	297		**314**

NORTHAMPTONSHIRE

Mr L.E. Holland c Pellew b Docker	63	– c Docker b Collins	9
Mr L.J. Davies b Lampard	20	– b Gregory	7
R. Haywood c Long b Gregory	3	– b Gregory	2
J. Seymour b Gregory	35	– c Gregory b Collins	9
C.N. Woolley c Long b Docker	39	– c Gregory b Trennery	51
F. Walden c Long b Gregory	21	– c Collins b Gregory	36
Mr A. Wright c Trennery b Collins	27	– c Gregory b Collins	23
W.A. Buswell b Gregory	0	– not out	12
Mr J.H. Beasley b Docker	4	– b Gregory	0
Mr E.H. Hawes not out	12	– c Taylor b Collins	4
Thomas c Taylor b Collins	0	– b Collins	1
B 14, l-b 7, n-b 1	22	B 12, l-b 1, w 2	15
	246		**169**

NORTHAMPTONSHIRE BOWLING

	Overs	Mdns	Runs	Wkts	Overs	Mdns	Runs	Wkts
Woolley	28	6	51	4	25	5	70	1
Thomas	11	2	31	0	15	2	65	1
Seymour	20	1	93	1	16	0	58	2
Hawes	4	0	23	0				
Wright	9.5	1	38	2	1	0	13	0
Holland	5	0	39	1				
Beasley	4	1	7	0	7	1	30	1
Davies					6	1	20	1
Walden					7.3	0	43	4
Haywood					2	0	7	0

AUSTRALIANS BOWLING

	Overs	Mdns	Runs	Wkts	Overs	Mdns	Runs	Wkts
Docker	17	3	57	3	6	0	29	0
Collins	16	4	34	2	19.3	8	26	5
Gregory	23	2	71	4	21	1	74	4
Lampard	18	0	62	1	4	0	13	0
Trennery					3	0	12	1

Umpires: Stockwin and Wrigley.

AIF TEAM v. NEW SOUTH WALES

Played at Sydney, January 31, February 2, 3, 1920, the Imperial Forces Team winning easily by 203 runs. The match was specially noteworthy for the wonderful all-round cricket of Gregory. In addition to scoring a century in each innings, he secured eight wickets for 130 runs, and caught three men out. His 102 occupied him only an hour and a half. He then deliberately threw his wicket away. [...] Mailey took ten wickets in the game for 167 runs, and greatly impressed the critics as a googley bowler. The AIF team, and Gregory in particular, had a tremendous reception at the finish.

AIF TEAM

H.L. Collins b Norman	0	c and b Mailey 129
J.M. Gregory c Carter b Norman 122		st Carter b Mailey 102
C.E. Pellew c E. Trennery b Hendry 1		c Carter b Mailey 10
A.W. Lampard c Mailey b E. Trennery 45		c E.Trennery b Mailey 18
J.M. Taylor c Mailey b E. Trennery 7		b Mailey 32
W.L. Trennery st Carter b Mailey 31		b E. Trennery 26
J.T. Murray lbw, b Mailey 0		c Trennery b Mailey 29
W.A. Oldfield c Mailey b Hendry 12		b Hendry 2
W.S. Stirling lbw, b Hendry 0		c Carter b Mailey 12
C.T. Docker c Carter b Mailey 38		lbw, b Mailey 1
C.S. Winning not out 2		not out 13
Byes, &c. 7		Byes, &c. 21
	265	395

NEW SOUTH WALES

H. Carter b Gregory 17		c Oldfield b Gregory 15
H.L. Hendry b Gregory 85		c Gregory b Collins 3
W. Bardsley c Oldfield b Collins 60		b Gregory 2
T.J.E. Andrews c Docker b Gregory 39		b Winning 65
A. Kippax c Winning b Gregory 17		run out 2
K.B. Docker lbw, b Lampard 0		c Lampard b C.T. Docker 27
A. Punch b Docker 30		c Oldfield b C.T. Docker 6
A.A. Ratcliffe c Oldfield b Gregory 22		c Winning b Gregory 12
R. Norman c Gregory b Winning 3		c Gregory b Lampard 24
E. Trennery run out 0		not out 15
A.A. Mailey not out 0		c Taylor b Winning 1
Byes, &c. 6		Byes, &c. 6
	279	178

NEW SOUTH WALES BOWLING

	Overs	Mdns	Runs	Wkts	Overs	Mdns	Runs	Wkts
Norman	16	3	66	2	15	0	81	1
Hendry	10	2	62	3	20	3	85	1
E. Trennery	14	1	85	2	9	0	69	1
Mailey	10.4	1	45	3	26.7	0	122	7
Andrews					2	0	17	0

AIF TEAM BOWLING

Lampard	12	0	70	1	2	0	8	1
Gregory	5.3	1	65	5	15	3	65	3
Collins	11	0	59	1	20	1	52	1
C.T. Docker	9	0	34	1	8	1	28	2
Winning	10	0	45	1	4.7	1	19	2

AUSTRALIANS IN ENGLISH CLUB CRICKET

By Flight Lieutenant Bruce Andrew, RAAF

Cricket has done much to foster the feeling of good fellowship and to maintain friendly relations between Australians and Englishmen during the second world-war. The Royal Australian Air Force cricketers, many of whom may never enjoy the privilege of visiting the old country again, finished the 1943 season unanimous in their appreciation of the way the game was played here. One well-known airman stated during the last match that he would like to do an extra tour of flying operations so that he could fit in another cricket season. When another player returned to the MCC pavilion after making a 'duck' he remarked: 'Well, I have had the honour of playing at Lord's. They can send me home now if they want to.' He had just completed his operational tour of duty as a bomber pilot.

There were really no big names among the RAAF cricketers who took part in representative, inter-Service, Dominion and club cricket in England in 1943. When war broke out many were schoolboys, some promising, others unknown. Of the Australians who appeared at Lord's in the Dominions XI and for the RAAF team, which, after losing to Sir Pelham Warner's team, finished the summer by gaining a great victory over the Royal Air Force side, composed solely of Test and county players, only four had inter-State experience.

From the Australian point of view, the find of the season was Flight Sergeant Keith Miller, the young Victorian. He revealed the ability and temperament of a champion and showed every promise of developing into one of Australia's best all-rounders. The fast bowler, Flying Officer A.W. Roper, played in the Sheffield Shield for several seasons for New South Wales, and he and Flying Officer S.G. Sismey, the wicket-keeper, also of NSW, were the most experienced players. Sismey displayed brilliant form behind the stumps, and his actions indicated that he had modelled himself on that fine stylist W.A. Oldfield, who between the two wars appeared in 55 Tests for Australia. Oldfield was a product of the successful AIF team of 1919, which was formed by the military authorities in England and became the nucleus of the 1920–21 Australia Test team. Another NSW representative, Flying Officer Keith Carmody, captained both the RAAF and Dominions teams. Before coming over here he was making his way in State cricket. An opening batsman, he closely resembled in style S.J. McCabe, with whom he played in Sydney club cricket. Apart from these few the RAAF men had not graduated beyond club or park cricket.

In England, cricket has been more than a game for them. Only those who have played with or against English clubs can appreciate the great difference between club cricket here and at home. We Australians love our cricket and thoroughly enjoy the way we play it, but we had to travel 12,000 miles to appreciate the real atmosphere of the great game which has contributed so much to war-time recreation. This may sound strange to English people who have seen Australian Test teams in action, but I am not thinking of big cricket. I refer to the club cricketers – the thousands of 'flannelled fools' – who keep the game alive without receiving any limelight.

In Australia these men play in open paddocks, on hard dirt wickets which have been scraped smooth, or on 22 yards of concrete laid down by local councils in public parks. Flags resembling small pennants are used to mark out the boundary, and in the cities and large towns the wickets are so close and the boundaries so overlap that the fieldsman in the outfield talk, in a whisper, to the slips or square-leg of an adjoining game.

Park matches form the nurseries for club cricket in Australia. It was from these surroundings that players such as Don Bradman, Jack Ryder, Fleetwood-Smith, Bill O'Reilly, Charlie Macartney and others found the first rung of the ladder to cricketing fame. From park competitions players graduate to club cricket. Then comes the Sheffield Shield, in which the four main cricketing States, Queensland, New South Wales, Victoria, and South Australia, meet each other twice in a season; form shown in these matches wins a place in Australia Test teams.

Australian club cricket is played on council-owned grounds – much larger than those used for your club cricket – with large grandstands and small crowds. At the end of the day's play most players go their own way, and unless a member of the team visits the ground for practice during the week, he may not see his team-mates until the match is resumed the following Saturday.

What a contrast to the atmosphere of your smaller, friendly-looking grounds, where the spectators sit in deck chairs or on the grass around the boundary! These surroundings give the player confidence and make him feel at home. When stumps are drawn he is one of a happy family fraternising in the club room over a mild-and-bitter or a pale ale. Licensing laws in Australia do not encourage this 'after the game' social spirit. Is it any wonder, then, that we park and club cricketers considered it a privilege to play in this country?

Australians are Saturday afternoon cricketers. Some people over here have the impression that we live on the cricket field. This is not so. A player is lucky if he gets 12 innings in a season. We are not as orthodox as English cricketers; our early experiences on dirt or concrete wickets and the absence of coaches account for that. 'Play your natural game' is the usual advice to young Australian players.

In England, 9, 10 or 11 usually go to the wicket in much the same way, and with the same idea, as the openers. In Australia the tail-enders revel in the long-handle game and their one idea is 'to have a go'. This does the game no harm, as a six by O'Reilly or Fleetwood-Smith provides as much pleasure and entertainment as a hook to the fence by Bradman or a late cut for four by McCabe. Still, as I said before, we Australians are glad we have had the opportunity of visiting the cradle of cricket. We greatly admire the game as it is played over here as well as your cricketers, and we appreciate all the hospitality we have received from everyone connected with it. (*1944*)

MISCELLANEA

Len Hutton, of Yorkshire and England, gave a bat to an Army unit, and the commanding officer presented it to Cecil Pepper of New South Wales for rapidly making a century against an English team in Palestine. Using this bat in Queensland, Pepper scored an amazing hundred in 24 minutes, his hits including ten 6's. (*1944*)

Flying-Officer A.E. Barras, who played cricket for the RAAF in England last summer, after being shot down over Libya, returned to Australia. Playing his first game for five years for Fitzroy, his old club, Barras took six wickets for 36 and scored 41. (*1944*)

FROM NOTES BY THE EDITOR

[…] In very different surroundings – Stalag Luft prison camp in East Prussia – Australia won a 'Test' match by three runs, the last England wicket falling to a wonderful catch off the last ball of the final over. The fieldsman at point lost his balance but rising with the ball in his right hand claimed victory as his reward. That catch gave J.E. Connolly, who was cricket secretary of Sydney University before the war, a match record of 13 wickets for 60 runs. At another prison camp, Stammlager, Australia won a triangular tournament, defeating England in the deciding match after a victory for each over New Zealand. […] (*1944*)

CALVERT, FLIGHT-SERGT. CLIVE P., a very promising all-rounder of the Royal Australian Air Force team, lost his life at the age of 21 on a mine-laying expedition over the Baltic Sea on December 16, 1944. He appeared in inter-state cricket for New South Wales, and during the 1944 summer he played in the one-day matches at Lord's for Australia against England. Possessing a crisp cut and powerful drive he was an attractive batsman. His best innings was 141 in two and a half hours for the RAAF against West Indies at Birmingham. His medium-fast bowling was also a great asset to the side.

CHRISTIE, PRIVATE ROBERT THOMAS of the Australian Imperial Forces, died of wounds on May 7, 1941, aged 24. A free-scoring batsman for Glenelg, he won *The Mail* Cup for the fastest hundred in Adelaide cricket by hitting up a century in 58 minutes in the last match of the 1938–39 season. Previously Don Bradman was credited with the fastest hundred, made in 80 minutes. Christie, prominent also in Australian football and baseball, excelled in games when at Sacred Heart College, Adelaide.

GREGORY, SERGEANT-OBSERVER ROSS G., RAAF, who stood out prominently among Australian batsmen during three seasons before the war, died when on air operations, as announced on June 24, 1942. Born on February 26, 1916, Ross Gregory became one of the youngest cricketers to play in a Test, sharing in recent years with A.A. Jackson, S.J. McCabe and D.G. Bradman the distinction of playing for Australia before coming of age; but Clem Hill still holds the record of appearing in a Test for Australia in his youth – 19 years 3 months – against England at Lord's in June 1896. The untimely end of Ross Gregory removed a batsman showing promise of a long career for Australia. After doing brilliant things as a boy, he was chosen for Victoria when still at school. Continuing to improve, he established himself in his State XI and against G.O. Allen's 1936–37 MCC team he made 128 for Victoria, his stand with I. Lee for 262 being a fourth wicket record against an England team. In State matches that season he averaged over 39, with 85 against South Australia his best score, and he helped Victoria carry off the Sheffield Shield. So it was no surprise that during that season he rose to Test match fame, playing in the last two engagements against England with marked success. He scored 23 and 50 (run out) at Adelaide, where Australia won by 148 runs, and 80 in the deciding encounter at Melbourne, where victory by an innings and 200 runs brought success in the rubber for Don Bradman's side. Only Bradman and S.J. McCabe recorded higher averages in that series of Tests, and Ross Gregory clearly possessed strong claims for a place in the team that came to England in 1938, but for some reason he was passed over. In 1938-39 he gave further evidence of consistency by averaging 44.72, with top score 77, for Victoria. That finished his cricket career; he joined up for the war directly on the declaration of hostilities, and his Air Force training in England took place during the next winter, so he never played in this country. Below medium height, Ross Gregory used his strong arms in brilliant front-of-the-wicket forcing strokes and pulled in confident style. His cut also earned praise, and quick footwork enabled him to defend with high skill. A slow leg-break bowler, deceptive in flight and varied pace, Ross Gregory took five wickets for 69 runs for Victoria against the MCC team captained by E.R.T. Holmes which toured Australia and New Zealand in 1935-36. With limited opportunities for taking part in the attack he failed to maintain that form with the ball, but sure hands made him valuable in the field.

ROACH, FLIGHT-SERGT. W.A., a left-hand opening batsman from Western Australia, who appeared in the two 1944 Whitsuntide matches at Lord's for Australia, was shortly afterwards killed during operations against the enemy. He was 29.

WALKER, FLYING OFFICER CHARLES W., the South Australian wicket-keeper, failed to return to England after a flight over Germany in the autumn of 1942. He was 33. As a player Walker reached his best form at the peak of Oldfield's career, and, though touring England with the 1930 and 1938 Australian teams, he never appeared in a Test match. Born at Hindmarsh (S.A.) on February 19, 1909, Walker was only just 20 when he stumped five and caught three in his first big match for South Australia against New South Wales in March 1929. His form against A.H.H. Gilligan's side in 1929-30 went further to prove his ability particularly in bringing off amazing catches and stumpings on the leg side. A neat cricketer, he was a useful batsman and often opened the innings for his State. When hostilities broke out, he became an air-gunner, and during leave in England he was always welcome at cricket grounds; in fact he kept wicket in several games for the RAF.

AUSTRALIAN SERVICES TEAM

By Norman Preston

By embarking on a programme which eventually involved them in nearly 50 fixtures, including five Victory matches against England, Australian Servicemen made a valuable contribution towards the recovery of cricket in all parts of the Mother Country. Above everything else the cricket provided enjoyment for all kinds of people seeking relaxation after six years of total war.

In the early months of 1945, no ideas of such a tour existed. The RAAF cricket XI was already established and the AIF, stationed at Eastbourne after service in the Middle East, were preparing for the rehabilitation of 6,000 of their prisoners-of-war still in German hands. They took a lease of the Saffrons ground as part of their programme for restoring POW's to full health. The organiser, Captain John Mallyon, arranged matches against various teams and meanwhile the RAAF drew up a separate list of games. Sir Pelham Warner, who did so much for cricket during the lean years, arranged his programme at Lord's with the Australians as frequent visitors, including two-day games against England at Whitsun and August Bank Holiday, and a single day game in July.

So the season began, but when VE Day came on May 8 those simple arrangements gradually grew like a snowball. The three games at Lord's between England and Australia were in turn extended to three days each, and the British Inter-Services Committee staged two more representative matches in the provinces at Sheffield and Manchester. At no time was there any suggestion that the games should count in the regular Test series, and no doubt this decision went a long way towards making the cricket so agreeable. In fact, all five games were contested by each side, under the admirable captaincy of W.R. Hammond and A.L. Hassett, in a spirit of fellowship and goodwill, which I, among many, would like to see continued when the real Tests come round again.

Adequate descriptions are given of all the games and therefore I do not propose to mention them here, except to say honours were evenly divided, Australia winning the first and third matches, England the second and last – both played out of London – the fourth being drawn. The Australians possessed only one man of Test experience, Hassett, and to him belonged the credit of knitting them into such a splendid team. [...] I would single out K.R. Miller, the tall Victorian, as the find of the season from Australia's point of view. Having the temperament for big cricket, he possessed the ability to play the right kind of innings according to the state of the game. Essentially a front of the wicket batsman, he was a great attraction wherever he went, and I firmly believe he is destined to become one of the great men of Australian cricket. As an opening bowler he was the liveliest seen in England during the summer. Besides Miller, S.G. Sismey, wicket-keeper, and the three slow bowlers, C.G. Pepper, D.R. Cristofani and R.S. Ellis may reach the top mark. Bearing in mind the bowling problem which beset D.G. Bradman in 1938, A.G. Cheetham and R.G. Williams, both tall and elegant in action, would have been welcome in some touring sides of the past. After the third Victory match, Cheetham returned home and left a gap which was never filled properly, as Miller strained a back muscle that prevented him being used consistently as a bowler. There were two repatriated prisoners-of-war in the party – R.G. Williams and D.K. Carmody. Despite spending nearly four years in a German prison camp after being shot down in a Maryland aircraft during the Libyan campaign, Williams soon found his form and he claimed Hutton as a victim four times in the five games with England. Carmody, released by the Russians after one year in Germany, failed to produce the form he showed before his capture. Within a week of getting back to England he joined the side; he might have done better as a batsman if he had rested longer. [...]

Flight Lieutenant Keith Johnson, a member of the Australian Board of Control, flew from Australia to manage the team, arriving the first week in June. A stranger to this country, he found the programme in only skeleton form; and that the tour proved such a success from every point of view was due to his hard work and courtesy. Before the team sailed for India, Johnson left the following message: [...] 'You are putting your bats away here now, and in other parts of the world they are taking them out, the village greens of other countries are ringing with the joyous shouting of youth at play, for the grand game is always being played in some part of our Cricket Empire. We look back with pride and pleasure to the grand country where the game was born and nurtured.'

ENGLAND V. AUSTRALIA

FIRST VICTORY MATCH

At Lord's, May 19, 21, 22, 1945. Australia won by six wickets. In a dynamic finish, true to the exhortation expressed in the post-war cricket plans, Pepper made the winning hit off the fourth ball of the last possible over just at seven o'clock. To the majority of the 18,000 people who saw the cricket this really fine climax gave intense pleasure and the Australian batsmen reached the pavilion amidst enthusiastic applause. The England team deserved equal praise for their splendid sportsmanship in doing their part in the speediest manner, changing positions quickly and starting each over without a suggestion of delay when the waste of seconds might have meant a drab draw. While giving Australia hearty congratulations for their triumph, it must be indicated clearly that the prevailing conditions favoured them. After heavy rain overnight England batted on a green pitch with the outfield slow. The immediate loss of Hutton from a poor stroke gave Robertson the opportunity to prove his worth, and for 85 minutes he mastered the well-varied attack. He and Washbrook added 53, Hammond showed his form until after lunch a fast ball took his off stump, Ames and Edrich put on 75, but Stephenson alone of the remainder caused trouble, the last three wickets falling at 267.

Australia made 82 for two wickets before the close, and on Whit-Monday, when some 30,000 watched the game, they found the pitch – completely covered during the week-end and so protected from much rain – after being mown in the morning according to custom, quite favourable to scoring. Also better reward came for scoring strokes. Hassett increased his 27 by 50 before hitting over a yorker. Batting in quiet, resolute fashion, with hooks and cuts his most effective strokes, Hassett maintained his reputation. An interruption by rain did not help the fielding side and the bowling was mastered, Miller and Stanford making 99 runs together, while Pepper gave an idea of his power in a stand for 73.

Miller accounted largely for Australia gaining the upper hand, his elegant, emphatic style fully meriting the hundred he earned before his first lifted stroke gave Ames a catch at deep mid-off. Batting three and a half hours, Miller hit only six 4's, but he was always getting runs with the soundness characteristic of most Australians. Williams and Price forced the pace with such effect that 88 runs came in fifty minutes for the ninth partnership. Williams, last out to a catch at the wicket, hit eleven 4's in his 53. A repatriated prisoner of war, Williams hit hard in front of the wicket and cut cleanly.

Rain fell as play ceased shortly before half-past six, and in the morning England, 188 behind, batted on turf drying in sunshine. Pepper used his height and strong finger spin and, with the ball keeping low, he dismissed Hutton at 52 and Washbrook at 75, but Robertson, in another admirable display, stayed two hours forty minutes, hitting two 6's to the on and five 4's before Sismey, standing back, caught him off the first delivery by Cheetham coming on with the new ball. Edrich and Robins further improved matters for England in a stand for 68 but, through haste for runs when victory was out of the question, both left at 286 and the remaining three wickets went for eight runs.

Wanting 107 runs with seventy minutes at their disposal, Australia soon lost Whitington and Miller – dismissed when starting for an impossible second run. Then Pepper joined Hassett and Hammond spread his field out so as to prevent fours, but singles came very frequently and often the boundary could not be saved. Fielding at deep mid-off, Hammond, running across behind the bowler, caught Hassett cleverly, and Cheetham lost his wicket when Pepper refused a sharp run. Then Price came in with twelve minutes left and 31 runs wanted. Hammond did not use the opportunity afforded by these wickets falling to change his bowling. He kept the onus of attack with his two fast bowlers, who stuck heroically to their work, but the effect of such unusual toil was shown when Stephenson, whose first match this was since 1941, got both hands to a high catch at short slip but could not hold the ball.

So Pepper escaped after a cut for four, and in the next over there came four singles and a six from a mighty on-drive into one of the grand-stand boxes. With the clock almost at seven, Price scored one from the second ball by Gover; Pepper followed with a couple of twos to leg, and the terrific strain was over: Australia victorious over a side lacking a left-handed batsman or bowler and generally unfortunate in all the circumstances of the match, hastily extended to three days as a cricket celebration of 'V' Day. About 17,000 people saw the finish. while altogether 67,660 paid the shilling admission during the three days, the proceeds of £1,935 3s. 6d. going to Red Cross and Australian charities. Entertainment tax absorbed £957 10s. 10d.

ENGLAND

L. Hutton c Sismey b Williams	1	– b Pepper	21
Flt.-Sgt. C. Washbrook st Sismey b Ellis	28	– lbw b Pepper	32
Capt. J.D. Robertson lbw b Ellis	53	– c Sismey b Cheetham	84
W.R. Hammond b Williams	29	– lbw b Ellis	33
Sqn.-Ldr. L.E.G. Ames c Price b Cheetham	57	– b Ellis	7
Sqn.-Ldr. W.J.Edrich b Miller	45	– Workman b Price	50
Sqn.-Ldr. R.W.V. Robins b Cheetham	5	– c Hassett b Pepper	33
Lt.-Col. J.W.A. Stephenson c Sismey b Price	31	– b Price	1
Lt.-Col. S.C. Griffith c Sismey b Cheetham	9	– not out	4
Lt. D.V.P. Wright b Price	0	– run out	1
A.R. Gover not out	0	– st Sismey b Pepper	1
B 1, l-b 6, w 1, n-b 1	9	B 18, l-b 8, n-b 1	27
	267		**294**

AUSTRALIA

Flt.-Sgt. J.A. Workman b Gover	1		
Capt. R.S. Whitington c Griffith b Wright	36	– lbw b Stephenson	0
W/O A.L. Hassett b Stephenson	77	– c Hammond b Gover	37
Sqn.-Ldr. S.G. Sismey c Wright b Edrich	37		
P/O K.R. Miller c Ames b Stephenson	105	– run out	1
F/O R.M. Stanford st Griffith b Stephenson	49		
Sgt. C.G. Pepper c Griffith b Stephenson	40	– not out	54
Capt. A.G. Cheetham c Hammond b Wright	0	– run out	0
W/O R.G. Williams c Griffith b Wright	53		
Sgt. C.F. Price c Robertson b Stephenson	35	– not out	10
F/O R.S. Ellis not out	1		
B 9, l-b 10, n-b 2	21	B 4, l-b 1	5
	455	Four wkts, dec.	**107**

ENGLAND BOWLING

Cheetham	13.1	1	49	3	17	2	44	1
Williams	19	2	56	2	21	7	47	0
Pepper	19	2	59	0	32.4	7	80	4
Ellis	31	8	59	2	17	3	33	2
Miller	9	2	11	1	9	1	23	0
Price	9	1	24	2	19	3	40	2

AUSTRALIA BOWLING

Gover	25	3	90	1	11.4	1	51	1
Stephenson	36	4	116	5	11	0	51	1
Edrich	17	2	61	1				
Wright	37.3	9	122	3				
Robins	10	0	45	0				

ENGLAND v. DOMINIONS

At Lord's, August 25, 27, 28, 1945. Dominions won by 45 runs with eight minutes to spare. One of the finest games ever seen produced 1,241 runs, including sixteen 6's, a century in each England innings by Hammond, and grand hundreds for the Dominions by Donnelly, the New Zealand left-hander, and Miller, of Australia. In addition, the result was a triumph for Constantine, who, in the absence of Hassett through illness, was chosen captain by the Dominions players just before the match began. Both sides experienced various changes of fortune and the issue remained in doubt till the end. Although Craig, a left-hander from South Australia, forced the pace from the beginning, the Dominions lost half their side for 109. Then Pepper and Donnelly added 120. Always master of the bowling, Donnelly hit two 6's and eighteen 4's, being last out. With Gimblett suffering from cramp, Hammond changed his order, and before the first day ended England lost Fishlock, Robertson and Phillipson for 28.

By twenty minutes to one on Monday six England wickets were down for 96 but Hammond and Edrich lifted their side out of trouble with a stand of 177 of which Edrich's share was 65. Against keen bowling Hammond never made a mistake. Three drives off Cristofani went into the pavilion for 6, and he also hit ten 4's, getting his 121 in two hours forty minutes. Edrich, missed in the slips off Williams when 17, scored freely to the on. After Hammond left the innings was soon over, the last three wickets falling at the same total. As Gimblett and Phillipson were unfit, England fielded two substitutes when the Dominions batted again. Fell and Craig opened with a stand of 49, and the second day closed with Donnelly and Miller together and the total 145 for three wickets.

The final stage will be remembered chiefly for the glorious driving of Miller. He outshone everyone by his dazzling hitting. In ninety minutes he raised his overnight 61 to 185, and in three-quarters of an hour of superb cricket he and Constantine put on 117. Though travelling at such a pace, Miller played faultlessly. One of his seven 6's set the whole crowd talking. It was a terrific on-drive off Hollies, and the ball lodged in the small roof of the broadcasting box above the England players' dressing-room. Besides his 6's Miller hit thirteen 4's, his 185 taking him only two and three-quarter hours. This was a wonderful finish to his season at Lord's, where in four first-class matches he scored 568 runs in eight innings, twice not out, with three centuries and an average of 94.68.

England wanted 357 in four and a half hours, and, thanks to Hammond they made a worthy challenge. Always seeking runs, the England captain was twice missed in the deep before completing 50, but, though tiring, he carried on freely, getting 102 out of 152 in two hours. His main strokes were one 6 and ten 4's. By hitting two separate hundreds in a match for the seventh time, Hammond set up an individual record. After he left there followed some daring batting by Davies and Griffith, who added 83 in fifty-eight minutes, but England for victory needed to get 74 in three-quarters of an hour when Phillipson joined Davies. Brilliant fielding by Constantine accounted for Phillipson, and next Pepper bowled Davies. Only fifteen minutes remained when the last man, Hollies, joined Wright. In tense excitement Ellis and Pepper each delivered a maiden with the fielders crowded round the batsmen. Constantine then brought back Cristofani, who bowled Wright, and the Dominions gained a grand victory. [...]

THE DOMINIONS

D.R. Fell c Griffith b Wright 12	– b Davies 28
H.S. Craig c Davies b Phillipson 56	– c Hammond b Davies 32
J. Pettiford b Davies 1	– b Wright 6
K.R. Miller lbw b Hollies 26	– c Langridge b Wright 185
M.P. Donnelly c and b Hollies 133	– b Wright 29
L.N. Constantine c Hollies b Wright 5	– c Fishlock b Hollies 40
C.G. Pepper c Hammond b Wright 51	– c Robertson b Hollies 1
D.R. Cristofani lbw b Edrich 6	– b Wright 5
R.G. Williams lbw b Wright 11	– c Hammond b Wright 0
R.S. Ellis b Wright 0	– st Griffith b Hollies 0
C.D. Bremner not out 1	– not out 0
L-b 3, w 2 5	B 1, l-b 8, n-b 1 10
	307	336

ENGLAND

L.B. Fishlock c Pettiford b Ellis 12	– run out 7
J.D. Robertson lbw b Constantine 4	– c Fell b Pettiford 5
James Langridge lbw b Cristofani 28	– b Pepper 15
W.E. Phillipson b Pepper 0	– run out 14
S.C. Griffith c Bremner b Williams 15	– c Pepper b Pettiford 36
W.R. Hammond st Bremner b Pepper 121	– st Bremner b Cristofani 102
H. Gimblett c Pettiford b Cristofani 11	– b Pepper 30
W.J. Edrich c Pepper b Cristofani 78	– c Pepper b Ellis 31
J.G.W. Davies lbw b Pepper 1	– b Pepper 56
D.V.P. Wright lbw b Pepper 0	– b Cristofani 0
E. Hollies not out 0	– not out 0
B 7, l-b 6, w 2, n-b 2 17	B 6, l-b 5, n-b 4 15
	287	311

ENGLAND BOWLING

	O	M	R	W	O	M	R	W
Phillipson	16	2	40	1	2	1	1	0
Edrich	9	1	19	1	3	0	13	0
Wright	30	2	90	5	30.1	6	105	5
Davies	22	9	43	1	13	3	35	2
Hollies	20.2	3	86	2	29	8	115	3
Langridge	6	1	24	0	8	0	57	0

THE DOMINIONS BOWLING

	O	M	R	W	O	M	R	W
Miller	1	0	2	0	5	0	28	0
Williams	22	4	49	1	2	0	11	0
Constantine	15	2	53	1	6	0	27	0
Pepper	18	3	57	4	33	13	67	3
Ellis	4	3	4	1	20	4	54	1
Cristofani	23.3	4	82	3	21.3	1	64	2
Pettiford	5	0	23	0	14	3	45	2

CRICKET UNDER THE JAPS

By Major E.W. Swanton, R.A.

It is strange, perhaps, but true, how many of us agreed on this: That we were never so thankful for having been cricketers as we were when we were guests of the Japanese. There were periods when we could play 'cricket' if our antics do not desecrate the word. There were occasions when we could lecture, and be lectured to, about it. It was a subject that filled countless hours in pitch-dark huts between sundown and the moment that continued to be euphemistically known as lights-out. And it inspired many a daydream, contrived often in the most gruesome setting, whereby one combated the present by living either in the future or the past.

In the days that followed shortly on the fall of Singapore, before work for prisoners had become widely organized, there was a certain amount of play on the padangs of Changi camp that really deserved the name of cricket. It is true that one never seemed able to hit the ball very far, a fact probably attributable about equally to the sudden change to a particularly sparse diet of rice, and the conscientious labours of generations of corporals in charge of sports gear, for whom a daily oiling of the bats had clearly been a solemn, unvarying rite. These Changi bats must have reached saturation point in the early thirties, and I never found one that came up lighter than W.H. Ponsford's three pounder. However, the pitches were true – matting over concrete – and there were even such refinements as pads and gloves. After most of us had been moved to Singapore City on the first stage of the journey up to Thailand, Lieut.-Colonel A.A. Johnson, of the Suffolk Regiment, promoted some excellent matches with the Australians, whose captain was none other than B.A. Barnett; I cannot write of these from first-hand knowledge, but this was, so to speak, Cricket de Luxe, and our jungle cricket bore little outward relation to it.

This first of the camps on the Thai-Burma railway in which we played cricket was Wampo. Christmas Day, 1942, was our first holiday, I think, since our arrival in October, and it was perhaps the fact of our so occupying the afternoon that caused our guards to receive subsequent requests to play cricket with suspicion, as having some religious significance and being therefore good for morale. (It was always the policy to keep prisoners' morale at the lowest level compatible with their being considered able to undertake whatever work was on hand. It was no doubt on this principle that, later on, the Allied chaplains were solemnly and sternly forbidden to pray for victory!)

This particular game was notable, I remember, for what is probably the fastest hundred of all time. It was scored in about five overs by a very promising young Eurasian cricketer called Thoy, who, with graceful ease, kept hitting the tennis ball clear over the huts! Nothing, of course, could have been more popular than the victory of the Other Ranks over the Officers, but the broad lesson of the match was that the merit of any contest depends on the preservation of the balance between attack and defence. (One could not help wondering, earlier in the war, when bombs were raining down on the Oval, whether the Surrey Committee were taking the hint.) For Jungle cricket our bat, surreptitiously made by the carpenter, was obviously too big.

Our cricket for the next twelve months was confined to theory and reminiscence, but lower down the line, at the base camps of Tarsao and Chungkai, various forms of play were improvised, while still later, at Nakom Patom, the hospital camp, the technique was exploited in front of large and happy crowds of men anxious to forget the tiresomeness of dysentery, beri-beri, and malaria.

Cricket at Nakom Patom reached its climax on New Year's Day, 1945, when a fresh, and certainly hitherto unrecorded, page was written in the saga of England v. Australia. The scene is not easy to put before you, but I must try. The playing area is small, perhaps sixty yards by thirty, and the batman's crease is right up against the spectators, with the pitch longways on. There are no runs behind the wicket, where many men squat in the shade of tall trees. The sides are flanked by long huts, with parallel ditches – one into the ditch, two over the hut. In fact all runs by boundaries, 1, 2, 4 or 6. An additional hazard is washing hung on bamboo 'lines'. Over the bowler's head are more trees, squaring the thing off, and in the distance a thick, high, mud wall – the camp bund – on which stands a bored and sulky Korean sentry. (Over the bund no runs and out, for balls are precious.) In effect, the spectators are the boundaries, many hundreds of them taking every inch of room. The dress is fairly uniform, wooden clogs, and a scanty triangular piece of loin-cloth known (why?) as a 'Jap-Happy'. Only the swells wear patched and tattered shorts. The mound at long-on is an Australian preserve, their 'Hill'. The sun beats down, as tropical suns do, on the flat beaten earth which is the wicket. At the bowler's end is a single bamboo stump, at the other five – yes, five – high ones. There is the hum of anticipation that you get on the first morning at Old Trafford or Trent Bridge, though there are no score cards, and no 'Three penn'orth of comfort' to be bought from our old friend 'Cushions'.

The story of the match is very much the story of that fantastic occasion at the Oval in August 1938. Flt.-Lieut. John Cocks, well known to the cricketers of Ashtead, is our Hutton; Lieut. Norman Smith, from Halifax, an even squarer, even squatter Leyland. With the regulation bat – it is two and a half inches wide and a foot shorter than normal – they play beautifully down the line of the ball, forcing the length ball past cover, squeezing the leg one square off their toes. There seems little room on the field with the eight Australian fielders poised there, but a tennis ball goes quickly off wood, the gaps are found, and there are delays while it is rescued from the swill basket, or fished out from under the hut. As the runs mount up the barracking gains in volume, and in wit at the expense of the fielders. When at last the English captain declares, the score is acknowledged to be a Thailand record.

With the Australian innings comes sensation. Captain 'Fizzer' Pearson, of Sedbergh and Lincolnshire, the English fast bowler, is wearing BOOTS! No other cricketer has anything on his feet at all, the hot earth, the occasional flint being accepted as part of the game. The moral effect of these boots is tremendous. Captain Pearson bowls with shattering speed and ferocity, and as each fresh lamb arrives for the slaughter the stumps seem more vast, the bat even punier. One last defiant cheer from the 'Hill' when their captain, Lieut.-Colonel E.E. Dunlop, comes in, another and bigger one from the English when his stumps go flying.

While these exciting things proceed one of the fielders anxiously asks himself whether they will brew trouble. 'Should fast bowlers wear boots? Pearson's ruse condemned – where did he get those boots? … boots bought from camp funds: Official denial … Board of Control's strong note …' headlines seem to grow in size. Then he remembers gratefully that here is no Press box full of slick columnists and Test captains, no microphones for the players to run to – in fact, no papers and no broadcasting. The field clears at last. As he hurries off to roll-call he thinks of a New Year's Day six years before when the bund was Table Mountain, the field was the green of Newlands, and he decides that even the South Africans who jostled their way cheerfully back into Cape Town that evening had not enjoyed their outing more than the spectators of this grotesque 'Cricket Match'.

There was much more 'cricket' at Nakom Patom of similar sort, and not a few who came to jeer stayed on to cheer. One was reminded how hitting a moving ball demands the observance of certain principles, whatever the circumstances, while, as for bowling, I defy anyone who does not obey the cardinal rules to pitch six running to a length with a tennis ball.

Talks on cricket were given at many camps, and there were cricket 'Quizzes' too, wherein a few so-called experts were showered with questions from all sides. These occasions were never lacking in humour, and there were generally enough Australians among the audience to give, as one might say, a bite to the thing. Sometimes the game was presented from a particular angle. Thus Len Muncer, of Middlesex, a sergeant in the Sherwood Foresters, described the life of a cricket professional, while Lieut.-Colonel D.V. Hill, of Worcestershire, showed the game from the point of view of a County captain. Admittedly in a prison camp there was not much in the way of alternative diversion. None the less the interest was wide enough and genuine enough to emphasize what a tremendously strong hold cricket has in England; a hold that among Australians is even stronger.

A few days after the Japanese surrender our camp at Kanburi began to assemble frequently for news bulletins. Emissaries, we heard, were flying hither and thither, instructions and encouragement were being relayed from Governments to POW's; the air was heavy with the most momentous happenings. Moreover, many of those present had had no news of the outside world for months, or longer; yet, no item commanded so much attention as the Test match at Manchester.

I had, by then, already taken my first walk for three and a half years as a free man. We found ourselves in a Thai village on the edge of the jungle. In the little café our hosts politely turned on the English programme. Yes, we were at Old Trafford, and a gentleman called Cristofani was getting a hundred […] (*1946*)

18

MOMENTS OF GLORY

Cricket offers just about everyone who plays it a glimpse of the possible: the unexpectedly well-hit stroke, unprecedentedly smart catch or unusually sharp delivery. For some who play first-class or Test cricket, there is the equivalent: that moment in which success comes as easily as it proves elusive on all other occasions. This section is devoted to such singular feats, by players who for whatever reason never rose again to equivalent heights.

In some cases, this condenses to a single delivery, as it did with Lincoln Hynes, for whom a knighthood was one thing, dismissing Donald Bradman for a duck in January 1936 quite another. In others, the moment spanned an innings, as with Alan Shiell, whose 212 against MCC in December 1965 was briefly the subject of headlines, but who found headlines simpler to make as a cricket writer in Adelaide; or two innings, like the enigmatic Bob Massie, hero of 1972's Lord's Test.

What a moment of glory has implied more often, however, has been tragedy. *Wisden* is sometimes like the recording angel in *Tristram Shandy* who, 'as he wrote it down, dropped a tear upon the word, and blotted it out forever'. None who watched New South Wales play South Australia at the SCG in January 1927 could have imagined that the young centurions Karl Schneider and Archie Jackson would both die at the ages of twenty-three. One can only wonder what 'Sunny Jim' Mackay, Charles Gregory, Frank O'Keeffe and Robert Rose might have accomplished with better health and fortune, and what fame Eddie Gilbert might have secured had he lived in more enlightened times.

Meteoric careers are less frequent in an age of longer life expectancy, better player emoluments and less capricious selection. Someone like Dr Harry Rock, with a first-class average of 95, could expect to play more than six first-class matches. But now and then, the phenomenon of the flash in the pan is repeated, as it was with Peter Taylor, whose 8 for 154 against England at Sydney in January 1987 in his seventh first-class match began a sequence of twenty-five Australian victories in the last forty Ashes Tests. Taylor never remotely paralleled the feat, but subsequently, and fittingly, became an Australian selector.

—GH

NEW SOUTH WALES V. SOUTH AUSTRALIA

Played at Sydney, Friday, Saturday, Monday, Tuesday, Wednesday, January 5, 6, 8, 9, 10, 1906. – In beating South Australia by nine wickets New South Wales were chiefly indebted to Mackay who played superbly, and made two separate hundreds. South Australia sadly missed Clement Hill's batting. Mackay's hitting when New South Wales went in to win the game, was exceptionally brilliant. Gehrs played far better than on any other occasion during the season.

SOUTH AUSTRALIA

N.H. Claxton c Waddy b Cotter	5	– b Cotter	1
F.T. Hack b Garnsey	32	– c Carter b Cotter	41
J. Darling b Cotter	14	– c Waddy b Noble	2
J.H. Pellew c Noble b Garnsey	36	– b Macartney	9
D.R.A. Gehrs c Garnsey b O'Connor	101	– c Macartney b Cotter	10
C.E. Dolling st Carter b O'Connor	13	– not out	83
J.E. Reedman c Carter b Cotter	31	– c Garnsey b O'Connor	8
R.F. Cowan c Cotter b Macarthey	3	– b O'Connor	2
J.F. Travers not out	6	– lbw, b Garnsey	16
H. Jarvis c Cotter b Garnsey	3	– absent	0
H.T. Wright c and b Garnsey	0	– b Garnsey	0
Byes, &c.	13	Byes, &c.	16
	257		**188**

NEW SOUTH WALES

V.T. Trumper c Jarvis b Reedman	16	– c Hack b Reedman	35
J.R.M. Mackay c Darling b Blaxton	105	– not out	102
M.A. Noble c Claxton b Reedman	43	– not out	37
A. Diamond c Gehrs b Claxton	15		
A. Cotter c Cowan b Claxton	0		
Rev. E.F. Waddy c Pellew b Claxton	4		
C.G. Macartney c Gehrs b Reedman	1		
S.J. Redgrave c Reedman b Travers	8		
H. Carter b Wright	40		
G.L. Garnsey not out	32		
J. O'Connor c Gehrs b Wright	2		
Byes, &c.	3	Byes, &c.	3
	269		**177**

NEW SOUTH WALES BOWLING

	Overs	Mdns	Runs	Wkts	Overs	Mdns	Runs	Wkts
Cotter	24	4	97	3	29	12	47	3
Garnsey	20.5	1	70	4	19.2	6	46	2
Macartney	14	2	25	1	22	13	21	1
Redgrave	5	0	15	0	2	1	3	0
O'Connor	12	3	25	2	16	4	35	2
Noble	6	2	12	0	8	3	20	1

South Australia Bowling

Wright	14.1	2	61	2	7	0	32	0
Reedman	26	0	98	3	8.4	1	48	1
Claxton	20	4	44	4	9	1	34	0
Cowan	2	0	6	0	3	1	16	0
Travers	25	6	57	1	6	0	26	0
Dolling					4	0	18	0

MACKAY, MR JAMES RAINEY MUNRO, who died in Walcha Hospital, New South Wales, on June 13, 1953, aged 71, was one of Australia's greatest cricketing sons. Only a magnificent constitution enabled him to live so long, for his doctor told him fifteen years before that he might pass away at any time. Born on September 9, 1881, he never came to England, and so was not so well known as some of the Australians who did. Yet he batted brilliantly for New South Wales in Inter-State games, and in 1905–6 was wonderfully successful. In successive innings he hit 90 v. South Australia, 194 v. Victoria, 105 and 102 not out v. South Australia, 18 and 50 v. Victoria. When the 1905 Australian team returned from England, they played a match for Jim Kelly's benefit against New South Wales, for whom Mackay scored 4 and 136. Against Queensland, not then in the Sheffield Shield tournament, he made 203.

Wisden of 1907 stated of this performance: 'The sensation of the season was the wonderful batting of J.R.M. Mackay ... who scored in six innings, once not out, 559 runs. In face of such form it would seem that a great mistake was committed in not bringing him to England in 1905 ... It was the general opinion that, for brilliancy, his batting has never been surpassed in Australia except by Trumper.' Shortly after, Mackay accepted a lucrative position in Johannesburg and was very successful in South African cricket. The question arose as to whether he should be a candidate for selection in the 1907 South African team to tour England, but it was felt that he had not lived long enough in the Union to qualify. This was a great disappointment to him, for he thus had the hard luck of just missing two visits to the Mother Country. He was known by the nick-name of 'Sunny Jim', a tribute to his disposition on and off the cricket field.

QUEENSLAND V. NEW SOUTH WALES

Played at Brisbane, Saturday, Monday, Tuesday, November 10, 12, 13, 1906. – Although without Trumper, Noble and Diamond, New South Wales beat Queensland by an innings and 301 runs. The match was rendered memorable by the fact that Charles Gregory, with his innings of 383, beat the record in Australia in good class cricket. He was batting for five hours and three-quarters, his hits including fifty-five 4's. His play was disfigured by three chances, but when he gave the first of them he had scored 282.

QUEENSLAND

R. Hartigan c Waddy b Garnsey	50	– c Bardsley b Barnes	61
G. Brown st Carter b Macartney	30	– c Redgrave b Barnes	32
C.E. Simpson b Macartney	8	– st Carter b Barnes	59
T.B. Faunce b Cotter	11	– c Redgrave b Garnsey	17
M.F. Dunn b Macartney	3	– c and b Garnsey	19
W.B. Hayes c and b Cotter	4	– run out	21
W.T. Evans run out	19	– c Garnsey b Barnes	43
J. Thomson c Cotter b Garnsey	3	– c Blaxland b Garnsey	43
F. Timbury c Waddy b Garnsey	5	– not out	2
M.F. McCaffrey c Waddy b Garnsey	0	– lbw, b Barnes	5
C. Barstow not out	0	– c Bardsley b Garnsey	0
B 4, l-b 8	12	B 9, l-b 4, w 1, n-b 1	15
	145		**317**

NEW SOUTH WALES

W. Bardsley b Barstow 12
C. Gregory c and b Hayes 383
R.N. Hickson run out 48
S.J. Redgrave run out 32
E.L. Waddy c Hartigan b McCaffrey 100
J.C. Barnes c Thomson b Timbury 13
M.H. Blaxland b Barstow 94

C.G. Macartney not out 21
A. Cotter c Hartigan b Hayes 34
H. Carter c Simpson b Hayes 1
G.L. Garnsey c Faunce b Hayes 10
B 10, l-b 4, w 1 15

763

NEW SOUTH WALES BOWLING

	Overs	Mdns	Runs	Wkts	Overs	Mdns	Runs	Wkts
Cotter	14	1	53	2	11	3	40	0
Garnsey	17	3	64	4	21	0	94	4
Macartney	5	2	14	3	10	0	31	0
Redgrave	2	1	2	0	12.5	0	105	5
Barnes					8	2	32	0

QUEENSLAND BOWLING

	Overs	Mdns	Runs	Wkts
Hayes	28.3	0	120	4
Timbury	29	6	123	1
McCaffrey	28	2	132	1
Barstow	27	2	115	2
Dunn	10	0	59	0
Hartigan	17	3	65	0
Brown	2	0	10	0
Simpson	11	1	59	0
Thompson	10	3	37	0
Evans	3	0	28	0

CHARLES W. GREGORY, died at St. Vincent's Hospital Darlinghurst, New South Wales, on November 14th, 1910. Born on September 13th, 1878, he was only in his thirty-third year. At one time it was confidently expected that he would rival his brother, Sydney Gregory, and make a great name for himself, but, though he did many brilliant things, he proved, on the whole, a disappointment and was never thought quite good enough to be picked for a tour in England. From some cause or other he generally failed on big occasions. One performance will cause his name to be remembered. For New South Wales against Queensland at Brisbane in November, 1906, he scored 383 – the second highest innings on record in a first-class match and the highest in Australia.

Australian XI v. Rest of Australia

(Frank Iredale's Testimonial Match)

Played at Sydney, Friday, Saturday, Monday and Tuesday, February 3, 4, 6, and 7, 1922. – This was the match of the Australian season. For some reason it was restricted to four days and had to be left unfinished. The takings, including boxes on the ground, came to £1,740 10s. 9d., and but for rain on the Saturday would have amounted to a good deal more. Frank Iredale is now secretary of the New South Wales Cricket Association. The bat beat the ball, 1,358 runs being scored and only twenty-nine wickets going down. Still in the first innings of the Rest, Gregory bowled right up to the form he had shown in England. Beyond everything else the feature of the match was the splendid batting of O'Keeffe, who scored 177 and 141.

Rest of Australia

C. Kelleway c Oldfield b Gregory	0	
F. O'Keeffe b McDonald	177 – b Macartney	141
V. Richardson c Oldfield b Gregory	8 – b Ryder	5
H.S. Love b Gregory	28 – c Mailey b McDonald	63
E.P. Barbour c Oldfield b Gregory	20 – c Andrews b Mailey	16
C.B. Willis c and b Gregory	133 – not out	34
A. Punch c Ryder b McDonald	4	
V.S. Ransford c Oldfield b Macartney	0	
A.W. Lampard not out	21 – lbw, b Ryder	32
J.D. Scott c Mailey b Gregory	0	
P.M. Hornibrook c Oldfield b Gregory	0	
Byes, &c.	2	Byes, &c. 11
	393	***302**

*Innings declared closed.

AUSTRALIA XI

H.L. Collins lbw, b Kelleway 41	– b Hornibrook 117
W. Bardsley c Love b Scott 25	
C.G. Macartney c Kelleway b O'Keefe 47	– b Hornibrook 9
T.J.E. Andrews run out 30	– c Love b Scott 45
J. Ryder c sub b Scott 62	– not out 63
J.M. Gregory c Love b Kelleway 1	– c Ransford b Hornibrook 6
J.M. Taylor c Love b Hornibrook 19	
W.A. Oldfield c and b Hornibrook 63	
W.W. Armstrong not out 77	
A.A. Mailey c Barbour b Hornibrook 6	
E.A. McDonald b Hornibrook 14	
Byes, &c. 18	Byes, &c. 20
403	**260**

AUSTRALIAN XI BOWLING

	Overs	Mdns	Runs	Wkts	Overs	Mdns	Runs	Wkts
Gregory	19	3	95	7	9	0	51	0
McDonald	19	1	95	2	14	1	52	1
Mailey	12	1	66	0	18	1	81	1
Armstrong	9	3	29	0				
Ryder	7	2	27	0	11	1	42	2
Andrews	5	0	35	0	4	0	25	0
Collins	3	0	6	0	8	1	14	0
Macartney	9	2	38	1	11	0	26	1

REST OF AUSTRALIA BOWLING

	Overs	Mdns	Runs	Wkts	Overs	Mdns	Runs	Wkts
Scott	24	4	109	2	13	1	71	1
Kelleway	17	1	68	2				
Hornibrook	30.3	5	107	4	21.2	1	106	3
Richardson	1	0	13	0				
O'Keeffe	7	0	41	1				
Barbour	9	0	47	0				
Lampard					5	0	29	0
Punch					6	0	34	0

O'KEEFFE, FRANK ALOYSIUS, born at Waverley, Sydney, on May 11, 1896, died on March 26, 1924, at the New End Hospital, Hampstead, of peritonitis, at the early age of 27. A brilliant batsman and field as well as a very useful slow right-handed bowler, a great future seemed in store for him. He had performed splendidly in Australia before coming to England, and would, had he lived, have been qualified for Lancashire by residence last June. Our climate, unfortunately, did not suit him, and he was never in the best of health while in this country. After playing for Waverley C.C. he appeared for Paddington for two years under M.A. Noble's captaincy and for New South Wales against Queensland in 1920–1 he scored 83 at Sydney and 4 and 72 at Brisbane. Settling in Melbourne, where he thought his skill would be better appreciated, he enjoyed a most successful season in 1921–2. In succession he made 87 and 79 for Victoria v. New South Wales at Sydney, 177 and 144 for Rest of Australia v. The Australian Eleven of 1921 in Iredale's benefit match on the same ground, and 180 for Victoria v. South Australia at Adelaide, where he and E.R. Mayne (85) put up 144 for the first wicket. Accepting an engagement with the Church C.C., in the Lancashire League, he was disappointing in 1922, but for the club a year later he scored 650 runs with an average of 40.62 and took 50 wickets for 14.38 runs each. He was a man of much personal charm, and his early death was regretted by a very large number of friends.

NEW SOUTH WALES V. VICTORIA

Played at Sydney, January 24, 26, 27, 28, 1925. – In an extraordinary match New South Wales, with only a moderate side, lost by seven wickets after putting together the huge total of 614 in the first innings. Both Rock, who shared with Morgan in an opening partnership of 202, and Kippax gave brilliant displays of batting. Victoria made a capital response to the great total, and then skilful bowling by Hartkopf and Hendry brought about such a collapse of the New South Wales batsmen that the visitors had a fairly light task in the last innings.

NEW SOUTH WALES

H.O. Rock c Tarrant b Hartkopf	235 – c Hartkopf b Blackie	51
G. Morgan b Hendry	87 – c Hartkopf b Wallace	3
A. Ratcliffe lbw, b Blackie	1 – c Hartkopf b Hendry	8
B.M. Salmon run out	31 – c Liddicutt b Blackie	9
A.P. Wells st Ellis b Hartkopf	9 – run out	14
A. Kippax not out	212 – st Ellis b Hartkopf	40
C.V. Morrissey c Ellis b Hartkopf	4 – b Hendry	0
C. Lawes b Hartkopf	0 – st Ellis b Hartkopf	1
A.D. Mayes run out	6 – not out	5
J.D. Scott b Wallace	1 – c Schneider b Hartkopf	4
N. Bosley st Ellis b Hartkopf	1 – c Mayne b Hendry	9
Byes, &c.	27	Byes, &c.	8
	614	**152**

VICTORIA

E.R. Mayne b Scott	12 – lbw, b Scott	1
W.M. Woodfull run out	81 – not out	120
H.L. Hendry c Mayes b Lawes	19 – c Scott b Morrissey	85
F.A. Tarrant c Ratcliffe b Scott	23 – not out	18
A.E. Liddicut b Scott	132 – c Ratcliffe b Morgan	28
A.E.V. Hartkopf c Wells b Morrissey	56	
K.J. Schneider b Scott	1	
J.L. Ellis run out	20	
C.B. Willis c Rock b Scott	100	
D. Blackie c Kippax b Lawes	23	
P.H. Wallace not out	0	
Byes, &c.	35	Byes, &c.	13
	502	**265**

VICTORIA BOWLING

	Overs	Mdns	Runs	Wkts	Overs	Mdns	Runs	Wkts
Wallace	24	0	103	1	5	0	16	1
Blackie	31	1	108	1	12	2	29	2
Hendry	33	2	129	1	9	0	23	3
Hartkopf	23.1	0	121	5	8	0	45	3
Tarrant	20	1	69	0	6	1	13	0
Liddicut	14	1	42	0	2	0	9	0
Schneider	3	0	15	0	2	0	9	0

NEW SOUTH WALES BOWLING

	Overs	Mdns	Runs	Wkts	Overs	Mdns	Runs	Wkts
Scott	33.1	3	149	5	11	0	44	1
Lawes	33	9	82	2	16	1	47	0
Morrissey	26	4	91	1	11	0	36	1
Kippax	14	3	58	0	9	0	47	0
Bosley	12	2	36	0	15.4	1	46	0
Mayes	16	3	51	0	10	3	15	0
Morgan					6	0	17	1

ROCK, Dr HARRY OWEN, who died in Sydney on March 10, 1978, aged 81, had a unique career. His six first-class matches, spread over three Australian seasons, 1924 to 1927, produced 758 runs with an average of 94.75; his four Sheffield Shield matches 560 runs, average 112. In his first match for New South Wales he scored 127 and 27 not out, and in his next 235 and 51. Then room had to be found for Collins, Bardsley, Taylor, Andrews and Kelleway and he was omitted! Two more Sheffield Shield matches and one against Western Australia, in which he scored 151, with a Test Trial match in 1926–7 completed his career. Qualifying as a doctor and practising in Newcastle, he was lost to Australian cricket. Otherwise he must surely have ranked among the great. Though slightly built, he was a tremendous driver and had a wonderful gift of placing the ball and a basic soundness of technique which enabled him, as an opening batsman, to score at a great pace without taking undue risks. He was a son of C.W. Rock, the Cambridge blue and Warwickshire player.

NEW SOUTH WALES v. SOUTH AUSTRALIA

Played at Sydney, January 8, 10, 11, 12, 1927. – In their return match with New South Wales, South Australia took an ample revenge for the defeat at Adelaide, a comparatively low scoring match ending in their favour by 340 runs. On the first day Arthur Richardson played very sound cricket for four hours and three-quarters, but otherwise, the South Australian batting was disappointing until Schneider, in the second innings, strengthened his side's advantage of 147 with a steady three-figure innings. O'Brien, McNamee, Grimmett, McKay and Lee bowled well at different periods of the game.

SOUTH AUSTRALIA

K.J. Schneider c Morgan b Fox	.9 – c Kippax b Macartney	.146
A.J. Richardson c O'Brien b Macartney	.189 – b Fox	.30
V.Y. Richardson b O'Brien	.29 – lbw, b McNamee	.55
D.E. Pritchard c and b O'Brien	.43 – lbw, b McNamee	.7
W.C. Alexander b Fox	.14 – b Fox	.26
C.V. Grimmett b McNamee	.3 – c Osborne b McNamee	.4
D.G. McKay b O'Brien	.17 – run out	.49
P.K. Lee b O'Brien	.5 – b McNamee	.23
N.L. Williams b O'Brien	.14 – c sub, b McNamee	.21
J.D. Scott b Macartney	.5 – not out	.7
G.P. Inkster not out	.4 – b Macartney	.12
Byes, &c.	.13 Byes, &c.	.19
	345	**399**

NEW SOUTH WALES

N.E. Phillips lbw, b A.J. Richardson	.15 – b Grimmett	.4
L.W. Gwynne c Inkster b McKay	.43 – c Inkster b Scott	.0
C.G. Macartney c and b McKay	.43 – c and b Grimmett	.0
A.F. Kippax c and b Scott	.32 – b Lee	.52
A. Jackson c Inkster b McKay	.0 – not out	.104
J.E. Hogg st Inkster b Grimmett	.20 – lbw, b Lee	.5
G. Morgan b Grimmett	.28 – c V.Y. Richardson b Scott	.10
R. Osborne b Grimmett	.7 – c Scott b Lee	.8
E. O'Brien b Grimmett	.1 – b Lee	.7
N. Fox lbw, b McKay	.2 – b Lee	.0
R. McNamee not out	.0 – c Schneider b Williams	.4
Byes, &c.	.7 Byes, &c.	.12
	198	**206**

NEW SOUTH WALES BOWLING

	Overs	Mdns	Runs	Wkts	Overs	Mdns	Runs	Wkts
Fox	16	1	79	2	21	0	99	2
McNamee	22	4	75	1	40	6	86	5
Phillips	6	0	16	0	4	0	19	0
O'Brien	21.7	0	99	5	16	0	69	0
Macartney	22	2	63	2	16.7	5	28	2
Morgan					14	2	70	0
Kippax					3	0	9	0

SOUTH AUSTRALIA BOWLING

	Overs	Mdns	Runs	Wkts	Overs	Mdns	Runs	Wkts
Scott	10	0	44	1	9	2	23	2
A.J. Richardson	7	1	25	1	2	1	4	0
Williams	9	2	20	0	9	0	49	1
Grimmett	15.4	0	70	4	10	2	50	2
McKay	11	2	32	4	6	0	32	0
Lee					7	0	36	5

SCHNEIDER, Mr KARL J., who died at Adelaide on September 5, 1928, of heart failure, had had a brief but brilliant career. Although very short, he was in quite the first flight of left-handed batsmen. He had not many strokes, but his footwork was excellent and he could hit hard: in addition a brilliant out-field, he could also bowl a useful slow ball. For four years he appeared in the Xavier College Eleven, at Melbourne, and for a little while he was also at Melbourne University. In club matches for the Melbourne C.C. in 1921–2 his average was 134.66, and during his last season in first-class cricket – 1927–8 – his figures were 10–0–143–520–52.00. When Victoria totalled 1059 against Tasmania in 1922–3 he made 56, assisting Ponsford, who set up a new record in scoring 429, to add 164 for the seventh wicket. Subsequently his chief triumphs were obtained for South Australia during the seasons 1926–7 and 1927–8, when he scored 146 and 108 v. New South Wales, 107 v. West Australia, 143 v. Victoria, and 114 v. Queensland. First with A.J. Richardson and later with G.W. Harris, he proved himself a splendid man to open the innings. Against Victoria at Melbourne in 1927–8 he and Harris figured in first wicket stands of 89 and 138. Just a year ago he took part in the Australian tour of New Zealand, where he continued to display capital form. In the match with Canterbury he scored 138, he and Oldfield, who made 137, pulling round the game by adding 229 together after six wickets had fallen for 135.

FOURTH TEST MATCH

Played at Adelaide, Friday, Saturday, Monday, Tuesday, Wednesday, Thursday, Friday, February 1, 2, 4, 5, 6, 7, 8, 1929. [...] England had no reason for changing their eleven, but Australia brought in Jackson for Richardson, the young New South Wales batsman enjoying the distinction of playing a three-figure innings in his first Test match. Before going further, it is only right to pay a great tribute to his performance. Accomplished, as will be told later, in circumstances calculated to daunt a player of mature experience, it was, in point of style and beauty of execution and stroke play, the best innings played against the Englishmen during the whole tour. Other achievements made the match memorable. Hammond followed his innings of 251 and 200 at Sydney and Melbourne respectively by making two separate hundreds; Hobbs and Sutcliffe once more gave the side a good start; Jardine played an invaluable innings in partnership with Hammond and, above all, White, sending down over 124 overs, obtained thirteen wickets for 256 runs, eight of them in the second innings. [...]

England's first innings lasted until after three o'clock on the second day yet, excellent as was a total of 334, there existed reason for anticipating when Hobbs and Sutcliffe had made 143 in two hours and three-quarters that the final score would be considerably higher. Both these men left at the same total, Grimmett going on when Hobbs was out and getting Sutcliffe second ball. To show the character of Hobbs's innings, his hits may be given in detail. These were two 4's, two 3's, eleven 2's and thirty-eight 1's. Still each man batted wonderfully well. Hammond, who had gone in at the fall of the first wicket, saw Jardine and Hendren quickly dismissed, and although Chapman helped to add 67, nobody else did anything. Taking out his bat, Hammond scored 72 of the last 88 runs, batting altogether for nearly four hours and a half. He hit nine 4's, his driving all through being splendid. Grimmett in this innings bowled better than in any other match against the Englishmen.

Going in on the second day just before half-past three, Australia made a deplorable start, three wickets falling for 19 runs. Off the fourth ball from Tate, Woodfull was magnificently caught at the wicket on the leg-side, Hendry left at six and White, going on at 16, bowled Kippax. It was then that Jackson revealed his great powers. The position did not seem to trouble him in the slightest, and he drove, cut and hit to leg with the utmost certainty and confidence. Ryder helped him to add 126, Bradman stayed while 82 were put on, and then 60 more came in fifty minutes before his superb innings ended at 287. Jackson batted for five hours and twenty minutes, gave no chance, and hit fifteen 4's, seven 3's and twenty-three 2's. In the end Australia, after being in over seven hours and a half, led by 35 runs. A word of praise is due to Tate for some fine bowling.

Going in on the fourth day just before half-past twelve, England lost Hobbs and Sutcliffe for 21, Hobbs, like Woodfull, being splendidly caught on the leg-side at the wicket with only one run scored. The position was serious, but Hammond and Jardine rose to the occasion in wonderful style. Both men forced the ball to the on-side with clever strokes, and were together at the close of play with the score at 206. They were not separated until a quarter to three on Wednesday afternoon, and by adding 262 runs established a record for the third wicket partnership in Test Matches. The stand lasted nearly five hours and fifty minutes, Jardine, when he looked certain to reach his hundred, being caught at silly mid-off. England had then pulled the game round but they proceeded to throw away their advantage, Hendren, Chapman and Larwood all leaving while the score was being raised to 302. Hammond was at length seventh out at 327, just before four o'clock. [...] After tea, Tate, hitting a 6 and five 4's, played an invaluable innings and England, all out for 383, set their opponents 349 to get. Before play ceased 24 runs were scored without loss, and on Thursday and Friday there came a fight which will long be remembered by those who saw it. The first wicket fell at 65, and soon after lunch on the Thursday three men were out for 74. A little later occurred an incident which looked like losing the game for England, Ryder, with his score at 26, offering the simplest of catches to White who, to everyone's surprise and his own obvious annoyance, dropped the ball. Kippax and Ryder added 137, Australia then being on top, but soon afterwards White made amends for his previous blunder by holding a hard return from Ryder high up with the left hand. The Australian captain had made a great effort for his side in a fine display of hard hitting. a'Beckett stayed for thirty-five minutes, Hammond making a sensational catch at second slip to dismiss him, and when play ceased for the day Australia, with six men out for 260, required 89 to win. When, next morning, Bradman and Oxenham carried the score to 308, victory for Australia appeared more than likely. These two had added 50 in 65 minutes. At 320, with Bradman run out, fortunes changed again. [...] Blackie went in amidst tense excitement and carefully played four balls from White. Then came one pitched just a little shorter; Blackie hooked it high into the long field in front of square leg where Larwood, running a few yards, brought off a fine catch and finished a wonderful struggle.

ENGLAND

J.B. Hobbs c Ryder b Hendry	74 – c Oldfield b Hendry	1
H. Sutcliffe st Oldfield b Grimmett	64 – c Oldfield b a'Beckett	17
W.R. Hammond not out	119 – c and b Ryder	177
Mr D.R. Jardine lbw, b Grimmett	1 – c Woodfull b Oxenham	98
E. Hendren b Blackie	13 – c Bradman b Blackie	11
Mr A.P.F. Chapman c a'Beckett b Ryder	39 – c Woodfull b Blackie	0
G. Duckworth c Ryder b Grimmett	5 – lbw, b Oxenham	1
H. Larwood b Hendry	3 – lbw, b Oxenham	5
G. Geary run out	3 – c and b Grimmett	6
M.W. Tate b Grimmett	2 – lbw, b Oxenham	47
Mr J.C. White c Ryder b Grimmett	0 – not out	4
B 3, l-b 7, w 1	11 B 6, l-b 10	16
	334	**383**

AUSTRALIA

W.M. Woodfull c Duckworth b Tate	1 – c Geary b White	30
A. Jackson lbw, b White	164 – c Duckworth b Geary	36
H.L. Hendry c Duckworth b Larwood	2 – c Tate b White	5
A.F. Kippax b White	3 – c Hendren b White	51
J. Ryder lbw, b White	63 – c and b White	87
D.G. Bradman c Larwood b Tate	40 – run out	58
E.L. a'Beckett b White	36 – c Hammond b White	21
R.K. Oxenham c Chapman b White	15 – c Chapman b White	12
W.A. Oldfield b Tate	32 – not out	15
C.V. Grimmett b Tate	4 – c Tate b White	9
D.J. Blackie not out	3 – c Larwood b White	0
L-b 5, w 1	6 B 9, l-b 3	12
	369	**336**

AUSTRALIA BOWLING

	Overs	Mdns	Runs	Wkts	Overs	Mdns	Runs	Wkts
A'Beckett	31	8	44	0	27	9	41	1
Hendry	31	14	49	2	28	11	56	1
Grimmett	52.1	12	102	5	52	15	117	1
Oxenham	34	14	51	0	47.4	21	67	4
Blackie	29	6	57	1	39	11	70	2
Ryder	5	1	20	1	5	1	13	1
Kippax					2	0	3	0

ENGLAND BOWLING

	Overs	Mdns	Runs	Wkts	Overs	Mdns	Runs	Wkts
Larwood	37	6	92	1	20	4	60	0
Tate	42	10	77	4	37	9	75	0
White	60	16	130	5	64.5	21	126	8
Geary	12	3	32	0	16	2	42	1
Hammond	9	1	32	0	14	3	21	0

Umpires: D. Elder and G. Hele.

JACKSON, Mr ARCHIBALD, the New South Wales and Australian Test cricketer, died at Brisbane on February 16, 1933, the day that England defeated Australia and regained the 'Ashes', at the early age of 23. His passing was not only a very sad loss to Australian cricket in particular but to the cricket world in general. A native of Scotland where he was born on September 5, 1909, he was hailed as a second Victor Trumper – a comparison made alike for his youthful success, elegant style and superb stroke play. Well set up, very active his feet, and not afraid to jump in to the slow bowlers and hit the ball hard, he accomplished far more in big cricket than Trumper had done at his age. He first attracted attention when at school in Balmain, Sydney, and later at the Roselle School. So quickly did he mature that, at the age of seventeen, he gained an assured place in the New South Wales team. In his first season of Sheffield Shield cricket he scored 464 runs at an average of 58; next year he achieved a feat no other batsman of his age had performed, by making two centuries in a match – 131 and 122 against South Australia. For a time Jackson had something of a reputation of being a second innings batsman, for often he failed at his first attempt and then made a good score in the second innings. This weakness, however, he overcame and he soon established himself as an opening batsman for New South Wales. Given his place in the Australian team when the MCC side, under the captaincy of Mr A.P.F. Chapman, toured Australia in 1928–29, Jackson, on his first appearance in Test cricket against England, made a hundred – the youngest player to do so. This was at Adelaide where in the Fourth Test Match, which England won by 12 runs, he scored 164. For sheer brilliance of execution his strokes during this delightful display could scarcely have been exceeded. He reached three figures with a glorious square drive off Larwood in the first over after lunch and was one of the very few Australian batsmen who during that tour could successfully jump in and drive J.C. White. An innings of 182 in the Australian Test Trial – regarded as the finest he ever played – made certain of inclusion in the team which visited England in 1930. Unfortunately, English cricket lovers did not in that tour see Jackson at his best. Although he scored over 1,000 runs he failed to reveal his true form until towards the end of the summer. Then, in the final Test Match at the Oval, he put together a score of 73 and helped Bradman in a partnership of 243 for the fourth wicket which still stands as a record in a Test Matoh between Australia and England. Jackson, of course, never saw Trumper play, but Kippax, in style and stance and in some strokes, was not unlike Trumper; and Jackson, consciously or unconsciously, and while giving full play to his natural tendencies, took Kippax as his model. He had a splendid return from the deep field and if not so fast a runner as Bradman, covered ground very quickly. His later years were marred by continued ill-health and his untimely end was not unexpected. While lying in hospital on what was to prove his death-bed he was married.

QUEENSLAND V. NEW SOUTH WALES

Played at Brisbane, November 6, 7, 9, 10, 1931. – Queensland, after being dismissed for 109, secured the wickets of Bill and Bradman before their opponents scored a run but afterwards their bowling was mastered and New South Wales won by an innings and 238 runs. Amos, with five wickets for 22, figured prominently in the early rout of Queensland and a magnificent innings by McCabe went far towards deciding the issue. Going in when three wickets had fallen for 31 and Kippax had retired injured, McCabe, batting through the rest of the innings, made 229 not out. Fingleton stayed over four hours. Queensland, 323 behind, collapsed again and altogether in the match nine batsmen were dismissed without scoring. Thurlow suffered that indignity twice.

QUEENSLAND

R. Higgins b Amos 3	– lbw, b McCabe 8
F.J. Gough b Fairfax 14	– lbw, b Fairfax 0
F.W. Sides c Oldfield b Amos 1	– not out 22
R.K. Oxenham b Amos 0	– c Bradman b Hunt 0
D. Hansen c Oldfield b Amos 20	– c Hird b Hunt....................0
K. Mossop not out 44	– c McCabe b Hunt 2
A. Hurwood lbw, b Amos 0	– c Oldfield b Campbell 9
L. Waterman c Oldfield b McCabe 18	– c Campbell b Fairfax 20
V.B. Suche c Bradman b Campbell 6	– c and b Hunt 12
H.M. Thurlow b Campbell 0	– c Bill b Campbell 0
E. Gilbert b McCabe 0	– lbw, b Campbell 5
B 2, w 1 3	B 4, l-b 3 7

109 85

NEW SOUTH WALES

O.W. Bill c Waterman b Gilbert 0	W.A. Oldfield b Hurwood 46
J.H. Fingleton b Oxenham 93	J.N. Campbell c Oxenham
D.G. Bradman c Waterman b Gilbert 0	b Hurwood 4
A.F. Kippax retired hurt 16	G.S. Amos lbw, b Gilbert 2
A. Fairfax b Gilbert 5	W.A. Hunt run out..................3
S.J. McCabe not out 229	B 17, l-b 9, n-b 5 31
S.F. Hird lbw, b Oxenham 3	

432

NEW SOUTH WALES BOWLING

	Overs	Mdns	Runs	Wkts	Overs	Mdns	Runs	Wkts
Amos	13	5	22	5	6	1	12	0
Fairfax	9	2	21	1	6	1	24	2
McCabe	9.5	1	23	2	5	1	4	1
Hunt	8	1	22	0	8	1	25	4
Campbell	5	0	18	2	3.5	1	13	3

QUEENSLAND BOWLING

Thurlow	22	4	69	0
Gilbert	20.7	2	74	4
Hurwood	25	5	95	2
Oxenham	27	7	79	2
Suche	14	1	50	0
Gough	5	0	34	0

GILBERT, EDWARD, who was the best remembered aboriginal cricketer to play first-class cricket in Australia, had been long absent from the scene of his sometimes sensational fast bowling feats of the 1930s and in ill health for many years before his death in the Wolston Park Hospital near Brisbane on January 9, 1978, aged 69. Nevertheless, this notably quiet but well spoken product of Queensland's Cherbourg Aboriginal Settlement has remained a legend down through the years. After successfully graduating through the Queensland Colts XI in 1930, Eddie Gilbert quickly reached the headlines in the 1931 Sheffield Shield match against NSW in Brisbane by his first over dismissals of Wendell Bill and Bradman without scoring. Both were caught by wicketkeeper Len Waterman within seven deliveries, but not before one ball rising from a green-top had flicked off Sir Donald's cap and another knocked the bat from his hands! Sir Donald has since recalled that the six deliveries he faced on this occasion were the fastest experienced during his career.

Lightly built and only a little over five feet seven inches in height, Gilbert possessed exceptionally long arms and could bowl at great pace off a run sometimes no longer than four paces. It was this, allied with a somewhat whippy forearm action, which led to suggestions that his right arm bent on occasions during a pronounced arc action which finished with his hand almost touching the ground and his head at knee level. Strong advocacy for Gilbert's Test selection was nullified by the suspect action, a view several times shared and acted on by senior umpires. Nevertheless, the same officials completely accepted his delivery on most other occasions. Several films were taken without conclusive decision and controversy continued throughout Gilbert's career which was undoubtedly affected by the publicity. He faded out of the game in 1936 after showing fine form while taking six wickets in his final match – against Victoria at the Brisbane Cricket Ground in 1936. In nineteen Shield matches, he took 73 wickets at an average of 29.75, while a further fourteen wickets were gained in Queensland matches against touring MCC, West Indies and South African sides.

NEW SOUTH WALES V. SOUTH AUSTRALIA

Played at Sydney, January 17, 18, 20, 1936. – Abandoned. Rain prevented play on the first day, and owing to the death of King George V, there was no cricket on the last day. When the game started after lunch on Saturday, McGilvray sent South Australia in, and White (8 for 31) nonplussed the batsmen on an awkward wicket. However, he did not have the satisfaction of disposing of Bradman who was out without scoring through Little showing smart anticipation in moving to fine short leg and holding a glide off Hynes. South Australia took nearly three hours over their 94. An improved wicket and perfect weather gave New South Wales every advantage on Monday. Fallowfield spent almost three hours in scoring 53, but Robinson, who placed his strokes beautifully, and Hynes showed more freedom.

SOUTH AUSTRALIA

C.L. Badcock c McGilvray b White 24
R. Parker c McGilvray b White 14
D.G. Bradman c Little b Hynes 0
A.J. Ryan c Little b White 2
M.G. Waite c Marks b White 0
E.J. Moyle b White 5
T. O'Connell c Marks b White 13

C.W. Walker c Robinson b White 7
R.G. Williams not out 10
F. Ward c Mudge b White 12
T.W. Wall run out 0
    B 2, l-b 2, w 1, n-b 2 7

94

NEW SOUTH WALES

L. Fallowfield c Williams b Ward 53
H. Mudge lbw, b Wall 8
R. Little c Walker b Ward 30
A.E. Marks lbw, b Ward 25
R. Robinson not out 94
L.C. Hynes run out 41

F. Easton c Walker b Williams 1
E.S. White not out 27
    L-b 3, n-b 4 7

Six wkts **286**

A. McGilvray, H.C. Chilvers, A. Cooper did not bat

NEW SOUTH WALES BOWLING

	Overs	Mdns	Runs	Wkts
Cooper	9	3	11	0
McGilvray	4	0	11	0
Hynes	11.3	2	25	1
White	19	8	31	8
Chilvers	3	0	9	0

SOUTH AUSTRALIA BOWLING

Wall	15	2	58	1
Williams	17	5	34	1
O'Connell	15	1	60	0
Ward	18	1	57	3
Ryan	23	12	41	0
Waite	8	1	29	0

Umpires: G. Borwick and H. Armstrong.

HYNES, SIR LINCOLN CARRUTHERS, died during the year at the age of 65. As a fast left-hander he did useful work for New South Wales in the 1930s. His proudest moment was when he had Bradman caught at leg-slip for 0. He was knighted in 1971 in recognition of his work for broadcasting, charities and hospitals. (*1978*).

SOUTH AUSTRALIA v. MCC

At Adelaide, December 23, 24, 27, 28, 1965. MCC won by six wickets. After a week up-country on a whistle-stop tour of four one-day games, MCC needed time to re-acclimatise themselves to first-class cricket and owed their win to the generous declaration of Favell. In his first State match since joining the team, as a reinforcement in Brisbane, Knight batted excellently and bowled usefully. South Australia lost their first five wickets for 133, but again young Shiell was in great form. In five hours he hit 202 not out with two 6's and nineteen 4's. Jarman, who hooked and square-cut strongly, was his partner in a stand of 146 in two and a half hours, and South Australia averaged 4.6 runs an over. MCC also scored briskly after recovering from the loss of four wickets for 87. Smith made his 108 with fifteen 4's in under two and a quarter hours, and Knight hit 79 inside two hours. Murray struck his batting form for the first time in two tours of Australia in first-class company and batted almost three hours for 110, in which were eleven 4's. Before South Australia declared, leaving MCC three hours and ten minutes in which to make 269, Chappell hit fourteen 4's in an innings of 113 in three hours, forty minutes. With Barber and Boycott hitting 138 in only 18 overs for the first wicket before falling in successive overs, MCC sailed home with more than half an hour to spare. Knight hit 46 in forty-one minutes and Cowdrey 63 not out in seventy-seven minutes.

SOUTH AUSTRALIA

*L.E. Favell cAllen b Knight	40	– b Knight 31
L. Marks c Parfitt b Jones	0	– c Murray b Higgs 11
I.M. Chappell st Murray b Allen	59	– not out 113
K.G. Cunningham c Barber b Higgs	0	– run out 46
H.N. Dansie run out	30	– c Boycott b Parfitt 43
A.B. Shiell not out	202	
†B.N. Jarman c Parfitt b Higgs	70	
G. Griffiths c and b Higgs	23	
D.J. Sincock not out	28	
B 3, l-b 2, n-b 2	7	B 4, l-b 3, w 1, n-b 1 9

1/3 2/58 3/48 4/122   (7 wkts, dec.) 459   1/34 2/79   (4 wkts, dec.) 253
5/133 6/279 7/330   3/181 4/253

D. Robins and A. Frost did not bat.

Bowling: FIRST INNINGS – Jones 14.1-1-78-1; Higgs 21-2-82-3; Knight 15-1-89-1; Allen 18-4-75-1; Barber 20-0-87-1; Parfitt 5-1-15-0; Barrington 1-0-5-0; Boycott 5-0-21-0. SECOND INNINGS – Jones 8-0-62-0; Higgs 10-1-29-1; Knight 7-0-17-1; Allen 13-2-35-0; Barber 10-1-41-0; Parfitt 5.2-1-32-1; Boycott 4-0-28-0.

MCC

G. Boycott c Chappell b Frost 0	– b Sincock .... .58
R.W. Barber c Griffiths b Robins .... .42	– c Cunningham b Chappell .... .77
P.H. Parfitt b Robins 6	– c Favell b Chappell 2
M.C. Cowdrey c Jarman b Sincock .... .18	– not out .... .63
*M.J.K. Smith c Cunningham b Sincock ... .108	– not out .... .15
K.F. Barrington st Jarman b Sincock .... .63	
†J.T. Murray c Sincock b Robins .... .110	
D.A. Allen b Chappell 1	
B.R. Knight b Robins .... .79	– c and b Griffiths .... .46
K. Higgs not out 4	
I.J. Jones b Chappell 0	
L-b 8, w 2, n-b 3 .... .13	B 7, l-b 1, n-b 1 9

1/0 2/13 3/66 4/87 5/223   **444**   1/138 2/138 3/152   (4 wkts) **270**
6/250 7/253 8/417 9/444   4/237

Bowling: FIRST INNINGS – Frost 21-2-89-1; Robins 18-1-69-4; Sincock 29-1-141-3; Chappell 17.1-3-77-2; Griffiths 7-0-44-0; Cunningham 1-0-6-0; Dansie 1-0-5-0. SECOND INNINGS – Frost 8-0-59-0; Robins 6-0-35-0; Sincock 8-0-59-1; Chappell 9-0-58-1; Griffiths 7-0-37-1; Dansie 1-0-5-0; Favell 0.3-0-8-0.

Umpires: C. Egar and F. Godson.

ENGLAND V. AUSTRALIA

SECOND TEST MATCH

At Lord's, June 22, 23, 24, 26, 1972. Australia won by nine wickets. Australia soon avenged their defeat at Manchester in a contest which will be remembered as Massie's match. The 25-year-old fast bowler from Western Australia surpassed all Australian Test bowling records by taking sixteen wickets for 137 runs; in all Tests only J.C. Laker, nineteen for 90 for England against Australia in 1956 and S.F. Barnes, seventeen for 179 for England against South Africa in 1913–14, stand above him. Moreover, Massie performed this wonderful feat on his Test debut, the previous best by a bowler on his first appearance for his country being as far back as 1890 when at The Oval, Frederick Martin, a left-arm slow–medium pacer from Kent, took twelve for 102 for England against Australia on a pitch that had been saturated by rain.

Not for the first time, particularly in recent years, England were badly let down by their specialist batsmen, who failed lamentably in all respects. From the start they allowed the Australian bowlers to take the initiative and their excessive caution met with fatal results. Illingworth won the toss for the seventh consecutive time and one must admit that the hard fast pitch – it remained true to the end – was ideal for men of pace. During the first three days, too, the atmosphere was heavy and ideally suited to swing. Massie maintained excellent length and direction and his late swing either way always troubled the England batsmen. The conditions would also have suited Arnold, but England's best bowler at Manchester was suffering from hamstring trouble and on the morning of the match was replaced by Price, who proved rather disappointing. That was England's only change, whereas Australia brought in Edwards and Massie, who had recovered from a strain. Both were making their Test debuts and for the first time Western Australia had four representatives in the Test XI.

One must also stress the important part Lillee played in Australia's victory. Perhaps he was inspired by his six for 66 in England's second innings at Manchester. Anyhow, although this time his reward was confined to two wickets in each innings he looked a far better bowler. He had tidied his long fast approach of 22 strides, he was truly fast and he sent down far fewer loose deliveries. Massie capitalised on the hostility of his partner.

A light drizzle delayed the toss and the start for twenty-five minutes. Australia lost little time in taking the initiative, Boycott, Luckhurst and Edrich being removed for 28 runs before any substantial resistance was offered. At times Massie bowled round the wicket, but Smith and d'Oliveira raised the score to 54 for three at lunch. Afterwards, d'Oliveira struck three fine boundaries only to be leg-before to Massie's slower ball, whereupon Greig proceeded to hit his third successive fifty for his country.

Greig and Knott enabled England to make a satisfactory recovery in their stand of 96, but immediately after tea at 146 Knott spooned Gleeson gently to mid-wicket where to everyone's amazement Francis dropped the catch. In the end both batsmen fell to casual strokes, but Illingworth and Snow played well so that at the close of a momentous and exciting first day England were 249 for seven.

Next morning the new ball was due after two overs and Massie snatched the remaining three wickets and led his team back to the pavilion. Of the 36 bowlers *Wisden* lists who have taken eight wickets in a Test innings, only A.E. Trott, for Australia against England at Adelaide in 1895 and A.L. Valentine, for West Indies against England at Manchester, 1950 had previously accomplished the performance on their Test debuts.

A superb century by G.S. Chappell made the second day memorable after Australia had received early shocks in the loss of Francis and Stackpole for seven runs. Ian Chappell set a noble example as captain, leading the recovery with an aggressive display. He used his favourite hook to some purpose while his brother remained strictly defensive. Ian struck one 6 near Smith before he fell to a fine running-in catch that Smith held rolling over near his ankles.

Snow, if not so fast as Lillee, bowled splendidly and soon induced a catch from Walters, but Greg Chappell, in for three hours before he hit his first boundary, now took charge, excelling with the off drive. Edwards gave valuable support, but with the light murky Illingworth brought on Gifford and then himself, tempting Edwards into indiscretion for Smith to bring off another fine running catch on the leg side. Chappell duly completed his hundred on the stroke of time and Australia wound up 71 behind with half their wickets intact.

On Saturday the gates were closed at 11.10 a.m. with 31,000 inside. Greg Chappell lasted another hour and a half, batting altogether for six and a quarter hours, and in his splendid upright style hit fourteen 4's. Australia, who did not wish to face a huge target in the fourth innings, went ahead through another gallant display of powerful hitting by Marsh. He struck two 6's and six 4's in his 50, which came in seventy-five minutes and Australia gained a useful lead of 36. Snow, five for 57, alone of the England bowlers excelled.

Only the most optimistic Australian could have anticipated the success which so soon attended the efforts of Lillee and Massie. The England collapse – half the side were out for 31 – began when a fast shortish ball from Lillee lifted and Boycott, instead of dodging, preferred to let it strike his body while his bat was lifted high. It bounced off his padded front left ribs over his shoulder and dropped behind him on to the off bail. It was most unlucky for Boycott as well as England. Obviously, the Australians, having captured so valuable a wicket so cheaply, now bowled and fielded like men inspired. Luckhurst had no positive answer to Lillee's pace and soon went, to be followed by Edrich who was compelled to flick at a late outswinger (to him) that would have taken his off stump.

Again, Smith, getting right behind the ball, kept up his end, but the remainder were bemused by Massie's accuracy and late swing which meant that at the end of a miserable Saturday for England they stood only 50 runs ahead with nine wickets down. It remained only for the weather to stay fine on Monday for Australia to gain their just reward. Gifford and Price put on 35 in the best stand of the innings but Australia needed only 81 to win and Stackpole saw them comfortably home. With 7,000 present on the last day, the match was watched by just over 100,000 (excluding television viewers) and the receipts of £82,914 were considered to be a world record for a cricket match with the possible exception of India.

ENGLAND

G. Boycott b Massie	11	– b Lillee 6
J.H. Edrich lbw b Lillee	10	– c Marsh b Massie 6
B.W. Luckhurst b Lillee	1	– c Marsh b Lillee 4
M.J.K. Smith b Massie	34	– c Edwards b Massie 30
B.L. d'Oliveira lbw b Massie	32	– c G.S. Chappell b Massie 3
A.W. Greig c Marsh b Massie	54	– c I.M. Chappell b Massie 3
†A.P.E. Knott c Colley b Massie	43	– c G.S. Chappell b Massie 12
*R. Illingworth lbw b Massie	30	– c Stackpole b Massie 12
J.A. Snow b Massie	37	– c Marsh b Massie 0
N. Gifford c Marsh b Massie	3	– not out 16
J.S.E. Price not out	4	– c G.S. Chappell b Massie 19
L-b 6, w1, n-b 6	13	W 1, n-b 4 5

1/22 2/23 3/28 4/84 5/97   **272**   1/12 2/16 3/18 4/25 5/31   **116**
6/193 7/200 8/260 9/265   6/52 7/74 8/74 9/81

Bowling: FIRST INNINGS – Lillee 28-3-90-2; Massie 32.5-7-84-8; Colley 16-2-42-0; G.S. Chappell 6-1-18-0; Gleeson 9-1-25-0. SECOND INNINGS – Lillee 21-6-50-2; Massie 27.2-9-53-8; Colley 7-1-8-0.

AUSTRALIA

K.R. Stackpole c Gifford b Price	5	– not out 57
B.C. Francis b Snow	0	– c Knott b Price 9
*I.M. Chappell c Smith b Snow	56	– c Luckhurst b d'Oliveira 6
G.S. Chappell b d'Oliveira	131	– not out 7
K.D. Walters c Illingworth b Snow	1	
R. Edwards c Smith b Illingworth	28	
J.W. Gleeson c Knott b Greig	1	
†R.W. Marsh c Greig b Snow	50	
D.J. Colley c Greig b Price	25	
R.A.L. Massie c Knott b Snow	0	
D.K. Lillee not out	2	
L-b 7, n-b 2	9	L-b 2 2

1/1 2/7 3/82 4/84 5/190　　　　**308**　1/20 2/51　　　　(2 wkts) **81**
6/212 7/250 8/290 9/290

Bowling: FIRST INNINGS – Snow 32-13-57-5; Price 26.1-5-87-2; Greig 29-6-74-1; d'Oliveira 17-5-48-1; Gifford 11-4-20-0; Illingworth 7-2-13-1. SECOND INNINGS – Snow 8-2-15-0; Price 7-0-28-1; Greig 3-0-17-0; d'Oliveira 8-3-14-1; Luckhurst 0.5-0-5-0.

Umpires: D.J. Constant and A.E. Fagg.

QUEENSLAND V. VICTORIA

At Brisbane, October 26, 27, 28, 29, 1973. Drawn. Bonus points: Victoria 7, Queensland 5. In a match described as the most exciting on the ground since the tied Test between Australia and the West Indies, Queensland batted in dreadfully bad light and failed to gain outright victory by seven runs with three wickets standing. The game was unusual in that both Chappell and the left-handed Sieler hit centuries in each innings. Victoria began badly by losing the wickets of Stackpole and Scholes to the first two balls of the game to the former test left arm pace bowler Dell: then Sieler and Rose set a new Victorian Shield record of 271 for the fifth wicket. It was Sieler's third first class century and Rose's first. Chappell batted with authority to enable Queensland to pass Victoria's first innings by one run and after Victoria's second poor start, Sieler and Rose made a stand of 185. Chappell and Majid Khan batted superbly for a century apiece but Victoria refused to concede defeat.

VICTORIA

*K.R. Stackpole b Dell	.0	– c Albury b Dell	.20
A.P. Sheahan c Trimble b Dell	.17	– b Dell	.19
J.W. Scholes c Trimble b Dell	.0	– c Dudgeon b Albury	.5
I.R. Redpath c Khan b Albury	.19	– c Seib b Dell	.1
A.J. Sieler c Chappell b Albury	.157	– b Dymock	.105
R.P. Rose not out	.118	– c and b Dymock	.88
†R.D. Robinson (did not bat)	–	b Albury	.21
R.J. Bright (did not bat)	–	not out	.20
M.H.N. Walker (did not bat)	–	not out	.3
L-b 1, n-b 2	.3	B 3, l-b 6, n-b 2	.11

1/0 2/0 3/33 4/43 (5 wkts, dec.) **314** 1/26 2/45 3/47 4/57 (7 wkts, dec.) **293**
5/314 5/241 6/250 7/283

A.G. Hurst and J.D. Higgs did not bat.

Bowling: FIRST INNINGS – Dell 19-2-71-3; Dymock 15-4-55-0; Albury 17-0-91-2; Francke 17-1-71-0; Chappell 4-1-8-0; Carlson 3-0-15-0; Khan 1-1-0-0. SECOND INNINGS – Dell 23-2-106-3; Dymock 16-4-53-2; Albury 14-3-29-2; Francke 14-0-56-0; Khan 15-4-38-0.

QUEENSLAND

S.C. Trimble c Sheahan b Higgs	.57	– lbw b Walker	.17
I.M. Seib c Higgs b Walker	.1	– c Robinson b Walker	.8
Majid J. Khan c Sheahan b Hurst	.4	– c Stackpole b Higgs	.100
*G.S. Chappell c Bright b Hurst	.180	– c Sheahan b Walker	.101
P.H. Carlson b Hurst	.27	– st Robinson b Higgs	.5
K.E. Dudgeon c Stackpole b Higgs	.7	– b Walker	.17
†J.A. Maclean c Walker b Higgs	.2	– c Bright b Hurst	.28
F.M. Francke c Stackpole b Higgs	.4	– not out	.1
W.D. Albury c Robinson b Hurst	.14	– not out	.2
G. Dymock b Higgs	.9		
A.R. Dell not out	.0		
B 1, l-b 7, n-b 2	.10	B 4, l-b 3	.7

1/6 2/10 3/134 4/191 5/222 6/224 **315** 1/19 2/30 3/215 4/237 (7 wkts) **286**
7/238 8/295 9/314 5/247 6/283 7/283

Bowling: FIRST INNINGS – Hurst 27-4-89-4; Walker 26-4-91-1; Sieler 11-0-34-0; Bright 10-2-39-0; Higgs 13.1-1-52-5. SECOND INNINGS – Hurst 12-0-53-1; Walker 21-1-97-4; Sieler 2-0-23-0; Bright 4-0-31-0; Higgs 12-0-75-2.

Umpires: P. Enright and T. Warwick.

ROSE, ROBERT PETER, died at Heidelberg, Melbourne, on May 12, 1999. Born at Eastern Hill, Melbourne, on February 6, 1952, Rose was member of one of Melbourne's most distinguished sporting families. His father, Bob, was an outstanding Australian Rules player and coach with Collingwood, for which club three of Robert's uncles turned out. His younger brother, Peter, is a well-known poet and the publisher at Oxford University Press who guided *The Oxford Companion to Australian Cricket* to its publication in 1996. A prominent schoolboy sportsman at Haileybury College, Robert played 26 games of Australian Rules with the Magpies before moving to Footscray when his father took the coaching job there in 1973.

As a cricketer, Rose made his first-grade debut for Collingwood in 1969–70 at the age of 17 as an opening batsman and, during the next season, his partnerships with Keith Stackpole made an important contribution to the club's first district premiership since 1912–13. In his first match for Victoria, against Western Australia at Melbourne, in December 1971, Rose displayed the technical substance of his batting by making 49 in 168 minutes at No. 6 in the second innings as his side battled to avoid outright defeat. Despite a generally quiet season in 1972–73, he took part in opening stands of 145 against New South Wales at Melbourne with Alan Sieler and, two matches later, 217 with Paul Sheahan against South Australia at Adelaide. Rose's batting was built around both a sound defence and an array of handsome strokes; these attributes, however, were cemented by a calm and mature temperament which led discerning critics to claim that he had a future in the national team. He displayed these attributes to the full against Queensland at Brisbane early in the 1973–74 season. In scoring 118 not out and 88 at No. 6, he twice joined Sieler in rescuing his side from parlous situations; in the first innings, they came together with the score at four for 43 and added a Victorian Sheffield Shield record fifth-wicket stand of 271 in 259 minutes. In the second innings, Victoria had declined to four for 57 before the pair added 184 in just over even time. As a result of a car accident near Bacchus Marsh in February 1974, Rose was left a quadriplegic. Despite the gravity of his situation, Rose and his family dealt with it through a courage and fortitude which gave a pure and shining ring to those much-abused words in the sporting lexicon.

FIFTH TEST MATCH

At Sydney, January 10, 11, 12, 14, 15, 1987. Australia won by 55 runs. When, with one over left, Sleep bowled Emburey to complete Australia's first Test win in more than a year, it was an unexpected as well as welcome victory. Indeed, at the start of the final twenty overs England appeared to have the better chance. Recovering from the loss of four wickets in eight overs, among them Botham first ball to Taylor in his maiden Test, they had been carried to within 90 runs of their target (320) by the pugnacity of Gatting with determined help from Richards in a stand of 131, a record for England's sixth wicket on the ground. Only once before, in 633 Tests, had England scored more than 300 runs to win – at Melbourne in 1928–29 when Hobbs and Sutcliffe shared one of their most celebrated partnerships, 105 on a rain-affected pitch. However, at 230 for five, with Australia faltering, the odds had swung their way. Even when Gatting was caught and bowled by Waugh, 4 short of his hundred and with only another 3 on England's total, it was not until Sleep dismissed Richards and Edmonds with successive balls in the eleventh over of the final twenty that Australia scented victory.

Small defended resolutely through seven overs until, with only fourteen balls remaining, Border at first slip, one of eight men round the bat, claimed a sharp, low catch off Reid. Then, with 12,684 spectators in a state of high excitement, Sleep penetrated Emburey's defence with a grubber to give Australia their first win in fifteen

Tests. Of Sleep's five for 72, his best figures in a Test, three were taken in his last five overs as England, through neither carelessness nor lack of fight, lost five for 31 in 70 tense minutes. If their leg-spinner delivered Australia's *coup de grâce*, however, there was no question that their hero was the 30-year-old Taylor, a sandy-haired off-spinner from Sydney's Northern District club who had played only six first-class matches in his life, and only one that season, restricted to few appearances for New South Wales by their three Test spinners.

So little was known about him that when Australia announced a twelve containing only one opening batsman there was speculation that he owed selection to an error in transmission, confusing him with M.A. Taylor, a dour left-handed opener who had been making runs for New South Wales. There was no substance to the allegations, and in a saga that developed along the lines of a story in *Boy's Own*, the unassuming Taylor gloriously vindicated the selectors' judgement with a performance of such merit that he was named player of the match. Figures of six for 78 in England's first innings and two for 76 in the second revealed him as a thoughtful bowler with more than average powers of spin. But well as he did in his specialist department, it was his batting – angular, left-handed and blessed with common sense – that made possible Australia's win. Going in at No. 9, he batted for 244 minutes in both innings while 142 runs were scored, enabling Jones to add 111 with his last three partners in the first innings and sharing a stand of 98 with Waugh in the second when Australia's needs were even greater. [...]

Jones, whose 184 not out (540 minutes, 420 balls, one six, twelve fours) was his first Test hundred on home soil, was Australia's other match-winner in a game that produced more runs on every day than the bowlers should have allowed on a pitch which helped spin as well as seam. Faulty umpiring contributed to that, Jones, when 5, being the fortunate recipient of a benefit-of-doubt decision when Richards dived to take a leg-glance and Gower, when 62, surviving an lbw appeal when Taylor, over the wicket, got through a back-foot defensive stroke with a straight ball which kept low. Lack of confidence appeared to be at the root of the umpires' difficulties. It was to Jones's credit that he made the most of his luck while Gower failed to, driving a half-volley to extra-cover early on the following morning.

That England trailed by no more than 68 on first innings, bowled Australia out for 251 in their second, and came within a whisker of saving the match after Sleep's removal of Richards and Edmonds was due in large measure to Emburey, who with the ball and bat was in the thick of things for more than fourteen hours of the 30. Handicapped by a strained groin for most of his 210-minute 69, he went on to take seven for 78, his best figures in Test cricket, in Australia's second innings and finally logged another 68 minutes' batting in the last session. Like Gatting, Small and Richards, he deserved better than to finish on the losing side.

Man of the Match: P.L. Taylor. *Attendance*: 96,429.

Man of the Series: B.C. Broad.

Close of play: First day, Australia 236-7 (D.M. Jones 119*, P.L. Taylor 0*); Second day, England 132-5 (D.I. Gower 62*, C.J. Richards 8*); Third day, Australia 74-2 (D.M. Jones 6*, A.R. Border 38*); Fourth day, England 39-1 (C.W.J. Athey 11*, D.I. Gower 7*).

AUSTRALIA

G.R. Marsh c Gatting b Small	.24	– (2) c Emburey b Dilley	.14
G.M. Ritchie lbw b Dilley	.6	– (1) c Botham b Edmonds	.13
D.M. Jones not out	.184	– c Richards b Emburey	.30
*A.R. Border c Botham b Edmonds	.34	– b Edmonds	.49
D.M. Wellham c Richards b Small	.17	– c Lamb b Emburey	.1
S.R. Waugh c Richards b Small	.0	– c Athey b Emburey	.73
P.R. Sleep c Richards b Small	.9	– c Lamb b Emburey	.10
†T.J. Zoehrer c Gatting b Small	.12	– lbw b Emburey	.1
P.L. Taylor c Emburey b Edmonds	.11	– c Lamb b Emburey	.42
M.G. Hughes c Botham b Edmonds	.16	– b Emburey	.5
B.A. Reid b Dilley	.4	– not out	.1
B 12, l-b 4, w 2, n-b 8	.26	B 5, l-b 7	.12

1/8 (2) 2/58 (1) 3/149 (4) 4/184 (5) **343** 1/29 (2) 2/31 (1) 3/106 (4) 4/110 (3) **251**
5/184 (6) 6/200 (7) 7/232 (8) 5/115 (5) 6/141 (7) 7/145 (8)
8/271 (9) 9/338 (10) 10/343 (11) 8/243 (6) 9/248 (9) 10/251 (10)

Bowling: FIRST INNINGS – Dilley 23.5-5-67-2; Small 33-11-75-5; Botham 23-10-42-0; Emburey 30-4-62-0; Edmonds 34-5-79-3; Gatting 1-0-2-0. SECOND INNINGS – Dilley 15-4-48-1; Small 8-2-17-0; Edmonds 43-16-79-2; Emburey 46-15-78-7; Botham 3-0-17-0; Gatting 2-2-0-0.

ENGLAND

B.C. Broad lbw b Hughes	.6	– c and b Sleep	.17
C.W.J. Athey c Zoehrer b Hughes	.5	– b Sleep	.31
*M.W. Gatting lbw b Reid	.0	– (5) c and b Waugh	.96
A.J. Lamb c Zoehrer b Taylor	.24	– c Waugh b Taylor	.3
D.I. Gower c Wellham b Taylor	.72	– (3) c Marsh b Border	.37
I.T. Botham c Marsh b Taylor	.16	– c Wellham b Taylor	.0
†C.J. Richards c Wellham b Reid	.46	– b Sleep	.38
J.E. Emburey b Taylor	.69	– b Sleep	.22
P.H. Edmonds c Marsh b Taylor	.3	– lbw b Sleep	.0
G.C. Small b Taylor	.14	– c Border b Reid	.0
G.R. Dilley not out	.4	– not out	.2
B 9, l-b 3, w 2, n-b 2	.16	B 8, l-b 6, w 1, n-b 3	.18

1/16 (2) 2/17 (3) 3/17 (1) 4/89 (4) **275** 1/24 (1) 2/91 (3) 3/91 (2) 4/102 (4) **264**
5/119 (6) 6/142 (5) 7/213 (7) 5/102 (6) 6/233 (5) 7/257 (7)
8/219 (9) 9/270 (10) 10/275 (8) 8/257 (9) 9/262 (10) 10/264 (8)

Bowling: FIRST INNINGS – Hughes 16-3-58-2; Reid 25-7-74-2; Waugh 6-4-6-0; Taylor 26-7-78-6; Sleep 21-6-47-0. SECOND INNINGS – Hughes 12-3-32-0; Reid 19-8-32-1; Sleep 35-14-72-5; Taylor 29-10-76-2; Border 13-6-25-1; Waugh 6-2-13-1.

Umpires: P.J. McConnell and S.G. Randell.

1 9

SMOKERS, NON-SMOKERS AND OTHERS

Wisden has traditionally been dedicated to games between teams at first-class domestic and international levels. But that has not prevented it from widening its gaze at times to encompass the spontaneous, the spectacular and the downright odd. This section features some unusual matches, now largely forgotten, included in the almanack's sweep.

Some might have been consigned to oblivion quite happily. *Wisden* has looked the other way on some of Australian cricket's embarrassments: our defeats by Holland in 1964, by Tobago in 1965, and by Eastern Canada in 1975 it reported only perfunctorily. But there was no hiding Australian failure against Philadelphia in 1893. And *Wisden*'s report of Jeff Thomson's appearance in the International Floodlit Sixes is about as inglorious a cricket interlude as can be imagined.

Other games here have survived as records, like the Smokers' 803 against Non-Smokers in March 1887, and Melbourne University's 1,094 against Essendon in March 1898, while the tie in Donald Bradman's benefit match in December 1948 remains one of only thirty anywhere in first-class cricket since World War II. Others suggest how heavily wedded cricket has grown to the idea of nation playing nation, because the alternatives seem surprising. These games feature us engaged with the rest of the planet, meeting the World XI of 1971–72, and playing among ourselves, both happily in the Bushfire Test of April 1967 and less happily when Australia skirmished with Australia A eight years ago. Then there's us as part of the planet, personified by the prodigies of Michael Bevan for the Rest of the World XI against the Asia XI in April 2000.

If there's a message here, it's that status doesn't always confer importance. Perhaps the most urgent game in this section was the least official: the twelve-a-side exhibition match staged before a restive crowd at Gujranwala by Pakistan and Australia in October 1994. After the official game's abandonment because of rain, the city's deputy commissioner entreated Mark Taylor: 'If you don't play some cricket, they'll kill us.'

Wisden's understated report records: 'Taylor said he had never heard a more pressing reason to play.'

—GH

SMOKERS V. NON-SMOKERS

Played at Melbourne, on the East Melbourne Ground, Thursday, Friday, Saturday, Monday, March 17, 18, 19, and 21, 1887. –This game did not count in the averages of the Englishmen, but it was remarkable for producing the highest total ever obtained in a first-class match, the Non-Smokers going in first, and scoring 803. The previous best was 775 by New South Wales against Victoria at Sydney in 1882. Though the East Melbourne Ground is small, the performance was an extraordinary one, Shrewsbury, Bruce, and Gunn batting splendidly. After four days' cricket the result was a draw. Score:

NON-SMOKERS

A. Shrewsbury, 1 3 1 1 1 2 2 4 4 1 4 4 4 4 4 2 2 2 4 4 4 1 2 1 3 4 4 4 4 3
    4 2 1 1 1 4 4 2 3 2 4 1 1 4 4 1 2 4 1 1 2 4 4 4 2 4 4 1 3 4 4 4 2 1 4
    4 1 1 1 4 4 2 4 4 2 4 4 2 2 1 4 1 1 1 1 2 4 4, c Duffy, b Briggs 236
W. Bruce, 1 1 4 4 1 4 2 4 3 6 4 4 4 4 2 1 1 2 3 4 2 3 4 1 3 4 3 2 1 2 4 1
    4 3 2 1 1 1 1 4 4 4 2 1 1 1 2 1 1 1 1 1 1 4, lbw, b Palmer 131
N.V. Bates, 4, b Palmer 4
W. Gunn, 3 4 4 1 4 4 2 4 4 4 3 1 1 3 2 4 2 1 1 1 1 4 2 1 4 1 1 4 3 3 2 1
    2 2 1 5 2 4 4 2 2 1 4 4 3 2 4 4 4 1 4 1 1 3 1 4 1 2, b Boyle 150
R.G. Barlow, 2 1 1 1 1 1 1 4 4 1 2 4 1 1 4, b Palmer 29
R. Houston, 3 1 2 1 1 4 4 1 1 1 1 4 2 2 1 4 2 1 1 1 1 2 4 1 1 3 1 1 1 1 2 1, c and b Briggs 57
H. Musgrove, 3 4 4 1 1 1 2 4 1 2 1 2 1 3 1 4 4 1 1 4 4 1 3 1 1 4 2 1, st Lewis, b Briggs 62
J. Worrall, 4 2 2 1 4 2 1 1 4 4 1 4 4 4 1 2 1 2 1 2 2 1 1 4 1 1 1 4 4 3 4 2 2 1, b Read 78
W.H. Cooper, 4 4 1 4 4 1 1 1 4 1 3 1 1 1 1 4 4 3 1 2, c and b Briggs 46
M. Sherwin, 3 1 1, not out 5
W. Barnes, absent 0
    Byes, &c. 5

                803

Fall of the wickets: 1-196, 2-204, 3-514, 4-524, 5-575, 6-656, 7-686, 8-788, 9-803.

SMOKERS

M. Read, st Sherwin, b Cooper 30		
G.E. Palmer, c Worrall, b Bruce 113	– c Houston, b Worrall 24	
J. Briggs, c Shrewsbury, b Bates 86	– st Sherwin, b Bates 54	
W. Flowers, run out 69	– b Houston 25	
G. Lohmann, c Briggs (sub.), b Bates 19	– lbw, b Gunn 2	
W. Scotton, c Bruce, b Bates 11	– handled ball 18	
H.F. Boyle, b Bruce 7	– not out 0	
G. Browning, b Bates 1		
F. Walters, st Sherwin, b Bates 0		
P. Lewis, c Houston, b Bates 2		
W. Duffy, not out 0		
B 12, l-b 2, w 2, n-b 2 18	B 9, l-b 2, n-b 1 12	
356	**135**	

SMOKERS' BOWLING

	First Innings					Second Innings			
	Overs	Mdns	Runs	Wkts		Overs	Mdns	Runs	Wkts
Briggs	55.1	11	141	4	Scotton	26	4	82	0
Palmer	54	10	189	3	Duffy	15	2	52	0
Boyle	31	14	60	1	Read	26	10	43	1
Lohmann	48	18	113	0	Walters	9	4	25	0
Flowers	38	12	93	0					

Briggs bowled a wide.

NON-SMOKERS' BOWLING

Bates	49	18	73	6		21	8	40	1
Cooper	29	5	85	1		4	0	18	0
Bruce	36.3	10	92	2		14	7	15	0
Worrall	15	7	30	0		12	5	22	1
Gunn	12	4	27	0		6	5	1	1
Houston	9	2	31	0		5	1	13	1
Barnes						8	3	14	0
Shrewsbury						1	0	0	0

Bruce bowled two wides, Shrewsbury one and Gunn two no-balls.

AUSTRALIANS V. PHILADELPHIA

Played at Philadelphia, Friday, Saturday, Monday, September 29, 30, October 2, 1893. – Having to enter on their first engagement directly after landing, and without any practice, the Australians were heavily handicapped, but the severe manner in which their bowling was punished was surprising. The Philadelphian score of 525 was put together in less than seven hours, and some spirited batting was shown by Bohlen and Noble, who added 180 runs for the fifth wicket. The Australians gave a fair display of cricket, and Bannerman carried his bat through the second innings, being in three hours and a half without making a mistake. The Philadelphians won in a single innings with 69 runs to spare.

PHILADELPHIA

G. Patterson, run out	.56
R.D. Brown, c Blackham, b Trumble	.23
W. Scott, run out	.8
A.M. Wood, b Bruce	.40
F.H. Bohlen, c Trott, b Bruce	.118
W.W. Noble, b Trumble	.77
C. Coates, sen., b Bruce	.15
J.W. Muir, b Coningham	.9
H.I. Brown, not out	.59
J.W. Ralston, run out	.47
J.B. King, c Lyons, b Bannerman	.36
B 17, l-b 12, w 4, n-b 4	.37

525

AUSTRALIANS

A.C. Bannerman, c H.I. Brown, b King 16	– not out	.79
J.J. Lyons, c Bohlen, b Patterson 12	– c Ralston, b Patterson	.30
G. Giffen, c Wood, b King 62	– c Bohlen, b R.D. Brown	.1
G.H.S. Trott, b King 0	– c Scott, b Muir	.58
W. Bruce, c Wood, b King 11	– c Bohlen, b Muir	.0
H. Graham, run out 25	– c Muir, b King	.2
S.E. Gregory, c King, b H.I. Brown 12	– c Coates, b Scott	.32
H. Trumble, c Wood, b H.I. Brown 1	– b King	.0
W.F. Giffen, not out 18	– c Ralston, b Scott	.2
A. Coningham, b King 9	– c Coates, b Scott	.30
J.M'C. Blackham, b H.I. Brown 22	– run out	.6
B 6, l-b 3, n-b 2 11	B 9, l-b 5, w 1, n-b 3	.18
	199	**258**

AUSTRALIAN BOWLING

	Overs	Mdns	Runs	Wkts	Overs	Mdns	Runs	Wkts
G. Giffen	33	7	114	0				
Trumble	55	30	104	2				
Trott	15	3	45	0				
Coningham	20	5	63	1				
Lyons	11	4	34	0				
Bruce	36	0	100	3				
Gregory	12	0	27	0				
Bannerman	31	2	1	1				

Bruce bowled three wides and Coningham one, and Trumble bowled four no-balls.

PHILADELPHIA BOWLING

King	25	6	78	5	32.3	5	90	2
Patterson	6	0	31	1	17	4	48	1
H.I. Brown	12.4	3	41	3				
Scott	2	0	20	0	11	1	41	3
R.D. Brown	4	0	18	0	1	0	10	1
Noble					5	2	29	0
Muir					9	4	14	2

MELBOURNE UNIVERSITY V. ESSENDON

Played on the University Ground, Melbourne, March 5, 12, 19, and 23, 1898.

To Melbourne University belongs the credit of having played an innings of 1094 – the highest authenticated total in the history of cricket. The match was played on the Melbourne University Ground, on Saturday March 5th, Saturday March 12th, Saturday March 19th, and Wednesday March 23rd, 1898. As showing the keenness with which the game was conducted it is recorded that several maiden overs were bowled when the University total stood at 998. The wickets fell as follows: 1 for 38; 2 for 156; 3 for 459; 4 for 542; 5 for 746; 6 for 828; 7 for 845; 8 for 968; 9 for 1025; 10 for 1094. The circumference of the Melbourne University Ground is 554 yards.

MELBOURNE UNIVERSITY

L. Miller c Ramsey b Smith 205
H.J. Stewart c and b Washington 23
C. Miller c Christian b Washington 57
E.C. Osborne b O'Shea 190
W. O'Hara hit wkt b Griffiths 7
J.J. Quirk b Sampford 179
E. Feilchenfeld c Gaunt b C.Christian 176
H. Bullivant not out 139
W.S. Ross b Griffiths 32
A. Gray b H. Christian 22
T. Lewers c C. Miller (sub) b Washington ...26
    B 31, l-b 2, w 5 38

1,094

ESSENDON

W. Griffiths c and b C. Miller 26
C. Ramsay b Feilchenfeld 2
M. O'Shea b Gray 1
C. Dalton c Gray b C. Miller 22
H. Christian b C. Miller 2
G. Washington b Ross 2
C. Christian not out 13
P. Barr b Ross 6
W. Smith absent 0
C. Sampford absent 0
J. Gaunt absent 0
    B 1, w 1 2

76

ESSENDON BOWLING

	Balls	Mdns	Runs	Wkts
Sampford	240	9	145	1
H. Christian	312	23	243	1
C. Christian	228	2	137	1
Gaunt	102	1	69	0
Griffiths	204	5	137	2
O'Shea	102	0	88	1
Washington	201	3	119	3
Smith	96	1	47	1
Dalton	60	1	42	0
Barr	30	0	26	0
Ramsay	6	0	3	0

MELBOURNE UNIVERSITY BOWLING

Gray	48	0	30	1
Feilchenfeld	36	4	5	1
C. Miller	30	0	34	3
Ross	19	0	5	2

BRADMAN TESTIMONIAL MATCH

D.G. BRADMAN'S XI v. A.L. HASSETT'S XI

At Melbourne, December 3, 4, 6, 7, 1948. The result was a tie. The match produced a magnificent farewell to Bradman by the Melbourne crowd. It also produced a riot of run-getting, 1,672 runs being scored in the four innings. Don Tallon, batting for Bradman's XI against Hassett's XI, levelled the scores from the last ball of the match. Tallon made 91 of 100 runs scored in the last hour. Lindwall on the first day 'stole the show' with his 104 in eighty-six minutes. He and Saggers put on 160 in eighty-four minutes. The stage was set for Bradman on the Saturday. When 97 he was missed by McCool, off W. Johnston, in a manner that pleased the crowd of nearly 53,000. Bradman reached 123 – his 117th and final century in first-class cricket. Meuleman, Hassett and Morris, as well as Bradman, Tallon and Lindwall, scored centuries in this most enjoyable match. Bradman received approximately £A10,000.

A.L. HASSETT'S XI

W.A. Brown c Tallon b Noblet	5	– b Raymer	43
S.G. Barnes c and b Johnson	32	– c Tallon b Ring	89
A.L. Hassett c Tallon b Loxton	35	– st Tallon b Ring	102
N. Harvey c Tallon b Raymer	34	– c and b Raymer	9
W. Langdon c Tallon b Loxton	60	– c Meuleman b Johnson	42
C.L. McCool c Johnson b Loxton	35	– c and b Loxton	29
R.R. Lindwall c and b Raymer	104	– b Noblet	11
R.A. Saggers c Meuleman b Ring	52	– c Morris b Ring	41
L. Johnson c Loxton b Ring	9	– not out	53
B. Dooland not out	9	– c Johnson b Bradman	1
W.A. Johnston c Bradman b Johnson	15	– st Tallon b Bradman	5
Extras	16	Extras	5
	406		**430**

D.G. BRADMAN'S XI

K. Meuleman c and b Johnson	100	– c Johnson b Lindwall	3
A.R. Morris c and b McCool	25	– c and b Barnes	108
R.A. Hamence st Saggers b McCool	58	– b Lindwall	45
D.G. Bradman c Harvey b Dooland	123	– c Saggers b Johnston	10
K.R. Miller b Johnson	2	– c Langdon b McCool	14
S.J. Loxton b Johnston	21	– c Hassett b Lindwall	15
V.N. Raymer c Lindwall b McCool	40	– b Johnson	11
I.W. Johnson c Johnson b McCool	22	– c Johnson b Dooland	29
D. Tallon lbw b McCool	11	– not out	146
D. Ring c McCool b Johnston	17	– b Dooland	6
G. Noblet not out	4	– not out	9
Extras	11	Extras	6
	434		Nine wkts **402**

D.G. BRADMAN'S XI BOWLING

	O.	M.	R.	W.	O.	M.	R.	W.
Noblet	17	1	56	1	14	1	47	1
Loxton	13	0	39	3	10	0	61	1
Johnson	17	2	125	2	16	0	40	1
Ring	24	2	109	2	18	0	150	3
Raymer	21	5	61	2	15	1	66	2
Hamence					3	0	13	0
Morris					3	0	36	0
Bradman					1.7	0	12	2

A.L. HASSETT'S XI BOWLING

	O.	M.	R.	W.	O.	M.	R.	W.
Lindwall	15	3	41	0	14	3	32	3
Johnson	12	1	46	2	14	0	53	1
McCool	19.4	1	101	5	8	0	74	1
Johnston	21	4	92	2	17	2	63	1
Dooland	16	0	95	1	16	1	105	2
Langdon	4	1	17	0				
Barnes	4	0	16	0	8	0	49	1
Hassett	1	0	2	0				
Brown	1	0	13	0	1	0	8	0
Harvey					3	0	12	0

AUSTRALIAN SOUTH AFRICAN TOURING TEAM
v. AUSTRALIAN N.Z. TOURING TEAM

At Melbourne, April 7, 8, 9, 10, 1967. Australian South African Touring Team won by seven wickets. The match between teams from the two overseas tours was staged by the Victorian Cricket Association, with some sponsorship, in aid of the Tasmanian Bushfires Relief Fund. Thomas was not available for Simpson's South African team, and Walters, who had missed that tour through National Service, was given special leave from the Army to appear.

AUSTRALIAN SOUTH AFRICAN TOURING SIDE

W.M. Lawry c Davies b Cunningham	.....33 – run out	30
*R.B. Simpson lbw b Connolly	............5 – lbw b Freeman	6
I.R. Redpath c Gleeson b Cunningham	......8 – not out	37
K.D. Walters c Davies b Freeman	..........5 – c Favell b Philpott	21
R.M. Cowper not out	................169 – not out	27
I.M. Chappell run out	58	
K.R. Stackpole c Sheahan b Connolly	0	
G.D. Watson st Jarman b Cunningham	98	
G.D. McKenzie c Jarman b Philpott	22	
†H.B. Taber not out	19	
B 6, l-b 6, w 1, n-b 9	22	L-b 1, w 1, n-b 2 4

1/23 2/40 3/58 4/68   (8 wkts, dec.) **439**   1/15 2/56 3/62   (3 wkts) **125**
5/177 6/180 7/357 8/405

J. Hubble did not bat.

Bowling: FIRST INNINGS – Connolly 28-3-72-2; Freeman 16-1-85-1; Cunningham 13-2-62-3; Gleeson 14-1-76-0; Philpott 17-0-86-1; Davies 9-0-33-0; O'Neill 1-0-3-0; SECOND INNINGS – Connolly 6-0-19-0; Freeman 12-0-43-1; Gleeson 3-0-16-0; Philpott 9-1-39-1; O'Neill 0.4-0-4-0.

AUSTRALIAN NEW ZEALAND TOURING SIDE

*L.E. Favell c Stackpole b Cowper	.........53 –c Simpson b Hubble	9
K.G. Cunningham retired hurt	............10 – absent hurt	0
A.P. Sheahan lbw b Watson	................9 – run out	51
N.C. O'Neill c Taber b Watson	.............0 – c Watson b Hubble	74
P.J. Burge b Watson	..........20 – lbw b Stackpole	4
G. Davies b Chappell	....................80 – c Watson b Hubble	31
†B.N. Jarman c Taber b Watson	...........25 – c Redpath b Stackpole	35
P.I. Philpott b Simpson	...................9 – c Redpath b Chappell	90
E.W. Freeman c Walters b Simpson	........24 – lbw b Chappell	0
J.W. Gleeson not out	...................6 – b Hubble	0
A.N. Connolly c Taber b Watson	..........15 – not out	1
B 4, l-b 7, n-b 1	12	B 2, l-b 3 5

1/40 2/44 3/81 4/138 5/177   **263**   1/25 2/86 3/127 4/145 5/204   **300**
6/204 7/234 8/242 9/263   6/288 7/289 8/290 9/300

Bowling: FIRST INNINGS – McKenzie 14-0-59-0; Hubble 6-0-39-0; Watson 9.2-0-26-5; Walters 4-0-18-0; Simpson 11-3-43-2; Cowper 8-1-31-1; Chappell 10-1-35-1. SECOND INNINGS – McKenzie 16-0-52-0; Hubble 14-0-71-4; Watson 11-1-22-0; Walters 4-0-13-0; Simpson 4-0-22-0; Cowper 13-3-34-0; Chappell 11.7-3-31-2; Stackpole 15-1-50-2.

A WORLD TEAM IN AUSTRALIA, 1971–72

The 1971–72 visit by a World Team for a tour including twelve first-class matches, with five representative matches against Australia came in place of the proposed tour by a South African team. The Springboks' visit, which would have been the fifth such official visit to Australia, was cancelled by the Australian Board of Control, following sustained political and moral pressures and in view of practical problems.

The 'Rest of the World', a multi-national team chosen by the Australian authorities, included two South African Test players, the brothers P.M. and R.G. Pollock (who were late arrivals) and H.M. Ackerman. There were also players from England, the West Indies, India, Pakistan and New Zealand. In the end, and after early vicissitudes, the tour was rated a considerable success. [...] The most distinguished innings of the season came from the captain, G.S. Sobers, when in Melbourne at New Year he scored 254 runs against Australia. It was an unforgettable display combining such elegance of stroke play, power and aggression that the crowds responded ecstatically. It was a throwback to the dominance of Sobers in other years.

On Monday, January 3, 1972, Sobers scored 139 not out in three hours, thirty-six minutes, and he hit twenty-one 4's. It was majestic batting. After a rest day, Sobers resumed his great innings on the Wednesday sedately but recovered his aggression until, obviously tired, he was dismissed for 254. He had batted for six hours and sixteen minutes, and hit two 6's off successive balls from O'Keeffe, and thirty-five 4's Sir Donald Bradman said of this innings: 'I believe Garry Sobers' innings was probably the best ever seen in Australia. The people who saw Sobers have enjoyed one of the historic events of cricket, they were privileged to have such an experience. [...] (*T.L. Goodman*)

AUSTRALIA V. A WORLD XI

At Melbourne, January 1, 2, 3, 5, 6, 1972. A World XI won by 96 runs.

WORLD XI

H.M. Ackerman b Lillee 0	– c Stackpole b Lillee 9
S.M. Gavaskar c G.S. Chappell b Lillee ..... .38	– c I.M. Chappell b Jenner .... .27
Zaheer Abbas c Stackpole b Massie 4	– c I.M. Chappell b Lillee .... .86
R.G. Pollock c Marsh b Lillee 8	– b Massie .... .28
*G.S. Sobers c Stackpole b Lillee 0	– c Walters b G.S. Chappell .... .254
A.W. Greig c Benaud b Massie .... .66	– c and b Jenner 3
†F.M. Engineer c Marsh b Lillee 5	– b Lillee .... .14
Intikhab Alam lbw b Jenner .... .38	– lbw b Watson .... .15
P.M. Pollock lbw b Jenner 3	– c O'Keefe b Jenner .... .54
N. Gifford not out 0	– not out 4
B.S. Bedi run out 7	– c Massie b Jenner 3
B 5, l-b 8, w 1, n-b 1 .... .15	L-b 13, w 3, n-b 1 .... .17

1/0 2/11 3/26 4/26 5/105   **184**   1/12 2/87 3/146 4/177 5/214   **514**
6/117 7/151 8/160 9/177   6/248 7/319 8/505 9/505

Bowling: FIRST INNINGS – Lillee 16.3-4-48-5; Massie 14-3-70-2; G.S. Chappell 10-2-17-0; Watson 3-1-10-0; Jenner 6-0-24-2. SECOND INNINGS – Lillee 30-3-133-3; Massie 25-4-95-1; G.S. Chappell3-1-12-1; Watson 16-2-37-1; Jenner 20.3-5-87-4; Walters 2-0-5-0; O'Keeffe 27-5-121-0; Stackpole 1-0-7-0.

AUSTRALIA

K.R. Stackpole c Ackerman b Greig	.32	– c Engineer b Greig .... .24
G.D Watson c R.G. Pollock b Greig	.16	– retired hurt .... .21
*I.M. Chappell b P.M. Pollock	.21	– run out .... .41
J. Benaud lbw b Intikhab	.24	– c Sobers b Intikhab .... .42
G.S. Chappell not out	115	– c Sobers b Bedi .... .12
K.D. Walters b Greig	.16	– c sub b Bedi 127
†R.W. Marsh b Greig	.4	– lbw b Bedi 0
K.J. O'Keeffe c Gavaskar b Intikhab	.1	– c Sobers b Intikhab 1
T.J. Jenner c Engineer b Sobers	.19	– c Gavaskar b Bedi .... .12
R.A.L. Massie c Engineer b Sobers	.34	– c and b Intikhab .... .23
D.K. Lillee c Bedi b Sobers	.0	– not out 1
B 1, l-b 2	.3	B 6, l-b 2, w 1, n-b 4 .... .13

1/58 2/58 3/78 4/104 5/133	**285**	1/35 2/117 3/133 4/157 5/158	**317**
6/141 7/146 8/188 9/285		6/163 7/201 8/313 9/317	

Bowling: FIRST INNINGS – P.M. Pollock 19-2-87-1; Sobers 14.6-0-16-3; Greig 16-4-41-4; Intikhab 12-0-45-2; Bedi 6-0-28-0; Gifford 4-0-14-0. SECOND INNINGS – P.M. Pollock 1-0-8-0; Sobers 8-0-48-0; Greig 14-1-71-1; Intikhab 24-5-83-3; Bedi 24-4-81-4; Gifford 5-1-13-0.

Umpires: J.R. Collins and M.G. O'Connell.

INTERNATIONAL FLOODLIT SIXES

A floodlit six-a-side competition, involving some of the best-known international players of the past two decades, ended in farce and confusion after just one of the scheduled two days when the players' demand for immediate cash payment was not met. A crowd estimated at 'a few dozen' attended the opening day, at The Oval on September 21, 1994, to watch players such as Derek Underwood and Jeff Thomson operating a form of the game based on the successful competition in Hong Kong. The *Times* headlined its report 'Rotten enterprise worthy of contempt'. (*1995*)

PAKISTAN V. AUSTRALIA

At Gujranwala, October 26, 1994. No result (abandoned).

Rain forced officials to call off the game but, fearing for their safety when the large crowd rioted, they persuaded the teams to play a 12-a-side exhibition match of 15 overs an innings. The deputy commissioner of Gujranwala told Taylor, the Australian captain, 'If you don't play some cricket they'll kill us.' Taylor said he had never heard a more pressing reason to play. About sixty people were hurt in the disturbances. Conditions were so damp that bowling was possible only from one end; Pakistan reversed their batting order and won by four wickets.

AUSTRALIA V. AUSTRALIA A

At Adelaide, December 11, 1994. Australia won by six runs. Toss: Australia. Backed by an increasingly vocal crowd, the A side were closing on a famous win, only for their lack of experience to scupper them: their last four fell for six runs in 11 balls, including three to McGrath. On a dry surface which made strokeplay difficult, Australia failed to hit a boundary after the 32nd over and owed much to the diligence of Taylor and Slater. In reply, Ponting – a rare talent, still eight days short of 20 – hoisted Warne for six on his way to 42. Afterwards Taylor, always an opponent of the A team concept, renewed his criticism, saying: 'I don't like playing against my own players and I don't like it when the crowd does not support us when we are playing at home.' ·

Man of the Match: G.D. McGrath. *Attendance*: 20,470

AUSTRALIA

*M.A. Taylor b Robertson 44	C.J. McDermott not out 10	
M.J. Slater c Hayden b Rowell 64	T.B.A. May run out 1	
M.E. Waugh b Hughes 0	G.D. McGrath c Langer b Reiffel 0	
D.C. Boon c Langer b Hughes 39	B 4, l-b 7, w 6 17	
M.G. Bevan c Emery b Robertson 4		
S.G. Law b Moody .0	1/93 2/94 3/132 (48.3 overs) **202**	
†I.A. Healy c Hayden b Reiffel 15	4/151 5/152 6/175	
S.K. Warne c Langer b Hughes 8	7/181 8/197 9/199	

Bowling: Rowell 10-0-41-1; Reiffel 9.3-2-34-2; Moody 7-0-36-1; Hughes 9-0-33-3; Martyn 3-0-20-0; Robertson 10-1-27-2.

AUSTRALIA A

D.S. Lehmann c Healy b McGrath 4	P.R. Reiffel lbw b McGrath 0	
M.L. Hayden c Taylor b Law 45	G.J. Rowell c Law b McGrath 0	
*D.R. Martyn b Warne 37	M.G. Hughes c Law b McGrath 1	
J.L. Langer c Law b Warne 1	B 1, l-b 5, w 4, n-b 2 12	
R.T. Ponting c Bevan b Warne 42		
T.M. Moody c sub (D.W. Fleming) b May . .5	1/10 2/71 3/77 (47.3 overs) **196**	
†P.A. Emery run out 30	4/108 5/117 5/157	
G.R. Robertson not out 19	7/190 8/190 9/190	

Bowling: McDermott 9-0-33-0; McGrath 9.3-0-43-4; Waugh 4-1-17-0; Warne 10-1-40-3; May 10-0-29-1; Law 5-0-28-1.

Umpires: S.J. Davis and P.D. Parker.

SAND MEN

As part of a 'Play the Aussie Team' competition sponsored by a brewery, Steve Waugh's Beach Boys (91) defeated Gold Coast pensioner Peter Dawson's Lite Ice All Stars (58) in an eight-over-a-side beach cricket game at Coogee in Sydney on January

17, 2000. Eight current Australian players were involved, being divided between the two teams, with a matting pitch, rubber ball, and plastic stumps and bats in use.

ASIA XI V. REST OF THE WORLD XI

At Dhaka, April 8, 2000 (day/night). Asia XI won by one run. Toss: Asia XI.

A crowd of 50,000 witnessed a feast of runs. Tendulkar and Ganguly set the tone. adding 114 runs from 17 overs. Both were dropped by Tufnell off his own left-arm spin, but he finally had Tendulkar caught at long-on, then accounted for Ganguly in identical fashion. Tendulkar hit 11 fours in 77 balls, Ganguly six fours and three sixes in 66. Further attractive contributions from Asia set a target of 321, which looked beyond the Rest of the World when they limped to 196 for seven. But Bevan, supported by Caddick, then put on 119 in 13 overs. Widely regarded as the world's best one-day batsman, Bevan produced some devastating strokeplay, while Caddick played admirably until carelessly failing to ground his bat with one ball to go. Needing six, Bevan managed four, and Asia won by a single run. He remained unbeaten on 185 from 132 bails, with five sixes and 19 fours. Television later suggested that one of those, a straight drive, should have been signalled as six.

Man of the Match: M.G. Bevan.

ASIA XI

S.T. Jayasuriya c Bevan b Hayward 12	A. Kumble not out 14
S.R. Tendulkar c Rose b Tufnell 80	W.P.U.J.C. Vaas run out 0
S.C. Ganguly c Rose b Tufnell 67	M. Muralitharan not out 0
P.A. de Silva c Gilchrist b Bevan 39	L-b 9, w 16, n-b 3 28
A. Jadeja c Johnson b Waugh 28	
Abdur Razzaq b Waugh 3	1/49 2/163 3/183 (9 wkts, 50 overs) **320**
†Moin Khan c and b Hayward 34	4/242 5/248 6/248
*Wasim Akram b Hayward 15	7/291 8/314 9/319

Bowling: Caddick 4-0-27-0; Hayward 7-0-39-3; Rose 6-0-44-0; Cairns 4-0-22-0; Tufnell 9-0-68-2; Klusener 4-0-22-0; Bevan 10-0-61-1; Waugh 6-0-28-2.

REST OF THE WORLD XI

N.C. Johnson c Jadeja b Wasim Akram 2	A.R. Caddick run out 23
*M.E. Waugh c and b Vaas 28	M. Hayward not out 0
J.H. Kallis lbw b Kumble 27	
M.G. Bevan not out 185	B 5, l-b 13, w 2, n-b 2 22
C.L. Cairns c and b Muralitharan 8	
L. Klusener c Jayasuriya b Muralitharan ..16	1/28 2/46 3/97 (8 wkts, 50 overs) **319**
†A.C. Gilchrist b Abdur Razzaq 1	4/134 5/180 6/186
F.A. Rose lbw b Abdur Razzaq 7	7/196 8/315

P.C.R. Tufnell did not bat.

Bowling: Wasim Akram 5-1-27-1; Vaas 10-1-57-1; Abdur Razzaq 10-0-68-2; Kumble 9-0-59-1; Muralitharan 9-1-45-2; Tendulkar 7-0-45-0.

Umpires: D.L. Orchard and S. Venkataraghavan. Referee: P.L. van der Merwe.

2 0

THE LONG STOP

Since inaugurating the custom in 1892, *Wisden* has published more than 10,000 obituaries. This sample of forty-five, from the slight and small to the worthier and weightier, reveals something of their range. There are a sprinkling of distinguished Test cricketers but the accent is on those figures whose only common bond, it might be felt, is commemoration in the world's oldest and yellowest cricket annual.

It is notable how closely *Wisden* followed antipodean cricket and its community from earliest times. It knew the story of George Gibson's bat. It recalled Ben Wardill's Wimbledon visit. It acknowledged supernumeraries like Rowley Pope, fan and friend to Ashes teams for more than half a century, and Bill Ferguson, scorer extraordinaire.

Wisden has also often taken pleasure in those cricketers and cricket aficionados distinguished in other fields, a trend celebrated in Jonathan Rice's essay 'Never a Famous Cricketer' in the almanack last year. Politicians have always been popular in this respect: thus, in these pages, Sir Robert Menzies, Doc Evatt, Sir Reginald Dallas Brooks, Sir Malcolm McEachern, and John Curtin, not to mention Curtin's political mentor Frank Hyett. They are joined here by businessmen Ray Ferrall and Roger Kimpton, soldier Colonel Alan Newton, educationalist Sir Brian Hone and psychologist Philip Le Couteur. Also guaranteed to interest the almanack have been those gifted in other games and pastimes, such as 'Snowy' Baker, Reg Bettington, Hec Oakley, 'Nip' Pellew and John Hill (a 'famous whip' who happened also to be Clem's father).

If you can't lead an especially remarkable life, there is always the chance that an unusual death will catch *Wisden*'s eye. This sample includes Frank Bryant, Jack Burge and Herbert Thompson, who died respectively watching, listening to and participating in their favourite game, along with bibliophile Arthur Gregory, mortally injured while returning from nephew Syd's funeral. There are the melancholy Percy McShane and Reginald Wood, the mysterious Andrew Newell, and the curious conjunction of Tasmania's Savigny brothers, both memorialised in the 1924 *Wisden*.

Not that *Wisden* is ghoulish. The almanack can be coy. 'Had he ordered his life more carefully,' reads the tribute to the benighted alcoholic Harry Graham, 'he might have had a much longer and more successful career.' Of Joey Palmer's waning fortunes, little is said: 'The latter part of his life was the reverse of prosperous but on this point there is no need to dwell.'

—*GH*

BAKER, MR REGINALD LESLIE, who died at Hollywood, California, on December 2, 1953, aged 69, was known as the greatest all-round athlete produced by Australia. He got his Blue at Sydney University for cricket and also for football, athletics and rowing. He took part in twenty-six different sports, representing Australia at Rugby football and taking part in international polo. 'Snowy' Baker, as he was generally known, fought and lost to the late J.W.H.T. Douglas, who became captain of the England cricket team, for the Olympic middle-weight boxing championship in London in 1908. Though born in Sydney he spent most of his life in America.

BRYANT, FRANK JOSEPH, who died in Perth on March 11, 1984, while watching the Sheffield Shield final, aged 76, was one of three brothers who played for Western Australia, on one occasion in the same match. In 32 first-class matches he scored 1,495 runs (average 26.69), including three centuries, the highest of them 155 for J. Ryder's touring team against Bombay in 1935–36. He became a popular and influential cricket administrator in Perth, welcoming many England sides there, besides managing Western Australia on numerous occasions as well as three Australian teams to New Zealand. A delegate to the Australian Cricket Board, he had much to do with Perth receiving Test status.

BURGE, MR THOMAS JOHN, who died at his home in Brisbane on January 7, 1957, aged 53, while listening to a radio commentary on a cricket match in which his son was batting, had been a member of the Australian Board of Control since 1952. He suffered a heart attack while his son was touring England in 1956. He was a life-member of the Queensland C.A. and managed the first Australian team to tour the West Indies in 1955.

CROCKETT, ROBERT W., the Australian umpire, died on December 12, 1935, aged 72. Born in Melbourne, he was closely connected with Melbourne cricket for many years, and was at work on the club's famous ground when he contracted a chill, as the result of which he passed away. 'Bob' Crockett 'stood' in most of the Test matches during a long period when England teams visited Australia, and was held in high regard by everyone for his accurate decisions. Recognised by cricketers the world over as one of the finest umpires of his time, his quiet demeanour, unfailing good humour and strict impartiality endeared him to all players with whom he came in contact. When failing sight compelled him to give up umpiring, he became a director in a company to make cricket bats at Melbourne out of Tasmanian willow. This experiment proved fairly satisfactory, and provided Crockett with a livelihood for many years. The bats are still being made. So many times did Crockett umpire at the end from which Blackie, the Victorian, bowled, and so many decisions did he give in favour of Blackie, that their combination gave rise to many jests. When the two met in the street, 'Rocketty' would welcome Crockett with 'How's that, Bob?' and the umpire answered with the 'out' signal, raising his hand high in the air. J.B. Hobbs coupled him with Frank Chester as the best umpires he knew, and the Surrey batsman had good opportunities of forming an opinion, because when he was in the MCC team captained by A.O. Jones in 1907, Crockett already held an honoured name for his unfailing care and accuracy. Crockett came to England with the Australian team in 1926 and umpired in one match – Public Schools Fifteen v. The Australians, at Lord's.

Mr P.F. Warner, when asked about Bob Crockett, said:— 'A very fine umpire: one of the best I have ever seen. He commanded the respect of everyone, and gained a reputation with English cricketers who, even if they doubted whether they were out, were quite satisfied when they realised that Crockett had made the decision.'

BETTINGTON, DR REGINALD HENSHAW BRINDLEY, who died in an accident – his car fell 100 feet on to a railway line – in New Zealand on June 24, 1969, aged 69, was a fine all-round sportsman. He was in the Oxford cricket XI for four years from 1920, being captain in 1923, played as a forward in the University Rugby matches of 1920 and 1922 and got his Blue at golf. He appeared for Middlesex, for Gentlemen v. Players and, after returning to Australia, captained New South Wales. In addition, he won both the New South Wales and Australian amateur golf championships.

Going from King's School, Parramatta, to Oxford in 1920, 'Reg' Bettington got his cricket Blue as a Freshman. He created a big impression with his leg-breaks and googlies, taking 56 wickets for the University for 15.12 runs each. In the Freshmen's match he dismissed eight men for 48 runs in an innings, took seven for 47 and five for 42 against Somerset, five for 48 against Essex and earned a similar analysis in the match at Oxford with Warwickshire. Yet he met with little success in the University match and he did not touch the same form in the following two seasons.

In 1923, when he became the first Australian to captain Oxford, however, he reaped a rich harvest of Cambridge victims. Helped by the effects of what *Wisden* described as 'the worst thunderstorm for twelve years', he took three wickets for 19 runs in the first innings and eight for 66 in the second, thus playing a leading part in the victory for Oxford by an innings and 227 runs – the most substantial in the series between the Universities. Among other outstanding analyses he achieved were six wickets for 71 runs against Hampshire at Oxford and five for 22 and four for 91 against Surrey at The Oval, and his full figures for the summer were 61 wickets for 16.55 each.

From the University he went to St. Bartholomew's Hospital where he qualified as a doctor, and in 1928 he assisted Middlesex. In 15 County Championship matches, he took 54 wickets for 29.44 runs apiece and made 605 runs at an average of 30.25. Against Somerset at Lord's he followed an innings of 95 by sending back six second-innings batsmen for 78 runs.

In all first-class cricket in England, he obtained 335 wickets for 22.15 runs each and, as a forthright batsman who once drove a ball into the Press Box at The Oval, he scored 3,072 runs, including five centuries, average 27.67.

For a number of years he was ear, nose and throat specialist to the Hawke's Bay Hospital Board, a post he held at the time of his death.

CURTIN, MR JOHN, Prime Minister of Australia, a cricket enthusiast, died on July 4, 1945, aged 60. Notwithstanding his many national activities he maintained a close interest in cricket and often mentioned the game in his speeches. Last year's *Wisden* quoted his memorable remarks regarding Lord's when he became a Freeman of London.

Early in the war he declared that games were not detrimental to the war effort, but a refresher, and he recommended that a series of Test matches between Australia and England should be played immediately after the war as an effective way of demonstrating to the world the characteristics of the British race. Mr Curtin visited Lord's in 1944, and just before the first 'Victory Test' last May he sent a message to MCC conveying his best wishes for the reopening of a series which he hoped would never again be interrupted.

Flight-Lieut. K. Johnston, a member of the Australian Board of Control, who was in England when the news came that Mr Curtin was dead, said that although a very busy man at Canberra, the headquarters of Australian politics, a long way from cricket centres, Mr Curtin seldom missed an opportunity of watching the game. He was often a spectator at West Australian matches. By his death, cricket in England and Australia lost a very valuable friend and supporter.

DALLAS BROOKS, GENERAL SIR REGINALD ALEXANDER, who died on March 22, 1966, aged 69, was in the Dover XI from 1912 to 1914 as a batsman and medium-paced bowler. In his last season he headed the School batting figures with 939 runs, of which he scored 187 in an innings against King's School, Canterbury, at an average of 62.62, and was also leading bowler with 36 wickets at 12.94 runs each. In 1919 and 1921 he appeared in a few matches for Hampshire, hitting 107 from the Gloucestershire bowling at Southampton in the first year. A fine all-round sportsman, he captained the Combined Services against touring teams from Australia, South Africa and New Zealand, led them at hockey, at which he played for England against Ireland and France, and captained the Royal Navy at golf. Joining the Royal Marines on his eighteenth birthday, he earned the D.S.O. in the First World War for his part in the St George's Day raid on Zeebrugge in 1918. He was Governor of Victoria from 1949 to 1963.

EVATT, DR HERBERT VERE, who died at Canberra following a long illness on November 3, 1965, aged 71, was a keen cricket enthusiast who contributed articles to *Wisden* in 1935 and 1938. At the age of 36, he was the youngest man ever to become a member of the Australian High Court Bench and he was Minister for External Affairs in 1941. Later he became Deputy Prime Minister of Australia.

FERRALL, RAYMOND ALFRED, died at Newstead, Launceston, on June 1, 2000, four days after his 94th birthday. A lifelong resident of Launceston, Sir Ray was born there on May 27, 1906 and educated at the city's grammar school, where he was awarded colours for cricket, football, rowing and athletics. A consistently heavy scorer with both the East and South Launceston clubs, he was a lithe and fit figure, whose batting was solid and technically correct and who accumulated runs by working the ball deftly and prizing his wicket dearly. Ferrall's first-class appearances were limited by his burgeoning business activities but they suggest that he would have enhanced a fragile batting side had he been able to play more regularly. In his first game, against Victoria, at Launceston over New Year 1933–34, he made 67 in 171 minutes, joining the flamboyant young Jack Badcock (274) in a second-wicket partnership of 175. A month later, at the MCG, he made 84 in what he always regarded as the innings of his life, this time adding 165 in 142 minutes for the second wicket with Badcock (104). Another month on and he batted with substance against the 1934 Australian touring team at Launceston. In the first innings he made 47, again teaming up with Badcock in a second-wicket partnership, this time of 108 in 92 minutes, and he followed this up with 39 in the second innings. A year later, in his final game for

Tasmania, he captained the side against Victoria in Melbourne. He later served as a Northern Tasmanian selector and spent terms as both board member and treasurer of the Northern Tasmanian Cricket Association. Ferrall was a major public and business figure who made an incalculable contribution to 20th century Tasmania. His standing can be gauged by the fact that he was one of the final three men to be considered as Tasmanian of the Century, a title eventually bestowed on long-serving premier, Eric Reece. Originally a journalist on the *Launceston Daily Telegraph*, he moved into a diverse range of business ventures, starting with his father's general store, which he converted into a successful food company specialising in flour and dried fruit. He subsequently accepted directorships in the fields of banking, building materials, newspapers, television and finance and was a founder of the Qintex Corporation, serving as a chairman whose probity and rectitude stood in stark contrast to his successor, Christopher Skase. From 1946 to 1980, he was Warden of the Port of Launceston Authority and during that period was also an Associate Commissioner of the Hydro Electric Commission of Tasmania. His service was recognised in 1980 by his being knighted for services to Tasmania; in the same year he was made a Freeman of the City of Launceston. The sagacious and witty Sir Ray was still writing a business column in the *Launceston Examiner* and in constant demand as a public speaker even after he passed the age of ninety.

FERGUSON, MR WILLIAM HENRY, who died at Bath on September 22, 1957, aged 77, was the best-known cricket scorer in the world. For 52 years, from the time he first visited England with Joe Darling's Australian side of 1905, he acted as scorer and baggage-master for England, South Africa, West Indies, New Zealand and, naturally, Australia, in no fewer than 43 tours. In all that time his boast was that he never lost a bag. 'Fergie', as he was affectionately known in the cricket world, scored in no fewer than 208 Test matches in every country where big cricket is played. He liked to relate how he first took up the job. The office in Sydney, his birthplace, where he was employed as a clerk, overlooked the harbour and he often felt the urge to travel. So in 1905 he 'thought up a nice toothache', went to see his dentist, M.A. Noble, the Test batsman, and brought up the question of scoring. Amused at the ingenious method of approach, Noble put forward 'Fergie's' name to the authorities, with the result that this short, slightly-built man began his travels which totalled well over half a million miles. His salary for the 1905 tour was £2 per week, from which he defrayed his expenses, and he paid his own passage.

For all his long connection with it, 'Fergie' never took much active part in the game, but figures, for which he always had a passion, fascinated him, and he loved to travel. Besides actual scoring, he kept diagrams of every stroke played, with their value, by every batsman in the matches in which he was concerned, and could account for every ball bowled – and who fielded it. Touring captains, including D.G. Bradman and D.R. Jardine, employed his charts to study the strengths and weaknesses of opposing batsmen.

When in England with the Australian team of 1948, 'Fergie' was presented to King George VI. That summer Bradman scored 2,428 runs. Said the King: 'Mr Ferguson, do you use an adding-machine when the Don is in?'

'Fergie', who received the British Empire Medal in 1951 for his services to cricket, emerged from two years' retirement to score for the West Indies last summer. A fall at an hotel in August prevented him from finishing the tour, and he spent some time in hospital, returning home only two days before his death. His autobiography, titled *Mr Cricket,* was published in May, 1957.

MR GEORGE GIBSON, a native of Jamaica, died at Carlton, Melbourne on September 5th, 1910, aged 83. His first appearance in a match of note was for Victoria v. New South Wales, on the Melbourne ground, in December, 1865, and his highest innings in a first-class game 41 – against the same colony in March, 1872 – for playing which, he was presented with a bat made from a willow-tree grown in his own garden. In addition to being a capable batsman, he was a good wicket-keeper.

HARRY GRAHAM, born at Carlton, Melbourne, November 29th, 1870, died at Dunedin, New Zealand, February 7th, 1911. Graham did many brilliant things as a batsman but scarcely gave himself a fair chance. Had he ordered his life more carefully he might have had a much longer and more successful career in first-class cricket. His natural powers were great. He did not play with quite a straight bat but he was a splendid hitter with any amount of dash and vigour. When he came to England for the first time in 1893 he was at his best, playing the innings of his life against England at Lord's. No one who saw the match will forget the way in which he and Gregory knocked off the England bowling after Australia had lost five wickets for 75. Graham was very successful all through the tour and headed the averages in all matches, just beating Lyons. However, he was not the same man in 1896 and had to be left out of many matches. He recovered his batting form at home and for a couple of seasons was almost as good as ever, playing two innings of over a hundred for Victoria against South Australia. Taking his career as a whole he was a player of immense possibilities only half fulfilled.

GREGORY, MR ARTHUR H., born at Sydney on July 7, 1861, died at Chatswood, Sydney, on August 17, 1929, aged 68. Returning from the funeral of S.E. Gregory he fell from a tramcar, and blood-poisoning supervened as a result of injuries to arm. He was a member of the most famous of Australian cricket families, and, although perhaps better known as a graceful and well-informed writer on the game, was a sound batsman, a good field and a fair leg-break bowler and had himself appeared for New South Wales. He was younger brother of E.J., D.W., and C.S. Gregory, and uncle of S.E., C.W., and J.M.

GREGORY, MR SYDNEY EDWARD, born on the site of the present cricket ground at Sydney, on April 14, 1870, died at Randwick, Sydney, on August 1, 1929, aged 59. It is given to few men to enjoy such a long and successful career in international cricket as that which fell to his lot, but he had cricket in his blood, for what the Graces and the Walkers were to the game in England, the Gregory family, it could be urged, was to that in Australia. Twelve years after his uncle Dave had come to England, as captain of the pioneer side of 1878, S.E. Gregory paid his first visit here as a member of the 1890 team under W.L. Murdoch, and he was chosen for every side up to and including that of 1912. On his first two visits here he did not quite realize expectations as a batsman – he completed his twentieth year on his way here in 1890 – but he jumped to the top in the Australian season of 1894–95, and when in England in

1896 he batted brilliantly, scoring over 1,400 runs in all matches and coming out at the head of the averages. Altogether he played in fifty-two Test Matches for Australia, a larger number than any other Australian cricketer. In the course of these he made four three-figure scores and obtained 2,193 runs with an average of 25.80. He captained the Australian team of 1912 – the year of the Triangular Tournament – but had a somewhat thankless task in filling that office. Dissatisfied with the financial terms offered, several of the leading Australian cricketers refused to make the trip and the side, as finally constituted, included, in the regrettable circumstances, several players who had little claim to figure as representatives of the best in Australian cricket. He himself scored over a thousand runs but the team, although beating South Africa twice, had only a moderate record.

Pronounced and numerous as were his triumphs in batting, Sydney Gregory will probably be remembered more for what he accomplished as a fieldsman for, while several men have equalled and some have beaten his achievements as a run-getter, the cricket field had seen no more brilliant cover-point. Clever in anticipation and quick to move, he got to and stopped the hardest of hits, gathered the ball cleanly and returned it with deadly accuracy. His work, indeed, was always an inspiration to his colleagues and a joy to the spectators. Small of stature – he was little more than 5 feet in height – Gregory overcame this disadvantage in a batsman by splendid footwork. He possessed a very finished style, strong wrists and a keen eye. Particularly attractive in his strokes on the offside, he also, thanks to his quickness of movement, used to take balls off the middle stump with remarkable facility. The latter stroke, no doubt, cost him his wicket on many occasions but it brought him a lot of runs and, when successful, had a demoralising effect upon the bowler. He could stonewall when the situation called for those methods but his natural tendency was always to attack and, even when the ball turned a lot, his dashing game often knocked a bowler off his length. In short his cricket, both as batsman and fieldsman, suggested the bright and happy temperament which Sydney Gregory possessed in such full measure.

GROUT, ARTHUR THEODORE WALLACE, who died in hospital in Brisbane on November 9, 1968, aged 41, kept wicket for Australia in 51 Test matches between 1957 and 1965. He entered hospital only two days before his death. A Brisbane doctor was afterwards reported as saying that Grout knew that he might collapse at any time during the last four years of his Test career and that he took part in the Australian tour of the West Indies only a few months after a heart attack in 1964. Yet 'Wally's' unfailingly cheerful demeanour gave no inkling that there might be anything amiss with him.

Few chances escaped the agile Grout behind the stumps. In Test cricket he dismissed 187 batsmen, 163 of them caught and 24 stumped. Of these, 23 fell to him in the series with the West Indies in Australia in 1960–61; 21 in England in 1961 and 20 against England in Australia in 1958–59. Only T.G. Evans, who played in 40 more Test matches for England, possesses a better record. On two occasions Grout claimed eight victims in a Test match and his six catches in one innings against South Africa at Johannesburg in 1957–58 set up a world's record which has since been equalled by J.D. Lindsay for South Africa and J.T. Murray for England. On five other occasions Grout disposed of five batsmen in an innings. Outside Test cricket, his greatest achievement was when he exceeded all previous wicket-keeping feats in first-class cricket; for

Queensland in the Sheffield Shield match at Brisbane in 1960, he sent back eight Western Australia batsmen, all caught, in one innings. That world's record still stands.

In addition to his wicket-keeping ability, Grout was also a distinctly useful late-order batsman, as he proved in that Test at Johannesburg in which he brought off his six catches. He and R. Benaud, in adding 89, set up a new record for the Australian eighth wicket against South Africa.

Tributes to Grout included:

S.C. Griffith (MCC Secretary): 'Among cricketers, he was regarded as one of the most kindly and generous of men. Speaking as a former wicket-keeper myself, I regarded him as among the most consistent performers behind the wicket I have ever played with or seen.'

Sir Donald Bradman: 'He was one of the finest wicket-keepers of all time.'

R.B. Simpson: 'He was the greatest wicket-keeper I ever saw.'

R. Benaud: 'He was able to read a match as well as any captain and was always of tremendous value to me in captaining the Australian side.'

W.W. Hall (West Indies fast bowler who played for Queensland in two Sheffield Shield series): 'He was the finest wicket-keeper I either played with or against in my ten years of big cricket.'

B.N. Jarman (successor to Grout as Australian wicket-keeper): 'I could not speak too highly of Wally as a wicket-keeper. He was one of the game's greatest characters. I never begrudged playing second fiddle to him.'

MR H.W. HEDLEY died in the Hospital at Melbourne on November 20th, 1911, at the age of 63. On the previous Saturday, though obviously ill, he was reporting the match between Victoria and the MCC's eleven. Mr Hedley was one of the best known cricket journalists in Australia, writing for many years in the *Melbourne Age* under the signature of 'Mid On'. He came to England with the Australian team of 1884, supplying his paper with full details of the tour.

HILL, MR CLEMENT, the Australian left-handed batsman, ranked among the finest cricketers in the world during a long period, died on September 5, 1945, aged 68. Born at Adelaide on March 18, 1877, the son of H.J. Hill, who scored the first century on Adelaide Oval, Clem Hill excelled his brothers – all good at the game – and when 16 he put together the remarkable score of 360 in an Inter-College match at Adelaide. This was the highest innings hit in Australia at that time, 1893, and young Clem Hill gave clear indication of the skill which matured without a check.

Soon after completing his 18th year he scored 150 not out and 56 for South Australia against A.E. Stoddart's team in 1895, and a year later, with Harry Trott as captain, he made the first of four visits to England. Third in the averages, he established himself as being worthy of a place in any eleven, and when next Stoddart took a side to Australia Hill exceeded the highest expectations by scoring 829 runs in twelve innings, his average of 75 far surpassing that of both K.S. Ranjitsinhji and A.C. MacLaren, the chief batsmen in the touring side. That season he scored 200 for South Australia against the visiting team, and his 188 at Melbourne in the fourth Test, when Australia began so badly as to lose six men for 57, was largely responsible for a victory by eight wickets. This innings was considered the finest that Clem Hill ever played.

Coming to England with the side under the captaincy of Joe Darling, another fine left-handed batsman, in 1899, he showed splendid form until taken ill early in July. He and Victor Trumper each scored 135 at Lord's, sharing the chief honours in beating England by ten wickets, and so helping largely to win the rubber: for this was the only decisive result in the five Tests. He headed the averages for the tour with 60.20. To prove that even such a splendid batsman may fail it is interesting to recall that in the second innings of the third Test at Leeds, the order of batting being altered, he fell the first victim of a hat-trick by J.T. Hearne; Hill was clean bowled, S.E. Gregory and M.A. Noble were both caught in the slips. From 1896 to 1912 he played in 49 Test matches, 41 against England, eight against South Africa; he captained Australia when South Africa were the visitors in 1910, and in the following season against the England touring side, led by J.W.H.T. Douglas owing to the illness of P.F. Warner.

As a rule Clem Hill, going in first wicket down, was at his best on the important occasion and in Test matches he scored 3,412 runs; average 39. He hit seven centuries against South Africa and four against England, besides 96, 99, 98 and 97. The innings of 98 and 97 were the highest scores for Australia at Adelaide in January 1902 and, with Trumble's all-round work, brought about the defeat of England by four wickets. These displays followed his 99 which helped in a victory by 229 runs at Melbourne – three consecutive scores just short of the century in Tests with England.

A specially brilliant batsman on hard pitches, Clem Hill scored 6,274 runs, average 52.28 in Sheffield Shield matches – a record until beaten by Don Bradman. His highest innings was 365 not out for South Australia against New South Wales at Adelaide in December 1900, his average that season being 103.33. In similar matches he made 206 not out at Sydney in 1895 and 205 at Adelaide in 1909.

While able to drive hard to the off or straight, usually with the ball kept down, Clem Hill scored chiefly on the leg side by skilful strokes perfectly timed and placed, the way in which he turned straight balls clear of fieldsmen being exceptional. Brilliant square and late cutting made Hill delightful to watch and in defence his style claimed admiration while his patience was unlimited. A splendid field particularly in the deep, Clem Hill brought off one catch that will never be forgotten by the spectators at the third Test match at Old Trafford in 1902. When England wanted eight runs for victory with two wickets in hand Dick Lilley made a square-leg hit which looked like carrying the pavilion rails, but as Hill ran from long-on the wind seemed to check the force of the hit. The ball fell almost straight and Hill, racing across its flight, with outstretched hands, held it, so accepting a chance that few fieldsmen would have thought worth attempting. Australia won by three runs, and the victory, following success at Sheffield, where Hill scored 119, by far the highest innings in the match, gave them the rubber, a triumph to which Hill's amazing catch contributed to an unknown degree. Rain ruined the first two Tests and England won the last by one wicket.

HILL, MR H. JOHN, father of the well-known Australian cricketing brotherhood which included Clement Hill, died in Adelaide on September 18, 1926. A good player in his day, he will be remembered chiefly for having been the first batsman to play a three-figure innings on the Adelaide Oval – 102 not out for North Adelaide v. Kent C.C. on January 26, 1878. A trustee of the South Australian Cricket Association for many years and a vice-president of that body since 1893, Mr Hill was also a famous whip and in 1874 he drove W.G. Grace's team to Kadina in one of his four-in-hands. Born in Adelaide on March 16, 1847, he was, at the time of his death, in his 80th year.

MR HARRY HILLIARD, one of the oldest Australian cricketers, and the last survivor but one of the first match between New South Wales and Victoria – at Melbourne in March, 1856 – died in Sydney (his native place) on March 19, 1914. He was born on November 7, 1826, and was thus in his 88th year. Altogether he played in five games against Victoria, with 20, at Sydney in January, 1857, as his highest score. Few men followed cricket more closely, and for very many years he watched the matches between the two States both in Melbourne and Sydney. In 1878 he visited England and saw the Australian team of that year win their memorable match with the MCC at Lord's – an event, almost needless to add, which occasioned him the greatest satisfaction.

HONE, SIR BRIAN, OBE, who died in Paris on May 28, 1978, aged 70, was the noted Australian educationalist who enjoyed a brief but successful first-class cricket career between 1928 and leaving his home city, Adelaide, as its 1930 Rhodes Scholar. In that time, Sir Brian scored 860 runs at an average of 50.58, including three excellent Sheffield Shield centuries. A determined player, possessed of a good defence, he won cricket and tennis Blues at Oxford and, on joining the staff of Marlborough College as head of the English Department, he played with success for Wiltshire in the Minor Counties Competition when the opportunity presented itself, topping the side's batting averages between 1937 and 1939. Returning to Australia as Headmaster of Sydney's Cranbrook School in 1940, Sir Brian became Headmaster of Melbourne Grammar School in 1950, a post he filled with distinction until retirement in 1970. He was later to be Deputy Chancellor of Monash University in 1973–1974 and Chairman of the Commonwealth Secondary Schools Libraries Committee between 1971 and 1974.

HYETT, MR FRANK, born on February 9, 1882, died in Melbourne of influenza in April 1919. He had been associated with the Brunswick and Carlton Clubs, and had appeared with success for Victoria. In his first match for the State he scored 108 not out v. Tasmania. He was well known in Labour circles as the Secretary of the Victorian Railway Union.

KIMPTON, ROGER CHARLES MacDONALD, died in Melbourne on November 30, 1999. Born at Toorak, Melbourne, on September 21, 1916, Kimpton was educated at Melbourne Grammar School before reading philosophy, politics and economics at Brasenose College, Oxford. In his second match for the university, against Gloucestershire at Oxford, he showed his rapid acclimatisation to English conditions by making 160 exhilarating runs in 165 minutes. He played for the university in each of the four seasons between 1935–1938, being awarded a blue in each season except 1936, when he missed the match against Cambridge because of a sprained ankle. He turned out for Worcestershire during the summer holidays, taking a century off the Derbyshire bowlers at Chesterfield in 1937. During that season he had represented the Gentlemen against the Players at Lord's, scoring a crisp 59; he had also played for the Gentlemen at Folkestone at the end of the previous season and made another century at a run a minute. Kimpton visited Jamaica with a combined Oxford and Cambridge team in August 1938, his 113 in two hours in the first of the two matches drawing favourable comparison with the panache of George Headley. He returned to the West Indies in 1955–56 with E.W. Swanton's team. Trim and slight in stature, Kimpton's batting was built on the fundamentals of confident footwork, powerful wrists and sure placement. This combination, and his determination to subjugate bowlers quickly and completely, gave his batting a powerful elegance which caused *Wisden* to compare him to Charlie Macartney. At the end of 1938, Kimpton returned to Australia to assume a role in the management of his family's milling business, and rejoined the Prahran club for whom he had played in 1933–34. During World War II, his flying skills were quickly utilised by the RAAF; ultimately, he became Commanding Officer of No. 75 Squadron, with its Kittyhawk aircraft, and was awarded the DFC for his distinguished record. Although he never played first-class cricket in Australia, he was lauded by commentators such as Gerald Brodribb and John Arlott as one of the late flowerings of thrillingly uninhibited Oxbridge batsmanship. Their praise was tinged with that sense of cricketing 'what might have been' had circumstances not dictated that he leave the game so early. This sense was made even sharper at Stourbridge, in July 1949, when, in borrowed gear, he filled in for Worcestershire in his solitary post-war first-class match in England and proceeded to make an unbeaten 93 in 80 minutes off the Nottinghamshire bowling – despite having his eyebrow stitched during his innings when it was cut by a ball which flew from a good length. His older brother, Stephen MacDonald Kimpton (1914–) played four matches for Oxford University in 1935 and headed the Prahran bowling averages each season from 1936–37 to 1939–40, taking 90 wickets with his accurate off-breaks.

LE COUTEUR, MR PHILIP RIDGEWAY, who died in Australia on June 30, 1958, aged 73, did fine work as an all-rounder for Oxford University where he was a Rhodes Scholar, in the early part of the century. From Melbourne University he went to Oxford in 1908 and appeared in the eleven in the three following seasons. He fared moderately in his first match against Cambridge, but in 1910 enjoyed pronounced success. He played an innings of 160, and, in taking six wickets for 20 and five for 46, bore a leading part in the dismissal of the Light Blues for 76 and 113 and their defeat in an innings with 126 runs to spare. Next season he took eight wickets for 99 in the second innings and helped Oxford to victory by 74 runs. In 1910 and 1911 he made six appearances for Gentlemen against Players. A batsman who excelled in back-play and on-side strokes, he also bowled leg-breaks skilfully with deceptive variation of pace. After leaving Oxford, he studied psychology for two years at the University of Bonn, returning in 1913 to Australia, where he became lecturer in philosophy at the University of Western Australia. He made two or three appearances for Victoria without achieving distinction.

SIR MALCOLM McEACHERN, a former Lord Mayor of Melbourne, died at Cannes on March 11th, 1910 aged 57. He was fond of cricket, but never gained any celebrity as a player. A few years ago he offered to provide a cup, valued at £250, for competition at cricket between England and Australia.

MR MICHAEL JOSEPH McMAHON, died at Drummoyne, New South Wales, on August 31st, 1908 in his eighty-second year. At one time he was proprietor of the largest sports depot in Sydney, and in 1870 he published 'McMahon's Cricket and Sports Manual' (134 pp.), which had been compiled by Mr Peter C. Curtis.

P.G. M'SHANE, one of the leading players of Victoria, a couple of decades ago, died in Melbourne on December 11th, 1903, in his forty-sixth year. In Boyle and Scott's *Cricketers' Guide* he is described as a 'Very fine left-hand bowler, with great command over the ball; splendid batsman, and has made some fine scores; good field.' He did excellent service for Victoria in Inter-State matches for a number of years. While engaged as curator to the St Kilda Club he had to be removed to Kew Asylum, suffering from a mental ailment, and though he was able to be removed temporarily, a relapse occurred from which he never recovered.

MENZIES, SIR ROBERT GORDON, the famous Australian statesman, who died at his home in Melbourne on May 15, 1978, aged 83, was a very great lover of cricket indeed and had much to say in his autobiography, *Afternoon Light*, on how much it had meant to him. A close friend of many of the Australian players, between 1965, when he was appointed Lord Warden of the Cinque Ports, and the breakdown of his health in 1971, he spent much of each summer in England and was constantly to be found watching, specially on Kent grounds. He was President of the Kent County Cricket Club in 1968 and was a member of I Zingari and of the Band of Brothers.

MOYES, ALBAN GEORGE, who died suddenly at his home in Sydney on January 18, 1963, aged 70, was a celebrated cricket radio-commentator and author. 'Johnny' Moyes, as he was generally known, played for South Australia in Sheffield Shield matches from 1912 to 1915, scoring 104 against Western Australia in the first season and, after service with the Australian Forces during the First World War, in which he won the M.C., assisted Victoria in 1920–21. As a team-selector for New South Wales in 1926–27, he helped Sir Donald Bradman to get his first chance in State Cricket. His services to sport earned him the M.B.E. At one time he was news editor of the *Sydney Daily Telegraph*.

MR ANDREW L. NEWELL, the well-known Australian cricketer, left home over a year ago [1908] and has not been seen or heard of since. He had been in indifferent health for some time and had been advised to take a month's holiday. It is probable that he lost his life over the sea cliffs in the vicinity of Ben Buckler, near Bondi. He was born on November 13th, 1870, and was a very useful all-round player identified with the Glebe Electorate C.C. of Sydney. He will be best remembered on account of his not-out innings of 68 for New South Wales in the return match with Stoddart's team at Sydney in February, 1898. He added 169 for the eighth wicket with S.E. Gregory (171) and 109 for the last in sixty-three minutes with Howell, who claimed 95 of the number. New South Wales, who had made 415 in their first innings, scored 574 in their second, and won by 239 runs.

NEWTON, COLONEL ALAN COLIN, Paymaster-in-Chief of the Australian Army when he retired from the Commonwealth Department of Defence, and probably Tasmania's most gifted all-round athlete, died in Sydney on March 27, 1979, aged

85. 'Picker' Newton achieved early fame in 1908 when he shared an undefeated opening partnership of 400 for Queen's College, Hobart, with the (later) Tasmanian
Rhodes Scholar, John Barnett; their record still stands. As a schoolboy, Newton took
seven wickets for 33 in his first 'A' Grade match, and gained initial representative
honours with a score of 68 in the same season, despite the expressed objection of selectors to his 'wearing knickerbockers' at the time. Originally associated with East
Hobart, Newton helped to form the harbourside Sandy Bay club in 1926 and was its
captain and committee chairman for most of the time until his Defence Department
duties took him first to Perth in 1936 and then to the Royal Military College,
Duntroon. He was honoured with Tasmanian Cricket Association life membership a
year later. During his 22 years as the outstanding all-round player in the Tasmanian
XI, his highest score was 117 at Launceston in 1922 against Victoria when, batting
number ten, he established a new state record partnership of 148 with H.C. Smith. In
all, he scored 1,108 runs and took 66 wickets for Tasmania. He was a most attractive
right-hand batsman, and his left-arm bowling ranged from fast-medium in-swing to
leg-breaks.

A keen tennis player, he won eight major championships, including the
Tasmanian singles titles of 1924 and 1925 and the state doubles championship on three
later occasions between 1930 and 1933.

This true amateur gave much time as a committeeman of the TCA, its Executive
Cricket Council, and as a state selector, as well as being Hon. Treasurer of the Lawn
Tennis Association. He wrote with authority on both sports as a local Hobart press
correspondent, using the *noms-de-plumes* 'Willow' and 'Volley'.

OAKLEY, HECTOR HERBERT, died at Sandringham, Melbourne, on December
19, 1998. Born in the Melbourne suburb of North Fitzroy on January 10, 1909, Hec
Oakley was educated at Wesley College, where he represented the school at cricket,
Australian Rules football and gymnastics. But for the perspicacity of his family doctor, however, he would not have been able to participate in any form of sport. As a
child, he slipped from his bicycle and injured his right knee on a stump of bamboo.
When the wound became seriously infected, a surgeon advised that the leg should be
amputated below the knee but the local doctor saved the situation by putting the leg
into plaster for some months. After an outstanding initial season in St Kilda's first-
grade team in 1929–30 when he scored two centuries and two nineties, he was selected
for the Victorian team for the last Sheffield Shield match of the season, against South
Australia at Adelaide when Keith Rigg was unavailable. He was the likely 12th man
for the game but, on the day before the match, Leo O'Brien was injured when he fell
while riding a horse. Despite being dismissed for a duck by Clarrie Grimmett in the
first innings, Oakley made a sparkling 43 in only 48 minutes in the second innings,
adding 77 for the seventh wicket with Ted a'Beckett (152), a partnership which laid
the foundations for a Victorian victory. Over the next three seasons he became a fixture in the side, his batsmanship being distinguished by a pleasant array of shots all
around the wicket and an ability to score speedily without sacrificing the fundamental soundness of his approach. During that time he scored three Sheffield Shield centuries, all against South Australia at the Melbourne Cricket Ground. In addition, he
played in each of Victoria's matches against the MCC in the Bodyline season of

1932–33, scoring 83 not out and 50; the former of these innings perhaps epitomised his skills as his runs came in only two hours as wickets fell around him. Oakley was dropped from the state side after the 1934–35 season but was restored to the team during 1938–39 when he was made captain for the two matches in Tasmania. In the latter of these games, he made his highest first-class score of 162. Opening the innings, he dominated proceedings to the extent that when he was third out at 281 he had only been at the crease for 175 minutes. For St Kilda, he made a club record 8,307 runs between 1929–30 and 1947–48, averaging 39.36 and including 17 centuries.

Oakley came from that time when a more leisurely and less commercialised fixture schedule meant that players could reach high levels of representation in a number of sports. He played on the forward line for Collegians in the Victorian Amateur Football Association, his left-footed kicking being a reminder of that so-nearly catastrophic accident in his boyhood. He was selected for the Victorian amateur side against South Australia in 1931. A gifted table tennis player, Oakley was Victorian singles champion five times between 1927 and 1940 and played for Australia against England in 1935. In addition, he was a highly proficient tennis player and was St Kilda singles champion five times between 1935 and 1952. Subsequently, he gave many years of substantial administrative service to each of the sports that he had played. He spent over 40 years with BHP, mainly in sales, ultimately becoming general marketing manager of Titan Manufacturing. Any picture of Hec Oakley would be incomplete without emphasising his membership of the Methodist and the Uniting Church and his committed participation in both the religious and social dimensions of the life of his church. His son, Ross, became the executive director, later the chief executive officer, of the Australian Football League in 1986.

GEORGE EUGENE PALMER, one of the greatest of Australia's many famous bowlers, died at Badaginnie, near Benalla, Victoria, on August 22, 1910. Born at Albury, New South Wales, on February 22, 1860, he was in his fifty-first year at the time of his death. Few bowlers have reached the top of the tree so early in life. His fame was established when at Melbourne, in March 1879, playing for Victoria against Lord Harris' eleven, he took six wickets, all bowled down, for 64 runs, and three wickets for 30. Among the batsmen who fell to him were Lord Harris and George Ulyett, twice each, Tom Emmett, and Vernon Royle. His bowling astonished the English team, but to one fine judge of cricket in Melbourne his success did not come as a surprise. Mr Hedley, of the *Melbourne Age*, has told the story of how the late Mr T.W.Wills – for many years the moving spirit of Victorian cricket – asked him one morning on the Melbourne ground if he would like to go out to the nets and see a better bowler than Frank Allan. From the day of his success against Lord Harris' team there was no doubt as to the position Palmer would take in Australian cricket, and for the next six years he had no superior except Spofforth. As all who follow cricket will remember he paid four visits to England, coming over with the teams of 1880, 1882, 1884, and 1886. Many English batsmen of those days maintain that they never met a bowler who was more difficult on a hard true wicket. In one way his effectiveness in fine weather told against him, as on soft wickets he did not get the same opportunities as Spofforth and Harry Boyle. During the latter part of the season of 1880, however, when Spofforth was laid aside by an injured hand, he had a chance of showing what he could do under all conditions, and his success was great. Still he was not so accurate as Spofforth, and afterwards Turner, on a sticky wicket, often doing too much and missing the stumps after beating the batsman. Palmer had many gifts as a bowler. His delivery was one of the best and most natural ever seen, he had a fine off-break and a good variety of pace, and his yorker was deadly. Moreover he bowled a quick leg-break with extraordinary skill. This leg-break, however, proved to some extent his undoing. While he kept it strictly in reserve it was an invaluable servant to him, but as time went on he bowled it more and more and his accuracy of pitch suffered. When he came to England for the last time in 1886 he was not nearly so good a bowler as he had been in his three previous visits. It must be said, however, that while his bowling declined, he developed into an excellent batsman. Following his return to Australia after the unsuccessful tour of 1886, he had the misfortune to fracture his knee-cap and not much more was seen of him in first-class cricket. The latter part of his life was the reverse of prosperous, but on this point there is no need to dwell. He married a sister of Blackham, the great wicket-keeper.

PELLEW, CLARENCE EDWARD ('NIP'), died in Adelaide on May 9, 1981, aged 87. The last survivor but one of Warwick Armstrong's great Australian side of 1921, which was perhaps the first to set the winning of the Tests above all other considerations, he stood out from the rest as having more the traditional approach of the English amateur. Flaxen-haired and seldom wearing a cap, he was an attacking batsman, a matter of some importance when Tests in England were confined to three days. He was a fine straight-driver and a great exponent of the off-drive played slightly late to send the ball between cover and third-man: he was also a competent player off his legs and a splendid runner between the wickets. But though he made two hundreds in the 1920–21 series and for his career in Sheffield Shield cricket had an average of 39.50, it is as an outfield that he is chiefly remembered. Credited with being able to run the 100 yards in 10.2 seconds and to throw a cricket ball over 100 yards, he might well, after sprinting 40 yards round the boundary save not one run but two or three, so swiftly did he get rid of the ball. In any discussion of the world's greatest outfields, he must be a candidate for a place.

After showing promise for South Australia in 1913–14 and making 97 against New South Wales in 1914–15, he went to the War and it was not until 1919, when he was a member of the AIF side in England, that he really became prominent. Starting with 105 not out against Cambridge University in his first match, he made 1,260 runs with an average of 38, including four centuries. Returning to Australia he made 271 in four and three quarter hours against Victoria, equalling a record set up by George Giffen 30 years before. In 1920–21 he played in four of the five Tests, scoring 115 in just over three hours in the second and hitting brilliantly in the third to get 104 in two hours. After this he was a trifle disappointing as a batsman in England in 1921, failing to reach 1,000 runs, but even so he was never omitted from the Test side. That was the end of his regular first-class career but, reappearing for South Australia in a few matches in 1928–29, he showed what a loss his premature retirement had been. From 1930 to the War, and again from 1958 to 1970, he was South Australia's state coach. Several members of his family had played for South Australia, and it was from one of them, J.H. Pellew, a very useful performer, that he inherited the nickname of 'Nip'.

POPE, DR ROWLAND JAMES, who died at Sydney on July 27, 1952, aged 88, was a frequent visitor to England with Australian teams, though not as a playing member. Born on February 18, 1864, he was educated at Hutchins School, Hobart, Tasmania, gaining a place in the eleven as a batsman and bowler of lobs, and he later played for Sydney University. Subsequently, while studying medicine, he was in the Edinburgh University side. In 1884–85, after hitting 170 not out for Melbourne Zingari against Richmond, he represented New South Wales in two matches against Victoria, and he appeared for a Combined XI of Australia and for his State against Alfred Shaw's team. An M.D. and F.R.C.S. of Edinburgh and an ophthalmic specialist, he became a member of MCC in 1887.

SAVIGNY, Mr J. H., who was found dead on the banks of the Lefroy River, where he had gone fishing, at Bishopsbourne, near Launceston, on February 11, 1923, was for several years one of the leading batsmen of Tasmania. He was aged 56 at the time of his death. For Launceston against Cornwall in December, 1901, he made 106 in his first innings and 153 in his second. When he scored 164 not out v. England at Launceston, in 1903–4, he and O.H. Douglas made 202 together for the first wicket. This was his best feat in first-class cricket, and he hit twenty-one 4's and was missed when 33 during the five hours his innings lasted.

SAVIGNY, MR WILLIAM HENRY, who died in Sydney on August 6, 1922, aged 58, was a capital batsman and for some time was prominent in Tasmanian cricket. For twenty-six years he was a master at the Sydney Grammar School, where a memorial tablet to his memory was unveiled on March 23, 1923.

MR ROBERT S. STILL, who introduced round-armed bowling into Australia in a match between the Australian and Victoria clubs at Sydney in March, 1843, died in July 1907, aged 85. All his early cricket was played in New South Wales, and he kept up the game for many years after settling in Tasmania. He was a good all-round cricketer. He visited England in 1878 and witnessed the triumph of the Australians in their match with the MCC at Lord's.

MR HERBERT S. THOMPSON, an old Sydney Grammar School boy, and a great lover of the game, died on March 2nd, 1907 in his fifty-third year. He collapsed suddenly whilst walking towards the pavilion on the conclusion of his innings in a match at Concord Park, and died two hours later.

WALMSLEY, WALTER THOMAS, who died suddenly in New Zealand on February 25, 1978, aged 61, was a much travelled Australian all-round cricketer who made good use of limited opportunities, including the establishment of long standing records in Queensland and Tasmania while embarking on a successful coaching career. After early years spent with the Sydney Western Suburbs Club, Walmsley gained further experience in Lancashire League before transferring to Tasmania as the coach of its Northern area. Walmsley scored 180 against the 1948 Indian touring side, this remaining as a State record for International matches. None the less valuable was a long unbeaten defensive innings of 41 which staved off Tasmania's defeat in Hobart two months later at the hands of the powerful 1948 Australian team, then *en route* to England.

Transferring to Brisbane as official QCA coach in the 1948–49 season, Walmsley became a valuable member of the Queensland Sheffield Shield team, his well flighted leg spinners gathering 95 wickets. In addition, he still holds the State's ninth and tenth wicket partnerships – the former being 152 scored with the late Wally Grout against NSW in 1956–57 and the last wicket stand with fellow spin bowler John Freeman against the same State a year later. A deeply dedicated cricketer, Walmsley effectively carried his experience into coaching duties in which he showed marked ability to impart the basic principles to his many charges in a most infectious manner. After transferring to reside in New Zealand, Wal Walmsley frequently returned to Australia to attend Test series – often accompanied by some members of his large family of children – his last visit being the January 1978 Australia v. India Test match at the Sydney Cricket Ground.

WARDILL, MAJOR BENJAMIN JOHNSON, born at Everton, Liverpool, October 15, 1842; died at Melbourne, October 17, 1911. Sec. to Melbourne C.C., 1878 to 1910, when he retired owing to ill-health. In 1878 there were only 400 members, but in 1910 between 5,000 and 6,000. He was Manager of the Australian teams in England in 1886, 1899 and 1902. Went to Australia at age of 19, and in his young days was a useful cricketer. Played for XXII of Victoria v. Parr's Team at Melbourne, and kept wicket for Victoria and the Melbourne C.C. For Victoria v. XVI of Tasmania, in 1865–6, he caught two and stumped two. Played for the Australians in 1886 v. XI of the South of England at Hastings and scored 17. He did much to popularise rifle-shooting in Australia, and was himself a splendid shot. Was one of the Victorians who visited Wimbledon in 1876 on their way to compete at the first Rifle Competition at Creedmore, U.S.A. during the Philadelphia Exhibition. Major Wardill was very fond of England, and came here more than once on visits after the tour of 1902. As manager for the Australians he had rather a trying experience in 1886, when the players did not get on well together, but he thoroughly enjoyed his subsequent trips.

WHITINGTON, RICHARD SMALLPIECE, who died in Sydney on March 13, 1984, aged 71, was a Sheffield Shield cricketer for South Australia before becoming a prolific producer of cricket books. In England he may be best remembered as Captain R.S. Whitington, a member of A.L. Hassett's Australian team that met 'England' in the Victory 'Tests' of 1945, his opening partner being Flight Sergeant J.A. Workman. 'Whitington, often troubled by hay fever, displayed a beautiful square cut and hooked well', wrote *Wisden*. He was not, however, a naturally attacking batsman. When Hassett's same team played a series of matches in India, on their way home to Australia, Whitington scored 155 in the Representative match in Calcutta. For South Australia he made three Sheffield Shield hundreds and scored 1,728 runs at 30.86. Of his twenty cricket books, several were written in conjunction with K.R. Miller, with whom he had played in the Victory 'Tests'. He also wrote biographies of W.J. O'Reilly, Lindsay Hassett, Victor Richardson and Miller himself, and he assembled the distinguished *Illustrated History of Australian Cricket*. Poker-faced and peripatetic, he was as likely to turn up at a Test match in Johannesburg as in Melbourne, and he was internationally read as a journalist as well as in his many books.

WILKIE, MR DANIEL, born in Melbourne, December 1, 1843; died about June 1917. One of the most genial of men. Slow underhand bowler. Captain of the Melbourne University XI. Made the first hundred ever hit for the East Melbourne C.C. Captain of East Melbourne 1861–75. Played for Victoria v. New South Wales. For Victoria v. XVI of Tasmania, at Launceston, 1865–6, his analyses were 7 wickets for 15 runs and 11 for 12 – altogether 18 for 27. Later played for the St Kilda C.C. He was the best-known of four cricketing brothers.

WOOD, REGINALD, who died in poverty in Manly, Sydney on January 6, 1915, aged 54, was in the Charterhouse XI of 1876, played six games for Lancashire as an amateur between 1880 and 1884 and played a Test match for England on the 1886–87 tour of Australia. Wood had emigrated to Melbourne and reappeared in first-class cricket for Victoria against Alfred Shaw's English team. Shaw had brought only 11 players, and the First Test at Sydney was marked by a fight between the England player, William Barnes, and the Australian captain, Percy McDonnell. Barnes injured his hand, apparently after missing McDonnell's face and punching a wall. Wood was then co-opted into the Test team: batting No. 10 he scored six and nought, did not bowl and took no catches. He played for Shaw's team against Victoria then disappeared from first-class cricket. He became professional at both East Melbourne and Sydney Albert but was later reported to be working 'in a lowly capacity, with sheep'. A correspondent in Australia said that at his death he had little more than the clothes he wore and his tuckerbag.

WOOLF, MR LOUIS SYDNEY, who played for Victoria against New South Wales in 1877, and lived to be the oldest representative of his State, died in August 1942. For South Melbourne he was prominent in club cricket, and played also for his University. A barrister, he often appeared for The Bar against The Army – popular matches in Australia early this century.

BELIEVE IT OR NOT

For a game that's inherently conservative, cricket revels in the unusual, and *Wisden Cricketers' Almanack* has never been averse to acting as a kind of 'Ripley's Believe It or Not' for its readers. Its 'Chronicle' has for the last decade contained a digest of notable press cuttings, while editions since 1996 have guided readers to happenings quaint and quirky concealed in their bulk with an 'Index of Unusual Occurrences'.

Wisden's affinity for curiosities, however, has been evident for far longer. This small selection begins 120 years ago with an evening in Nottingham where Billy Murdoch's Australians found themselves without lodgings in the wee hours of the morning – none too happily. Also included is a man-of-the-match award in the form of shares in a mine, a team that decided its batting order by drawing lots, a game of cricket between teams led by Australians on the West End stage, and a job lot of new balls that brought a Test to a standstill. As for individual feats, *Wisden* has reported on one bowler who sent a bail travelling more than 75 metres, another who claimed eight for nought in 34 balls, a third who gave up 38 in an over, plus a triple-century containing thirty-one sixes. The notion that nothing is new in cricket also gets a boost from the response of the Lord's crowd to Joe Darling's slow batting in August 1899, prompting the crowd to whistle the 'Dead March in Saul'. The idea of spicing one-day internationals with pop tunes seems banal by comparison.

—GH

THE AUSTRALIANS V. NOTTINGHAMSHIRE

Played at Nottingham, Thursday, Friday, Saturday, June 8, 9, 10, 1882. The only serious unpleasantness during the tour occurred during the progress of this match, and it must be admitted the Colonists had just cause for irritation. It appears that on arriving at Nottingham from Bradford, at about one o'clock in the morning, the Australians were unable to obtain the rooms which had been engaged for them, and in consequence did not get to bed until nearly three. This circumstance, as annoying as it was to tired travellers, would probably soon have been forgotten, but when the interval for luncheon arrived the Colonists found that no places had been reserved for them at the table, a piece of unaccountable carelessness on the part of the executive, which, coming after the mishap overnight, led to an unfriendly interchange of words between the Secretary of the County Club and Murdoch and other members of the team, and to a correspondence in the papers, which made the matter more regrettable. [...]

SHAW'S TEAM V. TWENTY-TWO OF MARYBOROUGH AND DISTRICT

Played at Maryborough, Thursday, Friday, February 5, 6, 1885. – The features of this match were the brilliant hitting of Ulyett and the successful bowling of Peel and Flowers for Shaw's Team, and of Halpin for Maryborough, the last named taking eight English wickets for 37 runs, in addition to making the top score for his side. He succeeded in carrying his bat right through the second innings, scoring 106, while the other batsmen made 72. For this performance the Yorkshireman received a present of 250 shares in the Gympie Mine, given by a resident of Maryborough for the highest score on the English side. [...]

MR VERNON'S TEAM V. EIGHTEEN OF WAGGA WAGGA

Played at Wagga Wagga, Tuesday, Wednesday, February 28, 29, 1888. – A single innings victory for the Englishmen, with five runs to spare. The order of going in was decided by drawing lots.

AUSTRALIANS V. MIDDLESEX

Played at Lord's, Monday, Tuesday, August 21, 22, 1899. [...] On the first day the game was marred by an unseemly demonstration on the part of spectators, happily without precedent at Lord's. Resenting the extreme caution with which Darling and Iredale were batting, a section of the crowd forgot their manners, cheering ironically when a run was obtained, and at one point whistling the 'Dead March in Saul'. [...]

from THE ROAR OF THE GREASEPAINT – THE SMELL OF THE LINSEED

By David Rayvern Allan

[...] The only time that county cricketers as a team have played the game on the West End stage was when the impresario Sir Oswald Stoll mounted a variety spectacle for his winter season of 1908 at the Coliseum. The billing read Surrey v. Middlesex, with four professionals from The Oval captained by Alan Marshal, against the same number from Lord's led by Albert Trott. J.T. Hearne and 19-year-old 'Patsy' Hendren were in the Middlesex side. The audience were given a scorecard to keep tabs on the official scorer who was on the stage itself. The painting on the backcloth was of a village green surrounded by trees, depicting a pastorally idyllic summer's day. The pitch was restricted to 15 yards and adapted rules applied; for instance, a hit meant a run had to be attempted. The runs scored at each performance were cumulative and each morning the revised score was posted outside the theatre. At one performance, the net which protected orchestra and audience from the four-ounce ball could not be raised for some reason and the game proceeded with those in the stalls acting as extra fielders. Fortunately, no one was hurt. At the end of a week, Middlesex just managed to beat Surrey. [...] (*1993*)

FROM CRICKET CONUNDRUMS

By Arthur Gilligan

[...] I have already mentioned that, if the umpires agree that a ball in use is unfit for play, they have the right to allow the substitution of another ball as much as possible similar to the one discarded.

I recall that, in the second Test Match between England and Australia at Melbourne in 1925, after only 15 runs were on the board – I was bowling at the time – I noticed that a great piece of leather had come off the ball. I immediately showed the ball to Umpire Bob Crockett, who consulted his colleague, and a brand new ball was brought out.

Before lunch that day we had no fewer than four new balls with the total no more than 87! When we adjourned, we discovered that, by mistake, a wrong packet of balls had been delivered to the ground and that we had No. 3 grade cricket balls instead of No. I. It was was agreed between 'Herby' Collins and myself to play out the first innings with both sides using the No. 3 grade variety, and it is interesting now to record that we used eight new balls before the score reached 200 and Australia had seven. I do not think that any similar incident can be brought to mind of the ball being changed so frequently in a Test or an other match. It came as quite a relief when we embarked upon the second innings. [...] (*1939*)

FROM NOTES BY THE EDITOR

[...] Just as the Almanack is going to press comes a letter from Hobart, stating that in a match there between New Town and North-West Hobart 'A' Grade on November 21 last, A.O. Burrows of New Town bowled one of his opponents with a ball which sent the bail 83 yards 1 foot 9 inches. The statement is vouched for by no fewer than half a dozen different men associated with the club or the other, among those being Joe Darling, the famous left handed batsman who captained Australia in this country in 1899, 1902 and 1905, and who is now president of the New Town Club. Previously the record was 70½ yards by A.F. Morcom for Bedfordshire against Suffolk at Luton in 1908. (*1926*)

MISCELLANY

At the end of March, a strip of turf from Melbourne was laid on the practice-ground at Lord's as an experiment to see how it fared in the English climate, with a possibility that such turf might be use to obviate the wearing of bowlers' footholds. (*1936*)

The MCC received a beautiful illuminated address from the Federal Capital Territory Cricket Association, commemorating 'the historic occasion of the first visit of an All-England cricket team to the national capital of the Commonwealth of Australia'. (*1938*)

OXFORD UNIVERSITY v. AUSTRALIANS

Played at Christ Church Ground, Oxford, May 4, 5, 6, 1938. Australians won by an innings and 487 runs. [...] On the last day when Walker had a damaged finger, Fingleton, who like Hassett hit during this match his first century in England, stumped three men.

FROM NOTES BY THE EDITOR

OLDEST TEST PLAYER

[...] The passing of F.A. MacKinnon raised a doubt as to who could be the oldest surviving Test player. Having heard in reply to a letter that Sir Timothy C. O'Brien was living in the Isle of Man, I found that his seniority for England was established by a matter of six days over that of Stanley Christopherson, born on November 11, 1861. But M.C. Kemp, born on September 7 of that same vintage year, seems to have become the oldest living University Blue. Actual seniority of all Test players belongs, however, to Australia, S.P. Jones, born on August 1, 1861, being strong and hearty, as my son, Norman Preston, when touring with the England team last winter, found him at Auckland, New Zealand. Sam Jones watched the cricket with keen zest, and told my son that he well remembered Charles, Sydney and Edgar Pardon. He came to England in 1882, 1886 and 1888, having first played for Australia in February 1882 at Sydney, when the England team, captained by Alfred Shaw, lost by five wickets. Talking to my son, Jones said he disliked modern batsmanship, even deploring the methods of Hobbs and Hammond compared with the old masters, Grace and Trumper. On his first visit to England he played in the historic Oval Test which Australia won by 7 runs. The sole survivor of that match, he remembers vividly how W.G. Grace, fielding point, ran him out. Of Grace, whom he described as a great sportsman and cricketer, he said, 'I never saw him leave alone any ball outside the off stump. He either cut or drove them.' Jones went to Auckland in 1904 as coach to the Grammar School, and stayed there, making only one visit to Sydney some twenty-three years ago. He has never seen Bradman play. [...] (*1948*)

AUSTRALIAN BOWLER'S FEAT

Geoffrey Jinkins of the North Melbourne club achieved an astounding bowling feat in a Grade One match. He was playing in the last fixture of the 1958–59 season against Prahran, the club which produced Sam Loxton. Owing to rain, no play was possible on the first day, Saturday, but on Monday North Melbourne gained an outright win by six wickets. The scores were Prahran 53 and 13; North Melbourne 52 and 15 for four wickets. In Prahran's first innings Jinkins took six wickets for 25 runs in eleven overs and in the second innings his analysis was eight wickets for no runs in 4.2 overs, a performance probably without parallel in senior cricket. (*1960*)

NINE CATCHES IN AN INNINGS

Les Andrews, keeping wicket in a first-grade match in Sydney, for Bankstown-Canterbury against Sydney University in November 1982, held nine catches during Sydney's innings of 236. So far as is known this constitutes a world record. The tenth wicket fell to a run out at the bowler's end. (*1983*)

CHRONICLE

In keeping with the tradition dating back to Bradman's time, the Australian captain, Allan Border, was presented with a whortleberry pie by the Castle Hotel, Taunton. Unfortunately, the whortleberry was out of season on the Quantocks and the tradition was maintained only when a local man came up with a supply from his freezer. (*The Times*, May 8, 1993)

More than 60 people offered to give a home to a stray mongrel who ran on to the pitch at Trent Bridge as Merv Hughes was about to deliver the first ball of the Third Test. Graham and Sally Bosnall from Derby, who adopted him, followed the example of the staff at the RSPCA shelter and called him Merv. (*Daily Telegraph*, July 12, 1993)

Corey Hojnacki, 9, scored 426 out of a total of 710 for Heinz Southern Districts against Silverton in the Dandenong and District C-Grade, adding 338 on Saturday to the 88 he scored a week earlier. He hit 31 sixes and 36 fours. Hojnacki's own bat had been stolen and he used his father's old 'Austral' bat. It's as thick as a tree trunk,' Hojnacki said. 'I only had to to block and the ball went for four.' (*Herald-Sun*, Melbourne, February 28, 1994)

The match between Methodists and Sandown Park in the Dandenong and District Cricket Association, Victoria, was declared a draw ten days after it finished, following four hearings, when local officials finally sought advice from MCC. Methodists lost their ninth wicket to the last available ball and Sandown claimed victory because they knew the last man was missing. (*Sunday Age*, Melbourne, March 13, 1994)

Blair Sellers, playing for South Melbourne in the Dowling Shield under-16 competition, hit a lofted drive that was stopped by the back of a seagull's head, turning a certain four into two. He was not unduly disturbed by this until he was bowled for 98. The seagull recovered. (*Sunday Age*, Melbourne, February 5, 1995)

Shane Warne, a four-year-old bay colt, beat 11 rivals to win the Pakistan Derby, the country's richest horse race, at Lahore. (*Dawn*, Karachi, March 1996)

RECORD FOR CLAYTON

Jon Clayton will enter cricket record books after hitting 38 runs from one over during the 1997–98 Country Carnival. Clayton, playing for South East, struck six sixes and a two from an over off Murray Districts medium-pacer Darren Nitschke. The sequence was as follows 6666266, the sixth delivery being a no-ball. Clayton, who was eventually dismissed for 80, said: 'Apart from the fifth ball, all the others were in the right spot so I thought I'd have a go. It was all pre-meditated.' (*1998–99*)